Lecture Notes in Artificial Intelligence   3558

Edited by J. G. Carbonell and J. Siekmann

Subseries of Lecture Notes in Computer Science

T0226138

Vicenç Torra   Yasuo Narukawa
Sadaaki Miyamoto (Eds.)

Modeling Decisions for
Artificial Intelligence

Second International Conference, MDAI 2005
Tsukuba, Japan, July 25-27, 2005
Proceedings

 Springer

Series Editors

Jaime G. Carbonell, Carnegie Mellon University, Pittsburgh, PA, USA
Jörg Siekmann, University of Saarland, Saarbrücken, Germany

Volume Editors

Vicenç Torra
Institut d'Investigació en Intel·ligència Artificial
Consejo Superior de Investigaciones Científicas
Campus UAB, 08193 Bellaterra, Catalonia, Spain
E-mail: vtorra@iiia.csic.es

Yasuo Narukawa
Toho Gakuen
3-1-10 Naka, Kunitachi, Tokyo, 186-0004, Japan
E-mail: narukawa@d4.dion.ne.jp

Sadaaki Miyamoto
University of Tsukuba
School of Systems and Information Engineering
Ibaraki 305-8573, Japan
E-mail: miyamoto@risk.tsukuba.ac.jp

Library of Congress Control Number: 2005928987

CR Subject Classification (1998): I.2, F.4.1, H.2.8, I.6

ISSN   0302-9743
ISBN-10   3-540-27871-0 Springer Berlin Heidelberg New York
ISBN-13   978-3-540-27871-9 Springer Berlin Heidelberg New York

Springer is a part of Springer Science+Business Media

springeronline.com

© Springer-Verlag Berlin Heidelberg 2005
Printed in Germany

Typesetting: Camera-ready by author, data conversion by Olgun Computergrafik
Printed on acid-free paper   SPIN: 11526018   06/3142   5 4 3 2 1 0

Preface

This volume contains papers presented at the 2nd International Conference on Modeling Decisions for Artificial Intelligence (MDAI 2005), held in Tsukuba, Japan, July 25–27. This conference follows MDAI 2004 (held in Barcelona, Catalonia, Spain), the proceedings of which were also published in the LNAI series (Vol. 3131).

The aim of this conference was to provide a forum for researchers to discuss about theory and tools for modeling decisions, as well as applications that encompass decision-making processes and information fusion techniques. In this second edition, special focus was given to applications related to risk, security and safety.

The organizers received 118 papers, from 14 different countries, 40 of which are published in this volume. Each submission received at least two reviews from the Program Committee and a few external reviewers. We would like to express our gratitude to them for their work. The plenary talks presented at the conference are also included in this volume.

The conference was supported by the Department of Risk Engineering of the University of Tsukuba, the Japan Society for Fuzzy Theory and Intelligent Informatics (SOFT), the Catalan Association for Artificial Intelligence (ACIA), the European Society for Fuzzy Logic and Technology (EUSFLAT) and the Generalitat de Catalunya (AGAUR 2004XT 0004).

Sabadell (Catalonia, Spain)   Vicenç Torra
Kunitachi (Japan)   Yasuo Narukawa
Tsukuba (Japan)   Sadaaki Miyamoto

April, 2005

Modeling Decisions for Artificial Intelligence – MDAI 2005

General Chair

Sadaaki Miyamoto, University of Tsukuba, Japan

Program Chairs

Vicenç Torra, IIIA-CSIC, Catalonia, Spain
Yasuo Narukawa, Toho Gakuen, Japan

Program Committee

G. Beliakov (Australia)
D.A. Bell (UK)
J. Domingo-Ferrer (Spain)
J. Dujmovic (USA)
M. Grabisch (France)
E. Herrera-Viedma (Spain)
K. Hirota (Japan)
M. Inuiguchi (Japan)
J. Kacprzyk (Poland)
Z.-Q. Liu (HongKong, China)
Y. Maeda (Japan)
L. Magdalena (Spain)
J.-L. Marichal (Luxemburg)
R. Mesiar (Slovakia)
K.-R. Muller (Germany)
T. Murofushi (Japan)
T. Onisawa (Japan)
E. Pap (Yugoslavia)
G. Pasi (Italia)
C. Sierra (Spain)
L. Sweeney (USA)
J. van den Herik (The Netherlands)
R.R. Yager (USA)

Organization Chairs

Yasunori Endo (University of Tsukuba, Japan)
Mika Sato-Ilic (University of Tsukuba, Japan)

Finance Chair

Yasunori Endo (University of Tsukuba, Japan)

Additional Referees

K. Fujimoto, J. Hoshino, P. Spronck, H.H.L.M. Donkers, M. Hagiwara, J. Laub,
J. Kohlmorgen, T. Suzuki, S.S. Park, J. Castellà, F. Sebé, C.A. Vallve-Guionnet,
A. Martinez Ballesté, J.M. Mateo-Sanz, G. Escalada, J. Castro, J. Ozawa,
H. Nobuhara, A. Valls, H. Sakai, Y. Yoshida, M. Hagiwara, D. Nettleton, J. Li,
Y. Saygin, A. Soria, S. Costantini, I. Kobayashi, J. Lang, S. Greco, L. Xie, Z. Ye,
J. Zeng, G. Luo, W. Feng, P. Wang, T. Fujimoto, T. Nakashima

Supporting Institutions

Department of Risk Engineering of the University of Tsukuba
Japan Society for Fuzzy Theory and Intelligent Informatics (SOFT)
Catalan Association for Artificial Intelligence (ACIA)
European Society for Fuzzy Logic and Technology (EUSFLAT)
Generalitat de Catalunya (AGAUR 2004XT 0004)

Table of Contents

Modeling Decisions for Artificial Intelligence: Theory, Tools and Applications

Vicenç Torra[1], Yasuo Narukawa[2], and Sadaaki Miyamoto[3]

[1] Institut d'Investigació en Intel·ligència Artificial
Campus de Bellaterra, 08193 Bellaterra, Catalonia, Spain
vtorra@iiia.csic.es
[2] Toho Gakuen, 3-1-10 Naka, Kunitachi, Tokyo, 186-0004 Japan
narukawa@d4.dion.ne.jp
Department of Risk Engineering
School of Systems and Information Engineering
University of Tsukuba, Ibaraki 305-8573, Japan
miyamoto@esys.tsukuba.ac.jp

Abstract. Aggregation operators, in particular, and information fusion techniques, in general are being used in several Artificial Intelligence systems for modeling decisions. In this paper we give a personal overview of current trends and challenges as well as describe our aims with respect to the MDAI conference series.

Keywords: Decision modeling, aggregation operators, information fusion, applications

1 Introduction

Methods for combining information (information fusion) have been used for different purposes for centuries. The election mechanisms (to select an alternative taking into account the preferences of different individuals) are a well known example. In fact, methods for this purpose were already proposed and studied [11] by R. Llull (S. XIII) and Cusanus (S. XV), and latter reconsidered by Condorcet and Borda (S. XVIII).

Current pervasive software systems have increased the importance of such techniques taking into account all the relevant information. Part of this information grows year by year [31] and is stored in a highly distributed environment. To further difficult the process, part of the information is *perishable* as becomes obsolete when the time passes (*e.g.*, sensory information in robots or traffic information in devices for route planning).

Several Artificial Intelligence-based applications embed aggregation operators and other information fusion tools to make such timely and appropriate decisions [26]. Existing applications include robotics where data from different sensors are fused, vision where image fusion is performed and machine learning with the so-called ensemble methods.

For all this, we can say that information fusion techniques are a basic element for decision making and that decision processes are increasingly situated in dynamic environments.

V. Torra et al. (Eds.): MDAI 2005, LNAI 3558, pp. 1–8, 2005.

2   Establishing a Framework

In this section we review several issues concerning the use of information fusion tools in artificial intelligence applications.

2.1   Usage of Information Fusion and Aggregation Operators

Although the number of applications is rather large and fusion serves different purposes, most usages of aggregation and fusion methods can be classified according to two rough categories [33]: methods (i) to make (better) decisions and (ii) to have a better understanding of the application domain.

Decision making: In this case, the final goal is to make a decision. Then, the decision can be either selected from a set of alternatives (*alternative selection*) or built from several ones (*alternative construction*). Aggregation and fusion are applied in both cases but in a different way:

Alternative selection: Aggregation and fusion is typically used when there are several criteria for selecting each alternative. This corresponds to a multi-criteria decision problem. Software agents in an electronic auction would correspond to this situation, as the agent has to select a concrete alternative and this selection is done on the basis of several different criteria: the best price or the best quality.

This situation is modeled with a set of preferences or utility functions (one for each criteria) or using a single but multivalued preference. Then, to determine the best alternative, the preferences are aggregated. The alternative that gets the best score (in such aggregated utility or preference) is selected. As the score determines the final selection, the aggregation function used shapes the outcome.

Alternative construction: In this case, the alternative is constructed from a set of (partial) alternatives. Therefore, the method to build the alternative corresponds to the fusion process. Algorithms for *ensemble methods* can be studied from this perspective. Note that in ensemble methods for regression, several models are built first and each method corresponds to an alternative for deciding the outcome for a particular instance; then, all such outcomes are combined to construct the final outcome.

Improving the understanding of the application domain: The   main motivation for using information fusion here is that the information supplied by a single source is limited with respect to the whole application domain (it is circumscribed to a subdomain) or not reliable enough (due to errors of the information source – either intentional or unintentional – or to the transmission chanel). Fusion is used to increase the area of application of the system and to increase its performance.

The use of aggregation operators and fusion helps the systems to improve their performance. Nevertheless, their use also causes difficulties as it is often the case that information is not comparable and, in some cases, inconsistent. Therefore, systems have to embed simple fusion techniques in larger software tools so that the final outcome is consistent.

2.2 Integration, Fusion and Aggregation

In the previous sections we have used the terms "integration", "fusion" and "aggregation" as if they were synonyms. For the sake of clarity, we define them below. They are presented topdown. The following three terms are considered:

Information integration: This is the most general term that corresponds to the whole process of using information from several sources to accomplish a particular task. Similarly, we also have integration when the information is obtained at different time instants (even in the case that it is obtained from the same information source).

Information fusion: The integration of information requires particular techniques for combining data. Information fusion is the actual process of combining data into a single datum.

Aggregation operators: These operators (see *e.g.* [4, 41]) correspond to particular mathematical functions used for information fusion. We use this term when the functions that aggregate the information can be clearly identified in the whole system and their properties studied. In general, we consider that aggregation operators are mathematical functions that combine N values in a given domain D (*e.g.* N real numbers) and return a value also in this domain (*e.g.* another real number). Denoting these functions by $\mathbb{C}$ (from $\mathbb{C}onsensus$), aggregation operators are functions of the form:

$$\mathbb{C} : D^N \to D$$

From this point of view, it is clear that all aggregation operators are information fusion methods. However, only information fusion methods with a *straightforward* mathematical definition are considered here as aggregation operators. Therefore, not all information fusion methods are aggregation operators. In particular, methods with a complex operational definition (*e.g.* complex computer programs) are not considered in this paper as such. Naturally, the division between both terms is rather fuzzy.

Information fusion and aggregation operators heavily depend on the type of data representation (numerical, ordinal, nominal scales), kind of information they have to fuse (either redundant or complementary), etc. Accordingly, they can be studied from different perspectives.

3 Trends and Challenges: Theory, Tools and Applications

In this section we consider trends and challenges of information fusion focusing on aggregation operators. This section has been divided into three parts corresponding to theory, tools and applications.

3.1 Theory

Formal aspects of aggregation operators have been studied for a long time. Rellevant topics include the characterization of operators as well as representatation theorems. For example, results show that some operators can equivalently be expressed in terms of fuzzy integrals with respect to fuzzy measures[17, 24].

Results on the parameters of the operators and, more specifically, on fuzzy measures should also be considered as a present trend. In particular, current research focus on the definition of new families of fuzzy measures with reduced complexity (*i.e.*, requiring less than 2^N parameters where N is the number of sources) as well as characterizations of fuzzy measures. Distorted probabilities [25] and p-symmetric fuzzy measures [18] are examples of such new families.

Another topic for research on formal aspects is the definition of new operators or new applications. In this setting, we can find dynamic operators (dynamic in the sense that their behavior changes with respect to time). A particular type of them are standard aggregation operators with dynamic weights [36].

Finally, there are several techniques that have been used for modeling decisions and for which further research is needed. Rough sets and clustering techniques [19] are some of them. In the particular case of rough sets, rough measures and integrals have been defined [28]. Extensions of fuzzy multisets (bags) [20, 21, 38] might be also relevant to model situations in which several non-overlapping decisions are considered.

3.2 Tools

In a recent paper (see [34] for details), three research topics were distinguished concerning tools:

Parameter learning: As most aggregation operators are parametric, a crucial element for having a good performance is that parameters are correctly tuned. When the operator is fixed, this problem can be considered as an optimization one. Therefore, following the machine learning jargon, either supervised, unsupervised and reinforcement learning approaches can be applied.

Most research has been done using supervised approaches (see *e.g.* [1, 33]), although recently a few unsupervised approaches have also been used in conjunction with some fuzzy integrals (see *e.g.* [17] for details on fuzzy integrals). This is, methods have been defined for learning fuzzy measures from data. [14, 15, 29, 30] are a few examples of such results.

Function/operator selection: Selection of the operator is another important issue. At present much research has been devoted to the characterization of existing methods. Open issues include the development of algorithms and methodologies to determine (automatically) the suitable function for a given problem (see *e.g.* [2]).

Architecture determination: The topic of architecture determination encompasses two different aspects. On the one hand, we have the more general aspect of architectures for information integration. On the other hand, we can consider architectures of operators. *I.e.*, complex/composite models defined in terms of aggregation operators. Hierarchical models (as the two-step Choquet integrals) are more complex examples of such architectures. The Bipolar model [9, 10] and the Meta-knowledge model [35] are examples of such architectures.

In relation to the second aspect, recent results have shown that models can be built so that any arbitrary function can be approximated at the desired level of detail [23, 32]. Nevertheless, the flexibility of such models is at the expenses of a higher cost in the process of defining the architecture and its parameters. Note that for defining such models we need detailed information about the sources, and about which pieces of information can be combined together to get meaningful partial results. For all this, the definition of hierarchical models (both the definition of the architecture and the particularization of the aggregation operators) is a difficult problem. Results on clustering and hierarchical clustering [13, 22] and on hierarchical fuzzy systems [37] can have a role here.

Another important issue that is related with the three topics mentioned above is whether a particular model is reliable. This is, whether the outcome of the system is sound and whether such outcome can be significantly changed due to small variations either in the inputs or on the parameters of the model. This issue, that has been studied by *e.g.* Dujmovic et al. [7] is important for the construction of real applications.

Related with the issue of reliability, there is some research on the behavior of a system with respect to its conjunctiveness (whether the system behaves in a conjunctive or disjunctive manner). Since the seminal work by Dujmovic [6], several research has been done in this area [8, 39, 40].

3.3 Applications

While, the issues pointed out above deal with theory and tools for aggregation operators, another aspect to be considered are the applications. As it has been said, the number of applications that use information fusion techniques within the artificial intelligence field has increased in the last years. Nevertheless, although some complex models have been studied in the literature, applications often use simple aggregation operators.

This is the case, for example, when numerical information is considered. In this case, most systems use operators as *e.g.* the arithmetic or the weighted mean. Voting techniques are often used for non numerical information. This is so, even in the case when several fuzzy integrals have been developed and have been proven (see *e.g.* [16, 42]) to be most suitable when the data to be aggregated is not independent.

So, an open field of research is the development of application with more complex models based on aggregation operators. Robotics and information retrieval [27] are some of the fields where information fusion methods can be used to improve the performance of current systems. As an example in the latter field, we can refer to the work by Bi et al. [3], a recent work on paper categorization that uses Dempster's rule to combine classifiers.

4   Modeling Decisions for Artificial Intelligence

MDAI conferences seek to foster the application of information fusion tools and methods as well as other decision models in artificial intelligence applications. Here, information fusion is considered at large, encompassing from basic aggregation operators (as the arithmetic mean) to more complex process for information integration. In this latter group we can find tools for data base integration as well as those knowledge intensive systems that have an extensive use of ontologies.

To complete this framework, MDAI conferences also sought research on theory and methods that can help on the construction of such complex applications.

With this aim, the first conference was initiated in Barcelona in 2004 and this second conference takes place in Tsukuba in 2005.

5   Conclusions and Future Work

In this paper we have given a personal perspective of the field of aggregation operators and their interaction with artificial intelligence. We have focused on aggregation operators for numerical values, although similar trends can be found when information is represented under other formalisms (*e.g.*, categories in ordinal scales or sequences). We have also described in this paper our aims for the MDAI conference series.

References

1. Beliakov, G., (2003), How to build aggregation operators from data, Int. J. of Intel. Systems 18:8 903-923.
2. Beliakov, G., Warren, J. (2001), Appropriate Choice of Aggregation Operators in Fuzzy Decision Support Systems, IEEE Transactions on Fuzzy Systems, 9:6, 773-784.
3. Bi, Y., Bell, D., Wang, H., Guo, G., Greer, K., (2004), Combining Multiple Classifiers Using Dempster's Rule of Combination for Text Categorization, Modeling Decisions for Artificial Intelligence, Lecture Notes in Artificial Intelligence 3131 127-138.
4. Calvo, T., Kolesárová, A., Komorníková, M., Mesiar, R., (2002), Aggregation operators: properties, classes and construction methods, in T. Calvo, G. Mayor, R. Mesiar, Aggregation Operators, Physica-Verlag, 3-104.
5. Chiclana, F., Herrera-Viedma, E., Herrera, F., Alonso, S., (2004), Induced ordered weighted geometric operators and their use in the aggregation of multiplicative preference relations, Int. J. of Intel. Systems, 19:3 233-255.
6. Dujmović, J. J., (1974), Weighted conjunctive and disjunctive means and their application in system evaluation, Journal of the University of Belgrade, EE Dept., Series Mathematics and Physics, 483 147-158.

7. Dujmovic, J. J., Fang, W. Y., (2004), Reliability of LSP Criteria, Modeling Decisions for Artificial Intelligence, Lecture Notes in Artificial Intelligence 3131 151-162.
8. Fernández Salido, J. M., Murakami, S., (2003), Extending Yager's orness concept for the OWA aggregators to other mean operators, Fuzzy Sets and Systems, 139 515-549.
9. Grabisch, M., Labreuche, C., (2005), Bi-capacities I: definition, Mobius transform and interaction, Fuzzy Sets and Systems, 151, 211-236.
10. Grabisch, M., Labreuche, C., (2005), Bi-capacities II: the Choquet integral Fuzzy Sets and Systems, 151, 237-259.
11. Hägele, G., Pukelsheim, F., (2001), Llull's writings on electoral systems, Studia Lulliana 41 3-38
12. Herrera-Viedma, E., (2004), Fuzzy Qualitative Models to Evaluate the Quality on the Web, Modeling Decisions for Artificial Intelligence, Lecture Notes in Artificial Intelligence 3131 15-26.
13. Höppner, F., Klawonn, F., Kruse, R., Runkler, T., (1999), Fuzzy cluster analysis, Wiley.
14. Kojadinovic, I., (2004), Unsupervised Aggregation by the Choquet integral based on entropy functionals: Application to the Evaluation of Students, Modeling Decisions for Artificial Intelligence, Lecture Notes in Artificial Intelligence 3131 163-174.
15. Kojadinovic, I., (2006), Unsupervised aggregation of commensurate correlated attributes by means of the Choquet integral and entropy functionals, Int. J. of Intel. Systems, accepted.
16. Kuncheva, L.I., (2003), "Fuzzy" versus "nonfuzzy" in combining classifiers designed by Boosting, IEEE Trans. on Fuzzy Systems, 11:6 729- 741.
17. Mesiar, R., Mesiarová, A., (2004), Fuzzy Integrals, Modeling Decisions for Artificial Intelligence, Lecture Notes in Artificial Intelligence 3131 7-14.
18. Miranda, P., Grabisch, M., P. Gil, (2002), p-symmetric fuzzy measures, Int. J. of Unc., Fuzz. and Knowledge-Based Systems, 10 (Supplement) 105-123.
19. Miyamoto, S., (1999), Introduction to fuzzy clustering, (in Japanese), Ed. Morikita, Tokyo.
20. Miyamoto, S., (2003), Information clustering based on fuzzy multisets, Inf. Proc. and Management, 39:2 195-213.
21. Miyamoto, S., (2004), Generalizations of multisets and rough approximations. Int. J. Intell. Syst. 19:7 639-652.
22. Miyamoto, S., Nakayama, K., (1986), Similarity measures based on a fuzzy set model and application to hierarchical clustering, IEEE Trans. on Syst., Man, and Cyb., 16:3 479-482.
23. Murofushi, T., Narukawa, Y., (2002), A characterization of multi-level discrete Choquet integral over a finite set (in Japanese). Proc. of 7th Workshop on Evaluation of Heart and Mind, pp. 33-36.
24. Narukawa, Y., Murofushi, T., (2003), Choquet integral and Sugeno integral as aggregation funcitons, in: Information Fusion in Data Mining , V. Torra, ed., (Springer), pp. 27-39.
25. Narukawa, Y., Torra, V., Fuzzy measure and probability distributions: distorted probabilities, IEEE Trans. on Fuzzy Systems, accepted.
26. Pal, N. R., Mudi, R. K., (2003), Computational intelligence for decision-making systems, Int. J. of Intel. Systems 18:5 483-486.
27. Pasi, G., (2003), Modeling users' preferences in systems for information access, Int. J. of Intel. Systems 18:7 793-808.

28. Pawlak, Z., Peters, J. F., Skowron, A., Suraj, Z., Ramanna, S., Borkowski, M., (2001), Rough Measures and Integrals: A Brief Introduction, Lecture Notes in Computer Science 2253 375-379.
29. Soria-Frisch, A., (2003), Hybrid SOM and fuzzy integral frameworks for fuzzy classification, in Proc. IEEE Int. Conf. on Fuzzy Systems 840-845.
30. Soria-Frisch, A., (2006), Unsupervised Construction of Fuzzy Measures through Self-Organizing Feature Maps and its Application in Color Image Segmentation, Int. J. of Approx. Reasoning, accepted.
31. Sweeney, L., (2001), Information Explosion, 43–74, in Confidentiality, Disclosure, and Data Access: Theory and Practical Applications for Statistical Agencies, P. Doyle, J. I. Lane, J. J. M. Theeuwes, L. M. Zayatz (Eds.), Elsevier.
32. Torra, V., (1999), On some relationships between hierarchies of quasi-arithmetic means and neural networks, Int'l. J. of Intel. Syst., 14:11 1089-1098.
33. Torra, V., (2004), OWA operators in data modeling and reidentification, IEEE Trans on Fuzzy Systems, 12:5 652- 660
34. Torra, V., (2005), Aggregation Operators and Models, Fuzzy Sets and Systems, in press.
35. Torra, V., Narukawa, Y., On the Meta-knowledge Choquet Integral and Related Models, Intl. J. of Intelligent Systems, in press.
36. Torra, V., Narukawa, Y.,. Lòpez-Orriols, J.M., Dynamic aggregation and time dependent weights, Int. J. of Unc., Fuzziness and Knowledge Based Systems, submitted.
37. Tunstel, E., Oliveira, M. A. A., Berman, S., (2002), Fuzzy Behavior Hierarchies for Multi-Robot Control, Int'l. J. of Intel. Systems, 17, 449-470.
38. Yager, R. R., (1986), On the theory of bags, Int. J. General Systems, 13 23-37.
39. Yager, R. R., (1988), On ordered weighted averaging aggregation operators in multi-criteria decision making, IEEE Trans. Syst., Man, Cybern., 18 183-190.
40. Yager, R.R., (2003), Noble reinforcement in disjunctive aggregation operators, IEEE Trans. on Fuzzy Systems, 11:6 754-767.
41. Xu, Z. S., Da, Q. L., (2003), An overview of operators for aggregating information, Int. J. of Intel. Systems 18:9 953-969.
42. Xu, K., Wang, Z., Heng, P.-A., Leung, K.-S., (2003), Classification by nonlinear integral projections, IEEE Trans on Fuzzy Systems 11:2 187- 201.

Capacities and Games on Lattices:
A Survey of Results

Michel Grabisch

Université Paris I - Panthéon-Sorbonne
LIP6, 8 rue du Capitaine Scott, 75015 Paris, France
Michel.Grabisch@lip6.fr

Capacities, introduced by Choquet [3], or *fuzzy measures*, introduced by Sugeno [20], are set functions vanishing on the empty set and being monotone w.r.t. set inclusion. They have been widely used in decision making and related areas, e.g., pattern recognition (see a compilation of applications in the monograph [17]). *Cooperative games* in characteristic form are set functions vanishing on the empty set, but not requiring monotonicity; they are sometimes called *non monotonic fuzzy measures*. They model the power or worth of coalitions of players.

Recently, many variations or generalizations have been proposed around the above definition of a game, and to a less extent for capacities also. The primary aim of such generalizations is to model reality in a more accurate way. A first example in game theory is the case of *ternary voting games* [6]. Compared to classical voting games, a ternary voting game allows for abstention. Similarly, *bi-cooperative games* proposed by Bilbao [1] model a situation where a coalition of players is playing against another coalition, the remaining players not participating to the game. Multichoice games [18] allow different levels of participation for each player, these levels being totally ordered. A rather different way has been explored by Gilboa and Lehrer with *global games* [8], where instead of coalitions, partitions of players are considered. Lastly we may cite Faigle and Kern [5], who introduced *games with precedence constraints*, which means that a coalition of players is valid only if it is consistent with some order relation among the players.

In the field of capacities, much less examples can be cited. *Bi-capacities* have been proposed by Grabisch and Labreuche [10, 11], and corresponds to monotone bi-cooperative games. They have been introduced for multicriteria decision making when scales are bipolar, i.e., on such scales, a neutral level separates good outcomes (or scores) from bad ones. A generalization of this idea consists in putting more remarkable levels on each scale, and this leads to k-ary capacities [12], which correspond to monotone multichoice games.

Mathematically speaking, all previous examples can be casted into the general framework of *capacities on lattices* and *games on lattices*. Classical games and capacities are defined on the Boolean lattice of subsets (or coalitions), denoted usually 2^N, where N is the set of players. Bi-cooperatives and bi-capacities are defined on the lattice 3^N, while multi-choice games and k-ary capacities are defined on $(k+1)^N$. More generally, the underlying lattice is supposed to be a

V. Torra et al. (Eds.): MDAI 2005, LNAI 3558, pp. 9–12, 2005.

product lattice $L = L_1 \times \cdots \times L_n$, where lattice L_i is distributive, and represents the set of all possible actions of player i.

This being taken for granted, it remains to define the usual tools associated with cooperative games and capacities. Let us examine them briefly.

The Choquet integral w.r.t bi-capacities is obtained by a symmetrization of the usual Choquet integral around the central point of the lattice 3^N, thus keeping the meaning of interpolation between particular points (namely, ternary alternatives) the usual Choquet integral has. The same idea can be used for k-ary capacities, but there is no definition for the general case of a product lattice.

The Möbius transform can be readily defined on L, by just taking the general construction given by Rota [19], which can be applied to any (locally finite) partially ordered set. However, the case of bi-capacities rises a discussion, as remarked by Fujimoto [7]. Taking the usual Möbius transform as in [10] leads to a rather odd expression for the Choquet integral (see [13]). The reason is that the Choquet integral is obtained by a symmetry around the central point, while the Möbius transform is rooted at the bottom of the lattice. Fujimoto proposed a kind of bipolar Möbius transform, rooted at the center of the lattice, which solves the problem. This rises the question of the right mathematical structure for bi-capacities, which may be not the one introduced in [10] (see a discussion about this in [14]).

The next topic of importance concerns the Shapley value and interaction index. The situation seems to be not simple here, and several definitions are possible. Already in 1992, Faigle and Kern proposed a Shapley value for games on lattices which corresponds to take an average of the so called marginal vectors over all maximal chains in the lattice [5]. Although mathematically appealing, this definition suffers from a highly combinatorial complexity, since the enumeration of maximal chains in a lattice is a ♯-P-complete problem. The proposition of Hsiao and Raghavan [18] is different since it uses weights on levels of actions, and so is more in the spirit of the so-called weighted Shapley values. Nevertheless, Tijs *at al.* showed that for some examples of multichoice games, there is no set of weights such that the two values coincide [2]. Grabisch and Labreuche have proposed a radically different approach in [15], taking the mean derivative of the game over the vertices of the lattice. This gives a value which is very similar to the original Shapley value, and which has a low complexity. An axiomatization of this value has been proposed in [16]. As for the classical case, the interaction is obtained in a recursive way from the Shapley value [9].

A last topic of importance is the notion of core of a capacity or game, that is to say, the set of additive measures (or games) dominating a given capacity. Many results exist in the classical case, for example the fact that the core is non empty for convex games, and if non empty, the Shapley value is the center of gravity of the core. Faigle [4], and van den Nouweland *et al.* [21] have proposed several definitions for the core, and more recently Xie and Grabisch [22]. Necessary and sufficient conditions for nonemptiness are known.

References

1. J.M. Bilbao, J.R. Fernandez, A. Jiménez Losada, and E. Lebrón. Bicooperative games. In J.M. Bilbao, editor, *Cooperative games on combinatorial structures.* Kluwer Acad. Publ., 2000.
2. R. Branzei, D. Dimitrov, and S. Tijs. *Models in cooperative game theory: crisp, fuzzy and multichoice games.* Springer Verlag, to appear.
3. G. Choquet. Theory of capacities. *Annales de l'Institut Fourier*, 5:131–295, 1953.
4. U. Faigle. Cores with restricted cooperation. *ZOR – Methods and Models of Operations Research*, pages 405–422, 1989.
5. U. Faigle and W. Kern. The Shapley value for cooperative games under precedence constraints. *Int. J. of Game Theory*, 21:249–266, 1992.
6. D. Felsenthal and M. Machover. Ternary voting games. *Int. J. of Game Theory*, 26:335–351, 1997.
7. K. Fujimoto. New characterizations of k-additivity and k-monotonicity of bicapacities. In *SCIS-ISIS 2004, 2nd Int. Conf. on Soft Computing and Intelligent Systems and 5th Int. Symp. on Advanced Intelligent Systems*, Yokohama, Japan, September 2004.
8. I. Gilboa and E. Lehrer. Global games. *Int. J. of Game Theory*, 20:129–147, 1991.
9. M. Grabisch. An axiomatization of the Shapley value and interaction index for games on lattices. In *SCIS-ISIS 2004, 2nd Int. Conf. on Soft Computing and Intelligent Systems and 5th Int. Symp. on Advanced Intelligent Systems*, Yokohama, Japan, September 2004.
10. M. Grabisch and Ch. Labreuche. Bi-capacities. In *Joint Int. Conf. on Soft Computing and Intelligent Systems and 3d Int. Symp. on Advanced Intelligent Systems*, Tsukuba, Japan, October 2002.
11. M. Grabisch and Ch. Labreuche. Bi-capacities for decision making on bipolar scales. In *EUROFUSE Workshop on Informations Systems*, pages 185–190, Varenna, Italy, September 2002.
12. M. Grabisch and Ch. Labreuche. Capacities on lattices and k-ary capacities. In *3d Int, Conf. of the European Soc. for Fuzzy Logic and Technology (EUSFLAT 2003)*, pages 304–307, Zittau, Germany, September 2003.
13. M. Grabisch and Ch. Labreuche. Bi-capacities. Part II: the Choquet integral. *Fuzzy Sets and Systems*, 151:237–259, 2005.
14. M. Grabisch and Ch. Labreuche. Bi-capacities: towards a generalization of Cumulative Prospect Theory, June 2005. Presented at Risk, Uncertainty and Decision Workshop, Heidelberg, Germany.
15. M. Grabisch and Ch. Labreuche. Derivative of functions over lattices as a basis for the notion of interaction between attributes. *Discrete Applied Maths.*, submitted.
16. M. Grabisch and F. Lange. A new approach to the Shapley value for games on lattices, June 2005. Presented at the 4th Logic, Game Theory and Social Choice meeting, Caen, France.
17. M. Grabisch, T. Murofushi, and M. Sugeno. *Fuzzy Measures and Integrals. Theory and Applications (edited volume).* Studies in Fuzziness. Physica Verlag, 2000.
18. C.R Hsiao and T.E.S. Raghavan. Shapley value for multichoice cooperative games, I. *Games and Economic Behavior*, 5:240–256, 1993.
19. G.C. Rota. On the foundations of combinatorial theory I. Theory of Möbius functions. *Zeitschrift für Wahrscheinlichkeitstheorie und Verwandte Gebiete*, 2:340–368, 1964.

20. M. Sugeno. *Theory of fuzzy integrals and its applications.* PhD thesis, Tokyo Institute of Technology, 1974.

21. A. van den Nouweland, S. Tijs, J. Potters, and J. Zarzuelo. Cores and related solution concepts for multi-choice games. *ZOR – Mathematical Methods of Operations Research*, 41:289–311, 1995.

22. L. Xie and M. Grabisch. The core of capacities on lattices. In *Proc. of the Int. Fuzzy Systems Association World Congress (IFSA)*, Beijing, China, July 2005.

Cryptosystems Based on Elliptic Curve Pairing

Eiji Okamoto and Takeshi Okamoto

Graduate School of Systems and Information Engineering
University of Tsukuba
1-1-1 Ten-nohdai, Tsukuba, Ibaraki, 305-8573, Japan
{okamoto,ken}@risk.tsukuba.ac.jp

Abstract. The purpose of this paper is to introduce pairing over elliptic curve and apply it to ID based key agreement schemes and privacy preserving key agreement schemes. The key words here are ID based scheme, pairing over elliptic curve and privacy reserving scheme. Elliptic curve is one of the popular research topics in cryptography because it has some useful features. One of them is a bilinear function such as Tate pairing. Bilinear function has excellent properties suitable to applications in cryptography. Some schemes are proposed using the bilinear function so far and ID based cryptosystems are the one of the most important applications. ID is any information like name, mail address, phone number, any public information can be used. Another recent problem is privacy. Careless use of ID may leak privacy of the person corresponding to the ID. In this paper we introduce pairing over elliptic curve and propose ID based key agreement schemes and privacy preserving key agreement scheme.

Keywords: ID based cryptosystem, pairing, privacy, key agreement scheme

1 Introduction

Recent rapid growth of e-business induces substantial increase of attacks against computers and network. To defend these attacks, various requirements for cryptography are requested from almost all areas. Among them simplicity for wide applications and privacy protection are two major requirements. To apply cryptography to large scale and complex e-business, simple protocol is necessary. ID based scheme is very simple, because any information can be used as a public key.

ID based cryptosystem was a very popular research topic in late 80's and many results were reported. The idea was proposed by A. Shamir first [12], then [2], [11] and others were proposed. However, they were not satisfying because two way communications are required or conspiracy among some number of users succeeds to break the scheme. In 1999, Ohgishi, Sakai and Kasahara proposed new scheme based on pairing on elliptic curves which does not have such kind of drawbacks [10].

V. Torra et al. (Eds.): MDAI 2005, LNAI 3558, pp. 13–23, 2005.

However, on the other hand, if we use the ID too much, privacy problems will occur. Since ID is a sort of name, the information relating to ID is accumulated in some server or could be searched easily. Hence privacy is one of the major concerns in recent cryptosystems.

Security takes off privacy sometimes. See surveillance cameras in the street, for example. They are very effective for security, but the degree of privacy decreases. In cryptography, situation is same. To increase security, trusted third party has to keep information on each user like public key sometime. This is one of the examples of privacy deprival.

The rest of this paper is organized as follows. In section 2, previous related works are introduced, pairing over elliptic curve, ID based scheme and privacy preserving cryptography. Section 3 introduces our result on implementation of Tate pairing. Section 4 proposes ID based key agreement scheme using pairing over elliptic curve, and section 5 proposes privacy preserving key agreement scheme.

2   Previous Work

In this section, previous work on pairing, ID based scheme and privacy are introduced.

2.1   Pairing

Paring have been used for many algorithm recently [7], because it has an important property, bilinearity. In this paper, we use bilinear pairing over elliptic curve.

G_1 is cyclic additional group, generated by P and order of P is q. G_2 is a cyclic multiplicative group, which have same prime order q. For simplicity, capital letter express an element of G_1, and small letter express an element of G_2 here.

$e : G_1 \times G_1 \rightarrow G_2$ is a bilinear pairing with properties below.
  - **Bilinearity** : $e(aP, bQ) = e(P, Q)^{ab}$ for any $P, Q \in G_1$, $a, b \in Z_q$.
  - **Non-degeneracy** : There must exist, $P, Q \in G_1$, with $e(P, Q) \neq 1$.
  - **Computability** : There is an efficient algorism to compute $e(P, Q)$, for any $P, Q \in G_1$.

This bilinear property has many applications and it was first used for discrete logarithm problem in [9]. Ohgishi, Sakai and Kasahara used the bilinear property to ID based cryptosystem and since then there have been proposed a lot of cryptosystems based on pairing. This was possible because the existence of Diffie-Hellman gap problem on the pairing.

Diffie-Hellman gap families have been applied to many cryptography schemes [8]. In this section, we recall the properties of Diffie-Hellman gap families.

Definition 1 *Computational Diffie-Hellman problem Let,* $a, b \in Z_q$
  - *Given: P, aP, bP*
  - *Find : abP*

Definition 2 *Decision Diffie-Hellman Problem Let,* $a, b \in Z_q$
- *Given:* x, aP, bP
- *Answer* $\begin{cases} 1 : If \quad x = abP \\ 0 : else \end{cases}$

Definition 3 *Gap Diffie-Hellman Families*
Gap Diffie-Hellman families is a group, such that, there exist efficient algorism to solve DDH problem, in that group. However, there is not any polynomial-time algorithm to solve CDH problem.
So basically, Gap Diffie-Hellman families means 'easy to solve DDH, but hard to solve CDH'.

2.2   ID Based Key Agreement Scheme

If entities use their identity based asymmetric key pairs in the protocol for authentication and determination of the established key instead of using traditional public/private key pairs, then the authenticated key agreement protocol is called *identity(ID) based.*

The first ID based cryptosystem was proposed by Shamir [12] in 1984 but he did not construct an ID based encryption scheme. Since then some actual schemes were proposed ([2], [11]).

In 1999, an efficient ID based encryption scheme based on pairing was proposed by Ohgishi, Sakai and Kasahara [10] and their scheme is considered the first practical ID based encryption scheme. Afterwards, pairing were used widely to get a huge number of ID based cryptographic protocols (e.g., [6], [7]).

Informally, there are three types of ID based authenticated key agreement protocols. If both entities share an exclusive secret key without transmitting information to each other previously, then this protocol is called *non-interactive.* If only one entity is needed to be on-line, that is, if only one entity is needed to transmit information to the other, then the protocol is called *one-way.* Otherwise, the protocol is called *two-way* or *one-round.* [10] is non-interactive type.

More simple key agreement schemes or group key agreement schemes are next direction to explore.

2.3   Privacy Enhanced Scheme

Anonymous cryptosystems are proposed so far but they are usually signature schemes. Ring signature is one of the examples of anonymous group signature. Some anonymous key agreement schemes are proposed also, but they are not so efficient. We are going to introduce privacy preserving simple key agreement schemes using pairing.

3   Speeding up of Pairing Based Schemes

Two pairings on elliptic curve are known, Weil pairing and Tate pairing. For cryptographic purpose Tate pairing is more useful, because the computation is easy. Here we use Tate pairing.

3.1   Pairing Computation

Since Miller's algorithm is most famous to compute Tate pairing, we adopt this algorithm in this paper. Let the line through points U, V on the elliptic curve $E(F_{p^k})$ be $g_{U,V} \in F_{p^k}(E)$. If $U = V$, $g_{U,U}$ is the line tangent at the point U. If U or V is a zero O, $g_{U,V}$ is a vertical line through another point. g_U is often used instead of $g_{U,-U}$.

First Miller's formula is given below.

Theorem *Miller's formula*
For $P \in E(F_{p^k})$, f_c is defined as the rational function satisfying $div(f_c) = c(P) - (cP) - (c-1)(O)$ for c. For any integers $a, b \in Z$

$$f_{a+b} = f_a \cdot f_b \cdot \frac{g_{aP,bP}}{g_{(a+b)P}}$$

Here $div(f)$ is a principal divisor.
Miller's algorithm is given using this Miller's formula.

Miller's Algorithm.

1. Pick up $Q' \in E(F_p^k)$ randomly, $S = Q + Q' \in E(F_p^k)$
2. Let the binary digit of m be $(m_t, \cdots, m_0)_2$, and $f = 1, V = P$
3. Iterate the operations below from $i = t - 1$ till $i = 0$.

$$f = f^2 \frac{g_{V,V}(S)g_{2V}(Q')}{g_{2V}(S)g_{V,V}(Q')}, V = 2V$$

if $m_i = 1$

$$f = f \frac{g_{V,P}(S)g_{V+P}(Q')}{g_{V+P}(S)g_{V,P}(Q')}, V = P + V$$

4. Return f

Speed up Techniques. Above Miller's algorithm is a basic algorithm. There are many techniques to speed up computation.

1. $Q' = O$ Miller's algorithm becomes
   1. Let the binary digit of m be $(m_t, \cdots, m_0)_2$, and $f = 1, V = P$
   2. Iterate the operations below from $i = t - 1$ till $i = 0$.

$$f = f^2 \frac{g_{V,V}(Q)}{g_{2V}(Q)}, V = 2V$$

if $m_i = 1$

$$f = f \frac{g_{V,P}(Q)}{g_{V+P}(Q)}, V = P + V$$

   3. Return f

2. **Omission of λ computation** One computation of λ is sufficient for two functions $g_{V,P}$ and $V = P + V$. Moreover, since P is fixed, pre-computation of λ is possible.

3. **Final powering** Powering with $\frac{(q-1)}{m}$ is necessary to get Tate pairing finally. When $z = \frac{(p^2-1)}{m} = \frac{(p+1)}{m} \cdot (p-1)$, to calculate $s = w^z \mod p$, first get $t = w^{\frac{(p+1)}{m}} \equiv u + iv$.

Since $(A + B)^p = A^p + B^p$ over F_p, $s = (u + iv)^{p-1} = \frac{(u+iv)^p}{u+iv} = (u^p + (iv)^p)/(u + iv)$. Moreover, $p \equiv 3 \mod 4$ and $i^p = -i$ implies $s = (u - iv)/(u + iv)$. Hence

$$s = \frac{(u^2 - v^2)}{(u^2 + v^2)} - \frac{2uvi}{(u^2 + v^2)}$$

.

4. **Coordinate transformation** Three coordinate transformations are known: Projective coordination system, Jacobian coordination system and Modified Jacobian coordination system. All are used to avoid divisions.

5. **Suitable selection of parameters** If m does not have many 1's in the binary digit, the number of operations in the Miller's algorithm decreases.

We implement Miller algorithm using these techniques. The result is in the table below.

Table 1. Comparison of speed up programs

Programs	Calculation speed[s]	Speed up ratio
Original Miller algorithm	0.124	-
$Q' = O$	0.083	34%
Only once calculation of λ	0.095	24%
Pre-computation of λ	0.093	25%
Simplification of final powering	0.115	8%
Coordination transformations	0.128	-3%
Suitable selection of parameters	0.096	23%
All applications of speed up techniques	0.037	71%

3.2   Elimination of Map to Point Hash

Recently, paring-based cryptosystems such as [1], [3] were proposed. Unfortunately there exists one drawback in those schemes, i.e., a special hash function called Map-To-Point [4] is used to compute some value from an ID information. This hash operation requires large amount of work and is much bigger than general hash functions such as SHA. Additionally the implementation is also difficult compared to the general hash function.

We propose new key agreement protocols. Our schemes are based on ID based cryptosystem [12] and use bilinear paring. Note that all the proposed schemes resolve the above problem.

Zhang et al. also construct such cryptosystems in [14] but their schemes are only related to signature and do not propose the key agreement protocol. So our approach is different from theirs.

Preliminary Key Setting. Let $\mathcal{H} : \{0,1\}^* \to \{0,1\}^\ell$ be a hash function . We set a user $\Omega \in \{A, B, \ldots\}$. The following setting is used to all our schemes.

Key Generation:
1. Pick up two elements P and $x \in \mathbb{Z}_q$.
2. Compute
$$\begin{cases} V = xP, \\ e_\Omega = \mathcal{H}(ID_\Omega), \\ S_\Omega = \frac{1}{x+e_\Omega}P. \end{cases}$$
3. CA sends S_Ω to Ω using private channel.
4. Ω checks whether
$$\hat{e}(e_\Omega P + V, S_\Omega) = \hat{e}(P, P)$$
holds or not.

Key: Parameter

- CA's key is $\begin{cases} \text{Public-Key} : V, \\ \text{Secret-Key} : x. \end{cases}$

- Ω's key is $\begin{cases} \text{ID Key} \quad\; : ID_\Omega, \\ \text{Secret-Key} : S_\Omega. \end{cases}$

One-Way Key Distribution. We assume that A who does not have a secret-key, sends a value to B to whom CA gives a secret-key. Consequently, A can distribute the work key to actual user B with enough security.

Key Agreement: (Scheme I)
1. A picks up a random number $r \in \mathbb{Z}_q$.
2. A computes
$$\begin{cases} X_A = r(e_B P + V), \\ K_{AB} = \hat{e}(P, P)^r. \end{cases}$$
3. A sends X_A to A.
4. B computes $K_{BA} = \hat{e}(X_A, S_B)$.

Note that $K_{AB} = K_{BA}$ since

$$\begin{aligned} K_{AB} &= \hat{e}(X_A, S_B) \\ &= \hat{e}(r(e_B P + V), \tfrac{1}{x+e_B}P) \\ &= \hat{e}(r(x+e_B)P, \tfrac{1}{x+e_B}P) \\ &= \hat{e}(P, P)^r \\ &= K_{BA}. \end{aligned}$$

One-Round Key Exchange. According to the difference of the complexity between off-line phase and on-line phase, our cryptosystem can be classified into two types.

Key Agreement: (Scheme II)
1. A picks up a random number $r_A \in \mathbb{Z}_q$.
2. B picks up a random number $r_B \in \mathbb{Z}_q$.

3. A computes $X_A = r_A (e_B P + V)$ and sends X_A to B.
4. B computes $X_B = r_B (e_A P + V)$ and sends X_B to A.
5. A computes $K_{AB} = \hat{e}(X_B, S_A)^{r_A}$.
6. B computes $K_{BA} = \hat{e}(X_A, S_B)^{r_B}$.

Note that $K_{AB} = K_{BA}$ since

$$
\begin{aligned}
K_{AB} &= \hat{e}(X_B, S_A)^{r_A} \\
&= \hat{e}(r_B(x + e_B)P, \tfrac{1}{x+e_A} P)^{r_A} \\
&= \hat{e}(P, P)^{r_A r_B} \\
&= K_{BA}.
\end{aligned}
$$

In the next scheme (Scheme III), each user explicitly uses the secret-key at first. In the following, an information related to the secret-key is removed by the verification method.

Key Agreement: (Scheme III)
1. A picks up a random number $r_A \in \mathbb{Z}_q$.
2. B picks up a random number $r_B \in \mathbb{Z}_q$.
3. A computes $X_A = r_A S_A$ and sends X_A to B.
4. B computes $X_B = r_B S_B$ and sends X_B to A.
5. A computes $K_{AB} = \hat{e}(X_B, (e_B P + V))^{r_A}$.
6. B computes $K_{BA} = \hat{e}(X_A, (e_A P + V))^{r_B}$.

Note that $K_{AB} = K_{BA}$ since

$$
\begin{aligned}
K_{AB} &= \hat{e}(X_B, (e_B P + V))^{r_A} \\
&= \hat{e}(\tfrac{r_B}{x+e_B} P, r_B(x + e_B)P)^{r_A} \\
&= \hat{e}(P, P)^{r_A r_B} \\
&= K_{BA}.
\end{aligned}
$$

4   An ID Based Non-interactive Tripartite Key Agreement Scheme

No secure tripartite key agreement protocol could provide authentication for entities without introducing certifications into the protocol or combining the protocol with a digital signature scheme so far. In addition, at least one-round of data transmission has been required for the current protocols. Moreover, most of the current protocols need a special hash function which requires large amount of computation. In this paper, we propose an ID based tripartite key agreement protocol which is non-interactive and requires no hash function.

System Setting:
Let P be a generator of G_1, where G_1 is an additive group of prime order q. The bilinear pairing is given by $\hat{e} : G_1 \times G_1 \longmapsto G_2$. $k \ll q$ is a security

parameter. This setting is assumed to be generated by the trusted authority, KGC. Moreover, $ID_i \in \mathcal{Z}_q^*$ is the identity information of entity i.

Key Generation:

KGC picks up k random numbers $d_0, d_1, \cdots, d_k \in \mathcal{Z}_q$, and generates a polynomial $f(x)$ of degree k where

$$f(x) = d_0 + d_1 x + \cdots + d_k x^k \in \mathcal{Z}_q[x].$$

KGC then computes $V_0 = d_0 P, V_1 = d_1 P, \cdots, V_k = d_k P$. KGC publishes $P, V_0, \cdots, V_k$ to the entities as the system's public information and keeps $d_0, \cdots, d_k$ secretly as his private key. After that, he computes

$$f_i = f(ID_i) = d_0 + d_1 ID_i + \cdots + d_k (ID_i)^k \bmod q$$

for the entity i with identity $ID_i \in \mathcal{Z}_q^*$ and sends f_i to i through a private secure channel.

Public-Key/Private-Key

For the three entities A, B, and C, their public/private keys are

$-$ A $\begin{cases} \text{Public-key}: ID_A \\ \text{Private-key}: f_A \end{cases}$

$-$ B $\begin{cases} \text{Public-key}: ID_B \\ \text{Private-key}: f_B \end{cases}$

$-$ C $\begin{cases} \text{Public-key}: ID_C \\ \text{Private-key}: f_C \end{cases}$

Key Agreement:

$-$ A computes

$$e_B = \Sigma_{i=0}^k (ID_B)^i V_i, \qquad e_C = \Sigma_{i=0}^k (ID_C)^i V_i,$$

and

$$k_{ABC} = (e_B, e_C)^{f_A},$$

$-$ B computes

$$e_C = \Sigma_{i=0}^k (ID_C)^i V_i, \qquad e_A = \Sigma_{i=0}^k (ID_A)^i V_i,$$

and

$$k_{BCA} = (e_C, e_A)^{f_B},$$

$-$ C computes

$$e_A = \Sigma_{i=0}^k (ID_A)^i V_i, \qquad e_B = \Sigma_{i=0}^k (ID_B)^i V_i,$$

and

$$k_{CAB} = (e_A, e_B)^{f_C},$$

Table 2. k-resilient tripartite IDNIKS

Key generation	Public-key/Private-key		Key agreement	
KGC : $d_i \longleftarrow_R \mathcal{Z}_q, 0 \le i \le k$ $f(x) \longleftarrow \Sigma_{i=0}^k d_i x^i$ $V_i \longleftarrow d_i P, 0 \le i \le k$ $f_A \longleftarrow f(ID_A)$ $f_B \longleftarrow f(ID_B)$ $f_C \longleftarrow f(ID_C)$	KGC $\begin{cases} \text{Public-key} : P, V_0, V_1, \cdots, V_k \\ \text{Private-key} : d_0, d_1, \cdots, d_k \end{cases}$ $A \begin{cases} \text{Public-key} : ID_A \\ \text{Private-key} : f_A \end{cases}$ $B \begin{cases} \text{Public-key} : ID_B \\ \text{Private-key} : f_B \end{cases}$ $C \begin{cases} \text{Public-key} : ID_C \\ \text{Private-key} : f_C \end{cases}$		$A \begin{cases} e_B &\longleftarrow \Sigma_{i=0}^k (ID_B)^i V_i \\ e_C &\longleftarrow \Sigma_{i=0}^k (ID_C)^i V_i \\ k_{ABC} &\longleftarrow (e_B, e_C)^{f_A} \end{cases}$ $B \begin{cases} e_C &\longleftarrow \Sigma_{i=0}^k (ID_C)^i V_i \\ e_A &\longleftarrow \Sigma_{i=0}^k (ID_A)^i V_i \\ k_{BCA} &\longleftarrow (e_C, e_A)^{f_B} \end{cases}$ $C \begin{cases} e_A &\longleftarrow \Sigma_{i=0}^k (ID_A)^i V_i \\ e_B &\longleftarrow \Sigma_{i=0}^k (ID_B)^i V_i \\ k_{CAB} &\longleftarrow (e_A, e_B)^{f_C} \end{cases}$	

Consistency:

$k_{ABC} = k_{BCA} = k_{CAB}$ holds since

$$\begin{aligned} k_{ABC} &= (e_B, e_C)^{f_A} \\ &= (\Sigma_{i=0}^k (ID_B)^i V_i, \Sigma_{i=0}^k (ID_C)^i V_i)^{f_A} \\ &= (f_A P, f_B P)^{f_A} \\ &= (P, P)^{f_A f_B f_C} \\ &= k_{BCA} \\ &= k_{CAB}. \end{aligned}$$

This is the first non-interactive key agreement protocol for three parties. In addition, the authentication is accomplished implicitly from the tripartite key. That is, no entity, say $s \notin \{A, B, C\}$, can compute K_{ABC} without knowing at least one of the private keys of f_A, f_B or f_C. The scheme is k-resilience, therefore, if KGC chooses a value k greater than the total number, n, of the entities, then even the cooperation of all the entities cannot recover the private key of KGC.

5   Privacy Preserving Group Key Agreement Scheme

In group key agreement schemes proposed, an outside party does not have any information about secret keys. Hence he cannot determine whether the correct key has been generated. In this section we address the problem and introduce a new group key agreement scheme. With our scheme an outside party cannot determine group key, but he can distinguish appropriate generation of the group key.

5.1   Key Distribution Protocol

Let secret key and public key of user A_i be s_i and $P_i = s_i P$, where P is a base point over elliptic curve. Key distribution protocol is given below.

1. Key generator generates a random number r.
2. Key generator sends rP_i to user A_i.
3. User A_i calculates a group key K using his secret key s_i and received data rP_i.

There are two methods to calculate a group key K as follows.

Method 1

$$K = e(rP_i, P)^{(1/s_i)} = e(P, P)^r$$

Method 2

$$K = s_i^{-1}rP_i = rP$$

5.2   Privacy Preserving Verification

Outside verifier checks if users A_1 and A_2 could get the same group key by checking the following equation holds or not.

$$e(rP_1, P_2) = e(rP_2, P_1)$$

He uses public key and the transmitted information over a public channel. If this equation holds, then verifier can assure that both users can get the same group key, because above equation equals to $K^{s_1 s_2}$ in the case of Method 1 for instance. However he cannot get the actual key K, so this is the privacy preserving key agreement scheme.

6   Conclusion

In this paper, we surveyed and proposed pairing based key agreement schemes. First we gave fast computation of pairing, then showed the method to eliminate map to point hash to save computation time. Next we proposed ID based non-interactive tripartite key agreement scheme, and finally showed privacy preserving key agreement scheme.

Using pairing, these schemes are simply constructed. For further use of pairing, faster computation is necessary in the future.

Acknowledgments

We would like to thank Mr. Raylin Tso, Mr. Tadahiko Ito and Mr. Seichi Matsuda for helpful discussions.

References

1. D. Boneh and M. Franklin, *Identity-based encryption from the Weil pairing*, Advances in cryptology –CRYPTO'01, Lecture Notes in Comput Sci. **2139** (2001), 213–229.

2. R. Blom, *An optimal class of symmetric key generation systems*, Advances in cryptology –Eurocrypt'84, Lecture Notes in Comput Sci. **209** (1984), 335–338.

3. D. Boneh, B. Lynn, and H. Shacham, *Short signatures from the Weil pairing*, Advances in cryptology – ASIACRYPT 2001, Lecture Notes in Comput Sci. **2248** (2001), 514-532.

4. P. Barreto, H. Kim, B. Lynn, and M. Scott, *Efficient lgorithms for Pairing-Based Cryptosystems*, Advances in cryptology – CRYPTO 2002, LLecture Notes in Comput Sci. **2442**, (2002), 354-368.

5. W. Diffie and M. E. Hellman, *New directions in cryptography*, IEEE Transactions on Information Theory. **22** (1976), 644–654.

6. C. Gentry and A. Silvergerg, *Hierarchical ID based cryptography*, Advances in cryptology –ASIACRYPTO'02, Lecture Notes in Comput Sci. **2501** (2002), 548–566.

7. F. Hess, *Efficient identity based signature schemes based on pairings*, Selected Areas in Cryptolography–SAC'02, Lecture Notes in Comput Sci. **2595** (2003), 310–324.

8. A. Joux, *A one-round protocol for tripartite Diffie-Hellman*, Algorithm Number Theory Symposium (ANTS), Lecture Notes in Comput Sci. **1838** (2000), 385–394.

9. A. Menezes, T. Okamoto and S. Vanstone, *Reducing elliptic curve logarithms to logarithms in a finite field*, The Annual ACM Symposium on Theory of Computing (STOC), ACM Press (1991), 80–89.

10. S. Ohgishi, R. Sakai and M. Kasahara, *IDNIKS using Weil-Tate pairing* Research Interest Group on Cryptography and Information Security (ISEC) The Institute of Electronics, Information and Communication Engineers, Japan (IEICE), (1999).

11. E. Okamoto and K. Tanaka, *Key distribution systems based on identification information*, Advances in cryptology –CRYPTO'87, Lecture Notes in Comput Sci. **293** (1987), 194–202.

12. A. Shamir, *Identity-based cryptosystems and signature schemes*, Advances in cryptology – CRYPTO'84, Lecture Notes in Comput Sci. **196** (1985), 47–53.

13. R. Sakai, K. Ohgishi and M. Kasahara, *Cryptosystems based on pairing*, Symp. on Cryptography and Information Security, Okinawa, Japan, Jan. 26–28, 2000.

14. F. Zhang, R. Safavi-Naini and W. Susilo, "An Efficient Signature Scheme from Bilinear Parings and Its Applications," PKC 2004, LNCS 2947, pp.277-290, 2004.

Building a Brain-Informatics Portal
on the Wisdom Web with a Multi-layer Grid:
A New Challenge for Web Intelligence Research

Ning Zhong

The International WIC Institute &
Department of Information Engineering
Maebashi Institute of Technology
460-1 Kamisadori-Cho, Maebashi-City 371-0816, Japan
zhong@maebashi-it.ac.jp

Abstract. Web Intelligence (WI) presents excellent opportunities and
challenges for the research and development of new generation of Web-
based information processing technology, as well as for exploiting Web-
based advanced applications. In this paper, we give a new perspective
of WI research: Web Intelligence meets Brain Informatics. We observe
that new instrumentation (fMRI etc.) and advanced IT are causing an
impending revolution in WI and Brain Sciences (BS). We propose a way
to build a Brain-Informatics portal by using WI technologies, which is
of great benefit to both WI and BS researches.

1 Introduction

The concept of Web Intelligence (WI for short) was first introduced in our papers and books [11, 23, 25–27, 29]. Broadly speaking, Web Intelligence is a new
direction for scientific research and development that explores the fundamental
roles as well as practical impacts of Artificial Intelligence (AI)[1] and advanced
Information Technology (IT) on the next generation of Web-empowered systems, services, and environments. The WI technologies revolutionize the way in
which information is gathered, stored, processed, presented, shared, and used by
virtualization, globalization, standardization, personalization, and portals.

In our previous paper [23], we gave perspectives of WI research:

> WI may be reviewed as applying results from existing disciplines (AI and
> IT) to a totally new domain; WI introduces new problems and challenges
> to the established disciplines; WI may be considered as an enhancement
> or an extension of AI and IT.

In this paper, we give a new perspective of WI research: *Web Intelligence meets
Brain Informatics.*

---

[1] Here the term of AI includes classical AI, computational intelligence, and soft computing etc.

V. Torra et al. (Eds.): MDAI 2005, LNAI 3558, pp. 24–35, 2005.

Brain Informatics (BI) is a new interdisciplinary field to study human information processing mechanism systematically from both macro and micro points of view by cooperatively using experimental brain/cognitive technology and WI centric advanced information technology. In particular, it attempts to understand human intelligence in depth, towards a holistic view at a long-term, global field of vision, to understand the principle, models and mechanisms of human multi-perception, reasoning and inference, problem solving, learning, discovery and creativity [34].

The paper investigates how to build a brain-informatics portal on the Wisdom Web with a multi-layer grid, which is of great benefit to both WI and Brain Sciences researches. The rest of the paper is organized as follows. Section 2 provides a new perspective of WI research in detail. Section 3 discusses multiple human brain data analysis. Section 4 describes how to develop a brain-informatics portal by using WI technologies. Finally, Section 5 gives concluding remarks.

2   A New Perspective of WI Research

New instrumentation (fMRI etc.) and advanced IT are causing an impending revolution in WI and Brain Sciences. This revolution is bi-directional:

- The WI based portal techniques will provide a new powerful platform for Brain Sciences.
- The new understanding and discovery of the human intelligence models in Brain Sciences will yield a new generation of WI research and development.

The first aspect means that WI technologies provide an agent based multi-database mining grid architecture on the Wisdom Web for building a brain-informatics portal [31, 34]. A conceptual model with three levels of workflows, corresponding to a grid with three-layers, namely data-grid, mining-grid, and knowledge-grid, respectively, is utilized to manage, represent, integrate, analyze, and utilize the information coming from multiple, huge data and knowledge sources. Furthermore, the Wisdom Web based computing will provide not only a medium for seamless information exchange and knowledge sharing, but also a type of man-made resources for sustainable knowledge creation, and scientific and social evolution. The Wisdom Web will rely on *grid-like agencies* that self-organize, learn, and evolve their courses of actions in order to perform service tasks as well as their identities and interrelationships in communities [11, 28]. The proposed methodology attempts to change the perspective of brain/cognitive scientists from a single type of experimental data analysis towards a holistic view at a long-term, global field of vision.

The second aspect of the new perspective on WI means that the new generation of WI research and development needs to understand multiple natures of intelligence in depth, by studying integrately the three intelligence research related areas: machine intelligence, human intelligence, and social intelligence, as shown in Fig. 1. Machine intelligence has been mainly studied as computer based technologies for the development of intelligent knowledge based systems; Human intelligence studies the nature of intelligence towards our understanding of intelligence; Social intelligence needs a combination of machine intelligence and human intelligence for establishing social networks that contain communities of people, organizations, or other social entities [28]. Furthermore, the Web is regarded as a social network in which the Web connects a set of people (or organizations or other social entities). People are connected by a set of social relationships, such as friendship, co-working or information exchange with common interests. In other words, it is a Web-supported social network or called virtual community. In this sense, the study of Web Intelligence is of social network intelligence (social intelligence for short).

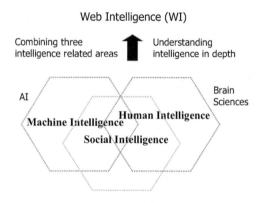

Fig. 1. The relationship between WI and other three intelligence related research areas

A good example is the development and use of a Web-based problem-solving system for portal-centralized, adaptable Web services [11, 20, 28, 29]. The core of such a system is the Problem Solver Markup Language (PSML) and PSML-based distributed Web inference engines, in which the following support functions should be provided since this is a must for developing intelligent portals.

- The expressive power and functional support in PSML for complex adaptive, distributed problem solving;
- Performing automatic reasoning on the Web by incorporating globally distributed contents and meta-knowledge automatically collected and transformed from the Semantic Web and social networks with locally operational knowledge-data bases;
- Representing and organizing multiple, huge knowledge-data sources for distributed Web inference and reasoning.

In order to develop such a Web based problem-solving system, we need to better understand how human being does complex adaptive (distributed) problem solving and reasoning, as well as how intelligence evolves for individuals and societies, over time and place [19, 20, 24].

More specifically, we will investigate ways by discussing the following issues:

- How to design fMRI/EEG experiments to understand the principle of human inference/reasoning and problem solving in depth?
- How to implement human-level inference/reasoning and problem solving on the Web based portals that can serve users wisely?

We will describe our endeavor in this direction, in particular, we will show that grid-based multi-aspect analysis in multiple knowledge and data sources on the Wisdom Web is an important way to investigate human intelligence mechanism, systematically.

3   Multiple Human Brain Data Analysis

As a crucial step in understanding human intelligence, we must first fully master the mechanisms in which human brain operates. The results reported, over the last decade, about studying human information processing mechanism, are greatly related to the progress of measurement and analysis technologies. Various noninvasive brain functional measurements are available recently, such as fMRI and EEG. If these measured data are analyzed systematically, the relationship between a state and an activity part will become clear. It is useful to discover more advanced human cognitive models based on such measurements and analysis. Hence, new instrumentation and new information technology are causing a revolution in both AI and Brain Sciences. The synergy between AI and Brain Sciences will yield profound advances in our understanding of intelligence over the coming decade [17, 19].

In recent papers [18, 32], we have reported an approach for modeling, transforming, and mining multiple human brain data obtained from visual and auditory psychological experiments by using fMRI and EEG. We observed that each method (fMRI and EEG) has its own strength and weakness from the aspects of time and space resolution. fMRI provides images of functional brain activity to observe dynamic activity patterns within different parts of the brain for a given task. It is excellent in the space resolution, but inferior time resolution. On the other hand, EEG provides information about the electrical fluctuations between neurons that also characterize brain activity, and measurements of brain activity at resolutions approaching real time. Hence, in order to discover new knowledge and models of human multi-perception activities, not only individual data source obtained from only single measuring method, but multiple data sources from various practical measuring methods are required.

It is also clear that the future of cognitive science and brain science may be affected by the ability to do large-scale mining of fMRI and EEG brain activations. The key issues are how to design the psychological and physiological experiments for obtaining various data from human information processing mechanism, as well as how to analyze such data from multiple aspects for discovering new models of human information processing. Although several human-expert centric tools such as SPM (MEDx) have been developed for cleaning, normalizing and visualizing the fMRI images, researchers have also been studying how the fMRI images can be automatically analyzed and understood by using data mining and statistical learning techniques. Megalooikonomou and colleagues proposed an interesting method for mining associations between lesioned structures and concomitant neurological or neuropsychological deficits [14–16]. Their method can deal with the morphological variability that exists between subjects, and is scalable so that large longitudinal studies can be performed. Tsukimoto and colleagues developed a novel method for mining classification rules by dividing brain images into meshes as condition attributes, and treating functions as classes [22]. Thus, such rules as "if mesh A and mesh B are active, then some function is positive" can be found. Their method consists of two steps: (1) a nonparametric regression is applied on the training data and (2) rules are extracted from the regression formula obtained by the regression analysis. Mitchell and colleagues classified instantaneous cognitive states using a Gaussian Naive Bayes classifier to predict the human subject's cognitive state given their observed fMRI data [17]. Furthermore, spectral analysis [1] and wavelet analysis [7] are the main stream as the frequency analysis methods of EEG brain waves.

We are concerned to extract significant features from multiple brain data measured by using fMRI and EEG in preparation for multi-aspect data mining that uses various data mining techniques for analyzing multiple data sources. Our purpose is to understand activities of human information processing by

- investigating the features of fMRI brain images and EEG brain waves for every state or part;
- studying the neural structures of the activated areas to understand how a peculiar part of the brain operates and how it is linked functionally to individual differences in performance.

As a step in this direction, we observe that fMRI brain imaging data and EEG brain wave data extracted from human information processing mechanism are *peculiar* ones with respect to a specific state or the related part of a stimulus. Based on this point of view, we propose a way of *peculiarity oriented mining* for knowledge discovery in multiple human brain data, without using conventional imaging processing to fMRI brain images and frequency analysis to EEG brain waves [18, 32, 35]. The proposed approach provides a new way for automatic analysis and understanding of fMRI brain images and EEG brain waves to replace human-expert centric visualization. The mining process is a multi-step one, in which various psychological experiments, physiological measurements, data cleaning, modeling, transforming, and mining techniques are cooperatively employed to investigate human information processing mechanism.

4   A Brain-Informatics Portal Architecture

In the paper [34], we proposed an agent based multi-database mining grid architecture on the Wisdom Web for a brain-informatics portal. As shown in Fig. 2, there are two main parts of the system based on such an architecture: the Wisdom Web and the multi-layer grid.

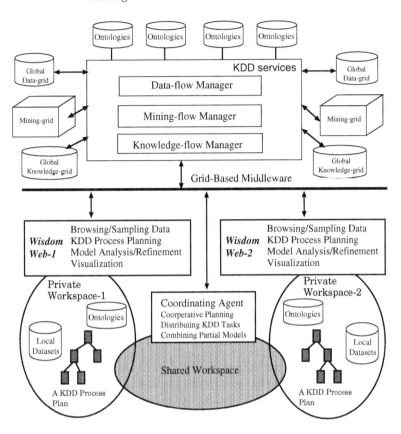

Fig. 2. A multi-database mining grid architecture on the Wisdom Web for a brain-informatics portal

The notion of the Wisdom Web was first introduced in [10, 11, 28]. We argue that the next paradigm shift in the Web is towards *wisdom* and developing the Wisdom Web will become a tangible goal for Web Intelligence research. The Wisdom Web based computing will provide not only a medium for seamless information exchange and knowledge sharing, but also a type of man-made resources for sustainable knowledge creation, and scientific and social evolution. The Wisdom Web will rely on *grid-like agencies* that self-organize, learn, and evolve their courses of actions in order to perform service tasks as well as their identities and interrelationships in communities.

A new platform as *middleware* is required to deal with multiple huge, distributed data sources for multi-aspect analysis in building an e-science portal on the Wisdom Web. Our methodology is to create a grid-based, organized society of data mining agents, called a *data mining grid* on the Grid computing platform (e.g. the Globus toolkit) [3, 4, 6]. This means:

– developing various data mining agents, for various services oriented multi-aspect data analysis;

- organizing the data mining agents into a grid with multiple layers such as data-grid, mining-grid, and knowledge-grid, under the OGSA (Open Grid Services Architecture) that firmly aligns with service-oriented architecture and Web services, to understand the user's questions, transform them to data mining issues, discover the resources and information about the issues, and get a composite answer or solution;
- using a conceptual model with three levels of workflows, namely data-flow, mining-flow, and knowledge-flow, corresponding to the three-layer grid, respectively, for managing data mining agents for multi-aspect analysis in distributed, multiple data sources and for organizing the dynamic, status-based e-science processes.

That is, the data mining grid is made of many smaller components that are called *data mining agents*. Each agent by itself can only do some simple thing. Yet when joining these agents on the multi-layer grid, more complex e-science tasks can be implemented.

4.1   The RVER Model and Ontologies

Based on the Wisdom Web and the Grid platform, a key question is how to represent and learn in a cluster of multiple data sources that are incompatible, not only in format but also in terms and wording used. We use the RVER (Reverse Variant Entity-Relationship) model to represent the conceptual relationships among various types of interesting data (including peculiar data) mined from multiple data sources [30]. Furthermore, the advanced rules hidden in inter-multiple data sources can be learned from the RVER model.

Besides the RVER model, ontologies are also used for description and integration of multi-data source and data mining agents in data mining (KDD) process planning [26, 27]. It is necessary to provide:

- a formal, explicit specification for integrated use of multiple data sources in a semantic way;
- a conceptual representation about the sorts and properties of data/knowledge and data mining agents, as well as relations between data/knowledge and data mining agents;
- a vocabulary of terms and relations to model the domain, and specifying how to view the data sources and how to use data mining agents;
- a common understanding of multiple data sources that can be communicated between data mining agents.

4.2   Multi-agent Support for the Wisdom Web

As stated above, the proposed brain-informatics portal is a multi-agent based one, in which at least the following four types of meta agents are required [9]:

- *Assistant agents*: assisting e-science users in various work, such as browsing and sampling data, planning data mining (knowledge discovery and data mining) process, analyzing/refining models on the Wisdom Web.

- *Interacting agents*: helping users in their cooperative work such as communication, negotiation, coordination, and mediation.
- *Mobile agents*: the mining tool that can move to global data grid services and execute within the data grids (multi-site and multi-owner data repositories).
- *System agents*: the administration of multiple data mining agents such as, to register and manage large numbers of components; to monitor events and status of the Workspaces as well as the AgentMeetingPlaces (see below), and to collect relevant measurement according predefined metrics.

In such a multi-agent architecture, an agent is a piece of software created by and acting on behalf of users (or some other agents). It is set up to achieve a modest goal, with the characteristics of autonomy, interaction, reactivity to environment, as well as pro-activeness.

Furthermore, within the architecture as shown in Fig. 2, the main components are interconnected and interoperated as follows:

- *Set up Workspaces*: In a large data mining process, we can perceive various groups of people working as a team. Each e-science person has his/her private Workspace, and the group has a share Workspace. There are controlling Workspaces where the managing, controlling and scheduling people (or their agents) work. They are responsible for the overall cooperative planning for the current e-science project (while other e-science people plan their own part of e-science tasks), for accessing to global databases, and for distributing real data analysis tasks to *computational grids* according to some resource allocation policy.
- *Create agents*: Various data mining agents are created dynamically according to the e-science task and the data mining process; Interacting agents are created for communication purpose; Mobile agents are created and sent to perform data mining tasks within data grids; and system agents are created by default to manage various components in the architecture.
- Communication between agent groups is via AgentMeetingPlaces (AMPs). Some system agents are created by default to manage the AMP (creation, deletion, and bookkeeping).
- Repositories can be global, local to one person or a group of people, or distributed. For the data and model repositories, we mention that: (1) Local databases and model repositories can be accessed from associated Workspaces; (2) Global data grids can be accessed only from controlling Workspaces where the controlling and scheduling people (or their agents) work. (3) Mobile agents can travel to global data grids and execute there.
- Within a Workspace, any existing data mining process models are allowed. For example, the planning and replanning techniques described in [26] can be applied to them.

4.3 Distributed PSML and Web Inference Engine

PSML needs to solve problems by constraints and situation based network reasoning in a large-scale distributed Web environment. The information on the brain-informatics portal can be organized on the data and knowledge grids with multi-layer and multi-level [8], as shown in Fig. 2. Here meta-knowledge is composed of experience knowledge and heuristic knowledge and is used for classifying and separating the query to sub-queries [20]. A query described with PSML will consist of two parts: one part is to describe the problem, and the other part presents constraints that will be useful to solve the problem. To express our idea clearly, we turn to introduce the structure of the nodes on the Web in distributed environment. Each node has an inference engine and a knowledge-base. There are three kinds of knowledge in the knowledge-base: meta-knowledge, constraint knowledge and domain knowledge, respectively. When a node in the distributed environment receives a query, the node classifies and separates the query into sub-queries with its meta-knowledge, solves some of them with its domain knowledge, and assigns others to its neighbors with its constraint knowledge. The constraint knowledge is formed by accumulated experience. Every neighbor handles the sub-queries in the similar way and the process continue until the nodes solve all sub-queries they received, and return the sub-answers recursively. When all the neighbors of the original node return answers of the sub-queries, the node combines them into the answer of the original query and returns it to the user. The answer may be incomplete because some sub-queries cannot be transferred to neighbors according to constraint knowledge.

As discussed in the papers [20, 21], ontologies represented in OWL can be easily translated to PSML. From the viewpoint of agents, the PSML functional support for complex adaptive, distributed problem solving is realized by using contents and meta-knowledge collection and transformation agents. These agents receive messages in PSML format and they are associated with the ontologies in the knowledge base that determine their domains of interest. It means that each agent is identified by its associated domain. Note that these agents are not isolated but cooperating together. When performing complex queries, a query needs to be decomposed into sub-queries. Then these sub-queries can be solved by using more agents that are distributed on the Web. Thus the decomposition of the query leads to design the distributed multi-agent cooperative system. The complex queries can be also formulated into distributed constraint satisfaction problems [12, 33].

There are also other problems needed to be considered such as uncertainty inference, combining various reasoning methods (e.g. deduction, inheritance, association, and case-based reasoning) in PSML more efficiently and effectively for complex adaptive, distributed problem solving.

5   Conclusion

In the paper, we gave a new perspective of WI research and proposed a way for building a Brain-Informatics portal on the Wisdom Web with a multi-layer grid. The proposed methodology attempts to change the perspective of brain/cognitive scientists from a single type of experimental data analysis towards a holistic view at a long-term, global field of vision. Furthermore, the new generation of

WI research and development needs to understand multiple natures of intelligence in depth. New instrumentation (fMRI etc.) and advanced IT are causing an impending revolution in WI and Brain Sciences.

Acknowledgments

I would like to thank Jiming Liu, Yiyu Yao, and Jinglong Wu who are my colleagues introduced Web Intelligence (WI) and Brain Informatics (BI) with me together. The contents of this paper include their contributions. I am very grateful to people who have joined or supported the WI community, members of the WIC advisory board, WIC technical committee, and WIC research centres, as well as keynote/invited speakers of WI-IAT conferences, in particular, N. Cercone, J. Bradshaw, B.B. Faltings, E.A. Feigenbaum, G. Gottlob, J. Hendler, W.L. Johnson, C. Kesselman, V. Lesser, J. McCarthy, T.M. Mitchell, S. Ohsuga, P. Raghavan, Z.W. Ras, A. Skowron, K. Sycara, B. Wah, P.S.P. Wang, M. Wooldridge, X. Wu, P.S. Yu, and L.A. Zadeh. I thank them for their strong support. Special thanks to V. Torra, S. Miyamoto, Y. Narukawa, and other organizers of MDAI 2005 for the kind invitation and the excellent organization.

References

1. J.P. Banquet, "Spectral Analysis of the EEG in Meditation", *Electroencephalography and Clinical Neurophysiology*, 35, (1973) 143-151.
2. J. Banfield and A. Raftery, "Model-based Gaussian and Non-Gaussian Clustering", Biometrics, 49 (1993) 803-821.
3. M. Cannataro and D. Talia, "The Knowledge Grid", *CACM*, 46 (2003) 89-93.
4. F. Berman, "From TeraGrid to Knowledge Grid", *CACM*, 44 (2001) 27-28.
5. S. Cerutti, G. Chiarenza, D. Liberati, P. Mascellani, and G. Pavesi, "A Parametric Method of Identification of Single Trial Event-related Potentials in the Brain", *IEEE Trans. Biomed. Eng.*, 35(9) (1988) 701-711.
6. I. Foster and C. Kesselman (eds.) *The Grid: Blueprint for a New Computing Infrastructure*, Morgan Kaufmann (1999).
7. R. Hornero, M. Martin-Fernandez, A. Alonso, A. Izquierdo, and M. Lopez, "A DSP Implementation of Wavelet Transform to Detect Epileptiform Activity in the EEG", *Proc. 8th Annual International Conference on Signal Processing Applications and Technology*, ICAPAT'97 (1997) 692-696.
8. J. Hu, and N. Zhong, "Organizing Dynamic Multi-level Workflows on Multi-layer Grids for e-Business Portals Development", *Proc. 2005 IEEE International Conference on e-Technology, e-Commerce and e-Service (EEE'05)*, IEEE Press (2005) 196-201.
9. C. Liu, N. Zhong, and S. Ohsuga, "A Multi-agent Based Architecture for Distributed KDD Process", Z.W. Ras and S. Ohsuga (eds.) *Foundations of Intelligent Systems*. LNAI 1932, Springer (2000) 591-600.
10. J. Liu, N. Zhong, Y.Y. Yao, and Z.W. Ras, "The Wisdom Web: New Challenges for Web Intelligence (WI)", *Journal of Intelligent Information Systems*, 20(1) Kluwer (2003) 5-9.

11. J. Liu, "Web Intelligence (WI): What Makes Wisdom Web?", *Proc. Eighteenth International Joint Conference on Artificial Intelligence (IJCAI'03)* (2003) 1596-1601.

12. J. Liu, X. Jin, and Y. Tang, "Multi-agent Collaborative Service and Distributed Problem Solving", *Cognitive Systems Research*, 5(3): 191-206, Elsevier, 2004.

13. J. McCarthy, "Roads to Human Level AI?", Keynote Talk at Beijing University of Technology, Beijing, China, September 2004.

14. V. Megalooikonomou, C. Davatzikos, and E.H. Herskovits, "Mining Lesion-Deficit Associations in a Brain Image Database", *Proc. Fifth International Conference on Knowledge Discovery and Data Mining (KDD'99)*, ACM Press (1999) 347-351.

15. V. Megalooikonomou, J. Ford, L. Shen, F. Makedon, and A. Saykin, "Data Mining in Brain Imaging", *Statistical Methods in Medical Research*, 9 (2000) 359-394.

16. V. Megalooikonomou and E.H. Herskovits, "Mining Structure-Function Associations in a Brain Image Database", K.J. Cios (ed.) *Medical Data Mining and Knowledge Discovery*, Physica-Verlag (2001) 153-179.

17. T.M. Mitchell, R. Hutchinson, M. Just, R.S. Niculescu, F. Pereira, and X. Wang, "Classifying Instantaneous Cognitive States from fMRI Data", *Proc. American Medical Informatics Association Annual Symposium* (2003) 465-469.

18. S. Motomura, N. Zhong, and J.L. Wu, "Brain Waves Data Mining for Human Multi-perception Activity Analysis", *Proc. Inter. Workshop on Advanced Technologies for e-Learning and e-Science (ATELS'04)* (2004) 65-72.

19. R.J. Sternberg, J. Lautrey, and T.I. Lubart, *Models of Intelligence*, American Psychological Association (2003).

20. Y. Su, L. Zheng, N. Zhong, C. Liu, and J. Liu, "Distributed Reasoning Based on Problem Solver Markup Language (PSML): A Demonstration through Extended OWL", *Proc. 2005 IEEE International Conference on e-Technology, e-Commerce and e-Service (EEE'05)*, IEEE Press (2005) 208-213.

21. K. Tomita, N. Zhong, and H. Yamauchi, "Coupling Global Semantic Web with Local Information Sources for Problem Solving", *Proc. First International Workshop on Semantic Web Mining and Reasoning (SWMR'04)* (2004) 66-74.

22. H. Tsukimoto and C. Morita, "The Discovery of Rules from Brain Images", *Proc. First Inter. Conf. on Discovery Science*, LNAI 1532, Springer (1998) 198-209.

23. Y.Y. Yao, N. Zhong, J. Liu, and S. Ohsuga, "Web Intelligence (WI): Research Challenges and Trends in the New Information Age", N. Zhong, Y.Y. Yao, J. Liu, S. Ohsuga (eds.) *Web Intelligence: Research and Development*, LNAI 2198, Springer (2001) 1-17.

24. L.A. Zadeh, "Precisiated Natural Language (PNL)", *AI Magazine*, 25(3) (Fall 2004) 74-91.

25. N. Zhong, J. Liu, Y.Y. Yao, and S. Ohsuga, "Web Intelligence (WI)", *Proc. 24th IEEE Computer Society International Computer Software and Applications Conference (COMPSAC 2000)*, (IEEE CS Press, 2000) 469-470

26. N. Zhong, C. Liu, and S. Ohsuga, "Dynamically Organizing KDD Process", *International Journal of Pattern Recognition and Artificial Intelligence*, Vol. 15, No. 3, World Scientific (2001) 451-473.

27. N. Zhong, "Representation and Construction of Ontologies for Web Intelligence", *International Journal of Foundations of Computer Science*, World Scientific, Vol.13, No.4 (2002) 555-570.

28. N. Zhong, J. Liu, and Y.Y. Yao, "In Search of the Wisdom Web", *IEEE Computer*, 35(11) (2002) 27-31.

29. N. Zhong, J. Liu, and Y.Y. Yao (eds.) *Web Intelligence*, Springer, 2003.

30. N. Zhong, Y.Y. Yao, and M. Ohshima, "Peculiarity Oriented Multi-Database Mining", *IEEE Transaction on Knowlegde and Data Engineering*, Vol.15, No. 4 (2003) 952-960.

31. N. Zhong, "Developing Intelligent Portals by Using WI Technologies", J.P. Li et al. (eds.) *Wavelet Analysis and Its Applications, and Active Media Technology*, Vol. 2, World Scientific (2004) 555-567.

32. N. Zhong, J.L. Wu, A. Nakamaru, M. Ohshima, and H. Mizuhara, "Peculiarity Oriented fMRI Brain Data Analysis for Studying Human Multi-Perception Mechanism", *Cognitive Systems Research*, 5(3), Elsevier (2004) 241-256.

33. N. Zhong, and J. Liu (eds.) *Intelligent Technologies for Information Analysis*, Springer, 2004.

34. N. Zhong, J. Hu, S. Motomura, J.L. Wu, and C. Liu, "Building a Data Mining Grid for Multiple Human Brain Data Analysis", *Computational Intelligence*, 21(2), Blackwell Publishing (2005) 177-196.

35. N. Zhong, S. Motomura, and J.L. Wu, "Peculiarity Oriented Multi-Aspect Brain Data Analysis for Studying Human Multi-Perception Mechanism", *Proc. SAINT 2005 Workshops (Workshop 8: Computer Intelligence for Exabyte Scale Data Explosion)*, IEEE Computer Society Press, (2005) 306-309.

Soft Computing in Human Centered Systems Thinking

Takehisa Onisawa

Graduate School of Systems and Information Engineering, University of Tsukuba
1-1-1, Tennodai, Tsukuba, 305-8573 Japan
onisawa@esys.tsukuba.ac.jp

Abstract. This paper describes human centered systems in which human evaluation, decision, interpretation, feelings, subjectivity play important roles. One of useful approaches to human centered systems thinking is soft computing techniques that permit uncertainty of information since a real world is complex and it is difficult and wasteful to deal with its information strictly. This paper also introduces some examples of human centered systems, a music composition support system, a story generation system from pictures, a facial caricature drawing system and a pedestrian navigation system.

1 Introduction

What are human centered systems? Many types of human centered systems can be considered. For example, networks systems are human centered systems in the sense that human is in the center of networks systems. In this paper, however, human centered systems are defined as systems in which human evaluation, human decision, human interpretation, human feelings, human subjectivity play central roles. Although conventional natural science has been developed based on concepts of objectivity, uniqueness, universality and reproducibility, human evaluation, interpretation, feelings, subjectivity cannot be necessarily dealt with based on these concepts since human information processing is performed based on subjectivity, ambiguity and fuzziness, and human decision making is sometimes dependent on the situation in which human is. Subjectivity, ambiguity, fuzziness and situation dependency are opposite to objectivity, uniqueness, universality and reproducibility. Therefore, the approach to human studies should not be based on the same paradigm which conventional natural science is based on.

The soft computing techniques [1] are proposed to deal with real world information, which permit inaccuracy of information at the sacrifice of its accuracy since real world is complex and it is difficult to deal with real world information in the way that seeks correctness and strictness of information completely. The soft computing techniques are considered as the total technology of fuzzy theory, genetic algorithms, neural network modeling, probabilistic reasoning, learning theory, etc. [2] Fuzzy theory, genetic algorithms, neural network modeling, probabilistic reasoning, learning theory have both advantages and disadvantages for dealing with real world information and the soft computing techniques complement their disadvantages [2]. The soft computing techniques become necessary as the approach that does not necessarily seek correctness and strictness of human information processing in human studies.

This paper discusses subjectivity, ambiguity, vagueness and situation dependence in human centered systems in which human evaluation, interpretation, feelings and subjectivity play central roles. This paper also claims that the approach to human

V. Torra et al. (Eds.): MDAI 2005, LNAI 3558, pp. 36–46, 2005.

centered systems thinking should be tolerant of subjectivity, ambiguity, vagueness and situation dependency in information and that human centered systems should reflect user's own evaluation, feelings, subjectivity. In this sense the soft computing techniques are appropriate for the human centered systems thinking. This paper also introduces some examples of human centered systems.

2 Human Centered Systems

Human interpretation or evaluation of information is not always the same and is dependent on human who receives it. Even if the same person receives the same information, his/her interpretation or evaluation is dependent on the situation in which human receives it. Let us consider human as a system and its input-output relation as shown in Fig.1. In this figure, image information, music information or text information is considered as input information. And human interpretation, evaluation, feelings are considered as system outputs. Even if same music information, same image information or same text information is inputted into this system (human), same output information is not always obtained since human subjectivity or a situation in which human receives the information is not always the same. Let f, X, Y, and S be an input-output relation of this system, its input information, its output information and its states, respectively. Let human subjectivity and/or human situation be considered as systems states. The input-output relation is expressed by

$$Y = f(X, S). \tag{1}$$

Although the input-output relation seems to be simple from the mathematical equation point of view, it is difficult to express S concretely since human subjectivity, evaluation, feelings, interpretation cannot be expressed easily by mathematical equations. This paper calls a system with Eq. (1) as human centered systems, where human feelings, subjectivity, situation are expressed by S. This chapter discusses subjectivity, ambiguity, vagueness, and situation dependency in human centered systems.

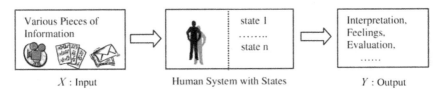

Various Pieces of Information	state 1 .... state n	Interpretation, Feelings, Evaluation, ...
X : Input	Human System with States	Y : Output

Fig. 1. Human as a System

2.1 Subjectivity

Objectivity is based on the standpoint that it is reasonable for everyone. Conventional natural science pursues objectivity. Even human intelligent information is dealt with objectively in artificial intelligence. According to the conventional information processing only objective information is considered even in a human system shown in Fig.1. However, if some information is assumed to be inputted into human itself, which is considered as a human system shown in Fig.1, it is reasonable to consider that human evaluation, decision, feelings, interpretation for inputted information are dependent on human who receives it since it is the problem of subjectivity.

Subjectivity is opposite concept of objectivity and based on the standpoint that it is reasonable only for some individual or some group whether it is good or not for other people or other group. Although a 175cm tall person recognizes a 185cm tall person as tall, a 200cm tall person recognizes a 185cm tall person as a short person. Then, does a 175cm tall person recognize a 180cm tall person as tall? It is a matter of subjective degree. There are many discussions on appropriateness that subjectivity is introduced to the science and engineering field. At the dawn of fuzzy theory [3], fuzzy theory met with severe criticisms from many researchers. That is, subjectivity should not be introduced to the science and engineering field. However, there are no systems that have no relation to human. It becomes necessary to consider human subjectivity in systems thinking. Especially, human subjectivity cannot help being excluded from human centered systems thinking since human subjectivity plays central roles in human centered systems. Even in Kansei information processing [4] or Kansei engineering [5] dealing with human feelings information, human subjectivity should be considered since human feelings information, i.e., Kansei information, is related to human subjectivity itself.

2.2 Ambiguity

The concept of objectivity is associated with that of uniqueness. Natural science has been developed based on uniqueness with an idea that we have only one objectively correct solution from one sense of values. The sense of values means, for example, a system of axioms in mathematics. We have only one interpretation about a theorem that is led from a system of axioms. If a theorem led from a system of axioms is interpreted from various points of view, mathematics is not developed. There is only one viewpoint from one sense of values.

On the other hand, the concept of subjectivity is associated with that of ambiguity. The concept of ambiguity means that the interpretation of image information, music information, or text information is dependent on a person or the situation of a person who gets these pieces of information. Diverse senses of values depending on subjectivity yield ambiguity. Therefore, it is unreasonable that human information interpretation is restricted by only one sense of values. Divers senses of values should be tolerated in such a human system as shown in Fig.1. Permission of ambiguity means permission of diverse senses of values. Only one sense of values yields uniqueness and we have only one objectively correct solution in problem solving. On the other hand, diverse senses of values permit various interpretations or different evaluations in problem solving. That is, we do not always have only one correct solution in problem solving or there is a possibility that we can have various types of correct solutions in problem solving. A local optimal solution should be accepted as a good solution in the system thinking that permits diverse senses of values so long as human is satisfied with it. The idea of only one objectively optimal solution should be excluded from human centered systems thinking.

Since human subjectivity, decision, evaluation, interpretation and feelings play central roles in human centered systems thinking, ambiguity yielding from diverse senses of values is permitted in human centered systems thinking. Fig.2 shows the concept of ambiguity, i.e., the concept of diverse senses of values.

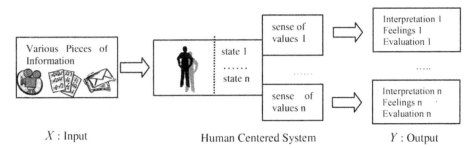

X : Input   Human Centered System Y : Output

Fig. 2. Concept of Diverse of Senses of Values

2.3 Vagueness

If an objective system has a clear causal relation or a clear input-output relation, the system has surely a regular effect for a cause or a regular output for an input according to its relation. This idea leads to the concept of universality. Then, let us consider human instead of the system. Is it reasonable that human has a regular input-output relation? Even if human has not a regular input-output relation, a human may have some input-output relation with his/her own peculiarity. However, human does not always make a decision, or have evaluation based on the same relation. Human sometimes makes a decision that is different from the one he/she does on the previous day. In this situation he/she seems to have an incoherent input-output relation. From his/her own points of view, however, he/she has input-output relations based on his/her own diverse senses of values. Then, where is vagueness from in a causal relation or in an input-output relation that human has? One is from human subjectivity. The other is from ambiguity that means diverse senses of values. Imprecision from error or inconsistency may be also related to vagueness. In either case it is difficult to express vagueness by the mathematical way.

It is necessary to permit vagueness having relation to subjectivity and diverse senses of values in human centered systems thinking since human subjectivity, evaluation, feelings, interpretation play central roles in human centered systems.

2.4 Situation Dependence

It is assumed that an objective system has some regular input-output relation under some fixed condition. Therefore, the system has an output corresponding to an input-output relation and an input. This is a basic idea of conventional natural science. However, the approach to information processing in a human system shown in Fig.1 is not well done in this framework since the framework does not permit subjectivity, ambiguity and vagueness, and, furthermore, since human subjectivity, evaluation, feelings, interpretation are dependent on situations in which a human system is. It is unreasonable that a human system is considered under only a fixed situation. Situations under which human as a system is have influence on a human state of mind. Not only an input but also situations have much influence on human as a system. This means that human centered systems are surely situation dependence.

If situations abovementioned are expressed by system state S, the situation dependence is expressed by Eq. (1). From the viewpoint of human centered systems, system state S is regarded as situations including senses of values, human subjectivity, feelings, etc. Therefore, even if input X is the same, output Y is dependent on system state S as Eq. (2) shows. From the conventional natural science framework point of view, the division of situations could analyze the system (1) since the conventional ways are based on analysis and synthesis. However, it is usually impossible to divide situations into in detail in human centered systems and many situations cannot be eliminated from the analysis since they have influence on the systems one another.

$$Y_1 = F(X, S_1)$$
$$Y_2 = F(X, S_2)$$
$$S_1 \neq S_2 \implies Y_1 \neq Y_2$$
(2)

3 Some Examples of Human Centered Systems

A system structure shown in Fig.3 is considered as one of human centered systems. This structure shows that a system in human centered systems learns human by the interaction with human about interpretation, evaluation of system's output, and then a system becomes the one reflecting human user's own individuality. In the conventional learning approach, some evaluation functions are prepared and a solution is obtained so that the values of evaluation functions become optimal. It is difficult, however, to define evaluation functions in human centered systems. Therefore, human centered systems have a system structure in which human plays a central role. As mentioned in Section 2, however, human has subjectivity, ambiguity, vagueness and situation dependence. Therefore, human centered systems should deal with these characteristics of human. The soft computing techniques are considered as one of suitable approaches to human centered systems in the sense that the techniques permit these characteristics. Several examples of human centered systems employing the soft computing techniques are introduced in this chapter, an interactive music composition support system [6], a story generation system from some pictures [7], facial caricature drawing system with words [8], and a pedestrian navigation system reflecting user's subjectivity and preference [9]. Some of them have the system structure shown in Fig.3. Other examples do not necessarily have this system structure and learning in these systems is performed offline. However, this paper calls all of them human centered systems.

3.1 Interactive Support System of Music Composition [6]

A human music composer is a system itself and a human user in Fig.3, who modifies a musical work composed by the system(himself/herself). In the sense of Fig.3, a human composer himself/herself is a human centered system. The music composition procedures of a human composer are modeled by the present interactive support system of music composition. A user has his/her image of a composed musical work. This image is an input in Fig.3. The interactive genetic algorithms [10] are applied to the music composition system. The music composition procedures in the present interactive support system of music composition are shown in Fig. 4. A human user

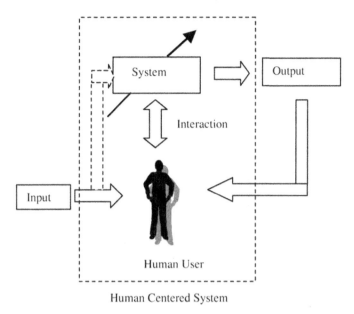

Human Centered System

Fig. 3. Human Centered System

listens to musical works presented by the system and evaluates them whether they fit his/her own image of a composed musical work. That is, the results of GA operations are evaluated not by fitness functions but by a human user. Therefore, composer's subjectivity and feelings are reflected to composed musical works. Chromosomes expressing information on musical works are evolved according to user's evaluation and finally become musical works fitting user's own image. Although musical composition is usually a work performed by only professional composers with technical knowledge of music, even an amateur at music can compose musical works fitting his/her image easily by the present system. It is confirmed that a variety of cheerful musical works are obtained in experiments trying to compose a cheerful work, and each work satisfies the composer himself/herself. Some score examples of composed musical works are presented in Fig. 5. The present system is a good example of human centered systems.

3.2 Story Generation System form Pictures [7]

Seeing pictures given in random order, even little children interpret them and make a story well based on their experience/knowledge. The present story generation system is realized on a computer as a model of human story generation from pictures. The story generation procedures are shown in Fig. 6. Inputs to the present system are information on pictures that are given in random order. The present system has user's own case database about the interpretation of pictures, which is based on his/her own experience/knowledge and dependent on a user. The system employs the case-based reasoning technique and makes stories from pictures given in random order. If stories generated from pictures do not fit user's feelings, new case database is added to the

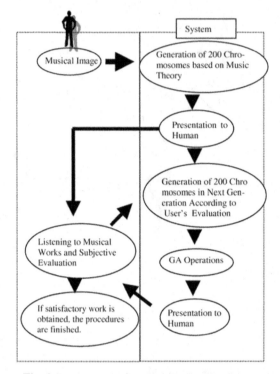

Fig. 4. Procedures in Composition Support System

Fig. 5. Score Examples of Composed Musical Works

system by the interaction. Therefore, the system becomes a user's own peculiar story generation system. That is, human subjectivity and feelings are reflected to stories generated from pictures since user's own case database reflects his/her own subjectivity and feelings. The present system is also one of human centered systems.

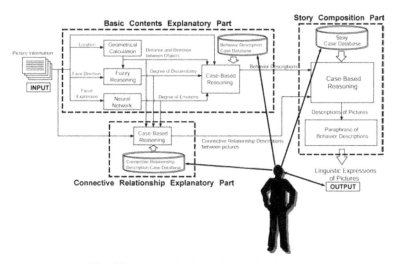

Fig. 6. Procedures in Story Generation System

3.3 Facial Caricature Drawing System with Words [8]

A montage is usually made based on a witness and facial caricature of a suspect is also drawn based on a witness. In this occasion, the witness is expressed with linguistic terms. That is, impressions of a suspect face and facial features are expressed with linguistic terms. A facial caricature artist interprets the meanings of linguistic terms expressed by an eyewitness and draws facial caricature. If drawn caricature does not fit witness's impressions of a suspect face and/or its facial features, a witness points out the part of caricature to be retouched with linguistic terms and the artist retouches the facial caricature. At the same time the artist learns the meanings of linguistic terms expressed by the eyewitness. A facial caricature artist draws facial caricature of a suspect learning the eyewitness. The present caricature drawing system models the procedures of facial caricature drawing based on an eyewitness.

There have been many studies on a face such as recognition of facial expression, facial caricature drawing. There are two types of studies on facial caricature drawing. One is the study that extracts facial features points by the image processing of a model's face image and draws facial caricatures using these points [11]. A facial caricature can be drawn exactly by this approach. However, even if various users draw a model's face by this approach, only the same caricature is obtained. Furthermore, it is difficult to reflect impressions of a model's face in a facial caricature only by the image processing since impressions are subjective and dependent on a person who looks at a face. The other study draws facial caricature based on linguistic terms expressing facial features and impressions of a model's face such as *a pretty face*, *a cheerful face*, *big eyes*. If a model's facial caricature is drawn by many facial caricature artists, various types of caricatures are drawn reflecting their impressions and facial features of a model's face. The present facial caricature drawing system is based on the latter idea and considers subjectivity in facial caricature drawing.

Fig.7 shows the structure of the facial caricature drawing system with words. Input to the present system is linguistic terms expressing impressions of a model's face and facial features by a facial caricature artist. The system draws a facial caricature based on the words. Fuzzy set theory is applied to the facial caricature drawing with words in order to express the meanings of the linguistic terms by fuzzy sets. Although an ideal facial caricature drawing system as an example of human centered systems should acquire the meanings of words by the interaction with the artist, the present system does not acquire them online. The present system has impression terms database and feature terms database of his/her own that are obtained by questionnaire, where impression terms express facial impressions and feature terms express facial features. The feedback shown in Fig.3 means the evaluation in the present facial caricature drawing system whether images of model's face are reflected on a facial caricature or not. If the caricature does not fit the images, an artist retouches it by words. An ideal facial caricature drawing system as an example of human centered systems should learn the meanings of impression terms and feature terms according to the words used in the retouching procedures. However, it is confirmed that even the present system can draw facial caricatures, which fit artist's images of models' faces well and by which it is known objectively whose faces are drawn. Therefore, the present system is an example of human centered systems in the sense that the system can draw facial caricatures which fit artist's images of models' faces well. Fig.8 shows the author's caricature.

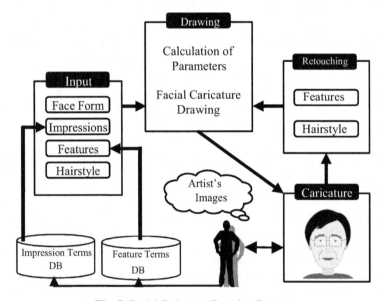

Fig. 7. Facial Caricature Drawing System

3.4 Pedestrian Navigation System [9]

A car navigation system usually shows the shortest distance route or the shortest time route from a starting point to a destination. A pedestrian navigation system, however, is required to have not only the guidance function to a destination but also some value-added function since human users do not always devote themselves entirely to their walking from a starting point to a destination and sometimes waste their time on stop on the way depending on the situation. That is, when they must be in appointed time for, e.g., meeting, they have the shortest distance course. However, when they have time to spare, they often walk window-shopping, or walk enjoying natural atmosphere. Therefore, the user's own pedestrian navigation system, which can show a suitable route according to the situation, is required.

In the present navigation system, fuzzy measures are used for the representation of user's subjectivity and preference in the route selection and fuzzy integrals are applied to choose a suitable route for a user's preference in a given situation. Fuzzy measures show the degree of user's preference for attributes of a route and the

Fig. 8. Facial Caricature of Author

results of fuzzy integrals show the degree of his/her preference on a route. Furthermore, the system shows the route by linguistic terms that express user's own cognitive distance based on user's own sensuous feeling of distance. Inputs to the pedestrian navigation system correspond to the present position, the destination and user's situation. The navigation system has the database of fuzzy measures expressing the degree of user's preference for attributes of a route, the database of user's preference for routes expressing user's subjective evaluation of road attributes such as *road pleasantness*, *road quietness*, and the database of user's own sensuous feeling of distance expressing user's own cognitive distance of a road, where fuzzy sets express the meaning of linguistic terms expressing user's own cognitive distance. These sorts of database should be acquired by online learning in the ideal pedestrian navigation system as an example of human centered systems. Although they are obtained by questionnaire, for example, fuzzy measures are identified using questionnaire data, the present pedestrian system is an example of human centered systems in the sense that the system shows a suitable route for a user according to the user's situation. Fig. 9 shows the structure of the present pedestrian navigation system. It is confirmed that experimental results show that the system can choose a suitable route fitting user's feelings and preference in the route selection according to their situations and that fuzzy measures show that which road attributes users attach great importance to in choosing the route.

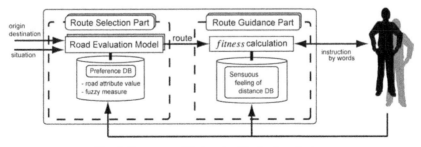

Fig. 9. Structure of Pedestrian Navigation System

4 Conclusions

This paper describes the concept of human centered systems thinking of which keywords are human subjectivity, ambiguity, vagueness, situation dependence. These keywords are quite opposite to the ones which conventional natural science has. Therefore, approaches to human centered systems thinking are not in the framework of conventional natural science that is based on objectivity, uniqueness, universality, and reappearance. This paper emphasizes that approaches in soft computing techniques are needed in human centered systems thinking. This paper also describes the structure of ideal human centered systems that learns human user himself/herself by online. That is, the system's outputs are evaluated by a human user and its evaluations are reflected to human centered systems themselves. Consequently, the system has outputs that have a peculiarity of user's own. Some examples of human centered systems are introduced, an interactive music composition support system, a story generation system from some pictures, a facial caricature drawing system with words and a pedestrian navigation system reflecting user's subjectivity and preference. These systems have outputs that have a peculiarity of user's own.

I hope that human centered systems thinking becomes important in a system design field such as universal design in which users themselves take part in a system design.

Reference

1. Zadeh L.A.: Applications of Fuzzy Technology and Soft Computing. Journal of Japan Society for Fuzzy Theory and Systems **5** (1993) 261-268
2. Li X, Ruan D., van der Wal A.J.: Discussion on Soft Computing at FLINS'96. International Journal of Intelligent Systems **13** (1998) 287-300
3. Zadeh L.A.: Fuzzy Sets. Information and Control **8** (1965) 338-353
4. Iguchi S., et al. : Kansei Information Processing. Ohmusha, Tokyo (1994)
5. Nagamachi M. :Kansei Engineering and Comfort – Preface. International Journal of Industrial Ergonomics **19** (1997) 79-80
6. Unehara M., Onisawa T.: Music Composition System with Human Evaluation as Human Centered Systems. Soft Computing, Springer-Verlag, Heidelberg **17** (2003) 167-178
7. Kato S., Onisawa T. : Explanation of Pictures Contents Considering Storyness. In: Proceedings of 2004 IEEE International Conference on Systems, Man & Cybernetics, The Hague, The Netherlands, IEEE (2004) 3377-3382
8. Onisawa T., Hirasawa Y.: Facial Caricature Drawing Using Subjective Image of a Face Obtained by Words. In: Proceedings of 2004 IEEE International Conference on Fuzzy Systems (FUZZ-IEEE), Budapest, Hungary, IEEE (2004) #1370
9. Akasaka Y., Onisawa T.: Construction of Pedestrian Navigation System and Its Evaluation. In: Proceedings of 2004 IEEE International Conference on Fuzzy Systems (FUZZ-IEEE), Budapest, Hungary, IEEE (2004) #1392
10. Takagi H.: Interactive Evolutionary Computations: Fusion of the Capabilities of EC Optimization and Human Evaluation. In: Proceedings of IEEE **89** (2001) 1275-1296
11. Sato M., Saigo Y., Hashima K., Kasuga M.: An Automatic Facial Caricaturing Method for 2D Realistic Portraits Using Characteristic Points. Journal of the 6th Asian Design International Conference, Tsukuba, Japan **1** (2203) E-40

Qualitative Model of Game Theory

Rafał Graboś

University of Leipzig, Dept. of Computer Science
Augustus Platz 10/11, 04109 Germany
grabos@informatik.uni-leipzig.de

Abstract. This paper studies the notion of qualitative game theory in the context of multi-agent decision making. We use logic programs with ordered disjunction (*LPOD*s), invented by Brewka, as representation and reasoning language for strategic form of games. Structure and rules of a game are represented as a *LPOD* in which preferences of players are encoded as ordered disjunctive rules. Solution of a game is defined in terms of equilibria such that preferred answer sets of a *LPOD* representing a game correspond exactly to respective types of equilibria of the game. We also discuss games in which rules have been changed or players are wrong informed about the rules of a game.

1 Introduction

Game theory is a field of study that bridges mathematics, artificial intelligence, statistics, economics, and psychology, among others. It can be interpreted as a part of multi-agent decision making, as opposed to one agent decision making. In this case game theory is the analysis of interactions of agents that are about making a decision, taking each other's actions into account.

Traditional game theory relies completely of the quantitative representation of a game, where preferences of players, reflecting their desirable strategy, have the form of a payoff function [15]. When uncertainty in a game occurs, it is usually represented by means of a probability distribution over a set of player types. The concept of solution of a game is defined quantitatively and is based either upon the notion of expected utility maximization and maximization of the worst case payoff or on the notion of an equilibrium, where an equilibrium is a joint behavior, providing a set of strategies for each player in a game.

In AI there is recently an interest in more qualitative models of decision making [4], [9], [14]. The motivations behind such approaches are as follows: qualitative information is easier to obtain from users; people usually formulate preferences in the form of human-like, intuitively readable expressions in a natural language etc. In order to deal with such postulates in the field of decision making, a symbolical system for representation and reasoning is needed. Some authors have proposed frameworks for qualitative decision making under uncertainty [9], [14]. However there are still fewer approaches w.r.t. the remaining areas of decision making, like multicriteria decision making, multiagent decision making etc[1].

In this paper we propose a qualitative counterpart of game theory in the context of logic programming with ordered disjunction, invented by Brewka as an extension of answer set programming [10] to represent a priority among literals and rules in a

---

[1] Exceptions are works of Benferhat et.al [1] and De Vos et.al [6], [7], [8].

V. Torra et al. (Eds.): MDAI 2005, LNAI 3558, pp. 47–58, 2005.
© Springer-Verlag Berlin Heidelberg 2005

program [2]. In general, logic programs with ordered disjunction (*LPODs*) encode possible solutions to a problem, being constraint satisfaction problem, and described by the program, where each clause is interpreted as a constraint. By that means many combinatorial, search and constraint satisfaction problems from the field of AI can be represented (diagnosis, planning, cryptography etc.) and solved by implemented systems[2].

From a practical perspective, ordered disjunction has been recognized as a useful tool for modeling and solving a wide range of knowledge representation problems [2], [3], for instance qualitative decision making under uncertainty [9], explaining unexpected observations that would otherwise lead to inconsistency [13], among others.

In our framework we use *LPODs* for representing a structure of a game, i.e. possible actions and players in a game and preferences of players of a game. Instead of a payoff function reflecting a player's preferred strategy, ordered disjunction is applied for encoding a priority among the possible strategies in a game, given the possible actions of the remaining players. We refer to the concepts of the dominant, Nash and Pareto equilibrium as well as define several new types of qualitative equilibria of a game. In order to obtain a concept of qualitative equilibrium, a notion of preferred answer set of *LPOD* is defined such that certain models of a program representing a game correspond exactly to the particular types of equilibria of the game.

We show that *LPODs* may be successfully used as a qualitative representation and reasoning tool for multiagent decision making problems, seen as strategic games. Due to the qualitative nature of the model, natural and human-like form of preferences is expressible; on the other hand several new equilibria are qualitatively defined.

In section 2 basic concepts of Game Theory are given. In section 3 we introduce the formal background, while in section 4 our approach is presented. In section 5 we give conclusions and future work.

2   Game Theory

Game theory was invented by the economists von Neumann and Morgenstern in the 1950s [15]. It is the study of situations involving competing interests, modeled in terms of the strategies, probabilities, actions, gains of opposing players in a game. There are 2 modules in GT: formal language describing the interaction among players and solution concepts.

2.1   Representation of a Game

Formally, game is a triple $G = \{N, A_{i \in N}, U_{i \in N}\}$ where:

- $N = \{1,\ldots,n\}$ is the set of players in a game
- A_i is the set of strategies available to player i,
- $u_i: A_1 \times \ldots \times A_n \to R$ is the utility function of player $i \in N$ called his strategy profile

We distinct between zero-sum and non zero-sum games - in the former all payoffs add up to zero while in the latter some outcomes have net results greater or less than

---

[2] http://saturn.hut.fi/pub/smodels/, http://www.dbai.tuwien.ac.at/proj/dlv/

zero. Moreover, strategic (normal) and extensive forms of a game are defined. Strategic game is described in terms of strategies and payoffs of the players only while extensive form of a game is represented as a tree encoding also the sequential dependencies in the game. In this paper only games in normal forms are investigated.

Sometimes agents are familiar with the sets of actions available to the remaining agents but they may not be aware of payoffs of these agents. We can distinguish between games with complete information, in which payoffs of each player are a common knowledge among all players, and games with incomplete information in which the knowledge about the payoffs of players remains private. In games with incomplete information beliefs about the types of players must be considered.

2.2 Solution Concepts

We distinguish between non-cooperative solutions in which each player takes the expected strategies of other players into account and cooperative solutions assuming cooperation among the players. Since in this paper we investigate non-cooperative solutions only, we present some definitions in more details. Maximin criterion is a strategy that maximizes the expected minimum payoff of a player. This procedure was proposed by von Neumann as a rational solution for 2 persons zero-sum game [15]. Since most of games are non zero-sum games, we refer to the notion of strategic equilibrium, known from the Game Theory literature. Equilibrium is a common strategy providing a set of strategies for each player in a game and may be interpreted as a description of behavior of rational players or as a recommendation for the players.

Since any normal form of a game can be translated to an extensive form game, concept of equilibrium in general is related to extensive form games. Below three types of equilibrium are informally defined:

- Dominant equilibrium: common strategy, when an individual strategy is the best for a corresponding player of a game, no matter what actions other players choose.
- Nash equilibrium: joint strategy, when any single agent by changing its decision can only reduce its payoff.
- Pareto equilibrium: joint option where any single agent by changing its decision can increase its payoff only by reducing the payoff of at least one another agent.

The Pareto optimal solution is interpreted from the point of view of players treated as a group, thus reflecting an interest of a group. The Nash equilibrium is the solution, pointing out the existence of outcomes which satisfy everyone's expectations. The Dominant equilibrium is the strongest notion and it is a subset of a set of Nash equilibria of a game. In one game many Nash and Pareto equilibria may exist.

2.3 Problems of Game Theory

The first difficulty of the traditional Game Theory when considering multi-agent environment is the knowledge acquisition problem. Numerical information about payoffs and probabilities may be hard to obtain while qualitative information is easier to elicit from both experts and laics. Additionally, due to the fact that preferences are a crucial issue for all decision making tasks, they should be expressed in intuitive and human-like forms,[0] as close to a natural language sentence as possible, in order to reduce the complexity of a decision process. In AI various symbolic approaches to decision making have been proposed, combining logic representations of a decision problem and reasoning mechanisms simulating decision rules [9], [14].

Another issue is expressivity and computational complexity of representation and reasoning language. In economy these problems are not addressed. However, in order to successfully automatize a decision process, these issues must be considered strongly relevant. One of the main ideas behind qualitative tools for decision making is that because of simplicity it can be made faster algorithms. Moreover, a qualitative model can serve to prune the computational space of a quantitative approach.

3   Formal Background

As logic programming with ordered disjunction (*LPOD*) is strictly related to answer set programming (*ASP*), basic knowledge about the *ASP* is given in the next section.

3.1   Answer Set Programming

Answer set programming is a new logic programming paradigm for knowledge representation and problem solving tasks in artificial intelligence [10]. Representation of a problem is purely declarative, suitable for many aspects of commonsense reasoning (diagnosis, configuration, planning etc.). Instead of a query technique (*Prolog*), it bases upon a notion of possible solution, called *answer set*.

Consider a propositional language *L*, with atomic symbols called atoms. A literal is an atom or negated atom (by classical negation ¬). The symbol *not* is called epistemic negation and the expression *not a* is true, if there is no reason to believe, that *a* is the case. The epistemic negation makes *ASP* a nonmonotonic system. Default rules, whose conclusions are defeasible in the light of certain knowledge, are represented by using epistemic negation. Knowledge which is not defeasible is represented by means of the rules without negation *not*. The symbol ∨ is called epistemic disjunction and it is interpreted as follows: at least one literal is believed to be true. Formally, the rule *r* is an expression of the form:

$$c_1 \vee \ldots \vee c_k \leftarrow a_1, \ldots, a_m, \text{ not } b_{m+1}, \ldots, \text{ not } b_n \tag{1}$$

where $k \geq 0$, $n \geq m \geq 0$, c_i, a_l, b_k are literals, $Body^-(r) = \{b_{m+1}, \ldots, b_n\}$, $Body^+(r) = \{a_1, \ldots, a_m\}$ are the conjunctions of literals and the disjunction $\{c_1 \vee \ldots \vee c_k\}$ is $Head(r)$ of the rule *r*. A rule with an empty *Head* ($\leftarrow Body$) is usually referred to as integrity constraint. A logic program is a finite set of the rules.

Intuitively the above rule *r* means that if $Body^+(r)$ of that rule is believed to be true and it is not the case that $Body^-(r)$ is believed to be true, then at least one literal of the *Head*(*r*) must be believed as true.

The semantics of *ASP* is defined by means of minimal set of literals satisfying all rules of the program. Let us assume now, that Lit_P is a set of all literals, being present in the extended logic program *P* and *I* is an interpretation of *P*, $I \subseteq Lit_P$. We say that a set of literals *I* satisfies a rule of the form (1), if $\{a_1, \ldots, a_m\} \subseteq I$ and $\{b_{m+1}, \ldots, b_n\} \cap I = \varnothing$ imply that $\{c_1, \ldots, c_k\} \cap I \neq \varnothing$.

The Gelfond-Lifschitz (*GL*) transformation of *P* with respect to *I* is a positive logic program *P′* which is obtained in two steps:

– deletion of all rules r of P, for which $Body^-(r) \cap I \neq \varnothing$
– deletion of the negative bodies ($Body^-(r)$) from the remaining rules of P

Then, I is an *answer set* of the logic program P, if I is a minimal model (no proper subset of I is a model of P') of the positive (without *not*) logic program P'; i.e. I is a minimal set satisfying every rule in P' or if I contains a pair of complementary literals l and $\neg l$, then $I = Lit_P$.

Since the symbol $\vee$ is interpreted as "or" disjunction, we present a second type of disjunction, called exclusive disjunction denoted by $|$. Intuitively, a rule of the form:

$$c_1 \mid \dots \mid c_k \leftarrow a_1, \dots, a_m , \text{ not } b_{m+1}, \dots, \text{ not } b_n \qquad (2)$$

is satisfied by a set of literals I if $\{a_1, \dots, a_m\} \subseteq I$ and $\{b_{m+1}, \dots, b_n\} \cap I = \varnothing$ imply that $|\{i \mid c_i \in I\}| = 1$. Therefore, such disjunctive rule with empty *Body* may be used as a generating rule (generation of possible answer sets) or as a constraint rule (restriction on answer sets to contain only one among particular literals). In Smodels [11] system, state-of-art implementation of stable model semantics, to the symbol $|$ the above semantics is given by default; however it's possible to use the standard disjunctive logic programming semantics as well.

Although answer set programs are basically propositional, it is possible to use rule schemata containing variables. These schemata are representations of their ground instances, and answer set solvers use intelligent ground instantiation techniques before the actual answer set computation takes place.

In general, programs under answer set semantics encode a problem, being constraint satisfaction problem, and described by the program, where each clause is interpreted as a constraint. By that means many combinatorial, search and constraint satisfaction problems from the field of AI can be represented (diagnosis, configuration, planning, cryptography etc.).

3.2 Logic Programs with Ordered Disjunction

Consider now an extended logic program (with two negations), where the ordered disjunction $\times$ is allowed in the *Head* part of a rule. A logic program with ordered disjunction (*LPOD*), proposed in [2], consist of rules of the form:

$$c_1 \times \dots \times c_k \leftarrow a_1, \dots, a_m , \text{ not } b_{m+1}, \dots, \text{ not } b_n \qquad (3)$$

where $k \geq 0$, $n \geq m \geq 0$, c_i, a_i, b_k are literals and the ordered disjunction $\{c_1 \times \dots \times c_k\}$ is a *Head*(r) of the rule r. The rule, let call it the preference rule, is originally to be read: if possible c_1, if c_1 is not possible, then $c_2, \dots$, if all of $c_1 \times \dots \times c_{k-1}$ are not possible, then c_k. The literals c_j are called choices of the rule.

Answer set semantics is submitted to the *LPOD*. In order to use a standard *ASP* semantics presented in the previous section, a split technique is applied, which results in a program without the ordered disjunction[3]. Then answer sets of such modified program are ranked according to degrees of satisfaction of ordered disjunctive rules. Note that in contrast to the standard *ASP* semantics, models are not always minimal.

To distinguish which answer set is preferred one, a notion of the degree of satisfaction of an ordered disjunctive rule by answer set is introduced.

---

[3] Details may be found in [3].

Let S be an answer set of an *LPOD* P. The ordered disjunctive rule r:

$$c_1 \times \ldots \times c_k \leftarrow a_1, \ldots, a_m, \text{ not } b_{m+1}, \ldots, \text{ not } b_n \qquad (4)$$

is satisfied by S to degree:

- *1, if $a_j \notin S$ for some j or $b_i \in S$, for some i*
- *d ($1 \leq d \leq k$), if $a_j \in S$ for all j, and $b_i \notin S$, for all i, and $d = min \{r \mid c_r \in S\}$*

Note that degrees of satisfaction are treated as penalties, the smaller the degree the better the answer set is. Moreover, a priority (meta-preferences) between preference rules can be expressed with a meaning: in case when it is not possible to satisfy all rules to the highest degree, the rules with higher priority are to be satisfied first.

Each solution to a problem, represented as an answer set of a *LPOD*, is ranked according to its satisfaction degree of ordered disjunctive rules and one global order is obtained. The following criteria to build this ranking was proposed in [3]: *cardinality* optimal criterion- maximizing the number of rules satisfied to the highest degree, *inclusion* optimal criterion, based on set inclusion of the rules satisfied to certain degree and Pareto optimal criterion, consisting of a selection of answer set, which satisfies all ordered disjunctive rules not worse than any other answer set does.

Example 1. Program $P_4 = \{b \times c \times a.\ a \times c \times b. \leftarrow a, b. \leftarrow a, c.\}$ has one cardinality optimal answer set: $S_1 = \{c, b\}$ satisfying all rules "best" (the first to degree 1 and the second to degree 2). The remaining answer sets: $S_2 = \{a\}$, $S_3 = \{b\}$ satisfy one rule to 1, and the other to degree 3. The Pareto and the inclusion winners are both S_1 and S_2.

Computational complexity of *LPODs* under Pareto and inclusion preferences is proved to be in the same complexity class as disjunctive logic programs, namely in Σ_P^2-complete, while in Δ^2_P under the cardinality criterion.

Psmodels is a prototype implementation of logic programming with ordered disjunction under the above criteria[4]. Since in this paper several new criteria, which are suitable for game theory applications are defined, they may be implemented in a similar way as presented in [3].

4 LPOD Representation of Qualitative Game Theory

4.1 System Architecture

We are interested in representing non cooperative, strategic games with complete and incomplete information as a *LPOD* and in determining equilibria for such games by means of preferred answer sets of a *LPOD* program. Let's assume that A_i denotes a set of literals representing strategies of a player i and N denotes a set of players. For a normal form of a game with complete information, a strategy profile of the player i is represented by a *LPOD* as a set of rules r of the form:

$$c_i^1 \times \ldots \times c_i^k \leftarrow a_1, \ldots, b_{n-1}. \qquad (5)$$

where c_i^k, a_m and b_n are literals, $k \leq |A_i|$, $n = |N|$, the head $\{c_i^1 \times \ldots \times c_i^k\}$, where $c_i^k \in A_i$ denotes an order over a set of strategies of player i and the body $\{a_1, \ldots, b_{n-1}\}$, where $a_1 \in A_1$ and $b_{n-1} \in A_{n-1}$, is a conjunction of strategies being a Cartesian product of $(A_1 \times \ldots \times A_{n-1})$.

---

[4] http://www.tcs.hut.fi/Software/smodels/priority/

Intuitively, depending on every possible strategy of the remaining players, each player of a game must preorder a set of strategies available to him. Note that although the literal c_i^k denotes a particular strategy and then it encodes a strict preference order among strategies by an ordered disjunctive rule, it is possible to express a weak order of the strategies as well. In this case, c_i^k represents a set of equally preferred strategies treated disjunctively. It is done in *LPODs* by means of an additional cardinality constraint rule such that its head contains literals corresponding to the strategies denoted by the c_i^k, while its body consists of the literal c_i^k itself.

Representation of a game G is a *LPOD P*, containing a set of rules r for all $i \in N$ and additional choice rules representing rules of a game.

4.2 Solution Concepts

In the current section we define several types of qualitative equilibria of a *LPOD*, representing a game as well as their application to some exemplary games.

4.2.1 Dominant and the Nash Equilibrium

Dominant equilibrium suggests the most preferred actions for each player in a game. Preferences of each player are independent of the behavior of the other agents, and there is no conflict among the preference of the players. Since in most games the dominant equilibrium almost never exists, we consider now the weaker form of a joint strategy, called the Nash equilibrium, defined informally in the previous sections. Note that every the dominant equilibrium is the Nash equilibrium but not vice versa[5].

Definition 1. *Given that S is an answer set of an LPOD P representing a game G, S is the Nash equilibrium of G if S is not-dominated answer set of the program P.*

We define now a notion of the not-dominated answer set of an LPOD P:

Definition 2. *Given that S_1 is an answer set of an LPOD P, S_1 is not-dominated answer set of P iff for all $r \in P$ and for any answer set S_2 of P, $degS_1(r) \leq degS_2(r)$.*

Example 2. Prisoner's dilemma: Bob and Al are picked up by the police and interrogated in separate cells. Both are allowed to choose among the following acts: confessing or not confessing. If both confess, both get five years in prison. If neither of them confesses, the police will be able to pin parts of the crime on Al and Bob, and both get one year. If one of the prisoners confesses but the other doesn't, the confessor will make a deal with the police and will go free while the other one will go to jail for ten years. The game may be represented in a form of a table, presented below:

Table 1. Prisoner's dilemma as a game in a normal form

Al / Bob	confess	don't confess
confess	(5, 5)	(0, 10)
don't confess	(10, 0)	(1, 1)

---

[5] For the dominant equilibrium, we proceed as follows: when a strategy profile of a player is independent on strategies of other players, we represent it as an ordered disjunctive rule r with the empty body. Then an answer set S_1 is the dominant equilibrium of an *LPOD* program P if and only if it is not dominated answer set for the program P consisting of the rules r only.

It is clear that $N = \{Al\ (A),\ Bob\ (B)\}$, $A_A = \{confess,\ don't\ confess\}$, $A_B = \{confess,\ don't\ confess\}$. Let us now represent this game as an *LPOD* P_1.
Bob's strategy profile:

$confess_B \times don't\_confess_B \leftarrow confess_A.$
$confess_B \times don't\_confess_B \leftarrow don't\_confess_A.$

Al's profile:

$confess_A \times don't\_confess_A \leftarrow confess_B.$
$confess_A \times don't\_confess_A \leftarrow don't\_confess_B.$

Choice rules:

$confess_A \mid don't\_confess_A.$
$confess_B \mid don't\_confess_B.$

The program P_1, encoding the prisoner's dilemma game, has one not-dominated answer set $S = \{confess_A,\ confess_B\}$ corresponding exactly to the Nash equilibrium of the game. Note that this answer set is also the dominant equilibrium of this game.

4.2.2 Pareto Equilibrium

The well-know fact is that in some games no the Nash or dominant equilibria may exist. However still we may be interested in finding "good enough" strategy when considering players as a group.

The Pareto efficient equilibrium is a strategy in which any agent can, by changing its decision, increase its level of satisfaction only by reducing the satisfaction's level of at least one another agent. Since many Pareto efficient solutions of a game may exist, we define some subclasses of a class of Pareto efficient solutions.

In [1] a notion of the Pareto preferred (p-preferred) answer set was defined. However it is easy to check that a set of p-preferred answer sets of an *LPOD* P is not equal to a set of the Pareto equilibrium of the game G represented by the program P. Thus, we define below a notion of Pareto efficient answer set of an *LPOD* P:

Definition 3. *Given that S_1 is an answer set of an LPOD P, S_1 is Pareto efficient iff there exists a rule $r \in P$ such that $degS_1(r) < degS_2(r)$ for any answer set S_2 of P.*
Then the following relation holds:

Proposition 1. *Given that S_1 is an answer set of an LPOD P representing a game G, if S_1 is Pareto equilibrium of G then S_1 is Pareto efficient answer set of the program P.*

Since by means of the Pareto efficient criterion it is not possible to find the Pareto equilibria of a game, we propose to modify the semantics of ordered disjunction. The ordered disjunctive rule r of the form:

$$c_1 \times \ldots \times c_k \leftarrow a_1, \ldots, a_m,\ not\ b_{m+1}, \ldots, not\ b_n \qquad (6)$$

is satisfied by an answer set S:

- *to degree d ($1 \leq d \leq k$), if $a_j \in S$ for all j and $b_i \notin S$ for all i and $d = min\ \{r \mid c_r \in S\}$*
- *if $a_j \notin S$ for some j or $b_i \in S$ for some i, then S is irrelevant w.r.t. r*

We define now the notion of the Pareto equilibrium in the context of *LPOD*:

Definition 4. *Given that S_1 is an answer set of an LPOD P representing a game G, S_1 is Pareto equilibrium of G iff there is no answer set S_2 of P such that:*

- *for any $r \in P$ for which S_1 and S_2 are relevant, $degS_2(r) < degS_1(r)$ and*
- *there exists $r' \in P$ for which S_2 is relevant, such that $degS_2(r') \leq degS_1(r'')$ for any $r'' \in P$ for which S_1 is relevant.*

Consider the next example of a game consisting of the following components: $N = \{1, 2\}$, $A_1 = \{a, b, c\}$, $A_2 = \{a, b, c\}$. The game is represented by the program P_2 and the players' strategy profiles are assumed to be as below:

Player's 1 strategy profile:

$$b_1 \times c_1 \times a_1 \leftarrow a_2.$$
$$b_1 \times a_1 \times c_1 \leftarrow b_2.$$
$$c_1 \times a_1 \times b_1 \leftarrow c_2.$$

Player's 2 strategy profile:

$$b_2 \times c_2 \times a_2 \leftarrow a_1.$$
$$c_2 \times a_2 \times b_2 \leftarrow b_1.$$
$$b_2 \times a_2 \times c_2 \leftarrow c_1.$$

Choice rules

$$a_1 \mid b_1 \mid c_1.$$
$$a_2 \mid b_2 \mid c_2.$$

For this game there is no dominant and no the Nash equilibrium, because there is no answer set not dominated for all preference rules of the program P_2. The set of the Pareto equilibria of the game represented by the program P_2 contains four answer sets satisfying the definition 4: $S_1 = \{c_2, b_1\}$, $S_2 = \{a_2, b_1\}$, $S_3 = \{b_2, a_1\}$, $S_4 = \{c_2, c_1\}$.

As exampled above, many the Pareto equilibria may exist in a game, which sometimes is not much informative. Thus, some interesting subsets of a set of the Pareto equlibria will be introduced: maximally efficient Pareto equilibrium, group equilibrium and social stable law. Besides, the inefficient Pareto equilibrium, namely pure equilibrium, will be informally defined. The notion of social stable law was introduced by [11], while the remaining solution concepts are novel.

4.2.3 Maximally Efficient and Group Equilibrium

Maximally efficient Pareto equilibrium intuitively may be seen as equilibrium in which at least one player of a game gets the maximal available payoff. Formally:

Definition 5. *Answer set S_l is maximally efficient equilibrium of a game G if S_l is Pareto equilibrium of G and there is at least one $r \in P$ such that for all i, $degS_l(r) < degS_i(r)$ and r is the rule which is relevant for S_l.*

The maximally efficient equilibria of the game encoded by P_2 are: $S_1 = \{c_2, b_1\}$, $S_2 = \{a_2, b_1\}$, $S_3 = \{b_2, a_1\}$, $S_4 = \{c_2, c_1\}$. Note that the above solutions are the Pareto equilibria of this game as well. However, this relation does not hold in general.

Although the Pareto solution concept is general, it may help to reduce the number of candidate strategies in a game. We can observe that some of the Pareto equilibria are "better" than others for some players. For instance, in the game exampled by the program P_3, two Pareto equilibria: $\{a_2, b_1\}$ and $\{a_1, b_2\}$ satisfy both players considered as a group better than other answer sets[6]. We introduce now a notion of group

---

[6] The problem of dividing such payoff among the members of a group is outside the scope of this paper.

equilibrium, being the second interesting subset of the Pareto efficient solutions. First we define the min-sum preferred answer set of an *LPOD P*:

Definition 6. *Given that S_1 and S_2 are answer sets of an LPOD P, S_1 is min-sum preferred to S_2 iff for all $r \in P$, $\sum_{r=1}^{n} degS_1(r) \leq \sum_{r=1}^{n} degS_2(r)$, where $n = |P|$ is equal to the number of rules in P.*

Intuitively, the group equilibrium is a strategy for players treated as a group, where a sum of payoffs of all players is maximal. Formally:

Definition 7. *Given that S is answer set of an LPOD P representing a game G, S is group equilibrium of G iff S is Pareto equilibrium of G and it is min-sum preferred answer set of P.*

For the game represented by the program P_2, two answer sets: $S_1 = \{a_2, b_1\}$, $S_2 = \{b_2, a_1\}$ are its group equilibria.

4.2.4 Pure Equilibrium

In the Game Theory literature a notion of Pareto inefficiency has been introduced. The strategy in which any agent can improve his position without reducing a level of satisfaction of other players, but at the same time she can not improve positions of all players, may be interpreted as the Pareto inefficient. We are interested in a variant of such strategy, which is Pareto inefficient, on the other hand warranting an equal payoff for all players. Formally:

Definition 8. *Given that S is an answer set of an LPOD P representing a game G, S is pure equilibrium of G iff:*

1. for all $r \in P$ w.r.t. which S is relevant, degS $(r) = const.$ and
2. S is the min-sum preferred answer set among all S satisfying the condition (1)

Given the game represented by the program P_2, two answer sets: $S_1 = \{a_2, c_1\}$ and $S_2 = \{c_1, a_2\}$ are the pure equilibria since they are the min-sum preferred answer sets among those satisfying all rules relevant to them to the equal degree.

In our framework, dominant and Nash equilibria are pure equilibria only for games with perfect information, i.e. games in which rules of games are a common knowledge. However, one can imagine a game in which some players are wrong informed about a structure of the game or rules of the game are changed suddenly.

Consider the program P_3 representing a game in which the player 2 was mistaken about the actions available to him. In fact, she can take only two actions: a or b, but not action c, while the player 1 is allowed to take all three actions $\{a, b, c\}$:
Strategy profile of the player 1:

$b_1 \times c_1 \times \ a_1 \leftarrow a_2.$
$a_1 \times \ b_1 \times c_1 \leftarrow b_2.$

Strategy profile of the player 2:

$b_2 \times c_2 \times \ a_2 \leftarrow a_1.$
$c_2 \times a_2 \times b_2 \leftarrow b_1.$
$b_2 \times a_2 \times \ c_2 \leftarrow c_1.$

Choice rules:

$a_1 \mid b_1 \mid c_1.$
$a_2 \mid b_2 \mid c_2.$
$\leftarrow c_2.$

Since action c is not allowed for the player 2 due to the rules of the game, we add the constraint rule at the end of the program P_3'. Now the Nash equilibria are the answer sets: $S_1 = \{a_1, b_2\}$ and $S_2 = \{a_2, b_1\}$, although S_2 is not the pure equilibrium of the game. Games with imperfect information, where some players may be mistaken about rules of a game and its representation in *LPOD* are the future topics of research.

4.2.5 Social Stable Law

In [12] the notion of a social law was introduced. The *social law* restricts the activities of the agents to a set of allowed actions which warranted the payoff defined by the law. More formally, a social stable law is the solution restricting set of strategies of players to a set of allowed actions warranting the payoff defined by the law ($l \leq k$, where k denotes a payoff) and any deviation is irrational, when agent is risk-averse.

Let's assume that a law is defined w.r.t. an *LPOD* as the restriction on answer sets for reaching a maximal level of satisfaction and denote it by $l \leq k$, where $1 \leq k \leq n$.

Definition 9. *Given that S is an answer set of an LPOD P representing a game G, S is a stable social law of G iff S is Pareto equilibrium of G and for all $r \in P$ w.r.t. which S is relevant, $degS(r) \leq l$.*

Consider the program P_2 and assume that a law $l \leq 2$. The stable social laws are the answer sets $S_1 = \{a_1, b_2\}$ and $S_2 = \{a_2, b_1\}$ since they satisfied the law and any deviation is irrational, (after changing the action by the first player, the second can change his move by decreasing the payoff of the first etc.). Note that the strategies: $\{a_1, c_2\}$ and $\{a_2, c_1\}$ are not the stable social laws, although they guarantee the minimal payoff, since they are not the Pareto equilibria of the game.

5 Conclusions and Related Work

In this paper we have proposed a qualitative counterpart of the game theory in the context of logic programming with ordered disjunction. We use a *LPOD* for representing the structure of a game, i.e. possible actions and players of a game, and preferences of players of a game. Instead of a payoff function reflecting a player's preferred strategy, ordered disjunction is applied for encoding a priority among the possible strategies, given the actions of the remaining players.

We investigate concepts of dominant, Nash and Pareto equilibrium as well as define several new types of qualitative equilibria. In order to obtain a concept of qualitative equilibrium, the notion of preferred answer set of a *LPOD* is defined such that certain models of a program, representing a game, correspond exactly to the particular types of equilibria. Moreover, games with incomplete information about as well as possible ways of handling changes of rules of the game are discussed.

The most similar to our framework are works of De Vos, Veremir [6], [7], [8], where Ordered Choice Logic Programming (OCLP), an extension of Choice Logic Programming (CLP), are proposed for representation and reasoning purposes. Notions of Nash equilibrium of normal games and subgame perfect equilibrium for extensive games are defined by means of stable models of CLP and OCLP, respectively.

Since we consider only games in normal forms, we can compare CLP with our approach. The main difference is due to different expressivities of CLP and LPOD; the former does not allow expressing priority among literals of a logic program. Therefore, only the notion of Nash equilibrium may be defined under CLP, while we investigate several types of equilibria. Moreover, we deal with games in which players may be mistaken about rules of the game or the rules have been changed.

In [12] the notion of stable social law was introduced as a solution concept for a normal form of a game. Authors showed that the social law corresponds to qualitative equilibrium for risk-averse agents and that it is useful when lack of simple conventions. In comparison to our approach, we use only qualitative representation of a decision problem, while the discussed framework is closer to the spirit of traditional game theory, where the payoff function for representing preferences of players is adopted.

In [5] a rule based qualitative decision and game theory based on belief (B) and desire (D) approach is proposed, where agents end up in equilibria by acting, as if they maximize a joint goal. Moreover, the notions of Nash, dominant and Pareto equilibrium are defined in terms of positive and negative goals being achieved by the agents.

Acknowledgements

The author is very grateful to Patryk Burek, Piotr Jańczuk and anonymous reviewers for useful comments and remarks.

References

1. Benferhat, S., et. al.: Towards a possibilistic logic handling of preferences. Applied Intelligence. 14 (2001) 303-317
2. Brewka, G.: Logic Programs with Ordered Disjunction. Proc. AAAI, Canada (2002) 100-105
3. Brewka, G.: Implementing Ordered Disjunction Using Answer Set Solvers for Normal Programs. Proc. JELIA'02, Italy (2002) 444-455
4. Doyle, J.,Thomason,R.: Background to qualitative decision theory. AI Mag. **20** (1997) 55-68
5. Dastani, M., Van der Torre, L.: What is a joint goal? Games with beliefs and defeasible desires. NMR'02, France (2002) 33-40
6. De Vos, M., Vermeir, D.: Choice Logic Programs and Nash Equilibria in Strategic Games. Proc. CSL'99, Spain (1999) 266-276
7. De Vos, M., Vermeir, D.: Logic Programming Agents and Game Theory. Proc. AAAI Spring Symposium on Answer Set Programming, USA, (2001) 27-33
8. De Vos, M., Vermeir, D.: Dynamic Decision Making in Logic Programming and Game Theory AI'02, Australia (2002) 36-57
9. Grabos, R.: Qualitative Model of Decision Making. Proc. AIMSA'04, Varna (2004) 480-489
10. Lifschitz, V.: Answer set programming and plan generation. AI 138 (2002) 39-54
11. Niemelä, I., Simons, P.: Smodels-an implementation of the stable model and well-founded semantics for normal logic programs. Proc. LPNMR'97, Germany (1997) 420-429
12. Tennenholtz, M.: On Stable Social Laws and Qualitative Equilibria. AI 102 (1998) 1-20
13. Osorio, M. et.al.: Generalized Ordered Disjunction and its Applications, not published
14. Tan, S. W., Pearl, J.: Qualitative Decision Theory. Proc. AAAI'94, USA (1994) 70–75
15. Von Neumann, J., Morgenstern, O.: Theory of Games and Economic Behavior. 2nd ed. Princeton University Press (1944)

Regularity Properties of Null-Additive Fuzzy Measure on Metric Spaces

Jun Li[1], Masami Yasuda[2], and Jinjie Song[3]

[1] Department of Applied Mathematics, College of Science
Communication University of China, Beijing 100024, China[*]
`lijun@seu.edu.cn`
[2] Dep of Math & Infor., Chiba University, Chiba 263-8522 Japan
`yasuda@math.s.chiba-u.ac.jp`
[3] Department of Computer Science and Engineering
Tianjin University of Technology, Tianjin 300191, China
`songjinjie@sidewave.com`

Abstract. We shall discuss further regularity properties of null-additive fuzzy measure on metric spaces following the previous results. Under the null-additivity condition, some properties of the inner/outer regularity and the regularity of fuzzy measure are shown. Also the strong regularity of fuzzy measure is discussed on complete separable metric spaces. As an application of strong regularity, we present a characterization of atom of null-additive fuzzy measure.

Keywords: Fuzzy measure, null-additivity, regularity

1 Introduction

Recently various regularities of a set function are proposed and investigated by many authors ([2, 4–7, 9, 11, 12]). As it is seen, the regularities play an important role in the nonadditive measure theory. In [4, 11] we discussed the regularity of a null-additive fuzzy measure and proved Egoroff's theorem and Lusin's theorem for fuzzy measures on a metric space.

In this paper, we shall continue to investigate further regularities of a fuzzy measure on metric spaces following the results by [4, 11]. Explicitly, under the null-additivity, the weekly null-additivity and the converse null-additivity condition, we shall discuss these relation among the inner regularity, the outer regularity and the regularity of fuzzy measures. Also we define the strong regularity of fuzzy measures and show our main result: the null-additive fuzzy measures possess a strong regularity on complete separable metric spaces. By using strong regularity we shall show a version of Egoroff's theorem and Lusin's theorem for null-additive fuzzy measures on complete separable metric spaces, respectively. Lastly, as an application of a strong regularity, we present a characterization of atom of a null-additive fuzzy measure.

---

[*] The first author wants to show his thanks to the China Scholarship Council.

V. Torra et al. (Eds.): MDAI 2005, LNAI 3558, pp. 59–66, 2005.

In preparation of the paper, authors are told two references [8] and [10] from anonymous referee. We find that there is another characterization of atom of null additive set functions in [10]. Also, in [8], a similar result of our main result is discussed. However, these results are not completely consistent with ours.

2   Preliminaries

Throughout this paper, we assume that $(X,\ d)$ is a metric space, and that $\mathcal{O}$, $\mathcal{C}$ and $\mathcal{K}$ are the classes of all open, closed and compact sets in (X, d), respectively. $\mathcal{B}$ denotes Borel σ-algebra on X, i.e., it is the smallest σ-algebra containing $\mathcal{O}$. Unless stated otherwise all the subsets mentioned are supposed to belong to $\mathcal{B}$.

A set function $\mu : \mathcal{B} \to [0, +\infty]$ is said to be (i) *continuous from below*, if $\lim_{n\to\infty} \mu(A_n) = \mu(A)$ whenever $A_n \nearrow A$; (ii) *continuous from above*, if $\lim_{n\to\infty} \mu(A_n) = \mu(A)$ whenever $A_n \searrow A$; (iii) *strongly order continuous*, if $\lim_{n\to+\infty} \mu(A_n) = 0$ whenever $A_n \searrow B$ and $\mu(B) = 0$; (iv) *null-additive*, if $\mu(E \cup F) = \mu(E)$ for any E whenever $\mu(F) = 0$; (v) *weakly null-additive*, if $\mu(E \cup F) = 0$ whenever $\mu(E) = \mu(F) = 0$; (vi) *converse-null-additive*, if $\mu(E - F) = 0$ whenever $F \subset E$ and $\mu(F) = \mu(E) < +\infty$; (vii) *finite*, if $\mu(X) < \infty$.

Refer to these definitions and their relations between them in [3] etc. We note here that, obviously, the null-additivity of μ implies weakly null-additivity.

Definition 1. A fuzzy measure on $(X, \mathcal{B})$ is an extended real valued set function $\mu : \mathcal{F} \to [0, +\infty]$ satisfying the following conditions:
(1) $\mu(\emptyset) = 0$;
(2) $\mu(A) \le \mu(B)$ whenever $A \subset B$ and $A, B \in \mathcal{F}$ (monotonicity).

We say that a fuzzy measure μ is continuous if it is continuous both from below and from above. Our fundamental assumtion in this paper is that μ is a "finite" fuzzy measure.

3   Regularity of Fuzzy Measure

Definition 2. ([12]) A fuzzy measure μ is called *outer regular* (resp. *inner regular*), if for each $A \in \mathcal{B}$ and each $\epsilon > 0$, there exists a set $G \in \mathcal{O}$ (resp. $F \in \mathcal{C}$) such that $A \subset G$, $\mu(G - A) < \epsilon$ (resp. $F \subset A$, $\mu(A - F) < \epsilon$). μ is called *regular*, if for each $A \in \mathcal{B}$ and each $\epsilon > 0$, there exist a closed set $F \in \mathcal{C}$ and an open set $G \in \mathcal{O}$ such that $F \subset A \subset G$ and $\mu(G - F) < \epsilon$.

Obviously, if fuzzy measure μ is regular, then it is both outer regular and inner regular.

Proposition 1. ([4]) *If μ is weakly null-additive and continuous, then it is regular. Furthermore, if μ is null-additive, then for any $A \in \mathcal{B}$,*

$$\mu(A) = \sup\{\ \mu(F) \mid F \subset A,\ F \in \mathcal{C}\ \}$$
$$= \inf\{\ \mu(G) \mid G \supset A,\ G \in \mathcal{O}\ \}$$

In the following we present some properties of the inner regularity and outer regularity of fuzzy measure, their proofs can be easily obtained:

Proposition 2. *If μ is weekly null-additive and strongly order continuous, then both outer regularity and inner regularity imply regularity.*

Proposition 3. *Let μ be null-additive fuzzy measure.*

(1) *If μ is continuous from below, then inner regularity implies*

$$\mu(A) = \sup\{\ \mu(F)\ |\ F \subset A,\ F \in \mathcal{C}\ \}$$

for all $A \in \mathcal{B}$;

(2) *If μ is continuous from above, then outer regularity implies*

$$\mu(A) = \inf\{\ \mu(G)\ |\ A \subset G,\ G \in \mathcal{O}\ \}$$

for all $A \in \mathcal{B}$.

Proposition 4. *Let μ be converse-null-additive fuzzy measure.*

(1) *If μ is continuous from below and strongly order continuous, and for any $A \in \mathcal{B}$,*

$$\mu(A) = \sup\{\ \mu(F)\ |\ F \subset A,\ F \in \mathcal{C}\ \},$$

then μ is inner regular.

(2) *If μ is continuous from above, and for any $A \in \mathcal{B}$,*

$$\mu(A) = \inf\{\ \mu(G)\ |\ A \subset G,\ G \in \mathcal{O}\ \},$$

then μ is outer regular.

Definition 3. μ is called *strongly regular*, if for each $A \in \mathcal{B}$ and each $\epsilon > 0$, there exist a compact set $K \in \mathcal{K}$ and an open set $G \in \mathcal{O}$ such that $K \subset A \subset G$ and $\mu(G - K) < \epsilon$.

The strongly regularity implies regularity, and hence inner regularity and outer regularity.

Proposition 5. *Let μ be null-additive and continuous from below. If μ is strongly regular, then for any $A \in \mathcal{B}$,*

$$\mu(A) = \sup\{\ \mu(K)\ |\ K \subset A,\ K \in \mathcal{K}\ \}.$$

Proposition 6. *Let μ be null-additive and order continuous. If for any $A \in \mathcal{B}$,*

$$\mu(A) = \sup\{\ \mu(K)\ |\ K \subset A,\ K \in \mathcal{K}\ \},$$

then μ is strongly regular.

In the rest of the paper, we assume that $(X,\ d)$ is complete and separable metric space, and that μ is finite continuous fuzzy measure. In the following we show the main result in this paper.

Theorem 1. *If μ is null-additive, then μ is strongly regular.*

To prove the theorem, we first prepare two lemmas.

Lemma 1. *Let μ be a finite continuous fuzzy measure. Then for any $\epsilon > 0$ and any double sequence $\{A_n^{(k)} \mid n \geq 1, k \geq 1\} \subset \mathcal{B}$ satisfying $A_n^{(k)} \searrow \emptyset \ (k \to \infty)$, $n = 1, 2, \ldots$, there exists a subsequence $\{A_n^{(k_n)}\}$ of $\{A_n^{(k)} \mid n \geq 1, k \geq 1\}$ such that*

$$\mu\left(\bigcup_{n=1}^{\infty} A_n^{(k_n)}\right) < \epsilon \quad (k_1 < k_2 < \ldots)$$

Proof. Since for any fixed $n = 1, 2, \ldots$, $A_n^{(k)} \searrow \emptyset$ as $k \to \infty$, for given $\epsilon > 0$, using the continuity from above of fuzzy measures, we have $\lim_{k \to +\infty} \mu(A_n^{(k)}) = 0$, therefore there exists k_1 such that $\mu(A_1^{(k_1)}) < \frac{\epsilon}{4}$; For this k_1, $(A_1^{(k_1)} \cup A_2^{(k)}) \searrow A_1^{(k_1)}$, as $k \to \infty$. Therefore it follows, from the continuity from above of μ, that

$$\lim_{k \to +\infty} \mu(A_1^{(k_1)} \cup A_2^{(k)}) = \mu(A_1^{(k_1)}).$$

Thus there exists $k_2 \ (> k_1)$, such that

$$\mu(A_1^{(k_1)} \cup A_2^{(k_2)}) < \frac{\epsilon}{2}.$$

Generally, there exist $k_1, k_2, \ldots, k_m$, such that

$$\mu(A_1^{(k_1)} \cup A_2^{(k_2)} \cup \ldots A_m^{(k_m)}) < \frac{\epsilon}{2}.$$

Hence we obtain a sequence $\{k_n\}_{n=1}^{\infty}$ of numbers and a sequence $\{A_n^{(k_n)}\}_{n=1}^{\infty}$ of sets. By using the monotonicity and the continuity from below of μ, we have

$$\mu\left(\bigcup_{n=1}^{+\infty} A_n^{(k_n)}\right) \leq \frac{\epsilon}{2} < \epsilon.$$

This gives the proof of the lemma.

Lemma 2. *If μ be continuous fuzzy measure, then for each $\epsilon > 0$, there exists a compact set $K_\epsilon \in \mathcal{K}$ such that $\mu(X - K_\epsilon) < \epsilon$.*

Proof. Since (X, d) is separable, there exists a countable dense subsets $\{x_i; i = 1, 2, \ldots\}$. For any for any $n, k \geq 1$, we put

$$\overline{S_k}(x_n) = \left\{x \ : \ x \in X, \ d(x, x_n) \leq \frac{1}{k}\right\},$$

then, for fixed $k = 1, 2, \cdots$, as $m \to +\infty$

$$\bigcup_{n=1}^{m} \overline{S_k}(x_n) \nearrow \bigcup_{n=1}^{\infty} \overline{S_k}(x_n) = X.$$

Thus, as $m \to +\infty$

$$X - \bigcup_{n=1}^{m} \overline{S_k}(x_n) \searrow \emptyset,$$

for fixed $k = 1, 2, \cdots$. Applying Lemma 1 to the double sequence $\{X - \bigcup_{n=1}^{m} \overline{S_k}(x_n) \mid m \geq 1, k \geq 1\}$, then there exists a subsequence $\{m_k\}_k$ of the positive integers such that

$$\mu \left(\bigcup_{k=1}^{+\infty} \left(X - \bigcup_{n=1}^{m_k} \overline{S_k}(x_n) \right) \right) < \epsilon$$

Put

$$K_\epsilon = \bigcap_{k=1}^{+\infty} \bigcup_{n=1}^{m_k} \overline{S_k}(x_n).$$

Thus, the closed set K_ϵ is totally bounded. From the completeness of X, we know that K_ϵ is compact in X and satisfies

$$\mu(X - K_\epsilon) = \mu \left(\bigcup_{k=1}^{+\infty} \left(X - \bigcup_{n=1}^{m_k} \overline{S_k}(x_n) \right) \right) < \epsilon.$$

Thus the lemma has proved.

Now we will show the proof of Theorem 1 by using the previous lemmas.

Proof of Theorem 1. Let $A \in \mathcal{B}$ and given $\epsilon > 0$. From Proposition 1 we know that μ is regular. Therefore, there exist a sequence $\{F^{(k)}\}_{k=1}^{\infty}$ of closed sets and a sequence $\{G^{(k)}\}_{k=1}^{\infty}$ of open sets such that for every $k = 1, 2, \ldots$, $F^{(k)} \subset A \subset G^{(k)}$,

$$\mu(G^{(k)} - F^{(k)}) < \frac{1}{k}.$$

Without loss of generality, we can assume that the sequence $\{F^{(k)}\}_{k=1}^{\infty}$ is increasing in k and the sequence $\{G^{(k)}\}_{k=1}^{\infty}$ is decreasing in k. Thus, $\{G^{(k)} - F^{(k)}\}_{k=1}^{\infty}$ is a decreasing sequence of sets with respect to k, and as $k \to \infty$

$$G^{(k)} - F^{(k)} \searrow \bigcap_{k=1}^{\infty} (G^{(k)} - F^{(k)}).$$

Denote $D_1 = \bigcap_{k=1}^{\infty} (G^{(k)} - F^{(k)})$, and noting that $\mu(D_1) \leq \mu(G^{(k)} - F^{(k)}) < 1/k$, $k = 1, 2, \ldots$, then $\mu(D_1) = 0$.

On the other hand, from Lemma 2 there exists a sequence $\{K^{(k)}\}_{k=1}^{\infty}$ of compact subsets in X such that for every $k = 1, 2, \ldots$

$$\mu(X - K^{(k)}) < \frac{1}{k},$$

and we can assume that $\{K^{(k)}\}_{k=1}^{\infty}$ is decreasing in k. Therefore, as $k \to \infty$

$$X - K^{(k)} \searrow \bigcap_{k=1}^{\infty}(X - K^{(k)}).$$

Denote $D_1 = \bigcap_{k=1}^{\infty}(X - K^{(k)})$, then $\mu(D_1) = 0$. Thus, we have

$$(X - K^{(k)}) \cup (G^{(k)} - F^{(k)}) \searrow D_1 \cup D_2$$

as $k \to \infty$. Noting that $\mu(D_1 \cup D_2) = 0$, by the continuity of μ, then

$$\lim_{k \to +\infty} \mu\left((X - K^{(k)}) \cup (G^{(k)} - F^{(k)})\right) = 0.$$

Therefore there exists k_0 such that

$$\mu\left((X - K^{(k_0)}) \cup (G^{(k_0)} - F^{(k_0)})\right) < \epsilon.$$

Denoting $K_\epsilon = K^{(k_0)} \cap F^{(k_0)}$ and $G_\epsilon = G^{(k_0)}$, then K_ϵ is a compact set and G_ϵ is an open set, and $K_\epsilon \subset A \subset G_\epsilon$. Since $G_\epsilon - K_\epsilon \subset (X - K^{(k_0)}) \cup (G^{(k_0)} - F^{(k_0)})$, we obtain

$$\mu(G_\epsilon - K_\epsilon) \le \mu(X - K^{(k_0)}) \cup (G^{(k_0)} - F^{(k_0)}) < \epsilon.$$

This shows that μ is strongly regular. *q.e.d.*

Corollary 1. *If μ is null-additive, then for any $A \in \mathcal{B}$ the following statements hold:*

(1) *For each $\epsilon > 0$, there exist a compact set $K_\epsilon \in \mathcal{K}$ such that $K_\epsilon \subset A$ and $\mu(A - K_\epsilon) < \epsilon$;*
(2) $\mu(A) = \sup\{ \mu(K) \mid K \subset A, \ K \in \mathcal{K} \}$.

By using the strongly regular of fuzzy measure, similar to the proof of Theorem 3 and 4 in [4], we can prove the following theorems. They are a version of Egoroff's theorem and Lusin's theorem on complete separable metric space, respectively.

Theorem 2. (Egoroff's theorem) *Let μ be null-additive continuous fuzzy measure. If $\{f_n\}$ converges to f almost everywhere on X, then for any $\epsilon > 0$, there exists a compact subset $K_\epsilon \in \mathcal{K}$ such that $\mu(X - K_\epsilon) < \epsilon$ and $\{f_n\}_n$ converges to f uniformly on K_ϵ.*

Theorem 3. (Lusin's theorem) *Let μ be null-additive continuous fuzzy measure. If f is a real measurable function on X, then, for each $\epsilon > 0$, there exists a compact subset $K_\epsilon \in \mathcal{K}$ such that f is continuous on K_ϵ and $\mu(X - K_\epsilon) \le \epsilon$.*

4   Atoms of Fuzzy Measure

In this section, as an application of strongly regularity, we shall show a characterization of atom of null-additive fuzzy measure on complete separable metric space.

Definition 4. ([2]) A set $A \in \mathcal{B}$ with $\mu(A) > 0$ is call an atom if for any $B \subset A$ then

(i) $\mu(B) = 0$, or
(ii) $\mu(A) = \mu(B)$ and $\mu(A - B) = 0$ holds.

Consider a nonnegative real-valued measurable function f on A. The *fuzzy integral* of f on A with respect to μ, denoted by $(S) \int_A f d\mu$, is defined by

$$(S) \int_A f d\mu = \sup_{0 \le \alpha < +\infty} [\alpha \wedge \mu(\{x : f(x) \ge \alpha\} \cap A)]$$

Theorem 4. *Let μ be null-additive and continuous. If A is an atom of μ, then there exists a point $a \in A$ such that the fuzzy integral satisfies*

$$(S) \int_A f d\mu = f(a) \wedge \mu(\{a\})$$

for any non-negative measurable function f on A.

Proof. It is similar to the proof of Theorem 8 in [2]. *q.e.d.*

Acknowledgement

The authors should express their thanks to referee who shows us two references [8] and [10].

References

1. I. Dobrakov, On submeasures I, *Dissertations Math.* 112(1974) 1−35.
2. Q. Jiang, H. Suzuki, Fuzzy measures on metric spaces, *Fuzzy Sets and Systems* 83(1996) 99−106.
3. J. Li, Order continuous of monotone set function and convergence of measurable functions sequence, *Applied Mathematics and Computation* 135(2003) 211−218.
4. J. Li, M. Yasuda, Lusin's theorem on fuzzy measure spaces, *Fuzzy Sets and Systems* 146(2004) 121−133.
5. Y. Narukawa, T. Murofushi, M. Sugeno, Regular fuzzy measure and representation of comonotonically additive functional, *Fuzzy Sets and Systems* 112(2000) 177−186.
6. Y. Narukawa, T. Murofushi, Conditions for Choquet integral representation of the comonotonically additive and monotone functional, *J. Math. Anal. Appl.* 282(2003) 201−211.

7. Y. Narukawa, T. Murofushi, Regular null-additive measure and Choquet integral, *Fuzzy Sets and Systems* 143(2004) 487−492.
8. Y. Narukawa, T. Murofushi, Choquet integral with respect to a regular non-additive measures, Proc. 2004 IEEE Int. Conf. Fuzzy Systems(FUZZ-IEEE 2004), (2004), 517-521.
9. E. Pap, *Null-additive Set Functions*, Kluwer, Dordrecht, 1995.
10. E. Pap, Regular null additive monotone set functions, Univ. u Novom Sadu Zb. rad Prorod. -Mat. Fak. Ser. mat. 25, 2(1995), 93-101.
11. J. Song, J. Li, Regularity of null-additive fuzzy measure on metric spaces, *Int. J. General Systems* 32(2003) 271−279.
12. J. Wu, C. Wu, Fuzzy regular measures on topological spaces, *Fuzzy Sets and Systems* 119(2001) 529−533.
13. Z. Wang, G. J. Klir, *Fuzzy Measure Theory*, Plenum, New York, 1992.

A Statistical Criterion of Consistency
in the Analytic Hierarchy Process

José Antonio Alonso[1] and Mª Teresa Lamata[2]

[1] Dpto. Lenguajes y Sistemas Informáticos. Universidad de Cádiz
Escuela Superior de Ingeniería, 11003-Cádiz, Spain
joseantonio.alonso@uca.es
[2] Dpto de Ciencias de la Computación e I.A, E.T.S de Ingeniería Informática
Universidad de Granada, 18071-Granada, Spain
mtl@decsai.ugr.es

Abstract. In this paper, we present a statistical criterion for accepting/rejecting the pairwise reciprocal comparison matrices in the Analytic Hierarchy Process. We have studied statistically the consistency in random matrices of different sizes. We are not agree with the traditional criterion of accepting matrices due to their inflexibility and because it is too restrictive when the size of the matrix increases. Our system is capable to adapt the acceptance requirements to different scopes and consistency's necessities. The advantages of our consistency system is the introduction of statistical relativity in the acceptance criterion and the simplicity of the used index, the eigenvalue (λ_{max}).

1 Introduction

Over the last three decades, a number of methods have been developed which use pairwise comparisons of the alternatives and criteria for solving discrete alternatives multicriteria decision making (MCDM [1]).

The Analytic Hierarchy Process (AHP) proposed by Saaty [2,3] is a very popular approach to MCDM, that involves qualitative data. It has been applied during the last twenty years in many situations of decision-making.

The AHP has been used on a wide range of applications in a lot of different fields. The method uses a reciprocal decision matrix obtained by pairwise comparisons such that the information is given in a linguistic form.

The method of pairwise comparisons was introduced by Fechner in 1860 [4] and worked out by Thurstone in 1927 [5]. Based in pairwise comparison, Saaty proposes the AHP [2,3] as a method for multicriteria decision-making. It provides a way of breaking down the general method into a hierarchy of sub-problems, which are easier to evaluate.

In the pairwise comparison method, criteria and alternatives, are presented in pairs of one or more referees (e.g., experts or decision-makers). It is necessary to evaluate individual alternatives, deriving weights for the criteria, constructing the overall rating of the alternatives and identifying the best one.

Let us denote the alternatives by $\{A_1, A_2,..., A_n\}$ (n is the number of compared alternatives), their current weights by $\{w_1, w_2,..., w_n\}$ and the matrix of the ratios of all weights by $W = [w_i/w_j]$.

V. Torra et al. (Eds.): MDAI 2005, LNAI 3558, pp. 67–76, 2005.

The matrix of pairwise comparisons $A = [\, a_{ij} \,]$ represents the intensities of the expert's preference between individual pairs of alternatives (A_i versus A_j, for all i,j=1,2,..,n). They are chosen usually from a given scale (9,8,…,1/8,1/9). Given n $\{A_1, A_2,…, A_n\}$ alternatives, a decision maker compares a pair of alternatives for all the possible pairs, n(n-1)/2, and a comparison matrix A is obtained, where the element a_{ij} shows the preference weight of A_i obtained by comparing with A_j.

The a_{ij} elements estimate the ratios w_i/w_j where w is the vector of current weights of the alternative, which is our goal. All the ratios are positive and satisfy the reciprocity property: $a_{ij} = 1/a_{ji}$ $\forall$i,j=1,2,..,n.

The a_{ij} elements estimate the ratios w_i/w_j where w is the vector of current weights of the alternative, which is our goal. All the ratios are positive and satisfy the reciprocity property: $a_{ij} = 1/a_{ji}$ $\forall$i,j=1,2,..,n.

This paper is divided into four sections. The first one introduces the AHP method. The second one shows the traditional way of measuring consistency and accepting or rejecting matrices in the AHP and the drawbacks we found in this approach. The third section develops our proposal. Our proposal is an alternative and statistical criterion of acceptance or rejection of AHP matrices due to its consistency. Finally, we present the conclusions of the paper.

2 Traditional Criterion of Consistency in the AHP. Drawbacks

The usual method for computing the ranking and weight of alternatives in the AHP is the eigenvector.

In the eigenvector method, the weight vector is the eigenvector corresponding to the maximum eigenvalue "λ_{max}" of the matrix A. According to the Perron-Frobenius Theorem, the eigenvalue "λ_{max}" is positive and real. Furthermore, the vector "w" can be chosen with all positive coordinates. It is a normalized solution of the following equation:

$$A\,w = \lambda_{max}\,w \qquad (1)$$

where "λ_{max}" is the largest eigenvalue of the matrix.

The traditional eigenvector method for estimating weights in the Analytic Hierarchy Process yields a way of measuring the consistency of the referee's preferences arranged in the comparison matrix. The consistency index (CI) is given by

$$CI = \frac{\lambda_{max} - n}{n-1} \qquad (2)$$

Saaty [2] has shown that if the referee is completely consistent then "$a_{ij} \cdot a_{jk} = a_{ik}$ ($\forall$ i,j,k)", "$\lambda_{max} = n$" and "$CI = 0$". Otherwise,, if the referee is not absolutely consistent "$\lambda_{max} > n$" and Saaty proposes the following index for measuring consistency :

$$CR = CI / RI \qquad (3)$$

where 'RI' is the average value of 'CI' for a random matrices using the Saaty's scale obtained by Forman[6]. A historical study of several used RIs and a way of estimation this index could be seen in Alonso and Lamata [10]. The main idea is that CR is a normalized value, because is divided by a arithmetic mean of a random matrices consistency indexes (*RI*).

Table 1. Random index for a several matrix dimensions. Forman (17672 to 77847 matrices)

n	1-2	3	4	5	6	7	8	9
RI	0,00	0.52	0.89	1.11	1.25	1.35	1.45	1.49

In the ideal case of total consistency "$\lambda_{max} = n$", the relations between the weights w_i and the judgments a_{ij} will be given by $\dfrac{w_i}{w_j} = a_{ij}$ for i,j = 1,2,...n.

In this exceptional case the two different matrices, – judgments and weights – are equal. However, it would be unrealistic to require these relations to hold in the general case.

Saaty suggests that a consistency index less or equal to 0.10 indicates that the decision maker has adequately structured the problem in question, but if the consistency index is greater than 0.10 then the response by subject can be considered as random.

But, is this really true? We don't agree with it, and the best way to illustrate it is by giving a pair of examples.

Suppose that two referees R_1 and R_2 express their preferences $P(A_i, A_j)$ about three alternatives $\{A_1, A_2; A_3\}$

$$R_1 \begin{cases} P(A_1, A_2) = 7 \\ P(A_2, A_3) = 1/5 \\ P(A_1, A_3) = 5 \end{cases} \quad \text{and} \quad R_2 \begin{cases} P(A_1, A_2) = 7 \\ P(A_2, A_3) = 1/5 \\ P(A_1, A_3) = 6 \end{cases}$$

We may see that a little difference in the appreciation concerning the preference between A_1 and A_3 yields that the $CR (R_1) = 0.0914$ (accepted), and $CR (R_2) = 0.12$ (rejected) to the second subject. We think otherwise that the two set of preferences are nearly the same,

$$P(A_1, A_2) > 1, P(A_1, A_3) > 1, P(A_3, A_2) > 1$$
$$P(A_1, A_2) \geq \text{Max}\{ P(A_1, A_3), P(A_3, A_2) \}$$
$$7 \geq \text{Max} \{5, 5\} \text{ for the first case}$$
$$7 \geq \text{Max} \{6, 5\} \text{ for the second one}$$

so, we accept the matrix in the first case and the second one will be rejected. We are absolutely disagree with this decision.

As a second example, this matrix

$$\begin{pmatrix} 1 & 5 & 9 \\ 1/5 & 1 & 6 \\ 1/9 & 1/6 & 1 \end{pmatrix}$$

is rejected because, $\lambda_{max} = 3.1632$ and $CR = 0.14 > 0.1$.

In this particular case, it is possible to proof that the transitivity property is not violated.

Therefore: A_1 is preferred (five times) to A_2, A_2 is preferred (six times) to A_3 and A_1 is preferred (nine times) to A_3. Being

$$9 \geq \max \{5, 6\}$$

it is not possible to use a value greater than 9 using the Saaty's scale. In our opinion this matrix must be accepted as a consistent matrix depending on the level of consistency needed.

Seeing these two clear examples, we absolutely disagree with this approach. The problem of accepting/rejecting matrices has been greatly discussed, especially the relation between the consistency and the scale used to represent the decision-maker judgments.

Lane and Verdini (1989) [7] have shown that using a 9-point scale, Saaty's CR threshold is so much restrictive due to the standard deviation of CI for randomly generated matrices is relatively small.

On the other hand Murphy in 1993 [8] have shown that the 9-point scale proposed by Saaty gives results which are outside the accepted consistency when n increases.

Salo and Hämäläinen (1993) [9] have shown that the CR threshold depends on the granularity of the scale, which is being used. Taking into account these ideas we want to introduce a relative and statistical criterion of matrix acceptance. The system can be adapted to whatever scale needed.

Kwiesielewicz [11] introduce the concept of contradictory judgments and Lamata and Pelaez [12,13] have studied different methods to study and improve consistency.

3   A New Statistical Criterion of Matrix Acceptance

The Analytic Hierarchy Process provides the decision-maker an index for measuring the consistency of pairwise reciprocal comparison matrices (CI). Although it is one of the most commonly used methods, it presents some disadvantages. One of these disadvantages is that this index is an absolute index. As we saw in the previous section, this fact causes reasonable consequences little, like accepting or rejecting matrices by minimum differences in the preferences or rejecting matrices that the common sense says to us that they are reasonably consistent.

In this paper we present a new criterion for acceptance and a new index for representing the consistency in pairwise reciprocal comparison matrices. This index and criterion allows the decision-maker to study the consistency of each matrix in a relative way. Using the index that we present, the user can decide about the matrix consistency using not only the matrix entries but also the level of consistency that the decision-maker needs in this particular case.

In this section, we study the AHP consistency problem with statistical criteria. We are going to use as a consistency index the maximum right eigenvalue (λ_{max}) of each studied matrix.

The main idea is that a matrix is consistent (or not) depending on the scope. In different situations, the decision-making could need different levels of consistency and he/she can represent them using percentiles. Therefore, one specific matrix is consistent or it is not (is accepted or not as a consistent matrix) depending on two different factors:

a) An index of consistency (λ_{max}) .
b) The level of consistency needed (percentile)

In that case, we can define the consistency of a specific matrix as a Boolean function with two parameters, CR and percentile.

$$F(\lambda_{max}, \text{percentile})$$

- Choosing the percentile by the decision-maker and knowing the number n of alternatives we get a value in Table 3 (λ_{max} T).
- Comparing the matrix CR to the entry λ_{max} T (percentile, n) of the table 3 and if

$$\lambda_{max} \leq \lambda_{max} T$$

the matrix is accepted, otherwise

$$\lambda_{max} > \lambda_{max} T$$

the matrix is rejected.

We are going to explain the algorithm that we use to generate the λ_{max} values table (λ_{max}T) and that we use to decided if one matrix must be accepted as a consistent one or not.

3.1 Algorithm for Obtaining the Table of λ_{max} Values Depending on Dimension and Percentiles

This algorithm is composed of the following sequence of steps:

1. Generation of the matrices that we are going to study.
2. λ_{max} calculus of each matrix (for all the matrices).
3. Generation of the λ_{max} table (λ_{max} T) depending on dimension and chosen percentiles.

3.1.1 Generation of the Matrices

We have generated 1,200,000 positive reciprocal pairwise comparison matrices (100,000 matrices for each dimension, from 3x3 to 14x14), whose entries were randomly generated using the scale 1/9, 1/8, ...1/2,1,2...8,9 and using a uniform distribution.

```
Algorithm Generation_of_AHP_matrices
   numbermatrices = 100000;
   dimensionfrom = 3;
   dimensionuntil = 14;
for dim= dimensionfrom to  dimensionuntil
   for i=1 to numbermatrices
       mats"dimxdim"(:,:,i)=
                   generates_AHP_single_matrix(dim);
   end
end
End_of_Algorithm Generation_ of_ AHP_ matrices
function   mat = generates_ahp_matrix(dim)
   for i=1 to dim
       for j=1 to dim
           if i>j
               new_value = calculate_AHP_value(random);
```

```
            mat (i,j)  =  new_value;
            mat (j,i)  =  1/new_value;
        end;
      end;
    end;
End_of_function_generates_ahp_matrix
function val = calculate_AHP_value (value)
  Saaty_values=[1/9,1/8,1/7,1/6,1/5,1/4,1/3,1/2,1,2,3
                ,4,5,6,7,8,9]
  ind = Int (value * 17) + 1
  val = Saaty_values[ind]
End_of_function_calculate_AHP_value
```

3.1.2 λ_{max} Calculus of Each Matrix (For All the Matrices)

We are going to calculate the maximum eigenvalue (λ_{max}) of all the matrices (1,200,000) we generated before.

```
Algorithm Calculus_λ    _all_matrices
                    max
    numbermatrices = 100000;
    dimensionfrom = 3;
    dimensionuntil = 14;
    for dim= dimensionfrom to  dimensionuntil
        for i=1 to numbermatrices
            LMAX"dimxdim"(i)  =   max(eig(mat))
        end
    end
End_of_Algorithm Calculus_λ    _all_Matrices
                           max
```

This function uses two Matlab functions, max and eig.

The λ_{max} (3x3) and λ_{max} (4x4) distributions seems to be a Weibull distribution. The rest of distributions are normal distributions. The mean and the standard deviation can be seen in Table 2.

Table 2. On show the mean and deviation of the λ_{max} values

n	3	4	5	6	7	8	9	10	11	12	13	14
$\overline{\lambda}_{max}$	4.051	6.644	9.434	12.241	15.05	17.837	20.598	23.370	26.142	28.903	31.658	34.408
Dstd	1.394	1.883	2.036	2.037	1.985	1.949	1.910	1.871	1.851	1.840	1.811	1.822

As you can see in Fig. 13 the least-squares adjustment line is $\overline{\lambda}_{max}$ = 2.7706 n − 4.356. The x-axis represents the matrix size and the y-axis presents the values of the correspondent values of $\overline{\lambda}_{max}$ (sizes 3 to 14). The correlation coefficient is 0.9999.

3.1.3 Generation of the λ_{max} Table Depending on Dimension and Percentiles

To develop the critical value of λ_{max} that allows us to accept the same percentile of matrices for all values of n, we use the percentile or percentage of the population of λ_{max} and we have used exactly the same scale that Saaty and Forman used to calculate the random index RI, as we present in the algorithm above and the λ_{max} values calculated previously.

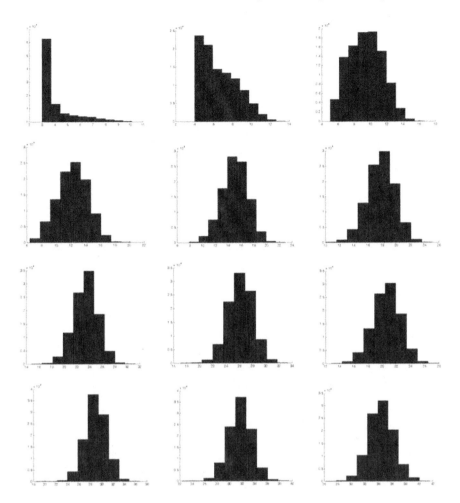

Fig. 1. to Fig 12. Represents the λ_{max} distribution histograms (matrices of dimension from 3x3 to 14x14)

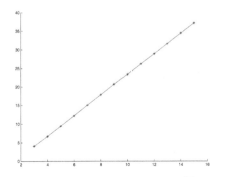

Fig. 13. The different points you can see are corresponding to $\overline{\lambda}_{max}$ of each size (from 3 to 14), and the line is the least-squares adjustment straight line

```
Algorithm Generation_table_LMAX_dimension_percentiles
    number_of_percentiles = 13
    percentiles = [0,1,5,10,15,20,25,30,35,40,45,50,100];
    numbermatrices = 100000;
    dimensionfrom = 3;
    dimensionuntil = 14;
    for dim= dimensionfrom to  dimensionuntil
      for p =1 to number_of_percentiles
        LMAXTablep_valuexdim(p,dim)=prctile
            (LMAX"dimxdim"(dim),percentiles(p));
      end
    end
End_of_Algorithm
Generation_table_LMAX_dimension_percentiles
```

For each percentile, $p \in [0,1]$, we show the population's value where the $(100p)\%$ of the population is on the left and $(100(1-p)\%)$ is on the right. If p is equal to 0, we get the minimum of the population, if p is equal to 1; we obviously get the maximum of the population.

Table 3. On show the λ_{max} values obtained for several percentiles and number of alternatives

p	Number of alternatives											
	3	4	5	6	7	8	9	10	11	12	13	14
Min	3.000	4.000	5.004	6.435	7.876	10.073	12.811	14.818	17.039	18.474	22.415	26.249
0.01	3.000	4.118	5.689	7.703	10.237	13.106	15.975	18.796	21.685	24.488	27.325	30.128
0.05	3.007	4.333	6.217	8.747	11.640	14.535	17.364	20.212	23.095	25.821	28.638	31.441
0.10	3.029	4.518	6.664	9.480	12.425	15.297	18.110	20.956	23.779	26.537	29.326	32.125
0.15	3.053	4.678	7.070	10.023	12.962	15.816	18.614	21.444	24.228	27.006	29.780	32.582
0.20	3.094	4.834	7.455	10.462	13.381	16.217	19.011	21.826	24.580	27.370	30.144	32.936
0.25	3.135	5.004	7.830	10.832	13.731	16.556	19.335	22.145	24.887	27.688	30.444	33.231
0.30	3.197	5.186	8.185	11.160	14.046	16.862	19.631	22.427	25.166	27.976	30.720	33.501
0.35	3.252	5.399	8.516	11.464	14.334	17.140	19.909	22.691	25.439	28.228	30.979	33.753
0.40	3.313	5.650	8.829	11.747	14.597	17.399	20.165	22.942	25.692	28.473	31.219	33.987
0.45	3.367	5.936	9.135	12.022	14.858	17.650	20.413	23.179	25.935	28.705	31.448	34.219
0.50	3.435	6.243	9.433	12.293	15.111	17.897	20.655	23.415	26.170	28.937	31.674	34.446
Max	10.111	13.595	16.615	20.215	22.904	25.074	27.981	31.276	33.373	36.672	39.433	41.551

3.2 Relation Between Our Acceptance System and Saaty's Acceptance System

Using the definition of Consistency Index (2) and the definition of the Consistency Ratio (3) and the traditional acceptance criterion

$$CR = CI / RI < 0.1 \qquad (4)$$

and taking into account the definition of RI, as a mean of CI

$$RI = \frac{\overline{\lambda_{max}} - n}{n - 1}$$

we can infer that

$$CR = \frac{\overline{\lambda_{max}} - n}{\overline{\lambda_{max}} - n} < 0.1$$

thus Saaty only accepts matrices as a consistent one, if and only if

$$\lambda_{max} < n + 0.1 \left(\overline{\lambda}_{max} - n \right).$$

Using the least-squares adjustment straight line we calculated before

$$\overline{\lambda}_{max} = 2.7706 \, n - 4.356 \tag{5}$$

we can conclude that the consistency criterion of Saaty using eigenvalue can be expressed as

$$\lambda_{max} < n + 0.1(17706n - 4.356) \tag{6}$$

and thus

$$max\lambda_{max} \, err = 0.1(1.7706n - 4.356) \tag{7}$$

must be the maximum error that Saaty´s accepts in the λ_{max}.

Table 4. On show the maximum λ_{max} accepted by Saaty depending on the number of alternatives (3 to 14)

n	3	4	5	6	7	8	9	10	11	12	13	14
λ_{max}	3.095	4.272	5.449	6.626	7.803	8.980	10.157	11.335	12.512	13.689	14.866	16.043

Comparing the values of Table 3 and Table 4 we notice that the criterion of Saaty is too much restrictive.

As we have said the criterion for accepting/rejecting matrices using this table (Table 3) is simple and clear. We accept a matrix as a consistent matrix if and only if its maximum eigenvalue (λ_{max}) is not greater than the value we can get from the table (the row of percentile and column of its dimension). The relativity of this criterion appears when you choose several percentiles for each different situations (or scopes), and its simplicity get using directly the λ_{max}.

It is important notice that, if we use the traditional AHP acceptance criterion, we cannot accept none of them (none of 100,000) of the matrices of dimension greater than 6x6. We are using exactly the same quality data (random matrices), and, in that situation, the traditional matrix acceptation depends not only of the data quality (consistency) but also the dimension of the matrices (number of alternatives concerned). Saaty haven't took into account this fact and the traditional acceptance criterion is absolute and, consequently, too restrictive when the number of alternatives increases.

4 Conclusions

As we have shown, the Saaty's AHP acceptance criterion is absolute and too restrictive when the number of alternatives increases. We have studied statistically the consistency in random matrices of different dimensions. We realized that the value of whatever consistency index depends not only of the consistency of the data (entries of the matrix) but also its dimension.

The AHP criteria haven't took into account this situation and, for that reason, is not appropriate to work with matrices of different dimensions. We took into account this situations, comparing the value of the used consistency index (λ_{max}) for different matrices of the same size.

Our system is able to accept different levels of consistency needed (to adapt the criterion to more or less restrictive situation), and uses a statistical criterion to decide if accepts or not a matrix as a consistent one. Our system compares the matrix level of consistency when the level of consistency of the rest of the matrices of the same dimension. This statistical criterion, taking into account the dimension of the matrices, and the different level of consistency needed, offer clear advantages compared with the traditional system, and we use a more simple consistency index than Saaty´s, the maximum eigenvalue of each matrix (λ_{max}).

Acknowledgments

This work was partially supported by the DGICYT under project TIC2002-03411.

References

1. Keeney, R., Raiffa, H.: Decisions with Multiple Objectives; Preferences and Values Trade-offs. Wiley. New York (1976)
2. Saaty, T.L.: The Analytic Hierarchy Process. New York (1980)
3. Saaty, T.L.: Fundamentals of Decision Making and Priority Theory with the Analytic Hierarchy Process. RWS Publications Pittsburgh (1994)
4. Fechner,G.T.: Elements of Psychophysics, Volume 1, Holt, Rinehart & Winston, New York, (1965); translation by H.E.Adler of Elemente der Psychophysik, Breitkopf und Hârtel, Leipzig (1980)
5. Thurstone, L.L.: A law of comparative judgments. Psychological Reviews 34, (1927) 273-286.
6. Forman, E.H.: Random indices for Incomplete Pairwise Comparison Matrices. European Journal of Operational Research 48, (1990) 153-155.
7. Lane, E.F., Verdini, W.A.: A consistency test for AHP decision makers. Decision Science 20, (1989) 575-590.
8. Murphy, C.K.: Limits of the Analytical Hierarchy Process from its consistency index. European Journal of Operational Research 65, (1993) 138-139
9. Salo A.A., Hämäläinen R.P.: On the measurement of preferences in the AHP", Research Report, Systems Analysis Laboratory, Helsinki University of Technology (1993)
10. Alonso. J.A, Lamata M.T.: Estimation of the Random Index in the Analytic Hierarchy Process. Proceedings of Information Processing and Management of Uncertainty in Knowledge-Based Systems (IPMU'04) Perugia Vol I, (2004) 317-322.
11. Kwiesielewicz. M., van Uden.E.: Inconsistent and contradictory judgements in pairwise comparison method in the AHP Computers & Operations Research 31, (2004) 713–719
12. Pelaez.J.I., Lamata.M.T.: A New Measure of Consistency for Positive Reciprocal Matrices. Computers and Mathematics with Applications 46, (2003) 1839-1845
13. Lamata.M.T., Pelaez.J.I.: A method for improving the consistency of judgements. International Journal of Uncertainty Fuzzyness and Knowledge-based Systems 10 (2002) 677-686

Evaluating the Airline Service Quality
by Fuzzy OWA Operators

Ching-Hsue Cheng[1], Jing-Rong Chang[1], Tien-Hwa Ho[2], and An-Pin Chen[2]

[1] Department of Information Management
National Yunlin University of Science and Technology
123, Section 3, University Road, Touliu, Yunlin 640, Taiwan
{chcheng,g9120806}@pine.yuntech.edu.tw
[2] Graduate School of Information Management, National Chiao Tung University
1001 Ta Hsueh Road, Hsinchu 300, Taiwan

Abstract. The OWA (Ordered Weighted Averaging) aggregation operators have been extensively adopted to assign the relative weights of numerous criteria. However, previous aggregation operators (including OWA) are independent of aggregation situations. To solve the problem, this study proposes a new aggregation model – dynamic fuzzy OWA operators based on situation model, which can modify the associated dynamic weight based on the aggregation situation and can work like a "magnifying lens" to enlarge the most important attribute dependent on minimal information, or can obtain equal attribute weights based on maximal information. We also apply proposed model to evaluate the service quality of airline.

1 Introduction

Information aggregation can be applied to many situations, including neural networks, fuzzy logic controllers, expert systems, and multi-criteria decision support systems [12]. In a vague condition, fuzzy set theory [30] can provide an attractive connection to represent uncertain information and can aggregate them properly. The existing aggregation operators are, in general, the t-norm [27], t-conorm [27], mean operators [9], Yager's operator [28,29] and γ-operator [32].

Multi-criteria decision making (MCDM) models are characterized to evaluate a finite set of alternatives. The main purpose of solving MCDM problems is to measure the overall preference values of the alternatives. Two reasons reveal the importance of obtaining relative weights in MCDM problems. First, numbers of approaches have been proposed to assess criteria weights, which are then used explicitly to aggregate specific priority scores [19,20,28,31]. Second, some experiments [2,18,25] demonstrate that different approaches for deriving weights may lead to different results [1,14].

When an attempt is made to solve the MCDM problem by aggregating the information of each attribute in many disciplines, a problem of aggregating criteria functions to form overall decision functions occurs owing to these criteria always being interdependent. One extreme is the situation in which we hope that all the criteria will be satisfied ("and" situation), while another situation is the case in which satisfying simple criteria satisfaction is that any of the criteria is all we desire ("or" situation) [28,29]. In 1988, Yager [28] first introduced the concept of OWA operators to solve this problem. The OWA operators have the ability to provide an aggregation lying

V. Torra et al. (Eds.): MDAI 2005, LNAI 3558, pp. 77–88, 2005.
© Springer-Verlag Berlin Heidelberg 2005

between these two extremes, so it more fit the thought of human being (between the "and" and "or situations) [28]. O'Hagan [15] is the first to use the concept of entropy in the OWA operation, but situation factor has not yet been taken into the consideration of this method. Mesiar and Saminger [13] have shown that in the class of OWA operators is on the domination over the t-norm and continuous Archimedean t-norms.

According to previous studies, t-norm and t-conorm are based on the theory of logic [27], and the mean operators [9] are based on the mathematical properties of averaging. Choi [5] has pointed out that even though Yager's operator [26] and γ-operator [32] are suggested as an aggregation method using parameter, at present, how to obtain feasible value of parameter is still missing. In the opinion of Choi [5], these types of aggregation operators [9,26,32] are independent of their situations and cannot reflect change in situations. To resolve this problem, this study proposes a Fuzzy OWA aggregation model based on the faster OWA operators, which has been introduced by Fuller and Majlender [7] and can work like a magnifying lens and adjust its focus based on the sparest information to change the dynamic attribute weights to revise the weight of each attribute based on aggregation situation, and then to provide suggestions to decision maker (DM). To verify the proposed model, this paper adopted the data of airline cases in Tsaur et al. [24]. This study also compares our results with method of Tsaur et al. [24] that have been applied to evaluate the service quality of three airlines.

The rest of this paper is organized as follows. Section 2 presents a basic concept of the OWA operator. Section 3 then introduces the proposed model and a generalized algorithm. The adjusted algorithm of proposed model and empirical example of airline service quality are introduced in section 4. Conclusions are finally made in section 5.

2 OWA Operator

The OWA operator [28,29] is an important aggregation operator within the class of weighted aggregation methods. Many related studies have been conducted in recent years. For example, Filev and Yager [6] derived a method for obtaining the OWA aggregating operator from aggregated data and developed methods for calculating the weights of the OWA operator. Torra then studied the learning of weights for the weighted mean, OWA, WOWA [22], and quasi-weighted means [21] operators. Carbonell et al. [3] have introduced the concepts of Extended Aggregation Function and Extended OWA operator. Torra [23] also discussed the application of OWA operators in two fields (i.e. model building and information extraction) of data mining. Fuller and Majlender [7] have used Lagrange multipliers to derive a polynomial equation to solve constrained optimization problem and to determine the optimal weighting vector. Meanwhile, Smolikova and Wachowiak [19] have described and compared aggregation techniques for expert multi-criteria decision-making method. Furthermore, Ribeiro and Pereira [16] have presented an aggregation schema based on generalized mixture operators using weighting functions, and have compared it with these two standard aggregation method: weighting averaging and ordered weighted averaging in the context of multiple attribute decision making. The main concepts of this approach are derived from the OWA operators of Yager [28,29] and Fuller and Majlender [7]. This section introduces the main content of their methods.

2.1 Yager's OWA

Yager [28] proposed an order weighted averaging (OWA) operator, which had the ability to get optimal weights of the attributes based on the rank of these weighting vectors after aggregation process (reference to Definition 1.).

Definition 1. An OWA operator of dimension n is a mapping $F: R^n \rightarrow R$, that has an associated weighting vector $W = [w_1, w_2, \dots, w_n]^T$ of having the properties

$$\sum_i w_i = 1, \quad \forall w_i \in [0,1] \ , \ i=1,\dots,n$$

and such that

$$f(a_1,\dots,a_n) = \sum_{j=1}^n w_j b_j \tag{1}$$

where b_j is the jth largest element of the collection of the aggregated objects $\{a_1,\dots,a_n\}$.

Yager [28,29] also introduced two important characterizing measures in respect to the weighting vector W of an OWA operator. The first one was the measure of orness of the aggregation, which was defined as

$$\text{Orness}(W) = \frac{1}{n-1} \sum_{i=1}^n (n-i) w_i \tag{2}$$

And, the second one, implying the measure of dispersion of the aggregation, was defined as

$$\text{Disp}(W) = -\sum_{i=1}^n w_i \ln W_i \tag{3}$$

And it measures the degree to which W takes into account all information in the aggregation.

O'Hagan [15] suggested a method which combines the principle of maximum entropy [8,10,17] and Yager's approach [28] to determine a special class of OWA operators having the maximal entropy of the OWA weights for a given level of *orness*. This approach was based on the solution of the following problem:

Maximize the function $\qquad -\sum_{i=1}^n w_i \ln W_i$

Subject to the constraints $\alpha = \dfrac{1}{n-1} \sum_{i=1}^n (n-i) w_i, \ 0 \le \alpha \le 1$

$$\sum_i w_i = 1, \quad \forall w_i \in [0,1] \ , \ i=1,\dots,n, \tag{4}$$

2.2 Fuller and Majlender's OWA

Fuller and Majlender [7] used the method of Lagrange multipliers to transfer Yager's OWA equation to a polynomial equation, which can determine the optimal weighting vector. By their method, the associated weighting vector is easily obtained by (5)-(7).

$$\ln w_j = \frac{j-1}{n-1} \ln w_n + \frac{n-j}{n-1} \ln w_1 \Rightarrow w_j = \sqrt[n-1]{w_1^{n-j} w_n^{j-1}} \tag{5}$$

$$\text{and } w_n = \frac{((n-1)\alpha - n) w_1 + 1}{(n-1)\alpha + 1 - n w_1} \tag{6}$$

$$\text{then } w_1\big[(n-1)\alpha+1-n\,w_1\big]^n = \big[(n-1)\alpha\big]^{n-1}\big[((n-1)\alpha-n)w_1+1\big] \tag{7}$$

So the optimal value of w_1 should satisfy equation (7). When w_1 is computed, we can determine w_n from equation (6) and then the other weights are obtained from equation (5). In a special case, when $w_1 = w_2 = \cdots\cdots = w_n = \frac{1}{n} \Rightarrow \text{disp(W)} = \ln n$ which is optimal solution to equation (5) for $\alpha = 0.5$.

3 New Dynamic OWA Aggregation Model

3.1 Dynamic Fuzzy OWA Model

After comparing the operators in [4,5,7,9,11,16,19,26,32] with the OWA operator, we find that the OWA operator has the rational aggregation result, and more closely fits the thoughts of human beings (between the "and" and "or" situations) [28]. Moreover, under the circumstances of maximal information entropy, the OWA operator can get the optimum result of the aggregation. However, it lacks the ability to reflect the aggregative situation during the aggregation process because the previous OWA operators use a common parameter (i.e. α), but do not view it as the situational factor. To maintain the useful character of the OWA (rational aggregation result) and correct the shortcomings (lack to reflect the aggregative situation), this study adds two main concepts:

1. Continuous improving aggregation result (attribute weights) and aggregating experts' opinions in sequential periods.
2. Changing the attribute weights based on situation (with situation parameter α).

Table 1. Main differences between proposed model and other aggregation methods

	Yager's OWA [28]	Fuller & Majlender's OWA [7]	Choi's operator [5]	Lee's two algorithm [11]	Chen's algorithm [4]	Tsaur et al. [24]	Proposed dynamic OWA
Aggregation operator	Yes	Yes	Yes	No	No	No	Yes
Situation parameter (α)	Partial*	Partial*	Yes	No	No	No	Yes
Feedback	No	No	No	No	No	No	Yes
Fuzzy Input	No	No	No	Yes	Yes	Yes	Yes

* The OWA operators use a common parameter (i.e. α), but they do not view it as the situational factor

After joining these two characters with fundamental OWA aggregation model, this work proposes a new fuzzy OWA aggregation model, and clarifies the main differences between the proposed model and other aggregation methods in Table 1. This new model not only has the ability to modify forecasting results of functions corresponding with the aggregative situation, but also can obtain associated attribute weights that rely on the OWA operator matching the model of human thoughts.

The first concept of modifying the aggregation dynamic attribute weights is the process, which is given to experts who want to evaluate the projects different weights.

In this way, experts will have different affects on integral result after evaluation. For example, if the evaluative time is regarded as a criterion to measure the degree of information quality, the newly-coming experts will be assigned a higher weight. This step can enable the newly-coming experts to have more influence on the attribute weights and individual project evaluation. Consequently, different attribute ratings can obtain dissimilar attribute weights and also different final proposed solutions for reference by decision makers.

Second, the concept of changing weights of each attribute "based on situation" is that the decision maker (or project manager) determines what is the value of parameter α from information entropy of actual aggregative situation. Therefore, the proposed model can be used to obtain attribute weights by rating them after OWA aggregation according to α. Main advantage of this concept is that the model can be treated as a magnifying lens to determine the most important attribute (assign weight =1) based on the sparest information (*i.e.* optimistic and $\alpha = 0$ or 1) situation. On the other hand, when α =0.5 (moderate situation), the proposed model can obtain attribute weights (equal weights of attributes) based on maximal information.

3.2 Algorithm for the Proposed Model

The steps of proposed algorithm are as follows:

Step 1. Build hierarchical structure model from determination problem and number (N) of attributes/criteria.

Step 2. Obtain opinions of domain experts and then collect their evaluative attribute weights of attributes in respect to the hierarchical structure model.

Step 3. List the feasible projects/alternatives, and request the experts to evaluate the grades of these projects.

Step 4. If no new expert is available, execute Step 5. If the experts do not have significant orderings, assign equal weight for evaluation. Otherwise, perform the OWA aggregation process to obtain the weights of experts for evaluation.

Step 5. The weights of each expert multiply their evaluative attribute weights to form the aggregative weights of attributes.

Step 6. Sort the attribute weights and execute OWA aggregation (by equation (5)-(7)) to obtain refined attribute weights.

Step 7. If the aggregative weights of sub-attributes are exist, to distribute the refined weight(s) of the sub-attributes of each attribute based on the ratio of weights of these sub-attributes given by the experts.

Step 8. Multiply the weights of the attributes by their project grades, and then rank their orderings to make reference solution to the decision maker.

4   Verification and Comparison

To verification proposed method, this section first introduces the context of data in airline service quality [24] and then presents the adjusted algorithm to fit this example. The results are also presented in section 4.3.

4.1 Data Contents

In Tsaur et al. [24], 450 questionnaires with 15 criteria were sent out to licensed tour guides in 29 general travel agencies. There were 211 surveys returned for a return rate of 47%. The questionnaire was composed of two parts: questions for evaluating the relative importance of criteria and airlines's performance corresponding to each criterion. Tsaur et al. [24] picked three major airlines as the objects of the empirical study. Airline A, the oldest airline in Taiwan, with more than 30 years history, gains the highest market share by nearly 30%. The market share of airline B, although is only 20%, is rapidly growing because of the positive image and reputation. Airline C is a rather young jetliner of operation history and the market share is just about 13%. By applying Analytic Hierarchy Process (AHP) in obtaining criteria weight and Technique for Order Preference by Similarity to Ideal Solution (TOPSIS) in ranking, Tsaur et al. found the most concerned aspect of service quality was tangible and the least was empathy (see Fig. 1).

4.2 Adjusted Algorithm

To verify the proposed model, this study assumes that a symbol $D(\tilde{A})$ denotes the defuzzification result of this fuzzy number $\tilde{A}$ by the centroid method [11], and uses the data in *Tsaur et al. [24]* as an example to explain each step. The adjusted steps based on section 3.2's algorithm are as follows:

Step 1. Build hierarchical structure model from determination problem and number of attributes (N).

> *For example, there are five aspects (first-level attributes/criteria) for airline service quality in Tsaur et al. [24] (i.e. N=5). The five aspects are Tangibility (AS_1), Reliability (AS_2), Responsiveness (AS_3), Assurance (AS_4), and Empathy (AS_5).*

Step 2. Collect attribute weights in respect to the hierarchical structure model by the domain experts (*Fig. 1 shows the results after AHP. We assume the weights of AS_1~AS_5 are W_1~W_5. For example, W_1 is equal to 0.245 according to Fig. 1*).

Step 3. List the feasible alternatives, and request the experts to evaluate the grades of these projects.

> *The three alternatives in this case are Airline A, B, and C. The original range of fuzzy measures in Tsaur et al. [24] is from 1 to 100. We have transferred the range to [0,1] and the transferred triangular fuzzy numbers (TFNs) of these alternatives under each criterion are shown in Table 2.*

Step 4. If no new expert is available, execute Step 5. If the experts do not have significant orderings, assign equal weight for evaluation. Otherwise, perform the OWA aggregation process to obtain the weights of experts for evaluation.

Step 5. The weights of each expert multiply their evaluative attribute weights to form the aggregative weights of attributes.

> *(In this example, steps 4 & 5 can be skipped.)*

Step 6. Sort the attribute/criteria weights and execute OWA aggregation OWA aggregation (by equation (5)-(7)) to obtain refined attribute weights (denoted as $W'_1 \sim W'_5$) under different α's values.

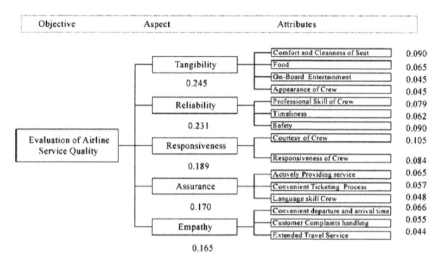

Fig. 1. Weights of five aspects and 15 criteria [24]

Table 2. Fuzzy performace measures (TFNs) of airlines

Service quality evaluation criteria	Airline A	Airline B	Airline C
Courtesy of attendants	(0.52,0.62,0.71)	(0.53,0.62,0.71)	(0.55,0.65,0.74)
Safety	(0.39,0.48,0.58)	(0.55,0.68,0.74)	(0.53,0.63,0.72)
Comfort and cleanness of seat	(0.52,0.61,0.70)	(0.54,0.63,0.72)	(0.56,0.66,0.75)
Responsiveness of attendants	(0.53,0.63,0.72)	(0.54,0.64,0.73)	(0.46,0.55,0.64)
Professional skills	(0.54,0.68,0.73)	(0.56,0.66,0.75)	(0.47,0.57,0.66)
Convenient departure time	(0.54,0.64,0.73)	(0.55,0.64,0.73)	(0.53,0.63,0.71)
Food	(0.53,0.63,0.71)	(0.51,0.61,0.69)	(0.52,0.61,0.70)
Actively providing service	(0.53,0.59,0.68)	(0.47,0.59,0.66)	(0.49,0.59,0.67)
Timeliness	(0.45,0.55,0.64)	(0.53,0.62,0.71)	(0.51,0.61,0.70)
Convenient ticketing process	(0.54,0.64,0.73)	(0.55,0.64,0.73)	(0.53,0.63,0.72)
Customer complaints handling	(0.44,0.54,0.63)	(0.46,0.56,0.65)	(0.45,0.55,0.65)
Language skill of airline attendant	(0.59,0.68,0.80)	(0.61,0.68,0.77)	(0.49,0.59,0.68)
On-board entertainment	(0.60,0.70,0.78)	(0.58,0.70,0.76)	(0.57,0.66,0.75)
Appearance of crew	(0.52,0.61,0.70)	(0.48,0.58,0.67)	(0.50,0.60,0.69)
Extended travel service	(0.50,0.59,0.68)	(0.54,0.61,0.70)	(0.49,0.59,0.68)

Table 3. The weights of aspects after OWA aggregation

	α =0.5	α =0.6	α =0.7	α =0.8	α =0.9	α =1.0
Tangibility (W'_1)	0.20000	0.28839	0.39617	0.53067	0.71044	1
Reliability (W'_2)	0.20000	0.23528	0.25740	0.25651	0.20720	0
Responsiveness (W'_3)	0.20000	0.19196	0.16724	0.12399	0.06043	0
Assurance (W'_4)	0.20000	0.15660	0.10859	0.05986	0.01679	0
Empathy (W'_5)	0.20000	0.12777	0.07060	0.02897	0.00514	0

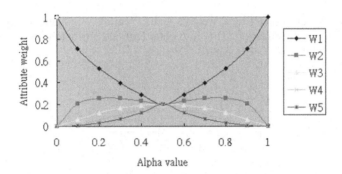

Fig. 2. The distribution of the refined weights

The ranking order of AHP weights in Fig. 1 is $W_1> W_2> W_3> W_4>W_5$. Then, the distribution of refined weights for each criterion after OWA is shown as Fig. 2, and the values are listed in Table 3.

Step 7. If the aggregative weights of sub-attributes are exist, to distribute the refined weight(s) of the sub-attributes of each attribute based on the ratio of weights of these sub-attributes. Equation (8) is apply to distribute the refined weight(s) of attributes of each aspects based on the ratio of weights of these attributes by AHP operation in Fig. 1 (denoted as W_{ij}, where $i=1,....,5$, $j=1,...,n(AS_i)$, $n(AS_i)$ is the number of attributes in aspect i). Then, the refined weights W'_{ij} are

$$W'_{ij} = \frac{W_{ij}}{W_i} \times W'_i \tag{8}$$

For example, W_{23} (weight of "safety") is 0.09, and $W'_2 =0.2574$ (the refined weight of "Reliability") when $\alpha =0.7$. Then, $W'_{23} =(0.09/0.231)*0.2574 =0.1003$.

Step 8. Multiply the weights of the attributes by their fuzzy performance measures, and then rank their orderings based on the results.
This step can be divided into two branch steps------

Step 8.1. Defuzzified the fuzzy performance measures in Table 2 by the centroid method [11]. Assume the TFNs in Table are $\tilde{r}_{ijk} = (a_{ijk}, b_{ijk}, c_{ijk})$ (where $i=1,...,5$, $j=1,...,n(AS_i)$, $k=1\sim3$, and k is the label of airline A, B, and C, respectively). Then, the defuzzified values of $\tilde{r}_{ijk}$ is

$$D(\tilde{r}_{ijk}) = \frac{1}{3} \times [a_{ijk}+b_{ijk}+c_{ijk}] \tag{9}$$

For example, $D(\tilde{r}_{111}) =(0.52+0.62+0.71)/3=0.6167$.

Step 8.2. Multiply the refined weights of attributes by their project grades. Finally, the aggregative result of Airline k is

$$Agg\_Result(k) = \sum_{i=1}^{5} \sum_{j=1}^{n(AS_i)} (W'_{ij} \times D(\tilde{r}_{ijk})) \tag{10}$$

4.3 Results and Discussion

Because the proposed model has the same results of α =0.5+ δ and α =0.5- δ (0≤ δ ≤0.5), it merely shows the data of α ≥0.5 to represent the total results. For example, the aggregation results are the same when α = 0.7 and α = 0.3. According to the entropy of information after OWA aggregation of the input data, the output weights of the aspects are summarized in Table 3 and Fig. 2. From the last column in Table 3, the proposed model can be viewed as a magnifying lens to determine the most important attribute based on the situation of sparest information (*i.e.* optimistic and α =0 or 1). In the second column of Table 3, when α =0.5 (moderate situation), the proposed model can obtain the attribute weights (equal weights) based on maximum information.

Similarly, we take α value from 0.5 to 1.0 as the parameter for execution according to our adjusted algorithm for the purpose of verification, and the results are presented in Table 4 and Fig. 3.

Table 4. The aggregation result of adjusted algorithm

	The proposed model						Tsaur et al. [24]
	α =0.5	α =0.6	α =0.7	α =0.8	α =0.9	α =1.0	
Airline A	0.61009	0.60641	0.60280	0.59889	0.59368	0.58191	0.3857*
Airline B	0.62280	0.62385	0.62558	0.62804	0.63132	0.63463	0.8155*
Airline C	0.60538	0.60669	0.60900	0.61234	0.61736	0.62544	0.5534*
Ranking	B>A>C	B>C>A	B>C>A	B>C>A	B>C>A	B>C>A	B>C>A

* The similarity to ideal solution

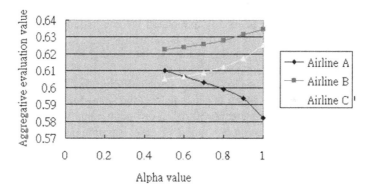

Fig. 3. The aggregative results under α = [0.5,1.0]

To verify the validity of the proposed model, this study compares the result of the proposed algorithm with the algorithm in Tsaur et al. [24]. The ranking orders of Airlines B and C are changed based on different α's values in Table 4 and Fig. 3. This is because the fuzzy performance measures of attributes are approximate in the Airlines A and C (see Table 2), and the overall evaluating results will easily affect by the refined weights (OWA weights).

Besides, when α's value is larger, the overall performance of Airline C becomes better, and the performance of Airline A becomes worse. This fact reveals that Airline

C perform better service quality than Airline A in the most important aspect (i.e. "Tangibility"). We also find Airline B has best service quality under all condition. The results show that if the alternative perform stable in each attribute, the evaluating results obtained by proposed model will also robust. The results in Fig.3 also show that the ranking of three airlines is B>A>C under $\alpha = [0.59, 1.0]$, which has the same order as results of Tsaur et al. [24]. The proposed model thus can be validated.

After the experiments in this section, we suggest the decision maker can adjust α 's value under the following situation:

1. No preference: When a decision maker has no preference toward the criteria, we can assign these attributes equal weight. Under this circumstance, the suggesting α 's value is 0.5. (If no preference, the results will be same with just using TOPSIS)
2. Partial preference: We suggest the range of α 's values is [0.6, 0.9], when a decision maker has collected criteria weights from domain experts and want to execute sensitivity analysis for making final decision based the opinions of experts.
3. Single preference: If the decision maker is confident and believe in the most important criterion, we suggest to assign $\alpha = 1.0$. This can enlarge the effect of this single preference criterion.

5   Conclusions

This study has proposed a dynamic fuzzy OWA model to deal with fuzzy MCDM problems. The proposed model can help users to solve MCDM problems under the situation of fuzzy or incomplete information. The advantages of this study are:

1. The proposed approach can modify associated weights based on the aggregation situation (preference level toward the criteria/attributes).
2. Continuous improving aggregation result (attribute weights) and aggregating experts' opinions in sequential periods.
3. The fuzzy OWA model can work like a "magnifying lens" to enlarge/find the most important attribute, which is dependent on the sparest information (*i.e.* optimistic case: situation parameter $\alpha = 0$ or 1), or obtain equal weights of attributes based on maximal information (*i.e.* moderate case: situation parameter $\alpha = 0.5$).

Acknowledgement

The authors acknowledge V. Torra and the referees for their suggestions. Their insight and comments led to a better presentation of the ideas expressed in this paper.

References

1. Beliakov, G., Warren, J.: Appropriate Choice of Aggregation Operators in Fuzzy Decision Support Systems. IEEE Transactions on Fuzzy Systems 9(6) (2001) 773-784
2. Borcherding, K., Epple, T., Winterfeldt, D.V.: Comparison of weighting judgments in multi-attribute utility measurement. Management Science 37(12) (1991) 1603-1619

3. Carbonell, M., Mas, M., Mayor, G.: On a class of Monotonic Extended OWA Operators. Proceedings of the Sixth IEEE International Conference on Fuzzy Systems (1997) (IEEE-FUZZ'97), Barcelona, Catalunya, Spain, 1695-1699

4. Chen, S.M.: Fuzzy group decision making for evaluating the rate of aggregative risk in software development. Fuzzy Sets and Systems **118** (2001) 75-88

5. Choi, D.Y.: A new aggregation method in a fuzzy environment. Decision Support Systems **25** (1999) 39-51

6. Filev, D., Yager, R.R.: On the issue of obtaining OWA operator weights. Fuzzy Sets and Systems **94** (1998) 157-169

7. Fuller, R., Majlender, P.: An analytic approach for obtaining maximal entropy OWA operator weights. Fuzzy Sets and Systems **124** (2001) 53-57

8. Jaynes, E.T.: Cleaning up mysteries: The original goal, Maximum Entropy and Bayesian Methods. Kluwer, Dordrecht (1989)

9. Klir, G.J.: Fuzzy Sets, Uncertainly and information. Prentice Hall (1988)

10. Klir, G.J., Wierman, M.J.: Uncertainty-Based Information, 2nded Edition. Physica-Verlag, Germany (1999)

11. Lee, H.M.: Group decision making using fuzzy sets theory for evaluating the rate of aggregative risk in software development. Fuzzy Sets and Systems **80** (1996) 261-271

12. Mendel, J.M.: Uncertain Rule-Based Fuzzy Logic Systems: Introduction and New Directions. Prentice Hall PTR, Upper Saddle River NJ (2000)

13. Mesiar, R., Saminger, S.: Domination of ordered weighted averaging operators over t-norms. Soft Computing **8** (2004) 562-570

14. Moshkovich, H.M., Schellenberger, R.E., Olson, D.L.: Data influences the result more than preferences: Some lessons from implementation of multiattribute techniques in a real decision task. Decision Support Systems **22** (1998) 73-84

15. O'Hagan, M.: Aggregating template or rule antecedents in real-time expert systems with fuzzy set logic. Proc. 22nd Annu. IEEE Asilomar Conf. On Signals, Systems, Computers, Pacific Grove, CA (1988) 681-689

16. Ribeiro, R.A., Pereira, R.A.M.: Generalized Mixture Operators using weighting functions: A comparative study with WA and OWA. European Journal of Operational Research **145** (2003) 329-342

17. Shannon, C.E.: A Mathematical Theory of Communication. Bell Systems Technical Journal **27** (1948) 379-423

18. Shoemaker, P.J.H., Carter, W.C.: An Experimental Comparison of different approaches to determining Weights in Additive Utility Models. Management Science **28** (1982) 182-196

19. Smolikova, R., Wachowiak, M.P.: Aggregation operators for selection problems. Fuzzy Sets and Systems **131** (2002) 23-34

20. Solymosi, T., Dombi, J.: A method for determining the weights of criteria: the centralized weights. European Journal of Operational Research **26** (1986) 35-41

21. Torra, V.: Learning weights for the Quasi-Weighted Mean. IEEE Transactions on Fuzzy Systems **10**(5) (2002) 653-666

22. Torra, V.: On the learning of weights in some aggregation operators. Mathware and Soft Computing **6** (1999) 249-265

23. Torra, V.: OWA operators in data modeling and re-identification. IEEE Transactions on Fuzzy Systems **12**(5) (2004) 652-660

24. Tsaur, S.-H., Chang, T.Y., Yen C.-H.: The evaluation of airline service quality by fuzzy MCDM. Tourism management **23** (2002) 107-115

25. Weber, M., Eisenfhr, F., von Winterfeldt, D.: The effects of splitting attributes on weights in multiattribute utility measurement. Management Science **34** (1988) 431-445

26. Yager, R.R.: Connectives and quantifiers in fuzzy sets. Fuzzy Sets and Systems **40** (1991) 39-75

27. Yager, R.R.: On a general class of fuzzy connectives. Fuzzy Sets and Systems **4** (1980) 235-242
28. Yager, R.R.: Ordered weighted averaging aggregation operators in multi-criteria decision making. IEEE Trans. Systems Man. and Cybernetics **18** (1988) 183-190
29. Yager, R.R., Kacprzyk, J.: The Ordered Weighted Averaging Operators. Kluwer Academic Publishers, Boston (1997)
30. Zadeh, L.A.: Fuzzy Sets. Information and Control **8** (1965) 338-353
31. Zhang, D., Yu, P.L., Wang, P.Z.: State-dependent weights in multicriteria value functions. Journal of Optimization Theory and Applications **74**(1) (1992) 1-21
32. Zimmermann, H.J., Zysno, P.: Latent connectives in human decision making. Fuzzy Sets and Systems **4** (1980) 37-51

An Adaptive Module
for the Consensus Reaching Process
in Group Decision Making Problems⋆

Enrique Herrera-Viedma[1], Francisco Mata[2],
Luis Martínez[2], and Luis G. Pérez[2]

[1] Dept. of Computer Science and A.I., University of Granada
18071 - Granada, Spain
`viedma@decsai.ugr.es`
[2] Dept. of Computer Science, University of Jaén, 23071 - Jaén, Spain
`{fmata,martin,lgonzaga}@ujaen.es`

Abstract. In the group decision making (GDM) framework we deal with decision problems where several decision makers try to achieve a common solution about a problem. In the literature, we can find two processes to carry out before obtaining a final solution: the consensus process and the selection one. The consensus process is a discussion process where the experts change their opinions in order to achieve a high agreement. The selection process searches the solution.

The consensus reaching process is a very important task for GDM problems regarding the necessity that the solution achieved will be assumed and shared by all experts involved in the GDM problem. It consists of several consensus rounds where the experts discuss and change their opinions in order to improve the level of agreement among them.

In this paper, we propose an optimization of the consensus reaching process in GDM problems by means of an adaptive module that applies different procedures to identify the experts' opinions that should be changed according to the level of agreement in each consensus round. Usually at the beginning the agreement is low, so the adaptive module will suggest to many experts to change their opinions. However, after several rounds, the agreement will be higher and hence the number of the changes will be smaller.

Keywords: Consensus, group decision-making, fuzzy preference relation

1 Introduction

In today's business environments, where outside competition is so great, the organizational survival depends on the internal cooperation. The internal cooperation among departments allows to reduce costs and increase the productivity of a company. Research indicates that collective decision making actually produces higher quality decisions than single decision making. So, the role of decision making is changing from a sole expert to teams or group of experts.

⋆ This work has been partially supported by the Research Project TIC2002-03348.

V. Torra et al. (Eds.): MDAI 2005, LNAI 3558, pp. 89–98, 2005.

A GDM problem may be defined as a decision making process with two or more experts, $E = \{e_1, e_2, \ldots, e_m\}$ $(m \geq 2)$, characterized by their own perceptions, attitudes and knowledge about the problem, try to choose a common solution from a set of alternatives $X = \{x_1, x_2, \ldots, x_n\}$ $(n \geq 2)$.

To solve a GDM problem are applied two processes to obtain the final solution (see Figure 1):

- A *Consensus process*: It is a discussion process where the experts exchange their opinions in order to reach the maximum agreement about the set of alternatives, X, before making a decision. Normally, this process is guided by the figure of a human moderator [3, 4, 8].
- A *Selection process*: It refers to how to obtain a solution set of alternatives from the opinions provided by the experts. Clearly, it is preferable that the set of experts have a high agreement about the alternatives before applying the selection process.

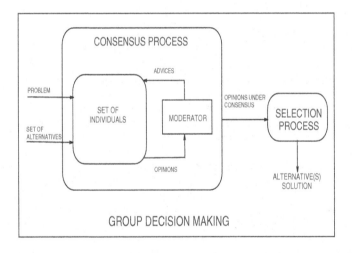

Fig. 1. Resolution process of a group decision-making problem

In this paper, we focus on the consensus process. The consensus is defined as a state of mutual agreement among members of a group where all opinions have been heard and addressed to the satisfaction of the group [11]. The consensus reaching process is defined as a dynamic and iterative process composed of several rounds, where the experts express and discuss about their opinions. Traditionally this process is coordinated by a human moderator, who computes the agreement among experts in each round using different consensus measures [2, 6]. If the agreement is not acceptable (i.e., if it is lower than a specified consensus threshold) then the moderator recommends to the experts to change their furthest opinions from the group opinion in an effort to make their preferences closer in the next consensus round [1, 14].

In the literature, some approaches have been proposed to deal with the consensus reaching process [7, 9, 10, 12, 13]. All these approaches always use the same procedure independently of the level of agreement achieved in the each round. We think that could be more appropriate to use different procedures according to the agreement in each round of the consensus reaching process. So, in the first rounds of the consensus process, the agreement is usually low and it seems logic that many experts should change the most of their opinions. However, after several rounds, the agreement should be higher and then just the furthest experts from the group opinion will change their opinions. Therefore, the procedures ought to be different according to the level of agreement in each round.

In this sense, we propose in this paper to include an adaptive module for the consensus reaching process in GDM problems, such that depending on the level of agreement in each round, it will use a different procedure to identify the experts' opinions that should change to improve the agreement. The goals of this adaptive module are to optimize the consensus reaching process decreasing the number of consensus rounds and the number of changes in experts' opinions.

The rest of the paper is set out as follows. A review of the concept of consensus reaching process is described in Section 2. The features and performance of the adaptive module is presented in Section 3, and finally, in Section 4 we draw our conclusions.

2   The Consensus Reaching Process

In decision making problems where several experts provide their opinions that are usually different. So, it is suitable to carry out a consensus process where the experts exchange their opinions in order to reach a good agreement about the alternatives of the problem before making a decision. In group decision making could happen that some experts may have complaints because their opinions have not been heard when the solution is obtained. Therefore they don't agree with the solution. The consensus reaching process tries that all experts' opinions are taking into account to obtain the solution.

The consensus reaching process is an iterative process where the experts accept to change their opinions following the advice given by the figure of a moderator (see Figure 1). The moderator plays a key role in this process. Normally the moderator is a person that does not participate in the discussion but knows the degree of agreement in each round of the consensus process. He/she is in charge of addressing the consensus process toward success, i.e, to achieve the highest agreement such that the number of experts outside of the consensus will be as small as possible.

To compute the agreement among the experts, it is necessary to measure the similarity among experts' opinions. To do so, the moderator uses two type of measures [5]:

a) *Consensus degrees.* These measures are used to calculate the global level of agreement among the experts' opinions and identify the experts' preferences where exist a great disagreement.

b) *Proximity measures.* These measures evaluate the distance between the experts' individual opinions and the group opinion. They allow to identify the furthest experts' preferences that should be changed.

In [5, 6], different examples of both types of measures for GDM problems, have been proposed.

In GDM problems, the experts usually use preference relations to express their opinions. A preference relation is defined as a matrix $\mathbf{P_{e_i}} = (p_i^{lk})$, where each element p_i^{lk} represents the preference of the alternative x_l on the alternative x_k provided by the expert e_i.

$$\mathbf{P_{e_i}} = \begin{pmatrix} p_i^{11} & \cdots & p_i^{1n} \\ \vdots & \ddots & \vdots \\ p_i^{n1} & \cdots & p_i^{nn} \end{pmatrix}$$

The preference relations allow to compute both consensus degrees and proximity measures at three different levels of representation:

Level 1: *Pairs of alternatives.* In this level both the consensus degree and the proximity (between each individual expert's opinion and the group opinion) on each pair of alternatives are calculated. So, given the preference p_i^{lk} on the pair of alternatives x_l, x_k:
- The consensus degree on that pair of alternatives will be represented as cp^{lk}.
- The proximity of that pair of alternatives for the expert e_i will be represented as pp_i^{lk}.

Level 2: *Alternatives.* In this level, the consensus degree and the proximity on each alternative are obtained. Given the alternative $x_l \in X$:
- The consensus degree on that alternative will be represented as ca^l.
- The proximity of that alternative for the expert e_i will be represented as pa_i^l.

Level 3: *Preference relation or experts.* The global consensus degree among all the experts and the proximity between each individual expert's opinion and the group opinion are calculated.
- The consensus degree among all experts will be represented as cr.
- The proximity of the expert e_i will be represented as pr_i.

Once we have presented the measures to assess the agreement, we show an overall schema of the different phases of a consensus reaching process (see Figure 2).

1. The experts provide their opinions.
2. The consensus measures to measure the agreement among experts are computed.
3. It is checked the level of agreement. If the consensus threshold is achieved, then the consensus reaching process will finish and the selection process will be applied to obtain the solution.

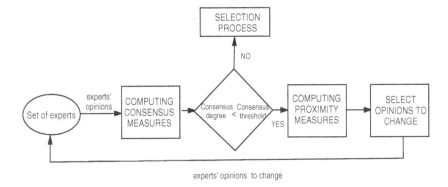

Fig. 2. Phases of the consensus reaching process

4. The proximity measures are computed to measure the distance among individual experts' opinion and group opinion.
5. The experts' opinion that should be changed are selected.

The value of the consensus threshold will depend on each problem and it will be fixed in advance. For instance, a value of 0.8 could be required if the consequences of the decision making are of a significant importance or in other cases a value a little bigger than 0.5 could be enough.

In the literature have been proposed several approaches for the consensus reaching process [9, 10, 12, 13], all of them follow a similar schema to the presented in the Figure 2, in which the process is always the same independently of the agreement in each discussion round. However, we think that the process should be different according to the achieved agreement in the current discussion round, i.e, low consensus implies the search of many values to be changed, however, a higher consensus implies only that search of the furthest experts regarding the group opinion. Therefore, we propose to modify the schema shown in the Figure 2. Such that, the processes after checking the agreement, will be carried out by means of an adaptive module, that according to the current agreement, will apply different operations in order to obtain the experts' opinions that should be changed to improve the agreement in the next discussion round. This scheme is shown in the Figure 3.

In Section 3 we make a detail description of this adaptive module.

3   The Adaptive Module for Consensus Reaching Process

The goal of the adaptive module is to adapt the search of the experts' opinions to change according to the agreement among the experts in each round of the consensus reaching process. To achieve this purpose, we propose that the adaptive module carries out two tasks (see Figure 4):

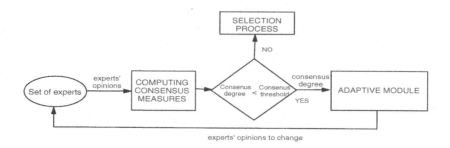

Fig. 3. Adapted consensus reaching process

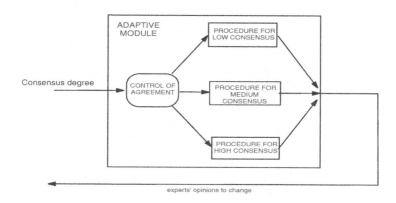

Fig. 4. Adaptive module for the consensus reaching process

1. *Control of agreement.* This module checks the level of agreement or consensus degree among the experts in order to choose a identification procedure to search the opinions to change.
2. *Application of identification procedures.* Depending on the global consensus degree (cr), three different identification procedures have been developed to identify the preferences that should be changed:
   (a) Procedure for low consensus.
   (b) Procedure for medium consensus.
   (c) Procedure for high consensus.
   Each one applies different consensus and proximity criteria to choose the preferences to be changed.

In the next subsections, the details of both tasks are described.

3.1   Control of Agreement

To control the agreement, we need to define rules or selection criteria such that, depending on the consensus degree, will select the appropriate identification procedure. A selection criterion could be the following one:

$$If \ \ cr < \gamma \cdot \theta_j \ \ Then \ldots$$

where θ_j is a value or percentage used to establish different levels of agreement that imply the different identification procedures to apply, and $\gamma \in [0, 1]$ represents the consensus threshold. In our case, as we propose three identification procedures we will need to define three values, $\theta_1, \theta_2, \theta_3 = 100\%$. The values of θ_j will depend on type of problem that we are dealing with.

The structure of the algorithm used to control the agreement is shown in the Table 1.

Table 1. Algorithm of control of the level of agreement

```
INPUTS:
        cr, θ₁, θ₂
BEGIN
        IF cr ≤ γ · θ₁
        THEN
                Execute procedure for low consensus
        ELSE
                IF cr ≤ γ · θ₂
                THEN
                        Execute procedure for medium consensus
                ELSE
                        Execute procedure for high consensus
                END-IF
        END-IF
END
```

3.2 Application of the Identification Procedures of Preferences

In our module we propose three different procedures to identify the preferences that the experts should to change in order to improve their agreement: procedure for low consensus, procedure for medium consensus, procedure for high consensus.

Each identification procedure analyzes the agreement from different points of view and uses both consensus degrees and proximity measures, as those presented in [3, 6, 8], according to its performance. Furthermore, each identification procedure returns a different set of preferences for each expert e_i, called $PREFECH_i^L$, $PREFECH_i^M$, and $PREFECH_i^H$, respectively. Each one of these sets represents the set of preferences that e_i should change to make their opinions closer to the collective opinion and to improve the agreement.

All identification procedures are described as follows:

Procedure for Low Consensus. This procedure is usually run at the beginning of the consensus process, i.e., when the agreement is low. For instance, we could consider that the agreement is low if the achieved consensus degree is smaller than the half of the wanted consensus threshold, $cr \leq \gamma \cdot \theta_1$, being $\theta_1 = 1/2$. In this situation, the experts' opinions are very different and it will be necessary to propose a lot of changes to improve the agreement.

The purpose of this procedure is to identify all the pairs of alternatives where there exists a high disagreement and suggest *all the experts* to change their preferences on them. In such a way, all the experts change their initial opinions and we avoid that in the first rounds some experts impose their preferences and can address the consensus reaching process toward their own opinions. This circumstance is known as "Tyranny of the Majority" [11].

To do so, the procedure for low consensus carries out the following operations:

1. To compute the consensus degree on all the pairs of alternatives,

$$\{cp^{lk}, \ l,k = 1, ..., n\}.$$

2. To identify the pairs of alternatives where the agreement is smaller than the specified consensus threshold,

$$M = \{(l,k) \mid cp^{lk} < \gamma\}.$$

3. For each e_i, to compute the set of preferences, $PREFECH_i^L$, that he/she should change to improve the agreement in the next consensus round.

$$PREFECH_i^L = \{p_i^{lk} \mid (l,k) \in M\}$$

Procedure for Medium Consensus. After several consensus rounds the agreement should have improved, for example $\gamma \cdot \theta_1 < cr \leq \gamma \cdot \theta_2$, being $\theta_1 = 1/2$ and $\theta_2 = 2/3$. In this situation, we think that it seems logic to reduce the number of proposed changes.

The purpose of this procedure is only focused on the *alternatives* where exist disagreement, to identify their pairs with smallest agreement and suggest to the furthest experts from the group opinion that change their preferences on those pairs of alternatives.

To do so, the procedure for medium consensus carries out the following operations:

1. To compute the consensus degree on all the pairs of alternatives,

$$\{cp^{lk}, \ l,k = 1, ..., n\}.$$

2. To compute the consensus degree at the level of alternatives,

$$\{ca^l, \ l = 1, ..., n\}.$$

3. To identify the alternatives in which there does not exist agreement,

$$X^M = \{x_l \mid ca^l < \gamma\}.$$

4. For each e_i, to compute the set of preferences, $PREFECH_i^M$. To do that, we use his/her proximity measures computed in the level of pairs of alternatives, pp_i^{lk}, and in the level of alternatives, pa_i^l,

$$PREFECH_i^M = \{p_i^{lk} \mid l \in X^M \wedge pa_i^l < \beta \wedge pp_i^{lk} < \beta\}.$$

being β a proximity threshold.

It is easy to demonstrate that $PREFECH_i^M \subseteq PREFECH_i^L$.

Procedure for High Consensus. If the consensus reaching process is successfully carried out, in the last consensus rounds the agreement will be close to the wanted consensus threshold, e.g., $cr \geq \gamma \cdot 2/3$. In this case, to improve the agreement it is necessary to suggest less changes than in the above identification procedure.

The procedure for high consensus carries out the following operations:

1. To compute the consensus degree on all the pairs of alternatives,

$$\{cp^{lk}, \ l, k = 1, ..., n\}.$$

2. To compute the consensus degree at the level of alternatives,

$$S\{ca^l, \ l = 1, ..., n\}.$$

3. To identify the alternatives in which there does not exist agreement,

$$X^M = \{x_l \mid ca^l < \gamma\}.$$

4. For each e_i, to compute the set of preferences, $PREFECH_i^H$. To do that, we use his/her proximity measures computed in the level of pairs of alternatives, pp_i^{lk}, and in the level of alternatives, pa_i^l, and in the level of preference relation, pr_i,

$$PREFECH_i^H = \{p_i^{lk} \mid l \in X^M \wedge pr_i < \beta \wedge pa_i^l < \beta \wedge pp_i^{lk} < \beta\}.$$

being β a proximity threshold.

It is easy to demonstrate that $PREFECH_i^H \subseteq PREFECH_i^M$.

Given that $PREFECH_i^H \subseteq PREFECH_i^M \subseteq PREFECH_i^L$, we should point out that our adaptive module goes looking for to reduce the number of changes to achieve the consensus situation and to get convergent consensus processes.

4   Conclusions

In the GDM problems to achieve consensus solutions is a desirable property. So, before solving a GDM problem could be suitable to develop a consensus process to make experts' preferences closer, such that, the solution obtained presents a high consensus degree.

In this paper we have presented a adaptive module to guide consensus reaching processes that chooses preferences to change in each consensus round depending on the agreement that there exist at each moment. In such a way, we get to reduce the number of changes to suggest experts in each round and to increase the convergence of the consensus processes.

References

1. Bryson, N.: Group decision-making and the analytic hierarchy process: exploring the consensus-relevant information content. Computers and Operational Research **23** (1996) 27-35
2. Kuncheva, L.I.: Five measures of consensus in group decision making using fuzzy sets. Proceedings of IFSA (1991) 141-144
3. Herrera, F., Herrera-Viedma, E., Verdegay, J.L.: Linguistic Measures Based on Fuzzy Coincidence for Reaching Consensus in Group Decision Making. Int. J. of Approximate Reasoning (1997) 309-334
4. Herrera, F., Herrera-Viedma, E., Verdegay, J.L.: A rational consensus model in group decision making under linguistic assessments. Fuzzy Sets and Systems, **88** (1997) 31-49
5. Herrera-Viedma, E., Herrera, F., Chiclana, F.: A Consensus Model for Multiperson Decision Making with Different Preference Structures. IEEE Transactions on Systems, Man and Cybernetics-Part A: Systems and Humans **32** (2002) 394-402
6. Herrera-Viedma, E., Mata, F., Martínez, L., Chiclana, F., Pérez, L.G.: Measurements of Consensus in Multi-granular Linguistic Group Decision Making. Modeling Decisions for Artificial Intelligence. Lecture Notes in Artificial Intelligence, Vol. 3131. Springer-Verlag, Berling Heidelberg New York (2004) 194-204
7. Herrera-Viedma, E., Martínez, L., Mata, F., Chiclana, F.: A Consensus Support System Model for Group Decision-making Problems with Multi-granular Linguistic Preference Relations. IEEE Transactions on Fuzzy Systems (2004). In Press.
8. Kacprzyk, J., Fedrizzi, M., Nurmi, H.: Group decision making and consensus under fuzzy preferences and fuzzy majority. Fuzzy Sets and Systems **49** (1992) 21-31
9. Karacapilidis, N.I., Pappis, C.P.: A framework for group decision making support systems: Combining AI tools and OR thecniques. European Journal of Operational Research **103** (1997) 373-388
10. Marakas, G.H.: Decision support systems in the 21th century. 2rd edn. Pearson Education, Inc., New Jersey, (2003)
11. Saint, S., Lawson, J. R.: Rules for Reaching Consensus. A Modern Approach to Decision Making. Jossey-Bass, San Francisco (1994)
12. Salo, A.A.: Interactive decision aiding for group decision support. European Journal of Operational Research **84** (1995) 134-149
13. Torra, V., Cortes, U.: Towards an automatic consensus generator tool: EGAC. IEEE Transactions on Systems, Man and Cybernetics **25** (1995) 888-894
14. Zadrozny, S.: An Approach to the Consensus Reaching Support in Fuzzy Environment. In: Kacprzyk, J., Nurmi, H., Fedrizzi, M. (eds.): Consensus under Fuzziness. Kluwer Academic Publishers, Boston, (1997) 83-109

Qualitative Reasoning Model for Tradeoff Analysis

Tom Wanyama and Behrouz Homayoun Far

Department of Electrical and Computer Engineering, University of Calgary
2500 University Drive, N.W., Calgary, Alberta, Canada, T2N 1N4
{twanyama,far}@ucalgary.ca

Abstract. In Multi-Criteria Decision Making problems such as choosing a development policy, selecting software products, or searching for commodities to purchase, it is often necessary to evaluate solution options in respect of multiple objectives. The solution alternative that performs best in all the objectives is the dominant solution, and it should be selected to solve the problem. However, usually the selection objectives are incomparable and conflicting, making it impossible to have a dominant solution among the alternatives. In such cases, tradeoff analysis is required to identify the objectives that can be optimized, and those that can be comprised in order to choose a winning solution. In this paper we present a tradeoff analysis model based on the principles of qualitative reasoning that provides visualization support for understanding interaction and tradeoff dependences among solutions evaluation criteria which affect the tradeoff among selection objectives. Moreover, the decision support system based on our tradeoff analysis model facilitates discovery of hidden solution features so as to improve the completeness and certainty of the user preference model.

1 Introduction

When dealing with complicated decision making problems such as choosing a development policy, selecting software products, or searching for commodities to purchase, decision makers often depend on computerized systems to assess the alternative solutions. The assessment is essentially carried out to determine the ability of each solution option to satisfy multiple selection objectives that reflect the needs and preferences of the decision maker. Usually, the selection objectives are incomparable and conflicting, making it impossible to have a dominant solution, and leading to a tradeoff problem.

There is a variety of tradeoff analysis models in the reviewed literature. However, most of them do not have the ability to adequately assist users to make tradeoffs because of the following reasons:

- They do not explicitly identify the tradeoff criteria, and their effect on each selection objective.
- Some of the tradeoff models can only handle a limited number of selection objectives, and/or criteria for evaluating solutions.
- Most tradeoff models require a fully specified value function for all the solution alternatives. However, the value functions of Multi Criteria Decision Making (MCDM) problems are difficult to establish because the user preference models are normally incomplete and uncertain. However, the preference models become more complete and more certain as the solution evaluation process progresses [10].

V. Torra et al. (Eds.): MDAI 2005, LNAI 3558, pp. 99–109, 2005.

In this paper, we present a tradeoff analysis model that is based on the principles of qualitative reasoning. The model has the following characteristics:

- Utilizes a visualization component to explicitly identify the tradeoff criteria, and specifies whether a tradeoff criterion optimizes or compromises a particular selection objective.
- It is not limited on the number of selection objectives or evaluation criteria that it can handle.
- It does not require a fully specified value function for the solution alternatives. Instead, it prompts the user on other criteria that can be included in the evaluation of the alternatives to increase on the completeness and certainty of the user preference model, which in turn increases the chances of extracting a dominant solution.

The paper is arranged as follows: Section 2 describes the tradeoff analysis work in the reviewed literature. Section 3 covers the framework in which our tradeoff analysis model operates, while Section 4 deals with the Qualitative Reasoning (QR) model for tradeoff analysis. Section 5 presents a tradeoff analysis Decision Support System (DSS) based on our tradeoff analysis model. In section 6 an example illustrating the application of our tradeoff analysis model is presented. Finally, conclusions are given in Section 7.

2   Related Work

Integer programming (IP) is the general method for determining solutions that satisfy multiple objectives with constraints. Generally, IP is a linear programming problem whose solution space is discrete. The method carries out the tradeoff process automatically, yielding the final optimal solution. In the context of MCDM, IP has two major drawbacks, these are;

1. It is difficult to find a global objective function relating all the different selection objectives. Such an objective function is required in order to apply IP.
2. It is practically inappropriate to entrust computers with the responsibility of making tradeoffs, because in most cases they are not aware of all the information required to make a satisfactory tradeoff. We believe that the tasks of computers should be limited to identifying the tradeoff criteria, specifying the strength of each tradeoff criterion, and identifying the selection objectives that each tradeoff criterion affects. The actual tradeoff should be left to the decision maker who is normally aware of the impossible-to-model information.

The Pareto Space for 2D tradeoff Analysis [6, 10] is a visual-based tradeoff model that consists of multi-criteria tradeoff analysis and a map of the solution space. This model is especially useful for under-constrained problems such as selecting a solution from a set of alternatives, where many solutions compete for attention. Users rely on visualization assistance in order to evaluate the solutions and make intelligent decisions. However, the visualization is only feasible for up to three criteria or selection objectives.

Tradeoff Map method [6] can handle tradeoff among more than three criteria, by combining color patterns, visual structures and interactivity. In the solution space, the y-coordinates represent the total sum of the scores of a solution in all the selection objectives. Thus the node with the largest y value represents the 'best' solution. To calculate the x-coordinates, weights are imagined, each corresponding to the score of the solution in each criterion.

The above three methods assume that user preference models are complete. However, in practice the models are normally incomplete and uncertain at the beginning of the tradeoff process, because users are often not aware of all the features of the solution alternatives for the problem that they are solving. To address the issue of incomplete and uncertain user preference models, Pu et al [10] proposed a tradeoff model based on the Constraint Satisfaction Problem (CSP) technique. The model proposes the tradeoff criteria automatically. Additionally, it assists users to discover hidden preferences in order to treat incompleteness and uncertainties in the user preference models. However, Pu et al [10] do not discuss the sources of the solution features that help users to discover their hidden preferences.

Although we use a totally different approach from that used by Pu et al, our model extends the functionalities of theirs by adding capability to visualize the relative strength of the tradeoff criteria, as well as the effect of every tradeoff criteria on each of the selection objectives. Moreover, we explicitly discuss the source of the solution attributes that help users to identify the hidden preferences.

3   Framework for Tradeoff

When solving a multi-objective MCDM problem, the decision maker starts by identifying the solution selection objectives, followed by defining the evaluation criteria with respect to each selection objective, as well as the user preference over the criteria (criteria weights). Moreover, the domain expert determines the strength of each solution alternative with respect to every evaluation criteria. Thereafter, the user preferences and the expert information on the solutions is used to estimate the performance of each solution alternative with respect to every selection objective. If there is a solution alternative that performs best in all the selection objectives then it is the dominant solution, and it should be selected for the purpose of solving the problem. However, usually there is no dominant solution because selection objectives tend to conflict, causing different solutions to be the best with respect to different selection objectives, which in turn leads to a tradeoff problem.

Before trading off, it is necessary to carryout tradeoff analysis in order to identify the tradeoff criteria, as well as how they affect each selection objective, and it is important to identify extra solution features that can help users to discover hidden evaluation criteria (preferences). Moreover, using the impossible-to-model information, the user should determine the objectives to optimize and those to compromise, because this establishes the tradeoff criteria whose weights are increased and those whose weights are reduced so that a dominant solution emerges.

3.1   Multi-criteria Evaluation of Solution Alternatives

Selection of a solution from a set of alternatives is facilitated by evaluating each alternative on a set of criteria, using a MCDM technique. The simplest MCDM model for estimating the performance of solution alternative k against the set of evaluation criteria is given by Equation 3.1. We used it as a starting point for developing and testing our QR model, and in the future we shall replace it with more flexible models such as Ordered weighted Averaging [11] and the Logic Scoring Preference model [8].

$$Score_k = \sum_{i=1}^{n} a_{ki} w_i.$$ (3.1)

Where, a_{ki} is the strength of solution alternative k in criterion i.

w_i is the weight of criterion i.

n is the total number of the evaluation criteria.

If the selection problem is characterized by multiple objectives, the performance of each solution is determined for every selection objective. The results are thereafter compared to determine whether there is a dominant solution, or tradeoff is required to extract a dominant solution.

3.2   Role of Experts in the Evaluation of Solutions and in Tradeoff Analysis

Equation 3.1 shows that the performance of a solution alternative against a set of evaluation criteria is determined by two types of parameters, namely; the strength a_{ki} of the alternative in each of the criteria, and the weight w_i of every criterion. Since w_i represents user preferences, it is subjective data that varies from user to user. On the other hand, a_{ki} is objective data which depends exclusively on the characteristics of an alternative solution.

We believe that it is the role of the domain experts to identify the attributes of solution alternative that can be used as evaluation criteria. Moreover, the experts should rank the solution alternatives on the attributes, hence providing the values of a_{ki} for each solution alternative. Having a complete set of solution attributes assists users to identify hidden criteria during tradeoff analysis. Moreover, generating the values of a_{ki} in advance leads to two advantages. Firstly, it reduces the time required by users to evaluate solution alternatives. Secondly, it improves the accuracy of the performance estimates of the solution alternatives. We refer to the set of the attributes of the solution alternatives and the corresponding rating of every alternative with respect to each criterion, as expert knowledge about the solutions.

4   Tradeoff Analysis Based on a QR Model

The one most important activity during tradeoff is tradeoff analysis, because the activity identifies the criteria that can be traded to optimize particular selection objectives, and compromise others. In this paper we present a tradeoff analysis model based on qualitative reasoning (QR).

QR captures the human common sense understanding of the behavior of systems and processes. The common sense understanding of systems and processes is based on common sense reasoning. Therefore, Table 1 shows the qualitative differential equations (QDE) derived from the common sense reasoning stated in text form, about the performance of solution alternatives with respect to different selection objectives.

Table 1. Common Sense Reasoning about the Performance of Solution Alternatives in respect of Competing Selection Objectives

Common Sense Reasoning about Evaluation of Solution Options	Qualitative Differential Equations (QDE)	Definition of Symbols
1. The performance of an alternative solution against the preferences of a user is determined by the strength of the solution in each evaluation criterion, as well as the weight which the user attaches to each of the criteria.	$Score = \sum_{i=1}^{n} a_i w_i$	$Score$ - Estimated Performance (score) of a solution with respect to preferences of a user n - Number of the evaluation criteria a_i - Strength of the solution in criteria i w_i -The weight the stakeholder attaches to criteria i
2. The performance difference between two solution alternatives is determined by their relative strength in each evaluation criteria	$\Delta Score_{AB} = Score_A - Score_B$ $= \sum_{i=1}^{n} (a_i - b_i) w_i$	$\Delta Score_{AB}$ - Performance difference between solution A and solution B with respect to the user preferences $Score_A$ - Performance of solution A $Score_B$ - Performance of solution B
3. When comparing performance of two solution alternatives (for example A and B) against preferences of a user, we encounter thee types of evaluation criteria	$p + q + r = n$	p - Number of criteria of type 1 q - Number of criteria of type 2 r - Number of criteria of type 3
3.1 Type 1: Criteria in which A is stronger than B	$w_i \subset (w_1 ...... w_p) \forall i : a_i > b_i$	a_i - Strength of the solution A in criteria i
3.2 Type 2: Criteria in which B is stronger than A	$w_j \subset (w_1 ...... w_q) \forall i : a_j < b_j$	b_i - Strength of the solution B in criteria i
3.3 Type 3: Criteria in which A is as strong as B	$w_k \subset (w_1 ...... w_r) \forall i : a_k > b_k$	
4. Assuming solution B performs better than A against the preferences of a user, to reduce the performance difference between the two solutions, do the following;	$Score_B > Score_A$	$Score_A$- As defined above $Score_B$- As defined above Δw_i - Change in weight of criteria i
4.1 Increase the weight of criteria in which A is stronger at a rate that increases with the relative strength of A in the criteria, with respect to B.	$\dfrac{\partial(\Delta w_i)}{\partial \alpha_i} = M^+(\alpha_i)$ $\alpha_i = a_i - b_i$	M^+ - Qualitative simulation symbol for strictly increasing functions α_i - Strength of A relative to B in criteria i
4.2 Reduce the weight of criteria in which B is stronger at a rate that increases with the relative strength of B in the criteria, with respect to A.	$\dfrac{\partial(\Delta w_j)}{\partial \beta_j} = M^+(\beta_j)$ $\beta_j = b_j - a_j$	β_j - Strength of B relative to A in criteria j
4.3 Do not worry about the criteria where A is as strong as B.	$w_k = Const . \forall a_k - b_k = 0$	
5. In the context of evaluation of solution options, a state is a set of criteria used to evaluate alternative solutions, the criteria weights, and the performance of the solutions against the criteria	$State = Set \{(c_1 ....c_n),$ $(w_1 .... w_n),$ $(Score_A, Score_B ....)\}$	$(c_1 ....c_n)$ - Set of evaluation criteria 1 to n $(w_1 .... w_n)$ - Set of Weights of criteria 1 to n respectively $(Score_A, Score_B ....)$ - Performance of solutions A, B, and so on, against the criteria weights above.

There is a variety of possible representations of the relationships among different parameters of a MCDM problem. We selected the presentation in Table 1 because of its simplicity [2, 3]. The mathematical representation of the QR statements 1 to 3 aims at determining the performance difference between the solutions *A* and *B* with respect to each evaluation criterion. The representation for statement 4 is based on the QR relationship +*M* that represents a monotonically increasing function, and the statement aims at determine the 'amount' by which each criteria weight should be adjusted, to make solution *A* better than solution *B*. The weight adjustment may be an increase, or a reduction depending on the type of the criterion associated with the weight (see QR statement 3).

5   Support System for Tradeoff Analysis

We have developed a Qualitative Reasoning System for Tradeoff Analysis called QR-Trade that is based on the tradeoff analysis model described in section 4. The system has a knowledge base which stores quantitative and qualitative information about the solution alternatives. The quantitative information is the a_{ki}-values (see, section 3.2) of the alternative solutions provided by the domain expert, while the qualitative information is the features of the solutions, as well as descriptions of how every alternative fulfills each feature. In Mohamed et al [1], we describe how such a knowledge base can be implemented and utilized in the domain of Commercial-Off-The-Shelf (COTS) software components selection.

If the solution selection problem is characterized by multiple objectives, the user starts by selecting the objective of interest from the Graphical User Interface (GUI) shown in Figure 1 (this step is not necessary in a single objective problem). Thereafter, solution features which can be used as criteria for the evaluation of the solutions, and are relevant to the selected objective appear in the "Solution Features" window. The user then selects a set of evaluation criteria from the features. Whenever a criterion is added to the set of evaluation criteria, a window which enables setting the user preference associated with the criterion opens up (see, "Set Criterion Preference" window in Figure 1). The solutions are evaluated by clicking "Evaluate", and the solution scores are displayed in the "Solution / Ranking" window in a manner that demonstrates the ranking of the solutions.

To carryout tradeoff analysis, the user selects the objective of interest, followed by the solution alternatives to study. The default setting of QR-Trade is such that the solution with a highest score in the objective is used to provide the baseline performance. Therefore, it is shown as the preferred solution, and the others are shown as the un-preferred solutions in the GUI. However, the user can select any other solution alternative to provide the baseline performance.

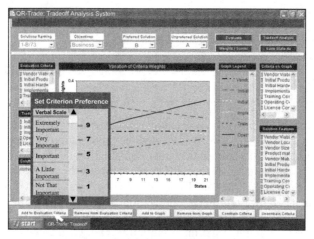

Fig. 1. The Main GUI of QR-Trade

Upon clicking "Tradeoff Analysis", the system produces graphs which reveal how the criteria weights can be varied to improve the performance of the un-preferred solution, while worsening that of the preferred solution. Table 2 presents the meaning of the graphical representation.

If a selection objective or solution alternative which a user is interested in does not exist, the issue is raised and discussed through the information sharing component of the decision support system which OR-Trade is part of. Then the expert information in the knowledge base can be modified accordingly. However, the focus of this paper

Table 2. Meaning Derived from Criteria Graphs

Nature Of Criterion Graph	Meaning Associated with Graph Gradient	Comment
Positive Gradient	The preferred solution is weaker than the un-preferred solution in the criterion	Preference over the two solutions is more likely to change if the user is willing to increase preference (weight) of the criterion
Negative Gradient	The preferred solution is stronger than the un-preferred solution in the criterion	Preference over the two solutions is more likely to change if the user is willing to reduce preference (weight) of the criterion
Zero Gradient	Both Solutions have the same strength in the criterion	Preference over the two solutions is not affected by changing preference (weight) of the criterion
General Comments: The larger the gradient of a graph the higher the effect of the criterion on changing user preference over the alternative solutions.		

is tradeoff analysis, therefore, we assume that the solution alternatives are available and the knowledge base has all the information required to evaluate those alternatives.

6 Example

An organization dealing in chinese food intends to change its business model from delivering food home based upon phone orders to building a webshop where orders can be placed. The system should be able to receive and process orders by telephone, email, SMS, and internet (Web site access). Moreover, it should process credit card payments

The team developing the software for the webshop intends to use a COTS to provide most of the functional requirements, then develop the extra requirements and interfaces inhouse. On noticing that the available COTS alternatives fulfil the same functionalities, the team decides to evaluate the alternatives basing on the quality and business concerns of the shop manager.

6.1 Solution Process

The MCDM model presented in section 3.1 was used to solve the problem. Firstly, the alternative COTS were graded in each COTS feature. The quality features were specified according to ISO/IEC 9126 software quality model [7], while the business concerns features were stipulated basing on the COTS cost (COCOTS) model [4], and on the information obtained from the CeBASE Lessons Learned Repository [5] about issue of concern during COTS selection. Figure 2 shows the strength of each COTS product in the features that were used as the evaluation criteria. In other words, the figure represents the expert (quantitative) information about the alternative (solutions) COTS products. We identify the COTS products as Product A, Product B, Product C, and Product D, because they are commercial products, and we do not have permission to publish their names.

Secondly, the preference of the shop manager over the evaluation criteria was acquired using the paired comparison method. The method is based upon organizing the evaluation criteria into a matrix, followed by cross-comparing each pair of criteria in terms of importance (i.e., The QR-Trade scale was used to compare two criteria at a time instead of using it to set the actual weight of the criteria). After the criteria grad-

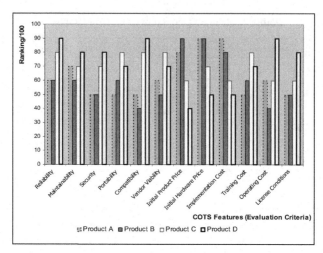

Fig. 2. Evaluation Criteria Weights

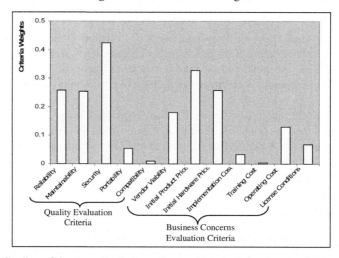

Fig. 3. Grading of the strength of alternative products in the various evaluation criteria

ing process, the geometric mean of the received grades for each criterion was calculated. The final criteria weights were obtained by normalizing the means for a sum of 1. Figure 3 shows the evaluation criteria and the associated criteria weights.

The system development team decided to evaluate each COTS product separately with respect to the quality objective; which is to select high quality product, and with respect to the business concerns objective; which is to select a low cost COTS with favorable long term acquisition conditions.

6.2 Results

Information in Figures 2 and 3 was utilized to determine a score for each COTS product according to how well it satisfies each selection objective, and Figure 4 shows the scores of the products for each of the objectives. From Figure 4, we notice that Product *B* is the best for the business concerns objective, while Product *D* is the best for the quality objective. This causes a selection dilemma that is resolved by tradeoff analysis to identify what is given up/gained if a particular solution is selected. It is upon the user to decide whether s/he is willing to make the identified tradeoff or not.

Tradeoff analysis was carried out using QR-Trade. It involved Product *B* (the best alternative for the business concerns objective), Product *D* (the best product for the quality objective) and Product *C*. Results shown in Figure 5 reveals that by choosing Product *C*, the user would get better quality than s/he would get with Product *B* at a cheaper price than that of Product *D*. Moreover, there are some quality criteria in which Product *C* is better than Product *D*.

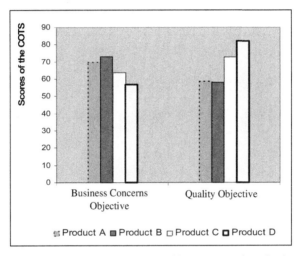

Fig. 4. Scores of alternative COTS products with respect to the selection objectives

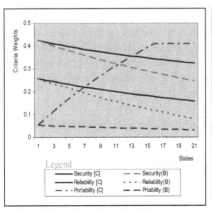

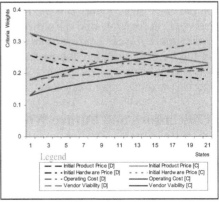

(a) Tradeoff Analysis for the Quality Objective   (b) Tradeoff Analysis for the Business Concerns Objective

Fig. 5. Tradeoff Analysis Involving Product B, Product C, and Product D

6.3 Discussion

It is not appropriate to select a solution from a set of alternatives based on the result of a MCDM model alone, because the aggregation process in MCDM techniques lead to loss of information. For example, from the scores in Figure 4 one cannot tell whether to choose Product *B* or Product *D*, because both are the best in the different incomparable selection objectives. However, tradeoff analysis enables identification of the tradeoff criteria, see Figures 5. These are the criteria that really affect the choice of a solution alternative.

QR-Trade identifies the tradeoff criteria, as well as the direction in which the criteria weights must be adjusted in order to achieve tradeoff. For example, Figure 5 indicates that tradeoff is only possible if the user is willing to accept paying a higher initial cost (i.e. high initial product price and high hardware price) than what the market can offer, in exchange for higher quality and better long term economic benefits.

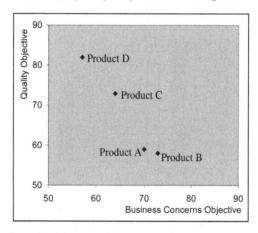

Fig. 6. Pareto Space for 2D tradeoff Analysis representation of results in figure 8

On the other hand, Figure 6 is the *Pareto Space for 2D Tradeoff Analysis* version of the results in figure 4. One can easily notice that unlike the representation in Figure 5, *Pareto Space for 2D Tradeoff Analysis* does not explicitly identify the criteria that affect the tradeoff, and how the preferences should be adjusted to achieve tradeoff. This is one of the major differences and strength of our tradeoff analysis model in comparison with the other models in the reviewed literature.

7 Conclusions and Future Work

This paper presents a tradeoff analysis model based on qualitative reasoning, as well as a tradeoff support tool based on the model. Throughout the paper we emphasize the importance of tradeoff analysis. Moreover, we relate tradeoff analysis to exploratory and discovery studies that aim at discovering extra evaluation criteria to improve completeness and certainty of the user preference model. Our tradeoff analysis support system (QR-Trade), utilizes visualization to stimulate the users thinking about the tradeoff criteria in particular, and the entire tradeoff process in general.

Besides the tradeoff analysis results, we believe that the user should review the qualitative description of the solutions performance in the tradeoff criteria before effecting the tradeoff, as this enables her/him to relate the tradeoff analysis results to the problem being solved. For this reason, QR-Trade has a knowledge base which stores both qualitative and quantitative information about the solutions. Finally, we explicitly discuss the role of the domain expert in the solution evaluation process, as well as in tradeoff analysis.

As future work, we intend to study the appropriateness of different type of mathematical functions, for our tradeoff analysis model. In addition, we would like to integrate tradeoff analysis into Group-Choice decision support.

References

1. Mohamed, T. Wanyama, G. Ruhe, A. Eberlein· and B. Far, "COTS Evaluation Supported By Knowledge Bases", *LNCS 3096*, pp.43-54, 2004.
2. Kuipers, "Commonsense Reasoning about Causality: Deriving Behavior from Structure", *Artificial Intelligence*, Vol. 24, Issue 1-3, pp. 169-203, December, 1984.
3. Kuipers, C. Chiu, D. T. D. Molle, D. Throop, "Higher-Order Derivative Constraints in Qualitative Simulation", *Artificial Intelligence*, Vol. 51, pp. 343-379, 1991.
4. B. W. Boehm, C. M. Abts, E. K. Bailey, "COCOTS Software Integration Cost Model: an Overview" *Proceedings of the California Software Symposium*, October, 1998.
5. CeBASE COTS lessons learned Repository, available at http://www.cebase,org
6. J. Petrie, T. A. Webster, and M. R. Cutkosky,, "Using Pareto Optimality to Coordinate Distributed Agents", *AIEDAM Special Issue on Conflict Management*, Vol. 9, pp. 269-281, 1995.
7. International Organization for Standardization: Software Products Evaluation – Quality Characteristics and Guidelines. Geneva, Switzerland: International Organization for Standardization (ISO), 1991.
8. J. J. Dujmovic, W. Y. Fang, "Reliability of LSP Criteria", *LNAI 3131*, pp. 151-162, 2004,
9. P. Pu, and D. Lalanne, "Design Visual Thinking Tools for Mixed Initiative Systems", *International Conference on Intelligent User Interfaces*. 2002.
10. P. Pu, P. Kumar, and B. Faltings, "User-Involved Tradeoff Analysis in Configuration Tasks", *Workshop notes, 3rd International Workshop on User-Interaction in Constraint Satisfaction, at the 9th International Conference on Principles and Practice of Constraint Programming*, 2003.
11. V. Torra, "The Weighted OWA operator", *International Journal of Intelligent Systems*, Vol. 12, pp. 153-166, 1997.

Evaluation of Control Performance
of Multi-stage Fuzzy Reasoning
in Anti-lock Braking System for Railways
Using Fuzzy Reasoning

Tetsuya Asanome[1], Toshiaki Nonaka[2], Yasunori Endo[3],
Shin-ichi Nakazawa[4], and Hiroshi Yoshikawa[5]

[1] Graduate School of Systems and Information Engineering, University of Tsukuba
Ibaraki 305-8573, Japan
asanome@edu.esys.tsukuba.ac.jp
[2] Odakyu Electric Railway Corporation, Tokyo 160-8309, Japan
[3] Faculty of Systems and Information Engineering, University of Tsukuba
Ibaraki 305-8573, Japan
[4] Railway Technical Research Institute, Tokyo 185-8540, Japan
[5] Mitsubishi Electric Corporation, Hyogo 661-8661, Japan

Abstract. Anti-lock braking system (ABS) for railways is mentioned as one of the way of reducing the risk for railways. Recently, ABS for railways is put in practical use, for example, ABS using multi-stage fuzzy reasoning. In this paper, we propose the new types of ABS using one-stage fuzzy reasoning, and compare the control performances of the proposed ABSs with the present ABS in respect of braking distance, wheel damages, and the frequency of action of valves through the numerical simulations. Moreover, we show the effect for the prevention of hunting.

1 Introduction

In recent years, risk analysis in various fields occupies the very important position and the methods of risk analysis are proposed in each field. In railway industry, the methods of risk analysis are also proposed from various points. For example, one of the methods of risk avoidance is anti-lock braking system (ABS) for railways. The ABS for railways is the equipment for preventing skid and lock of wheels.

Wheel may skid and/or lock when the brake is put on in the rain. The following two problems arise by the skid and lock for railways.

– Extension of braking distance
– Occurrence of the running noise by wheel damages

The former problem not only prevents a sudden stop for safety but causes disruption of the train schedule. On the other hand, the latter can be considered to increase the number of the maintenance parts and have the great trouble with the residents who live along the railways. These problems can be regarded as

V. Torra et al. (Eds.): MDAI 2005, LNAI 3558, pp. 110–121, 2005.

great risks for human life or environment of living. Research and development to such problems have been studied actively and the effective results are obtained by some of the authors [1].

By the way, ABSs of mechanical brake for railways are put in practical use. ABS using fuzzy reasoning (fuzzy ABS) is mentioned as one of the ABSs, and the effect of the fuzzy ABS is shown through numerical simulations and running tests (e.g. [1]). On the other hand, there are some problems, e.g. how to construct or how to choose the operators in fuzzy reasoning etc. One of the significant problems is that control performances of multi-stage fuzzy reasoning for fuzzy ABS have not been considered sufficiently.

Multi-stage fuzzy reasoning consists of some 'one-stage fuzzy reasoning' and inputs the output from the previous fuzzy reasoning to the following fuzzy reasoning. In the multi-stage fuzzy reasoning, it is known that the fuzziness is amplified rather than only one-stage fuzzy reasoning [2]. Therefore, the multi-stage fuzzy reasoning is hardly put in practical use in comparison with one-stage fuzzy reasoning in general. However, it is experientially known that the fuzzy ABS using multi-stage fuzzy reasoning is effective in the prevention of hunting. The hunting is the movement that supplying and exhausting the pressure of a brake cylinder (BC) are repeated for a short time and the movement is known to be uncomfortable to ride.

In this paper, we evaluate the control performances of multi-stage fuzzy reasoning in fuzzy ABS quantitatively in respect of braking distance etc. through the numerical simulations, and confirm the effect on the prevention of hunting by comparing the charts.

2   Braking System for Railways

The braking system supplies braking force to the train sets according to operation of driver or command from automatic train control (ATC) etc. and passenger load (Fig. 1). The role of braking system is reducing the translational kinetic energy of train sets and rotational kinetic energy of each axle by the braking force.

The brake is classified into various methods according to how to put on. Mechanical brake classified in the adhesion brake is shown as follows.

2.1   Mechanical Brake

Compressed air which is supplied to a BC pushes a brake shoe (or a brake pad) onto wheel tread (or brake disk). As a result, friction force is generated between a brake shoe and wheel tread and traction occurs on the contact area between a rail and a wheel as anti-force (Fig. 2). The traction is friction force which occurs by skid generated by wheel rolling on the rail. The friction force increase according to the increase of braking force while skid is microscopic. But the friction force reaches a limit point if skid increases gradually. The friction force until a limit point is called adhesion force.

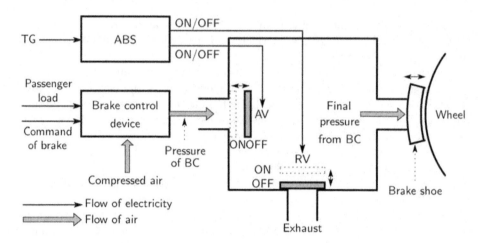

Fig. 1. Mechanical braking system for railways

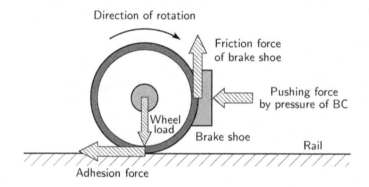

Fig. 2. The relation of braking force and adhesion force

2.2   ABS

Wheel may skid or lock when the brake is put on strongly in the state that the rail is wet. Skid is the state that the velocity of each axle is lower than the velocity of the train sets, and lock is the state that the velocity of an axle is zero. Tacho-generator (TG) is equipped on each axle and observes the velocity of each axle. ABS supplies or exhausts the pressure of BC quickly by active valve (AV) and release valve (RV) if the skid is detected, and aims at the prevention of skid in putting on brake. Concretely, AV is the valve which shut off the compressed air inputted to BC in the state 'ON', and RV is the valve which exhaust the compressed air in the state 'ON'. The action of ABS is shown as follows.

1. State with non-skid
   In this state, the mode is set to 'supply' ((AV, RV)=(OFF, OFF)) to increase the pressure of BC.

2. State with skid

   If the skid is detected, the mode is set to 'exhaust' ((AV, RV)=(ON, ON)) to decrease the pressure of BC quickly.

3. State of changing from 2 to 1

   If the skid has been decreased, the mode is set to 'keep' ((AV, RV) = (ON, OFF)) to keep the pressure of BC. After that, if the state is with non-skid, the mode is reset to 'supply' and the pressure of BC is increased to the pressure of command.

3   The Construction of the Present Fuzzy ABS

We show the flow of the present fuzzy ABS as follows (show Fig. 3) [1].

FL 1 *Velocity of each axle*
The velocity of each axle is calculated by using sine wave outputted from TG of each axle (①, ②).

FL 2 *Reference velocity of each car*
The reference velocity is the maximum value in the velocity of each axle and the velocity calculated virtually by using a constant deceleration (③).

FL 3 *Velocity difference (ΔV) and deceleration (β) of each axle*
ΔV and β of each axle are calculated by using the velocity of each axle and the reference velocity, where (ΔV of each axle) = (reference velocity $-$ velocity of each axle), and (β of each axle) = ((last time value $-$ this time value) of the velocity of each axle)/ sampling time (④).

FL 4 *Grades of ΔV and β of each axle*
The grades of ΔV and β of each axle are calculated in the condition part of the first stage of multi-stage fuzzy reasoning (Fig. 4, ⑤).

FL 5 *Skid Degree (SD)*
SD is calculated from the rule 'ΔV & $\beta \Rightarrow$ SD' in the conclusion part of the first stage of multi-stage fuzzy reasoning (Table 1, Fig. 5, 6, ⑥). **FL 4** and **FL 5** are the first stage of multi-stage fuzzy reasoning (⑤, ⑥).

FL 6 *Determination of action of AV and RV (second stage of multi-stage fuzzy reasoning)*

1. SD calculated in **FL 5** is inputted into the condition part of the second stage of multi-stage fuzzy reasoning (Fig. 8).
2. ON/OFF time of each valve is calculated by using the rule 'SD $\Rightarrow$ ON/OFF time'.
3. The action of each valve is determined by using ON/OFF time of each valve (Table 2, ⑦).

FL 7 *Setting of control area*
Control area in which the valves begin to act is set up so that valves are not operated until ΔV reaches the value which is established according to reference velocity (Fig. 7, ⑧).

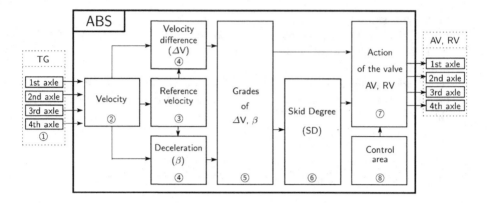

Fig. 3. The construction of the present fuzzy ABS using multi-stage fuzzy reasoning

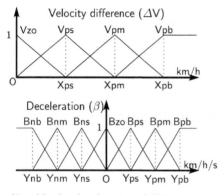

V**: Membership function of ΔV
B**: Membership function of β
nb: negative big, nm: negative medium
ns: negative small, pb: positive big
pm: positive medium, ps: positive small
zo: zero

Fig. 4. Membership functions of ΔV and β in the first stage

Table 1. Rule sets in the first stage

ΔV \ β	Bnb	Bnm	Bns	Bzo	Bps	Bpm	Bpb
Vzo	NB	NM	ZO	ZO	ZO	ZO	ZO
Vps	NM	NM	NS	ZO	PS	PS	PS
Vpm	NS	NS	NS	ZO	PS	PS	PM
Vpb	ZO	ZO	ZO	ZO	PM	PM	PB

NB: Negative Big, NM: Negative Medium
NS: Negative Small, PB: Positive Big
PM: Positive Medium, PS: Positive Small
ZO: Zero

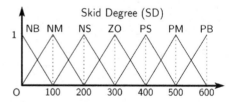

Fig. 5. Membership functions of SD in the first stage

4   The Problems of the Present Fuzzy ABS and the Improvement Methods

4.1   The Problems of the Present Fuzzy ABS

We show the problems of the present fuzzy ABS as follows and propose the new types of ABS using one-stage fuzzy reasoning to solve the problems.

1. The effect of ON/OFF time of each valve
   In the present fuzzy ABS, the action of each valve is determined after the

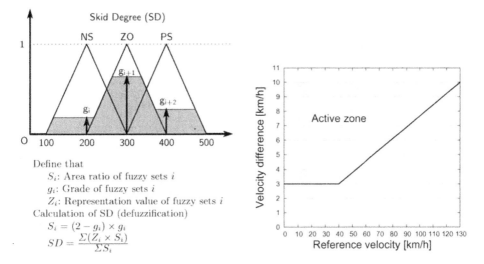

Define that
S_i: Area ratio of fuzzy sets i
g_i: Grade of fuzzy sets i
Z_i: Representation value of fuzzy sets i
Calculation of SD (defuzzification)
$$S_i = (2 - g_i) \times g_i$$
$$SD = \frac{\Sigma(Z_i \times S_i)}{\Sigma S_i}$$

Fig. 6. Calculation of SD in the first stage   **Fig. 7.** Control area

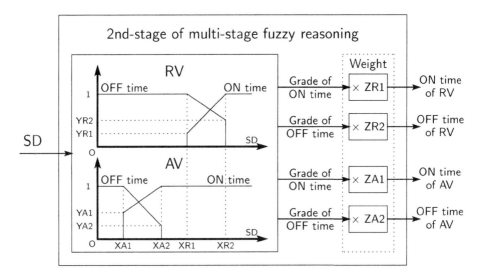

Fig. 8. The construction of second stage ('SD $\Rightarrow$ ON/OFF time')

ON/OFF time is calculated by using the SD. But it is not studied how to determine the action of each valve without ON/OFF time.

2. The effect of multi-stage fuzzy reasoning for prevention of hunting
   In the present fuzzy ABS, the multi-stage fuzzy reasoning is used to reduce the frequency of hunting. But it is not well-known how effective the multi-stage fuzzy reasoning shows for braking distance, wheel damages, and the frequency of action of valves.

Table 2. How to determine the action of valves: 'ON/OFF time $\Rightarrow$ ON/OFF'. The action of each valve is determined by this table. '$*$' means arbitrary value, and 'dt' means a sampling time

Input					Output
ON time	OFF time	Pre. Action	counter	Action	counter
> 0	$= 0$	$*$	$*$	ON	0
$= 0$	> 0	$*$	$*$	OFF	0
> 0	> 0	ON	> 0	ON	max(min(ON time, counter)$-$dt, 0)
> 0	> 0	ON	$= 0$	OFF	OFF time
> 0	> 0	OFF	> 0	OFF	max(min(OFF time, counter)$-$dt, 0)
> 0	> 0	OFF	$= 0$	ON	ON time

4.2   The Proposed ABS 1

In the present fuzzy ABS, fuzzy reasoning is used in the case that the action of valves is determined from SD (SD $\Rightarrow$ ON/OFF of valves). On the other hand, in the proposed ABS 1, condition branch is used in the same case.

FL 1~5, 7
   The same procedures to the present ABS (①~⑥, ⑧).
FL 6 *Determination of action of AV and RV (⑦)*
   The action of valves is determined from the following formulas.

$$(AV, RV) = \begin{cases} (OFF, OFF); \begin{cases} 0 \le SD \le V_A - DIFF \\ dS \le 0 \, \& \, |SD - V_A| < DIFF \end{cases} \\ (ON, OFF); \begin{cases} dS > 0 \, \& \, |SD - V_A| < DIFF \\ V_A + DIFF \le SD \le V_R - DIFF \\ dS \le 0 \, \& \, |SD - V_R| < DIFF \end{cases} \\ (ON, ON); \begin{cases} dS > 0 \, \& \, |SD - V_R| < DIFF \\ V_R + DIFF \le SD \le 600 \end{cases} \end{cases}$$

where V_A, V_R, $DIFF$, SD, dS, '&', and '{' are the threshold of AV, the threshold of RV, a constant distance from the threshold, this time value of SD, SD difference (this time value $-$ last time value of SD), 'AND', and condition branch respectively, for example, (AV, RV) = (OFF, OFF) if $(0 \le SD \le V_A - DIFF)$ or $(dS \le 0 \, \& \, |SD - V_A| < DIFF)$.

4.3   The Proposed ABS 2

In the proposed ABS 2, SD is not calculated from ΔV and β, but the action of valves is determined directly (ΔV & $\beta \Rightarrow$ ON/OFF). So the proposed ABS 2 is the ABS in which one-stage fuzzy reasoning is used as well as the proposed ABS 1.

Table 3. Rule sets of fuzzy reasoning in the proposed ABS 2. There are three modes in ABS, 'supply'(1), 'keep'(2), and 'exhaust'(3). In the cell with '*', the mode changes according to the reference velocity. On the left side of '/', the region of high reference velocity is shown. On the right side, the region of low reference velocity is shown

β / ΔV	Bnb	Bnm	Bns	Bzo	Bps	Bpm	Bpb
Vzo	1	1	1/2*	2	2	2	2
Vps	1	1	1/2*	2	2	2	3
Vpm	1	1/2*	2	2	2	2/3*	3
Vpb	1/2*	2	2	2	2	3	3

Table 4. Conditions of simulations

Item	Value	Unit
Initial velocity	100	km/h
Sampling time	0.02	s
Wheel load	4000	kg
Friction force by brake shoes	11000	N
Friction coefficient by brake shoes	0.33	-
Wheel radius	0.43	m
Moment of inertia / an axle	60	kg·m^2
Waste time of the pressure of BC	0.05	s
Time constant of the pressure of BC	0.8	s
Number of axle / train sets	4 axles(1 car)	
Unit of AV, RV control	4 axles(1 car)	

FL 1~4, 6 (FL 6 is same to FL 7 in the present ABS)
The same procedures to the present ABS (①~⑤, ⑧).
FL 5 *Determination of the action of AV and RV* (⑦)

1. Algebraic sum is used as fuzzy operator 'and' in each cell of Table 3.
2. The sum of the grades in each cell is calculated for each mode.
3. The mode which has the biggest grade in three modes (supply, keep, and exhaust) is chosen, and the action of valves is determined from the chosen mode.

5   Numerical Simulations

5.1   Method and Result

In Table 4, we show the conditions of the numerical simulations in the present ABS and the proposed ABS 1, 2. The parameters in Table 4 follow the actual vehicles in the conventional lines and the experimental values. Moreover, we show the parameters of ABS in Table 5.

Table 5. Parameters of ABS (Fig. 4, 8)

Xzo	Xps	Xpm	Xpb	Ynb	Ynm	Yns	Yzo	Yps	Ypm	Ypb
0	5	15	25	-40	-30	-25	0	5	15	25

XA1	XA2	XR1	XR2	YA1	YA2	YR1	YR2	ZA1	ZA2	ZR1	ZR2
1	250	350	600	0.50	0.50	0.27	0.33	0.6	0.2	0.3	0.6

Table 6. Result of simulation

Item	Present ABS	Proposed ABS 1	Proposed ABS 2
Braking distance [m]	326.4	323.8	328.0
Wheel damages [kN·m]	482.7	572.6	431.2
Frequency of the action of AV [times]	34	44	36
Frequency of the action of RV [times]	32	24	30

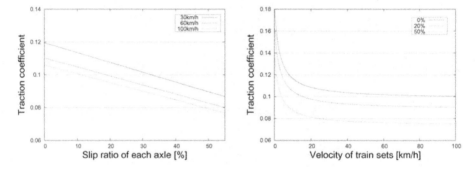

Fig. 9. Traction coefficient model. Left figure shows the change of traction coefficient according to slip ratio of each axle in the condition of three kinds of velocity. Right figure shows the change of traction coefficient according to velocity of train sets in the condition of three kinds of slip ratio

The traction coefficient model shown in Fig. 9 is taken into consideration about the matters which running tests and experiments which are performed until now show qualitatively. Moreover, the noise is added in consideration of the wheel load variation by wheel shaking, the rough of contact area, dirt, and water film thickness etc.

We show the results of numerical simulations for the traction coefficient model of Fig. 9 in Fig. 11~13, and show the comparison of braking distance, wheel damages [3], and the frequency of the action of valves (sum of all axles) in Table 6. Wheel damages is defined by the following formula.

$$Q = \sum_{i=1}^{n} \int_0^T (F_{bi} - \frac{J_i}{R_i} \frac{d\omega_i}{dt}) \cdot (-v + R_i\omega_i)dt$$

where n, T [s], F_{bi} [N], J_i[kg·m^2], R_i [m], v [km/h], and ω_i [rad/s] are the number of axle of train sets, time after brake is started to put on until train sets stop,

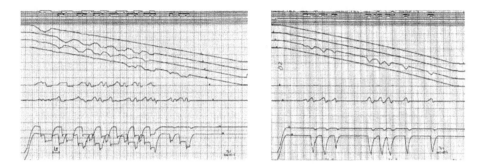

Fig. 10. Example charts in the running tests (left: present ABS, right: proposed ABS 1). These charts show the pulse waveforms of the action of valves, the velocity of each axle, SD, and the pressure of BC from a top to order

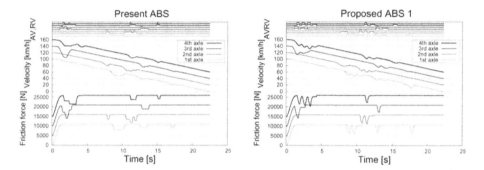

Fig. 11. Chart of simulation result in the present ABS

Fig. 12. Chart of simulation result in the proposed ABS 1

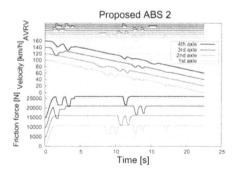

Fig. 13. Chart of simulation result in the proposed ABS 2

friction force by a brake shoe of the i-th axle, moment of inertia of the i-th axle, wheel radius of the i-th axle, velocity of train sets, and angular velocity of the i-th axle. The direction of braking force is defined as positive.

The pulse waveforms in the upper part of Fig. 11~13 show the action of RV of 4th axle, AV of 4th axle, RV of 3rd axle, $\cdots$, AV of 1st axle from a top to order. In addition, we prepared three traction coefficient models other than Fig. 9 and performed the same numerical simulations to each. We obtained the almost same results for these models.

5.2   Discussion

Compared with the present ABS, the proposed ABS 1 shortened braking distance by $2.5 \sim 3$m (2.7m on average), but increased wheel damages by $31 \sim 90$kN·m (48kN·m on average). The cause of these phenomena is considered the difference in design policy. In the present ABS, one skid time is shortened preferentially in order to prevent a lock completely. On the other hand, the proposed ABS 1 allows skid by $(V_A , V_R)=(272, 410)$ which are the parameters of the formula of condition branch in **FL 6** of **4.2**. As a result, the proposed ABS 1 shortened braking distance and increased wheel damages. Moreover, hunting occurs frequently in the proposed ABS 1 (Fig. 12). At this point, the multi-stage fuzzy reasoning in present ABS is effective.

On the other hand, in the proposed ABS 2, braking distance is practically equal, but the wheel damages decrease by $52 \sim 172$kN·m (126kN·m on average). The cause of these phenomena is considered the existence of the mode 'keep' during the mode 'exhaust'. For example, a big skid occurred after two seconds from starting to put on brake (Fig. 11). At this time, the mode shifted from 'exhaust' to 'keep' once in the present ABS. But the mode sometimes go back to 'exhaust' because the situation for skid is not improved. On the other hand, the proposed ABS 2 continued the mode 'exhaust' without shifting to the mode 'keep' (Fig. 13). As a result, the situation for skid is improved earlier than the present ABS and the difference appeared in wheel damages because such a situation continued. Moreover, hunting occurs frequently in the proposed ABS 2 (Fig. 13). At this point, the multi-stage fuzzy reasoning in the present ABS is effective for the prevention of hunting as well as the proposed ABS 1.

Therefore, the proposed ABS 1 is effective in 'shortening of braking distance', the proposed ABS 2 is effective in 'reduction of wheel damages', and the present ABS using multi-stage fuzzy reasoning is effective in 'prevention of hunting'. The effect of multi-stage fuzzy reasoning can be also confirmed from the example charts (Fig. 10) of the running tests performed by using the type 3000 commuter train of Odakyu Electric Railway in February, 2004.

6   Conclusion

In this paper, we discussed how to determine the action of valves in the second stage of multi-stage fuzzy reasoning of the present ABS. As a result, we proposed more effective ABS than the present ABS in respect of shortening of braking distance and reduction of wheel damages. On the other hand, we showed that multi-stage fuzzy reasoning used in the present ABS was effective from a viewpoint of prevention of hunting.

In the forthcoming paper, we will discuss theoretically how the fuzziness in multi-stage fuzzy reasoning raise the effect to prevention of hunting.

References

1. T. Nonaka, Y. Endo, H. Yoshikawa: "Improvement of Control Performance of Anti-Lock Braking System with Fuzzy Reasoning for Rolling Stock" , Journal of Japan Society for Fuzzy Theory and Intelligent Informatics Vol.16, No.5, pp.431–440 (2004).
2. M. Mizumoto : "Fuzzy Reasoning (2)", Journal of Japan Society for Fuzzy Theory and Intelligent Informatics Vol.4, No.3, pp.35–46 (1992).
3. T. Nonaka, T. Ohyama, Y. Endo, H. Yoshikawa: "Anti-Lock Braking System for Train Sets on Railways (1st Report, Formation of Dynamics Model and Methods of Evaluation for Controls)" , Transactions of the Japan Society of Mechanical Engineers, C (to be published).

One-Way and Two-Party Authenticated ID-Based Key Agreement Protocols Using Pairing

Takeshi Okamoto, Raylin Tso, and Eiji Okamoto

Risk Engineering Major
Graduate School of Systems and Information Engineerin
University of Tsukuba
1-1-1 Tennodai, Tsukuba, Ibaraki, 305-8573, Japan
{ken,okamoto}@risk.tsukuba.ac.jp
raylin@cipher.risk.tsukuba.ac.jp

Abstract. Cryptography is the ancient science of encrypting messages so that only the sender and receiver can recover them. To achieve this goal, an agreed key between the sender and receiver is required. In asymmetric cryptosytems, so far, only a few ID-based key agreement protocols are *one-way* and most of them can only provide authentication for only one entity to the other. In this paper, two ID-based one-way key agreement protocols are proposed. The advantage of our protocols is that the authentication of the sender and receiver is established at the same time although the key distribution is only one pass. In addition, transmitted data size in our schemes is very small and the parameter for key agreement consists of just one. In this paper, an additional security attribute for key agreement protocols is defined and the rigorous security of our protocols is estimated. The performance evaluation is also analyzed by comparing our schemes with the previous schemes.

Keywords: Cryptography, authentication, ID-based, key agreement, pairing

1 Introduction

Cryptography is the ancient science of encrypting messages so that only the sender and receiver can understand them. It is now available to everyone and every field of financial activities thanks to the development of modern computers, which can perform more mathematical operations in a second than a human being could do in a lifetime. In order to achieve the goal of encrypting a message by a sender and recover the message by a receiver, an agreed key called a *session key* between the two entities is necessary. Key establishment protocols are designed for this purpose. Formally, key establishment protocols are designed so that two or more entities can establish a session key in order to communicate with confidentiality over an open network or to achieve a cryptographic goal such as data integrity. In general, if one entity generates a session key and securely

V. Torra et al. (Eds.): MDAI 2005, LNAI 3558, pp. 122–133, 2005.

transmits it to the other entity, this is usually called *key transport*. On the other hand, if both entities contribute information from which a joint secret key is derived, this is usually known as *key agreement*.

The first key agreement protocol based on asymmetric cryptography was the Diffie-Hellman protocol [4]. Its security is based on the intractability of the Diffie-Hellman problem and the discrete logarithm problem. Unfortunately, this protocol is insecure against *man-in-the-middle attack*[1] because it does not attempt to authenticate the communication entities. A key agreement protocol is called an *authenticated* key agreement protocol [3, 7, 9] if it enables a group of entities within a large and completely insecure public network to establishment a common secret key and furthermore ensures that they are indeed sharing this key with each other. To achieve this goal, usually an authenticated public/private key pair for each entity is required.

If entities use their identity-based asymmetric key pairs in the protocol for authentication and determination of the established key instead of using traditional public/private key pairs, then the authenticated key agreement protocol is called *identity(ID)-based*.

The first ID-based cryptosystem was proposed by Shamir [12] in 1984 but he did not construct an ID-based encryption scheme. In 2001, an efficient ID-based encryption scheme based on pairing was proposed by Boneh and Franklin [1] and their scheme is considered the first practical ID-based encryption scheme. Afterwards, pairing were used widely to get a huge number of ID-based cryptographic protocols (e.g., [5, 6]). In addition, many constructions have also been given for ID-based key agreement protocols (e.g., [8, 13, 15, 18]) because of the reason that in the conventional method, the existing symmetric cryptography is much faster than asymmetric one. Hence asymmetric cryptography is often used only as a key exchange protocol to exchange a secret key between each users.

Informally, there are three types of ID-based authenticated key agreement protocols. If both entities share an exclusive secret key without transmitting information to each other previously, then this protocol is called *non-interactive*. If only one entity is needed to be on-line, that is, if only one entity is needed to transmit information to the other, then the protocol is called *one-way*. Otherwise, the protocol is called *two-pass* or *one-round*. We emphasize that one-way key agreement protocol is the most suitable protocol for (network) environments than non-interactive or two-pass protocols. The detail remarks on these three types of protocols will be discussed in the next section.

On the other hand, we notice that up to the present, only a few ID-based key agreement protocols are one-way [15, 16]and these protocols can only provide authentications for only one entity (i.e., receiver) instead of both. Therefore, these protocols have to combine with some signature schemes in order to verify the identity of a sender, which not only complicate the key agreement protocols but also decrease the computational efficiency of the protocols.

---

[1] In cryptography, a man-in-the-middle attack is an attack in which an attacker is able to read, insert and modify at will, messages between two parties without either party knowing that the link between them has been compromised. The attacker must be able to observe and intercept messages going between the two victims.

In this paper, we propose two ID-based one-way key distribution protocols using pairing. The main feature of these protocols is that the authentication of both entities (i.e., sender and receiver) is established at the same time although the key agreement is only one pass. Therefore, a signature scheme is not necessary in our one-way protocols. In addition, our protocols have the following features.

- The message flows in our new protocols consist of only one parameter.
- The key generation center (KGC) is able to recover the agreed session keys from the message flow and from its private key. This would enable law enforcement agencies to decrypt messages encrypted with the session keys, after having obtained the necessary warrants.
- Our protocols provide enhanced security, which makes these protocols more secure than many other two-pass protocols and signcryption[2] schemes (e.g., [11, 17]).

The standards for evaluating the security of our protocols are the desirable secure attributes proposed in [2]. These attributes are originally defined for two-pass key agreements so we will modify some of these attributes in order for them to evaluate one-way key distribution protocols. In addition. we will define a new security attribute called *random number compromise security* which has been less considered in many key agreement protocols and signcryption schemes. We will show that our protocols possess all the security attributes proposed in [2] and also the random number compromise security.

We emphasize the main contributions of this paper. First, we propose two ID-based key distribution protocols which provide authentications for both entities although the schemes are one way and the massage flows in our protocols consist of only one parameter. Also, we defined a new security attribute called random number compromise security which is important but has been less considered so far. Our protocols possess this security attribute and those proposed in [2] so our protocols provide enhanced security and are more secure than many of the previously proposed schemes.

The remainder of this paper is organized as follows. Section 2 makes remarks on the three types of ID-based key agreement protocols. Section 3 explains the definitions of the desirable attributes of two-pass key agreement protocols, modified desirable attributes of one-way key agreement protocols and our newly proposed security attribute. In Section 4, we give some preliminaries about bilinear maps and Diffie-Hellman assumptions. Section 5 presents our newly proposed schemes and the security concerns of our schemes. Section 6 shows the comparative results of their performance and security with some previously proposed schemes. Finally, our conclusion is formulated in Section 7.

2 Comparison Remarks on the Three Types of the ID-Based Key Agreement Protocols

As we have mentioned in Introduction, there are informally three types of authenticated ID-based key agreement protocols: non-interactive protocols, one-

---

[2] A scheme which can achieve both confidentiality and authenticity at the same time.

way protocols and two-pass protocols. This section makes comparison remarks on these three types of protocols.

First, we see the non-interactive protocols. The first non-interactive ID-based key agreement protocol based on pairing was proposed by R. Sakai, K. Ohgishi and M. Kasahara [14] in the year of 2000. In this protocol, the established key consists of only one private key and one ID-based public key. A drawback of this protocol is that it always establishes the same (secret) key for the same entities (e.g., Alice and Bob) in each run of the protocol. Consequently, the established key usually cannot be used as a session key but only used for the sender (Alice) to encrypt a session key she chosen, and to send it to the receiver (Bob) secretly over insecure channels. This causes other problems. First, the session key is completely chosen by Alice which may be not desirable for Bob in general. Second, if a private key of one entity has been disclosed, then the established key as well as all the session keys encrypted by the established key will be disclosed. On the other hand, about the communication cost, even Alice and Bob use the established key as the session key which can be established non-interactively, the message encrypted by the session key cannot be transmitted non-interactively (i.e., Alice has to be on-line in order to send the encrypted message for the current session). Therefore, at least once (instead of zero) of message transmission is required for Alice in total.

Second, let's see the two-pass key agreement protocols. In this protocol, two random parameters (one from Alice and one from Bob) have to be exchanged between Alice and Bob before the key generation. After the (session) key generation phase, a message encrypted by the established session key will be transmitted from Alice to Bob for the current session. Consequently, at least three times of message transmission are required in total.

Finally, let's consider the one-way key agreement protocol. In this protocol, once of message transmission is required for the generation of the session key and once is required for sending a ciphertext encrypted by the session key for the current session. Since these two messages are both transmitted from the sender, Alice, they can be in fact transmitted at the same time. In other words, key establishment and message encryption can be done at once. Therefore, the total times of transmission required in one-way scheme is only once, the same as that of the non-interactive key agreement protocol. Moreover, the established keys varies in each run of the protocol even if the two entities remains unchanged.

Since the communication cost is the critical consideration for designing a key agreement protocol and a protocol with high security but a minimal number of passes and rounds is always desirable. We conclude from these comparison remarks that one-way protocols are the most suitable protocols for the (network) environment.

3   Desirable Attributes

Some desirable security attributes of key agreement protocols have been identified by Blake-Wilson, Johnson and Menezes in [2]. Those attributes are outlined as follows:

1. **Known-key security:** Each run of the protocol should result in a unique secret session key. The compromise of one session key should not compromise other session keys.
2. **Unknown key-share:** An entity A must not be coerced into sharing a key with any entity C if A thinks that she is sharing the key with another entity B.
3. **Key control:** Neither entity should be able to force the session key to be a preselected value.
4. **Key-compromise impersonation:** Suppose A's private key is disclosed. Clearly an adversary that knows this value can now impersonate A since it is precisely this value that identifies A. However, it may be desirable that this loss doesn't enable an adversary to impersonate other entities in the presence of A.
5. **Forward security:** If private keys of one or more entities are compromised, the secrecy of previously established session keys should not be affected.

We emphasize that not all these attributes are suitable for evaluating the security of one-way key agreement protocols. For example, the compromise of a receiver B's private key in a one-way key protocol will always compromise the secrecy of previously established session keys. In addition , any adversary E who knows B's private key can also impersonate a sender A in the presence of B and share an agreement key with B. Therefore, B will mistakenly believes that he is sharing the key with A. These are owing to the reason that the session key is computed from B's private key and some other public values. Consequently, in order to evaluate the security of one-way key distribution protocols, we have to re-define the attributes 4 and 5 as follows:

4. **Sender's key-compromise impersonation:** The compromise of sender A's private key will allow an adversary to impersonate A, but it should not enable the adversary to impersonate other entities in the presence of A.
5. **Sender's forward security:** If private keys of senders are compromised, the secrecy of previously established session keys should not be affected.

In addition, a new security attribute called *random number compromise security* is defined for the first time in this paper which has been less considered in most of the previously established schemes up to the present.

6. **Random number compromise security:** The compromise of a random number or a random element selected by the sender A should not compromise A's private key or the established session keys.

In most of the key agreement schemes or signcryption schemes, a random number or a random element chosen by each entity respectively (or by the sender only, if the scheme is a signcryption scheme or a one-way key agreement scheme) is required for the key generation. The random number/element is masked by some other parameters and sent from one entity A to the other entity B and/or from B to A, respectively. We note that in many of the current schemes, an adversary E who knows the random number(s)/element(s) can consequently compute the session key between A and B, or even worse, the sender A or both entities's private keys. For example, the compromise of random numbers in [1, 8, 15] and Schemes I and II in [16] will compromise the established session key, and the compromise of random numbers in [10, 11, 17, 18] and Scheme III in [16] will compromise the sender A's private key and the established session key both. As a result, in these schemes, the random number selected by each entity should be protected with higher secrecy than that of his/her private key for security purpose. It seems a little unreasonable so we hope to propose a one-way scheme such that even the random number has been disclosed, it will not affect the scheme or sender A's private key.

4 Preliminaries

4.1 Bilinear Maps

Let G_1 be an additive group of prime order q and G_2 be a multiplicative group of the same order, in which the discrete logarithm problem is assumed to be hard. Concretely, we can think of G_1 as a group of points on an elliptic curve over F_q, and G_2 as a subgroup of the multiplicative group of a finite field F_{q^k} for some $k \in Z_q^*$. Let P be a generator of G_1 and let $\hat{e} : G_1 \times G_1 \longmapsto G_2$ be a mapping with the following properties:

1. **Bilinearity:** A mapping $\hat{e}$ is bilinear if $\hat{e}(aP, bQ) = \hat{e}(P, Q)^{ab}$ for all $P, Q \in G_1$ and for all $a, b, \in Z_q^*$.
2. **Non-degeneracy:** A mapping is non-degenerate if $\hat{e}(P, Q) = 1\ \forall Q \in G_1$ implies $P = \mathcal{O}$, where $\mathcal{O}$ denotes the point at infinity..
3. **Computability:** A mapping is efficiently computable if $\hat{e}(P, Q)$ can be computed in polynomial-time for all $P, Q \in G_1$.

4.2 Diffie-Hellman Assumptions

To construct the bilinear pairing, we can use the Weil pairing or the Tate pairing associated with supersingular elliptic curves.

With the group G_1 described in Section 4.1, we can define the following hard cryptographic problems:

- **Discrete Logarithm (DL) Problem:** Given $P, Q \in G_1$, find an integer n such that $P = nQ$ whenever such integer exists.
- **Computational Diffie-Hellman (CDH) Problem:** Given a triple $(P, aP, bP) \in G_1$ for $a, b \in Z_q^*$, find the element abP.
- **Decision Diffie-Hellman (DDH) Problem:** Given a quadruple $(P, aP, bP, cP) \in G_1$ for $a, b, c \in Z_q^*$, decide whether $c = ab \bmod q$ or not.
- **Gap Difffie-Hellman (GDH) Problem:** A class of problems where the CDH problem is hard but DDH problem is easy.

5   Proposed Schemes

In this section, we describe our newly proposed schemes. All the parameters are assumed the same as those in Section 4. The identity, $ID_i \in \{0,1\}^*$, of each user i is select by the user which can be any information representing the user, for example, his/her e-mail address. In addition, the following settings are assumed to be generated by a key generation center (KGC) which is trusted by all users.

- $l \in Z_q^*$: a secret number selected by KGC,
- $\mathcal{H}$: a hash function mapping any string $\{0,1\}^*$ to the additive group G_1,
- $\mathcal{H}(ID_i)$: the public key of user i,
- S_i: the private key of user i where $S_i = l\mathcal{H}(ID_i)$,

5.1   Scheme I

Parameter Distribution:
- A picks up a random number $r \in Z_q^*$, computes $X_A = r\mathcal{H}(ID_A)$ and sends X_A to B using public channels.

Established Key:
- A computes $k_{AB} = \hat{e}(S_A, \mathcal{H}(ID_B))^r \oplus \hat{e}(S_A, \mathcal{H}(ID_B))$.
- B computes $k_{BA} = \hat{e}(X_A, S_B) \oplus \hat{e}(\mathcal{H}(ID_A), S_B)$.

where $\oplus$ is the additional operation[3] in G_2

Consistency: $k_{AB} = k_{BA}$ holds since

$$k_{AB} = \hat{e}(S_A, \mathcal{H}(ID_B))^r \oplus \hat{e}(S_A, \mathcal{H}(ID_B))$$
$$= \hat{e}(\mathcal{H}(ID_A), \mathcal{H}(ID_B))^{rl} \oplus \hat{e}(\mathcal{H}(ID_A), \mathcal{H}(ID_B))^l$$
$$= \hat{e}(X_A, S_B) \oplus \hat{e}(\mathcal{H}(ID_A), S_B)$$
$$= k_{BA}$$

Security Analysis

We give a brief security analysis to show that Scheme I possesses all the security attributes described in Section 3.

1. **Known-key security:**
   Analysis: Each run of the protocol between the two entities A and B produces a unique session key which depends on the value of r. Also note that r and the private keys for A and B still remain secret even if the session key of a session has been compromised. Therefore, an adversary cannot derive other session key k_{AB} as A did since he doesn't know S_A and r of that session. Also, he cannot derive k_{BA} as B did since he doesn't know S_B.

---

[3] The additional operation in G_2 can be predefined by the entities or PKG previously. They can also modify the scheme into $k_{AB} = k_{BA} \in \{0,1\}^*$. In this case, an additional hash function $\mathcal{H}' : G_2 \longmapsto \{0,1\}^*$ is required such that $k_{AB} = \mathcal{H}'(\hat{e}(S_A, \mathcal{H}(ID_B))^r) \oplus \mathcal{H}'(\hat{e}(S_A, \mathcal{H}(ID_B))) = \mathcal{H}'(\hat{e}(X_A, S_B)) \oplus \mathcal{H}'(\hat{e}(\mathcal{H}(ID_A), S_B)) = k_{BA}$ where $\oplus$ is the $Exclusive - OR$ operation.

2. **Unknown key-share:**
   Analysis: Note that $\hat{e}(S_A, \mathcal{H}(ID_B)$ and $\hat{e}(\mathcal{H}(ID_A), S_B)$ are exactly the shared key of SOK Scheme [14]. It is easy to see that SOK Scheme possesses the desirable attribute of unknown key-share providing that the private keys S_A and S_B are kept secret. Consequently, Scheme I inherits this property from theirs.

3. **Key control:**
   Analysis: It is easy to see that B cannot control the session key since X_A is selected by A. A still cannot do this since it is computationally impossible to find a $r \in G_1$ for a preselected value c of k_{AB}.

4. **Sender's key-compromise impersonation:**
   Analysis: Without the knowledge of r, an adversary E learned S_A of A cannot compute a session key k_{AB} as $\hat{e}(S_A, \mathcal{H}(ID_B))^r \oplus \hat{e}(S_A, \mathcal{H}(ID_B))$. E also cannot compute k_{BA} as $\hat{e}(X_A, S_B) \oplus \hat{e}(\mathcal{H}(ID_A), S_B)$ if he doesn't know B's private key S_B. This explains that an adversary E learned the private key S_A of sender A cannot share a common session key with A while allowing A mistakenly believe that he shares the session key with B. Consequently, it is impossible for a adversary E to impersonate B to A even if he knows the private key S_A of A.

5. **Sender's forward security:**
   Analysis: Note that without the knowledge of r, an adversary cannot derive a session key k_{AB} even if he has learned the private key S_A of sender A. The only way to learn the information r is from the equation $X_A = r\mathcal{H}(ID_A)$ while it is computational infeasible if the order q of G_1 is large enough.

6. **Random number compromise security:**
   Analysis: To compute a session key or the private key of A or B from the random number r and public information in this protocol is equivalent to solve the SOK scheme form only public information.

One may think that the random number r can be public information because the compromise of r will not affect the scheme. We make r as secret information in order to achieve the security attributes of Sender's key-compromise impersonation and Sender's forward security in this scheme.

5.2 Scheme II

Additional settings are required in this scheme.
- P: a generator of G_1 which is known to all users.
- V: the public key of KGC where $V = lP$.
- $\mathcal{H}_1: G_1 \longrightarrow Z_q^*$ a hash mapping.

Parameter Distribution:
- A picks up a random number $r \in Z_q^*$, computes $R_A = rP$ and sends R_A to B using public channels.

Established Key:

– A computes $h = \mathcal{H}_1(R_A)$ and the established key for A is

$$k_{AB} = \hat{e}(hS_A + rV, \mathcal{H}(ID_B)).$$

– B computes $h = \mathcal{H}_1(R_A)$ and the established key for B is

$$k_{BA} = \hat{e}(h\mathcal{H}(ID_A) + R_A, S_B).$$

Consistency: $k_{AB} = k_{BA}$ holds since

$$\begin{aligned}
k_{AB} &= \hat{e}(hS_A + rV, \mathcal{H}(ID_B)) \\
&= \hat{e}(h\mathcal{H}(ID_A) + rP, \mathcal{H}(ID_B))^l \\
&= \hat{e}(h\mathcal{H}(ID_A) + R_A, S_B) \\
&= k_{BA}
\end{aligned}$$

Security Analysis

The security of Scheme II can be analyzed using the same consideration of that of Scheme I which shows that Scheme II also also possesses all the security attributes described in Section 3. $h = \mathcal{H}_1(R_A)$ applied in Scheme II is to prevent an adversary E from predetermining the value a of $\hat{e}(a, S_B)$ from B' viewpoint. Since if E can determine the value a, then he can impersonate the sender A and share a key with B. For example, letting a of $\hat{e}(a, S_B)$ equals $\mathcal{H}(ID_E)$, then B will compute the agreement key $k_{BA} = \hat{e}(\mathcal{H}(ID_E), S_B) = \hat{e}(S_E, \mathcal{H}(ID_B))$ which can also be computed by E. Consequently, E shares a key with B but letting B mistakenly believe that he is sharing the key with the entity A. Also, random number r is made secret for satisfying the security attributes of Sender's key-compromise impersonation and Sender's forward security.

Since from sender's point of view, Scheme I is more efficient than Scheme II but from receiver's point of view, Scheme II is more efficient than scheme I. It is hard to conclude that which scheme is more efficient or better than the other.

5.3   Key Escrow

Key escrow is essential in situations where confidentiality as well as an audit trail is a legal requirement. For example, law enforcement agencies, after having obtained the necessary warrants, would be able to decrypt messages encrypted with the session keys.

It is easy to see that in Scheme I and Scheme II, if necessary, PKG is able to recover the agreed session keys from the message flow and from its private key.

6   Performance Evaluation

This section compares the security attributes and efficiency performance of our schemes with some one-way based schemes (key agreement schemes and sign-cryption schemes) proposed in [7, 11, 14, 15]. Although scheme in [11] is a sign-cryption scheme which consists of the processes of key agreement, signature

Table 1. Comparison of Efficiency

	Amount of work		
	Sender	Receiver	Total
Scheme I	1P + 1EC. + 1Exp.	2P	3P + 1EC. + 1Exp.
Scheme II	1P + 3EC.	1P + 1EC.	2P + 4EC.
II of [7]	3EC.	2EC.	5EC.
NR [11]	1P + 2EC. + 1Exp.	3P + 1Exp. + Ver.	4P + 2EC. + 2Exp. + Ver.
SOK [14]	1P + Enc.	1P + Dec.	2P + Enc. + Dec.
TBO [15]	1P + 2EC. + Sign.	1P + Ver.	2P + 2EC. + Sign. + Ver.

Table 2. Comparison of Security

	Known-key security	Sender's key-compromise impersonation	Sender's forward security	Random number compromise security
Scheme I	√	√	√	√
Scheme II	√	√	√	√
II of [7]	√			√
NR [11]	√	√	√	
SOK [14]				N/A
TBO [15]	√	N/A	N/A	

and encryption. One-way ID-based key agreement protocols can also achieve the same goal by encrypting a message using the established session key and some symmetric cryptosystems, and combines a signature scheme if the key agreement protocol does not provide authentication of the sender or both entities. Therefore, we can compare all these schemes on the same level. Table 1 gives the comparison result of efficiency in terms of computational cost. SOK Scheme[14] is non-interactive in key-generation. Therefore, in order for the session key of the scheme to be varied in each session, the secret key established by SOK Scheme is assumed to be used for encrypting a session key selected by the sender. As a result, an additional process (i.e., Encryption) for a sender and an additional process (i.e., Decryption) are required. Scheme II in [7] and TBO Scheme [15] are both one-way key agreement schemes

For abbreviation, in Table 1, we denote "P" pairing operation, "EC." elliptic curve scalar multiplication and "Exp." the exponential operation in G_2. "Sign." denotes the computation cost for signature and "Ver." denotes the computation cost for verification. "Enc." is the computation cost for encrypting a session key and "Dec." is that for recovering the session key.

Table 2 shows the possession of required security attributes in each schemes. Unknown key-share and Key control attributes are omitted since all these schemes are possessed. Also, "N/A" means "not applicable".

We conclude from these tables that:

- since TBO Scheme can only provide authentication of receivers, a signature scheme is required which scarifies the efficiency of the scheme.
- SOK Scheme and II of [7] are efficient but possess less security attributes.
- our schemes are more efficient than [11] and also possess the most security attributes than all these schemes.

7   Conclusion

In this paper, we proposed two ID-based one-way key distribution protocols using bilinear pairing. The most import feature of our schemes is that our schemes can provide authentications of both entities at the same time although the key distribution is only one pass. In addition, they are useful in application because the small transmitted data size (the message flows in our new protocols consist of only one parameter). In this paper, a new security attribute called random number compromise security is defined which is important but has been less considered in current schemes.

Finally, we end this conclusion by comparing our one-way and two-party authenticated ID-based key agreement protocols with signcryption schemes. In recent years, signcryption schemes have been investigated by many researchers because they think that a signcryption scheme is more efficient than traditional signature-then-encryption schemes. We note that our protocols and signcryption schemes are very similar. First, both schemes need only once of data transmission. The difference is that the message in a signcryption scheme transmitted from a sender to a receiver is a construction of three-tuples (C, U, V). C is the cipher text, U is the parameter for key recovery and V is the parameter for authentication. On the other hand, in our schemes, transmitted message is a construction of only two-tuples (C, X) where C is the cipher text encrypted by the session key and X is the random number for a receiver to derive the session key and to authenticate the sender at the same time. In other words, key agreement and entities' authentication are done simultaneously according to only one parameter, X. Consequently, one-way and two-party authenticated ID-based key agreement schemes like our schemes are superior to signcryption schemes from this point of view.

References

1. D. Boneh and M. Franklin, *Identity-based encryption from the Weil pairing*, Advances in cryptology –CRYPTO'01, Lecture Notes in Comput Sci. **2139** (2001), 213–229.
2. S. Blake-Wilson, D. Johnson and A. Menezes, *Key agreement protocols and their security analysis*, Proceedings of the sixth IMA international Conference on u Cryptography and Coding, Lecture Notes in Comput Sci. **1355** (1997), 30–45.
3. S. Blake-Wilson and A. Menezes, *Authenticated Diffie-Hellman key agreement Protocols*, Selected Areas in Cryptolgraphy–SAC'98, Lecture Notes in Comput Sci. **1556** (1999), 339–361.
4. W. Diffie and M. E. Hellman, *New directions in cryptography*, IEEE Transactions on Information Theory. **22** (1976), 644–654.
5. C. Gentry and A. Silverberg, *Hierarchical ID-based cryptography*, Advances in cryptology –ASIACRYPTO'02, Lecture Notes in Comput Sci. **2501** (2002), 548–566.
6. F. Hess, *Efficient identity based signature schemes based on pairings*, Selected Areas in Cryptolography–SAC'02, Lecture Notes in Comput Sci. **2595** (2003), 310–324.
7. L. Law, A. Menezes, M. Qu, J. Solinas and S. Vanstone, *An efficient protocol for authenticated key agreement*, Designs, Codes and Cryptogr. **28** (2003), no. 2, 119–134.

8. N. McCullagh and P. S. L. M. Barreto, *A new two-party identity-based authenticated key agreement*, Cryptology ePrint Archive, Report 2004/122, available at **http://eprint.iacr.org/2004/122/**.

9. A. Menezes, M. Qu and S. Vanstone, *Some new key agreement protocols providing mutual implicit authentication*, Proceedings of Selected Areas in Cryptography–SAC'95 (1995), 22–32.

10. J. Malone-lee, *Identity-based signcryption*, Cryptology ePrint Archive, Report 2002/098, available at **http://eprint.iacr.org/2002/098/**.

11. D. Nalla, K. C. Reddy, *Signcryption scheme for identity-based cryptosystems*, Cryptology ePrint Archive, Report 2003/066, available at **http://eprint.iacr.org/2003/066/**.

12. A. Shamir, *Identity-based cryptosystems and signature schemes*, Advances in cryptology – CRYPTO'84, Lecture Notes in Comput Sci. **196** (1985), 47–53.

13. N.P. Smart, *An identity based authenticated key agreement protocol based on the Weil pairing*, Electron. Lett. **38** (2002), 630–632, Cryptology ePrint Archive, Report 2001/111, available at **http://eprint.iacr.org/2001/111/**.

14. R. Sakai, K. Ohgishi and M. Kasahara, *Cryptosystems based on pairing*, Symp. on Cryptography and Information Security, Okinawa, Japan, Jan. 26–28, 2000.

15. R. Terada, W. D. Benis Jr. and E. Okamoto, *An IBE scheme to exchange authenticated secre keys*, Symp. on Cryptography and Information Security, Sendai, Japan, January 27-30 (2004), 1529–1533.

16. T. Okamot, K. Harada and E. Okamoto, *ID-based agreement protocols using pairing*, Symp. on Information Theory and Its Application–ISITA'04, Parma, Italy, Oct. 2004.

17. Y. Zheng, *Digital signcryption or how to achieve cost(signature & encryption) << cost(signature)+cost(encryption)*, Advances in cryptology –CRYPTO'97, Lecture Notes in Comput Sci. **1294** (1997), 165–179.

18. F. Zhang, S. Liu and K. Kim, *ID-based one round authenticated tripartite key agreement protocol with pairings*, Cryptology ePrint Archive, Report 2002/122, available at **http://eprint.iacr.org/2002/122/**.

Noise-Robust Watermarking
for Numerical Datasets

Francesc Sebé, Josep Domingo-Ferrer, and Agustí Solanas

Rovira i Virgili University of Tarragona
Dept. of Computer Engineering and Maths
Av. Països Catalans 26, E-43007 Tarragona, Catalonia
{francesc.sebe,josep.domingo,agusti.solanas}@urv.net

Abstract. Watermarking has been used on multimedia for a variety of applications, among which intellectual property protection stands out. However, and in spite of a growing need, very few attempts have been made at using watermarking to protect the intellectual property of alphanumerical databases. We present in this paper a watermarking system for numerical databases, which is the first one of its kind to preserve means and variances of attributes in the database. Given a watermarked dataset and a candidate watermark, the recovery algorithm makes a decision whether the candidate watermark is embedded or not in the dataset. The probabilities of false positive and false negative can be made arbitrarily small by proper choice of a security parameter. We give an analytical expression for the information or data utility loss caused by watermark embedding. The proposed system can be made arbitrarily robust against noise addition. We also give empirical results showing a noise addition attack trying to remove the watermark must cause a distortion (and thus a loss of data utility) much larger than the watermark itself.

Keywords: Database watermarking, Watermark recovery decision, Intellectual property protection.

1 Introduction

Watermarking techniques have been widely used on multimedia data in order to transparently embed messages by including hidden information (*e.g.* the watermark) into the cover data (*e.g.* still images, sound streams or video streams)[KP00] Multimedia watermarking has a variety of uses [CMB00], the most typical being intellectual property protection: to prove ownership or to help tracing illegal copies of the cover data. Such is the case when the watermark contains a digital signature hidden by using a secret key[PK95][LVL97].

In contrast to its wide use over multimedia data, watermarking has found little application for protecting the copyright of numerical data or any kind of alphanumerical data, for that matter. The reason is not lack of need, for there are virtually no alternative approaches; rather, it might be that there are more constraints to care about when dealing with (numerical or alphanumerical) data than when dealing with multimedia. Specifically for numerical data, there are two

V. Torra et al. (Eds.): MDAI 2005, LNAI 3558, pp. 134–143, 2005.

main differences with multimedia that prevent straightforward use of multimedia watermarking techniques:

1. A number of statistics must be preserved for the watermarked data to stay analytically useful; at the very least, averages and variances of attributes should be preserved.
2. Numerical data are position-independent, that is, there is no clear connection between a numerical datum and its position in the dataset (unlike for an image, where a pixel value bears some relationship of similarity to the values of the surrounding pixels); in fact, a numerical dataset can be re-ordered and still be the same dataset.

Having pointed out the above differences, there are also similarities between numerical and multimedia watermarking: the watermark should be able to resist different kind of spiteful attacks such as additive noise attacks, bit flipping attacks, rounding attacks, subsampling attacks an so on[VPP+01].

The literature on data watermarking is very scarce: the main contribution is [AJK03] by Agrawal *et al.*, who proposed a watermarking system over databases which was able to resist a great number of attacks but did not preserve the average nor the variance values of the original data.

1.1 Contribution and Plan of This Paper

In this paper we tackle the problem of inserting a watermark into a numerical dataset while preserving the average and the variance of the original data. At the same time, we prove that the proposed watermarking system is robust against additive noise attacks. To do that, we present a method for *deciding* whether a watermark is embedded or not into a data vector. The probabilities of false positive and false negative decision can be made arbitrarily small. Also, the system can be made arbitrarily robust against noise addition.

The paper is organized as follows. Section 2 gives an overview of our watermarking system. Section 3 presents the proposed algorithms while defining the way in which their parameters must be computed to meet the aforementioned constraints. In Section 4 the robustness of the proposed algorithms against additive noise attacks is proven. Empirical results are given in Section 5. Finally, conclusions and future work are summarized in Section 6.

2 Watermarking System Overview

We assume that all attributes to be watermarked in the dataset are numerical and continuous.

2.1 Algorithms

In our proposal, a watermarking system is composed of two algorithms:

- *Mark embedding:* This is an algorithm taking as input the original unmarked dataset X, the watermark K and a positive number M which is a security parameter. Its output is a dataset X' embedding K that is slightly different from X.

$$Embed(X, K, M) \rightarrow X'$$

- *Mark recovery:* This is an algorithm taking as input a dataset $\hat{X}$ and a watermark K. Its output is a value $\hat{M}$ whose interpretation is: if $\hat{M} > \frac{M}{2}$ we decide that K is embedded into $\hat{X}$; otherwise we decide that it is not.

$$Recover(\hat{X}, K) \rightarrow \hat{M}$$

$$\begin{cases} If \ \hat{M} > \frac{M}{2} \rightarrow K \ is \ in \ \hat{X} \\ If \ \hat{M} \leq \frac{M}{2} \rightarrow K \ is \ not \ in \ \hat{X} \end{cases}$$

2.2 Properties

We require our watermarking system to meet the properties below.

- *Imperceptibility:* The watermarked dataset X' should be similar to the original X in order to stay useful. This means that its statistical properties should be preserved as much as possible. In our system we ensure that the mean and variance of all attributes are preserved, *i.e.* $\overline{X_i'} = \overline{X_i}$ and $S_{X_i'}^2 = S_{X_i}^2$, for all pairs of corresponding attributes (X_i, X_i'), where X_i is in X and X_i' in X'.
- *Low false positive probability:* The probability of recovering a watermark K from a dataset X which does not embed K should be low. In our system, this means that

$$P\left[Recover(X, K) > \frac{M}{2}\right] < \epsilon$$

where ϵ can be made arbitrarily small by choosing an appropiate parameter M.
- *Correctness:* Given a watermarked dataset X', $Recover(X', K)$ should always return a value greater than $\frac{M}{2}$. In our system $Recover(X', K)$ always returns M.
- *Robustness:* Given a watermarked dataset X', obtaining an attacked dataset X'' so that $Recover(X'', K) < \frac{M}{2}$ without knowledge of K implies a high degradation on the quality of X''. In this paper, we focus on noise addition attacks and we prove that, for a noise addition attack to have a non-negligible probability of success, the mean square error between X' and X'' is much higher than the one between X and X'.

3   Our Watermarking System

For the sake of clarity, we will describe our system in reverse order. First, the mark recovery algorithm will be specified. Understanding how the mark is recovered gives insight on how the mark should be embedded, which makes the subsequent mark embedding algorithm easier to understand.

3.1 Mark Recovery

As previously mentioned, recovery takes two parameters as input: a dataset $\hat{X}$ and the watermark K. Without loss of generality, we assume the dataset to consist of a single attribute, that is, $\hat{X} = \{\hat{x}_1, \ldots, \hat{x}_n\}$, where $\hat{x}_i$ is a scalar. If the dataset has several attributes, mark recovery (and embedding) is independently performed for each attribute.

The algorithm is next detailed:

Algorithm 1 (Recover($\hat{X}, K$))

1. *Generate a binary sequence* $S = \{s_1, \ldots, s_n\}$, $s_i = \{-1, 1\}$, $p(s_i = 1) = p(s_i = -1) = 1/2$ *using a pseudo-random generator* G *seeded by* K.
2. *Compute* $\hat{M}$ *as*

$$\hat{M} = \frac{1}{n} \sum_{i=1}^{n} s_i \hat{x}_i$$

3. *Return* $\hat{M}$.

As previously said, we decide that K is embedded into $\hat{X}$ if $\hat{M} > \frac{M}{2}$. We wish our system to have a low false positive probability. The following lemma and corollary address this subject.

Lemma 1. *Given a random dataset* $X = \{x_i\}$ *and a pseudo-random binary sequence* $S = \{s_i\}$, *with* $s_i = \{-1, 1\}$ *and* $p(s_i = 1) = p(s_i = -1) = 1/2$, *it holds that*

$$\frac{1}{n} \sum_{i=1}^{n} s_i x_i \sim N\left(0, \frac{E[X^2]}{n}\right)$$

where $N(\mu, \sigma^2)$ *denotes a Gaussian distribution with* μ *mean and* σ^2 *variance.*

Proof: By the independence of X and S, we have $E[SX] = E[S]E[X]$. Now, since $E[S] = 0$, it holds that $E[SX] = 0$

Next, $Var[SX] = E[(SX)^2] - (E[SX])^2 = E[S^2X^2] - (E[S]E[X])^2$, since $E[S] = 0$ and $s_i^2 = 1$, we conclude that $Var[SX] = E[X^2]$.

Now, from the Central Limit Theorem, we have that

$$\frac{\sum_{i=1}^{n}(s_i x_i) - nE(SX)}{\sqrt{Var[SX]n}} = \frac{\frac{\sum_{i=1}^{n}(s_i x_i)}{n} - E(SX)}{\sqrt{\frac{Var[SX]}{n}}} = \frac{\frac{\sum_{i=1}^{n}(s_i x_i)}{n}}{\sqrt{\frac{E[X^2]}{n}}}$$

follows a $N(0, 1)$ distribution. Thus,

$$\frac{1}{n} \sum_{i=1}^{n} s_i x_i \sim N\left(0, \frac{E[X^2]}{n}\right)$$

$\square$

Corollary 1. *Given a random dataset X and a watermark K, the probability $P\left[Recover(X, K) > \frac{M}{2}\right]$ can be made arbitrarily small by increasing M.*

Proof. Since $\frac{1}{n}\sum_{i=1}^{n} s_i x_i \sim N\left(0, \frac{E[X^2]}{n}\right)$ and $M > 0$, from the Chebyshev bound we have that

$$P\left[\frac{1}{n}\sum_{i=1}^{n} s_i x_i > \frac{M}{2}\right] \leq \frac{2E[X^2]}{M^2 n}$$

It can be seen that this upper bound can be made arbitrarily small by increasing M. $\square$

3.2   Mark Embedding

Next we describe the mark embedding algorithm. It takes as input a dataset $X = \{x_1, \ldots, x_n\}$, a secret key K and a security parameter M. It generates as output a dataset X' meeting $Recover(X', K) = M$

Algorithm 2 (Embed(X, K, M))

1. *Generate a binary sequence $S = \{s_1, \ldots, s_n\}$, $s_i = \{-1, 1\}$, $p(s_i = 1) = p(s_i = -1) = 1/2$ using a pseudo-random generator G seeded by K.*
2. *Using a random seed, generate a pseudo-random sequence $T = \{t_1, \ldots, t_n\}$ whose elements t_i follow a Gaussian $N(0, 1)$ distribution*
3. *Let us denote by $X' = \{x'_1, \ldots, x'_n\}$ the resulting watermarked dataset. Its elements are computed as*

$$x'_i = a x_i + b + s_i |t_i| \lambda$$

where $|\cdot|$ denotes the absolute value operator.

Next, we describe how to choose parameters a, b and λ.

Parameter Choice. Our objective is to embed K into X while meeting the imperceptibility and correctness properties. This is achieved by obtaining a watermarked dataset X' that is slightly different from X. To do that, we wish the following:

1. The mean of X should be preserved by X', that is,

$$\overline{X'} = \overline{X} \tag{1}$$

2. The variance of X should be preserved by X', that is,

$$S^2_{X'} = S^2_X \tag{2}$$

3. Correctness is met in the above sense; to ensure that, we force that $Recover(X', K) = M$. By construction of the recovery algorithm, this is equivalent to

$$\frac{1}{n} \sum_{i=1}^{n} s_i x_i' = M \tag{3}$$

In this way, we will choose parameters a, b, λ so that the aforementioned constraints are met.

According to Constraint (1) we must equal $\overline{X'}$ and $\overline{X}$. Now,

$$\overline{X'} = \frac{1}{n} \sum_{i=1}^{n} x_i' = \frac{1}{n} \sum_{i=1}^{n} (ax_i + b + s_i |t_i| \lambda)$$

$$= \frac{a}{n} \sum_{i=1}^{n} x_i + b + \frac{\lambda}{n} \sum_{i=1}^{n} s_i |t_i| = a\overline{X} + b + \lambda \overline{S|T|}$$

Now equalling with $\overline{X}$, we obtain a first equation:

$$\overline{X} = a\overline{X} + b + \lambda \overline{S|T|} \tag{4}$$

According to Constraint 2 we must preserve the variance of X into X'. Now,

$$S_{X'}^2 = S_{ax_i + b + s_i |t_i| \lambda}^2 = a^2 S_X^2 + \lambda^2 S_{S|T|}^2$$

By equalling with S_X^2, we obtain a second equation:

$$S_X^2 = a^2 S_X^2 + \lambda^2 S_{S|T|}^2 \tag{5}$$

Finally, according to Constraint 3 we must force $Recover(X', K) = M$.

$$Recover(X', K) = \frac{1}{n} \sum_{i=1}^{n} s_i x_i' = \frac{1}{n} \sum_{i=1}^{n} s_i (ax_i + b + s_i |t_i| \lambda)$$

$$= \frac{a}{n} \sum_{i=1}^{n} s_i x_i + \frac{b}{n} \sum_{i=1}^{n} s_i + \frac{\lambda}{n} \sum_{i=1}^{n} |t_i| = a\overline{XS} + b\overline{S} + \lambda \overline{T}$$

By equalling the above expression to M, we obtain a third equation

$$M = a\overline{XS} + b\overline{S} + \lambda \overline{T} \tag{6}$$

We can now solve the system formed by Equations (4), (5) and (6) for a, b and λ.

3.3 Information Loss

By construction, the previous choice of a, b and λ guarantees that the mean and variance of X are preserved into X'. The information loss can be measured as the mean square error between elements of X and X', *i.e.*

$$E[(X - X')^2] = \frac{1}{n} \sum_{i=1}^{n} (x_i - x_i')^2$$

We can rewrite $E[(X - X')^2]$ as

$$E[(X - aX - b - S|T|\lambda)^2] = E[((1 - a)X - b - S|T|\lambda)^2]$$

$$= E[((1 - a)^2 X^2 + 2(a - 1)(b + S|T|\lambda)X + (b + S|T|\lambda)^2)]$$

$$= E[((1 - a)^2 X^2 + 2(a - 1)bX + 2(a - 1)\lambda S|T|X + b^2 + 2b\lambda S|T| + S^2|T|^2\lambda^2)]$$

$$= (1 - a)^2 E[X^2] + 2(a - 1)bE[X] + 2(a - 1)\lambda E[T]E[X] + b^2 + 2b\lambda E[T] + \lambda^2 E[T^2]$$

Since $T \sim N(0, 1)$, we have that $E(T) = 0$ and $E(T^2) = 1$. Thus, the information or data utility loss can be written as

$$E[(X - X')^2] = (1 - a)^2 E[X^2] + 2(a - 1)bE[X] + b^2 + \lambda^2 \qquad (7)$$

So far, the approach followed has been to compute a, b, λ from the system of equality constraints (4), (5) and (6) and then compute the information loss using Expression (7). If the information loss obtained is too high or reducing information loss has a very high priority, then one might sacrifice to some extent mean and variance preservation and also reduce robustness by allowing $Recover(X', K)$ to output a number less than M. With this alternative approach, one would compute a, b, λ minimizing Expression (7) subject to constraints for mean-variance preservation and robustness relaxed as follows:

- Change Equation (4) by just requiring that $\overline{X'} \in \{\overline{X} \pm \varepsilon_{\overline{X}}\}$ for some $\varepsilon_{\overline{X}} > 0$;
- Change Equation (5) by just requiring that $S_{X'}^2 \in \{S_X^2 \pm \varepsilon_{S_X^2}\}$ for some $\varepsilon_{S_X^2} > 0$;
- Change Equation (6) by just requiring that $\frac{1}{n} \sum_{i=1}^{n} s_i x_i' > M/2$

4 Robustness Against Noise Addition

Let us now study the effect of noise addition on watermark recovery.

4.1 Probability of Watermark Removal

Lemma 2. *Given a watermarked dataset X' and an altered version obtained through noise addition $X'' = X' + D$, where D is the noise, its holds that*

$$\frac{1}{n} \sum_{i=1}^{n} s_i x_i'' \sim N\left(M, \frac{E[D^2]}{n}\right)$$

Proof: First, $E[SX''] = E[S(X' + D)] = E[SX' + SD] = E[SX'] + E[SD] = M + E[S]E[D]$, since $E[S] = 0$, we conclude that $E[SX''] = M$.

Second, $Var[SX''] = Var[S(X' + D)] = Var[SX'] + Var[SD]$. Since $Var[SX'] = 0$ we have $Var[SX''] = Var[SD]$.

Now, $Var[SD] = E[S^2D^2] - E[SD]^2 = E[D^2] - (E[S]E[D])^2$. Since $E[S] = 0$, we obtain $Var[SD] = E[D^2]$.

From the Central Limit Theorem, we have that

$$\frac{\sum_{i=1}^{n}(s_i x_i'') - nE(SX'')}{\sqrt{Var[SX'']n}} = \frac{\frac{\sum_{i=1}^{n}(s_i x_i'')}{n} - E(SX'')}{\sqrt{\frac{Var[SX'']}{n}}} = \frac{\frac{\sum_{i=1}^{n}(s_i x_i'')}{n} - M}{\sqrt{\frac{E[D^2]}{n}}}$$

follows a $N(0,1)$ distribution. Thus,

$$\frac{1}{n}\sum_{i=1}^{n} s_i x_i'' \sim N\left(M, \frac{E[D^2]}{n}\right)$$

$\square$

Corollary 2. *Given a watermarked dataset X' and an altered version obtained through noise addition $X'' = X' + D$, where D is the noise, the probability $P\left[Recover(X'', K) < \frac{M}{2}\right]$ can be made arbitrarily small by increasing M.*

Proof. Since $\frac{1}{n}\sum_{i=1}^{n} s_i x_i'' \sim N\left(M, \frac{E[D^2]}{n}\right)$ and $M > 0$, from the Chebyshev bound we have that

$$P\left[\frac{1}{n}\sum_{i=1}^{n} s_i x_i'' < \frac{M}{2}\right] \leq \frac{2E[D^2]}{M^2 n}$$

It can be seen that this upper bound can be made arbitrarily small by increasing M. $\square$

4.2 Information Loss

A noise addition attack introduces a distortion on the attacked dataset.

Given a watermarked dataset X' and its attacked version $X'' = X' + D$, we will measure its distortion as the mean square error between X' and X'',

$$\frac{1}{n}\sum_{i=1}^{n}(x_i' - x_i'')^2$$

Its average corresponds to $E[(X' - X'')^2]$. Thus, it is

$$E[(X' - X' - D)^2] = E[D^2]$$

5   Numerical Example

We have used a dataset extracted from the 1995 U.S. Current Population Survey extracted using the U. S. Bureau of the Census Data Extraction System. This dataset contains 1080 records and 13 numerical attributes. Among these attributes, we have used PTOTVAL (total personal income). The 1080 values that PTOTVAL takes over the 1080 records are our data vector X. Table 1 shows the performance of our system against a Gaussian noise addition attack $N(0, \sigma_D^2)$.

Table 1. Performance figures

M	$IL(X, X')$	$100*P[false\ positive]$	σ_D^2	$IL(X', X'')$	$100 * P[mark\ removal]$	$\frac{IL(X', X'')}{IL(X, X')}$
100	13693.117	30.85%	10^4	10022.434	0.00%	0.732
100	13693.117	30.85%	10^6	1002243.426	5.05%	73.193
100	13693.117	30.85%	10^8	100224342.622	43.64	7319.323
200	59125.869	16.11%	10^4	10022.434	0.00%	0.170
200	59125.869	16.11%	10^6	1002243.426	0.05%	16.951
200	59125.869	16.11%	10^8	100224342.622	37.45%	1695.101
300	137444.551	6.81%	10^4	10022.434	0.00%	0.073
300	137444.551	6.81%	10^6	1002243.426	0.00%	7.292
300	137444.551	6.81%	10^8	100224342.622	31.21%	729.198

We can clearly observe that the distortion produced by the noise necessary to remove the watermark is much greater than the one produced by the insertion of the watermark on the original data. As an extreme case, when the noise added to remove the watermark is 7319.323 times larger than the noise caused by watermark embedding, the attacker has only probability 0.4364 of success in removing the watermark.

6   Conclusion and Future Work

The literature on watermarking alphanumerical data is quite scarce. This is surprising, because there is an increasing demand for copyright protection of databases. We have presented a spread-spectrum watermarking technique for numerical data which has the interesting feature of preserving means and variances of attributes; to the best of our knowledge, ours is the first data watermarking algorithm to do so.

Based on the whole watermarked dataset, the recovery algorithm makes a decision whether a particular watermark K is embedded in the data. The probabilities of false positive and false negative can be made arbitrarily small by proper choice of the security parameter M, even after a noise addition attack.

An analytical expression of the information loss (distortion) caused by watermark embedding on the original data has been given. As mentioned above, robustness against noise addition attacks can be arbitrarily increased by tuning M. Empirical results have been presented showing that removing a watermark via noise addition is only possible at the cost of completely damaging the utility of the attacked dataset.

The proposed system has been described for univariate datasets. In case of multivariate datasets, it can be independently applied to the various attributes. Future research will involve:

- Refining the proposed system to withstand other attacks beyond noise addition and bit-flipping (which is a special case of noise addition). In particular, we aim at making correct watermark recovery decisions in presence of the attacks mentioned in [AJK03]: subsetting, mix-and-match, etc.
- Extending the system to non-numerical data types, that is, categorical attributes.

Acknowledgments

The authors are partly supported by the Spanish Ministry of Science and Education through project SEG2004-04352-C04-01 "PROPRIETAS".

References

[AJK03]   R. Agrawal, P. J. Haas, and J. Kiernan. Watermarking relational data: Framework, algorithms and analysis. *VLDB journal*, vol. 12, no. 2, pp. 157-169, 2003.

[CMB00]   I. J. Cox, M. L. Miller, and J. A. Bloom. Watermarking applications and their properties. In *Proceedings of ITCC'2000*, pp. 6–10. IEEE Computer Society, 2000.

[KP00]   S. Katzenbeisser and F. A. P. Petitcolas. *Information Hiding: techniques for steganography and digital watermarking*. Artech House, 2000.

[LVL97]   G. C. Langelaar, J. C. A. VanderLubbe, and R. L. Lagendijk. Robust labeling methods for copy protection of data. In *Proceedings of SPIE 3022, Storage and Retrieval for Image and Video Databases V*, pp. 298–309, 1997.

[PK95]   I. Pitas and T. H. Kaskalis. Applying signatures on digital images. In *IEEE Workshop on Nonlinear Signal and Image Processing*, Thessaloniki, Greece, pp. 460–463, 1995.

[VPP+01] S. Voloshynovskiy, S. Pereira, T. Pun, J.J. Eggers, and J.K. Su. Attacks on digital watermarks: Classification, estimation-based attacks and benchmarks. *IEEE Communications Magazine*, vol. 30, no. 8, pp. 118–127, 2001.

Possibilistic Approach to Kernel-Based Fuzzy c-Means Clustering with Entropy Regularization

Kiyotaka Mizutani[1] and Sadaaki Miyamoto[2]

[1] Graduate School of Systems and Information Engineering
University of Tsukuba, Ibaraki 305-8573, Japan
`kiyotaka@soft.risk.tsukuba.ac.jp`
[2] Department of Risk Engineering, School of Systems and Information Engineering
University of Tsukuba, Ibaraki 305-8573, Japan
`miyamoto@risk.tsukuba.ac.jp`

Abstract. The fuzzy c-means (FCM) is sensitive to noise or outliers because this method has the probabilistic constraint that the memberships of a data point across classes sum to one. To solve the problem, a possibilistic c-means clustering (PCM) has been proposed by Krishnapuram and Keller. An advantage of PCM is highly robust in a noisy environment. On the other hand, some clustering algorithms using the kernel trick, e.g., kernel-based FCM and kernel-based LVQ clustering, have been studied to obtain nonlinear classification boundaries. In this paper, an entropy-based possibilistic c-means clustering using the kernel trick has been proposed as more robust method. Numerical examples are shown and effect of the kernel method is discussed.

1 Introduction

The method of the fuzzy c-means (FCM) [1] has been known to be the well-known technique of data clustering whereby a set of data is classified using mutual distance between a pair of objects. Since the classification is done without providing standard from outside, clustering is also called unsupervised classification [3].

The FCM uses the probabilistic constraint that the memberships of a data point across classes sum to one. This constraint is used to generate the membership update equations for an iterative algorithm. The memberships resulting from FCM and its derivatives, however, do not always correspond to the intuitive concept of degree of belonging or compatibility. Moreover, the FCM is sensitive to the data including noise or outliers. To solve such a problem, Krishnapuram and Keller [8] relax this probabilistic constraint and have proposed a possibilistic approach to fuzzy c-means clustering (PCM).

On the other hand, the kernel trick has attracted great attention with the development of the Support Vector Machine (SVM) [15] and has been successfully applied into many learning machines, e.g., the Kernel Principal Component Analysis (KPCA) [14] and the Kernel Fisher Discriminant analysis (KFD) [10]. Moreover, Miyamoto et al. have proposed a kernel-based fuzzy c-means [12] and Inokuchi et al. have proposed a kernel-based LVQ clustering [7] to obtain

V. Torra et al. (Eds.): MDAI 2005, LNAI 3558, pp. 144–155, 2005.

nonlinear classification boundaries. A common principal of these methods is to construct nonlinear variants of linear algorithms by substituting inner products by kernel functions. The resulting kernel-based algorithm can be interpreted as running the original algorithm on feature space mapped objects.

In this paper, we propose a kernel-based possibilistic c-means clustering (KPCM) to get more robust solution in a noisy environment. We consider an entropy-based objective function [11, 13] in FCM, instead of the standard objective function which has been proposed by Bezdek [1]. Because the entropy-based method is available for both the probabilistic constraint and possibilistic constraint. Numerical examples are shown and we discuss the effectiveness of the kernel method.

2   Fuzzy and Possibilistic c-Means Clustering

Let $\boldsymbol{R}^p$ be p-dimensional real Euclidean space and $x_1, \ldots, x_n \in \boldsymbol{R}^p$ be objects to be clustered, where $x_k = (x_k^1, \ldots, x_k^p), k = 1, \ldots, n$. The Euclidean norm in the data space $\boldsymbol{R}^p$ is denoted by $\| \cdot \|$.

2.1   Fuzzy c-Means

Assume, as usual in the fuzzy c-means (FCM) [1], $U = (u_{ik}), i = 1, \ldots, c, k = 1, \ldots, n$, be the matrix of memberships in which c is the number of clusters; $v_i = (v_i^1, \ldots, v_i^p), i = 1, \ldots, c$, is the center for the cluster i. We put $V = (v_1, \ldots, v_c)$ for simplicity.

The constraint of U in FCM is

$$M_{prb} = \{(u_{ik}) : \sum_{i=1}^{c} u_{ik} = 1, u_{ik} \geq 0, \forall i, k\},$$

and this constraint M_{prb} is called probabilistic partition [5, 13].

An objective function J of the two variables U and V is assumed for FCM, specifically,

$$J_s(U, V) = \sum_{i=1}^{c} \sum_{k=1}^{n} (u_{ik})^m d_{ik} \quad (m > 1) \tag{1}$$

where

$$d_{ik} = \|x_k - v_i\|^2,$$

and the subscript s implies that the objective function is for the standard fuzzy c-means [1].

In addition to the standard fuzzy c-mean, an entropy method has been proposed by Miyamoto and Mukaidono [11] that uses an additional term of entropy for fuzzification. This entropy regularization method has been generalized and its close relationship to the Gaussian mixture method has been uncovered by Ichihashi *et al.* [6]. An entropy type criterion has also been considered [13]:

$$J_e(U,V) = \sum_{i=1}^{c}\sum_{k=1}^{n} u_{ik}d_{ik} + \lambda^{-1}\sum_{i=1}^{c}\sum_{k=1}^{n} u_{ik}\log u_{ik}/\alpha \qquad (2)$$

where λ and α are a positive parameter and the subscript e implies that the objective function is for the entropy-based fuzzy c-means.

In the following alternative optimization algorithm of **FCM**, the above objective functions are used as J (i.e., $J = J_s, J = J_e$) and the constraint of U is used as $M = M_{prb}$.

Algorithm FCM.

FCM0. Set an initial value of $\bar{V}$.

FCM1. Fix $\bar{V}$ and minimize with respect to U:

$$\min_{U \in M} J(U,\bar{V})$$

and let the optimal solution be new $\bar{U}$.

FCM2. Fix $\bar{U}$ and minimize with respect to V:

$$\min_{V} J(\bar{U},V)$$

and let the optimal solution be new $\bar{V}$.

FCM3. If the solution is convergent, stop; else go to **FCM1**.

End of FCM.

The optimal solutions for J_s are omitted, as they are well-known. When the entropy-based objective function J_e is used, the optimal solution of V is

$$v_i = \frac{\displaystyle\sum_{k=1}^{n} u_{ik}x_k}{\displaystyle\sum_{k=1}^{n} u_{ik}}, \qquad (3)$$

and the optimal solution of U is

$$u_{ik} = \frac{\exp(-\lambda d_{ik})}{\displaystyle\sum_{j=1}^{c} \exp(-\lambda d_{jk})}. \qquad (4)$$

2.2   Possibilistic c-Means

Krishnapuram *et al.* [8] have proposed using the following constraint instead of M_{prb}:

$$M_{pos} = \{(u_{ik}) : \sum_{i=1}^{c} u_{ik} > 0, u_{ik} \geq 0, \forall i, k\},$$

which is called possibilistic partition [5, 13]. Additionaly, they have proposed the following objective function:

$$J_{pos}(U, V) = \sum_{i=1}^{c} \sum_{k=1}^{n} (u_{ik})^m d_{ik} + \sum_{i=1}^{c} \eta_i \sum_{k=1}^{n} (1 - u_{ik})^m \tag{5}$$

where η_i is a positive parameter.

The clustering algorithm in possibilistic approach, which is called **PCM** in this paper, is the same as **FCM**, but the equation of the optimal solution of U is different since M_{pos} is used as the constraint of U. We omit the optimal solutions for J_{pos} here, as they are well-known.

Notice that the combination of J_s and M_{pos} produces a trivial solution and therefore useless; the combination of J_{pos} and M_{prb} is not analytically solvable in general. However, J_e can be obtained the optimal solutions in both M_{prb} and M_{pos}. Therefore we consider the entropy-based objective function J_e in this paper.

The optimal solution of V for M_{pos} is the same as (3), but the optimal solution U is used as follows:

$$u_{ik} = L \exp(-\lambda d_{ik}) \tag{6}$$

where $L = \alpha e^{-1}$. For simplicity, we put $\alpha = e$ and it is assumed $L = 1$ in this paper.

3   Kernel-Based Clustering

The kernel trick is a well-known technique as a general way to get the nonlinear classification boundaries [4, 7, 12]. Here we consider the application of kernel trick to the possibilistic clustering.

3.1   Kernel Trick

A high-dimensional feature space used in SVM [15] is denoted by H here which is called the feature space, whereas the original space $\boldsymbol{R}^p$ is called the data space. H is in general an infinite dimensional inner product space. Its inner product is denoted by $\langle \cdot, \cdot \rangle$; the norm of H is denoted by $\| \cdot \|_H$.

Notice that in the kernel trick, a mapping $\Phi \colon \boldsymbol{R}^p \to H$ is employed and x_k is transformed into $\Phi(x_k)$. An explicit representation of $\Phi(x_k)$ is not usable in general but the inner product $\langle \Phi(x_k), \Phi(x_\ell) \rangle$ is expressed by a kernel function:

$$K(x_k, x_\ell) = \langle \Phi(x_k), \Phi(x_\ell) \rangle.$$

The following two kernel functions have often been employed:

$$K(x_k, x_\ell) = \exp(-cnst\|x_k - x_\ell\|^2), \tag{7}$$

$$K(x_k, x_\ell) = (1 + \langle x_k, x_\ell \rangle)^d. \tag{8}$$

The first is called the Gaussian kernel, while the second is called the polynomial kernel. In this paper the Gaussian kernel is used in numerical examples.

3.2   Kernel-Based Fuzzy and Possibilistic c-Means Clustering

We put the dissimilarity measure in a high-dimensional feature space as follows:

$$D_{ik} = \|\Phi(x_k) - w_i\|_H^2. \tag{9}$$

We consider the next objective function which is the entropy-based objective function:

$$J_{ke}(U, W) = \sum_{i=1}^{c} \sum_{k=1}^{n} u_{ik} D_{ik} + \lambda^{-1} \sum_{i=1}^{c} \sum_{k=1}^{n} u_{ik} \log u_{ik}/\alpha \tag{10}$$

where $W = (w_1, \ldots, w_c)$ is cluster centers in a high-dimensional feature space.
The solutions in the **FCM** alternative minimization algorithm are

$$u_{ik} = \frac{\exp(-\lambda D_{ik})}{\displaystyle\sum_{j=1}^{c} \exp(-\lambda D_{jk})}, \tag{11}$$

$$w_i = \frac{\displaystyle\sum_{k=1}^{n} u_{ik} \Phi(x_k)}{\displaystyle\sum_{k=1}^{n} u_{ik}}. \tag{12}$$

However, solutions of (11) and (12) can not directly be obtained, since an explicit form of $\Phi(x_k)$ is unavailable.

This problem is solved by eliminating W by substituting (12) into (9):

$$D_{ik} = \|\Phi(x_k) - w_i\|_H^2$$
$$= K_{kk} - \frac{2}{U_i} \sum_{j=1}^{n} u_{ij} K_{jk} + \frac{1}{U_i^2} \sum_{j=1}^{n} \sum_{\ell=1}^{n} u_{ij} u_{i\ell} K_{j\ell} \tag{13}$$

where

$$U_i = \sum_{k=1}^{n} u_{ik}$$

and

$$K_{j\ell} = K(x_j, x_\ell) = \langle \Phi(x_j), \Phi(x_\ell) \rangle.$$

The following algorithm **KFCM** is a fuzzy c-means in which the kernel function is used for **FCM**. We use the initial cluster centers $y_1, \ldots, y_c \in X$ randomly selected from the data set X instead of w_i. In that case the initial distance is given by

$$D_{ik} = \|x_k - y_i\|_H^2 = K(x_k, x_k) - 2K(x_k, y_i) + K(y_i, y_i). \tag{14}$$

Algorithm KFCM.

KFCM1. Select randomly $y_1, \ldots, y_c \in X$. Calculate D_{ik} by Eq.(14).

KFCM2. Calculate $U = (u_{ik})$ by Eq.(11).

KFCM3. If the solution $U = (u_{ik})$ is convergent, stop. Else update the dissimilarity measure D_{ik} by Eq.(13). Go to **KFCM2**.

End of KFCM.

Notice that in **FCM**, w_i is not explicitly calculated but calculations of (13) and (11) are repeated until convergence. Hence the convergence in **FCM** should be based on U, not W.

When we consider the possibilistic approach to kernel-based clustering, we only have to replace the equation of optimal solution U in **KFCM2** as the following equation:

$$u_{ik} = \exp(-\lambda D_{ik}), \tag{15}$$

and then, we call this algorithm **KPCM**.

4   Fuzzy Classification Function

Fuzzy classification rules are naturally derives as functions that interpolate the memberships; the functions are defined in the whole space. We call them fuzzy classification functions. Such functions have implicitly been employed in literature in fuzzy clustering [9]. A reason why we explicitly define the classification functions is that theoretical properties of the classifications rules are made clear.

The next formula calculates fuzzy classification functions: $U_i^{prb}(x)$ for the FCM (the entropy-based fuzzy c-means clustering) and $U_i^{pos}(x)$ for the PCM (the entropy-based possibilistic c-means clustering).

$$U_i^{prb}(x) = \frac{\exp(-\lambda d_i(x))}{\displaystyle\sum_{j=1}^{c} \exp(-\lambda d_j(x))}, \tag{16}$$

$$U_i^{pos}(x) = \exp(-\lambda d_i(x)) \tag{17}$$

where

$$d_i(x) = \|x - v_i\|^2.$$

Notice that v_i after convergence should be used.

When kernel-based method is used, the fuzzy classification functions are as follows:

$$U_i^{prb}(x) = \frac{\exp(-\lambda D_i(x))}{\displaystyle\sum_{j=1}^{c} \exp(-\lambda D_j(x))}, \tag{18}$$

$$U_i^{pos}(x) = \exp(-\lambda D_i(x)) \tag{19}$$

where

$$D_i(x) = \|\Phi(x) - w_i\|_H^2.$$

We have

$$D_i(x) = K(x,x) - \frac{2}{U_i} \sum_{j=1}^n u_{ij} K(x,x_j) + \frac{1}{U_i^2} \sum_{j=1}^n \sum_{\ell=1}^n u_{ij} u_{i\ell} K_{j\ell}. \qquad (20)$$

Notice that u_{ik} after convergence should be used. Note moreover that

$$K(x,x_j) = \exp(-cnst\|x - x_j\|^2),$$

when the Gaussian kernel is employed.

5   Numerical Examples

In this section, we show two numerical examples to illustrate the effectiveness of our proposed method.

The first example, which is used in [8], involves two well-separated clusters of seven points each. The data points are numbered as shown in Fig. 1. Two outliers (data points of No.15 and No.16) are added, i.e., one lies in (50,40) and the other one lies in (50,80).

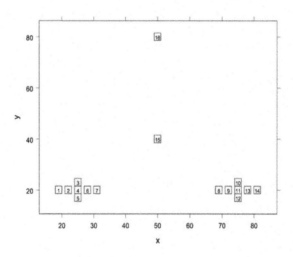

Fig. 1. A simple example of a data set with two outliers (No.15 and No.16)

Table 1 shows the membership values in each methods, i.e., FCM($\lambda = 0.001$), PCM($\lambda = 0.001$), KFCM($\lambda = 5.0, cnst = 0.1$) and KPCM($\lambda = 5.0, cnst = 0.001$), and cluster centers in FCM and PCM. Fuzzy classification functions of each cluster of FCM, PCM, KFCM and KPCM are shown in Fig. 2, Fig. 3, Fig. 4 and Fig. 5. In this example, the most desirable result is that No.4 and

Table 1. Clustering result for Fig.1

	FCM		PCM		KFCM		KPCM	
	Clust.1	Clust.2	Clust.1	Clust.2	Clust.1	Clust.2	Clust.1	Clust.2
1	0.805	0.195	0.710	0.149	0.920	0.080	0.855	0.000
2	0.783	0.217	0.786	0.192	0.983	0.017	0.961	0.000
3	0.758	0.242	0.855	0.243	0.974	0.026	0.961	0.000
4	0.758	0.242	0.855	0.243	0.992	0.008	0.999	0.000
5	0.758	0.242	0.838	0.238	0.974	0.026	0.961	0.000
6	0.732	0.268	0.912	0.302	0.983	0.017	0.961	0.000
7	0.704	0.296	0.957	0.368	0.920	0.080	0.855	0.000
8	0.296	0.704	0.368	0.957	0.077	0.923	0.000	0.855
9	0.268	0.732	0.302	0.912	0.017	0.983	0.000	0.961
10	0.242	0.758	0.243	0.855	0.026	0.974	0.000	0.961
11	0.242	0.758	0.243	0.855	0.008	0.992	0.000	0.999
12	0.242	0.758	0.238	0.838	0.026	0.974	0.000	0.961
13	0.217	0.783	0.192	0.786	0.017	0.983	0.000	0.961
14	0.195	0.805	0.149	0.710	0.077	0.923	0.000	0.855
15	0.500	0.500	0.610	0.610	0.487	0.522	0.002	0.002
16	0.500	0.500	0.028	0.028	0.480	0.520	0.000	0.000
Centers	v1(38.6, 25.0)		v1(37.4, 21.7)					
	v2(61.4, 25.0)		v2(62.6, 21.7)					

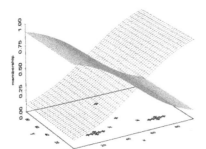 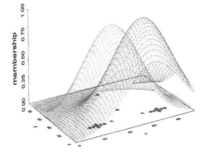

Fig. 2. Fuzzy classification functions in FCM. The symbol × represents the center of cluster

Fig. 3. Fuzzy classification functions in PCM. The symbol × represents the center of cluster

No.11 have the highest membership value, because those data points are located to center of each cluster. However, No.1 and No.14 in FCM, No.3 and No.10 in PCM have the highest membership value in each cluster. It can be considered that the cluster centers deviated by influence of noise data.

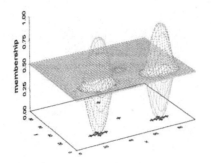 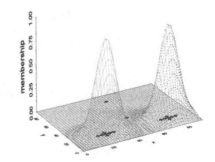

Fig. 4. Fuzzy classification functions in KFCM   **Fig. 5.** Fuzzy classification functions in KPCM

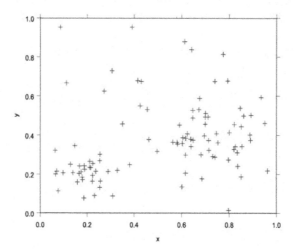

Fig. 6. An original data set in the second example

Consequently, KFCM and KPCM have much better robustness than FCM and PCM when the data sets contains outliers, since No.4 and No.11 have the highest membership value in each cluster. Furthermore, it can be seen that the difference of a fuzzy classification rule in each method is obvious by the fuzzy classification functions.

Fig. 6 shows another example with an artificially generated 100 points on two dimensional space. This data set has been formed by two classes which were generated by the normal random-number, and noise data were added to the circumference by the uniform random-number. In this example, we will discuss the effectiveness of the proposed method by comparing KFCM with KPCM.

The result by **KFCM** is shown in Fig. 7 and the result by **KPCM** is shown in Fig. 8. These figures are shown that counters of membership and fuzzy classification functions.

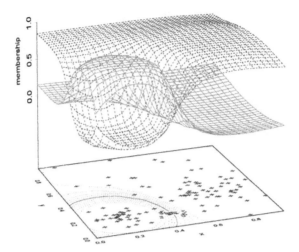

Fig. 7. Counters by the algorithm **KFCM** and fuzzy classification functions of the kernel-based fuzzy c-means. Parameters are $(\lambda = 5, cnst = 20)$

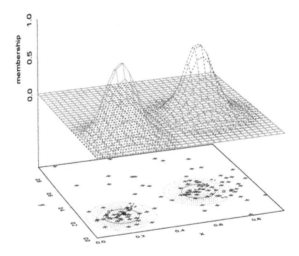

Fig. 8. Counters by the algorithm **KPCM** and fuzzy classification functions of the kernel-based possibilistic c-means. Parameters are $(\lambda = 5, cnst = 20)$

Fig. 7 shows that the original data were classified into two classes nonlinearly, i.e., it is classified into two classes depending on the density of the object. However, it cannot be said a too preferable result in KFCM because it is classified so that the noise data may belong to either class by a probabilistic constraint.

In contrast, Fig. 8 shows that the original data were classified into two classes without receiving the influence of the noise data. It can be seen that the result of KPCM is more desirable than a result of KFCM in this example.

6   Conclusion

We have considered a method of possibilistic approach to kernel-based clustering to get more robust solution in a noisy environment and we have shown the effectiveness of the proposed method in numerical examples. The entropy-based objective function was used as an objective function because of getting the optimal solution of U in both constraints of M_{prb} and M_{pos}.

Possibilistic clustering has a character that each prototype converges independently. Therefore, the following new algorithm can be considered in the possibilistic clustering. First, algorithm is started by using many initial prototypes, and after that, the cluster number c and classification are decided by evaluating prototypes after convergence. There is a method of using the Minimum-Spanning-Tree (MST) as a technique for evaluating prototypes. The details are omitted here, which we will show in near future.

Moreover, Davé *et al.* has mentioned a potential function method in [2], and we would consider the unified method of probabilistic partition and possibilistic partition that applies this idea to the present method.

References

1. J.C. Bezdek, *Pattern Recognition with Fuzzy Objective Function Algorithms*, Plenum, New York, 1981.
2. R.N. Davé, R. Krishnapuram, Robust clustering methods: a unified view, *IEEE Trans. Fuzzy Syst.*, Vol.5, No.2, pp. 270-293, 1997.
3. R.O. Duda, P.E. Hart, D.G. Stork, *Pattern Classification, 2nd Ed.*, Wiley, New York, 2001.
4. M. Girolami, Mercer kernel based clustering in feature space, *IEEE Trans. on Neural Networks*, Vol.13, No.13, pp. 780-784, 2002.
5. F. Höppner, F. Klawonn, R. Kruse, T. Runkler, *Fuzzy Cluster Analysis*, Wiley, Chichester, 1999.
6. H. Ichihashi, K. Honda, N. Tani, Gaussian mixture PDF approximation and fuzzy c-means clustering with entropy regularization, *Proc. of the 4th Asian Fuzzy System Symposium*, May 31-June 3, 2000, Tsukuba, Japan, pp. 212-221, 2000.
7. R. Inokuchi, S. Miyamoto, LVQ clustering and SOM using a kernel function, *Proc. of the IEEE International Conference on Fuzzy Systems (FUZZ-IEEE 2004)*, July 25-29, 2004, Budapest, Hungary, pp.182-185, 2004.
8. R. Krishnapuram, J.M. Keller, A possibilistic approach to fuzzy clustering, *IEEE Trans. on Fuzzy Syst.*, Vol.1, No.2, pp. 98-110, 1993.
9. Z.Q. Liu, S. Miyamoto (eds.), *Soft Computing and Human-Centered Machines*, Springer, Tokyo, 2000.
10. S. Mika, G. Rätsch, J. Weston, B. Schölkopf, K.-R. Müller, Fisher discriminant analysis with kernels, Y.-H. Hu et al. (Eds.), *Neural Network for Signal Processing IX* , IEEE, pp. 41–48, 1999.
11. S. Miyamoto, M. Mukaidono, Fuzzy c - means as a regularization and maximum entropy approach, *Proc. of the 7th International Fuzzy Systems Association World Congress (IFSA'97)*, June 25-30, 1997, Prague, Czech, Vol.II, pp. 86–92, 1997.
12. S. Miyamoto, D. Suizu, Fuzzy c-means clustering using kernel functions in support vector machines, *J. of Advanced Computational Intelligence and Intelligent Informatics*, Vol.7, No.1, pp. 25–30, 2003.

13. S. Miyamoto, D. Suizu, O. Takata, Methods of fuzzy c-means and possibilistic clustering using quadratic term, *Scientiae Mathematicae Japonicae,* Vol.60, No.2, pp. 217–233, 2004.
14. B. Schölkopf, A. Smola, K.-R. Müller, Nonlinear component analysis as a kernel eigenvalue problem, *Neural Computation,* Vol.10, pp. 1299–1319, 1998.
15. V. Vapnik, *Statistical Learning Theory,* Wiley, New York, 1998.

Fuzzy *c*-Means Clustering in the Presence of Noise Cluster for Time Series Analysis

Arnold C. Alanzado[1] and Sadaaki Miyamoto[2]

[1] Graduate School of Systems and Information Engineering,
University of Tsukuba, Ibaraki, 305-8573, Japan
`arnold@soft.risk.tsukuba.ac.jp`
[2] Department of Risk Engineering,
School of Systems and Information Engineering,
University of Tsukuba, Ibaraki, 305-8573, Japan
`miyamoto@risk.tsukuba.ac.jp`

Abstract. Cluster analysis for time series is becoming increasingly important in many real applications. Clustering plays an important role in extracting information from the noise in economic and financial time series. In this paper we consider the use of fuzzy *c*-means clustering method in the context of econometric analysis of time-series data. We discuss and demonstrate a methodology for model identification and estimation that is based on the fuzzy *c*-means algorithm in the presence of noise cluster that is widely used in the context of pattern recognition. The effect of noise on time-series prediction is important to quantify for accurate forecasting. The noise clustering approach is based on the concept of first defining a noise cluster and then defining a similarity or dissimilarity measure for the noise cluster.

1 Introduction

Time-series is a series of values of a variable at successive times. The samples of the variable are ordered in time. Usually the variables are sampled uniformly so that the interval between any two samples is the same. Examples occur in a variety of fields, ranging from economics to engineering and methods of analyzing time series constitutes an important area in statistics [1].

Cluster analysis for time series has become increasingly important in a wide range of applications, such as economic and financial time series analysis. Clustering plays an important role in extracting information from the noise in economic and financial time series. Although the term clustering is different in different fields, it refers to automatic unsupervised classification method in data analysis. Clustering algorithms can be classified into different categories based on the type of input they deal with, the type of clusters they consider or the methods they use to construct the result, and each has its own advantages and disadvantages, from *k*-means clustering algorithm to Fuzzy *c*-means algorithm [2].

The most famous clustering method is the fuzzy *c*-means clustering. The *c*-means clustering does not mean here a specific algorithm but a class of algorithms. There have been a number of new methods of fuzzy *c*-means proposed but the main ideas are very similar to the traditional or standard fuzzy *c*-means clustering

In this paper we consider the use of fuzzy *c*-means clustering method in the context of econometric analysis of time-series data. We discuss a methodology for model

V. Torra et al. (Eds.): MDAI 2005, LNAI 3558, pp. 156–163, 2005.

identification and estimation that is based on the fuzzy *c*-means algorithm in the presence of noise cluster. The noise clustering approach is based on the concept of first defining a noise cluster and then defining a similarity or dissimilarity measure for the noise cluster. The noise is considered to be a separate class represented by an extra centroid that has a constant distance δ from all feature vectors.

2 Background on Clustering

Clustering is a descriptive task that seeks to identify homogeneous groups of objects based on the values of their attributes. The groups may be mutually exclusive or overlapping groupings. The objective of clustering is to create groups of objects that are close to each other and distant from other groups of objects. If distant correspond to similarity, clustering forms groups of objects that are maximally similar

There are many different types of clustering algorithms, each has his own advantages and disadvantages. However, almost all the common clustering algorithms can be divided into two groups. They are probabilistic clustering and possibilistic clustering [3].

The main property of probabilistic clustering is that they all obey the constraint:

$$\sum_{i=1}^{c} u_{ik} = 1, k = 1, \cdots, n, \tag{1}$$

where, u_{ik} is the membership value of object k towards concept i, c is the number of clusters, and n is the number of objects. On the other hand, possibilistic clustering does not obey the constraint shown above. It is the reverse of probabilistic clustering, and it gives intra-cluster information.

3 Fuzzy *c*-Means Algorithm

In fuzzy clustering we need to determine the portioning of the sample data for each input variable into a number of clusters. These clusters have "fuzzy" boundaries. Each object is bound to each cluster to a certain degree, $\mu \in [0,1]$, also known as membership.

The idea of fuzzy clustering came from the Hard C-Means (HCM) founded by Ruspini [4]. He introduced a notion of fuzzy partition to describe the cluster structure of a data set and suggested an algorithm to compute the optimum fuzzy partition. Dunn [5] generalized the minimum-variance clustering procedure to a Fuzzy ISODATA clustering technique. Bezdek [2] generalized Dunn's approach to obtain an infinite family of algorithms known as the Fuzzy *c*-Means (FCM) algorithms. One approach to fuzzy clustering is the fuzzy *c*-Means [2]. Before Bezdek, Dunn [5] had developed the fuzzy *c*-Means Algorithm. The idea of Dunn's algorithm is to extend the classical within groups sum of squared error objective function to a fuzzy version by minimizing this objective function. Bezdek generalized this fuzzy objective function by introducing the weighting exponent m, $1 \le m \le \infty$.

Fuzzy *c*-means clustering is a probabilistic clustering. The basic idea of fuzzy *c*-means is very similar to *k*-means algorithm. It assumes the number of cluster *c*, is known a priori, and tries to minimize the objective function. The clustering problem is posed as an optimization problem in which a given objective function needs to be optimized.

Objective function methods allow most precise formulation of the clustering criterion. Optimizing the objective function is performed to find the optimal partitions of data.

$$J_1(U,V) = \sum_{i=1}^{c} \sum_{k=1}^{n} (u_{ik})^m D_{ik} \tag{2}$$

The main property of fuzzy is that it obeys the constraint:

$$M = \{U = (u_{ik}) : \sum_{j=1}^{c} u_{jk} = 1, \ 0 \leq u_{ik} \leq 1, \ i=1,\cdots,c, \ k=1,\cdots,n\} \tag{3}$$

where u_{ik} is the membership value of object k towards concept i, c is the number of clusters, and n is the number of objects.

A similarity measure is required to construct an objective function. A standard way of expressing similarity is through a set of distances between pairs of data points. Objects with smaller distances are given the same class label, while those with larger distances are put into different classes. The term D_{ik} is assumed to be the square of the Euclidean distance between the individual x_k and the center $v_i = (v_i^1, \cdots, v_i^p)$ of the cluster i:

$$D_{ik} = \|x_k - v_i\|^2 \tag{4}$$

$V = (v_1, \cdots, v_c)$: the vector collecting all cluster centers.

The conditions for local minimum for the objective function J_1 are derived using Lagrangian multipliers and the results are:

$$\bar{u}_{ik} = \left[\sum_{j=1}^{c} \left(\frac{D_{ik}}{D_{jk}} \right)^{\frac{1}{m-1}} \right]^{-1} \ ; \tag{5}$$

and

$$\bar{v}_i = \frac{\sum_{k=1}^{n} (u_{ik})^m x_k}{\sum_{k=1}^{n} (u_{ik})^m}. \tag{6}$$

Minimization of J_1 is performed by alternating optimization technique. The algorithm becomes a numerical procedure for finding those membership degrees that optimizes the objective function.

Algorithm of fuzzy c-means

FCM1 Set initial value for $\bar{V}$.

FCM2 Find optimal solution $\bar{U}$:

$$J(\bar{U},\bar{V}) = \min_{U \in M} J(U,\bar{V})$$

FCM3 Find optimal solution $\overline{V}$:

$$J(\overline{U}, \overline{V}) = \min_{V \in R^{pc}} J(\overline{U}, V)$$

FCM4 Check stopping criterion and if convergent, stop. Otherwise go to FCM2.

The fundamental idea of fuzzy *c*-means is to alter the objective function and the constraint. Different options for $J(U, V)$ and M produce various methods of fuzzy *c*-means.

4 Noise Clustering Approach

There is a great problem on FCM and many other probabilistic clustering algorithm. This is the problem of outliers or noisy data. A strange value that stands out because it is not like the rest of the data in some sense is commonly called noisy point or outlier. Outliers are vectors, or called data point, in the data domain which are so distant from the rest of the other vectors in the data set. Such as in the case of the i.i.d (idependent, identically, distributed) variable. An outlier in this situation is usually detected by its distance from the rest of the data, suitably measured. This idea already has an implicit assumption that the whole data are the same probability distribution, and observations not compatible with this distributional assumption are deemed outliers [6].

The idea of noise clustering approach was proposed by Davé [7] to deal with noisy data for fuzzy clustering methods. A noise cluster, cluster number 0 with membership $u_{0k}, k = 1, \cdots, n$, is introduced, with the hope that all noisy point can be dumped into this cluster. The objective function is given by

$$J_2(U, V) = \sum_{i=1}^{c} \sum_{k=1}^{n} (u_{ik})^m D_{ik} + \sum_{k=1}^{n} (u_{0k})^m \delta^2 \tag{7}$$

in which the constraint is

$$M = \{U = (u_{ik}) : \sum_{j=0}^{c} u_{jk} = 1, 0 \le u_{ik} \le 1, i = 0, \cdots, c, k = 1, \cdots, n\} \tag{8}$$

Ichihashi *et al.* [8] propose a generalized objective function using K-L information with additional variables. A variation of which has been proposed by Miyamoto and Alanzado [9] to handle noise clusters.

$$J_3(U, V, \alpha) = \sum_{i=1}^{c} \sum_{k=1}^{n} u_{ik} D_{ik} + \sum_{k=1}^{n} u_{0k} \delta^2 + \lambda^{-1} \sum_{i=0}^{c} \sum_{k=1}^{n} u_{ik} \log \frac{u_{ik}}{\alpha_i} \tag{9}$$

with the constraint (8) and

$$A = \{\alpha = (\alpha_i) : \sum_{i=0}^{c} \alpha_i = 1, \ \alpha_i \ge 0, \ i = 1, \cdots, c\}. \tag{10}$$

for which the algorithm FCMA1-FCMA5 is used.

Algorithm of FCMA (FCM with additional variables)

FCMA1 Set initial value for $\overline{U}, \overline{V}$.

FCMA2 Find new optimal solution $\overline{\alpha}$:

$$J(\overline{U}, \overline{V}, \overline{\alpha}) = \min_{\alpha \in A} J(\overline{U}, \overline{V}, \alpha)$$

FCMA3 Find new optimal solution $\overline{V}$:

$$J(\overline{U},\overline{V},\overline{\alpha})=\min_{V\in R^{pc}} J(\overline{U},V,\overline{\alpha})$$

FCMA4 Find new optimal solution $\overline{U}$:

$$J(\overline{U},\overline{V},\overline{\alpha})=\min_{U\in M} J(U,\overline{V},\overline{\alpha})$$

FCMA5 Check stopping criterion and if convergent, stop. Otherwise go to FCMA2.

The conditions for local minimum for the objective function J_3 are derived using Lagrangian multipliers and the results are:

$$u_{ik} = \frac{\alpha_i e^{-\lambda D_{ik}}}{\sum_{j=1}^{c} \alpha_j e^{-\lambda D_{jk}} + \alpha_0 e^{-\lambda \delta^2}} \tag{11}$$

for $i=1,\cdots,c$, and

$$u_{0k} = \frac{\alpha_0 e^{-\lambda \delta^2}}{\sum_{j=1}^{c} \alpha_j e^{-\lambda D_{jk}} + \alpha_0 e^{-\lambda \delta^2}} \tag{12}$$

$$v_i = \frac{\sum_{k=1}^{n} u_{ik} x_k}{\sum_{k=1}^{n} u_{ik}} \tag{13}$$

$$\alpha_i = \frac{1}{n} \sum_{k=1}^{n} u_{ik} \tag{14}$$

for $i=0,\cdots,c$.

5 Time-Series Clustering

A time series is the simplest form of temporal data and is a sequence of real numbers collected regularly in time, where each number represents a value.

Clustering time series analysis has been researched and used for a long time motivated by several research challenges including similarity search as well as the challenge to develop new methods to recognize dynamic change in time series. Many clustering algorithms have been applied to time series data based on the actual value of each time point. K-means clustering is the most commonly used clustering algorithm, with the number of clusters K specified by the user. Euclidean distance is the most common method for determining similarity in time series clustering.

Outlier detection has become an important part of time series analysis and influences modeling, testing and inference. Outliers can lead to model misspecification, biased parameter estimation, poor forecasting and inappropriate decomposition of the series [10]

The analysis of time series is an important area of statistics and there is a clear need to understand the nature of outliers and to have available methods to detect, or accommodate, them [11].

6 Fuzzy Time-Series Clustering Algorithm

Like most clustering method we assume that the relationship among a set of n objects is described by an n x n matrix containing a measure of similarity or dissimilarity between the ith and the jth data points. It is referred to as a distance function between a pair of points.

Definition of a good distance function is the most critical step in any distance based clustering method.

In our work we describe a new distance metric based on econometric model. For a single input variable the fuzzy relationship is of the form

$$y = f(x) + \varepsilon \tag{15}$$

where ε is a random disturbance term. If the disturbance term has a zero mean, the fuzzy function y, represents the conditional mean of the output variable. To which we adopt a non-parametric kernel regression. If the chosen estimation procedure is the least squares, then

$$y_{ij} = \beta_{i0} + \beta_{i1} x_{ij} + \varepsilon_{ij} \; ; \quad j = 1, \ldots, n_i; \quad i = 1, \ldots, c \tag{16}$$

Thus the predicted conditional mean of y has the form of

$$\hat{y}_k = \frac{\left[\sum\limits_{i=1}^{c} (\beta_{i0} + \beta_{i1} x_k) \mu_{ik} \right]}{\left[\sum\limits_{i=1}^{c} \mu_{ik} \right]} \quad ; k = 1, \ldots, n \tag{17}$$

where μ_{ik} is the degree of membership of the k'th value of x in the i'th fuzzy cluster, and b_{im} is the least squares estimator of β_{im} (m=0,1) obtained using the i'th fuzzy partition of the sample.

The fuzzy predictor of the conditional mean of y is a weighted average of the linear predictors based on the fuzzy portioning of the input data, with the weights (membership values) varying continuously through the sample.

For our fuzzy time series clustering algorithm the similarity metric is define by

$$D_{ik} = \left(y_{ik} - \hat{y}_k \right)^2 \tag{18}$$

The objective function is given as

$$J_4(U, V, \alpha) = \sum_{i=1}^{c} \sum_{k=1}^{n} u_{ik} \left(y_{ik} - \hat{y}_k \right)^2 + \sum_{k=1}^{n} u_{0k} \, \delta^2$$

$$+ \lambda^{-1} \sum_{i=0}^{c} \sum_{k=1}^{n} u_{ik} \log \frac{u_{ik}}{\alpha_i} \tag{19}$$

The method of fuzzy c-means uses an alternative minimization of the objective function J_4 to find the optimum value of U and V. An additional variable $\alpha = (\alpha_1, \ldots, \alpha_c)$ with the constraint A is used for controlling the sizes of the clusters. Algorithm FCMA is used to find the conditions for the local minimum. The local minimum is the same as that of the noise clustering approach discussed in the previous section with the parameter δ as an arbitrary value.

7   Illustrative Examples

We applied the fuzzy model describe above and the result is shown in the figures below. For illustration purposes we modify the data and noisy points are added to serve as outliers or noisy data. Figure 1 and Figure 2 shows the result using our proposed algorithm. The initial values of the memberships are assumed to be random. The objective function J_4 and the algorithm FCMA is used to cluster this data. From the resulting memberships, each point has crisply been reallocated to the cluster of the maximum membership. The noisy points are clustered into the noise cluster.

It is immediate to see the method has worked effectively and the noise points have been well separated in these examples.

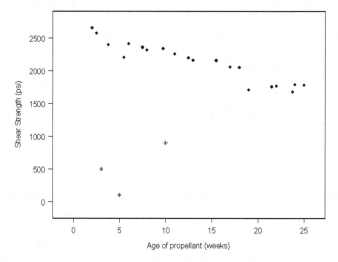

Fig. 1. Shear strength versus propellant age data with noise points added

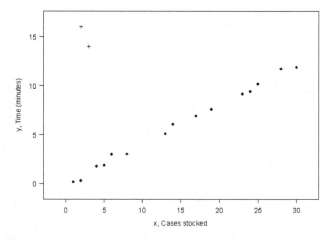

Fig. 2. Scatter diagram of shelf-stocking data with noise points added

8 Conclusion and Future Works

An alternative fuzzy clustering technique has been proposed in this paper. We have developed a modification of the well-known fuzzy *c*-means objective function to handle the noise cluster utilizing the concept of non-parametric kernel regression model. In our experiment the proposed method worked effectively. The noise points have been well separated from the other cluster.

Future studies include application to larger data sets with multiple input variables with noise present. The effectiveness of the method should moreover be investigated.

References

1. Chris Chatfield, The Analysis of Time Series, An Introduction, 5th ed. Chapman and Hall, London, 1996
2. J. C. Bezdek, *Pattern Recognition with Fuzzy Objective Function Algorithms*, Plenum Press, New York, 1981
3. R.N. Davé, R. Krishnapuram, Robust clustering methods: a unified view, *IEEE Trans. Fuzzy Syst.*, Vol. 5, No.2, pp. 270-293, 1997
4. E. H. Ruspini, A New Approach to Clustering, *Information Control* 15: 22-32, 1969.
5. J. C. Dunn, Fuzzy Relative of the ISODATA Process and Its Use in Detecting Compact Well- Separated Clusters, *Journal of Cybernetics* 3: 32-57, 1973.
6. V. Barnet and T. Lewis, *Outliers in statistical data, 3rd ed.* John Wiley, Chichester, 1994.
7. R. N. Davé, "Characterization and detection of noise in clustering", *Pattern Recognition Letters.*, Vol. 12, pp. 657-664, 1991
8. K. Miyagishi, Y.Yasutomi, H. Ichihashi, K. Honda, Fuzzy Clustering with regularization by K-L information. *16th Fuzzy System Symposium*, Akita, Sept. 6-8, 2000, pp.549-550 (in Japanese).
9. S. Miyamoto and A.C. Alanzado, Fuzzy *C*-Means and Mixture Distribution Models in the Presence of Noise Clusters. *International Journal of Image and Graphics*, Vol. 2, No. 4, pp 573-586, 2002.
10. Kaiser, R. and Maravall, A. Seasonal outliers in time series, Banco de Espana - Servicio de Estudios paper number 9915, 1999
11. Vic Barnett and Toby Lewis, Outliers in Statistical Data, Chichester : Wiley, 1978.

Quantification of Multivariate Categorical Data Considering Clusters of Items and Individuals

Chi-Hyon Oh[1], Katsuhiro Honda[2], and Hidetomo Ichihashi[2]

[1] Faculty of Liberal Arts and Sciences, Osaka University of Economics and Law
6-10 Gakuonji, Yao, Osaka, 581-8511, Japan
[2] Graduate School of Engineering, Osaka Prefecture University
1-1 Gakuen-cho, Sakai, Osaka, 599-8531, Japan

Abstract. This paper proposes a simultaneous application of homogeneity analysis and fuzzy clustering which simultaneously partitions individuals and items in categorical multivariate data sets. Taking the similarity between the loss of homogeneity in homogeneity analysis and the least squares criterion in principal component analysis into account, the new objective function is defined in a similar formulation to the linear fuzzy clustering.

1 Introduction

Simultaneous approaches to multivariate data analysis and fuzzy clustering have been applied to knowledge discovery from large-scale databases because the local model derived in each cluster effectively reveals local features of nonlinearly distributed high-dimensional data sets. Fuzzy c-Varieties (FCV) clustering proposed by Bezdek et al. [1][2] is regarded as a simultaneous approach to principal component analysis (PCA) and fuzzy clustering since the FCV partitions a dataset into several linear clusters using linear varieties as prototypes of clusters and basis vectors of prototypical linear varieties are often identified with local principal component vectors.

Honda et al. [3][4] proposed a modified linear fuzzy clustering algorithm in which the objective function was regarded as the least squares criterion for local PCA. While the objective function of the FCV algorithm consists of distances between data points and prototypical linear varieties, the same solution can be derived from the least squares criterion that achieves "component-wise" lower rank approximation of the data matrix. The algorithm can be used, however, only when the data matrix consists of numerical variables.

Homogeneity analysis [5][6] is a quantification technique for representing the structure of nonnumerical multivariate data and minimizes departures from perfect homogeneity measured by the Gifi loss function. Minimization of the Gifi loss function is based on the approximation of a matrix, so the algorithm is similar to that of PCA with the least squares criterion [7].

In this paper, we propose a quantification method for multivariate categorical data considering their local structures. Extraction of the local structures is

V. Torra et al. (Eds.): MDAI 2005, LNAI 3558, pp. 164–171, 2005.

achieved by the fuzzy clustering. To partition items and individuals of multivariate categorical data into clusters, we introduce memberships of both elements into the Gifi loss function. The proposed method implements the homogeneity analysis and fuzzy clustering simultaneously. We demonstrate the feasibility of our method in numerical examples.

2   Quantification of Multivariate Categorical Data Considering Clusters of Items and Individuals

2.1   Homogeneity Analysis

Suppose that we have collected data on n individuals $i(i = 1, \cdots, n)$ on m items $j(j = 1, \cdots, m)$ with K_j categories $k(k = 1, \cdots, K_j)$. Categories of each item are often nominal. These nonnumerical variables are represented by indicator matrices. Let G_j denote the $(n \times K_j)$ indicator matrix corresponding to item j and its entries be binary variables as follows:

$$g_{ijk} = \begin{cases} 1 \text{ ; if individual } i \text{ belongs to category } k \text{ of item } j. \\ 0 \text{ ; otherwise.} \end{cases} \tag{1}$$

$$\boldsymbol{G}_j = \begin{pmatrix} g_{1j1} & \cdots & g_{1jk} & \cdots & g_{1jK_j} \\ \vdots & \ddots & \vdots & \ddots & \vdots \\ g_{ij1} & \cdots & g_{ijk} & \cdots & g_{ijK_j} \\ \vdots & \ddots & \vdots & \ddots & \vdots \\ g_{nj1} & \cdots & g_{njk} & \cdots & g_{njK_j} \end{pmatrix}. \tag{2}$$

These matrices are collected in $(n \times K)$ partitioned matrix $G = [G_1, G_2, \cdots, G_m]$, where $K = \sum_{j=1}^{m} K_j$ is the total number of categories.

The goal of quantifying categorical data is to represent these individuals in a P dimensional space $p(p = 1, \cdots, P, \quad P < m)$. Homogeneity analysis [5][6] is basic non-linear multivariate analysis whose objective is to represent the structure of nonnumerical multivariate data by assigning scores to individuals and categories of items. Let $\boldsymbol{Y}_j$ denote the $(K_j \times P)$ matrix containing the multiple category quantification of item j and $\boldsymbol{X}$ be an $(n \times P)$ matrix containing resulting P individual scores as follows:

$$\boldsymbol{X} = \begin{pmatrix} x_{11} & x_{12} & \dots & x_{1P} \\ x_{21} & x_{22} & \dots & x_{2P} \\ \vdots & \vdots & \ddots & \vdots \\ x_{n1} & x_{n2} & \dots & x_{nP} \end{pmatrix}, \tag{3}$$

$$\boldsymbol{Y}_j = \begin{pmatrix} y_{j11} & y_{j12} & \cdots & y_{j1P} \\ y_{j21} & y_{j22} & \cdots & y_{j2P} \\ \vdots & \vdots & \ddots & \vdots \\ y_{jK_j1} & y_{jK_j2} & \cdots & y_{jK_jP} \end{pmatrix}. \tag{4}$$

Homogeneity analysis is based on the principle that a scale consisting of nominal variables is homogenizable if all items can be quantified so that the resulting scale is homogeneous, i.e., all items in the scale are linearly related. Departures from perfect homogeneity are measured by the Gifi loss function:

$$\sigma = \frac{1}{m} \sum_{j=1}^{m} \text{tr}\{(\boldsymbol{X} - \boldsymbol{G}_j \boldsymbol{Y}_j)^\top (\boldsymbol{X} - \boldsymbol{G}_j \boldsymbol{Y}_j)\}, \tag{5}$$

where "tr" represents the trace of the matrix (the sum of diagonal entries).

To avoid trivial solutions, the loss function is minimized under the following conditions:

$$\boldsymbol{1}_n^\top \boldsymbol{X} = \boldsymbol{0}^\top, \tag{6}$$

$$\boldsymbol{X}^\top \boldsymbol{X} = n\boldsymbol{I}_P, \tag{7}$$

where $\boldsymbol{1}_n$ represents a n dimensional vector all of whose entries are one and $\boldsymbol{I}_P$ does a P dimensional identity matrix.

2.2 Simultaneous Application of Fuzzy Clustering and Homogeneity Analysis

In this subsection, we propose an approach that performs fuzzy clustering and homogeneity analysis simultaneously. Items and individuals are partitioned fuzzily into C clusters $c(c = 1, \cdots, c)$ by introducing memberships w_{cj} and u_{ci}. w_{cj} denotes the membership degree of the j-th item to the c-th cluster and u_{ci} does that of the i-th individual to the c-th cluster. Scores to quantify the multivariate categorical data are assigned items and individuals of each cluster as follows:

$$\boldsymbol{X_c} = \begin{pmatrix} x_{c11} & x_{c12} & \cdots & x_{c1P} \\ x_{c21} & x_{c22} & \cdots & x_{c2P} \\ \vdots & \vdots & \ddots & \vdots \\ x_{cn1} & x_{cn2} & \cdots & x_{cnP} \end{pmatrix}, \tag{8}$$

$$\boldsymbol{Y_{cj}} = \begin{pmatrix} y_{cj11} & y_{cj12} & \cdots & y_{cj1P} \\ y_{cj21} & y_{cj22} & \cdots & y_{cj2P} \\ \vdots & \vdots & \ddots & \vdots \\ y_{cjK_j1} & y_{cjK_j2} & \cdots & y_{cjK_jP} \end{pmatrix}. \tag{9}$$

The objective function with regularization by entropy [8] is defined as follows:

$$\tilde{\sigma} = \frac{1}{m} \sum_{c=1}^{C} \sum_{j=1}^{m} w_{cj} \text{tr}\{(\boldsymbol{X_c} - \boldsymbol{G}_j \boldsymbol{Y_{cj}})^\top \boldsymbol{U}_c (\boldsymbol{X_c} - \boldsymbol{G}_j \boldsymbol{Y_{cj}})\}$$

$$+ \lambda_u \sum_{c=1}^{C} \sum_{i=1}^{n} u_{ci} \log u_{ci} + \lambda_w \sum_{c=1}^{C} \sum_{j=1}^{m} w_{cj} \log w_{cj}. \tag{10}$$

The second and third terms in Eq.(10) represent entropy maximization as a regularization which was introduced in Fuzzy c-Means by Miyamoto et al. [8] for the first time. It enables us to obtain fuzzy clusters. λ_u and λ_w are the weighting parameters which specify the degree of fuzziness.

To derive a unique solution, Eq.(10) is minimized under the following conditions:

$$\boldsymbol{u}_c^\top \boldsymbol{X}_c = \boldsymbol{0}^\top, \tag{11}$$

$$\boldsymbol{X}_c^\top \boldsymbol{U}_c \boldsymbol{X}_c = (\sum_{i=1}^{n} u_{ci}) \boldsymbol{I}_P, \tag{12}$$

where $U_c = \text{diag}(u_{c1}, \cdots, u_{cn})$. If the number of clusters is one i.e., $c = 1$, Eqs.(11) and (12) equal to Eqs.(6) and (7).

The optimal solution is derived based on the iterative least squares. From the necessary condition for the optimality $\partial \tilde{\sigma} / \partial \boldsymbol{Y}_{cj} = O$, the updating rule for $\boldsymbol{Y}_{cj}$ is derived as

$$\hat{\boldsymbol{Y}}_{cj} = (\boldsymbol{G}_j^\top \boldsymbol{U}_c^\top \boldsymbol{G}_j)^{-1} \boldsymbol{G}_j^\top \boldsymbol{U}_c^\top \boldsymbol{X}_c. \tag{13}$$

From $\partial \tilde{\sigma} / \partial \boldsymbol{X}_c = O$, we have

$$\hat{\boldsymbol{X}}_c = \frac{\sum_{j=1}^{m} w_{cj} \boldsymbol{G}_j \boldsymbol{Y}_{cj}}{\sum_{j=1}^{m} w_{cj}}. \tag{14}$$

As for memberships of individuals, from $\partial \tilde{\sigma} / \partial u_{ci} = O$, we have

$$\hat{u}_{ci} = \exp(B_{ci} - 1), \tag{15}$$

where

$$B_{ci} = \frac{-1}{\lambda_u m} \sum_{j=1}^{m} \sum_{p=1}^{P} w_{cj} (x_{cip} - \sum_{k=1}^{K_j} g_{ijk} y_{cjkp})^2. \tag{16}$$

When we consider the probabilistic constraint [9] for memberships of individuals ($\sum_{c=1}^{C} u_{ci} = 1$), the new membership of the individual is calculated as

$$\hat{u}_{ci} = \frac{\exp(B_{ci})}{\sum_{l=1}^{C} \exp(B_{li})}. \tag{17}$$

Identically, from $\partial \tilde{\sigma} / \partial w_{cj} = 0$, we have

$$\hat{w}_{cj} = \exp(A_{cj} - 1), \tag{18}$$

where

Table 1. Artificial data set

Individual	I1	I2	I3	I4	I5	I6
1	a	a	a	a	a	a
2	b	a	a	a	a	b
3	b	b	a	a	a	c
4	b	b	b	a	a	d
5	b	b	b	b	a	e
6	b	b	b	b	b	a
7	c	b	b	b	b	b
8	c	c	b	b	b	c
9	c	c	c	b	b	d
10	c	c	c	c	b	e
11	c	c	c	c	c	a
12	d	c	c	c	c	b
13	d	d	c	c	c	c
14	d	d	d	c	c	d
15	d	d	d	d	c	e
16	d	d	d	d	d	a
17	e	d	d	d	d	b
18	e	e	d	d	d	c
19	e	e	e	d	d	d
20	e	e	e	e	d	e
21	e	e	e	e	e	a

Individual	I1	I2	I3	I4	I5	I6
22	a	a	b	e	c	a
23	b	a	b	e	c	b
24	c	a	c	e	c	b
25	d	a	c	d	c	b
26	e	a	c	d	e	b
27	a	b	c	d	e	b
28	b	b	c	d	e	c
29	c	b	d	d	e	c
30	d	b	d	c	e	c
31	e	b	d	c	a	c
32	a	c	d	c	a	c
33	b	c	d	c	a	d
34	c	c	e	c	a	d
35	d	c	e	b	a	d
36	e	c	e	b	d	d
37	a	d	e	b	d	d
38	b	d	e	b	d	e
39	c	d	a	b	d	e
40	d	d	a	a	d	e
41	e	d	a	a	b	e
42	a	e	a	a	b	e

$$A_{cj} = \frac{-1}{\lambda m} \sum_{j=1}^{n} \sum_{p=1}^{P} u_{ci}\left(x_{cip} - \sum_{k=1}^{K_j} g_{ijk} y_{cjkp}\right)^2. \qquad (19)$$

The probabilistic constraint for memberships of items ($\sum_{j=1}^{m} w_{cj} = 1$) is different from that for memberships of individuals. For u_{ci}, the total amount of memberships of the i-th individual to the clusters has to be one. On the other hand, the total membership of the c-th cluster to the items should be one. Consequently, the new membership of the item is calculated as

$$\hat{w}_{cj} = \frac{\exp(A_{cj})}{\sum_{l=1}^{m} \exp(A_{cl})}. \qquad (20)$$

The optimal solution is derived based on the alternating least squares. Therefore, the proposed algorithm can be written as follows:

The Quantification Method of Multivariate Categorical Data Considering Clusters of Items and Individuals

Step 1:   Set values of parameters C, λ_u, λ_w, and termination threshold ϵ. Initialize $\boldsymbol{X}_c$ and $\boldsymbol{U}_c$ randomly, and normalize them so that the probabilistic constraint and Eqs.(6), (7) hold.

Table 2. Membership values of individuals

Individual	Cluster 1	Cluster 2		Individual	Cluster1	Cluster2
1	0.000	1.000		22	1.000	0.000
2	0.000	1.000		23	1.000	0.000
3	0.000	1.000		24	1.000	0.000
4	0.000	1.000		25	1.000	0.000
5	0.000	1.000		26	1.000	0.000
6	0.000	1.000		27	1.000	0.000
7	0.000	1.000		28	1.000	0.000
8	0.000	1.000		29	1.000	0.000
9	0.000	1.000		30	1.000	0.000
10	0.000	1.000		31	1.000	0.000
11	0.000	1.000		32	1.000	0.000
12	0.000	1.000		33	1.000	0.000
13	0.000	1.000		34	1.000	0.000
14	0.000	1.000		35	1.000	0.000
15	0.000	1.000		36	1.000	0.000
16	0.000	1.000		37	1.000	0.000
17	0.000	1.000		38	1.000	0.000
18	0.000	1.000		39	1.000	0.000
19	0.000	1.000		40	1.000	0.000
20	0.000	1.000		41	1.000	0.000
21	0.000	1.000		42	1.000	0.000

Step 2:   Calculate $\boldsymbol{Y}_{cj}$ using Eq.(13).
Step 3:   Calculate $\boldsymbol{X}_c$ using Eq.(14).
Step 4:   Normalize $\boldsymbol{X}_c$ so that Eqs.(6), (7) hold.
Step 5:   Update membership w_{cj} using (20).
Step 6:   Update memberships u_{ci} using (17).
Step 7:   If $\max |u_{ci}^{NEW} - u_{ci}^{OLD}| < \epsilon$, then stop. Otherwise, return to *Step 2*.

3   Numerical Experiment

In numerical experiment, we apply the proposed method to an artificial data set. The data set is shown in Table 1. The rows represent the individuals and the columns are the items. The data set consists of 42 individuals. The number of items is six and each item has 5 categories. In Table 1, individuals 1 through 21 are linearly related in categories 1 through 5 and individuals 22 trough 42 are in categories 2 through 6.

We tried to extract those local structures of the data set by our proposed method with $C = 2$ and $P = 2$. The results are shown in Table 2 and Table 3. Table 2 and Table 3 show memberships of individuals and items. In Table 2 and Table 3, we underlined larger memberships of individuals and items. We assume that individuals and items are more likely to belong to the cluster to which they

Table 3. Membership values of items

Item	Cluster 1	Cluster 2
1	0.025	0.193
2	0.193	0.196
3	0.196	0.196
4	0.197	0.196
5	0.196	0.193
6	0.193	0.025

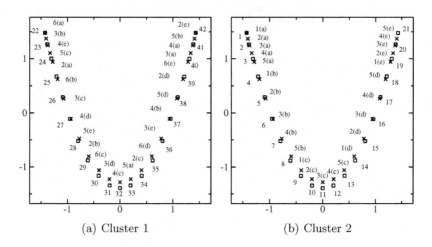

(a) Cluster 1   (b) Cluster 2

Fig. 1. Combined category and individual quantification plots

have larger memberships. From Table 2 and Table 3, we can see that individuals and items are properly divided into two clusters.

Figs. 1 shows the combined category and individual quantification plots. The figures are the combined 2-D plots of category scores y_{cjk} and individual scores x_{ci} and show that individuals and categories can be linearly arranged and the combined plots make it possible to recognize the relationship intuitively.

4   Conclusions

In this paper, we proposed the quantification method of multivariate categorical data considering clusters of items and individuals. The objective function was defined by introducing memberships of individuals and items to the Gifi loss function of homogeneity analysis. The proposed method was applied to the artificial data set which had two local substructures. The results showed that the proposed method successfully extracted those substructures and quantified individuals and items of the data set simultaneously.

Tsuchiya [10] proposed the construction of multi unidimensional scales by classifying a set of qualitative variables into groups. The comparative study

with Tsuchiya's method and the application of the proposed method to the
actual data set are left for future work.

References

1. Bezdek, J. C.: Nonlinear oscillations and Recognition with Fuzzy Objective Function Algorithms. Plenum Press (1981)
2. Bezdek, J. C., Coray, C., Gunderson, R., Watson, J.: Detection and characterization of cluster substructure 2. fuzzy c-varieties and convex combinations thereof. SIAM J. Appl. Math. **40** (1981) 358–372
3. Honda, K., Sugiura, N., Ichihashi, H., Araki, S.: Collaborative filtering using principal component analysis and fuzzy clustering. Web Intelligence: Research and Development, Lecture Notes in Artificial Intelligence, **2198** (2001) 394–402
4. Honda, K., Ichihashi, H.: Linear fuzzy clustering techniques with missing values and their application to local principal component analysis. IEEE Trans. on Fuzzy Systems, **12, 2** (2004) 183–193
5. Gifi, A.: Nonlinear Multivariate Analysis. Wiley (1990)
6. Bond, J., Michailidis, G.: Homogeneity analysis in Lisp-Stat. J. Statistical Software, **1, 2** (1996)
7. Honda, K., Nakamura, Y., Ichihashi, H.: Simultaneous application of fuzzy clustering and quantification with incomplete categorical data. J. Advanced Computational Intelligence and Intelligent Informatics, **8, 4** (2004) 183–193
8. Miyamoto, S., Mukaidono, M.: Fuzzy c-means as a regularization and maximum entropy approach. Proc. the 7th International Fuzzy Systems Association World Congress, **2** (1997) 86–92
9. Höppner, F., Klawonn, F., Kruse, R., Runkler, T.: Fuzzy Cluster Analysis. Jhon Wiley & Sons (1999)
10. Tsuchiya T.: A quantification method for classification of variables. Japanese J. Behaviormetrics **22, 2** (1995) 95–109 (in Japanese)

A New Approach to Fuzzification
of Memberships in Cluster Analysis

Katsuhiro Honda and Hidetomo Ichihashi

Graduate School of Engineering, Osaka Prefecture University
1-1 Gakuen-cho, Sakai, Osaka, Japan
honda@cs.osakafu-u.ac.jp

Abstract. Fuzzy c-Means (FCM) is the fuzzy version of the c-Means clustering, in which memberships are fuzzified by introducing an additional parameter into the linear objective function of weighted sum of distances between data points and cluster centers. Regularization of hard c-Means clustering is another approach to fuzzification and several regularization terms such as entropy and quadratic terms have been adopted. This paper generalizes the concept of fuzzification and proposes a new approach to fuzzy clustering. In the proposed approach, the linear weights of the hard c-Means clustering are replaced with non-linear ones by using regularization techniques. The numerical experiments demonstrate that the clustering algorithm has the features of both of the standard FCM algorithm and the regularization approaches.

1 Introduction

c-Means clustering algorithm [1] partitions data sets into well-separated clusters by minimizing within-group-sum-of-errors, i.e., the sum of squared distances between data points and prototypes of clusters. In the (hard) c-Means clustering, each data point belongs to one of clusters with their prototypical mean vectors. The concept has been enhanced into fuzzy clustering, in which the responsibility of each data point is shared amongst all of the prototypes instead of being assigned to only one prototypical mean. In order to derive fuzzy partition, the objective function of c-Means algorithm was enhanced to non-linear functions. Bezdek proposed the (standard) FCM algorithm [2] by replacing linear membership weights with non-linear weights, and the prototypes were calculated as the generalized means. Another approach to fuzzification of cluster analysis is the techniques based on the regularization of the objective function of the hard c-Means clustering. Miyamoto and Mukaidono [3] considered the singularity in the hard clustering which implies the case where proper partition is not obtained by the Lagrangian multiplier method, and introduced a regularization term, such as entropy term [3] and quadratic term [4], with a positive parameter into the objective function.

In this paper, a new approach to fuzzy clustering is proposed by combining the concept of the standard FCM algorithm and the regularized methods. The new approach transforms the objective function of the hard c-Means into

V. Torra et al. (Eds.): MDAI 2005, LNAI 3558, pp. 172–182, 2005.

non-linear functions with respect to memberships by replacing the linear membership weights with regularized weights. In this paper, two types of regularized weights are introduced. One is the linear combination of normal memberships and entropy terms, and the technique is a hybrid of the standard FCM algorithm and the entropy regularization approach. The other is the linear combination of normal memberships and quadratic terms, and the clustering algorithm has the features of both of the standard FCM algorithm and the quadratic regularization approach. The characteristic features of the new approach are demonstrated in several numerical experiments.

2 Fuzzy c-Means and Regularized Objective Functions

2.1 c-Means and Fuzzy c-Means

Let $\boldsymbol{x}_i = (x_{i1}, \cdots, x_{im})^\top$, $i = 1, \cdots, n$ denote m dimensional observations of n samples. c-Means clustering uses mean vector $\boldsymbol{b}_c$ as the prototype of the c-th cluster and estimates membership of each sample by minimizing the following within-group-sum-of-errors.

$$L_{cm} = \sum_{c=1}^{C} \sum_{i=1}^{n} u_{ci} d_{ci}^2$$

$$= \sum_{c=1}^{C} \sum_{i=1}^{n} u_{ci} (\boldsymbol{x}_i - \boldsymbol{b}_c)^\top (\boldsymbol{x}_i - \boldsymbol{b}_c), \tag{1}$$

where u_{ci} represents the membership of the i-th data point to the c-th cluster and is given as

$$u_{ci} = \begin{cases} 1 \text{ ; the } i\text{-th data point belongs to the } c\text{-th cluster} \\ 0 \text{ ; otherwise} \end{cases}$$

and

$$\sum_{c=1}^{C} u_{ci} = 1, \qquad i = 1, \cdots, n. \tag{2}$$

The clustering algorithm is a 2-step iterative algorithm composed of calculation of memberships u_{ci} and mean vectors $\boldsymbol{b}_c$ [1].

In fuzzy clustering, the constraint on the memberships is generalized to $u_{ci} \in [0, 1]$ so that membership matrix $U = (u_{ci})$ represents a fuzzy partition. Equation (1) is, however, a linear function with respect to memberships and the optimal memberships are given as the extremal points ($u_{ci} \in \{0, 1\}$). Then, Bezdek proposed Fuzzy c-Means (FCM) algorithm [2], in which an additional parameter is introduced into the linear objective function of weighted sum of distances between data points and cluster centers.

$$L_{fcm}^s = \sum_{c=1}^{C} \sum_{i=1}^{n} u_{ci}^\theta d_{ci}^2, \tag{3}$$

where θ is an additional weighting exponent. If $\theta = 1$, the clustering model is reduced to the (hard) c-means model. The larger the θ, the fuzzier the memberships. So, the weighting exponent is usually set to be $\theta > 1$ and is called the "fuzzifier". For deriving a clustering partition, an iterative algorithm is used. From the necessary conditions for the optimality, the new prototypes are derived as the weighted centers of clusters, and the memberships are calculated under the constraint of Eq.(2). Because the memberships are obtained by a formula similar to the updating rule for posterior probabilities in the EM algorithm with probabilistic mixture models, the constraint is called the "probabilistic constraint" [5].

The FCM algorithm is summarized as follows:

Algorithm: Fuzzy c-Means (FCM)

Step 1 Initialize memberships $u_{ci}, c = 1, \cdots, C, i = 1, \cdots, n$ randomly, and normalize the memberships so that they satisfy the probabilistic constraint. Choose termination threshold ε.

Step 2 Update $b_c, c = 1, \cdots, C$ as

$$b_c = \frac{\sum_{i=1}^{n} u_{ci}^{\theta} x_i}{\sum_{i=1}^{n} u_{ci}^{\theta}}. \tag{4}$$

Step 3 Update $u_{ci}, c = 1, \cdots, C, i = 1, \cdots, n$ as

$$u_{ci} = \begin{cases} \left[\sum_{l=1}^{C} \left(\frac{d_{ci}^2}{d_{li}^2} \right)^{\frac{1}{\theta-1}} \right]^{-1} & ; I_i = \emptyset \\ 1/|I_i| & ; I_i \neq \emptyset, c \in I_i \\ 0 & ; I_i \neq \emptyset, c \notin I_i \end{cases}, \tag{5}$$

where I_i is the set of indices such that d_{ci}^2 is zero, i.e., $I_i = \{c : d_{ci}^2 = 0\}$.

Step 4 If

$$\max_{c,i} | u_{ci}^{NEW} - u_{ci}^{OLD} | < \varepsilon,$$

then stop. Otherwise, return to Step 2.

This standard formulation is often called the "standard FCM algorithm" and its characteristic features are summarized as follows [6]: If we use the membership calculation rules of Eq.(5) as fuzzy classification rules u_c, the maximum value ($u_c = 1$) is given on the cluster center, and u_c moves toward $1/C$ as $||x|| \to \infty$.

2.2 Fuzzy Clustering with Regularized Objective Function

Another approach for fuzzification of the memberships is the regularization of the objective function of the hard c-Means clustering. Miyamoto and Mukaidono [3] introduced a regularization term with a positive parameter λ into the objective function. Using the entropy term, the objective function of the FCM clustering based on the regularization technique is defined as

$$L_{fcm}^e = \sum_{c=1}^{C} \sum_{i=1}^{n} u_{ci} d_{ci}^2 + \lambda \sum_{c=1}^{C} \sum_{i=1}^{n} u_{ci} \log u_{ci}, \tag{6}$$

where the entropy term works like the weighting exponent in the standard FCM algorithm, and transforms the linear programming problem into the non-linear optimization problem with respect to memberships u_{ci}. The parameter λ plays a role for tuning the degree of fuzziness of membership values. The larger the λ, the fuzzier the memberships. This fuzzification technique is called "regularization by entropy".

The updating rules for memberships and cluster centers are derived as follows:

$$u_{ci} = \frac{\exp(-\frac{1}{\lambda}d_{ci}^2)}{\sum_{l=1}^{c} \exp(-\frac{1}{\lambda}d_{li}^2)}, \tag{7}$$

$$b_c = \frac{\sum_{i=1}^{n} u_{ci} x_i}{\sum_{i=1}^{n} u_{ci}}. \tag{8}$$

From the classification aspect, the fuzzy classification function have different features from that of the standard FCM algorithm [6]. For example, u_c does NOT have the maximum value ($u_c = 1$) on the cluster center and u_c moves toward 1 as $\|x\| \to \infty$. So the maximum membership value might be given for the data point that is not so near the cluster center.

The regularization approach can also be performed by using other regularization terms. Miyamoto and Umayahara [4] proposed the following objective function, in which quadratic term is used as the regularization term.

$$L_{fcm}^q = \sum_{c=1}^{C} \sum_{i=1}^{n} u_{ci} d_{ci}^2 + \frac{1}{2}\lambda \sum_{c=1}^{C} \sum_{i=1}^{n} u_{ci}^2, \tag{9}$$

The parameter λ tunes the degree of fuzziness of membership values. The larger the λ, the fuzzier the memberships. This fuzzification technique is called "regularization by quadratic term".

While the updating rule for cluster centers b_c is given in the same formula as the FCM with regularization by entropy, the optimal membership is not expressed by a simple formula because the membership of data point x_i to the c-th cluster might be negative value in the case that x_i is far from b_c and another center is near. So, the membership values are calculated by an algorithm. Suppose that the cluster index is transformed so that the following condition is satisfied.

$$d_{1i}^2 \leq d_{2i}^2 \leq \cdots \leq d_{Ci}^2. \tag{10}$$

The updating rule is given as

$$u_{ci} = \begin{cases} \frac{1}{|I_i|}\left(\sum_{l \in I_i} \frac{d_{li}^2}{\lambda} + 1\right) - \frac{d_{ci}^2}{\lambda} & ; c \in I_i \\ 0 & ; \text{otherwise} \end{cases}$$

where I_i is the set of indices such that u_{ci} is positive, i.e.,

$$I_i = \left\{ c : \frac{1}{|I_i|}\left(\sum_{l=1}^{c} \frac{d_{li}^2}{\lambda} + 1\right) - \frac{d_{ci}^2}{\lambda} > 0 \right\}. \tag{11}$$

The characteristics of the quadratic regularization method are similar to those of the entropy regularization method. However, a remarkable feature is that the classification function is piecewise linear [6]. When a center is sufficiently far from x and another center is nearer to x than b_c, $u_c = 0$.

3   A New Approach to Fuzzification of Memberships

A new approach to fuzzification of memberships in cluster analysis is proposed in this section. Although the standard FCM algorithm and the regularized FCM algorithms are proposed based on different concepts, both of the fuzzification procedures can be summarized as transformation of the linear objective function into non-linear functions. The standard FCM algorithm directly transformed Eq.(1) by replacing u_{ci} with u_{ci}^θ while the regularized FCM algorithm added non-linear terms as the regularization terms. In the following, a generalized approach is considered by mixing the two fuzzification approaches.

The basic concept is similar to the standard FCM algorithm. In the new approach, u_{ci} of Eq.(1) is replaced with a non-linear term by adding a regularization term.

3.1   Fuzzification with Entropy Term

First, the standard FCM algorithm is mixed with the entropy regularization method. By replacing u_{ci} with $u_{ci} + \lambda u_{ci} \log u_{ci}$, the objective function of the hard c-Means clustering is transformed as follows:

$$L_{fcm}^{se} = \sum_{c=1}^{C} \sum_{i=1}^{n} (u_{ci} + \lambda u_{ci} \log u_{ci}) d_{ci}^2, \tag{12}$$

where the memberships should satisfy the probabilistic constraint. When $\min\{d_{ci} : c = 1, \cdots, C\} > 0$, necessary condition for the optimality of Lagrangian function

$$(1 + \lambda \log u_{ci} + \lambda) d_{ci}^2 - \gamma_i = 0 \tag{13}$$

derives the new membership as follows:

$$u_{ci} = \exp\left(\frac{\gamma_i}{\lambda d_{ci}^2} - \frac{1+\lambda}{\lambda}\right), \tag{14}$$

where γ_i is the Lagrangian multiplier that normalizes the membership so that the probabilistic constraint is satisfied. In Eq.(14), γ moves toward 0 as $\min\{d_{ci} : c = 1, \cdots, C\} \to 0$. Therefore, if $\min\{d_{ci} : c = 1, \cdots, C\} = 0$ and λ is small positive, u_{ci} should be given as

$$u_{ci} = \begin{cases} \frac{1}{|I_i|}\left(1 - (C - |I_i|)\exp\left(-\frac{1+\lambda}{\lambda}\right)\right) & ; c \in I_i \\ \exp\left(-\frac{1+\lambda}{\lambda}\right) & ; c \notin I_i \end{cases} \tag{15}$$

where I_i is the set of indices such that d_{ci}^2 is zero.

Here, in Eq.(14), it is difficult to calculate the optimal value of γ_i directly. In the numerical experiments, we calculated γ_i by using the Newton-Raphson method in each iteration step.

On the other hand, necessary condition $\partial L_{fcm}^{se}/\partial b_c = 0$ derives the optimal cluster centers as

$$b_c = \frac{\sum_{i=1}^{n}(u_{ci} + \lambda u_{ci}\log u_{ci})x_i}{\sum_{i=1}^{n}(u_{ci} + \lambda u_{ci}\log u_{ci})}. \tag{16}$$

3.2 Fuzzification with Quadratic Term

Another possible approach to fuzzification of membership is the mixture of the standard FCM algorithm and the quadratic regularization, in which u_{ci} is replaced with $u_{ci} + \lambda u_{ci}^2$. The objective function is defined as follows:

$$L_{fcm}^{sq} = \sum_{c=1}^{C}\sum_{i=1}^{n}\frac{u_{ci} + \lambda u_{ci}^2}{1+\lambda}d_{ci}^2. \tag{17}$$

Using the Lagrangian multiplier method, the optimal membership is given from the following equation.

$$\frac{1 + 2\lambda u_{ci}}{1+\lambda}d_{ci}^2 - \gamma_i = 0, \tag{18}$$

where γ_i is the Lagrangian multiplier. Here, the probabilistic constraint derives the updating rule as

$$u_{ci} = \left(\sum_{l=1}^{C}\frac{d_{ci}^2}{d_{li}^2}\right)^{-1}\left(1 + \frac{C}{2\lambda}\right) - \frac{1}{2\lambda}. \tag{19}$$

However, Eq.(19) is not the optimal solution because u_{ci} can be negative. So, the membership is updated by an algorithm in the same way as the quadratic regularization method.

Suppose that the cluster number is transformed so that the following condition is satisfied.

$$d_{1i}^2 \leq d_{2i}^2 \leq \cdots \leq d_{Ci}^2. \tag{20}$$

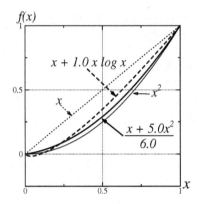

Fig. 1. Comparison of weight functions

The updating rule is given as

$$u_{ci} = \begin{cases} \left(\sum_{l=1}^{\phi} \frac{d_{ci}^2}{d_{li}^2} \right)^{-1} \left(1 + \frac{\phi}{2\lambda} \right) - \frac{1}{2\lambda} & ; \ 0 \le c \le \phi \\ 0 & ; \ \text{otherwise} \end{cases}$$

where ϕ is given as

$$\phi = \min \left\{ \phi : \left(\sum_{l=1}^{\phi} \frac{d_{ci}^2}{d_{li}^2} \right)^{-1} \left(1 + \frac{\phi}{2\lambda} \right) - \frac{1}{2\lambda} \le 0 \right\}. \tag{21}$$

The updating rule for cluster centers are derived from necessary condition $\partial L_{fcm}^{sq}/\partial b_c = \mathbf{0}$ as

$$b_c = \frac{\sum_{i=1}^{n} (u_{ci} + \lambda u_{ci}^2) x_i}{\sum_{i=1}^{n} (u_{ci} + \lambda u_{ci}^2)}. \tag{22}$$

3.3   Comparison of Non-linear Weights

Here, the characteristics of the proposed non-linear weights are discussed by comparing the weight functions shown in Fig. 1. $f(x) = x$ is the weight function of the hard c-Means clustering, in which the membership values are given by solving linear programming problems. $f(x) = x^2$ is the weight function of the standard FCM clustering, in which weighting exponent θ is often set to be 2.0. The coefficients in the proposed methods are set to be 1.0 for entropy terms and 5.0 for quadratic terms. It can be said that the weight function with quadratic terms is similar to that of the standard FCM clustering, and they derive the same clustering results with $\lambda \to \infty$. On the other hand, the weight function with entropy terms has a different type of curve, in which the minimum value is negative. Therefore, the fuzzification technique allows classification function not to have $u_c = 1$ on cluster center because the memberships of the data points that are far from a cluster center have positive values in the cluster.

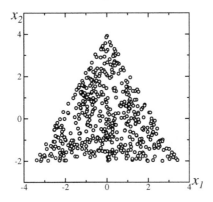

Fig. 2. Artificial data set

4   Numerical Experiments

This section shows the results of numerical experiments for comparing the characteristic features of the proposed fuzzification methods with the conventional algorithms. The experiments were performed by using an artificial data set consisting of 500 samples with 2-D observations. Figure 2 shows the 2-D plots of the data set. The data set was partitioned into 4 clusters using the FCM algorithm with various fuzzification techniques.

The derived fuzzy classification functions are shown in Figs. 3-6, in which the gray scale shows the maximum membership value, i.e., the membership degree belonging to the nearest cluster center ($\circ$). Figure 3 represents that the standard FCM algorithm assigns the maximum membership value ($u_c = 1$) on the cluster centers and the value moves toward $1/C$ as $||\boldsymbol{x}|| \to \infty$. Figure 4 shows the feature of the regularized FCM algorithm, e.g., because u_c does not have the maximum value ($u_c = 1$) on the cluster center, the center cluster ($c = 1$) has no area where $u_c = 1$. A remarkable feature of the regularized methods is that u_c moves toward 1 as $||\boldsymbol{x}|| \to \infty$. So, large memberships are often assigned to the data points that are far from the centroid of the whole data set.

The results of the proposed fuzzification methods are shown in Figs. 5 and 6. These figures indicate that the parameter λ tunes the degree of fuzziness. The larger the λ, the fuzzier the memberships. λ works as the fuzzification parameter and can be called the "fuzzifier". The features of the memberships derived by the proposed techniques are summarized as follows: While the maximum value of membership ($u_c = 1$) is not assigned on the cluster centers, u_c moves toward $1/C$ as $||\boldsymbol{x}|| \to \infty$. In this sense, the proposed techniques are hybrid versions of the standard FCM algorithm and the regularized FCM algorithms.

Especially, the proposed fuzzification method using entropy term performs not only attraction of data to clusters but also repulsion between different clusters. Table 1 shows the comparison of cluster centers derived by the hard c-

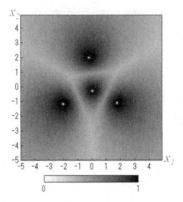

Fig. 3. Fuzzy classification function by standard FCM (FCM^s) with $\theta = 2.0$

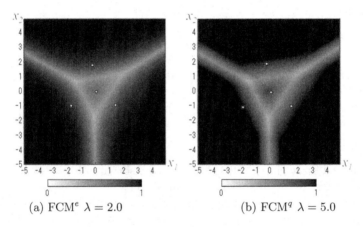

(a) FCM^e $\lambda = 2.0$ (b) FCM^q $\lambda = 5.0$

Fig. 4. Fuzzy classification function by FCM with regularized methods (entropy regularization: FCM^e, quadratic regularization: FCM^q)

Means algorithm and various fuzzification techniques. The distances between cluster centers derived by FCM^{se} is larger than those of other techniques. It is because, in Eq.(16), the weight of each data point $(u_{ci} + \lambda u_{ci} \log u_{ci})$ can be negative when u_{ci} is small. If the weight is negative, the cluster center moves far away from the data point. In this way, the new fuzzification technique makes it possible to derive a different type of fuzzy partition.

5 Conclusion

This paper proposed a new approach to fuzzification of memberships in cluster analysis. The new approach can be regarded as a hybrid of the standard FCM algorithm and the regularized FCM algorithm. Numerical experiments revealed

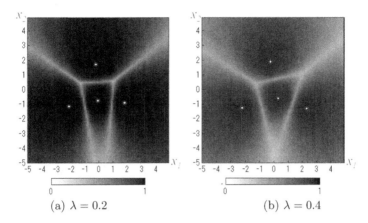

(a) $\lambda = 0.2$ (b) $\lambda = 0.4$

Fig. 5. Fuzzy classification function by proposed method using entropy term (FCM^{se})

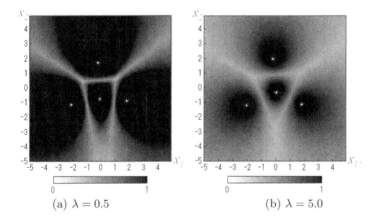

(a) $\lambda = 0.5$ (b) $\lambda = 5.0$

Fig. 6. Fuzzy classification function by proposed method using quadratic term (FCM^{sq})

that the fuzzy classification function derived by the proposed method has several features of conventional ones. One of the proposed techniques has a new feature of repulsion between different clusters that may be used for avoiding trivial solutions in possibilistic clustering [7]. Future work includes extension of the proposed techniques to possibilistic clustering [8]. Another potential extension is to combine the standard FCM algorithm with other regularization techniques such as regularization by K-L information [9] or fuzzy entropy [10], which have been compared with the EM algorithm for probabilistic mixture models [11] or other statistical models.

Table 1. Comparison of cluster centers

	$c = 1$		$c = 2$		$c = 3$		$c = 4$	
	x_1	x_2	x_1	x_2	x_1	x_2	x_1	x_2
c-Means	0.08	-0.59	-0.17	1.78	-2.05	-1.10	1.92	-0.93
$FCM^s(\theta = 2.0)$	0.09	-0.23	-0.16	2.05	-1.99	-1.14	1.83	-1.06
$FCM^e(\lambda = 2.0)$	0.13	-0.02	-0.14	1.81	-1.64	-0.97	1.47	-0.92
$FCM^q(\lambda = 5.0)$	0.13	-0.05	-0.17	1.91	-1.82	-1.07	1.56	-0.99
$FCM^{se}(\lambda = 0.2)$	-0.02	-0.71	-0.16	1.77	-2.09	-1.10	1.88	-0.86
$FCM^{se}(\lambda = 0.4)$	**0.32**	**-0.55**	**-0.22**	**1.94**	**-2.20**	**-1.21**	**2.34**	**-1.25**
$FCM^{sq}(\lambda = 0.5)$	-0.02	-0.71	-0.17	1.77	-2.09	-1.10	1.87	-0.85
$FCM^{sq}(\lambda = 5.0)$	0.07	-0.26	-0.16	2.05	-2.02	-1.15	1.87	-1.07

References

1. MacQueen, J.B.: Some Methods of Classification and Analysis of Multivariate Observations. Proc. 5th Berkeley Symposium on Math. Stat. and Prob. (1967) 281–297
2. Bezdek, J.C.: Pattern Recognition with Fuzzy Objective Function Algorithms. Plenum Press (1981)
3. Miyamoto, S., Mukaidono, M.: Fuzzy c-Means as a Regularization and Maximum Entropy Approach. Proc. 7th Int. Fuzzy Syst. Assoc. World Cong. **2** (1997) 86–92
4. Miyamoto, S., Umayahara, K.: Fuzzy Clustering by Quadratic Regularization. Proc. 1998 IEEE Int. Conf. Fuzzy Syst. (1998) 1394–1399
5. Höppner, F., Klawonn, F., Kruse, R., Runkler, T.: Fuzzy Cluster Analysis, Jhon Wiley & Sons (1999)
6. Liu, Z.-Q., Miyamoto S. (eds.): Soft computing and Human-Centered Machines, Springer-Verlag (2000)
7. Timm, H., Kruse, R.: A Modification to Improve Possibilistic Fuzzy Cluster Analysis. Proc. 2002 IEEE Int. Conf. Fuzzy Syst. (2002) 1460–1465
8. Krishnapuram, R., M. Keller, J.: A Possibilistic Approach to Clustering. IEEE Trans. Fuzzy Syst. **1** (1993) 98–110
9. Ichihashi, H., Miyagishi, K., Honda, K.: Fuzzy c-Means Clustering with Regularization by K-L Information. Proc. 2001 IEEE Int. Conf. Fuzzy Syst. (2001) 924–927
10. Yasuda, M., Furuhashi, T., Matsuzaki, M., Okuma, S.: Fuzzy Clustering Using Deterministic Annealing Method and Its Statistical Mechanical Characteristics. Proc. 2001 IEEE Int. Conf. Fuzzy Syst. (2001)
11. Honda, K., Ichihashi, H.: Regularized Linear Fuzzy Clustering and Probabilistic PCA Mixture Models. IEEE Trans. Fuzzy Syst. (2005) (in press)

Dynamic Clustering Based on Universal Gravitation Model

Yasunori Endo[1] and Hayato Iwata[2]

[1] Faculty of Systems and Information Engineering, University of Tsukuba
1-1-1 Tennodai, Tsukuba, Ibaraki, 305-8573 Japan
endo@risk.tsukuba.ac.jp
[2] KOEI Co., Ltd.
1-18-12, Minowa-cho, Kohoku-ku, Yokohama, 223-8503 Japan

Abstract. Hard/fuzzy c-means and agglomerative hierarchical method are famous and useful clustering algorithms. The former are algorithms using "global information of data", the latter is one using "local information of data". One of main results in this paper is proposal for new clustering algorithm (Dynamic Clustering; DC), which has the advantage of them.

In DC, clusters are updated by some model introduced in advance. That is, the clusters are moved according to the model, and merged. Here, merging two clusters means that two clusters contact each other. The model is called option of DC. In this paper, two options of DC are proposed, *i.e.*, interaction power model(IP) and unit weight model(UW). Moreover, the way to determine sampling time, which is one of the parameters in DC, is discussed for precise merging of data and shortening of calculation time. Furthermore, through numerical examples, it is shown that DC gives good classification for the data which is difficult to be classified by the former clustering algorithms.

1 Introduction

Clustering is a method to classify the objects into some groups by using similarity (or dissimilarity) defined between them. In clustering, no test data is used so that it belongs to unsupervised classification.

Hard/fuzzy c-means [1, 2] and agglomerative hierarchical method [2] are famous and useful clustering algorithms. In hard/fuzzy c-means, the representative point of each cluster is defined such that the sum of dissimilarities between each data and the representative point of clusters is the smallest. Each data belongs to the cluster that the dissimilarity between the data is the smallest of all clusters.

On the other hand, each data is regarded as a cluster in the agglomerative hierarchical method. The pair of the two clusters that the similarity is the biggest of all pairs is merged one by one.

The difference between these methods are as follows:

- In hard/fuzzy c-means, the clustering result depends on the "global" distribution state greatly. For example, it is hard to get the good classification

V. Torra et al. (Eds.): MDAI 2005, LNAI 3558, pp. 183–193, 2005.

of the data set such that some clusters are surrounded by the other cluster. On the other hand, the clustering result is not affected greatly by loss of data information. That is, there is generally almost no difference between the clustering result for the data set in which some data are removed and the complete set. From the above, we can say that hard/fuzzy c-means is "the clustering using global information of data sets".

- In agglomerative hierarchical method, we only use neighborhood of cluster so that the results of clustering don't depend on the distribution state greatly. However, loss of data information influences the classification and the clustering result is often influenced by the small change of data sets. From the above, we can say that the agglomerative hierarchical method is "the clustering using local information of data sets".

In this paper, we call these two methods static clustering. Static clustering is effective for various type of data but it is known that there is data set that it is hard to classify. For example, there are some errors in the clustering result of Fig.7 by fuzzy c-means (FCM) [1, 2]. Then, it is desirable to construct a clustering algorithm with the advantages of both of hard/fuzzy c-means and the agglomerative hierarchical method and in which the disadvantages of the both are solved.

Since, we propose a framework of dynamic clustering (DC) and some options of it in this paper. This clustering is based on the gravitation power model.

In the case that some objects are in the space, each object receives the universal gravitation power from the others, moves, and finally, they should make some flocks. From the viewpoint of clustering, this state means that data set makes the subsets. The universal gravitation power occurs all objects so that it can be regarded as the global information of the distribution state. That is, by introducing the concept of the universal gravitation model to the data space, we can construct a new clustering algorithm which treats the global information of data set by making the data move based on the introduced model and merge the close data each other.

We verify the availability of the proposed algorithm through numerical examples.

2   Dynamic Clustering Algorithm

2.1   Proposed Algorithm

In the universal gravitation model, a object receives the power from all the others and moves in the space. We regard the objects as the data to be classified and assume that the cluster C_i ($M(C_i)$ is the representative point of C_i) receives the power f_{ij} from the cluster C_j ($M(C_j)$ is the representative point of C_j). In Fig. 1, we illustrate that C_1 receives the power f_{12}, f_{13}, f_{14} from the other clusters. Finally F_1 in Fig. 1 means the resultant force.

Under the assumptions, we can regard the distance between the objects as dissimilarity, and the approach or collision of the objects as merging clusters.

In this paragraph, we propose a new clustering algorithm, dynamic clustering (DC). Basic flow of DC is as follows:

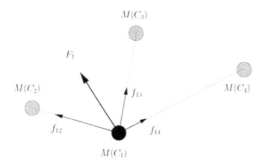

Fig. 1. Interaction power which C_i receives

1. Each data is assigned to the representative point of each cluster. One model is introduced in data space.
2. All point is moved by using the introduced model in the sampling time Δt.
3. If a representative point of a cluster collides with another one, these clusters are merged.

The above procedure is repeated until the number of clusters reaches the target cluster number. It can be said that the procedure changes neighborhood system of clusters of "local information" by using the interaction power between data of "global information". In this algorithm, the similarity is used for updating coordinates of the representative points of clusters, just as acceleration in physics.

We should consider two notes. The first note is determination of the value Δt. The longer Δt is, the worse the accuracy of calculation becomes. On the other hand, the less Δt is, the longer the calculation time becomes. The second note is about colliding two representative points. In general, two points don't collide perfectly and pass each other. For avoiding the situation, we set up a threshold Δx. If the distance of two representative points is less than Δx, it is considered that the two points collide.

Here, we show the framework of DC as follows.

Algorithm 1 (Framework of DC)

Let data set, target cluster number, family of sets of clusters, the representative point of the cluster C_k and the velocity vector of the cluster C_k be $X = \{x_1, x_2, \ldots, x_n\} \subset \Re^\lambda$, c, $\mathcal{C} = \{C_l\}$ $(l = 1, \ldots, |\mathcal{C}|)$, $c_k \in \Re^\lambda$ and $v_k \in \Re^\lambda$, respectively.

Step. 1 *Determine parameters and initialize variables as follows:*

$$C_k := \{x_k\} \ (k = 1, \ldots, n)$$
$$M^{(0)}(C_k) := x_k$$
$$|C_k| := 1$$
$$v_k^{(0)} := 0$$
$$l := 0$$

Merge initial clusters C_k according to Algorithm 2.

Step. 2 *According to the applied model, calculate the acceleration $a_k^{(l)}$ of the cluster C_k.*

Step. 3 *Update the representative point $M^{(l+1)}(C_k)$ ($k = 1, \ldots, |\mathcal{C}|$) as follows:*

$$M^{(l+1)}(C_k) := M^{(l)}(C_k) + v_k^{(l)} \cdot \Delta t \tag{1}$$

Step. 4 *Merge clusters according to Algorithm 2. If $|\mathcal{C}| \neq c$, DC is finished.*

Step. 5 *Update the velocity v_k as follows:*

$$v_k^{(l+1)} := a_k^{(l)} \cdot \Delta t \tag{2}$$

Go back to Step. 2 *with $l := l + 1$.* ∎

In the next place, we describe Algorithm 2 to merge clusters in Step.4 of Algorithm 1. The basic procedure is to merge all the pairs of clusters that the similarity is smaller than the threshold Δx. The operation corresponds with nearest neighbor method (NN) with the merging level less than Δx.

Algorithm 2 (Merging Clusters)

Step. 1 *Calculate the dissimilarity $d(C_r, C_q)$. In this paper, $d(C_r, C_q) = \|M(C_r) - M(C_q)\|^2$.*

Step. 2 *If $d(C_q, C_r) = \min_{i,j} d(C_i, C_j) > \Delta x$, go to* Step. 4, *else merge $C' = C_q \cup C_r$, add C' to $\mathcal{C}$ and delete C_q, C_r from $\mathcal{C}$.*

Step. 3 *If $|\mathcal{C}| \neq c$,*

$$d(C', C_i) = \min(d(C_q, D_i), d(C_r, C_i)) \tag{3}$$

for all $C_i \in \mathcal{C}$ ($C_i \neq C'$), go back to Step. 2.

Step. 4 *If there are new clusters by merging, update the representative points of new clusters. In case that clusters $C_{i_1}, \ldots, C_{i_s}$ are merged into C', i.e., $C' = \{C_{i_1} \cup \cdots \cup C_{i_s}\}$, the representative point $M(C')$ of C' is updated by the following equation:*

$$M(C') = \frac{\sum_{C_j \in B} |C_j| M(C_j)}{\sum_{C_j \in B} |C_j|} \tag{4}$$

Here, $B = \{C_{i_1}, \ldots, C_{i_s}\}$. ∎

When $C_{i_1}, C_{i_2} \ldots C_{i_s}$ are merged, the representative point of new cluster C' is defined as follows

$$M(C') = \frac{\sum_{C_j \in B} |C_j| M(C_j)}{\sum_{C_j \in B} |C_j|} \tag{5}$$

$$B = \{C_{i_1}, C_{i_2}, \ldots, C_{i_s}\} \tag{6}$$

Here, we mention initializing the velocity. In Step. 5 of Algorithm 1, the velocity since then is ignored and new one is afresh calculated in Eq.(2). The reason is to prevent divergence of the representative points by increase of velocity.

From the above-mentioned, the proposed algorithm characterizes data distribution by interaction power and apply NN under the condition that the merged level is less than Δx. In the case that Δx is given as the maximum value of the dissimilarity in the initial distribution, the action of the proposed algorithm corresponds with NN.

2.2 Dynamic Determination of Sampling Time

In the process of DC, the cluster which should be merged is not frequently merged when the velocity increase extremely. This depends on the value of sampling time Δt. In this paragraph, we show the solution of this problem.

We think that Δt should be determined by considering distribution of clusters in order to solve the problem. In the the first place, we show new algorithm DC' as follows, which is the revision of DC.

Algorithm 3 (DC')

Let data set, target cluster number, family of sets of clusters, the representative point of the cluster C_k and the velocity vector of the cluster C_k be $X = \{x_1, x_2, \ldots, x_n\} \subset \Re^\lambda$, c, $\mathcal{C} = \{C_k\}$ $(k = 1, \ldots, |\mathcal{C}|)$, $c_k \in \Re^\lambda$ and $v_k \in \Re^\lambda$, respectively.

Step. 1 *Determine parameters and initialize variables as follows:*

$$C_k := \{x_k\} \ (k = 1, \ldots, n)$$
$$M^{(0)}(C_k) := x_k$$
$$|C_k| := 1$$
$$v_k^{(0)} := 0$$
$$l := 0$$

Merge initial clusters C_k according to Algorithm 2.

Step. 2 *According to the applied model, calculate the acceleration $a_k^{(l)}$ of the cluster C_k.*

Step. 3 *Update the representative point $M^{(l+1)}(C_k)$ $(k = 1, \ldots, |\mathcal{C}|)$ as follows:*

$$M^{(l+1)}(C_k) := M^{(l)}(C_k) + v_k^{(l)} \cdot \Delta t^{(l)} \tag{7}$$

Step. 4 *Merge clusters according to Algorithm 2. If $|\mathcal{C}| \neq c$, DC' is finished.*

Step. 5 *Update the velocity $v_k^{(l+1)}$ as follows:*

$$v_k^{(l+1)} := a_k^{(l)} \cdot \Delta t^{(l)} \tag{8}$$

Step. 6 *Calculate $\Delta t^{(l+1)}$ and go back to Step. 2 with $l := l + 1$.*   ■

The difference between DC and DC' is calculation of $\Delta t^{(l+1)}$ in Step. 6 of the above algorithm.

In the next place, we show the method to update Δt in Step. 6 of the algorithm. In the first place, we think the following condition:

$$\max_{i,j \ i\neq j} (\|v_{ij}^{(l)}\|)\Delta t^{(l)} \leq \min_{i,j \ i\neq j} \|M^{(l)}(C_i) - M^{(l)}(C_j)\| \tag{9}$$

This is the sufficient condition for Δt to prevent to pass the representative point each other.

$$v_{ij}^{(l)} = v_j^{(l)} - v_i^{(l)} \tag{10}$$

Here, $v_{ij}^{(l)}$ is the relative velocity. From Eq. (9), we get

$$\Delta t^{(l)} \leq \sqrt{\frac{\min_{i,j \in I, i \neq j} \| M^{(l)}(C_i) - M^{(l)}(C_j) \|}{\max_{i \in I} \| v_{ij}^{(l)} \|}} \tag{11}$$

Hence, we can prevent to pass the representative point each other by determining Δt in Step. 6 of Algorithm 3 as follows:

$$\Delta t = \alpha \sqrt{\frac{\min_{i,j \in I, i \neq j} \| M(C_i) - M(C_j) \|}{\max_{i \in I} \| v_{ij}^{(l)} \|}} \tag{12}$$

Here, $0 < \alpha < 1$. α influences results of clustering.

3   Options of Dynamic Clustering

In this section, we show two options of DC, interaction power model and unit weight one.

3.1   Interaction Power Model

We assume that mass of the point $x_i \in \Re^\lambda$ and $x_j \in \Re^\lambda$ are m_i and m_j, respectively. The vector F_{ij} of the universal gravitation between x_i and x_j is represented as follows:

$$F_{ij} = G \frac{m_i m_j (x_j - x_i)}{\| x_j - x_i \|^3} \tag{13}$$

Here, G is the universal gravitation constant.

In general, we define the similarity s_{ij} between x_i and x_j when we classify a set $\{x_i\}$ into some subsets. The similarity represents the strength of the relation between these points and satisfy the following conditions generally.

Condition 1 (Similarity)

1. $s_{ij} \geq 0$
2. $s_{ij} = s_{ji}$
3. $\| x_i - x_j \| \leq \| x_i - x_k \| \iff s_{ij} \geq s_{ik}$ ∎

From this standpoint, the norm of the universal gravitation can be regarded as one of the similarities. Because we can know that the norm $\| F_{ij} \| = G \frac{m_i m_j}{\| x_j - x_i \|^2}$ is directly proportional to the reciprocal number of the square of the distance between x_i and x_j, so that $\| F_{ij} \|$ satisfy the above conditions.

Then, we propose a similarity based on the universal gravitation. Let representative points of clusters C_i and C_j be $M(C_i)$ and $M(C_j)$, respectively. We define the interaction power between these clusters as follows:

$$f_{ij} = G \frac{|C_i||C_j|}{\| M(C_j) - M(C_i) \|_p^q} \cdot s_{ij} \tag{14}$$

Here, $|C_i|$ and $|C_j|$ mean the numbers of the clusters. We regard them as the mass of the cluster. Moreover s_{ij} is the unit vector from C_i to C_j, that is,

$$s_{ij} = \frac{M(C_j) - M(C_i)}{\|M(C_j) - M(C_i)\|_2} \tag{15}$$

$\|M(C_j) - M(C_i)\|_p$ is shown as following equation.

$$\|M(C_j) - M(C_i)\|_p = (\sum_{l=1}^{\lambda} \|M_l(C_j) - M_l(C_i)\|^p)^{\frac{1}{p}} \tag{16}$$

Here, the resultant force which C_i receives is shown as follows:

$$f_i = \sum_{j=1(j\neq i)}^{|C|} f_{ij} \tag{17}$$

It is not necessary that the similarity is exactly same as the universal gravitation and it is sufficient that the similarity satisfy the above conditions. Hence, we can introduce the parameter q instead of 2 to give proposed algorithm flexibility. In this case, the norm of the interaction power $\|f_{ij}\|$ is represented as $G\frac{|C_i||C_j|}{\|M(C_j)-M(C_i)\|_p^q}$.

We illustrate the relation of the parameter q and the norm $\|f_{ij}\|$ in Fig. 2.

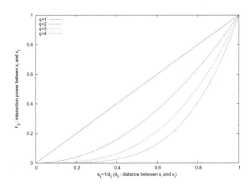

Fig. 2. Interaction power

We call DC' introduced this model DC'-Interaction Power (DC'-IP). In this case, Eq. (2) can be re-written as follows:

$$v_i := a_i \Delta t$$

$$= G \sum_{j=1 \ (j\neq i)}^{|C|} \frac{|C_j|}{\|M(C_j) - M(C_i)\|_p^q} \cdot \Delta t \cdot s_{ij} \tag{18}$$

from

$$a_i = \frac{f_i}{|C_i|}$$

$$= G \sum_{\substack{j=1 \ (j \neq i)}}^{|\mathcal{C}|} \frac{|C_j|}{\|M(C_j) - M(C_i)\|_p^q} \cdot s_{ij} \tag{19}$$

3.2   Unit Weight Model

In unit weight model, the mass of the clusters is ignored, that is,

$$f_{ij} = \frac{1}{\|M(C_j) - M(C_i)\|_p^q} s_{ij} \tag{20}$$

From this equation, we get a_k as follows.

$$a_i = \sum_{\substack{j=1 \ (j \neq i)}}^{1} \frac{1}{\|M(C_j) - M(C_i)\|_p^q} s_{ij} \tag{21}$$

We call DC' introduced this model DC'-Unit Weight (DC'-UW). In this case, Eq. (2) can be re-written as follows:

$$v_i := a_i \Delta t$$

$$= \sum_{\substack{j=1 \ (j \neq i)}}^{|\mathcal{C}|} \frac{1}{\|M(C_j) - M(C_i)\|_p^q} \cdot \Delta t \cdot s_{ij} \tag{22}$$

4   Numerical Examples

4.1   Example Data

We use six data sets (from Fig. 3 to Fig. 8). These data sets contain the characters that it is hard to classify by the former clustering algorithms. The character of each data set is as follows:

- Data 1 : Two clusters intersect orthogonally each other. (Fig. 3)
- Data 2 : Large cluster is close to small cluster. (Fig. 4)
- Data 3 : Line-type cluster is next to oval-type cluster. (Fig. 5)
- Data 4 : Line-type cluster is between two oval-type clusters. (Fig. 6)
- Data 5 : The cluster is surrounded by other two clusters. (Fig. 7)
- Data 6 : The cluster is surrounded by other four clusters. (Fig. 8)

These data sets are classified by FCM, NN method, Ward method, and DC'-UWDC'-IP. The specification of the computer is as follows: OS: RedHat Linux 9.0, CPU: Celeron 700 MHz, Memory: 512 MB.

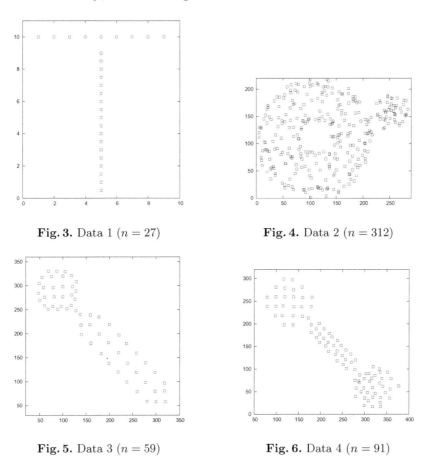

Fig. 3. Data 1 $(n = 27)$

Fig. 4. Data 2 $(n = 312)$

Fig. 5. Data 3 $(n = 59)$

Fig. 6. Data 4 $(n = 91)$

4.2   Consideration

Table 1 shows the numbers of classification errors of each algorithm. The parameters of DC'-IP and DC'-UW are shown in Table 2 and Table 3.

From Table 1, the classifications of DC'-IP, DC'-UW don't have most errors, on the other hand, the results of the other static algorithms have many errors. Especially, although DC' contains the processing of NN, the number of errors of DC' is more greatly smaller than that of NN. From the results, we can say that it is effective to consider both "local information" and "global information".

Moreover, introducing the dynamic determination of sampling time in the above section reduces the calculation time. Table 4 shows the calculation time of Data 1 and Data 3.

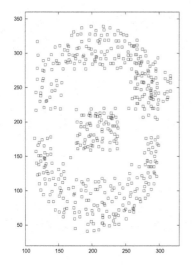

Fig. 7. Data 5 ($n = 509$)   **Fig. 8.** Data 6 ($n = 249$)

Table 1. Number of error about each data set

	Data 1	Data 2	Data 3	Data 4	Data 5	Data 6
FCM	6	93	6	0	59	62
NN method	8	46	21	66	75	249
Ward method	10	99	0	0	144	68
DC-IP	0	0	0	0	0	0
DC-UW	0	0	0	0	0	12

Table 2. The parameters of DC'-IP

	Data 1	Data 2	Data 3	Data 4	Data 5	Data 6
Δx	0.5	5.0				
p	2.0					
q	$1.0 \sim 4.0$	$1.0 \sim 4.0$	4.0	$3.0 \sim 4.0$	3.0	$2.0 \sim 3.0$
G	10.0					
α	0.5					

Table 3. The parameters of DC'-UW

	Data 1	Data 2	Data 3	Data 4	Data 5	Data 6
Δx	0.5	5.0				
p	2.0					
q	$1.0 \sim 4.0$	$1.0 \sim 4.0$	1.0, 3.0	$1.0 \sim 4.0$	1.0	2.0
α	0.5					

Table 4. Calculation time without/with dynamic determination of sampling time

	Data 1	Data 3
without	0.121 sec	1.454 sec
with	0.011 sec	0.952 sec

5 Conclusion

In this paper, we proposed dynamic clustering and its options (DC-IP, DC-UW). From the numerical examples, we inspected that DC is effective for some data set that it is hard for other former algorithm to classify.

However, there are some problems. One of the problems is that the calculation time of DC is much larger than that of the other algorithms. Also, another is that there is no method how to decide the parameters.

About the former, we have tried to apply Particle-Particle, Particle-Cell method [4] to DC [5]. The latter will be discussed in the forthcoming paper.

References

1. J. C. Bezdec: 'Pattern Recognition with Fuzzy Objective Function Algorithms', Plenum, New York(1978).
2. Miyamoto, S.: 'Introduction of Cluster Analysis', Morikita Shuppan (1999) (in Japanese).
3. Iwata, H. and Endo, Y.: "Dynamic Clustering Using Interaction Power between Data", Proc. of Second Rough Set Workshop, pp.59–62 (2003) (in Japanese).
4. M. Saito : "Molecular Dynamic Simulations of Proteins in Water without the Truncation of Longrange Coulomb Interactions" Trans.of Molecular Simulation,Vol8, pp.321–333 (1992)
5. Ide, Y. and Endo, Y.: "High-speed Computation of Dynamic Clustering Algorithm" Institute of Electronics,Information and Communication Engineers, p.248 (2004)(in Japanese).
6. Watanabe, K.: 'Recognition and Pattern', Iwanami Shinsho, (1978) (in Japanese).

Extracting Classification Rules
with Support Rough Neural Networks

He Ming and Feng Boqin

Department of Computer Science and Technology
Xi'an Jiaotong University, Xi'an, 710049, China
ming_he1314@sina.com

Abstract. Classification is an important theme in data mining. Rough sets and neural networks are two technologies frequently applied to data mining tasks. Integrating the advantages of two approaches, this paper presents a hybrid system to extract efficiently classification rules from a decision table. The neural network system and rough set theory are completely integrated to into a hybrid system and use cooperatively for classification support. Through rough set approach a decision table is first reduced by removing redundant attributes without any classification information loss. Then a rough neural network is trained to extract the rules set form the reduced decision table. Finally, classification rules are generated from the reduced decision table by rough neural network. In addition, a new algorithm of finding a reduct and a new algorithm of rule generation from a decision table are also proposed. The effectiveness of our approach is verified by the experiments comparing with traditional rough set approach.

1 Introduction

One important issue of data mining is classification attracting great attentions by researchers [1]. Rough sets and neural networks are two technologies frequently applied to data mining tasks [2,3]. The common advantage of the two approaches is that they do not need any additional information about data like probability in statistics or grade of membership in fuzzy set theory [4,5].

Neural networks are considered the most powerful classifier for their low classification error rates and robustness to noise. However, neural networks have two obvious disadvantages when applied to data mining problems [8,9]. The first is that neural networks require long time to train the huge amount of data of large databases. Secondly, neural networks do not provide us with a clear interpretation of knowledge it contains. The knowledge of neural networks is buried in their structures and weights. It is often difficult to extract rules from a trained neural network.

Rough set theory introduced by Pawlak in 1982 is a mathematical tool to deal with vagueness and uncertainty of information [6]. It has been proved to be very effective in many practical applications. However, in rough set theory, the deterministic mechanism for the description of error is very simple [7]. Therefore, using sorting rules developed by rough sets may lead to a burdensome situation where a new case does not match any of the sorting or classification rules.

The combination of rough sets and neural networks is very natural for their complementary features. One of the application methods combining the rough set theory and neural networks is to incorporate rough set methods into construction of the neu-

V. Torra et al. (Eds.): MDAI 2005, LNAI 3558, pp. 194–202, 2005.

ral networks by using so called rough neurons. Each rough neuron stores the upper and lower bounds of the input and output values. Depending on the nature of the application, two rough neurons in the network can be connected to each other using either two or four connections. A rough neuron can also be connected to a conventional neuron using two connections. A rough neural network consists of a combination of rough and conventional neurons connected each other [10]. More recent work considers rough neural networks with neurons, which construct rough set and output the degree of accuracy of approximation [11].Purely rough membership function neural networks were introduced by Peters et al. in 2000[12] in the context of rough set and rough membership function [13]. The design of rough neural networks based on rough membership function was introduced by Peters et al. in 2001 [14].

This paper uses rough patterns for classification using neural networks. Each value in a rough pattern is a pair of upper and lower bound. Conventional neural network models generally use a precise input pattern in their estimations. In this paper, the conventional neural network models are modified to accommodate rough patterns. Rough neurons used in this paper provide an ability to use rough patterns. The composite models of rough set components and neural network, which take advantage of each method's generic characteristics, were constructed to extract classification rules from large databases. Rough set approach, by which redundant attributes in multi-attribute information system can be removed without any information loss, is utilized as a preprocessor to improve prediction capability by neural network. The stream-lined information system by rough set approach is fed into neural network for training. At the prediction step, we apply the rules developed by rough sets first, and then we apply the neural network to the objects that does not match any of the rules. The effectiveness of our hybrid approach was verified with experiments that compared traditional discriminant analysis and neural network approach with the hybrid approach.

This paper is organized as follows. Section 2 briefly describes basic notions of rough set theory and some relevant techniques. Basic concepts of rough neural network and some relevant techniques are introduced in section 3. In Section 4, a hybrid system and the algorithms to generate classification rules from decision table are proposed. In Section 5, some experimental results are presented and analyzed, and conclusions in Section 6.

2 Basic Concepts of Rough Set

Formally, an information system is a 4-tuple $S=<U,A,V,f>$, where U is a is a finite set of objects, called the universe, A is a finite set of attributes, $V=\bigcup_{a\in A} V_a$ is a domain of attribute a, and $f:U\times A\to V$ is called an information function such that $f(x,a)\in V_a$, for $\forall a\in A, \forall x\in U$.

In the classification problems, an information system S is also seen as a decision table assuming that $A=C\cup D$ and $C\cap D=\varnothing$, where C is a set of condition attributes and D is a set of decision attributes.

Let $S=<U,A,V,f>$ be an information system, every $B\subseteq A$ generates an indiscernibility relation $IND(B)$ on U, which is defined as follows:

$$IND(B)= \{(x, y)\,|\,(x,y){\in}U^{2},(f(x,a){=}f(y,a),\forall a{\in}B\}\,.$$

$U/IND(B)=\{C_1, C_2, \ldots,C_K\}$ is a partition of U by B, every C_i is an equivalence class. For every $x\in U$, the equivalence class of x in relation $U/IND(B)$ is defined as follows:

$$[x]_{IND(B)}=\{y{\in}U:f(y,a)=f(x,a),\forall a{\in}B\}\,.$$

Let $B\subseteq A, X \subseteq U$. The B-lower approximation of X (denoted by $B\_(X)$) and B-upper approximation of X(denoted by $B^-(X)$) are defined as follows:

$$B\_(X) = \{y\,|\,y{\in}U \wedge [y]_{IND(B)} \subseteq X\},$$

$$B^-(X) = \{y\,|\,y{\in}U \wedge [y]_{IND(B)} \cap X \neq \varnothing\}.$$

$B\_(X)$ is the set of all objects from U which can be certainly classified as elements of X employing the set of attributes B. $B^-(X)$ is the set of all objects from U which can be possibly classified as elements of X employing the set of attributes B.

Let $P,Q{\in}A$, the positive region of classification $U/IND(Q)$ with respect to the set of attributes P, or in short, P- positive region of Q, is defined as

$$POS_P(Q) = \bigcup_{x{\in}U\,/\,IND(Q)} P\_(X).$$

$POS_P(Q)$ contains all objects in U that can be classified to one class of the classification $U/IND(Q)$ by attributes P. The dependency of Q on P is defined as

$$\gamma_P(Q) = \frac{card(POS_P(Q))}{card(U)}.$$

An attribute a is said to be dispensable in P with respect to Q, if $\gamma_P(Q) = \gamma_{P-\{a\}}(Q)$; otherwise a is an indispensable attribute in P with respect to Q.

Let $S=<U, C\cup D,V,f>$ be a decision table, the set of attributes $P(P{\subseteq}C)$ is a reduct of attributes C, which satisfies the following conditions:

$$\gamma_P(D)=\gamma_C(D) \text{ and } \gamma_P(D){\neq}\gamma_{P'}(D),\ \forall P'{\subset}P.$$

A reduct of condition attributes C is a subset that can discern decision classes with the same discriminating capability as C, and none of the attributes in the reduct can be eliminated without decreasing its discriminating capability.

3   Rough Neural Networks [10]

A rough neural network consists of conventional neurons and rough neurons connected to each other. A rough neuron r in rough neural networks can be viewed as a pair of neurons, one for the upper bound called $\overline{r}$ and the other for the lower bound called $\underline{r}$ .A rough neuron is connected to another rough neuron through two or four connections. Fig. 1 depicts three types of connections between rough neurons. The overlap between the upper and lower neurons indicates that upper and lower neurons exchange information. Two rough neurons in Fig. 1(a) are fully connected. A rough neuron r is said to be fully connected to another rough neuron s, if $\overline{r}$ and $\underline{r}$ are connected to both $\bar{s}$ and $\underline{s}$. If a rough neuron r is fully connected to s, then there are four connections from r to s. In Fig. 1(b) and 1(c), there only two connections from r to s. If the rough neuron r excites the activity of s (i.e. increase in the output of r will result in the increase in the output of s), then r will be connected to s as shown in Fig. 1(b). On the other hand, if r inhibits the activity of s (i.e. increase in the output of r corresponds to the decrease in the output of s), then r will be connected to s as shown in Fig. 1(c).

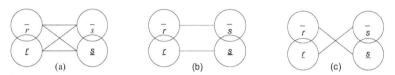

Fig. 1. Three Different Types of Connections between Two Rough Neurons

This paper uses multi-layered, feed-forward, and backpropagation design to describe the methodology of rough neural networks. Rough neural networks used in this study consist of one input layer, one output layer and one hidden layer of rough or conventional neurons. The input layer neurons accept input from the external environment. The outputs from input layer neurons are fed to the hidden layer neurons. The hidden layer neurons feed their output to the output layer neurons which send their output to the external environment. The output of a rough neuron is a pair of upper and lower bounds, while the output of a conventional neuron is a single value.

The input of a conventional, lower, or upper neuron is calculated using the weighted sum as:

$$input_j = \sum \omega_{ij} \times output_i . \tag{1}$$

Where i and j are either the conventional neurons or upper/lower neurons of a rough neuron. If two rough neurons r and s are fully connected as shown in Fig. 1(a), then the input of a rough neuron s is calculated as:

$$input_{\bar{s}} = \sum_i w_{\bar{r}\bar{s}} \times output_{\bar{r}} + w_{\underline{r}\bar{s}} \times output_{\underline{r}} . \tag{2}$$

$$input_{\underline{s}} = \sum_i w_{\underline{r}\underline{s}} \times output_{\underline{r}} + w_{\bar{r}\underline{s}} \times output_{\bar{r}} . \tag{3}$$

Where $w_{\bar{r}\bar{s}}$ and $w_{\bar{r}\underline{s}}$ ($w_{\underline{r}\bar{s}}$ and $w_{\underline{r}\underline{s}}$) are the weights between upper/lower neurons of r and upper/lower neurons of s, respectively.

The output of a rough neuron r is calculated using a transfer function as:

$$Output_{\bar{r}} = \max(f_U(input_{\bar{r}} - \theta_{\bar{r}}), f_L(input_{\underline{r}} - \theta_{\underline{r}})). \tag{4}$$

$$Output_{\underline{r}} = \min(f_U(input_{\bar{r}} - \theta_{\bar{r}}), f_L(input_{\underline{r}} - \theta_{\underline{r}})). \tag{5}$$

Where $\theta_{\bar{r}}$ and $\theta_{\underline{r}}$ are the thresholds of upper and lower neurons of a rough neuron r respectively. In this paper, $\theta_{\bar{r}}$ and $\theta_{\underline{r}}$ are both zero, f_U and f_L are the transfer functions of upper and lower neurons of a rough neuron r respectively. This study uses the sigmoid transfer function given as:

$$f_U(u) = f_L(u) = \frac{1}{1+e^{-gain \times u}}. \qquad (6)$$

Where *gain* is a system parameter determined by the system designer to specify the slope of the sigmoid function around input value of zero. There are several other functions for determining the output from a neuron. The sigmoid transfer function is chosen because it produces a continuous value in the 0 to 1 range.

If two rough neurons are partially connected, then the excitatory or inhibitory nature of the connection is determined dynamically by polling the connection weights. The network designer can make initial assumptions about the excitatory or inhibitory nature of the connections. If a partial connection from a rough neuron r to another rough neuron s is assumed to be excitatory, $w_{\overline{r}\overline{s}} < 0$ and $w_{\underline{r}\underline{s}} < 0$, then the connection from rough neuron r and s is changed from excitatory to inhibitory by assigning $w_{\overline{r}\underline{s}} = w_{\underline{r}\underline{s}}$ and $w_{\overline{r}\underline{s}} = w_{\overline{r}\overline{s}}$. The links $(\underline{r},\underline{s})$ and $(\overline{r},\overline{s})$ are disable while $(\underline{r},\overline{s})$ and $(\overline{r},\underline{s})$ are enabled. On the other hand, if the neuron r is assumed to have an inhibitory partial connection to s and $w_{\overline{r}\underline{s}} > 0$ and $w_{\underline{r}\overline{s}} > 0$, then the connection between rough neuron r and s is changed from inhibitory to excitatory by assigning $w_{\underline{r}\underline{s}} = w_{\overline{r}\underline{s}}$ and $w_{\overline{r}\overline{s}} = w_{\overline{r}\underline{s}}$. The links $(\underline{r},\overline{s})$ and $(\overline{r},\underline{s})$ are disable while links $(\underline{r},\underline{s})$ and $(\overline{r},\overline{s})$ are enabled.

The training and testing stage in the development of a rough neural network is similar to the conventional neural network. During the training stage the network uses inductive learning principle to learn from a set of examples called the training set. In supervised learning, the desired output from output layer neurons for the examples in the training set is known. The network attempts to adjust weights of connections between neurons to produce the desired output. During this process, the error in the output is propagated back from one layer to the previous layer for adjusting weights of the connections.

The weights of the connections are modified iteratively. The network is presented with the training set repeatedly and is allowed to change weights after one (or more) iteration(s). The weights are modified using a learning equation. This study uses the generalized delta rule for modifying the weights of the connections using the following equation:

$$w_{ji}(t+1) = w_{ji}(t) + \alpha \times output_j \times error_i \times f'(input_i). \qquad (7)$$

Where $f'(input_i)$ is the derivative of the transfer function evaluated at $input_i$ and α is the learning parameter which represents the speed of learning. For the sigmoid transfer function used in this study,

$$f'(input_i) = input_i \times (1 - input_i). \qquad (8)$$

The error in equation (7) is calculated as:

$$error_i = desired\_output_i - output_i. \qquad (9)$$

As mentioned before, in the testing stage, the network is tested for another set of examples for which the output from the output layer neurons is known. After the neural net model is tested successfully, it is used for predictions.

4   Hybrid System Development

4.1   The Structure of Hybrid System

The process of our hybrid approach of rough sets and neural networks for mining classification rules is outlined in Fig.2 (We did not show all the possible arrows to indicate that loops can, and do, occur between any two steps in the process), which consists of four major phases:

(1) Data cleaning and preprocessing: includes basic operations, such as removing noise or outliers if appropriate, collecting the necessary information to model or account for noise, deciding on strategies for handling missing values.
(2) Construct decision table: Creating a target information system and focusing on data samples on which discovery is to be performed.
(3) Attribute reduction by rough sets: Using rough set approach, a reduct of condition attributes of decision table is obtained. Then a deduct table is derived from the decision table by removing those attributes that are not in the reduct.
(4) Rules extraction from reduced decision table by rough neural network: Through rough neural network the final knowledge interpreted by a rule set is generated from the reduced decision table.

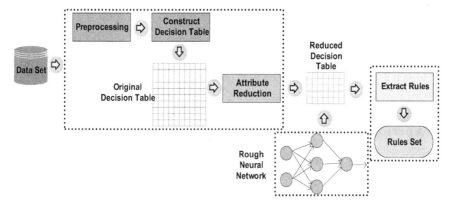

Fig. 2. The process of hybrid approach

4.2   The Algorithm

We develop our algorithms of attribute reduction and rule extraction. Even if the initial number of attributes is very large, using the measure can effectively delete irrelevant and redundant attributes in a relatively short time.

More than one reduct of condition attributes may exist for a decision table. Which is the best one depends on the optimality criterion associated with the attributes. Here we assume that the context of decision table is the only information source. Our objective is to find a reduct with minimal number of attributes. Based on the definition of the binary discernibility matrix, we propose our rough set attribute reduction (RSAR) algorithm of finding a reduct of a decision table, which is outlined below.

RSRA Algorithm

Input: A decision table $S=<U,C\cup\{d\},V,f>$, $U=\{u_1, u_2, ..., u_n\}$, $C=\{c_1, c_2,..., c_m\}$.

Output: A reduct of S, denoted as Redu.

1. Calculate the signification of condition attributes C in S relative to d, denoted as SIG_C;
2. Calculate the core of C relative to d, denoted as *Core*;
3. Let Redu=C;
4. For j=1 to |Redu- *Core*| do
5. For each attribute $c_j \in$ Redu-*Core*, calculate SIG $c_j = \gamma_{Redu}(d) - \gamma_{Redu-c_j}(d)$;
6. If SIG c_j=0 then Redu= Redu-$\{c_j\}$;
7. End for;
8. End.

The General Algorithm

Input: A decision table $S=<U,C\cup\{d\},V,f>$, $U=\{u_1, u_2, ..., u_n\}$, $C=\{c_1, c_2,..., c_m\}$.

Output: A rule set Rule.

1. Apply the RSRA algorithm, get a reduct of S, denote as Redu;
2. Remove the attribute that are not in Redu form S;
3. Construct the rough neural network over the reduced decision table;
4. Apply the rough neural network extract the rule set Rule form the reduced decision table;
5. Do step 4 until there is no change for significantly better result of classification with this network;
6. Do step 2-5 until satisfiable quality is obtained.
7. End.

5   Experiments

We did a series of experiments to generate rules from classification problems that involve real world problems. First, for comparing with traditional approaches, we applied our approach to three standard datasets from the UCI repository [15] that was used in [16].

In this paper, the rule set accuracy and the comprehensibility was used as the criteria of evaluation of the rule extraction approaches [17]. The accuracy of rule set was indicated by the accuracy of the rules generated on the testing set, and the comprehensibility of rule set includes two measures, the number of rules and the average number of conditions of each rule.

5.1   Three UCI Classification Problems

For comparing with traditional rough set based approaches (RS), we applied our approach to three standard datasets from the UCI datasets that was used by [16].Similar to [16], we randomly separate each dataset into two parts: two thirds as training set and the rest one third as testing set. The continuous attributes were also initially discreted using the equal width binding method. We also tested 20 times for each case and present the averages of the results in Table 1. The data of RS columns were given in [16] and they have no standard deviations. We can see that rough neural network (RNN) outperforms RS in accuracy in all three datasets and the rule set of RNN is more concise than that of RS. It is because RNN can filter effectively the noise in the data, which make generated rules more accurate and simpler.

Table 1. Comparison of performance of the rules generated by RN and RS

	Breast		Diabetes		German	
	RS	RNN	RS	RNN	RS	RNN
Average accuracy (%)	92.38	94.00	73.22	74.00	70.48	72.53
Average no. of rules	7.80	5.50	6.00	6.82	4.70	4.41
Average no. of conditions	1.60	2.10	1.50	2.21	1.40	2.27

6 Conclusion

Extracting classification rules is an important task of data mining. In this paper from a new perspective we have presented a hybrid approach integrating rough sets and neural networks to mine classification rules from datasets. Through rough set approach a decision table is first reduced by removing redundant attributes without any classification information loss. Then a rough neural network is trained to extract the rules set form the reduced decision table. Finally, classification rules are generated from the reduced decision table by rough neural network. In addition, a new algorithm of finding a reduct and a new algorithm of rule generation from a decision table were also proposed.

The present hybrid approach was applied to a series of classification problems that involve real world problems. The experimental results comparison with rough set based approach shows that our approach can generate more concise and more accurate rules.

Several related works maybe contribute to the more satisfactory results. First, adding the prior knowledge of attributes to the rough set attribute reduction phase and the neural network feature selection phase may be an affective way. Secondly, more attributes that have very little influence on classification can be removed by rough sets in the rough set attribute reduction phase. It can further relax the burden of neural network training. Finally, integrating with other rule generation techniques, such as decision tree method and genetic algorithm, is also an important issue in future studies.

References

1. Chen, M., Han, J., Yu, P.: Data mining: An overview from a database perspective, IEEE Transactions on Knowledge and Date Engineering 8 (6) (1996) 866–883
2. Bengio,Y., Buhlmann, J., Embrechts, M., Zurada, J.: Introduction to the special issue on neural networks for data mining and knowledge discovery, IEEE Transactions on Neural Networks 11 (3) (2000) 545–549
3. Ziarko,W.: Introduction to the special issue on rough sets and knowledge discovery, Computational Intelligence 11 (2) (1995) 223–226
4. Yahia, M., Mahmod, R., Sulaiman, N., Ahmad, F.: Rough neural expert systems, Expert Systems with Applications 18 (2) (2000) 87–99

5. Phuong, N., Phong, L., Santiprabhob, P., Baets, B.: Approach to generation rules for expert systems using rough set theory, in: IFSA World Congress and 20th NAFIPS International Conference, (2001)877–882
6. Pawlak, Z., Grzymala-Busse, J., Slowinski, R., Ziarko, W.: Rough sets, Communications of the ACM 38 (11) (1995) 88–95
7. Bazan, J., Skowron, A., Synak, P.: Dynamic reducts as a tool for extracting laws from decisions tables, in: Proceedings of the Symposium on Methodologies for Intelligent Systems, (1994)346–355
8. Lu, H., Setiono, R., Liu, H.: Effective data mining using neural networks, IEEE Transactions on Knowledge and Data Engineering 8 (6) (1996) 957–961
9. Craven, M., Shavlik J.: Using neural networks for data mining, Future Generation Computer Systems 13 (1997) 211–229.
10. Lingras, P.J.: Rough neural networks, in: Proceedings of the 6th International Conference on Information Processing and Management of Uncertainty in Knowledge-based Systems (IPMU'96), Granada, Spain, (1996) 1445–1450
11. Peters, J.F., Skowron, A., Han, L., Ramanna, S.: Towards rough neural computing based on rough membership functions: theory and application, in: Ziarko &Yao, Y., Proceedings of the 2nd International Conference on Rough Sets and Current Trends in Computing(RSCTC'2000), (2000)572–579
12. Peters, J.F., Pedrycz, W.: Software Engineering: An Engineering Approach, Wiley, J. & Sons, New York, (2000)
13. Pawlak, Z., Skowron, A.: Rough membership functions, in: Yager, R., Fedrizzi, M., & Kacprzyk, J, Advances in the Dempster-Shafter Theory of Evidence, Wiley, J. & Sons, New York, (1994)251–271
14. Peters, J.F., Han, L., Ramanna, S.: Rough neural computing in signal analysis, Computational Intelligence, 17 (3) (2001)493–513
15. Murphy, P.M., D.W. Aha: UCI repository of machine learning databases, machine-readable data repository, Irvine, CA, University of California, Department of Information and Computer Science, 1992.
16. Swiniarski, R.W., Skowron A.: Rough set methods in feature selection and recognition, Pattern Recognition Letters 24 (2003) 833–849.
17. Chen, X., Zhu, S., Ji, Y.: Entropy based uncertainty measures for classification rules with inconsistency   tolerance, in: Proceedings of the IEEE International Conference on Systems, Man and Cybernetics, (2000), 2816–2821.

On a Tool for Rough Non-deterministic Information Analysis and Its Perspective for Handling Numerical Data

Hiroshi Sakai[1], Tetsuya Murai[2], and Michinori Nakata[3]

[1] Department of Mathematics and Computer Aided Science, Faculty of Engineering
Kyushu Institute of Technology, Tobata, Kitakyushu 804, Japan
sakai@mns.kyutech.ac.jp

[2] Division of Systems and Information Engineering, Graduate School of Engineering
Hokkaido University Kita-ku, Sapporo 060, Japan
murahiko@main.ist.hokudai.ac.jp

[3] Faculty of Management and Information Science, Josai International University
Gumyo, Togane, Chiba 283, Japan
nakatam@ieee.org

Abstract. *Rough Non-deterministic Information Analysis* (*RNIA*) is a framework for handling rough sets based concepts, which are defined in not only *Deterministic Information Systems* (*DISs*) but also *Non-deterministic Information Systems* (*NISs*), on computers. This paper at first reports an overview of a tool for *RNIA*. Then, we enhance the framework of *RNIA* for handling numerical data. Most of *DISs* and *NISs* implicitly consist of categorical data, and multivariate analysis seems to be employed for numerical data. Therefore, it is necessary to investigate rough sets based information analysis for numerical data, too. We introduce numerical patterns into numerical values, and define equivalence relations based on these patterns. Due to this introduction, it is possible to handle the precision of information, namely it is possible to define fine information and coarse information. These fine and coarse concepts cause more flexible information analysis, including rule generation, from numerical data.

1 Introduction

Rough set theory offers a new mathematical approach to vagueness and uncertainty, and the rough sets based concepts have been recognized to be very useful [1,2,3,4]. This theory usually handles tables with deterministic information, which we call *Deterministic Information Systems* (*DISs*). Many applications of this theory to information analysis, data mining, rule generation, machine learning and knowledge discovery have been investigated [5,6,7,8,9,10,11].

Non-deterministic Information Systems (*NISs*) and *Incomplete Information Systems* have been proposed for handling information incompleteness in *DISs* [12,13,14,15,16,17,18]. In [12,13], the necessity of non-deterministic information is shown. In [14,15], Lipski showed a question-answering system besides

V. Torra et al. (Eds.): MDAI 2005, LNAI 3558, pp. 203–214, 2005.

an axiomatization of logic. The relation between rough logic and incomplete information is clarified in [16], and relational algebra with null values is also discussed in [17,18].

For every NIS, we usually suppose that there exists a DIS with unknown real information in a set of all derived $DISs$. Let DIS^{real} denote this deterministic information system from NIS. Of course, it is impossible to know DIS^{real} itself without additional information. However, if a formula α holds in every derived DIS from a NIS, α also holds in DIS^{real}. This formula α is not influenced by the information incompleteness in a NIS. If a formula α holds in some derived $DISs$ from a NIS, there exists such a possibility that α holds in DIS^{real}. We call the former the *certainty* (of the formula α for DIS^{real}) and the latter the *possibility*, respectively. In $NISs$, such two modalities for DIS^{real} have been employed, and several work on logic in $NISs$ has been studied [12,14,15,16].

At first in this paper, we focus on the issues in the following, which occupy the most important part of $RNIA$ [19].

(1) The consistency of an object in $NISs$ and an algorithm for handling it on computers. Furthermore, the manipulation of equivalence relations.
(2) Data dependency in $NISs$ and an algorithm for handling it on computers.
(3) Rules in $NISs$ and an algorithm for handling them on computers.

Then, we cope with $DISs$ with numerical values. In previous $RNIA$, we implicitly supposed that both $DISs$ and $NISs$ consist of only categorical values. As for numerical data, multivariate analysis may be more familiar than rough sets based information analysis. In such situation, we try to extend current $RNIA$ handling only categorical values to new $RNIA$ handling both categorical values and numerical values.

2   Rough Sets Based Information Analysis

Let us see an outline of rough sets based information analysis according to Table 1, which is a part of a table in [2]. Table 1 shows a relation between attributes $Head(ache)$, $Temp(erature)$ and Flu over a set $Patient$ of objects. This table may be too small, but it will be sufficient to know rough sets based concepts.

Table 1. Exemplary deterministic information system

Patient	Head(ache)	Temp(erature)	Flu
p1	no	very_high	yes
p2	yes	very_high	yes
p3	no	normal	no

We identify a tuple with a set of implications, for example
    imp1: [Head,no] $\Rightarrow$ [Flu,yes],
    imp2: [Head,no] $\wedge$ [Temp,very_high] $\Rightarrow$ [Flu,yes]
are extracted from patient p1, and
    imp3: [Head,no] $\Rightarrow$ [Flu,no]

is extracted from $p3$. We usually call a pair $[A, val]$ a *descriptor* for an attribute A and an attribute value val. Implication $imp1$ contradicts $imp3$, because the same condition $[Head, no]$ concludes the different decisions $[Flu, yes]$ and $[Flu, no]$. However, $imp2$ is consistent with implications from any other tuple. Most of rough sets based rules are defined by means of this concept of *'consistency'* [1,2,3,4,5]. We usually define rules in a DIS by consistent implications.

Three measures, *support*, *accuracy* and *coverage* are also applied to defining rules in $DISs$ [4,5,6,7]. Implication $imp1$ occurs once in Table 1. This ratio $1/3$ is named *support*. A formula $[Head, no]$ occurs twice and $[Flu, yes]$ occurs once under the condition of $[Head, no]$. This ratio $1/2$ means the degree of the consistency of $imp1$. This is named *accuracy*. Similarly, a formula $[Flu, yes]$ occurs twice and $[Head, no]$ occurs once under the condition of $[Flu, yes]$. The ratio, i.e., $1/2$, is named *coverage*.

Equivalence relations in $DISs$ are usually employed to generate rules [1,2,3, 4,5,6,7]. We see that *two objects belong to the same equivalence class*, if the attribute values of them are the same. In Table 1, both $p1$ and $p3$ satisfy $[Head, no]$, so $p1$ and $p3$ belong to the same class. Patient $p2$ only satisfies $[Head, yes]$, so $p2$ belongs to another class. In this way, we have equivalence classes $h1=\{p1, p3\}$ and $h2=\{p2\}$ on an attribute $Head$. We similarly have equivalence classes $t1=\{p1, p2\}$ and $t2=\{p3\}$ on $Temp$, and $f1=\{p1, p2\}$ and $f2=\{p3\}$ on Flu.

The concept of the consistency is examined by the inclusion of equivalence classes [1,2,3]. The relation $h1 \not\subset f1$ implies that $p1, p3 \in h1$ are inconsistent for attributes $Head$ and Flu, and the relation $t1 \subset f1$ implies $p1, p2 \in t1$ are consistent for attributes $Temp$ and Flu.

The concept of data dependency between attributes is also examined by equivalence classes. For attributes $CON=\{Head, Temp\}$ and $DEC=\{Flu\}$, we have equivalence relations $eq(CON)=\{\{p1\}, \{p2\}, \{p3\}\}$ and $eq(DEC)=\{\{p1, p2\}, \{p3\}\}$, respectively. For every $X \in eq(CON)$, there exists $Y \in eq(DEC)$ such that $X \subset Y$. Therefore, every object is consistent with other object. In this case, the degree of dependency from CON to DEC is 1. Generally, the degree of dependency is defined by a ratio that the amount of consistent objects by total amount of objects. Three measures *support*, *accuracy* and *coverage* are obtainable by equivalence relations, too. The *support* of $imp1$ is $|h1 \cap f1|/3=|\{p1\}|/3=1/3$, and the *accuracy* is $|h1 \cap f1|/|h1|=|\{p1\}|/|\{p1, p3\}|=1/2$.

3   Rough Non-deterministic Information Analysis

3.1   Basic Definitions on DISs and NISs

A *Deterministic Information System* (DIS) is a quadruplet $(OB, AT, \{VAL_A| A \in AT\}, f)$, where OB is a finite set whose elements are called *objects*, AT is a finite set whose elements are called *attributes*, VAL_A is a finite set whose elements are called *attribute values* and f is such a mapping that $f : OB \times AT \rightarrow \cup_{A \in AT} VAL_A$ which is called a *classification function*. Such a relation that $f(x, A)=f(y, A)$ for every $A \in ATR \subset AT$ is an equivalence relation over OB.

For two equivalence relations eq_1 and eq_2, a formula $eq_1 \subset eq_2$ implies that there exists a set $Y \in eq_2$ such that $X \subset Y$ for any $X \in eq_1$.

Let us consider two disjoint sets $CON \subset AT$ which we call *condition attributes* and $DEC \subset AT$ which we call *decision attributes*. An object $x \in OB$ is *consistent* with an object y, if $f(x, A)=f(y, A)$ for every $A \in CON$ implies $f(x, A)=f(y, A)$ for every $A \in DEC$. An object $x \in OB$ is *consistent*, if x is consistent with any $y \in OB$.

A *Non-deterministic Information System* (NIS) is a quadruplet $(OB, AT, \{VAL_A | A \in AT\}, g)$, where $g : OB \times AT \rightarrow P(\cup_{A \in AT} VAL_A)$ (a power set of $\cup_{A \in AT} VAL_A$) [12,14]. Let us consider a $NIS=(OB, AT, \{VAL_A | A \in AT\}, g)$, a set $ATR \subset AT$ and a mapping $h : OB \times ATR \rightarrow \cup_{A \in ATR} VAL_A$ such that $h(x, A) \in g(x, A)$. We call a $DIS=(OB, ATR, \{VAL_A | A \in ATR\}, h)$ a *derived DIS (for ATR) from NIS*. For a derived DIS from a NIS and a set $ATR \subset AT$, it is possible to define an equivalence relation over OB. We name this equivalence relation a *possible equivalence relation* (*pe*-relation).

3.2   An Overview of RNIA

$NISs$ were proposed by Pawlak, Orłowska and Lipski in order to handle information incompleteness in $DISs$ [12,13,14,15,16]. In $NISs$, some attribute values are given as a set of values, and we interpret this set as that '*The actual value exists in this set but it is unknown due to the information incompleteness.*'

Table 2. A non-deterministic information system

Patient	Head(ache)	Temp(erature)	Flu
p1	no	very_high	yes
p2	{yes, no}	{high, very_high}	yes
p3	no	{normal, high}	{yes, no}

In Table 2, there are 16 derived $DISs$, and Table 1 is a derived DIS from NIS in Table 2. According to the interpretation to $NISs$, there exists a derived DIS with real information in these 16 derived $DISs$. Two modalities *certainty* and *possibility*, which are defined by means of all derived $DISs$, are introduced into $NISs$.

(Certainty) If a formula α holds in every derived DIS from a NIS, α also holds in the unknown real DIS.

(Possibility) If a formula α holds in some derived $DISs$ from a NIS, there exists such a possibility that α holds in the unknown real DIS.

We have coped with several issues related to these two modalities, for example the definability of a set in $NISs$ [20,21], the consistency of an object in $NISs$, data dependency in $NISs$ [22], rules in $NISs$ [19,23], reduction of attributes in $NISs$ [24], etc. An important problem is how to compute two modalities depending upon all derived $DISs$ from a NIS. A simple method, such that every definition is sequentially computed in all derived $DISs$ from a NIS, is not suitable. Because the number of derived $DISs$ from a NIS increases in exponential order. This problem is uniformly solved by means of applying either *inf* and *sup* information or *possible equivalence relations* [19,23].

4   Real Execution by a Tool for RNIA

This section shows real executions on Table 2 by a tool. Programs are implemented on a workstation with 450 MHz UltraSparc CPU in prolog and C.

4.1   Definability of a Set and Pe-relations

```
% more data.pl [Operation 1]
object(3,3).
data(1,[no,very_high,yes]).
data(2,[[yes,no],[high,very_high],yes]).
data(3,[no,[normal,high],[yes,no]]).
total_cases(16).
```

In Operation 1, the contents in data file are displayed. The statement *object*(3, 3) implies that there are 3 objects and 3 attributes. Every tuple of data is denoted by means of a list structure. According to this syntax, it is possible to handle any *NIS*.

```
% tool.prolog [Operation 2]
?-translate. [Operation 3]
File Name for Read Open:'data.pl'.
EXEC_TIME=0.024(sec)
yes
?-pe. [Operation 4]
<< Attribute 1: Possible Case 2 >>
[1] [[1,2,3]] 1      [2] [[1,3],[2]] 1
<< Attribute 2: Possible Case 4 >>
[1] [[1,2],[3]] 2    [2] [[1],[2,3]] 1    [3] [[1],[2],[3]] 1
<< Attribute 3: Possible Case 2 >>
[1] [[1,2,3]] 1      [2] [[1,2],[3]] 1
EXEC_TIME=0.037(sec)
yes
```

In Operation 3, the contents in each attribute are translated into internal expressions, and are stored in files 1.*rs*, 2.*rs* and 3.*rs*. In Operation 4, all *pe*-relations of each attribute are generated, and *pe*-relations are stored in files 1.*pe*, 2.*re* and 3.*pe*. The first response implies that there exist two *pe*-relations $\{\{p1, p2, p3\}\}$ and $\{\{p1, p3\}, \{p2\}\}$ on *Head*. In this way, it is possible to obtain all *pe*-relations. In this execution, we employ an algorithm of checking the definability of a set. Since a set *OB* is definable for any equivalence relation, so every *pe*-relation is obtained as a side effect of checking the definability of a set *OB* [20,21].

4.2 Manipulation of Pe-relations and Data Dependency

```
% merge [Operation 5]
Merging 1.pe... 2.pe...
EXEC_TIME=0.010(sec)
% depratio [Operation 6]
File Name for Condition:12.pe
File Name for Decision:3.pe
----- Dependency Check ------------------------
CRITERION 1(Num_of_Consistent_DISs / Num_of_All_DISs)
    Number of Derived DISs:16
    Number of Derived Consistent DISs:15
    Degree of Consistent DISs:0.938
CRITERION 2(Total_Min_and_Max_Degree)
    Minimum Degree of Dependency:0.333
    Maximum Degree of Dependency:1.000
----- Consistency Ratio for Every Object -----
    Consistent ratio of the object 1:1.000(=16/16)
    Consistent ratio of the object 2:0.938(=15/16)
    Consistent ratio of the object 3:0.938(=15/16)
EXEC_TIME=0.040(sec)
```

In Operation 5, pe-relations 12.pe on attributes $\{Head, Temp\}$ are generated by using two pe-relations 1.pe and 2.pe. It is possible to generate a new equivalence relation from two different equivalence relations [2]. We have extended this property in equivalence relations to new property in pe-relations. We name this algorithm *merge algorithm*, and this algorithm can generate all pe-relations on any set of attributes [20,21]. According to pe-relations, it is possible to know the degree of data dependency [22]. The response in Operation 6 shows that there are 16 derived $DISs$, and 15 derived $DISs$ are consistent. In 15 derived $DISs$, the degree of dependency from $\{Head, Temp\}$ to $\{Flu\}$ is 1. In only one derived DIS, objects $p2$ and $p3$ are inconsistent.

4.3 Minimal Certain Rule Generation

This subsection shows an example to generate minimal certain rules from Table 2. Intuitively, a minimal certain rule is a minimal implication, which consists of only definite information and is consistent in all derived $DISs$ [23,24].

```
% more attrib.pl [Operation 7]
decision([3]).   decval([yes]).   condition([1,2]).
% tool.prolog [Operation 8]
?-translate_attrib. [Operation 9]
File Name for Read Open:'data.pl'.
Decision Definition File:'attrib.pl'.
File Name for Write Open:'data.rs'.
EXEC_TIME=0.014(sec)
yes
```

```
?-init. [Operation 10]
DECLIST:<inf=[1,2]>
Certain Rules come from [1]
EXEC_TIME=0.000(sec)
yes
?-minimal. [Operation 11]
<<Minimal Certain Rules from object 1>>
   Descriptor [2,very_high] is a core for object 3
   [2,very_high]=>[3,yes][8/8(=4/4,2/2),DGC:Only Core Descriptors]
   [(0.333,0.666),(1.0,1.0),(0.333,1.0)]
EXEC_TIME=0.002(sec)
yes
```

In Operation 7, the type of a rule is defined in file *attrib.pl*, namely a minimal certain rule in the form of *Condition* $\Rightarrow$ $[3, yes]$ is specified. It is possible to handle any type of a rule by changing this file. In Operation 9, internal expressions depending upon *attrib.pl* are generated. According to Operation 10, it is possible to generate certain rules from only object *p1*. In Operation 11, a minimal certain rule $[Temp, very\_high] \Rightarrow [Flu, yes]$ is obtained. This rule appears 8 derived *DISs* and is consistent in 8 derived *DISs*. The minimum and maximum of *support*, *accuracy* and *coverage* are also displayed. The minimum of *accuracy* is 1, which implies this rule is consistent in 8 derived *DISs*, too.

4.4   Execution Time for Other NISs

We omit the discussion on the computational complexity of algorithms, and we show execution time for other *NISs*. Table 3 gives the definitions of *NISs*, which are automatically generated by using a random number program. According to Table 4, this tool can easily handle *NISs* as large as NIS_3.

Table 3. Definitions of NISs

NIS	$|OB|$	$|AT|$	$|VAL_A|$	$derived\_DISs$
NIS_1	30	5	5	7558272
NIS_2	50	5	10	120932352
NIS_3	100	5	10	1451188224

Table 4. Execution time(sec) of programs: In *merge*, 123.pe is generated from 1.*pe*, 2.*pe* and 3.*pe*. In *depratio*, the degree of dependency from 1st, 2nd and 3rd attributes to 5th attribute.

NIS	$translate$	pe	$merge$	$depratio$	$translate\_attrib$	$init$	$minimal$
NIS_1	0.308	1.415	0.690	0.080	0.178	0.019	0.120
NIS_2	0.548	8.157	0.110	0.060	0.251	0.012	0.118
NIS_3	1.032	16.950	2.270	0.130	0.614	0.200	1.335

5   Perspective of Rough Sets Based Information Analysis for Numerical Data

5.1   An Exemplary Data with Numerical Values

Let us consider Table 5. There are numbered four persons, and Table 5 stores a relation between *Sex*, *Height* and *Weight*.

Table 5. Exemplary deterministic information system with numerical values

Person	Sex	Height(cm)	Weight(kg)
1	male	162	64.3
2	female	162	64.5
3	female	164	65.8
4	male	175	72.8

According to regression analysis in Microsoft Excel, we obtained a regression line from *Height* to *Weight*

`Weight=0.6445×Height-39.982.`

However, we may soon see such an implication that

`imp4:If Height is in the 160s, the Weight is in the 60s.`

In some cases, this implication may be more informative than the regression line. In rough set theory, we try to obtain not the former regression line but the latter implication.

5.2   Rough Sets Based Information Analysis: A Usual Case

In Table 5, there exists an equivalence relation on each attribute respectively in the following:

`eq({Sex})={{1,4},{2,3}}, eq({Height})={{1,2},{3},{4}},`
`eq({Weight})={{1},{2},{3},{4}}.`

In this case, $eq(\{Sex\}) \not\subset eq(\{Weight\})$ and $eq(\{Height\}) \not\subset eq(\{Weight\})$ hold, so we do not recognize data dependency from *Sex* to *Weight* nor *Height* to *Weight*. According to typical rough set theory, the combination of attributes is usually considered. Namely, $eq(\{Sex, Height\})=\{\{1\}, \{2\}, \{3\}, \{4\}\}$ is generated, and $eq(\{Sex, Height\}) \subset eq(\{Weight\})$ is examined. After this, four implications are extracted as rules from Table 5. For example,

`imp5:[Sex,male]∧[Height,162]⇒[Weight,64.3]`

is extracted from object 1. However, this *imp5* handles so special case that *imp5* has less generality.

5.3   A Proposal of Meaningful Figures in Numerical Values

Now in this subsection, we propose a concept of *meaningful figures* in numerical values. Let us consider an irrational number $\pi=3.14\cdots$. For students in elementary schools, $\pi=3.14$ will be sufficient for calculating the area of a circle.

On the other hand, π=3.14 may be insufficient for researchers of numerical analysis. We give another example. Let us suppose the real total price is \$14976.5 for buying a car. In this case, we may see \$15000 is enough for buying this car. The \$0.5 in \$14976.5 must be meaningless. According to these two examples, it seems important to think the concept of meaningful figures in numerical data. In Table 5, an implication is derived due to the restriction of 160s and 60s. In the subsequent sections, we introduce this concept of meaningful figures into rough set theory.

5.4 Numerical Patterns and Equivalence Relations

In order to handle the concept of meaningful figures, we introduce two symbols @ and #, which represent numeric from 0 to 9. We implicitly employ 10-adic numbers for expressing numerical data. Of course, it is possible to employ 2-adic and 8-adic numbers, too.

A numerical pattern is a sequence of @ and #, for example @@@, @@#, @##, @@.@ and @#.#. Here, '.' denotes a decimal point, and @ does not occur after #. We see @@@, @@#, @## and ### have the same *type*. Three patterns @@.@, @@.# @#.# have the same type, too. Intuitively, @ denotes a significant figure and # denotes a figure, which we do not care. For example, two values of weight 64.3Kg and 64.5Kg are different for a pattern @@.@. However, two values are the same for a pattern @@.#. In order to discriminate two values, we must apply a pattern @@@. According to such patterns, we define the meaningful figures in numerical values.

Clearly, it is possible to introduce an *order* ($<_p$) on *precision* into a set of patterns with the same type. The order is
$$@@@ <_p @@\# <_p @\#\# <_p \#\#\# \text{ and } @@.@ <_p @@.\# <_p @\#.\#$$
The pattern @@@ is the most precise, and the pattern ### is the least precise.

Such patterns cause different kinds of equivalence relations for the same data. For a set ATR of attributes and a numerical pattern pat, let $eq(ATR, pat)$ denote an equivalence relation according to pat. In Table 5, we have the following:

eq(Height,@##)={{1,2,3,4}}   eq(Weight,@#.#)={{1,2,3},{4}}
eq(Height,@@#)={{1,2,3},{4}}   eq(Weight,@@.#)={{1,2},{3},{4}}
eq(Height,@@@)={{1,2},{3},{4}} eq(Weight,@@.@)={{1},{2},{3},{4}}

Generally, we have the following property.

Property. Let $PATT$ denote a set of patterns (on a set ATR of attributes) with the same type. For $pat_1, pat_2 \in PATT$, let us suppose $pat_1 <_p pat_2$. Then, $eq(ATR, pat_1) \subset eq(ATR, pat_2)$ holds.

The concept of precision has already been introduced into rough set theory, and, $eq(ATR, pat_1)$ is called *more fine* and $eq(ATR, pat_2)$ is called *more coarse* in [1]. Even though there exist less work dealing with fine information and coarse information, recently such fine and coarse information is picked up [25,26,27]. Equivalence relations $eq(ATR, pat)$, which depends upon numerical pattern pat, give a real instance of the framework defined in [25,26].

5.5   Rule Generation from Numerical Data: An Example

This subsection gives an example of rule generation depending upon fine information and coarse information.

Let us suppose the condition attribute be $\{Height\}$ and the decision attribute be $\{Weight\}$. If we apply typical rough set theory, two equivalence relations, i.e., $eq(Height, @@@)$ and $eq(Weight, @@.@)$ are employed. In this case, $eq(Height, @@@) \not\subset eq(Weight, @@.@)$ holds, and object 1 and 2 are inconsistent. Here, as we have already shown in subsection 5.2, another attribute is picked up for generating more fine equivalence relation.

However, there exist other two cases, which depends upon patterns, in the following.

(Case 1) Let us consider a pattern $@@.\#$ for $\{Weight\}$. In this case, $eq(Height, @@@) \subset eq(Weight, @@.\#)$ holds, so every implication in the form of $[Height, @@@] \Rightarrow [Weight, @@.\#]$ is consistent. Thus, an implication

> imp6: [Height,162] $\Rightarrow$ [Weight,64.#]

is consistent. We see this implication expresses a property in Table 5.

(Case 2) Let us consider a pattern $@\#.\#$ for $\{Weight\}$. In this case, $eq(Height, @@@) \subset eq(Weight, @\#.\#)$ and $eq(Height, @@\#) \subset eq(Weight, @\#.\#)$ hold, and an implication

> imp7: [Height,16#] $\Rightarrow$ [Weight,6#.#]

is also consistent. This $imp7$ is the implication in subsection 5.1.

Since $@@.\# <_p @\#.\#$ holds in the decision part, we see $imp7$ is more precise than $imp6$. In this way, it is possible to define *more precise rules* and *less precise rules*. When we know an overview of data, less precise rules may be more useful. On the other hand, when we know a special property of data, less precise rules may be meaningless. More precise rules are required. To add such rule generation based on numerical patterns will enhance current rough sets based rule generation.

5.6   Rule Generation Based on Numerical Patterns: A Summary

According to previous discussion, we give a summary in the following.

A Summary

(1) Fix a set DEC of decision attributes, and generate $eq(DEC, pat_i)$ $(1 \leq i \leq n, pat_i <_p pat_{i+1})$.
(2) Fix a set of CON of condition attributes, and generate $eq(\{A\}, pat_j)$ $(1 \leq j \leq m, pat_j <_p pat_{j+1}, A \in CON)$.
(3) For $eq(DEC, pat_i)$, find a set $CON^* \subset CON$ and PAT^* such that
$eq(CON^*, PAT^*) = \cap_{A \in CON^*} eq(\{A\}, pat_j) \subset eq(DEC, pat_i)$.
We name an implication $\wedge_{A \in CON^*}[A, pat_j] \Rightarrow [DEC, pat_i]$ a *consistent pattern*, and the instance of $\wedge_{A \in CON^*}[A, pat_j] \Rightarrow [DEC, pat_i]$ becomes a consistent implication.

Key Problem

The key problem in the above rule generation is a way to find CON^* and PAT^*.

There are two manipulations for current CON and PAT.
(1) We fix CON and we change some numerical patterns in PAT.
(2) We fix PAT and we add or delete attributes in CON.

Let us consider an equivalence relation $eq(CON)$, and let $CON^-=CON\text{-}\{A\}$ ($A \in CON$) and $CON^+=CON \cup \{A\}$ ($A \notin CON$). Then, clearly $eq(CON^+) \subset eq(CON) \subset eq(CON^-)$ holds. In rough set theory, the above CON^+ is employed as a more precise equivalence relations, and the above CON^- is employed as a less precise equivalence relations. However, it is possible to adjust $eq(CON)$ by changing PAT. This way, which depends upon fine information and coarse information, proposes new method to rule generation from numerical data.

6   Concluding Remarks

An overview of a tool and a framework of Rough Non-deterministic Information Analysis ($RNIA$) is presented at first. We follow rough sets based concepts in $DISs$ and propose a framework of $RNIA$. $NISs$, which were proposed by Pawlak, Orłowska and Lipski, have been recognized to be one of the most important framework for handling incomplete information. Therefore, $RNIA$ will also be an important framework for rough sets based information analysis under incomplete information.

Then, we introduced numerical patterns into $DISs$, and proposed a framework for handling numerical data. We will add programs to handle numerical data in $DISs$, and will enhance the $RNIA$.

Acknowledgment

This work is partly supported by the Grant-in-Aid for Scientific Research (C) (No.16500176) from The Japanese Ministry of Education, Science, Sports and Culture.

References

1. Z.Pawlak, *Rough Sets: Theoretical Aspects of Reasoning about Data*, Kluwer Academic Publishers, Dordrecht, 1991.
2. Z.Pawlak, Some Issues on Rough Sets, *Transactions on Rough Sets*, Springer-Verlag, vol.1, pp.1-58, 2004.
3. J.Komorowski, Z.Pawlak, L.Polkowski and A.Skowron, Rough Sets: a tutorial, *Rough Fuzzy Hybridization*, Springer, pp.3-98, 1999.
4. A.Nakamura, S.Tsumoto, H.Tanaka and S.Kobayashi, Rough Set Theory and Its Applications, *Journal of Japanese Society for AI*, vol.11, no.2, pp.209-215, 1996.
5. S.Tsumoto, Knowledge Discovery in Clinical Databases and Evaluation of Discovered Knowledge in Outpatient Clinic, *Information Sciences*, vol.124, pp.125-137, 2000.
6. L.Polkowski and A.Skowron (eds.), *Rough Sets in Knowledge Discovery 1, Studies in Fuzziness and Soft Computing*, vol.18, Physica-Verlag, 1998.
7. L.Polkowski and A.Skowron (eds.), *Rough Sets in Knowledge Discovery 2, Studies in Fuzziness and Soft Computing*, vol.19, Physica-Verlag, 1998.

8. J.Grzymala-Busse, A New Version of the Rule Induction System LERS, *Fundamenta Informaticae*, vol.31, pp.27-39, 1997.
9. W.Ziarko, Variable Precision Rough Set Model, *Journal of Computer and System Sciences*, vol.46, pp.39-59, 1993.
10. N.Zhong, J.Dong, S.Fujitsu and S.Ohsuga, Soft Techniques to Rule Discovery in Data, *Transactions of Information Processing Society of Japan*, vol.39, pp.2581–2592, 1998.
11. Rough Set Software, *Bulletin of Int'l. Rough Set Society*, vol.2, pp.15–46, 1998.
12. E.Orłowska and Z.Pawlak, Representation of Nondeterministic Information, *Theoretical Computer Science*, vol.29, pp.27-39, 1984.
13. E.Orłowska (Ed.), *Incomplete Information: Rough Set Analysis*, Physica-Verlag, 1998.
14. W.Lipski, On Semantic Issues Connected with Incomplete Information Data Base, *ACM Trans. DBS*, vol.4, pp.269-296, 1979.
15. W.Lipski, On Databases with Incomplete Information, *Journal of the ACM*, vol.28, pp.41-70, 1981.
16. A.Nakamura, A Rough Logic based on Incomplete Information and Its Application, *Int'l. Journal of Approximate Reasoning*, vol.15, pp.367-378, 1996.
17. E.Codd, A Relational Model of Data for Large Shared Data Banks, *Communication of the ACM*, vol.13, pp.377-387, 1970.
18. M.Nakata and S.Miyamoto, Databases with Non-deterministic Information, *Bulletin of Int'l. Rough Set Society*, vol.7, pp.15-21, 2003.
19. H.Sakai and A.Okuma, Basic Algorithms and Tools for Rough Non-deterministic Information Analysis, *Transactions on Rough Sets*, Int'l. Rough Set Society, vol.1, pp.209-231, 2004.
20. H.Sakai and A.Okuma, An Algorithm for Finding Equivalence Relations from Tables with Non-deterministic Information. *Lecture Notes in AI*, Springer-Verlag, vol.1711, pp.64–72, 1999.
21. H.Sakai, Effective Procedures for Handling Possible Equivalence Relations in Nondeterministic Information Systems, *Fundamenta Informaticae*, vol.48, pp.343-362, 2001.
22. H.Sakai, Effective Procedures for Data Dependencies in Information Systems, *Rough Set Theory and Granular Computing, Studies in Fuzziness and Soft Computing*, Springer, vol.125, pp.167–176, 2003.
23. H.Sakai, A Framework of Rough Sets based Rule Generation in Non-deterministic Information Systems, *Lecture Notes in AI*, Springer-Verlag, vol.2871, pp.143-151, 2003.
24. H.Sakai, An Interactive Tool for Generating Minimal Certain Rules in Nondeterministic Information Systems, *Proc. International Workshop on Fuzzy Systems and Innovational Computing*, Japan Society for Fuzzy Theory and Intelligent Informatics, D4-2, pp.1-6, 2004.
25. T.Murai, G.Resconi, M.Nakata, Y.Sato, Operations of Zooming In and Out on Possible Worlds for Semantic Fields, E.Damiani et al.(eds), *Knowledge-Based Intelligent Information Engineering Systems and Allied Technologies(KES2002)*, IOS Press, pp.1083-1087, 2002.
26. T. Murai, G. Resconi, M. Nakata, Y. Sato, Granular Reasoning Using Zooming In & Out, *Lecture Notes in Computer Science*, Springer-Verlag, vol.2639, pp.421-424, 2003.
27. Y.Yao, C.Liau, N.Zhong, Granular Computing Based on Rough Sets, Quotient Space Theory, and Belief Functions, *Lecture Notes in AI*, Springer-Verlag, vol.2871, pp.152-159, 2003.

Several Approaches to Attribute Reduction in Variable Precision Rough Set Model

Masahiro Inuiguchi

Department of Systems Innovation
Graduate School of Engineering Science, Osaka University
1-3, Machikaneyama, Toyonaka, Osaka 560-8531, Japan
inuiguti@sys.es.osaka-u.ac.jp
http://www-inulab.sys.es.osaka-u.ac.jp

Abstract. In this paper, we discuss attribute reduction in variable precision rough set model. We consider several kinds of reducts preserving some of lower approximations, upper approximations, boundary regions and the unpredictable region. We show relations among those kinds of reducts. Moreover we discuss logical function representations of the preservation of lower approximations, upper approximations, boundary regions and the unpredictable region as a basis for reduct calculation. By those discussions, the great difference between the analysis using variable precision rough sets and the classical rough set analysis is emphasized.

1 Introduction

The rough sets (RSs) provide an approach to analysis of decision tables [4]. It treats inconsistent information contained in the tables properly. By the approach we may find the minimal attribute sets called reducts to classify objects without deterioration of classification quality and induce minimal length decision rules inherent in the given tables. The usefulness and effectiveness of the RS approach is shown in data mining, knowledge discovery, pattern recognition, decision analysis, and so on.

When the given decision table includes errors or lacks some important information, the classical RS analysis is not very effective. To overcome the shortcoming, variable precision rough set (VPRS) model [8] has been proposed as an extension of the classical RS model. While the classical RS model does not permit any errors in classification of objects in the lower approximations defined under a given decision table, VPRS model permits some errors. Because of this permission, the analysis becomes more effective when the given decision table includes errors or lacks some important

The permission of errors brings the diversification of the generalization of the classical RS analysis. Despite of the diversification, the conceivable approaches based on VPRS model have not yet considerably discussed and only some approaches have been proposed as a generalization of the classical RS analysis.

In this paper, we discuss attribute reduction in VPRS model. Reducts are useful since they indicate minimally necessary condition attributes. Using them

V. Torra et al. (Eds.): MDAI 2005, LNAI 3558, pp. 215–226, 2005.

we can evaluate the importance of attribute in classification of objects. While several kinds of reducts were discussed in the classical RS model [3, 6], only one kind of reducts is often investigated in VPRS model. In the classical RS model, reducts preserving lower approximations, reducts preserving upper approximations and reducts preserving boundary regions are discussed. Relations among those kinds of reducts are investigated and the equivalence between the last two reducts is shown [3, 6]. Moreover, logical functions characterizing the preservations of lower approximations and upper approximations are given. Every prime implicant of such a logical function corresponds to a reduct and all reducts can be obtained by enumerating all prime implicants [3, 5].

On the other hand, in VPRS model, a kind of reducts called β-reducts [1, 9] is only discussed. Neither reducts preserving lower approximations, reducts preserving upper approximations nor reducts preserving boundary regions have been yet investigated considerably.

In this paper, we consider several kinds of reducts defined by lower approximations, upper approximations, boundary regions and so on in VPRS model. We discuss the relations among them. Through this discussion, we show that the relations among those are different from those in the classical RS model. Moreover, we investigate logical functions characterizing the preservation of lower approximations, upper approximations, boundary regions and so on. The reducts may be obtained exactly or approximately as prime implicants of such logical functions.

In the following section, we briefly review the classical RS model and attribute reduction. After the introduction of VPRS model, we define several kinds of reducts in the framework of VPRS model in Section 3. We discuss the relations among reducts defined in this paper. In Section 4, we investigate logical functions characterizing the preservation of lower approximations, upper approximations, boundary regions and so on.

2   Classical Rough Sets and Reducts

2.1   Classical Rough Sets Under Decision Tables

The classical rough sets can be defined under any equivalence relation. In this paper we restrict ourselves to discussions of rough sets under decision tables. A decision table is characterized by 4-tuple $\mathcal{I} = \langle U, C \cup \{d\}, V, \rho \rangle$, where U is a finite set of objects, C is a finite set of condition attributes, d is a decision attribute, $V = \bigcup_{a \in C \cup \{d\}} V_a$ and V_a is a domain of the attribute a, and $\rho : U \times C \cup \{d\} \to V$ is an information function such that $\rho(x, a) \in V_a$ for every $a \in C \cup \{d\}$, $x \in U$.

Given a set of attributes $A \subseteq C \cup \{d\}$, we can define an equivalence relation I_A referred to as an indiscernibility relation by

$$I_A = \{(x, y) \in U \times U \mid \rho(x, a) = \rho(y, a), \ \forall a \in A\}. \tag{1}$$

From I_A, we have an equivalence class,

$$[x]_A = \{y \in U \mid (y, x) \in I_A\}. \tag{2}$$

When $A = \{d\}$, we define

$$\{D_j, \ j = 1, 2, \ldots, p\} = \{[x]_{\{d\}} \mid x \in U\}, \ D_i \neq D_j \ (i \neq j). \tag{3}$$

D_j is called a decision class. There exists some $v_j \in V_d$ such that $\rho(x, d) = v_j$ for each $x \in D_j$.

For a set of condition attributes $A \subseteq C$, the lower and upper approximations of D_j are defined as follows:

$$\underline{A}(D_j) = \{x \mid [x]_A \subseteq D_j\}, \quad \overline{A}(D_j) = \{x \mid [x]_A \cap D_j \neq \emptyset\}. \tag{4}$$

A pair $(\underline{A}(D_j), \overline{A}(D_j))$ is called a rough set (RS) of D_j. The boundary region of D_j is defined by $BN_A(D_j) = \overline{A}(D_j) - \underline{A}(D_j)$. Since $[x]_A$ can be seen as a set of objects indiscernible from $x \in U$ in view of condition attributes in A, $\underline{A}(D_j)$ is interpreted as a collection of objects whose membership to D_j is noncontradictive in view of condition attributes in A. $BN_A(D_j)$ is interpreted as a collection of objects whose membership to D_j is doubtful in view of condition attributes in A. $\overline{A}(D_j)$ is interpreted as a collection of possible members.

We have the following properties:

$$\underline{A}(D_j) \subseteq D_j \subseteq \overline{A}(D_j), \ j = 1, 2, \ldots, p, \tag{5}$$

$$U = \bigcup_{j=1,2,\ldots,p} \overline{A}(D_j), \tag{6}$$

$$A \subseteq B \Rightarrow \underline{A}(D_j) \subseteq \underline{B}(D_j), \ \overline{A}(D_j) \supseteq \overline{B}(D_j), \ j = 1, 2, \ldots, p, \tag{7}$$

$$\overline{A}(D_j) = D_j \cup BN_A(D_j), \ j = 1, 2, \ldots, p, \tag{8}$$

$$BN_A(D_j) = \overline{A}(D_j) \cap \bigcup_{i \neq j} \overline{A}(D_i), \ j = 1, 2, \ldots, p, \tag{9}$$

$$\underline{A}(D_j) = \overline{A}(D_j) - \bigcup_{i \neq j} \overline{A}(D_i), \ j = 1, 2, \ldots, p, \tag{10}$$

$$\underline{A}(D_j) = D_j - BN_A(D_j), \ j = 1, 2, \ldots, p. \tag{11}$$

The accuracy $\alpha_A(D_j)$ and the quality $\gamma_A(D_j)$ of approximation are defined as follows:

$$\alpha_A(D_j) = \frac{|\underline{A}(D_j)|}{|\overline{A}(D_j)|}, \qquad \gamma_A(D_j) = \frac{|\underline{A}(D_j)|}{|D_j|}, \tag{12}$$

where $|X|$ shows the cardinality of X. For a partition $\mathcal{D} = \{D_j, \ j = 1, 2, \ldots, p\}$, the quality of approximation is defined by

$$\gamma_A(\mathcal{D}) = \sum_{j=1}^{p} |\underline{A}(D_j)| \Big/ |U|. \tag{13}$$

2.2 Attribute Reduction

Attribute reduction is useful for many purposes. It shows minimally necessary attributes to classify objects and reveals important attributes. A set of minimally necessary attributes is called a reduct. In the classical RS analysis, reducts preserving lower approximations are frequently used. Namely a set of condition attributes, $A \subseteq C$ is called a reduct if and only if it satisfies (L1) $\underline{A}(D_j) = \underline{C}(D_j)$, $j = 1, 2, \ldots, p$ and (L2) $\nexists a \in A$, $(A - \{a\})(D_j) = \underline{C}(D_j)$, $j = 1, 2, \ldots, p$. Since we discuss several kinds of reducts, we call this reduct, a lower approximation preserving reduct or an L-reduct for short. An L-reduct can be seen as a reduct preserving the quality of approximation of a partition $\mathcal{D}$, $\gamma_C(\mathcal{D})$, and also as a reduct preserving the qualities of approximation of decision classes, $\gamma_C(D_j)$, $j = 1, 2, \ldots, p$.

We consider reducts preserving upper approximations and boundary regions [3, 6]. A set of condition attributes, $A \subseteq C$ is called an upper approximation preserving reduct or a U-reduct for short if and only if it satisfies (U1) $\overline{A}(D_j) = \overline{C}(D_j)$, $j = 1, 2, \ldots, p$ and (U2) $\nexists a \in A$, $\overline{(A - \{a\})}(D_j) = \overline{C}(D_j)$, $j = 1, 2, \ldots, p$. On the other hand, a set of condition attributes, $A \subseteq C$ is called a boundary region preserving reduct or a B-reduct for short if and only if it satisfies (B1) $BN_A(D_j) = BN_C(D_j)$, $j = 1, 2, \ldots, p$ and (B2) $\nexists a \in A$, $BN_{(A-\{a\})}(D_j) = BN_C(D_j)$, $j = 1, 2, \ldots, p$.

There are the following relations among L-reducts, U-reducts and B-reducts:

R1) A U-reduct is also a B-reduct and vice versa.

R2) There exists a U-reduct B for an L-reduct A such that $B \supseteq A$ and there exists an L-reduct A for a U-reduct B such that $B \supseteq A$.

R3) There exists a B-reduct B for an L-reduct A such that $B \supseteq A$ and there exists an L-reduct A for a B-reduct B such that $B \supseteq A$.

Those relations can be proved easily from (8)–(11). Since a U-reduct (or equivalently, B-reduct) preserves the lower approximations, it can be seen as a reduct preserving the accuracies of approximations of decision classes, $\alpha_C(D_j)$, $j = 1, 2, \ldots, p$. Since B-reduct is equivalent to U-reduct, we concentrate L-reduct and U-reduct in what follows.

To obtain a part or all of reducts, many approaches have been proposed in the literature [2, 4, 5]. Among them, we mention an approach based on discernibility matrices [5]. In this approach, we construct a logical function which characterizes the preservation of the lower approximations (resp. upper approximations) to obtain L-reducts (resp. U-reducts). Each reduct is obtained as a prime implicant of the logical function. For the detailed discussion of discernibility matrix, see reference [5].

3   Variable Precision Rough Sets and Several Reducts

3.1   Variable Precision Rough Sets

The larger a decision table is, the more frequent the inconsistency occurs. Such an increase of inconsistency may be caused by the lack of knowledge on condition attributes related to the decision attribute and/or by a noise in observation of attribute values. In such cases, the classical RS approaches would not be very useful because it does not permit any errors in classification of objects in the lower approximations.

To overcome such shortcoming of the classical RS analysis, the variable precision rough set (VPRS) model has been proposed [8]. In definitions of lower and upper approximations in VPRS model, the following rough membership value for a condition attribute set $A \subseteq C$ plays an important role:

$$\mu_{D_j}(x|A) = \frac{|[x]_A \cap D_j|}{|[x]_A|}, \tag{14}$$

where we assume a decision table $\mathcal{I} = \langle U, C \cup \{d\}, V, \rho \rangle$.

Given an allowable error ratio $\beta \in [0, 0.5)$, lower and upper approximations of D_j with respect to a condition attribute set $A \subseteq C$ in VPRS model are defined as

$$\underline{A}_\beta(D_j) = \{x \in U \mid \mu_{D_j}(x|A) \geq 1 - \beta\}, \quad \overline{A}_\beta(D_j) = \{x \in U \mid \mu_{D_j}(x|A) > \beta\}. \tag{15}$$

A pair $(\underline{A}_\beta(D_j), \overline{A}_\beta(D_j))$ is called a variable precision rough set (VPRS) of D_j with error ratio β. The boundary region of D_j with error ratio β is defined by $BN_A^\beta(D_j) = \overline{A}_\beta(D_j) - \underline{A}_\beta(D_j)$. When $\beta = 0$, the VPRS model of D_j with error ratio β is the same as the classical RS model. $\underline{A}_\beta(D_j)$ is a collection of objects which has the probability of its membership to D_j not less than $1 - \beta$. On the other hand, $\overline{A}_\beta(D_j)$ is a collection of objects which has the probability of its membership to D_j more than β. We call $\underline{A}_\beta(D_j)$ and $\overline{A}_\beta(D_j)$ β-lower and β-upper approximations of D_j, respectively.

We have the following properties:

$$\underline{A}_\beta(D_j) \subseteq \overline{A}_\beta(D_j), \ j = 1, 2, \ldots, p, \tag{16}$$

$$\frac{1}{p} > \beta \Rightarrow U = \bigcup_{j=1,2,\ldots,p} \overline{A}_\beta(D_j), \tag{17}$$

$$\overline{A}_\beta(D_j) = \underline{A}_\beta(D_j) \cup BN_A(D_j), \ j = 1, 2, \ldots, p, \tag{18}$$

$$\underline{A}_\beta(D_j) = \overline{A}_\beta(D_j) - BN_A(D_j), \ j = 1, 2, \ldots, p. \tag{19}$$

Note that $\underline{A}_\beta(D_j) \subseteq D_j$ and $D_j \subseteq \overline{A}_\beta(D_j)$ do not always hold. As shown in (17), the union of β-upper approximations of all decision classes does not always equal to U but when $1/p > \beta$. From this fact we may define β-unpredictable region by

$$UNP_A^\beta(\mathcal{D}) = U - \bigcup_{j=1,2,\ldots,p} \overline{A}_\beta(D_j), \tag{20}$$

where $\mathcal{D}$ is a partition $\{D_1, D_2, \ldots, D_p\}$. The properties corresponding to (7), (9) and (10) are not always satisfied in VPRS model. As demonstrated by those, the properties of VPRS model are very different from those of the classical RS model.

3.2   Several Kinds of Reducts in VPRS Model

We can also introduce the concept of reduct into VPRS model. So far, β-reduct has been discussed. To define β-reduct, we use the quality of classification defined by

$$\gamma_A^\beta(\mathcal{D}) = \sum_{j=1}^{p} |\underline{A}_\beta(D_j)| \Big/ |U|. \tag{21}$$

The β-reduct is a condition attribute set $A \subseteq C$ such that (β1) $\gamma_A^\beta(\mathcal{D}) = \gamma_C^\beta(\mathcal{D})$ and (β2) $\not\exists B \in A$, $\gamma_B^\beta(\mathcal{D}) = \gamma_C^\beta(\mathcal{D})$.

Since the quality of classification in VPRS model corresponds to the quality of approximation in the classical RS model, the β-reduct in VPRS model corresponds to the reduct preserving the quality of approximation, i.e., L-reduct, in the classical RS model. However, (7) does not hold, β-reduct does not always preserve β-lower approximations of D_j, i.e., it is possible that an object belongs to $\underline{C}_\beta(D_j)$ can belong to $\underline{A}_\beta(D_i)$ ($i \neq j$) for a β-reduct A in some cases. The unsatisfaction of (7), (9) and (10) brings the diversity of definitions of reducts. In this paper, we restrict ourselves to reducts defined by the combinations of β-lower approximations, β-upper approximations, β-boundary regions and the β-unpredictable region. We discuss relations among them and the logical function representation of the preservation of those regions.

We can define L^β-reducts, U^β-reducts and B^β-reducts as direct extensions of L-reducts, U-reducts and B-reducts discussed in the previous section as follows:

L^β-**reduct**: A set of condition attributes, $A \subseteq C$ is called an L^β-reduct if and only if it satisfies (LB1) $\underline{A}_\beta(D_j) = \underline{C}_\beta(D_j)$, $j = 1, 2, \ldots, p$ and (LB2) $\not\exists B \subseteq A$, $\underline{B}_\beta(D_j) = \underline{C}_\beta(D_j)$, $j = 1, 2, \ldots, p$.

U^β-**reduct**: A set of condition attributes, $A \subseteq C$ is called a U^β-reduct if and only if it satisfies (UB1) $\overline{A}_\beta(D_j) = \overline{C}_\beta(D_j)$, $j = 1, 2, \ldots, p$ and (UB2) $\not\exists B \subseteq A$, $\overline{B}_\beta(D_j) = \overline{C}_\beta(D_j)$, $j = 1, 2, \ldots, p$.

B^β-**reduct**: A set of condition attributes, $A \subseteq C$ is called a B^β-reduct if and only if it satisfies (BB1) $BN_A^\beta(D_j) = BN_C^\beta(D_j)$, $j = 1, 2, \ldots, p$ and (BB2) $\not\exists B \subseteq A$, $BN_B^\beta(D_j) = BN_C^\beta(D_j)$, $j = 1, 2, \ldots, p$.

The preservation of β-lower approximations and that of β-upper approximations are meaningful since β-lower approximations and β-upper approximations are often used in the analysis. On the other hand the preservation of β-boundary regions is not well interpreted. In the classical RS model, the preservation of the boundary regions implies the protection of ambiguity expansion. However, the ambiguity expansion cannot be protected only by preserving β-boundary regions but by preserving β-boundary regions and β-unpredictable region in VPRS model. From this point of view, the following BUN^β-reducts are meaningful.

BUN^β-**reduct**: A set of condition attributes, $A \subseteq C$ is called a BUN^β-reduct if and only if it satisfies (BUN1) $BN_A^\beta(D_j) = BN_C^\beta(D_j)$, $j = 1, 2, \ldots, p$, $UNP_A^\beta(\mathcal{D}) = UNP_C^\beta(\mathcal{D})$ and (BUN2) $\not\exists B \subseteq A$, $BN_B^\beta(D_j) = BN_C^\beta(D_j)$, $j = 1, 2, \ldots, p$, $UNP_B^\beta(\mathcal{D}) = UNP_C^\beta(\mathcal{D})$.

Moreover, we consider the following reducts:

LU^β-**reduct**: A set of condition attributes, $A \subseteq C$ is called an LU^β-reduct if and only if it satisfies (LU1) $\underline{A}_\beta(D_j) = \underline{C}_\beta(D_j)$, $\overline{A}_\beta(D_j) = \overline{C}_\beta(D_j)$, $j = 1, 2, \ldots, p$ and (LU2) $\not\exists B \subseteq A$, $\underline{B}_\beta(D_j) = \underline{C}_\beta(D_j)$, $\overline{B}_\beta(D_j) = \overline{C}_\beta(D_j)$, $j = 1, 2, \ldots, p$.

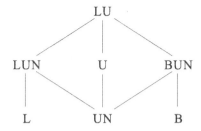

Fig. 1. Relations among 7 kinds of reducts in VPRS model

LUN$^\beta$-reduct: A set of condition attributes, $A \subseteq C$ is called a B$^\beta$-reduct if and only if it satisfies (LUN1) $\underline{A}_\beta(D_j) = \underline{C}_\beta(D_j)$, $j = 1, 2, \ldots, p$, $UNP_A^\beta(\mathcal{D}) = UNP_C^\beta(\mathcal{D})$ and (LUN2) $\not\exists B \subseteq A$, $\underline{B}_\beta(D_j) = \underline{C}_\beta(D_j)$, $j = 1, 2, \ldots, p$, $UNP_{A-\{a\}}^\beta(\mathcal{D}) = UNP_C^\beta(\mathcal{D})$.

UN$^\beta$-reduct: A set of condition attributes, $A \subseteq C$ is called a UN$^\beta$-reduct if and only if it satisfies (UN1) $UNP_A^\beta(\mathcal{D}) = UNP_C^\beta(\mathcal{D})$ and (UN2) $\not\exists B \subseteq A$, $UNP_B^\beta(\mathcal{D}) = UNP_C^\beta(\mathcal{D})$.

The idea of UN$^\beta$-reduct is to consider reducts protecting the expansion of β-unpredictable region since the unpredictability is most unacceptable. The ideas of the other two kinds of reducts are simply combinations of the preserving properties.

From (18) to (21) and from definitions, we know the following facts:

F1) An LU$^\beta$-reduct is a reduct preserving β-lower approximations and β-upper approximations at the same time. Moreover, it is a reduct preserving β-upper approximations and β-boundary regions at the same time.

F2) A U$^\beta$-reduct is a reduct preserving β-upper approximations and β-boundary approximations at the same time.

F3) An LU$^\beta$-reduct preserves β-boundary regions and the β-unpredictable region.

F4) A U$^\beta$-reduct preserves the β-unpredictable region.

From those observations, we obtain relations among 7 kinds of reducts as shown in Figure 1. In Figure 1, names of reducts are abbreviated to their first characters. Reducts located in the upper part of Figure 1 preserve the regions much more. Therefore, such reducts are larger in the sense of set inclusion than the other reducts located in the lower part. A line segment connecting two kinds of reducts implies that, for each reduct of the upper kind say A, there exists a reduct of the lower kind which is included by A. Form Figure 1, we know that an LU-reduct preserves regions most. On the other hand, a UN-reduct does not preserve many regions.

3.3   Logical Function Representation of the Preservation of Regions

L- and U-reducts in the classical RS model are characterized by prime implicants of certain logical functions [3, 5]. Each logical function is defined by a decision matrix and characterizes the preservation of the lower or upper approximations. In this section, we discuss the logical function representations with respect to 7 kinds of reducts in VPRS model. To do this, we discuss the representability by a logical function of the preservation of β-lower approximations, β-upper approximations, β-boundary regions and the β-unpredictable region since others can be obtained by taking the conjunction of those logical functions.

For convenience, we define the following functions of $x \in U$:

$$\partial_\beta^{\mathrm{L}}(x) = \{D_j \mid x \in \underline{C}_\beta(D_j)\}, \quad \partial_\beta^{\mathrm{U}}(x) = \{D_j \mid x \in \overline{C}_\beta(D_j)\}. \tag{22}$$

We also define $\partial_\beta^{\mathrm{B}}(x) = \partial_\beta^{\mathrm{U}}(x) - \partial_\beta^{\mathrm{L}}(x)$. Using those functions, we obtain the following equivalence relations:

$$I_\beta^{\mathrm{L}} = \{(x,y) \in U \times U \mid \partial_\beta^{\mathrm{L}}(x) = \partial_\beta^{\mathrm{L}}(y)\}, \tag{23}$$

$$I_\beta^{\mathrm{U}} = \{(x,y) \in U \times U \mid \partial_\beta^{\mathrm{U}}(x) = \partial_\beta^{\mathrm{U}}(y)\}, \tag{24}$$

$$I_\beta^{\mathrm{B}} = \{(x,y) \in U \times U \mid \partial_\beta^{\mathrm{B}}(x) = \partial_\beta^{\mathrm{B}}(y)\}, \tag{25}$$

$$I_\beta^{\mathrm{UN}} = \{(x,y) \in U \times U \mid \partial_\beta^{\mathrm{U}}(x) = \partial_\beta^{\mathrm{B}}(y) = \emptyset \text{ or } (\partial_\beta^{\mathrm{U}}(x) \neq \emptyset \text{ and } \partial_\beta^{\mathrm{B}}(y) \neq \emptyset)\}. \tag{26}$$

Note that the preservation of β-lower approximations, β-upper approximations, β-boundary regions and the β-unpredictable region is equivalent to the preservation of partitions $U|I_\beta^{\mathrm{L}}$, $U|I_\beta^{\mathrm{U}}$, $U|I_\beta^{\mathrm{B}}$ and $U|I_\beta^{\mathrm{UN}}$, respectively. For those partitions, each elementary set can be characterized by rough membership functions, $\mu_{D_j}(\cdot|C)$, $j = 1, 2, \ldots, p$. For example, consider an elementary set Y_k of $U|I_\beta^{\mathrm{B}}$ such that $x \in Y_k$. Then Y_k is a set of objects $y \in U$ satisfying

$$\mu_{D_j}(y|C) \in (\beta, 1 - \beta), \forall D_j \in \partial_\beta^{\mathrm{B}}(x) \text{ and}$$
$$(\mu_{D_j}(y|C) \leq \beta \text{ or } \mu_{D_j}(y|C) \geq 1 - \beta), \forall D_j \notin \partial_\beta^{\mathrm{B}}(x). \tag{27}$$

The concept of discernment-freeness is important for the discussion of the representability by a logical function. Given a partition $\mathcal{Y} = \{Y_1, Y_2, \ldots, Y_m\}$ whose elementary set Y_k is represented by $Y_k = \{x \in U \mid Cond_i(\mu_{D_l}(x|C)), l = 1, 2, \ldots, p\}$, where $Cond_i(\mu)$ means that μ satisfies some condition. Then $\mathcal{Y}$ is said to be discernment-free within elementary sets if and only if the following formula is valid:

$$\forall Y_k \in \mathcal{Y}, \ \forall Z \subseteq Y_k, \ \forall l \in \{1, 2, \ldots, p\}; \ Cond_i(\mu_{D_l}(Z|C)), \tag{28}$$

where $\mu_{D_l}(Z|C)$ is defined by

$$\mu_{D_j}(Z|C) = \left| D_l \cap \bigcup_{x \in Z} [x]_C \right| \Big/ \left| \bigcup_{x \in Z} [x]_C \right|. \tag{29}$$

We obtain the following assertions:

A1) $U|I_\beta^L$ is discernment-free within elementary sets.

A2) $U|I_\beta^U$ is discernment-free within elementary sets.

Those assertions can be proved easily from the following property: for $z_k \in U$, $k = 1, 2, \ldots, t$, we have

$$\min_{k=1,2,\ldots,t} \mu_{D_l}(z_k|C) \leq \mu_{D_l}(Z|C) = \sum_{k=1}^{t} \frac{|[z_k]_C|}{|[z_1]_C| + \cdots + |[z_t]_C|} \mu_{D_l}(z_k|C)$$
$$\leq \max_{k=1,2,\ldots,t} \mu_{D_l}(z_k|C),$$

where $Z = \{z_k \mid k = 1, 2, \ldots, t\}$.

Since the partition corresponding to the preservation of β-lower approximations is discernment-free within elementary sets, we do not need to discern objects belonging to the same elementary set of $U|I_\beta^L$. We can define a discernibility matrix with the following (i, j) component $\delta_{ij}^{L^\beta}$:

$$\delta_{ij}^{L^\beta} = \begin{cases} \{a \in C \mid \rho(u_i, a) \neq \rho(u_j, a)\}, & \text{if } \partial_\beta^L(u_i) \neq \partial_\beta^L(u_j), \\ *, & \text{otherwise.} \end{cases} \tag{30}$$

The preservation of β-lower approximations is characterized by the following logical function:

$$F^{L^\beta} = \bigwedge_{i,j:i<j} \bigvee \delta_{ij}^{L^\beta}. \tag{31}$$

Thus, all L^β-reducts can be obtained as prime implicants of F^{L^β}.

Similarly, the preservation of β-lower approximations is characterized by

$$F^{U^\beta} = \bigwedge_{i,j:i<j} \bigvee \delta_{ij}^{U^\beta}, \tag{32}$$

where the (i, j) component $\delta_{ij}^{U^\beta}$ of a discernibility matrix is defined by

$$\delta_{ij}^{U^\beta} = \begin{cases} \{a \in C \mid \rho(u_i, a) \neq \rho(u_j, a)\}, & \text{if } \partial_\beta^U(u_i) \neq \partial_\beta^U(u_j), \\ *, & \text{otherwise.} \end{cases} \tag{33}$$

Thus, all U^β-reducts can be obtained as prime implicants of F^{U^β}.

For the preservation of boundary regions and the unpredictable region, we cannot obtain the logical functions easily because the partitions $U|I_\beta^B$ and $U|I_\beta^{UN}$ are not discernment-free within elementary sets. When a partition $\mathcal{Y} = \{Y_1, Y_2, \ldots, Y_m\}$ with $Y_k = \{x \in U \mid Cond_k(\mu_{D_l}(x|C)), \ l = 1, 2, \ldots, p\}$ is not discernment-free within elementary sets, we should enumerate all minimal subsets $Z_k \subseteq Y_k$ for each elementary set Y_k such that $Cond_k(\mu_{D_l}(Z|C))$, $l = 1, 2, \ldots, p$ does not hold, and keep the discernibility among the objects in every minimal subset Z_k as well as the discernibility between objects belonging to different elementary sets in order to preserve partition $\mathcal{Y}$. This enumeration is computationally expensive. Then we consider two approximate logical functions: one is a logical function characterizing a sufficient condition of the preservation and the other is a logical function characterizing a necessary condition.

First let us discuss a logical function characterizing a necessary condition. As described before, to have the necessary and sufficient condition, we should enumerate all minimal subsets $Z_k \subseteq Y_k$ for each elementary set Y_k such that $Cond_k(\mu_{D_l}(Z|C))$, $l = 1, 2, \ldots, p$ does not hold. In order to reduce the effort for this enumeration, we restrict consideration of all subsets $Z \subseteq Y_k$ for each elementary set Y_k to of all pairs of objects u_i and u_j belonging to Y_k for each elementary set Y_k. Then we keep the discernibility between objects u_i and u_j in every pair such that $Cond_k(\mu_{D_l}(\{u_i, u_j\}|C))$, $l = 1, 2, \ldots, p$ does not hold, as well as the discernibility between objects belonging to different elementary sets, in order to represent a necessary condition for preservation of partition $\mathcal{Y}$.

From this consideration, we can define the (i, j) component $\check{\delta}_{ij}^{B^\beta}$ of a discernibility matrix as follows to represent a necessary condition for preservation of β-boundary regions:

$$\check{\delta}_{ij}^{B^\beta} = \begin{cases} \{a \in C \mid \rho(u_i, a) \neq \rho(u_j, a)\}, & \text{if } (\partial_\beta^B(u_i) = \partial_\beta^B(u_j) = \emptyset \text{ and} \\ & \quad \exists D_l \in \mathcal{D}, \ \mu_{D_l}(\{u_i, u_j\}|C) \in (\beta, 1 - \beta)) \\ & \quad \text{or } \partial_\beta^B(u_i) \neq \partial_\beta^B(u_j). \\ *, & \text{otherwise.} \end{cases}$$

(34)

Note that any two objects u_i and u_j such that $\partial_\beta^B(u_i) = \partial_\beta^B(u_j) \neq \emptyset$ are discernment-free to preserve $U|I_\beta^L$. Any two objects u_i and u_j such that $\partial_\beta^B(u_i) \neq \partial_\beta^B(u_j)$ should be discernible. Any subset of objects u such that $\partial_\beta^B(u) = \emptyset$ is not always discernment-free. In (34), we consider only pairs of such objects u_i and u_j and if $\exists D_l, \mu_{D_l}(\{u_i, u_j\}|C) \in (\beta, 1 - \beta)$ holds, we should discern them.

Using $\check{\delta}_{ij}^{B^\beta}$, a logical function characterizing a necessary condition for preserving β-boundary regions is obtained as

$$\check{F}^{B^\beta} = \bigwedge_{i,j:i<j} \bigvee \check{\delta}_{ij}^{B^\beta}.$$

(35)

Any prime implicant of $\check{F}^{B^\beta}$ gives a subset of some B^β-reduct.

In similar way, we can obtain a logical function characterizing a necessary condition for preserving the β-unpredictable region as

$$\check{F}^{UN^\beta} = \bigwedge_{i,j:i<j} \bigvee \check{\delta}_{ij}^{UN^\beta},$$

(36)

where $\check{\delta}_{ij}^{UN^\beta}$ is the (i, j) component of a discernibility matrix defined by

$$\check{\delta}_{ij}^{UN^\beta} = \begin{cases} \{a \in C \mid \rho(u_i, a) \neq \rho(u_j, a)\}, & \text{if } (\partial_\beta^U(u_i) \neq \emptyset \text{ or } \partial_\beta^U(u_j) \neq \emptyset) \text{ and} \\ & \quad \forall D_l \in \mathcal{D}, \ \mu_{D_l}(\{u_i, u_j\}|C) \leq \beta, \\ *, & \text{otherwise.} \end{cases}$$

(37)

Table 1. Logical functions related to 7 kinds of reducts

reduct	logical function(s)	exact/approx.
L	F^{L^β}	exact
U	F^{U^β}	exact
LU	$F^{L^\beta} \wedge F^{U^\beta}$	exact
B	$(\check{F}^{B^\beta}, F^{L^\beta} \wedge F^{U^\beta})$	approximate
UN	$(\check{F}^{UN^\beta}, F^{U^\beta})$	approximate
LUN	$(F^{L^\beta} \wedge \check{F}^{UN^\beta}, F^{L^\beta} \wedge F^{U^\beta})$	approximate
BUN	$(\check{F}^{B^\beta} \wedge \check{F}^{UN^\beta}, F^{L^\beta} \wedge F^{U^\beta})$	approximate

Any prime implicant of $\check{F}^{UN^\beta}$ gives a subset of some UN^β-reduct.

Now let us discuss a logical function characterizing a sufficient condition. Let us define an equivalence relation I_β^{LU} defined by $I_\beta^{LU} = I_\beta^L \cap I_\beta^U$. Then a partition $\mathcal{S} = U|I_\beta^{LU}$ is discernment-free within elementary sets. Therefore, the indiscernibility of objects in a set composed of members from different elementary sets of $\mathcal{S}$ may destroy the structure of an arbitrary partition $\mathcal{Y}$. Then by discerning any two objects from two different elementary sets of $\mathcal{S}$, we can preserve the partition corresponding to B-reducts.

Hence, the logical function characterizing a sufficient condition for preserving β-boundary regions is obtained as

$$\hat{F}^{B^\beta} = \bigwedge_{i,j:i<j} \bigvee \hat{\delta}_{ij}^{B^\beta}, \tag{38}$$

where the (i,j) component $\hat{\delta}_{ij}^{B^\beta}$ of a discernibility matrix is defined by

$$\hat{\delta}_{ij}^{B^\beta} = \begin{cases} \{a \in C \mid \rho(u_i, a) \neq \rho(u_j, a)\}, \text{ if } \partial_\beta^L(u_i) \neq \partial_\beta^L(u_j) \\ \qquad\qquad\qquad\qquad \text{ or } \partial_\beta^B(u_i) \neq \partial_\beta^B(u_j), \\ \qquad *, \qquad\qquad\qquad \text{ otherwise.} \end{cases} \tag{39}$$

Any prime implicant of $\hat{F}^{B^\beta}$ gives a super set of some B^β-reduct. Note that $\hat{F}^{B^\beta} = F^{L^\beta} \wedge F^{U^\beta}$ because $\partial_\beta^L(u_i) = \partial_\beta^L(u_j)$ and $\partial_\beta^B(u_i) = \partial_\beta^B(u_j)$ imply $\partial_\beta^U(u_i) = \partial_\beta^U(u_j)$.

By the same discussion based on assertion A2, the logical function characterizing a sufficient condition for preserving β-unpredictable region is obtained just as $\hat{F}^{UN^\beta} = F^{U^\beta}$. Any prime implicant of $\hat{F}^{UN^\beta}$ gives a super set of some UN^β-reduct.

The obtained logical functions are shown in Table 1. In the case of approximate logical functions, the first function in the parenthesis characterizes a necessary condition of the preservation and the second function characterizes a sufficient condition. The logical functions related to LU^β-reducts, LUN^β-reducts and BUN^β-reducts can be obtained by taking the conjunctions of logical functions related to L^β-reducts, U^β-reducts, B^β-reducts and UN^β-reducts. Note that

$\hat{F}^{\mathrm{B}^{\beta}} \wedge \hat{F}^{\mathrm{UN}^{\beta}} = (F^{\mathrm{L}^{\beta}} \wedge F^{\mathrm{U}^{\beta}}) \wedge \hat{F}^{\mathrm{UN}^{\beta}} = F^{\mathrm{L}^{\beta}} \wedge F^{\mathrm{U}^{\beta}}$. This is why we have $F^{\mathrm{L}^{\beta}} \wedge F^{\mathrm{U}^{\beta}}$ as the logical function characterizing a sufficient condition for the preservation of UN^{β}-reducts.

4   Concluding Remarks

In this paper we discuss 7 kinds of reducts preserving lower approximations, upper approximations, boundary regions and the unpredictable region in VPRS model. We show relations among them. The relations are very different from those in the classical RS model. We investigate logical function representations of preservation of lower approximations, upper approximations, boundary regions and the unpredictable region, which are useful in calculations of reducts. We show the exact representations for lower approximations and upper approximations and the approximate representations for the others.

By the nature of VPRS model, we may define reducts replacing the preservation with the enlargement/the diminishment. In this case analysis would be more complex. As a similar model to VPRS model, variable precision Bayesian rough set model is proposed [7]. Our discussion can be applied to this model, too. Those would be topics of our future research.

References

1. Beynon, M.: Reducts within the variable precision rough sets model: A further investigation, *European J. Operational Research* **134** (2001) 592–605.
2. Grzymala-Busse, J. W..: LERS – A system for learning from examples based on rough sets. in: Słowinski, R. (ed.) *Intelligent Decision Support: Handbook of Applications and Advances of the Rough Sets Theory*, Kluwer Academic Publishers, Dordrecht (1992) 3–18.
3. Inuiguchi, M., Tsurumi, M.: On utilization of upper approximations in rough set analysis, *Pro. Int. Workshop of Fuzzy Syst. & Innovational Comput.* (2004) CD-ROM
4. Pawlak, Z.: *Rough Sets: Theoretical Aspects of Reasoning About Data*, Kluwer Academic Publishers, Boston, MA (1991)
5. Skowron, A., Rauser, C. M.: The discernibility matrix and functions in information systems. in: Słowinski, R. (ed.) *Intelligent Decision Support: Handbook of Applications and Advances of the Rough Sets Theory*, Kluwer Academic Publishers, Dordrecht (1992) 331–362.
6. Ślęzak, D.: Various approaches to reasoning with frequency based decision reducts: a survey. in: Polkowski, L., Tsumoto, S., Lin, T. Y.(Eds.), *Rough Set Methods and Applications*, Physica-Verlag, Heidelberg (2000) 235–285.
7. Ślęzak, D., Ziarko, W.: Attribute reduction in the Bayesian version of variable precision rough set model, *Electr. Notes Theor. Comput. Sci.* **82**(4) (2003)
8. Ziarko, W.: Variable precision rough set model. *J. Comput. Syst. Sci.* **46**(1) (1993) 39–59.
9. Ziarko, W: Analysis of uncertain information in the framework of variable precision rough sets. *Foundations of Comput. Dec. Sci.* **18** (1993) 381–396.

Checking Whether or Not Rough-Set-Based Methods to Incomplete Data Satisfy a Correctness Criterion

Michinori Nakata[1] and Hiroshi Sakai[2]

[1] Faculty of Management and Information Science
Josai International University
1 Gumyo, Togane, Chiba, 283-8555, Japan
nakatam@ieee.org
[2] Department of Mathematics and Computer Aided Sciences
Faculty of Engineering, Kyushu Institute of Technology
Tobata, Kitakyushu, 804-8550, Japan
sakai@mns.kyutech.ac.jp

Abstract. Methods based on rough sets to data containing incomplete information are examined for whether a correctness criterion is satisfied or not. It is clarified that the methods proposed so far do not satisfy the correctness criterion. Therefore, we show a new formula that satisfies the correctness criterion in methods by valued tolerance relations.

1 Introduction

Rough sets, introduced by Pawlak[11], give suitable methods to knowledge discovery from data. This is because rough sets can handle granularity of data. Usually, approaches based on rough sets are applied to complete data not containing uncertainty and imprecision. However, there ubiquitously exists uncertainty and imprecision in the real world[10].

Researches handling uncertainty and imprecision are actively done on the field of databases[10], but are not so much on the field of knowledge discovery. Some pioneering work was done by Slowiński and Stefanowski[14] and Grzymala [3] to handle incomplete information by using rough sets. Recently, several investigations have been made on this topic.

Kryszkiewicz applies rough sets to data containing incomplete information by assuming a missing value expressing *unknown* as indiscernible with an arbitrary value[6–8]. An indiscernibility relation under the assumption is called a tolerance relation. In this method an object in which some attribute values are missing is indiscernible with every object for the attributes. The tolerance relation is reflexive, symmetric, but not always transitive. Stefanowski and Tsoukiàs apply rough sets to a table containing incomplete information by making an indescernibility relation from the assumption that an object with an exact attribute value is similar to another object with the attribute value being missing, but the converse does not hold, and missing values are similar to each other[15, 17]. They call

V. Torra et al. (Eds.): MDAI 2005, LNAI 3558, pp. 227–239, 2005.

the indiscernibility relation a similarity relation. The similarity relation is only reflexive. The above two approaches handle incomplete information by deriving an indiscernibility relation from making assumptions on indiscernibility of missing values and then by applying the conventional method of rough sets to the indiscernibility relation.

Furthermore, Stefanowski and Tsoukiás make an indiscernibility relation by introducing the probabilistic degree that two objects cannot be discerned under the premise that an attribute can equally take an arbitrary value included in the corresponding domain when the attribute value is a missing value[15–17]. This method does not make any assumptions on indiscernibility of missing values. The indiscernibility relation is called a valued tolerance relation and each element is a value in the interval [0, 1]. In the method, they use Reichenbach implication in calculating an inclusion degree of two indiscernible sets.

On the other hand, a method based on possible worlds is proposed[12, 13]. This method is to apply the conventional methods based on rough sets to every possible table derived from an incomplete table, and then to aggregate the obtained results.

Active researches are done into incomplete information in the field of databases[10]. Some extensions have to be made to operators in order to directly deal with incomplete information. In order to check whether or not the extended operators create correct results in query processing, a correctness criterion is used[1, 4, 5, 18]. The correctness criterion is as follows:

Results obtained from applying an extended operator to incomplete relations are the same as ones obtained from applying the corresponding conventional operator to possible relations derived from those incomplete relations.

Directly dealing with tables containing incomplete information can be regarded as equivalent to extending the conventional method applied to tables not containing incomplete information. In rough-set-based approaches this correctness criterion is checked as follows:

- Derive a set of possible tables from a table containing incomplete information.
- Aggregate the results obtained from applying the conventional method to each possible table.
- Compare the aggregated results with ones obtained from directly applying the extended method to the table.

Here, a possible table derived from a table is that of each missing value in the table being replaced by an element containing in the corresponding domain. When two results coincide, the correctness criterion is satisfied.

In this paper, we examine the correctness of methods proposed so far according to this criterion through calculating a degree of dependency. The paper is organized as follows. In section 2, approaches based on rough sets are briefly addressed. In section 3, methods handling incomplete information are comparatively studied. In section 4, we describe how to satisfy the correctness criterion in methods by valued tolerance relations. In section 5, conclusions are addressed.

2   Approaches Based on Rough Sets

The data are stored in a table, called an information table, where the rows are labeled by *objects* and columns by attributes, and entries are attribute values. First, we suppose that data about objects contain no incomplete information. When a set of attributes in a table t is denoted by $\mathcal{A}(=\{A_1, \ldots, A_n\})$, the indiscernibility relation $IND(X)$ for a subset $X \subseteq \mathcal{A}$ of attributes is

$$IND(X) = \{(o, o') \in t \times t \mid \forall A_i \in X \quad o[A_i] = o'[A_i]\},$$

where $o[A_i]$ and $o'[A_i]$ are attribute values of objects o and o' that are contained in t, respectively. The indiscernibility relation is an equivalence relation. Suppose that the family of all equivalence classes obtained from the indiscernibility relation $IND(X)$ is denoted by $\mathcal{E}(X)$ ($= \{E(X)_1, \ldots, E(X)_m\}$), where $E(X)_i$ is an equivalence class. Since every value of attributes contained in X is exact, $E(X)_i \cap E(X)_j = \emptyset$ with $i \neq j$. Thus, the objects are uniquely partitioned. The indiscernible set $S(X)_o \in \mathcal{E}(X)$ for a value $o[X]$ of an object o is

$$S(X)_o = \{o' \in t \mid \forall A_i \in X \quad o[A_i] = o'[A_i]\}.$$

The lower approximation $\underline{IND(Y, X)}$ and the upper approximation $\overline{IND(Y, X)}$ of $IND(Y)$ by $IND(X)$ are expressed by means of using indiscernible sets as follows:

$$\underline{IND(Y, X)} = \{o' \in t \mid \exists o \in t \quad S(X)_{o'} \subseteq S(Y)_o\},$$
$$\overline{IND(Y, X)} = \{o' \in t \mid \exists o \in t \quad S(X)_{o'} \cap S(Y)_o \neq \emptyset\}.$$

Now, the objects are restricted in ones contained in one table. Thus, the above formulas are reduced to

$$\underline{IND(Y, X)} = \{o \in t \mid S(X)_o \subseteq S(Y)_o\},$$
$$\overline{IND(Y, X)} = \{o \in t \mid S(X)_o \cap S(Y)_o \neq \emptyset\}.$$

When an object o contains incomplete information for some attributes, it does not always take the same actual value as another object o', even if both objects have the same description. To what degree the object o takes the same actual value as the object o' is obtained. The degree is called an indiscernibility degree of the object o with the object o'. The above indiscernible set $S(X)_o$ is replaced as follows:

$$S(X)_o = \{o'(EQ(o[X], o'[X])) \mid (EQ(o[X], o'[X]) \neq 0) \wedge (o \neq o')\} \cup \{o(1)\},$$

where $EQ(o[X], o'[X])$ is an indiscernibility degree of o with o' over X. In an indiscernible set each object has a degree that is contained in the interval $[0, 1]$.

When the degree is equal to 1, the object surely belongs to the indiscernible set. In addition,

$$EQ(o[X], o'[X]) = \bigotimes_{A_i \in X} EQ(o[A_i], o'[A_i]).$$

where the operator $\bigotimes$ depends on the properties of incomplete attribute values. When the incomplete attribute values are expressed in probability distributions, the operator is product. On the other hand, when the incomplete attribute values are expressed in a possibility distribution, the operator is min. The lower approximation $\underline{IND(Y, X)}$ and the upper approximation $\overline{IND(Y, X)}$ of $IND(Y)$ by $IND(X)$ are expressed by means of using indiscernible sets as follows:

$$\underline{IND(Y, X)} = \{o(\kappa(S(X)_o \subseteq S(Y)_o)) \mid \kappa(S(X)_o \subseteq S(Y)_o) > 0\},$$
$$\overline{IND(Y, X)} = \{o(\kappa(S(X)_o \cap S(Y)_o \neq \emptyset)) \mid \kappa(S(X)_o \cap S(Y)_o \neq \emptyset) > 0\},$$

where $\kappa(F)$ denotes a degree to which F is satisfied.

A measure called *quality of approximation* is used to estimate to what extent the approximation is correct. This measure means to what degree a dependency of attributes Y to attributes X holds[11]; in other words, to what degree a table t satisfies a dependency $X \Rightarrow Y$. The degree is

$$\kappa(X \Rightarrow Y)_t = |\underline{IND(Y, X)}|/|t|,$$

where $|t|$ is the cardinality of a table t, which is equal to the total number of objects in the table t. This degree can be also calculated by means of summing a degree to which each object o in the table t satisfies $X \Rightarrow Y$. The degree $\kappa(X \Rightarrow Y)_o$ to which an object o satisfies $X \Rightarrow Y$ is expressed by

$$\kappa(X \Rightarrow Y)_o = \kappa(S(X)_o \subseteq S(Y)_o).$$

Using the degree,

$$\kappa(X \Rightarrow Y)_t = \Sigma_{o \in t} \kappa(X \Rightarrow Y)_o / |t|.$$

In the next section, we calculate a degree $\kappa(X \Rightarrow Y)_o$ of a dependency $X \Rightarrow Y$ for each object o under the rough-set-based methods. This means to obtain a degree with which each object o belongs to the lower approximation $\underline{IND(Y, X)}$.

3   Comparative Studies on Methods Handling Incomplete Information

3.1   Tables and Possible Tables

We suppose that table t containing incomplete information is given as follows:

$$t$$

O	A	B
1	x	a
2	x	a
3	@	b
4	@	a

Here, column O denotes the object identity and @ denotes a missing value that means *unknown*. Possible tables obtained from table t are those that every missing value @ is replaced by an element consisting of the corresponding domain. Suppose that domains $dom(A)$ and $dom(B)$ of attributes A and B are $\{x, y\}$ and $\{a, b\}$, respectively. The following four possible tables are derived:

$Poss(t)_1$

O	A	B
1	x	a
2	x	a
3	x	b
4	x	a

$Poss(t)_2$

O	A	B
1	x	a
2	x	a
3	x	b
4	y	a

$Poss(t)_3$

O	A	B
1	x	a
2	x	a
3	y	b
4	x	a

$Poss(t)_4$

O	A	B
1	x	a
2	x	a
3	y	b
4	y	a

We check which object satisfies a dependency $A \Rightarrow B$ in these possible tables. For $Poss(t)_1$, indiscernible sets of the objects for attribute A are,

$$S(A)_{o_1} = S(A)_{o_2} = S(A)_{o_3} = S(A)_{o_4} = \{o_1, o_2, o_3, o_4\}.$$

Indiscernible sets of the objects for attribute B are,

$$S(B)_{o_1} = S(B)_{o_2} = S(B)_{o_4} = \{o_1, o_2, o_4\}, \quad S(B)_{o_3} = \{o_3\}.$$

The contribution of each object $o_i (i = 1, 4)$ is,

$$\kappa(A \Rightarrow B)_{o_i} = \kappa(S(A)_{o_i} \subseteq S(B)_{o_i}) = 0.$$

Thus, there exists no object that contributes to $A \Rightarrow B$ in $Poss(t)_1$. Similarly, only the fourth object contributes to $A \Rightarrow B$ in $Poss(t)_2$. All the objects contribute to $A \Rightarrow B$ in $Poss(t)_3$. The first and second objects contribute to $A \Rightarrow B$ in $Poss(t)_4$. Collectively speaking at every object, the first object satisfies $A \Rightarrow B$ in $Poss(t)_3$ and $Poss(t)_4$; the second in $Poss(t)_3$ and $Poss(t)_4$; the third in $Poss(t)_3$; the fourth in $Poss(t)_2$ and $Poss(t)_3$. One of the possible tables is the actual table, but it is unknown which table is the actual one. In this point, they can be regarded as probabilistically equal; namely, each of them has the same probabilistic degree $1/4$. Thus, contributions of each object o_i to $A \Rightarrow B$ are as follows:

$$\kappa(A \Rightarrow B)_{o_1} = 0 \times 1/4 + 0 \times 1/4 + 1 \times 1/4 + 1 \times 1/4 = 1/2,$$
$$\kappa(A \Rightarrow B)_{o_2} = 0 \times 1/4 + 0 \times 1/4 + 1 \times 1/4 + 1 \times 1/4 = 1/2,$$
$$\kappa(A \Rightarrow B)_{o_3} = 0 \times 1/4 + 0 \times 1/4 + 1 \times 1/4 + 0 \times 1/4 = 1/4,$$
$$\kappa(A \Rightarrow B)_{o_4} = 0 \times 1/4 + 1 \times 1/4 + 1 \times 1/4 + 0 \times 1/4 = 1/2.$$

We examine whether or not the same value $\kappa(A \Rightarrow B)_{o_i}$ for each object o_i is obtained by means of using the methods proposed so far in the following subsections.

3.2   Methods by Tolerance Relations

Kryszkiewicz[6–8] assumes a missing value as indiscernible with an arbitrary value contained in the corresponding domain. Under this assumption about indiscernibility of missing values, two objects are indiscernible when there is a probability that an object is equal to another object. Obtained indiscernibility relations, called tolerance relations, are reflexive and symmetric. The indiscernibility relations $IND(A)$ and $IND(B)$ for attributes A and B in table t are, respectively,

$$IND(A) = \begin{pmatrix} 1\,1\,1\,1 \\ 1\,1\,1\,1 \\ 1\,1\,1\,1 \\ 1\,1\,1\,1 \end{pmatrix}, \quad IND(B) = \begin{pmatrix} 1\,1\,0\,1 \\ 1\,1\,0\,1 \\ 0\,0\,1\,0 \\ 1\,1\,0\,1 \end{pmatrix}.$$

Indiscernible sets of the objects for attribute A are,

$$S(A)_{o_1} = S(A)_{o_2} = S(A)_{o_3} = S(A)_{o_4} = \{o_1, o_2, o_3, o_4\}.$$

Indiscernible sets of the objects for attribute B are,

$$S(B)_{o_1} = S(B)_{o_2} = S(B)_{o_4} = \{o_1, o_2, o_4\}, \quad S(B)_{o_3} = \{o_3\}.$$

The contribution of each object $o_i(i = 1, 4)$ is,

$$\kappa(A \Rightarrow B)_{o_i} = \kappa(S(A)_{o_i} \subseteq S(B)_{o_i}) = 0.$$

The obtained values $\kappa(A \Rightarrow B)_{o_i}$ are not equal to ones obtained from possible tables.

3.3   Methods by Similarity Relations

Stefanowski and Tsoukiàs[15, 17] make an indiscernibility relation under the assumption that an exact value is similar to a missing value, but the converse is not so, and the missing values are similar to each other. Under this assumption the probability from exact values is absolutely accepted, but the probability from missing values is not so at all. Obtained indiscernibility relations, called similarity relations, are only reflexive. The indiscernibility relation $IND(A)$ for attribute A in table t is

$$IND(A) = \begin{pmatrix} 1\,1\,1\,1 \\ 1\,1\,1\,1 \\ 0\,0\,1\,1 \\ 0\,0\,1\,1 \end{pmatrix}.$$

$IND(B)$ is unchanged. Indiscernible sets of the objects for attribute A are,

$$S(A)_{o_1} = S(A)_{o_2} = \{o_1, o_2, o_3, o_4\}, \quad S(A)_{o_3} = S(A)_{o_4} = \{o_3, o_4\},$$

The indiscernible sets of the objects for attribute B are unchanged. The contribution of each object $o_i (i = 1, 4)$ is,

$$\kappa(A \Rightarrow B)_{o_i} = \kappa(S(A)_{o_i} \subseteq S(B)_{o_i}) = 0.$$

The obtained values $\kappa(A \Rightarrow B)_{o_i}$ are not equal to ones obtained from possible tables.

3.4   Methods by Valued Tolerance Relations

Stefanowski and Tsoukiàs[15–17] do not impose any assumptions on indiscernibility of missing values. Under their approach, when an attribute value is a missing value, the actual value is one of elements in the domain of the attribute and which element is the actual value does not depend on a specified element; in other words, each element has the same probability for that the element is the actual value. Obtained indiscernibility relations are reflexive and symmetric, but consists of values in the interval $[0, 1]$, which are called valued tolerance relations. The indiscernibility relation $IND(A)$ for attribute A in table t is

$$IND(A) = \begin{pmatrix} 1 & 1 & 1/2 & 1/2 \\ 1 & 1 & 1/2 & 1/2 \\ 1/2 & 1/2 & 1 & 1/2 \\ 1/2 & 1/2 & 1/2 & 1 \end{pmatrix}.$$

$IND(B)$ is unchanged. The indiscernible sets of the objects for attribute A are,

$$S(A)_{o_1} = \{o_1(1), o_2(1), o_3(1/2), o_4(1/2)\},$$
$$S(A)_{o_2} = \{o_1(1), o_2(1), o_3(1/2), o_4(1/2)\},$$
$$S(A)_{o_3} = \{o_1(1/2), o_2(1/2), o_3(1), o_4(1/2)\},$$
$$S(A)_{o_4} = \{o_1(1/2), o_2(1/2), o_3(1/2), o_4(1)\}.$$

An indiscernible set of the objects for attribute B is unchanged.

Suppose that an object o belongs to sets S and S' with probabilistic degrees $P_{o,S}$ and $P_{o,S'}$, respectively. The degree $\kappa(S \subseteq S')$ that the set S is included in another set S' is,

$$\kappa(S \subseteq S') = \prod_{o \in S} \kappa(o \in S \rightarrow o \in S') = \prod_{o \in S} (1 - P_{o,S} + P_{o,S} \times P_{o,S'}).$$

In this formula, the inclusion degree of two sets is calculated by means of using Reichenbach implication ($u \rightarrow v = 1 - u + u \times v$). Now, S and S' are $S(A)_{o_i}$ and $S(B)_{o_i}$, respectively, and $P_{o_i, S(A)_{o_i}}$ and $P_{o_i, S(B)_{o_i}}$ are $EQ(o_i[A], o_j[A])$ and

$EQ(o_i[B], o_j[B])$, respectively. Thus, the contributions of the objects are as follows:

$$\kappa(A \Rightarrow B)_{o_1} = \kappa(S(A)_{o_1} \subseteq S(B)_{o_1})$$
$$= 1 \times 1 \times (1 - 1/2 + 1/2 \times 0) \times (1 - 1/2 + 1/2 \times 1) = 1/2.$$

Similarly,

$$\kappa(A \Rightarrow B)_{o_2} = \kappa(S(A)_{o_2} \subseteq S(B)_{o_2}) = 1/2,$$
$$\kappa(A \Rightarrow B)_{o_3} = \kappa(S(A)_{o_3} \subseteq S(B)_{o_3})$$
$$= (1 - 1/2 + 1/2 \times 0) \times (1 - 1/2 + 1/2 \times 0)$$
$$\times 1 \times (1 - 1/2 + 1/2 \times 0) = 1/8,$$
$$\kappa(A \Rightarrow B)_{o_4} = \kappa(S(A)_{o_4} \subseteq S(B)_{o_4})$$
$$= (1 - 1/2 + 1/2 \times 1) \times (1 - 1/2 + 1/2 \times 1)$$
$$\times (1 - 1/2 + 1/2 \times 0) \times 1 = 1/2.$$

The obtained value $\kappa(A \Rightarrow B)_{o_3}$ is not equal to one obtained from possible tables.

4   Methods Satisfying the Correctness Criterion

We have to examine why the methods proposed so far cannot satisfy the correctness criterion. The methods by tolerance relations and similarity relations impose some assumptions on indiscernibility of missing values. It is clear that the assumptions are not compatible with methods by possible tables. Thus, these methods cannot satisfy the correctness criterion. On the other hand, the method by valued tolerance relations, which is proposed by Stefanowski and Tsoukiàs[15–17], do not impose any assumptions on indiscernibility of missing values. We have to elucidate why this method by Stefanowski and Tsoukiàs cannot satisfy the correctness criterion.

Stefanowski and Tsoukiàs calculates the inclusion degree of two sets where each element belongs with a probabilistic degree as follows:

- Calculate to what probabilistic degree every element belonging to a set also belongs to another set by using Reichenbach implication.
- Multiply the obtained degrees together.

The process shows that the total inclusion degree is obtained through aggregating the inclusion degrees separately obtained for each element. This is valid under the condition that an inclusion degree for an element is determined independently of another element. Is this valid in the present situation?

In the previous section, the degree $\kappa(A \Rightarrow B)_{o_3}$ of a dependency $A \Rightarrow B$ for the third object o_3 does not coincide with the degree obtained from using possible tables. We observe when the third object is indiscernible with the first for attribute A, simultaneously it is indiscernible with the second. In short, the first and the second objects have to be dealt with together. This strongly suggests that the condition described above is not valid in the present situation.

Furthermore in order to examine this, we go into issues for using implication operators. In Reichenbach implication, a probability $Prob(a \rightarrow b)$ of a sentence $a \rightarrow b$ is equal to $1 - Prob(a) + Prob(a) \times Prob(b)$, when probabilities that a sentence a is valid and that a sentence b is valid are given with $Prob(a)$ and $Prob(b)$, respectively. This comes from the following. When the sentence a is valid with a probability $Prob(a)$, $a \rightarrow b$ is valid with $Prob(a) \times Prob(b)$; when a is invalid, $a \rightarrow b$ is valid regardlessly of b; namely, $a \rightarrow b$ is valid with $1 - Prob(a)$ when a is invalid. Thus, $Prob(a \rightarrow b)$ is $1 - Prob(a) + Prob(a) \times Prob(b)$ generally. Is it correct in the present situation that $a \rightarrow b$ is valid regardlessly of b when a is invalid?

The fact that an object o_i belongs to $S(X)_{o_j}$ with a probabilistic degree $EQ(o_j[X], o_i[X])$ means that o_j is equal to o_i for a set X of attributes with the degree $EQ(o_j[X], o_i[X])$. In the method by Stefanowski and Tsoukiàs using an implication, Reichenbach implication, the degree that $o_i \in S(X)_{o_j} \rightarrow o_i \in S(Y)_{o_j}$ is valid is $1 - EQ(o_j[X], o_i[X]) + EQ(o_j[X], o_i[X]) \times EQ(o_j[Y], o_i[Y])$, when o_j is equal to o_i for sets X and Y of attributes with probabilistic degrees $EQ(o_j[X], o_i[X])$ and $EQ(o_j[Y], o_i[Y])$, respectively. This calculation means that the dependency $X \Rightarrow Y$ is valid with a probabilistic degree $1 - EQ(o_j[X], o_i[X])$ regardlessly of a set Y of attributes when o_j is not equal to o_i for a set X of attributes with a probabilistic degree $1 - EQ(o_j[X], o_i[X])$. However, this is not correct if there exists another object o_k that is equal to o_j with a probabilistic degree for a set X of attributes, but that is not to o_i at all for X, as is shown in the following example.

We suppose that table t' containing incomplete information is given as follows:

$$t'$$

O	A	B
1	x	a
2	y	a
3	@	b
4	@	a

In table t' only the attribute value $o_2[A]$ is different from table t in subsection 3.1. Notice there exists another object o_2 that is equal to o_3 with a probabilistic degree, but that is not at all equal to o_1 for attribute A. Results obtained from using possible tables are:

$$\kappa(A \Rightarrow B)_{o_1} = 1/2,$$
$$\kappa(A \Rightarrow B)_{o_2} = 1/2,$$
$$\kappa(A \Rightarrow B)_{o_3} = 0,$$
$$\kappa(A \Rightarrow B)_{o_4} = 1/2.$$

The indiscernibility relations $IND(A)$ for attribute A in table t' is as follows:

$$IND(A) = \begin{pmatrix} 1 & 0 & 1/2 & 1/2 \\ 0 & 1 & 1/2 & 1/2 \\ 1/2 & 1/2 & 1 & 1/2 \\ 1/2 & 1/2 & 1/2 & 1 \end{pmatrix}.$$

$IND(B)$ is the same as in table t. The indiscernible sets of the objects for attribute A are,

$$S(A)_{o_1} = \{o_1(1), o_3(1/2), o_4(1/2)\},$$
$$S(A)_{o_2} = \{o_2(1), o_3(1/2), o_4(1/2)\},$$
$$S(A)_{o_3} = \{o_1(1/2), o_2(1/2), o_3(1), o_4(1/2)\},$$
$$S(A)_{o_4} = \{o_1(1/2), o_2(1/2), o_3(1/2), o_4(1)\}.$$

The indiscernible sets of the objects for attribute B are the same as in table t. We focus on the contribution of the third object o_3.

$$\kappa(A \Rightarrow B)_{o_3} = \kappa(S(A)_{o_3} \subseteq S(B)_{o_3})$$
$$= (1 - 1/2 + 1/2 \times 0) \times (1 - 1/2 + 1/2 \times 0) \times 1$$
$$\times (1 - 1/2 + 1/2 \times 0) = 1/8.$$

In the example, the contribution of the fact that o_3 is equal to o_1 for attribute A with a probabilistic degree $EQ(o_3[A], o_1[A])$ is calculated by means of $1 - EQ(o_3[A], o_1[A]) + EQ(o_3[A], o_1[A]) \times EQ(o_3[B], o_1[B])$. The fact that o_3 is not equal to o_1 for attribute A means that o_3 is equal to another object o_2 for attribute A, because the domain of A consists of only two elements $\{x, y\}$. Thus, when o_3 is not equal to o_1 for attribute A with a probabilistic degree $1 - EQ(o_3[A], o_1[A])$, o_3 has to be unconditionally equal to o_2 for attribute B. However, this is not valid in table t'. In other words, we cannot separate the two facts that o_3 is equal to o_1 with a probabilistic degree $EQ(o_3[A], o_1[A])$ and o_3 is equal to o_2 with a probabilistic degree $1 - EQ(o_3[A], o_1[A])(=EQ(o_3[A], o_2[A]))$. These two facts link with each other disjunctively. We simultaneously have to deal with the two facts.

From considering the above viewpoint, we propose a new formula for calculating $\kappa(X \Rightarrow Y)_{o_i}$.

Let $ps(X)_{o_i,l}$ be an element of the power set $PS(X)_{o_i}$ of $S(X)_{o_i} \setminus o_i$.

$$\kappa(X \Rightarrow Y)_{o_i} = \kappa(S(X)_{o_i} \subseteq S(Y)_{o_i})$$
$$= \sum_l \kappa(\wedge_{o' \in ps(X)_{o_i,l}} (o_i[X] = o'[X]) \wedge_{o' \notin ps(X)_{o_i,l}} (o_i[X] \neq o'[X]))$$
$$\times \kappa(\wedge_{o' \in ps(X)_{o_i,l}} (o_i[Y] = o'[Y]))),$$

where $\kappa(f)$ is a probabilistic degree that a formula f is valid and $\kappa(f) = 1$ when there is no f.

In this formula, all the elements in an indiscernible set are simultaneously handled. The first term denotes a probabilistic degree with which objects are indiscernible and the others are discernible for a set X of attributes. The second term denotes a probabilistic degree with which the objects that are indiscernible for X are also indiscernible for a set Y of attributes. Therefore, a probabilistic degree of inclusion for two sets is correctly calculated.

Proposition
Using the new formula, the method by valued tolerance relations satisfies the correctness criterion for a degree of dependency.

In order to exemplify the above things, we recalculate the degree of dependency $A \Rightarrow B$ for the object o_3 in table t. For the object o_3,

$$S(A)_{o_3} \backslash o_3 = \{o_1(1/2), o_2(1/2), o_4(1/2)\}.$$

For the power set $PS(X)_{o_3}$ of $S(A)_{o_3} \backslash o_3$,

$$PS(X)_{o_3} = \{\emptyset, o_1(1/2), o_2(1/2), o_4(1/2), \{o_1(1/2), o_2(1/2)\},$$
$$\{o_1(1/2), o_4(1/2)\}, \{o_2(1/2), o_4(1/2)\}, \{o_1(1/2), o_2(1/2), o_4(1/2)\}\}.$$

We calculate only for the element $\emptyset$, because $\kappa(o_3[B] = o_i[B]) = 0$ for $i = 1, 2$, and 4. For the element $\emptyset$,

$$\kappa((o_3[A] \neq o_1[A]) \wedge (o_3[A] \neq o_2[A]) \wedge (o_3[A] \neq o_4[A])) = 1/4.$$

Thus,

$$\kappa(X \Rightarrow Y)_{o_3} = 1/4 \times 1 + 0 + 0 + 0 + 0 + 0 + 0 + 0 = 1/4.$$

This value is equal to one obtained from possible tables. Similarly, for each object o_i with $i = 1, 2, 4$, the same results are derived as in subsection 3.4. Thus, the obtained results coincide with ones from possible tables.

5   Conclusions

We have adopted a correctness criterion to extended methods directly handling incomplete information, which are methods by tolerance relations, by similarity relations, and by valued tolerance relations. The correctness criterion is that an extended method has to derive the same results as the method by possible tables. We have examined the extended methods for calculating a degree of dependency, a measure of *quality of approximation*, in tables containing incomplete information for whether they satisfy the correctness criterion or not.

The methods by tolerance relations and by similarity relations impose assumptions on indiscernibility of missing values. The assumptions are not compatible with methods by possible tables. Therefore, these methods do not satisfy the correctness criterion.

The method by valued tolerance relations does not impose any assumptions on indiscernibility of missing values. However, the method does not simultaneously handle all the elements in an indiscernible set. Therefore, the method does not satisfy the correctness criterion.

To save the situation, we have proposed a new formula in which all the elements in an indiscernible set are simultaneously dealt with. Using the new formula, the method by valued tolerance relations satisfies the correctness criterion for a degree of dependency.

In this paper we use such examples that missing values are expressed in a uniform probability distribution over the corresponding domain. When some information is obtained for a missing value, it is reflected in the probability distribution expressing the missing value. As a result, all possible tables are not equally probable. Considering this point, our method also gives the same results as the method by possible tables. In addition, our approach can be also developed when missing values are expressed in a possibility distribution[9].

Acknowledgment

The authors wish to thank the anonymous reviewers for their valuable comments. This research has partially been supported by the Grant-in-Aid for Scientific Research (C), Japanese Ministry of Education, Science, Sports, and Culture, No. 16500176.

References

1. Abiteboul, S., Hull, R., and Vianu, V. [1995] Fundations of Databases, Addison-Wesley Publishing Company, 1995.
2. Gediga, G. and Düntsch, I. [2001]Rough Approximation Quality Revusited, Artificial Intelligence, **132**, 219-234.
3. Grzymala-Busse, J. W. [1991]On the Unknown Attribute Values in Learning from Examples, in Ras, M. Zemankova, (eds.), Methodology for Intelligent Systems, ISMIS '91, Lecture Notes in Artificial Intelligence 542, Springer-Verlag, 368-377.
4. Imielinski, T. [1989]Incomplete Information in Logical Databases, Data Engineering, **12**, 93-104.
5. Imielinski, T. and Lipski, W. [1984]Incomplete Information in Relational Databases, Journal of the ACM, **31**:4, 761-791.
6. Kryszkiewicz, M. [1998]Properties of Incomplete Information Systems in the framework of Rough Sets, in L. Polkowski and A. Skowron, (ed.), Rough Set in Knowledge Discovery 1: Methodology and Applications, Studies in Fuzziness and Soft Computing 18, Physica Verlag, 422-450.
7. Kryszkiewicz, M. [1999]Rules in Incomplete Information Systems, Information Sciences, **113**, 271-292.
8. Kryszkiewicz, M. and Rybiński, H. [2000]Data Mining in Incomplete Information Systems from Rough Set Perspective, in L. Polkowski, S. Tsumoto, and T. Y. Lin, (eds.), Rough Set Methods and Applications, Studies in Fuzziness and Soft Computing 56, Physica Verlag, 568-580.

9. Nakata, M. and Sakai, H. [2005] Rough-set-based Approaches to Data Containing Incomplete Information: Possibility-based Cases, in proceedings of the Fifth Congress of Logic Applied to Technology, IOS Press, in press.
10. Parsons, S. [1996] Current Approaches to Handling Imperfect Information in Data and Knowledge Bases, IEEE Transactions on Knowledge and Data Engineering, **83**, 353-372.
11. Pawlak, Z. [1991] Rough Sets: Theoretical Aspects of Reasoning about Data, Kluwer Academic Publishers 1991.
12. Sakai, H. [1998]Some Issues on Nondeterministic Knowledge Bases with Incomplete Information, in: Proceedings of RSCTC'98, Polkowski, L. and Skowron, A., eds., Lecture Notes in Artificial Intelligence Vol. 1424, Springer-Verlag 1998, pp. 424-431.
13. Sakai, H. [1999]An Algorithm for Finding Equivalence Relations from Table Nondeterministic Information, in N. Zhong, A. Skowron, S. Ohsuga, (eds.), New Directions in Rough Sets, Data Mining and Granular-Soft Computing, Lecture Notes in Artificial Intelligence 1711, pp. 64-72.
14. Słowiński, R. and Stefanowski, J. [1989]Rough Classification in Incomplete Information Systems, Mathematical and Computer Modelling, **12**:10/11, 1347-1357.
15. Stefanowski, J. and Tsoukiàs, A. [1999]On the Extension of Rough Sets under Incomplete Information, in N. Zhong, A. Skowron, S. Ohsuga, (eds.), New Directions in Rough Sets, Data Mining and Granular-Soft Computing, Lecture Notes in Artificial Intelligence 1711, pp. 73-81.
16. Stefanowski, J. and Tsoukiàs, A. [2000]Valued Tolerance and Decision Rules, in W. Ziarko and Y. Yao, (eds.), Rough Sets and Current Trends in Computing, Lecture Notes in Artificial Intelligence 2005, Springer-Verlag, pp. 212-219.
17. Stefanowski, J. and Tsoukiàs, A. [2001]Incomplete Information Tables and Rough Classification, Computational Intelligence, **17**:3, 545-566.
18. Zimányi, E. and Pirotte, A. [1997] Imperfect Information in Relational Databases, in Uncertainty Management in Information Systems: From Needs to Solutions, A. Motro and P. Smets, eds., Kluwer Academic Publishers, 1997, pp. 35-87.

Fuzzy Model Based Environmental Stiffness Identification in Stable Force Control of a Robot Manipulator

Chang-Woo Park[1], Jongbae Lee[1], Minkee Park[2], and Mignon Park[2]

[1] Precision Machinery Research Center, Korea Electronics Technology Institute
401-402 B/D 193,Yakdae-Dong, Wonmi-Gu, Puchon-Si, Kyunggi-Do, 420-734, Korea
drcwpark@keti.re.kr
[2] Dept. of Electrical and Electronic Eng., Yonsei Univ.

Abstract. In this paper, we propose a new force control method in contact tasks using a fuzzy model. The contact force that is exerted on the environment by the link is some general function of the displacement, and not necessarily linear. First, a new identification method of a fuzzy model is proposed and then a nonlinear function of contact force is modeled by a proposed identification algorithm of a fuzzy model. The system stability for the proposed force control method is proved theoretically using a Lyapunov direct method. Finally it is shown that the proposed method is useful for the force control of manipulator by simulation.

1 Introduction

Though force control has long been recognized as an essential robot capability, actual implementation has been delayed due to instability. Stability is an essential property of any control system and there have been a large number of papers discussing the stability problems associated with force control [1][2][3][4]. One of the reasons for the difficulties of the stable force control is that the characteristic of the environment a robot contacts is uncertain, and it complicates the total characteristic of the controlled system. Therefore it is necessary to estimate the environmental stiffness to improve the performance of force control[5][6]. To motivate the concept of new force control method, consider the problem of force control for the system, where the manipulator with mass m is assumed to be in contact with the environment which is located at static position zero. The control problem is to specify input force so that the manipulator moves to a desired contact position. In the conventional method, the force exerted on the environment is given by $f = k_e x$, where k_e is a positive constant used to denote the environmental stiffness[7]. That is, we assume that the environmental stiffness can be modeled as a linear spring with a spring constant denoted by k_e. But contact force f that is exerted on the environment by the link is not necessarily linear and some general function of the displacement x, such that $f = g(x)$.

Usually, environmental stiffness becomes progressively stiffer as they are deflected and it is necessary to determine a spring function $f = g(x)$. In this paper, the function is estimated using the fuzzy modeling methodology. We propose a new identification method of a fuzzy model and then develop a nonlinear relationship between interaction forces and manipulator position using a fuzzy model. By control-

V. Torra et al. (Eds.): MDAI 2005, LNAI 3558, pp. 240–251, 2005.

ling the manipulator position and specifying its relationship to the interaction forces, we can ensure that the manipulator is able to maneuver in a constrained environment while maintaining appropriate contact force. The system stability for n degree-of-freedom manipulator is proved theoretically using the Lyapunov direct method. As a result, we show that the manipulator is force-controlled with the guarantee of stability. The transient and steady-state response is examined by simulation.

2 Fuzzy Models

In order to illustrate a fuzzy model, we use the method suggested by Takagi and Sugeno[8]. The fuzzy model suggested by Takagi and Sugeno in 1985 is the nonlinear model represented by the following equations:

$$R^i : \text{If } x_1 \text{ is } A_1^i \text{ and } x_2 \text{ is } A_2^i, \cdots x_m \text{ is } A_m^i$$
$$\text{then } y^i = a_0^i + a_1^i x_1 + \cdots + a_m^i x_m \tag{1}$$

$$\hat{y} = \frac{\sum_{i=1}^{c} w^i y^i}{\sum_{i=1}^{c} w^i}, \qquad w^i = \prod_{j=1}^{m} A_j^i(x_j) \tag{2}$$

where R^i (i = 1,2,...n) represents the i-th implication, x_j (j=1,2,...,m) is an input variable, and y^i is the output from the i-th implication. a_j^i is a consequent parameter and $A_1^i, A_2^i, \cdots, A_m^i$ are fuzzy variables. As shown in Eq.(1) and (2), this fuzzy model describes the nonlinear input-output relation with piecewise linear equations for the divided input space [11].

The identification of a fuzzy model using input output data is divided into two kinds: structure identification and parameter identification. The former consists of premise structure identification and consequent structure identification. The latter also consists of premise parameter identification and consequent parameter identification. The consequent parameters are the coefficients of linear equations. In this paper, we suggest a new identification method based on the Takagi-Sugeno fuzzy model. In order to avoid complex calculations in this model we propose a new method to identify the structure and parameters of a fuzzy model using the Hough transform and pattern clustering method. In consequent part identification, it is important to come up with linear equations from input-output data considering both linearity and continuity. We identify consequent parts by the Hough transform method, which is used to find out a set of linear equations considering linearity. For premise part identification, input space should be partitioned to determine which rule corresponds to which set of consequent parameters from input output data. The input space is partitioned by clustering method considering the continuity of input output data included in the linear equations. Finally, we suggest a gradient descent algorithm to fine-tune the premise and consequent parameters from input-output data. In order to find out piecewise linear equations from the input-output data, we employ the Hough transform method[9]. In case of a single input and output system, the input and output can be mapped into one point in a 2-dimensional plane. Then the Hough transform method can be used to find straight linear segments and identify the parameters of the fuzzy model. Consider a point (x_i, y_i), which represents a input-output pair of the system and the general equation of a straight line in slope-intercept form, $y_i = ax_i + b$. There is an infinite number of lines that pass through (x_i, y_i), but they all satisfy the equation $y_i = ax_i + b$ for varying values of a and b. However, if we write this equation as $b = -x_i a + y_i$, and consider the ab plane (also called a parameter space), then we have the equation of a single line for a fixed pair (x_i, y_i). Furthermore, the second point (x_j, y_j) will also have a line in the parameter space associated with it, and this line will intersect the line associated with (x_i, y_i) at (a', b'), where a' is the slope and b' the intercept of the line containing both (x_i, y_i) and in the (x_j, y_j) plane. In fact, all points contained on this line will have lines in the parameter space that intersect at (a', b'). Because the slope and intercept can approach infinity as the line approaches a vertical position, the normal representation of a line as Eq.(3) is used in forming accumulator cells in the $\rho\theta$ plane:

$$\rho = x\cos\theta + y\sin\theta \tag{3}$$

ρ and θ are used to represent a straight line instead of a and b.

The result of the Hough transform is accumulated at the cells in the $\rho\theta$ plane and the cells with relatively high value are selected as candidates for the linear pieces of the fuzzy model. Although the Hough transform is usually applied to 2-dimensional data (especially in the image processing field), it is applicable to any function of the form $g(\mathbf{x}, \mathbf{c}) = 0$, where $\mathbf{x}$ is a vector of coordinates and $\mathbf{c}$ is a vector of coefficients. Therefore, the Hough transform method can be employed in case of a multi-input and multi-output system. By thresholding with a fixed value, several cells can be selected within a very small area in the $\rho\theta$ plane, which can cause an undesirably large number of lines corresponding to an linear-like group of input-output data. In order to avoid these problems, the cells at the local maximum points of the accumulator cells in the $\rho\theta$ plane are chosen to set the initial consequent parameters.

For premise structure identification, input space should be partitioned. According to the parameters obtained by Hough transform, input space is partitioned by clustering method, which considers the continuity of the input-output data. Once the input space is partitioned, each area is used to form a fuzzy rule of the model. The sample closest to a linear segment is to be included in the initial cluster of the segment. Each segment forms a initial set of clustering. When all the input-output sample are assigned to the initial clusters, the initial cluster centers and deviations are calculated. In the case that the number of clusters and partitions is unknown, an adaptive sample set construction is one of the common approaches. The whole procedure consists of the following steps[10]:

1) Take the first sample as representative of the first cluster:
   $\mathbf{z}_1 = \mathbf{x}_1$ where $\mathbf{z}_1$ is the first cluster center.
2) Take the next sample and compute its distance to all the existing clusters.

(a) Assign $\mathbf{x}$ to $\mathbf{z_i}$ if $d_i(\mathbf{x}, \mathbf{z_i}) \leq \theta\tau$ $0 \leq \theta \leq 1$

where τ is the membership boundary for a specified cluster. Its value is properly set by the designer.

(b) Do not assign $\mathbf{x}$ to $\mathbf{z_i}$ if $d_i(\mathbf{x}, \mathbf{z_i}) > \tau$

(c) No decision will be made on $\mathbf{x}$ if $\mathbf{x}$ falls in the intermediate region for $\mathbf{z_i}$.

3) (a) Each time a new $\mathbf{x}$ is assigned to $\mathbf{z_i}$, compute $\mathbf{z_i}(t+1)$ and $\mathbf{C}(t+1)$ according to the following expressions:

$$\mathbf{z_i}(t+1) = (1/t+1)[t\mathbf{z_i}(t) + \mathbf{x}]$$

$$\mathbf{C_i}(t+1) = (1/t+1)[t\mathbf{C}(t) + (\mathbf{x} - \mathbf{z_i}(t+1))^2]$$

where t is the number of pattern samples already assigned to $\mathbf{z_i}$ and $\mathbf{x}$ is the $(t+1)$ th such sample. $\mathbf{z_i}(t)$ and $\mathbf{C}(t)$, the variance, were already computed from the t samples.

(b) Form a new cluster $\mathbf{z_j}$ if $d(\mathbf{x}, \mathbf{z_i}) > t$.

4) Repeat steps 2 and 3 until all pattern samples have been assigned. There might be some reassignment of $\mathbf{x}'$s when all $\mathbf{x}'$s are passed again in order. This is because the means and variances have been adjusted with each $\mathbf{x}$ assigned to $\mathbf{z_i}$.

5) After the training is considered complete (that means that   no longer changes $\mathbf{x}$ its class belongings, or some number of $\mathbf{x}$'s are unassigned each time), we can let the system go free to do the clustering on a large number of pattern samples. No indeterminate region will exist this time. All $\mathbf{x}$'s falling in the indeterminate region may be assigned to the nearest class according to the minimum distance rule. All those $\mathbf{x}$'s can be considered unclassified if their distances to all cluster centers are greater than τ.

After input space is partitioned using the clustering method, the center and variance of the clusters are used to form the premise parameters of the fuzzy model. In this paper, all membership functions are Gaussian functions (bell-type) expressed as follows:

$$A_j^i(x) = \exp\left\{\frac{-(x - p_{j1}^i)^2}{P_{j2}^i}\right\} \tag{4}$$

where p_{j1}^i is the center of the cluster corresponding to the j-th linguistic variable in the i-th fuzzy rule and p_{j2}^i is the standard deviation of the cluster.

After initially identifying the structures and parameters of the model, we adjust the parameters so that the error between the model output and the system data decreases. We suggest Theorem 1 and Theorem 2, derived by gradient descent approach, as appropriate algorithms to fine-tune the parameters of a fuzzy model: Theorem 1 is the fine-tuning algorithm for the premise parameters and Theorem 2, for the consequent parameters.

Theorem 1. If the fuzzy model is represented by Eq.(5) and its output is inferred by Eq.(6):

$$R^i : \text{If } x_1 \text{ is } A_1^i(p_{11}^i, P_{12}^i) \text{ and } x_2 \text{ is } A_2^i(p_{21}^i, p_{22}^i) \text{ and } \cdots$$
$$\text{and } x_m \text{ is } A_m^i(p_{m1}^i, P_{m2}^i), \tag{5}$$
$$\text{then } j^i = a_0^i + a_1^i x_1 + \cdots + a_m^i x_m$$

$$\hat{y} = \frac{\displaystyle\sum_{i=1}^{c} w^i y^i}{\displaystyle\sum_{i=1}^{c} w^i} \quad , \qquad w^i = \prod_{j=1}^{m} A_j^i(x_j) \tag{6}$$

where p_{jk}^i is the k-th variable which constructs the linguistic variable of the j-th premise part in the i-th rule, then the premise parameter of the fuzzy model can be fine-tuned by the following method:

$$p_{jk}^i(t+1) = p_{jk}^i(t) + \Delta p_{jk}^i \tag{7}$$

$$\Delta p_{jk}^i = \gamma(y_{des} - \hat{y})(y - \hat{y}) \frac{1}{\displaystyle\sum_{i=1}^{m} w^i} \frac{\partial \omega^i}{\partial p_{jk}^i} \tag{8}$$

where γ denotes the learning rate, y_{des} denotes the desired output and $\hat{y}$ denotes output obtained from a fuzzy model.

Proof. Given sample data $(\mathbf{x}, \mathbf{y}_{des})$, we define the difference between y_{des} and $\hat{y}$ as error e,

$$e = y_{des} - \hat{y} = y_{des} - \frac{\displaystyle\sum_{i=1}^{m} \omega^i y^i}{\displaystyle\sum_{i=1}^{m} \omega^i} \tag{9}$$

The premise parameter should be adjusted to reduce the squared error. Therefore, from the gradient descent algorithm we obtain:

$$\Delta p_{jk}^i = -\gamma \frac{\partial}{\partial p_{jk}^i}\left(\frac{e^2}{2}\right) = -\gamma e \frac{\partial e}{\partial p_{jk}^i}$$

$$= \gamma(y_{des} - \hat{y}) \frac{\dfrac{\partial}{\partial p_{jk}^i}\left(\sum_{i=1}^{c} w^i y^i\right) \times \sum_{i=1}^{c} w^i - \sum_{i=1}^{c} w^i y^i \times \dfrac{\partial}{\partial p_{jk}^i}\left(\sum_{i=1}^{c} w^i\right)}{\left(\displaystyle\sum_{i=1}^{c} w^i\right)^2}$$

$$= \gamma(y_{des} - \hat{y}) \frac{\partial w^i}{\partial p_{jk}^i}\left\{ \frac{y^i}{\left(\displaystyle\sum_{i=1}^{c} w^i\right)^2} - \frac{\displaystyle\sum_{i=1}^{c} w^i y^i}{\displaystyle\sum_{i=1}^{c} w^i} \frac{1}{\displaystyle\sum_{i=1}^{c} w^i} \right\}$$

$$= \gamma(y_{des} - \hat{y})(y^i - \hat{y}) \frac{1}{\displaystyle\sum_{i=1}^{c} w^i} \frac{\partial w^i}{\partial p_{jk}^i}$$

The calculation of Eq.(8) depends on the type of membership function used in fuzzy inference. If the Gausian function, Eq.(4), is employed as a membership function, the learning method for the premise parameters is as follows:

$$\frac{\partial w^i}{\partial p_{j1}^i} = \frac{\partial A^i}{\partial p_{j1}^i} = \frac{2}{p_{j2}^i} \frac{x_j - p_{j1}^i}{p_{j2}^i} \exp\left\{-\left(\frac{x_j - p_{j1}^i}{p_{j2}^i}\right)^2\right\} \tag{10}$$

$$\frac{\partial w^i}{\partial p_{j2}^i} = \frac{\partial A^i}{\partial p_{j2}^i} = \frac{2}{p_{j2}^i}\left\{\frac{x_j - p_{j1}^i}{p_{j2}^i}\right\}^2 \exp\left\{-\left(\frac{x_j - p_{j1}^i}{p_{j2}^i}\right)^2\right\} = \frac{x_j - p_{j1}^i}{p_{j2}^i} \frac{\partial w^i}{\partial p_{j1}^i} \tag{11}$$

Theorem 2. If the fuzzy model is represented by Eq.(5) and its output is inferred by Eq.(6), then the consequent parameter can be fine-tuned by the following learning method:

$$a_i^j(t+1) = a_i^j(t) + \Delta a_i^j \tag{12}$$

$$\Delta a_i^j = \gamma(y_{des} - \hat{y})(y^i - \hat{y})\frac{1}{\displaystyle\sum_{i=1}^{c} w^i} w^i x_j \tag{13}$$

where γ denotes learning rate, y_{des} denotes desired output and $\hat{y}$ denotes output to be obtained from the fuzzy control.

Proof. The consequent parameter can be adjusted to reduce the squared error e^2 in the same way as that of premise parameters by a gradient descent algorithm.

$$\Delta a_j^i = -\gamma\frac{\partial}{\partial a_j^i}\left(\frac{e^2}{2}\right) = -\gamma\frac{\partial e}{\partial a_j^i} = \gamma(y_{des} - \hat{y})\frac{1}{\displaystyle\sum_{i=1}^{c} w^i} w^i x_j$$

3 Force Control of a Manipulator

In this section, we propose a new force control method for a n-link robot manipulator. If the end effector of the manipulator is in contact with the environment, the force interactions will occur between them. If the interaction forces are measured in the joint space, the manipulator dynamic equation can be written as

$$\mathbf{T} = \mathbf{M(q)\ddot{q}} + \mathbf{V_m(q,\dot{q})\dot{q}} + \mathbf{G(q)} + \mathbf{F(\dot{q})} + \mathbf{T_e} \tag{14}$$

where $\mathbf{q}$ is the joint variable n-dimensional vector and $\mathbf{T}$ is the n-dimensional vector of generalized forces. $\mathbf{M(q)}$ denotes the inertia matrix, $\mathbf{V_m(q,\dot{q})}$ the coriolis/centripetal vector, $\mathbf{G(q)}$ the gravity vector, and $\mathbf{F(\dot{q})}$ a friction term. $\mathbf{T_e}$ is an $n \times 1$ vector in joint space coordinates which denotes the force exerted on the environment.

The forces are commonly transformed into the joint-space via Jacobian matrix. Let $\mathbf{x}$ be the $n \times n$ task space and its derivative with respective to time becomes

$$\dot{\mathbf{x}} = \mathbf{J(q)\dot{q}} \tag{15}$$

where $\mathbf{J(q)}$ is an $n \times n$ task Jacobian matrix. Using the principle of virtual work and Eq.(15), we obtain the following relationship

$$\mathbf{T_e} = \mathbf{J^T(q)f} \tag{16}$$

Finally, substituting Eq.(16) into Eq.(14) yields the following robot manipulator equation:

$$\mathbf{T} = \mathbf{M(q)\ddot{q}} + \mathbf{V_m(q,\dot{q})\dot{q}} + \mathbf{G(q)} + \mathbf{F(\dot{q})} + \mathbf{J^T(q)f} \tag{17}$$

where $\mathbf{f}$ is the $n \times 1$ vector of contact forces and torques in task space.

Eq.(17) represents the robot manipulator dynamics in a form which includes the environmental interaction forces, and a new force controller for the n-link robot manipulator can be formulated as follows:

The force exerted on the environment is defined as

$$\mathbf{f} = \mathbf{g(x)}, \tag{18}$$

where $\mathbf{f} = [f_1, f_2, f_3, \cdots, f_n]^T$, $\mathbf{x} = [x_1, x_2, x_3, \cdots, x_n]^T$, $\mathbf{g(x)} = [g_1(x_1), g_2(x_2), g_3(x_3), \cdots, g_n(x_n)]^T$. $\mathbf{g(x)}$ is an $n \times 1$ vector function which represents the relationship between the interaction forces and manipulation position and actually a nonlinear function represented by the following fuzzy model:

$$R_k^i : \text{If } x_k \text{ is } A_k^i \text{ then } g_k^i = a_{k0}^i x_k + a_{k1}^i \qquad (\text{for } i = 1, \cdots, c) \tag{19}$$

$$f_k = g_k(x_k) = \frac{\displaystyle\sum_{i=1}^{c} A_k^i(x_k) g_k^i}{\displaystyle\sum_{i=1}^{c} A_k^i(x_k)} \tag{20}$$

where R_k^i represents the i-th implication for k-axis output $f_k = g_k(x_k)$, x_k is an input variable to represent k-axis displacement, g_k^i is the output from the i-th implication, a_{k0}^i are consequent parameters of the fuzzy model, and a_{k1}^i is the fuzzy variable for premise parts.

The multi-dimensional force controller is the PD-type controller

$$\mathbf{T} = \mathbf{J^T(q)}(-\mathbf{K_v \dot{x}} + \mathbf{K_p \tilde{x}})\mathbf{G(q)} + \mathbf{F(\dot{q})} \tag{21}$$

where $\mathbf{K_v}$ and $\mathbf{K_p}$ are $n \times n$ diagonal, constant, positive definite matrix, and task space tracking error is defined as

$$\tilde{\mathbf{x}} = \mathbf{x_d} - \mathbf{x} \tag{22}$$

where $\mathbf{x_d}$ is an $n \times 1$ vector which is used to denote the desired constant end-effector position.

Substitution of Eq.(18) and Eq.(21) into Eq.(17) yields the closed-loop dynamics

$$\mathbf{M(q)\ddot{q}} + \mathbf{V_m(q,\dot{q})} = \mathbf{J^T(q)}\{-\mathbf{K_v \dot{x}} + \mathbf{K_p \tilde{x}} - \mathbf{g(x)}\} \tag{23}$$

Using the mathematical model previously defined and the Lyapunov direct method, the stability of the system given by Eq.(23) is proved theoretically.

Proof. A scalar function for a Lyapunov function candidate is defined as

$$V = \frac{1}{2}\dot{\mathbf{q}}^{\mathrm{T}}\mathbf{M}(\mathbf{q})\dot{\mathbf{q}} + \frac{1}{2}\tilde{\mathbf{x}}^{\mathrm{T}}\mathbf{K}_{\mathbf{p}}\tilde{\mathbf{x}} + \sum_{k=1}^{n}\int^{x_{k}} g_{k}(y)dy \tag{24}$$

where $g_k(y)$ is a positive definite function, so that $V > 0$. Differentiating Eq.(24) with respective to time yields

$$\dot{V} = \dot{\mathbf{q}}^{\mathrm{T}}\mathbf{M}(\mathbf{q})\ddot{\mathbf{q}} + \frac{1}{2}\dot{\mathbf{q}}^{\mathrm{T}}\dot{\mathbf{M}}(\mathbf{q})\dot{\mathbf{q}} + \tilde{\mathbf{x}}^{\mathrm{T}}\mathbf{K}_{\mathbf{p}}\dot{\tilde{\mathbf{x}}} + \sum_{k=1}^{n} g_{k}(x_{k})\dot{x}_{k} \tag{25}$$

From Eq.(23)

$$\ddot{\mathbf{q}} = \mathbf{M}^{-1}(\mathbf{q})\{\mathbf{J}^{\mathrm{T}}(\mathbf{q})(-\mathbf{K}_{\mathbf{v}}\dot{\mathbf{x}} + \mathbf{K}_{\mathbf{p}}\tilde{\mathbf{x}} - \mathbf{g}(\mathbf{x})) - \mathbf{V}_{\mathbf{m}}(\mathbf{q},\dot{\mathbf{q}})\dot{\mathbf{q}}\} \tag{26}$$

Substituting Eq.(26) into Eq.(25) and utilizing Eq.(15) yields

$$\dot{V} = \frac{1}{2}\dot{\mathbf{q}}^{\mathrm{T}}\dot{\mathbf{M}}(\mathbf{q})\dot{\mathbf{q}} + \dot{\mathbf{q}}^{\mathrm{T}}\mathbf{M}(\mathbf{q})\mathbf{M}^{-1}(\mathbf{q})\{\mathbf{J}^{\mathrm{T}}(\mathbf{q})[-\mathbf{K}_{\mathbf{v}}\dot{\mathbf{x}} + \mathbf{K}_{\mathbf{p}}\tilde{\mathbf{x}} - \mathbf{g}(\mathbf{x})] - \mathbf{V}_{\mathbf{m}}(\mathbf{q},\dot{\mathbf{q}})\dot{\mathbf{q}}\}$$
$$+ \tilde{\mathbf{x}}^{\mathrm{T}}\mathbf{K}_{\mathbf{p}}\dot{\tilde{\mathbf{x}}} + \sum_{k=1}^{n} g_{k}(x_{k})\dot{x}_{k} \tag{27}$$

$$\therefore \quad \dot{V} = \frac{1}{2}\dot{\mathbf{q}}^{\mathrm{T}}\dot{\mathbf{M}}(\mathbf{q})\dot{\mathbf{q}} - \dot{\mathbf{q}}^{\mathrm{T}}\mathbf{J}^{\mathrm{T}}(\mathbf{q})\mathbf{K}_{\mathbf{v}}\dot{\mathbf{x}} + \dot{\mathbf{q}}^{\mathrm{T}}\mathbf{J}^{\mathrm{T}}(\mathbf{q})\mathbf{K}_{\mathbf{p}}\tilde{\mathbf{x}} - \dot{\mathbf{q}}^{\mathrm{T}}\mathbf{J}^{\mathrm{T}}(\mathbf{q})\mathbf{g}(\mathbf{x})$$
$$= -\dot{\mathbf{q}}^{\mathrm{T}}\mathbf{J}^{\mathrm{T}}(\mathbf{q})\mathbf{K}_{\mathbf{v}}\mathbf{J}(\mathbf{q})\dot{\mathbf{q}}, \tag{28}$$

which is nonpositive since $\frac{1}{2}\dot{\mathbf{M}}(\mathbf{q}) - \mathbf{V}_{\mathbf{m}}(\mathbf{q},\dot{\mathbf{q}})$ is skew-symmetric and $\dot{\mathbf{x}}^{\mathrm{T}}\mathbf{g}(\mathbf{x}) = \sum_{k=1}^{n} g_{k}(x_{k})\dot{x}_{k}$. Since the matrices $\mathbf{J}(\mathbf{q})$ and hence $\mathbf{J}^{\mathrm{T}}(\mathbf{q})\mathbf{K}_{\mathbf{v}}\mathbf{J}(\mathbf{q})$ are nonsingular, $\dot{V}$ can only remain zero along trajectories where $\dot{\mathbf{q}} = 0$ and hence $\ddot{\mathbf{q}} = 0$. Substituting $\dot{\mathbf{q}} = 0$ and $\ddot{\mathbf{q}} = 0$ into Eq. (23) yields

$$\lim_{t \to 0}[\mathbf{K}_{\mathbf{p}}\tilde{\mathbf{x}} - \mathbf{g}(\mathbf{x})] = 0 \tag{29}$$

Therefore, the steady state manipulator position satisfies the following equation:

$$\mathbf{x} = \mathbf{x_d} - \mathbf{K_p^{-1}}\mathbf{g}(\mathbf{x}) \tag{30}$$

The stability analysis above shows that the system cannot get stuck at a position which does not satisfy Eq.(30) and also means that the robot manipulator will stop moving when the task space coordinates are given by Eq.(30). Therefore, V is valid Lyapunov function of the closed loop system, and the result follows.

To obtain the steady-state force exerted on the environment, we substitute Eq.(30) into Eq.(18) to yield

$$g_i(x_{di} - \frac{f_{di}}{K_\pi}) = f_{di} \tag{31}$$

where $\mathbf{f_d}$ is the steady state force exerted on the environment and the subscript i is used to represent the i-th axis component of $\mathbf{x_d}$, and $\mathbf{K_{p'}}$. Because $\mathbf{K_v}$ is diagonal,

Eq.(30) can be converted into Eq.(31). Using Eq.(31) we can obtain a desired position from a desired force and the desired force is created by commanding a desired position that is slightly inside the contact force.

4 Simulations

In the previous section, the system stability was discussed. In this section, stability and response characteristic are simulated for the environment model obtained by fuzzy modeling method and they are compared with a conventional method.

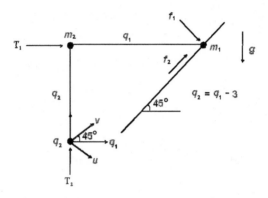

Fig. 1. Manipulator moving along slanted surface

We simulate a force controller for the robot manipulator system given in Fig.1. The control objective is to move the end effector to a desired final position of $v_d = 2m$ while exerting a final desired normal force of $f_{d1} = 4N$. We neglect the surface friction and joint friction. The robot link masses are assumed to be unity, and the initial end-effector position is given by

$$v(0) = 0m, \quad u(0) = 0m \tag{32}$$

T, Q, G, M and **x** are defined as follows:

$$\mathbf{T} = \begin{bmatrix} T_1 \\ T_2 \end{bmatrix}, \; \mathbf{q} = \begin{bmatrix} q_1 \\ q_2 \end{bmatrix}, \; \mathbf{G} = \begin{bmatrix} 0 \\ (m_1 + m_2)g \end{bmatrix}$$

$$\mathbf{M} = \begin{bmatrix} m_1 & 0 \\ 0 & m_1 + m_2 \end{bmatrix}, \; \mathbf{J} = \frac{1}{\sqrt{2}}\begin{bmatrix} 1 & -1 \\ 1 & 1 \end{bmatrix}, \; \mathbf{x} = \begin{bmatrix} u \\ v \end{bmatrix} \tag{33}$$

To accomplish the control objective, the force controller is given by

$$\mathbf{T} = \mathbf{j}^T(\mathbf{q})(-\mathbf{K}_v + \mathbf{K}_p \tilde{\mathbf{x}}) + \mathbf{G}(\mathbf{q}) \tag{34}$$

where $\tilde{\mathbf{x}} = \begin{bmatrix} u_d - u \\ v_d - v \end{bmatrix}$. The gain matrices K_v and K_p have been taken to be $-\mathbf{K}_v = K_v \mathbf{I}$ and $-\mathbf{K}_p = K_p \mathbf{I}$. For this simulation, we select $K_p = K_v = 10$.

Assume that the normal force satisfies the relationship

$$f_1 = g(u) \tag{35}$$

where $g(u)$ is obtained from a fuzzy modeling method. Fig.2 shows the relationship between interaction forces and manipulation position which is obtained from experiments. As shown in Fig.2, an environment stiffness becomes progressively stiffer as they deflected and the contact force that is exerted on the environment by the link is not linear. Fig.3 shows the linear segments obtained by the Hough Transform method from the measured force-displacement data. Fig.4 is the input and output of the constructed fuzzy model only after initial parameter setting by means of the Hough Transform and clustering method with the measured force-displacement data shown in Fig.2. This figure shows that there is some degree of error between the original system and the coarsely modeled system. To minimize error and adjust the system parameters, fine-tuning is accomplished by the gradient descent method. During the learning procedure, the premise and consequent parameters settle down and error decreases. Fig.6 is the input-output graph of the fuzzy model tuned by the gradient descent algorithm. It shows that the suggested fuzzy modeling method models the given system successfully.

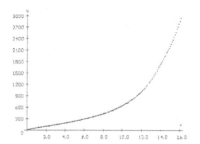

Fig. 2. Measured force/displacement data

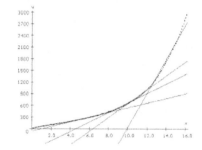

Fig. 3. Line segments by Hough transform

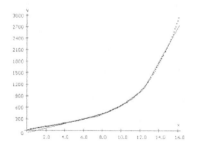

Fig. 4. Fuzzy model before fine-tuning

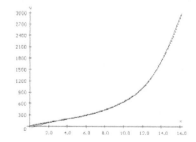

Fig. 5. Fuzzy model after fine-tuning

To satisfy the control objective that $f_{d1} = 4N$, we utilize Eq.(31). Substituting the values of f_{d1} and K_p into Eq.(31) yields $U_d = 0.42m$. The simulation result for the new force controller is given in Fig.6. It shows that the manipulator is force controlled with the guarantee of stability.

To satisfy the control objective that $f_{f1} = 4N$, we utilize the following equation:

$$f_{d1} = K_p U_d \tag{36}$$

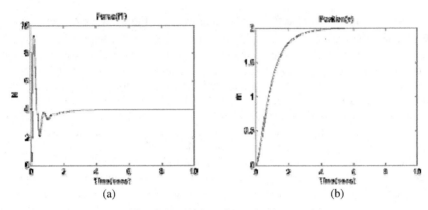

Fig. 6. Simulation of new force control

Substituting the values of f_{d_1} and K_p into Eq.(36) yields $U_d = 0.4m$. The simulation results of the stiffness controller for the manipulator system (Fig.2) is given in Fig.7. Because the actual contact force that is exerted on the environment is not linear, the stiffness controller is simulated for the nonlinear model of the contact force $f = g(x)$, which is obtained from the fuzzy model. As indicated by the simulation result, there exists some steady state error compared with the new force control method.

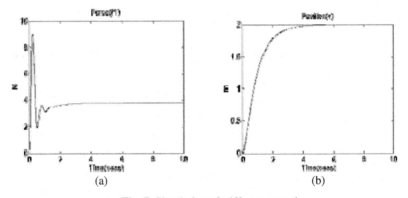

Fig. 7. Simulation of stiffness control

5 Conclusions

In this paper, we have developed a new force control method in contact tasks using a fuzzy model. A nonlinear function of contact force is easily modeled using a fuzzy modeling algorithm and system stability for the proposed method is proved theoretically using the Lyapunov direct method. Simulation result shows that the proposed method reduces the steady state error of the conventional method. As a result, we have showed that the manipulator is force controlled with the guarantee of stability.

References

1. D.E. Whitney,: Historical Perspective And State of The Art in Robot Force Control, IEEE Int. Conf. Robotics Autom, St. Louis, MO, pp. 262-268 (1985)
2. Y. Shoji, M. Inara, and T. Fukuda,: Stable force control of 1 degree-of-freedom manipulator in contact tasks, IEEE Int. Conf. IROS, Yokohama, Japan, pp. 1511-1515 (1993)
3. Y. Shoji, M. Inara, and T. Fukuda,: Stable force control of multi degree-of-freedom linear manipulator with collision phenomena, IEEE Int. Conf. IROS, Osaka, Japan, pp. 1109-1114 (1991)
4. D.M. Dawson, F. L. Lewis, and J. F. Dorsey,: Robust force control of a robot manipulator, Int. J. Robotics Res., vol. 11, no. 4, pp. 312-319 (1992)
5. K. Kiguchi and T. Fukuda,: Position/force control of robot manipulators for geometrically unknown objects using fuzzy neural networks, IEEE Trans. Ind. Electron. vol. 47, no. 3, pp. 641-649 (2000)
6. An, C.H., and Hollerbach J.M.: Dynamic stability issues in force control of manipulators, IEEE Int. Conf. Robotics Autom, Raleigh, NC, pp. 890-896 (1987)
7. J. Kenneth Salisbury,: Active Stiffness Control of A Manipulator in Cartesian Coordinates, 19th IEEE Conf. Decision and Control, pp.95-100 (1980)
8. T. Takagi and M. Sugeno,: Fuzzy Identification of Systems and Its Applications to Modeling and Control, IEEE Trans. Systems, Man and Cybernetics, vol. SMC-15, no. 1, pp. 116-132 (1985)
9. D.H. Ballard,: Generating the Hough Transform to Detect Arbitrary Shapes, Pattern Recognition, vol. 13, no. 2, pp. 111-122 (1981)
10. Sing-Tze Bow,: Pattern Recognition and Image Preprocessing, Dekker (1992)
11. C.W. Park and M. Park,: "Adaptive parameter estimator based on T-S fuzzy models and its application to indirect adaptive fuzzy control design", Information Sciences, An International Journal, vol. 159, pp. 125-139 (2004)

Omnidirectional Adaptive Behavior Control for Autonomous Mobile Robot

Yoichiro Maeda and Wataru Shimizuhira

Dept. of Human and Artificial Intelligent Systems
Faculty of Engineering, Univ. of Fukui
3-9-1, Bunkyo, Fukui 910-8507 Japan
{maeda,wsimizuhira}@ir.his.fukui-u.ac.jp

Abstract. We propose a multiple omnidirectional vision system with three omnidirectional cameras and its calculation method for the measurement of the object position and the self-localization in RoboCup soccer robots. On the identification of the self-position, we try to improve the accuracy of the measurement by correcting the absolute position based on the measurement error of landmarks in the origin of the absolute coordinate. Furthermore, we propose the omnidirectional behavior control method for collision avoidance and object chasing motion by using fuzzy reasoning in an autonomous mobile robot with MOVIS. In this paper, we also report some experimental results to confirm the efficiency of the proposed method by using a soccer robot in dynamic environment.

1 Introduction

In the research on multiple autonomous mobile robots such as RoboCup, some methods for obtaining the environmental information over all circumferences used an omnidirectional vision sensor, were proposed [1, 2]. In case of the research using the omnidirectional camera, only one camera is almost used in general, but the object image in the mirror is compressed according to the distance. If the height of the object is uncertain, the accurate distance measurement is generally impossible. To solve these problems, a vision system which two omnidirectional cameras are perpendicularly fixed was proposed by H.Koyasu [3], T.Matsuoka [4] and J.Gluckman [5] and the other system which two omnidirectional cameras are horizontally fixed was proposed by R.Miki [6]. In our laboratory, we have developed a multiple omnidirectional vision system (called MOVIS) which three omnidirectional cameras are arranged on an autonomous soccer robot like as a horizontal and equilateral triangle [7]. As a result, the stereo-vision system by the principle of the triangulation is made by each two cameras. The purpose of this research is to realize the object recognition and the position measurement of the robot accurately in real time. Furthermore, we propose the real-time object position measurement and the self-localization method for the autonomous soccer robot with MOVIS.

On the other hand, there are some researches for the autonomous behavior under the complicated environment by using fuzzy reasoning. In the research of

V. Torra et al. (Eds.): MDAI 2005, LNAI 3558, pp. 252–263, 2005.

the behavior control in the RoboCup middle-size league, a control system based on the fuzzy potential method was proposed by R.Tsuzaki [8], a multi-layered learning system was proposed by Y.Takahashi [9]. Generally, it is well known that an operator is easy to express his control knowledge by using fuzzy reasoning. However, if we are going to describe adaptive behaviors in the complicated environment with fuzzy rule, we must construct too many rules and take a lot of times to tune them. Therefore, we also propose a multi-layered fuzzy behavior control method that element behaviors of the robot are individually controlled with the behavior decision fuzzy rule in lower-layer, and combined them with the behavior selection fuzzy rule in higher-layer [10, 11]. The goal of the work is to acquire the surrounding environment information overall circumferences under the complicated environment, and to realize the omnidirectional adaptive behavior in an autonomous mobile robot. To confirm the efficiency of the proposed method, we performed the measurement and robot control experiment by using an actual autonomous soccer robot.

2   Research Subjects on RoboCup Soccer Robot

RoboCup is the most famous soccer robot competition in the world and was originally established as an international joint project to promote AI, robotics, and related field [12]. Technologies generated in RoboCup are able to be applied for socially significant problems and industries. RoboCup is a very attractive research area for AI and robotics researchers because there are many research subjects to realize actual soccer robots.

We are now developing the autonomous soccer robots to participate in the RoboCup world competition. Appearance of all robots of our team FC-Soromons is shown in Fig.1. In our laboratory, the high performance vision system to ac-

Fig. 1. Appearance of Team FC-Soromons

quire the surrounding environment information and the flexible behavior control method like human by using soft computing framework are main research topics. The team FC-Soromons is composed of four robots including three field-player and one goalkeeper robots. These robots are used for the subject of our research to confirm the efficiency of the proposed vision system and control method mentioned in the following sections.

3   Multiple Omnidirectional Vision System

To acquire the surrounding information in dynamic environment, we developed the multiple omnidirectional vision system (MOVIS). Measurement of the distance and direction to an object by only vision sensor without active sensors (for example, sonar, infrared sensor, laser range finder, etc.) becomes possible by using MOVIS.

3.1   Basic Architecture of MOVIS

Three omnidirectional cameras (M_1, M_2, and M_3) with same performances respectively are used in MOVIS. In this system, the omnidirectional cameras are horizontally arranged in the equilateral triangle on a soccer robot as shown in Fig.2. The center of gravity of the robot and the equilateral triangle vertically exist in the same point. By the line extended from the center of gravity of the equilateral triangle to each vertex point, the range of the acquisition of images are divided into three areas which each two cameras perform as the stereo vision within 120 degrees (for example in Fig.3, M_1 & M_2, M_2 & M_3, and M_3 & M_1). Measurement by two cameras in each area provides the precise distance information by the principle of triangulation.

Outline of the overall measurement process of MOVIS is shown in Fig.4. The measurement of the object position and the self-localization method used in MOVIS are described in this section.

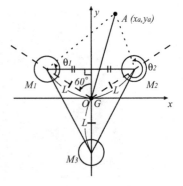

Fig. 2. Appearance of MOVIS   Fig. 3. Structure of MOVIS

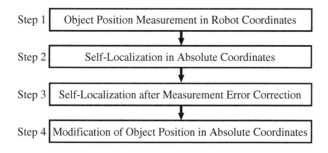

Fig. 4. Measurement Process of MOVIS

Measurement of Object Position. In the position measurement, an object position $A(x_a, y_a)$ in Fig.3 is obtained by using omnidirectional camera M_1 and M_2 in the robot coordinates. In the view point of $\overline{M_1 M_2}$, a slant angle of $\overline{AM_1}$ is $(\theta_1 - \frac{\pi}{6})[= \lambda_1]$, that of $\overline{AM_2}$ is $(\theta_2 - \frac{5\pi}{6})[= \lambda_2]$. The distance between the center of gravity of the robot and the center of camera is assumed as L. As a result, a position (x_a, y_a) of the object A in the robot coordinates is calculated by the following equations.

$$x_a = \frac{\sqrt{3}}{2} L \cdot \frac{\tan \lambda_2 + \tan \lambda_1}{\tan \lambda_2 - \tan \lambda_1} \tag{1}$$

$$y_a = \frac{1}{2} L + \sqrt{3} L \cdot \frac{\tan \lambda_2 \cdot \tan \lambda_1}{\tan \lambda_2 - \tan \lambda_1} \tag{2}$$

Self-localization of Robot Position. In this research, a half field of RoboCup middle-size robot league was constructed for the measurement experiment, and corner poles were used as a landmark for the self-localization. The coordinate axis in the absolute coordinates is shown in Fig.5. Positions of the corner pole p and q are assumed a width Fw and a depth Fd respectively from the origin of the field. Moreover, the position of the center of gravity of the robot is assumed as (X_r, Y_r) and the slant angle of x axis of the robot coordinates in the absolute coordinates is assumed as β.

In the robot coordinates, assuming that positions of corner pole p and q obtained from the position measurement are $p(x_p, y_p)$ and $q(x_q, y_q)$ respectively, the slant angle β is shown in the equation (3) and a center of the gravity position (X_r, Y_r) of the robot in the absolute coordinates is shown in equations (4) and (5). By the landmark position $p(x_p, y_p)$ in the robot coordinates and β obtained by the equation (3), the self-localization position (X_r, Y_r) in the absolute coordinates is calculated.

$$\beta = \tan^{-1} \frac{y_q - y_p}{x_p - x_q} \tag{3}$$

$$X_r = -x_p + Fw \cdot \cos \beta + Fd \cdot \sin \beta \tag{4}$$

$$Y_r = -y_p - Fw \cdot \sin \beta + Fd \cdot \cos \beta \tag{5}$$

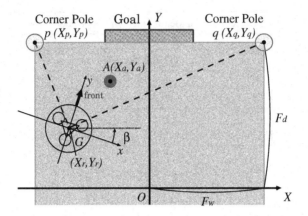

Fig. 5. Self-Localization in Absolute Coordinates

Measurement Error Correction. Assuming that the robot is fixed at the origin point, the robot coordinates coincide with the absolute coordinates. After the measurement of the self-localization, we assume that positions of right and left corner pole are $(\tilde{x}_p, \tilde{y}_p)$ and $(\tilde{x}_q, \tilde{y}_q)$ respectively including the measurement error. In this case, we replace x_p, y_p, x_q and y_q in equations (3) to (5) to x'_p, y'_p, x'_q and y'_q in the equation (6). The absolute robot position obtained by self-localization including the measurement error in the origin point in equations (3) to (5) was modified by using x'_p, y'_p, x'_q and y'_q instead of x_p, y_p, x_q and y_q.

$$x'_p = -x_p \cdot \frac{Fw}{\tilde{x}_p}, \quad y'_p = y_p \cdot \frac{Fd}{\tilde{y}_p}, \quad x'_q = x_q \cdot \frac{Fw}{\tilde{x}_q}, \quad y'_q = y_q \cdot \frac{Fd}{\tilde{y}_q} \quad (6)$$

Moreover, assuming that the absolute position of an object A is (X_a, Y_a), the position (x_a, y_a) of an object A in the robot coordinates is obtained from equations (1) and (2). After the measurement error correction, by the modified β' and self-localization position (X'_r, Y'_r), we can obtain the modified object position X_a and Y_a from equations (7) and (8).

$$X_a = (x_a + X'_r) \cos \beta' - (y_a + Y'_r) \sin \beta' \quad (7)$$

$$Y_a = (x_a + X'_r) \sin \beta' + (y_a + Y'_r) \cos \beta' \quad (8)$$

4   Multi-layered Fuzzy Behavior Control

Generally, adaptive behaviors of a robot under the complicated environment are divided into some sub-tasks in many cases. Hierarchical control systyem is very useful for combining these sub-tasks. Some recent works on hierarchical fuzzy systems [13–15] were proposed. In this research, we propose a multi-layered fuzzy behavior control that each behavior of a robot is controlled with lower-layered fuzzy rules and they are combined with higher-layered fuzzy rules.

4.1 Multi-layered Fuzzy Control Architecture

Fuzzy reasoning is one of the useful method to describe adaptive behaviors for an autonomous mobile robot. However, it is not easy to realize the omni-directional adaptive behavior in an autonomous mobile robot even if the vision sensor such as an omnidirectional camera is able to acquire the environmental information overall circumferences under the complicated environment. Furthermore, when we describe adaptive behaviors in the complicated environment with fuzzy inference rules, we have to construct too many rules and take a lot of times to tune them. Accordingly, we propose the multi-layered fuzzy behavior control for an autonomous mobile robot in this research.

First of all, robot behaviors are divided into some basic sub-tasks and individually controlled by the behavior decision fuzzy rules in a lower-layer. Then, one of the lower-layer fuzzy rules is selected by the behavior selection fuzzy rule in a higher-layer. Accordingly, the control of a robot is able to be realized by combining lower-layered fuzzy rules with higher-layer fuzzy rules. Outline of the multi-layered fuzzy behavior control method in case of the soccer robot is shown in Fig.6. By the MOVIS mentioned in the previous section, the environmental information overall circumferences is measured. As input variables to the behavior decision fuzzy rules, we used the distance and direction to an obstacle in the collision avoidance fuzzy rule and the direction to a goal and the distance and direction to a ball in the ball control fuzzy rule. And these fuzzy rules output the steering angle and the velocity of the robot. Same input variables are also used in the behavior selection fuzzy rule.

4.2 Behavior Decision Fuzzy Rule

Collision avoidance and ball control fuzzy rules in the behavior decision fuzzy rule are described with the simplified fuzzy reasoning. In the collision avoidance fuzzy rule, we divided spatial states for the robot as shown in Fig.7. The antecedent part of the rule indicates the direction and distance to an obstacle measured by MOVIS and the consequent part indicates the steering angle and the velocity

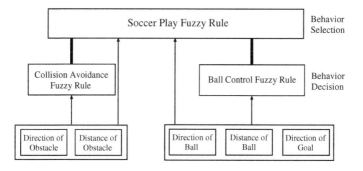

Fig. 6. Outline of Multi-Layered Fuzzy Behavior Control

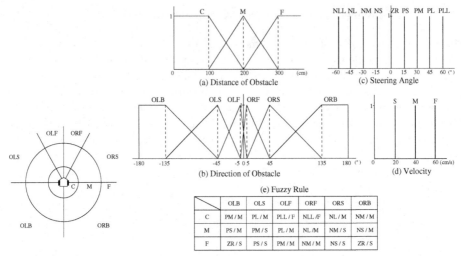

Fig. 7. State Division
(Collision Avoidance)

Fig. 8. Collision Avoidance Fuzzy Rule

to control the robot in Fig.8. Ball control fuzzy rule is the motion rule that the robot is controlled to move so that the ball exists between the goal and the robot. The state division and fuzzy rules are shown in Fig.9 and 10. Fig.10 shows the distance and direction to a ball and the direction to a goal overall circumferences in the antecedent part, and the steering angle and the velocity to control the robot in the consequent part.

4.3   Behavior Selection Fuzzy Rule

The behavior selection fuzzy rule for soccer playing is described to combine output values of behavior decision fuzzy rules. Fig.11 shows the ball and the obstacle distance overall circumferences in the antecedent part, and the weight of the collision avoidance between the collision avoidance and the ball control behavior in the consequent part. In the antecedent part, the distance to an obstacle and the distance to a ball are divided into three labels. In the consequent part, the weight of the collision avoidance behavior is divided into six labels. For example, if a ball exists in the far area and an obstacle exists in the near area, then the singleton value of the fuzzy weight α for the collision avoidance becomes extremely strong (WVL in Fig.11) so as to take the collision avoidance behavior specially. The weight value for the ball control behavior is calculated as $(1-\alpha)$.

5   Experiments

We actually performed the measurement experiment by MOVIS and the shoot experiment by a soccer robot with the multi-layered fuzzy behavior control

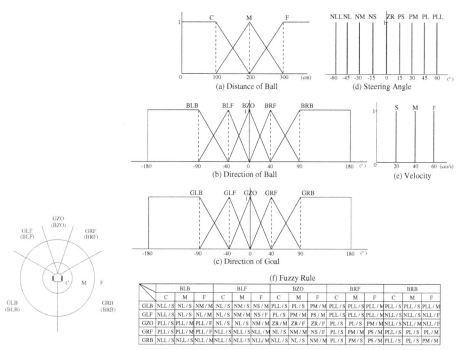

Fig. 9. State Division (Ball Control)

Fig. 10. Ball Control Fuzzy Rule

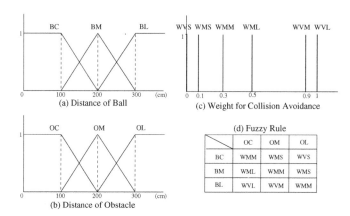

Fig. 11. Behavior Selection Fuzzy Rule

method. The experiment was executed by using three IEEE1394 digital omnidirectional cameras and a notebook PC with Celeron 600A MHz CPU and Vine Linux 3.0.

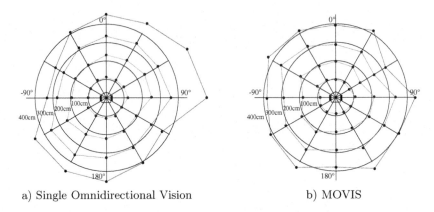

a) Single Omnidirectional Vision   b) MOVIS

Fig. 12. Results of Measurement Experiment

5.1   Measurement Experiment of MOVIS

In order to confirm the precision of MOVIS, we performed the measurement experiment of the ball direction and distance from the robot with MOVIS. We measured the direction and distance to a ball (θ, d) in 48 circular lattice points at 1m interval from 1m to 4m and 30 degrees interval from -180 to 180 degrees so as to be 0 degree in front of the robot. θ means the direction (positive in right-hand side) from the robot front and d the distance from the robot position.

By using the geometric relation of a single omnidirectional vision, the center of gravity of a ball is measured from the camera image. The measurement result is shown in Fig.12 a). Black point means the measurement result for each circular lattice point. In this measurement, the error of θ became less than approx 1 degree in all points, and it is able to prove that the direction is exactly measurable regardless of the distance of an object. However, the error of d was too large when the ball was far, and some maximum errors of over 100cm were measured in $(60degrees, 400cm)$ or $(90degrees, 400cm)$. It is considered because the information is compressed around the image acquired by an omnidirectional vision.

Results for same measurement using MOVIS are shown in Fig.12 b). For the error of θ, there are small errors partly, but the measurement is almost correct. For the distance, the error of about 10cm appeared in near objects and the error of about 40cm appeared in far objects. Moreover, the error became the largest in the direction in 60 degrees, -60 degrees and 180 degrees because the triangle used for the camera layout is distorted in the end of the measurement area by the stereo vision with dual cameras. As a result, we confirmed the measurement by MOVIS is more accurate than the measurement by a single omnidirectional vision about 63% in the average of errors.

5.2   Control Experiment of Soccer Robot

The main body and the system architecture of a soccer robot which we constructed for the RoboCup competition are shown in Fig.13 and 14. This robot

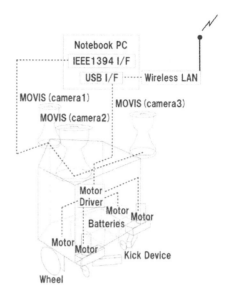

Fig. 13. Experimental Robot   **Fig. 14.** Robot System Architecture

has MOVIS composed of three omnidirectional cameras on the top of its body. Moreover, a miniature half field (5m width and 4m depth) of RoboCup middle-size league was constructed as the experimental measurement environment, and a ball and an obstacle were arranged at the fixed points on the field, respectively.

In this environment, at first the behavior decision fuzzy rules for the collision avoidance and the ball control were independently constructed previously. Next, we performed the shoot experiment which the robot carries a ball to the goal while avoiding an obstacle using the behavior selection fuzzy rule as shown in Fig.15 b). Furthermore, a comparative experiment used a linear weight k instead of fuzzy weight α for the collision avoidance in the behavior selection fuzzy rule was also performed as shown in Fig.15 a). In this experiment, we assumed that $k = L_b/(L_o + L_b)$ where L_o and L_b mean the distance to an obstacle and a ball, respectively.

We confirmed that each behavior is adaptively realized as shown in the result of the experiment. Moreover, in the shoot experiment using the multi-layered fuzzy behavior control, we also confirmed that it is possible to combine the collision avoidance behavior (repulsive motion) and ball approaching behavior (attractive motion) successfully. In the comparative experiment, the adaptive behavior was not realized. As the reason for this result, we considered that, when the distance of an obstacle and a ball is almost similar, weights of two behaviors also become nearly equal and keep the balance each other and the robot becomes not to take into account the information of the goal in this experiment.

a) In Case of Linear Weight k b) In Case of Fuzzy Weight α

Fig. 15. Results of Shoot Experiment

6   Conclusions

In this paper, we proposed the multiple omnidirectional vision system (MOVIS) with three omnidirectional cameras and its calculation method for the measurement of the object position and the self-localization in an autonomous mobile robot. We also proposed the multi-layered fuzzy behavior control method that each element behavior of the robot is individually controlled with the behavior decision fuzzy rule in the lower-layer and combined by the behavior selection fuzzy rule in the higher-layer.

The measurement experiment by MOVIS and the control experiment by an autonomous soccer robot were carried out by using the proposed method. As a result, we confirmed that the measurement of MOVIS is remarkably more accurate than that of a single omnidirectional vision and the strategic behavior including the collision avoidance and the ball control with the huge number of states is easily constructed by the fuzzy inference rule. We consider that the proposed methods for MOVIS and the fuzzy behavior control are also adaptable and useful for the other application of autonomous mobile robots.

References

1. Price, A.R. and Jones, T.: An Innovative Approach to Vision, Localization and Orientation Using Omnidirectional Radial Signature Analysis. RoboCup-98: Robot Soccer World Cup II (1998)
2. Bonarini, A.: The Body, the Mind or the Eye, First?. RoboCup-99: Robot Soccer World Cup III, pp.210-221 (1999)
3. Koyasu, H., Miura, J. and Shirai, Y.: Estimation of Ego-Motion and Its Uncertainty for a Mobile Robot Using Omnidirectional Stereo. Proc. of the 20th Annual Conference of the Robotics Society of Japan, CD-ROM, 3A24 (2002) [in Japanese]
4. Matsuoka, T., Motomura, A. and Hasegawa, T.: Real-time Self-Localization Method in a Dynamically Changing Environment. Proc. of the 2003 IEEE/RSJ International Conference on Intelligent Robots and Systems, pp.1234-1239 (2003)

5. Gluckman, J., Nayar, K. and Thoresz, J.: Real-Time Omnidirectional and Panoramic Stereo. Proc. of Image Understanding Workshop, Vol.1, pp.299-303 (1998)
6. Miki, R., Yamazawa, K., Takemura, H. and Yokoya, N.: A Remote Surveillance System Using Omnidirectional Sensors. Technical Report of IEICE, PRMU98-177, pp.7-14 (1999) [in Japanese]
7. Shimizuhira, W. and Maeda, Y.: Self-Localization Method Used Multiple Omnidirectional Vision System. Proc. of SICE Annual Conference 2003, pp.2796-2799 (2003).
8. Tsuzaki, R. and Yosida, K.: Motion Control Based on Fuzzy Potential Method for Autonomous Mobile Robot with Omnidirectional Vision. Journal of the Robotics Society of Japan, Vol.21, No.6, pp.656-662 (2003) [in Japanese]
9. Takahashi, Y., Hikita, K. and Asada, M.: Incremental Purposive Behavior Acquisition based on Self-Interpretation of Instructions by Coach. Proc. of the 2003 IEEE/RSJ International Conference on Intelligent Robots and Systems, pp.686-693 (2003)
10. Shimizuhira, W., Fujii, K. and Maeda, Y.: Fuzzy Behavior Control for Autonomous Mobile Robot in Dynamic Environment with Multiple Omnidirectional Vision System. Proc. of IEEE/RSJ International Conference on Intelligent Robots and Systems (IROS 2004), CD-ROM, SA2-M3 (2004)
11. Shimizuhira, W. and Maeda, Y.: Behavior Control Method by Multi-Layered Fuzzy Rule for Autonomous Mobile Robot with Multiple Omnidirectional Vision System. The Fourth International Symposium on Human and Artificial Intelligence Systems (HART 2004), pp.283-288 (2004)
12. Kitano, H., Asada, M., Noda, I. and Matsubara, H.: RoboCup: Robot World Cup. IEEE Robotics and Automation Magazine, Vol. 5, No.3, pp.30-36 (1998)
13. Tunstel, E., Oliveira, M.A.A.de and Berman, S.: Fuzzy behavior hierarchies for multi-robot control. Int. J. of Intel. Systems 17, pp.449-470 (2002)
14. Magdalena, L.: On the role of context in hierarchical fuzzy controllers. Int. J. of Intel. Systems 17, pp.471-493 (2002)
15. Torra, V.: A review of the construction of hierarchical fuzzy systems. Int. J. of Intel. Systems 17, pp.531-543 (2002)

Pairwise Matching of Spots in 2-DE Images Using Hopfield Network[*]

Young-Sup Hwang[1], Hoon Park[1], and Yoojin Chung[2]

[1] Division of Computer & Information
Sun Moon University, 336-708, Asan, Korea
{young,hpark}@sunmoon.ac.kr
[2] Dept. of Computer Engineering, Hankuk Univ. of Foreign Studies
89 Wangsan Mohyun, Yongin Kyounggi-do, 449-791, Korea
chungyj@hufs.ac.kr

Abstract. Matching spots between two-dimensional electrophoresis (2-DE) images is a bottleneck in the automation of proteome analysis. Because the matching problem is an NP-hard problem, the solution is usually a heuristic approach or a neural network method. So a Hopfield neural network approach is applied to solve this problem. An energy function is designed to represent the similarity of spots together with its neighbor spots. Experiment showed that Hopfield neural network with appropriate energy function and dynamics could solve the matching problem of spots in 2-DE images.

1 Introduction

Two-dimensional electrophoresis (2-DE) is used to separate thousands of polypeptides according to their electronic charge and molecular weights in complex protein solutions [1]. After staining process, proteins are visualized into spots that have various sizes, shapes and intensities. Analyzing this gel image reveals which proteins exist. The analysis of gel image contains image preprocessing, spot detection, spot matching and data analysis. Spot matching is a process to find spots in several gel images that are formed from the same protein. Newly developed protein can be found out from a spot that has no corresponding spots in the other images. By inspecting sizes and shapes of matched spots, the change of a protein can also be found out.

The Spots in gel images have some non-linear transformations occurred from sample preparation, electrophoresis, temperature condition and non-uniform movement in some gel area. This non-linearity makes it difficult to match spots just by overlapping the images.

Akutsu proved that matching spots between 2-D images in non-linear transformation is an NP-hard problem [2]. The time required to solve an NP-hard

---

[*] This work was supported by grant No. R01-2003-000-10860-0 from the Basic Research Program of the Korea Science & Engineering Foundation.
This work was supported by the Sun Moon University Research Grant of 2002.

V. Torra et al. (Eds.): MDAI 2005, LNAI 3558, pp. 264–271, 2005.

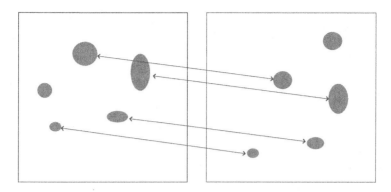

Fig. 1. Matching spots in gel images. Each spot lies in a non-linearly transformed positions. A spot in the left image disappeared and a new spot appeared in the right image

problem grows exponentially as the size of the problem grows. So a probabilistic or heuristic approach is used instead of finding the correct solution. One of the largely used methods is a neural network approach such as Hopfield network.

Panek and Vohradsky matched spots by comparing neighborhoods [3]. They gave spots binary codes according to the relative position between neighborhoods. The codes of a consecutive segment differs just one bit. These segment codes forms a descriptive matrix. They used similarity of descriptive matrix as a matching measure. CAROL system is designed to match spots locally or globally by using computational geometry [4]. It uses only the geometrical properties that are extracted from the detected spots in preprocessed images. Geometrical data are coordinates and intensity that are given in real numbers. It reduces search space by using a local search strategy based on a Delaunay net.

To match spots more correctly, commercial software package uses landmark spots [5]. Landmark spots are representative spots that came from the same protein. Usually landmarks are selected manually. Manual operation takes much time and humans are liable to make errors. So matching problem becomes the bottelneck in the automation of proteome analysis.

This study uses Hopfield network to match spots [6, 7]. If we set each neuron in the network to represent a match between spots and an energy function to be minimum when matches are correct, the stable states will give an optimal matching solution. The basic principle of Hopfield network and its application to spot match is described in Section 2. Experimental results are given in Section 3. Conclusion is in Section 4.

2   Hopfield Network

The two-dimensional binary Hopfield network was used to find matching spots between two gel images. The network consists of $N_l \times N_r$ neurons. N_l is a number of spots in a left image and N_r in a right image. The state of each neuron (0 or 1) represents whether the two spots match, i.e., came from the same protein. To match spots correctly, it is desirable to consider not only just the two spots but also neighborhood spots. It is because two spots that are closest could be a mismatching case. For example, spot (488.3, 1219.9) and spot (488.0, 1219.7) in Fig. 4 are very close but are not from the same protein. If we consider pair of spots, the probability of correct match rises. So we designed the network as to reflect match between two pairs of spots. Figure 2 shows the connection between

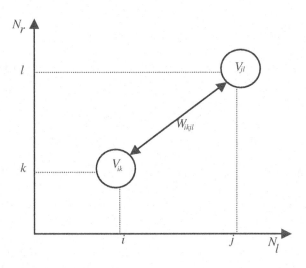

Fig. 2. The connection of neurons in a Hopfield network. The spot pair (i, j) in a left image and (k, l) in a right image are considered

neurons. In the figure, (i, j) are the two spots in left image and (k, l) are in right image. The energy of a 2-D binary Hopfield network is

$$E = -\frac{1}{2} \sum_i^{N_l} \sum_k^{N_r} \sum_j^{N_l} \sum_l^{N_r} W_{ikjl} V_{ik} V_{jl} - \sum_i^{N_l} \sum_k^{N_r} I_{ik} V_{ik} \qquad (1)$$

where V_{ik} and V_{jl} are binary neurons for the spot pair (i, k) and (j, l). If the value of a neuron is 1, the spot pair came from the same protein; it represents a match. If the value is 0, it represents a mismatch. $W_{ikjl} (= W_{jlik})$ is a connection weight between two neurons, V_{ik} and V_{jl} . The weight to neuron itself (W_{ikik}) is 0. I_{ik} is an initial input to the neuron. A change in the state of a neuron V_{ik} denoted by ΔV_{ik} will cause an energy change of ΔE_{ik}:

$$\Delta E_{ik} = - \left[\sum_j^{N_l} \sum_l^{N_r} W_{ikjl} V_{jl} I_{ik} \right] \Delta V_{ik} . \qquad (2)$$

The above equation describes the dynamics of the network that was shown by Hopfield to be always negative with the following stochastic updating rule:

$$V_{ik} = 0 \ \text{if} \ \left[\sum_j^{N_l} \sum_l^{N_r} W_{ikjl} V_{jl} I_{ik}\right] > 0$$

$$V_{ik} = 1 \ \text{if} \ \left[\sum_j^{N_l} \sum_l^{N_r} W_{ikjl} V_{jl} I_{ik}\right] < 0 \tag{3}$$

$$\text{no chnage if} \ \left[\sum_j^{N_l} \sum_l^{N_r} W_{ikjl} V_{jl} I_{ik}\right] = 0 \ .$$

To solve the spot-matching problem, the cost function given below is minimized:

$$E = -\frac{1}{2} \sum_i^{N_l} \sum_k^{N_r} \sum_j^{N_l} \sum_l^{N_r} C_{ikjl} V_{ik} V_{jl} - \sum_i^{N_l} \left[1 - \sum_k^{N_r} V_{ik}\right]^2 + \sum_k^{N_r} \left[1 - \sum_l^{N_l} V_{ik}\right]^2 \tag{4}$$

The minimum of this function will be the favorable and steady state of the matching. The first term in (4) represents the compatibility degree of the matching between a spot pair (i, j) in the left image and a spot pair (k, l) in the right one. The second and third term reinforce the uniqueness constraint, that is, one-to-one matching. The compatibility measure C is a non-linear function:

$$C_{ikjl} = \frac{2}{1 + e^{\lambda(X-\theta)}} - 1 \tag{5}$$

where X is

$$X = A|\Delta d| + B|\Delta D| \ . \tag{6}$$

X is based on two types of comparisons for the two spot pairs. The first comparison, Δd, is the difference in the disparities of the matched spot pairs (i, k) and (j, l), i.e., the intra-distance difference. If the spots are a valid matching pair, the difference should be very small. The other comparison, ΔD, is the difference between the distance from i to j and the distance from k to l, which is small when the spots are correctly matched. ΔD is the inter-distance difference. A and B are constants such that $A + B = 1$. The non-linear function in the equation scales the compatibility measure smoothly between +1 and -1, where λ is a parameter that sets the slope of the function. The parameter λ controls the position where the non-linear function crosses the x-axis. Equation 4 can be rearranged to get

$$E = -\frac{1}{2} \sum_i^{N_l} \sum_k^{N_r} \sum_j^{N_l} \sum_l^{N_r} (C_{ikjl} - \delta_{ij} - \delta_{kl}) V_{ik} V_{jl} - \sum_i^{N_l} \sum_k^{N_r} 2V_{ik} \tag{7}$$

where $\delta_{ij} = 1$ if $i = j$, otherwise 0; similarly $\delta_{kl} = 1$ if $l = k$, otherwise 0. The connection weight between two neurons is defined as $W_{ikjl} = (C_{ikjl} - \delta_{ij} - \delta_{kl})$. A state change in a neuron will result in an energy change, given by

$$\Delta E_{ik} = -\left[\sum_j^{N_l} \sum_l^{N_r} (C_{ikjl} - \delta_{ij} - \delta_{kl}) V_{jl} + 2\right] \Delta V_{ik} \ . \tag{8}$$

This expression is equivalent to (2), which is always negative if the state of each neuron is updated randomly and asynchronously according to the Hopfield updating rule:

$$V_{ik} = 0 \quad \text{if} \left[\sum_j^{N_l} \sum_l^{N_r} (C_{ikjl} - \delta_{ij} - \delta_{kl}) V_{jl} + 2 \right] > 0$$

$$V_{ik} = 1 \quad \text{if} \left[\sum_j^{N_l} \sum_l^{N_r} (C_{ikjl} - \delta_{ij} - \delta_{kl}) V_{jl} + 2 \right] < 0 \tag{9}$$

$$\text{no chnage if} \left[\sum_j^{N_l} \sum_l^{N_r} (C_{ikjl} - \delta_{ij} - \delta_{kl}) V_{jl} + 2 \right] = 0 \; .$$

3   Experimental Results

Gel images from the study of germination of S. granaticolor were used to get spot data [8]. PDQuest [9], a gel image analysis tool, detected spots and searched matches. Experts corrected the matches. The resulting data have the coordinates of spots and labels. A part of a gel image is given in Fig. 3, because the whole image is too big to show all the details.

Fig. 3. A part of a gel image. Usually image quality is not good because it came from a real biological experiment

A spot (i in (9)) to match was selected randomly. Then its partner k was also selected randomly around its neighborhood, within a limited distance. Because the spots far apart from the examining spot don't help to determine matching and they require too much time to compute. j and l were selected similarly. We set $A = 0.4, B = 0.6, \lambda = 7.0$ and $\theta = 27$. More weight was assigned to B since ΔD is more stable than Δd. λ and θ were selected empirically. Table 1 and Fig. 4 shows 12 spot pairs that came from the same protein, i.e., matching pairs. The 8-th left spot and the 9-th right spot are very close to each other but they are not the same proteins. No.2 and No.3 are similar as before. Fig. 5 shows how each neuron fires at each iteration. The figure also shows the proposed Hopfield neural network can find spot matches accurately after several loops.

Table 1. Experimental data

No.	Left image x	y	Right image x	y
1	132.2	601.7	186.2	640.7
2	361.3	647.1	406.3	697.6
3	393.6	741.2	433.3	795.3
4	509.7	895.9	540.0	948.9
5	489.9	1014.9	518.9	1067.4
6	295.8	1173.8	333.5	1213.9
7	193.4	1411.3	231.5	1441.5
8	461.6	1175.7	488.0	1219.7
9	488.3	1219.9	513.5	1258.0
10	351.8	1711.4	367.2	1746.0
11	483.9	1975.1	485.7	2003.4
12	403.7	1900.9	411.5	1931.1

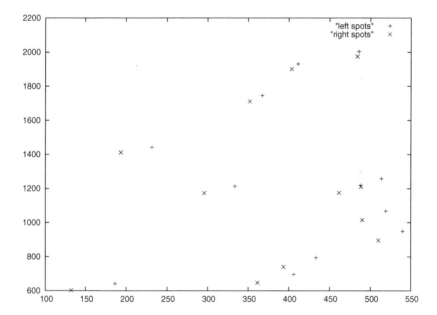

Fig. 4. Experimental data. No. 9 (488.3, 1219.9) in the left image and No. 8 (488, 1219.7) in the right image are very close. But considering neighborhood spots, No. 8 in the right image matches No.8 (461.6, 1175.7) in the left image. Spot numbers are from Table 1

There are hundreds or thousands of spots in a typical gel image. Matching thousand spots using Hopfield network requires much computing time. If we can use a neuro-computer or a parallel computer, neural network can be simulated faster. A faster method to overcome the time-complexity are under being investigated.

```
000000000000  000000000000  000000000000  000000000000  000000000000
000000000000  000000000000  000000000000  000000000000  000000000000
000000000000  000000000000  000000000000  000000000000  000000000000
000000000000  000000000000  000000000000  000000000000  000000000000
000000000000  000000000000  000000000000  000000000000  000000000000
000010000000  000010000000  000010000000  000010000000  000010000000
000000000000  000000000000  000000000000  000000000000  000000000000
000000000000  000000000000  000000000000  000000000000  000000000000
000000000000  000000000000  000000000000  000000010000  000000010000
000000000000  000000000000  000000000000  000000000000  000000000100
000000000000  000000000000  000000000000  000000000000  000000000000
000000000000  000000000000  000000000000  000000000000  000000000000

000000000000  000000000000  100000000000  100000000000  100000000000
000000000000  000000000000  000000000000  010000000000  010000000000
000000000000  000000000000  000000000000  000000000000  001000000000
000000000000  000000000000  000000000000  000000000000  000000000000
000000000000  000000000000  000000000000  000000000000  000000000000
000010000000  000010000000  000010000000  000010000000  000010000000
000000000000  000000000000  000000000000  000000000000  000000000000
000000000000  000000000000  000000000000  000000000000  000000000000
000000010000  000000010000  000000010000  000000010000  000000010000
000000000100  000000000100  000000000100  000000000100  000000000100
000000000010  000000000010  000000000010  000000000010  000000000010
000000000000  000000000001  000000000001  000000000001  000000000001

100000000000  100000000000  100000000000  100000000000  100000000000
010000000000  010000000000  010000000000  010000000000  010000000000
001000000000  001000000000  001000000000  001000000000  001000000000
000100000000  000100000000  000100000000  000100000000  000100000000
000000000000  000010000000  000010000000  000010000000  000010000000
000010000000  000010000000  000001000000  000001000000  000001000000
000000000000  000000000000  000000000000  000000100000  000000100000
000000000000  000000000000  000000000000  000000000000  000000010000
000000010000  000000010000  000000010000  000000010000  000000010000
000000000100  000000000100  000000000100  000000000100  000000000100
000000000010  000000000010  000000000010  000000000010  000000000010
000000000001  000000000001  000000000001  000000000001  000000000001

100000000000  100000000000
010000000000  010000000000
001000000000  001000000000
000100000000  000100000000
000010000000  000010000000
000001000000  000001000000
000000100000  000000100000
000000010000  000000010000
000000001000  000000001000
000000000100  000000000100
000000000010  000000000010
000000000001  000000000001
```

Fig. 5. The neurons status of each iteration. The value (i,j) in each table means whether the left spot i and the right spot j match(1) or not(0)

4   Conclusion

2-DE image analysis is central in the proteomics. Finding spots from the same protein between 2-DE images is a bottleneck in the analysis, because current commercial softwares need a manual inspection. Spots came from the same protein in several gel images are not in the same location but they are in an area within a limited distance. The location points are non-linearly transformed from each other. The non-linear transformation is natural considering its biological experiment process. Because of non-linearity, spot matching is a difficult problem having exponential time complexity. Thus spot matching problem was solved by the Hopfield network with a redesigned energy function. The energy function was designed to be minimum when spots are one-to-one matched. Since the closest spot could be a wrong match, a pair of spots are considered. A compatibility measure was introduced to compare the intra-difference and the inter-distance between the spot pair in each image and between the two images. Experimental results showed that the network can find matches in sample real data which has nearest spots from other proteins. However matching thousands of spots requires too much time to compute. So a faster way of matching is being studied. And other matching algorithm in image processing such as by Torra[10] or by Newton[11] could also be a good candidate solution to this problem.

References

1. Pennington, S. R. and Dunn, M. J.: Proteomics, from protein sequence to function. BIOS, Scientific Publishers. (2001)
2. Akutsu T. and et. al.: Matching of spots in 2D electrophoresis images. Point matching under non-uniform distortions. Lecture Notes in Computer Science. **164** (1999) 212–222
3. Josef Panek and Jiri Vohradsky: Point pattern matching in the analysis of two-dimensional gel electropherograms. Electrophoresis **20** (1999) 3483–3491
4. Pleissner et. al.: New algorithmic approaches to protein spot detection and pattern matching in two-dimensional electrophoresis gel databases. Electrophoresis **20** (1999) 755–765
5. Dowsey, A.W., Dunn M. J. and Yang, G. Z.: The role of bioinformatics in two-dimensional gel electrophoresis Electrophoresis **3** (2003) 1567–1596
6. Hopfield, J. and Tank, D.W.: Neural computation of decisions in optimization problems. Biological Cybernetics **52** (1985) 141–152
7. Nasrabadi, N. M. and Choo, C.Y.: Hopfield Network for Stereo Vision Correspondence. IEEE Transactions on Neural Network **3** (1992) 5–13
8. Jan Bobek, Petr Halada, Jakub Angelis, Jiri Vohradsky, and Karel Mikul: Activation and expression of proteins during synchronous germination of aerial spores of Streptomyces granaticolor. Proteomics **4:12** (2004) 3864–3880
9. Rosengran, R.T. and et. al.: Comparison of PDQuest and Progenesis software packages in the analysis of two-dimensional electrophoresis gels. Proteomics **3** (2003) 1936–1946.
10. Torra, V.: OWA operators in data modeling and reidentification, IEEE Transactions on Fuzzy Systems, **12:5** (2004) 652–660.
11. Newton, E.M., Sweeney, L. and Malin, B.: Preserving privacy by de-identifying face images, IEEE Transcations on Knowledge and Data Engineering, **17:2**, (2005), 232–243.

A New Concept of a Similarity Measure for Intuitionistic Fuzzy Sets and Its Use in Group Decision Making

Eulalia Szmidt and Janusz Kacprzyk

Systems Research Institute, Polish Academy of Sciences
ul. Newelska 6, 01–447 Warsaw, Poland
{szmidt,kacprzyk}@ibspan.waw.pl

Abstract. We propose a new measure of similarity for intuitionistic fuzzy sets[1], and use it to analyze the extent of agreement in a group of experts. The proposed measure takes into account two kinds of distances – one to an object to be compared, and one to its complement. We infer about the similarity of preferences on the basis of a difference between the two types of distances. We show that infering without taking into account a distance to a complement of an object can be misleading.

1 Introduction

Similarity assessment plays a fundamental role in inference and approximate reasoning in virtually all applications of fuzzy logic. For different purposes different measures of similarity are to be used. Importance of the problem motivates researchers to compare and examine the effectiveness and properties of the different measures of similarity for fuzzy sets (e.g. Zwick at al. [36], Pappis and Karacapilidis [15], Chen at al. [4], Wang at al. [33], Bouchon-Meunier at al. [3], Cross and Sudkamp [5]).

The analysis of similarity is also a fundamental issue while employing intuitionistic fuzzy sets which may be viewed as a generalization of conventional fuzzy sets (Atanassov [1], [2]).

In this article we introduce and apply a new measure of similarity to compare intuitionistic fuzzy preferences given by individuals (experts), and evaluate an extent of a group agreement. Like in our previous work (Szmidt and Kacprzyk [31]) we propose here a similarity measure which is not a standard similarity measure in the sense that it is not only a dual concept to a (general) distance measure (Tversky [32]). In commonly used similarity measures, the dissimilarity behaves like a distance function. Such a standard approach – formulated for objects meant as crisp values was later extended and used to evaluate the similarity of fuzzy sets (Cross and Sudkamp [5]). Distances were also proposed to measure

---

[1] There is currently a discussion on the appropriateness of the name *intuitionistic fuzzy set* introduced by Atanassov. However, this is beyond the scope of this paper which is just concerned with an application of the concept.

V. Torra et al. (Eds.): MDAI 2005, LNAI 3558, pp. 272–282, 2005.
© Springer-Verlag Berlin Heidelberg 2005

the similarity between intuitionistic fuzzy sets (Dengfeng and Chuntian [7]). The measure we propose is not that kind of similarity as it does not measure just a distance between individual intuitionistic fuzzy preferences being compared. The new measure answers the question if the compared preferences are more similar or more dissimilar. So the essence of the proposed measure is the same as in (Szmidt and Kacprzyk [31]). The difference is that the proposed measure needs less calculations (Section 3).

In Szmidt [16], Szmidt and Kacprzyk [19, 20, 22, 25, 26, 30] we use intuitionistic fuzzy sets to solve group decision problems, and to determine soft measures of consensus. These works are an intuitionistic fuzzy extension of an important direction in group decision making and consensus evaluation that has practically started with Loewer and Laddaga's [14] collection of papers which have indicated a need for the softening of the very meaning of consensus. This discussion has triggered, and provided a justification for many fuzzy extensions – cf. Kacprzyk and Fedrizzi [9], [10], [11]).

As intuitionistic fuzzy sets have become a popular research topic, they have also found applications in group decision making and consensus formation, notably because they seem to be an adequate and efficient model to deal with situations with abstention votes, in particular along the lines of recent views on abstention (cf. Kang [13]). In this area the works by Szmidt [16], Szmidt and Kacprzyk [19], [20, 22, 25, 26, 30] are worth mentioning.

We have a set of n options, $S = \{s_1, \ldots, s_n\}$, and a set of m individuals, $I = \{1, \ldots, m\}$. In the classic fuzzy approach (cf. Kacprzyk [8], Kacprzyk, Fedrizzi and Nurmi [12]), each individual k provides his or her individual fuzzy preference relation, R_k, given by $\mu_{R_k} : S \times S \to [0, 1]$. An individual fuzzy preference relation may be represented by a matrix $[r_{ij}^k]$ such that $r_{ij}^k = \mu_{R_k}(s_i, s_j)$; $i, j = 1, \ldots, n$; $k = 1, \ldots, m$; $[r_{ij}^k] + [r_{ji}^k] = 1$. Notice that we do not use fuzzy preference structures in the sense od De Baets and Fodor [6].

Here, we use intuitionistic fuzzy preference relations. Each individual k provides his or her *(individual) intuitionistic fuzzy preference relation*, giving not only R_k (given, as previously, by its membership function μ_{R_k}) but also

- ν_{R_k} – a non-membership function, $\nu_k : S \times S \to [0, 1]$, conveniently represented by a matrix $[\nu_{ij}^k(s_i, s_j)]$; $i, j = 1, \ldots, n$; $k = 1, \ldots, m$.

Such a representation of individual preferences, with additional parameters, can better reflect the imprecision of testimonies (expressing individual preferences), and is our starting point to assess an extent of agreement in a group.

2   A Brief Introduction to Intuitionistic Fuzzy Sets

As opposed to a fuzzy set in X(Zadeh [34]) , given by

$$A^{'} = \{< x, \mu_{A'}(x) > | x \in X\} \tag{1}$$

where $\mu_{A'}(x) \in [0,1]$ is the membership function of the fuzzy set A', an intu-itionistic fuzzy set (Atanassov [2]) A is given by

$$A = \{< x, \mu_A(x), \nu_A(x) > | x \in X\} \tag{2}$$

where: $\mu_A : X \to [0,1]$ and $\nu_A : X \to [0,1]$ such that

$$0 \le \mu_A(x) + \nu_A(x) \le 1 \tag{3}$$

and $\mu_A(x)$, $\nu_A(x) \in [0,1]$ denote a degree of membership and a degree of non-membership of $x \in A$, respectively.

Obviously, each fuzzy set may be represented by the following intuitionistic fuzzy set

$$A = \{< x, \mu_{A'}(x), 1 - \mu_{A'}(x) > | x \in X\} \tag{4}$$

For each intuitionistic fuzzy set in X, we will call

$$\pi_A(x) = 1 - \mu_A(x) - \nu_A(x) \tag{5}$$

an *intuitionistic fuzzy index* (or a *hesitation margin*) of $x \in A$ and, it expresses a lack of knowledge of whether x belongs to A or not (cf. Atanassov [2]). It is obvious that $0 \le \pi_A(x) \le 1$, for each $x \in X$.

In our further considerations we will use the notion of the complement ele-ments, which definition is a simple consequence of a complement set A^C

$$A^C = \{< x, \nu_A(x), \mu_A(x) > | x \in X\} \tag{6}$$

The application of intuitionistic fuzzy sets instead of fuzzy sets means the introduction of another degree of freedom into a set description. Such a gener-alization of fuzzy sets gives us an additional possibility to represent imperfect knowledge what leads to describing many real problems in a more adequate way. Applications of intuitionistic fuzzy sets to group decision making, negotiations and other situations are presented in Szmidt [16], Szmidt and Kacprzyk [20], [22], [23], [25], [28], [30], [29] (because of the different approaches presented in the cited above works, we are not able to discuss details here, and refer the interested reader directly to them).

2.1   Distances Between Intuitionistic Fuzzy Sets

In Szmidt [16], Szmidt and Baldwin [17, 18], Szmidt and Kacprzyk [24] it is shown why when calculating distances between intuitionistic fuzzy sets it is expedient to take into account all three parameters describing intuitionistic fuzzy sets. One of the reasons is that when taking into account two parameters only, for elements from classical fuzzy sets (which are a special case of intuitionistic fuzzy sets) we obtain distances from a different interval than for elements belonging to intuitionistic fuzzy sets. It practically makes it impossible to consider by the same formula the two types of sets.

In our further considerations we will use the normalized Hamming distance between intuitionistic fuzzy sets A, B in $X = \{x_1, x_2, \ldots, x_n\}$ Szmidt [16], Szmidt and Baldwin [17, 18], Szmidt and Kacprzyk [24]:

$$l_{IFS}(A, B) = \frac{1}{2n} \sum_{i=1}^{n} (|\mu_A(x_i) - \mu_B(x_i)| +$$
$$+ |\nu_A(x_i) - \nu_B(x_i)| + |\pi_A(x_i) - \pi_B(x_i)|) \tag{7}$$

For (7) we have:

$$0 \leq l_{IFS}(A, B) \leq 1. \tag{8}$$

3   A Similarity Measure

We propose here a new similarity measure for intuitionistic fuzzy sets. We use a geometric interpretation of intuitionistic fuzzy sets which was described in details by Szmidt ([16]), Szmidt and Baldwin ([17, 18]), Szmidt and Kacprzyk ([24],[27]). Here we remind only that

- the geometrical interpretation is based on the definition of an intuitionistic fuzzy set introduced by Atanassov [1], [2], and it does not introduce any additional assumptions,
- any combination of the values of the membership, nonmembership and hesitation function $[(\mu, \nu, \pi)]$ that define an intuitionistic fuzzy set can be represented inside the triangle ABD (Figure 1).

Therefore, each element belonging to an intuitionistic fuzzy set can be represented as a point (μ, ν, π) belonging to the triangle ABD (Figure 1). Point A represents elements fully belonging to an intuitionistic fuzzy set ($\mu = 1$), point B represents elements fully not belonging to an intuitionistic fuzzy set ($\nu = 1$), point D represents elements with hesitation margin $\pi = 1$, i.e. about which we are not able to say if they belong or do not belong to an intuitionistic fuzzy set. Any other combination of the values characterizeing an intuitionistic fuzzy set can be represented inside the triangle ABD.

In the simplest situations we assess a similarity of any two elements X and F belonging to an intuitionistic fuzzy set (or sets). The proposed measure states whether X is more similar to F than to F^C, where F^C is a complement of F. In other words, the proposed measure answers the question if X is more similar or more dissimilar to F.

Definition 1.

$$Sim(X, F) = l_{IFS}(X, F^C) - l_{IFS}(X, F) =$$
$$= (|\mu(X) - \mu(F^C)| + |\nu(X) - \nu(F^C)| + |\pi(X) - \pi(F^C)|) +$$
$$- (|\mu(X) - \mu(F)| + |\nu(X) - \nu(F)| + |\pi(X) - \pi(F)|) =$$
$$= (|\mu(X) - \mu(F^C)| + |\nu(X) - \nu(F^C)|) +$$
$$- (|\mu(X) - \mu(F)| + |\nu(X) - \nu(F)|) \tag{9}$$

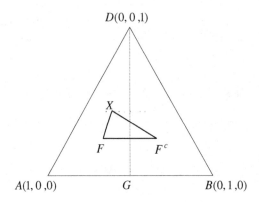

Fig. 1. The triangle ABD explaining a ratio-based measure of similarity

where: $l_{IFS}(X, F)$ is a *distance*(X, F) from $X(\mu_X, \nu_X, \pi_X)$ to $F(\mu_F, \nu_F, \pi_F)$,
$l_{IFS}(X, F^C)$ is the *distance*(X, F^C) from $X(\mu_X, \nu_X, \pi_X)$ to $F^C(\nu_F, \mu_F, \pi_F)$,
F^C is a complement of F,
the distances $l_{IFS}(X, F)$ and $l_{IFS}(X, F^C)$ are calculated from (7).

It is worth mentioning that although when calculating the distances for intuitionistic fuzzy sets it is expedient to take into account all the three functions (memberships, non-memberships, and the intuitionistic fuzzy indices) – see Section 2.1, in the similarity measure (9) the third components (the intuitionistic fuzzy indices) disappear (as the intuitionistic fuzzy indices for F and F^C are the same).

For (9) we have

$$- 1 \leq Sim(X, F) \leq 1 \qquad (10)$$

$$Sim(X, F) = Sim(F, X) \qquad (11)$$

The similarity has typically been assumed to be symmetric. Tversky [32], however, has provided some empirical evidence that the similarity should not always be treated as a symmetric relation. We stress this to show that a similarity measure (9) may have some features which can be useful in some situations but are not welcome in others (see Cross and Sudkamp [5]), Wang and Kerre [33]).

It is worth noticing that:

- $Sim(X, F) = 1$ means the identity of X and F (it occurs only when $l_{IFS}(X, F) = 0$ and $l_{IFS}(X, F^C) = 1$),
- $Sim(X, F) = 0$ means that X is to the same extent similar to F and to F^C (it occurs only when $l_{IFS}(X, F) = l_{IFS}(X, F^C)$),
- $Sim(X, F) = -1$ means the complete dissimilarity, (it occurs only when $l_{IFS}(X, F) = 1$ and $l_{IFS}(X, F^C) = 0$).

In other words, when applying the measure (9) to analyze the similarity of two objects, one should be interested in the values $0 < Sim(X, F) \leq 1$. The values of

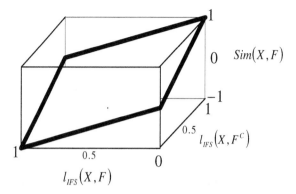

Fig. 2. Values of the proposed similarity measure $Sim(X, F)$ for different possible values of $l_{IFS}(X, F^C)$ and $l_{IFS}(X, F)$

the proposed similarity measure (9) for different possible values of $l_{IFS}(X, F^C)$ and $l_{IFS}(X, F)$ are illustrated in Figure 2 (the bold surface inside the cubicoid).

Now we will show that a measure of similarity defined as mentioned above, (9), between $X(\mu_X, \nu_X, \pi_X)$ and $F(\mu_F, \nu_F, \pi_F)$ is more powerful then a simple distance between them.

Example 1. Let X and F be two elements belonging to an intuitionistic fuzzy set (with the coordinates (μ, ν, π)), $X = (0.5, 0.4, 0.1)$, $F = (0.4, 0.5, 0.1)$, so $F^C = (0.5, 0.4, 0.1)$, and from (9) we have

$$l_{IFS}(X, F) = \frac{1}{2}(|0.5 - 0.4| + |0.4 - 0.5| + |0.1 - 0.1|) = 0.1 \qquad (12)$$

what means that the distance is small – and just taking this into account, we would say that X and F are similar. However

$$l_{IFS}(X, F^C) = \frac{1}{2}(|0.5 - 0.5| + |0.4 - 0.4| + |0.1 - 0.1|) = 0 \qquad (13)$$

what means that X is just the same as F^C. The similarity measure (9) is less than zero (it is equal to $0 - 0.1 = -0.1$) i.e., X is more similar to F^C than to F. In other words, a small distance between X and F does not guarantee that X and F are similar. Only when we also know the distance between X and F^C, we can conclude about similarity of X and F. $\qquad \square$

So, to summarize:

– when a distance between two (or more) objects/elements, or sets, is large, then it means for sure that the similarity does not occur.
– when a distance is small, we can say nothing for sure about the similarity just on the basis of a distance between the two objects [when we do not take into account complements of the objects as in (9)]. The distance between objects can be small and the compared objects can be more dissimilar than similar.

4   An Analysis of Agreement in a Group of Experts

Now, we will use a new concept of similarity to evaluate the extent of agreement between experts. As already mentioned, Loewer and Laddaga's [14] special issue has advocated, among others, that the very concept of consensus, i.e. a full and unanimous agreement, should be softened because in practice people mean by consensus a situation when, for instance, "most of the individuals agree as to most of the options". Many works have been published along this line, notably in Kacprzyk and Fedrizzi [10, 11] a new measure of consensus was proposed. In this paper that line of reasoning is adopted but in the intuitionistic fuzzy setting, using a different perspective based on the use of a similarity measure.

So, if all of the considered pairs of experts' preferences are

- just the same, we say about full agreement meaning consensus in a traditional sense – the proposed measure of similarity (9) is equal to 1,
- quite opposite, we say about full disagreement – similarity (9) is equal to -1),
- to the same extent similar as dissimilar – the proposed measure (9) is equal to 0,
- similar to some extent – similarity (9) is from the open interval $(0, 1)$),
- dissimilar to some extent – similarity (9) is from the open interval $(-1, 0)$),

Preferences given by each individual are expressed via intuitionistic fuzzy sets (describing intuitionistic fuzzy preferences). So we start from a set of data which consists of two types of matrices describing individual preferences. The first type of matrices is the same as for classical fuzzy sets, i.e. membership functions $[r_{ij}^k]$ given by each individual k concerning each pair of options ij. But, additionally, it is necessary to take into account non-membership functions $[\nu_{ij}^k]$.

In general, the extent of similarity for two experts k_1, k_2 considering n options is given as

$$
Sim^{k_1,k_2} = \frac{1}{A} \sum_{i=1}^{n-1} \sum_{j=i+1}^{n} Sim^{k_1,k_2}(i,j) =
$$

$$
= \frac{1}{A} [\sum_{i=1}^{n-1} \sum_{j=i+1}^{n} (\mid \mu_{ij}(k_1) - \nu_{ij}(k_2) \mid + \mid \nu_{ij}(k_1) - \mu_{ij}(k_2) \mid]
$$

$$
- [\sum_{i=1}^{n-1} \sum_{j=i+1}^{n} (\mid \mu_{ij}(k_1) - \mu_{ij}(k_2) \mid + \mid \nu_{ij}(k_1) - \nu_{ij}(k_2) \mid] \qquad (14)
$$

where

$$
A = \frac{1}{2C_n^2} = \frac{1}{n(n-1)} \qquad (15)
$$

When we have m experts, we examine the similarity of their preferences pairwise (14), and next we find an agreement of all experts

$$
Sim = \frac{1}{m(m-1)} \sum_{p=1}^{m-1} \sum_{r=p+1}^{m} Sim^{k_p,k_r} \qquad (16)
$$

where Sim^{k_p,k_r} is given by (14).

Example 2. Suppose that there are 3 individuals ($m = 3$) considering 3 options ($n = 3$), and the individual intuitionistic fuzzy preference relations are:

$$\mu^1(i,j) = \begin{bmatrix} - & .1 & .5 \\ .9 & - & .5 \\ .4 & .3 & - \end{bmatrix} \quad \nu^1(i,j) = \begin{bmatrix} - & .9 & .4 \\ .1 & - & .3 \\ .5 & .5 & - \end{bmatrix}$$

$$\mu^2(i,j) = \begin{bmatrix} - & .1 & .5 \\ .9 & - & .5 \\ .2 & .2 & - \end{bmatrix} \quad \nu^2(i,j) = \begin{bmatrix} - & .9 & .2 \\ .1 & - & .2 \\ .5 & .5 & - \end{bmatrix}$$

$$\mu^3(i,j) = \begin{bmatrix} - & .2 & .1 \\ .8 & - & .6 \\ .2 & .3 & - \end{bmatrix} \quad \nu^3(i,j) = \begin{bmatrix} - & .8 & .2 \\ .2 & - & .3 \\ .1 & .6 & - \end{bmatrix}$$

To find the extent of agreement in the group, we calculate the similarity $Sim^{p,r}(i,j)$ for each pair of experts (p,r) and each pair of options (i,j).

First, we calculate the similarity for each pair of experts concerning the first and the second option. For example, for the second and the third experts:

$F^2(1,2) = (0.1, 0.9, 0)$ - preferences of the second expert,
$F^3(1,2) = (0.2, 0.8, 0)$ - preferences of the third expert,
$F^{3,C}(1,2) = (0.8, 0.2, 0)$ - the complement of $F^3(1,2)$, i.e., opposite preferences of the third expert.

From (9) and (14) we have

$$Sim^{2,3}(1,2) = l(F^2(1,2), F^{3,C}(1,2)) - l(F^2(1,2), F^3(1,2)) = 0.6 \quad (17)$$

Similar calculations for experts (1,2) and (1,3) give respectively

$$Sim^{1,2}(1,2) = l(F^1(1,2), F^{2,C}(1,2)) - l(F^1(1,2), F^2(1,2)) = 0.8 \quad (18)$$

$$Sim^{1,3}(1,2) = l(F^1(1,2), F^{3,C}(1,2)) - l(F^1(1,2), F^3(1,2)) = 0.6 \quad (19)$$

From (17)–(19) we obtain an average similarity for the three considered experts considering options $(1,2)$, namely

$$Sim(1,2) = \frac{1}{3}(0.6 + 0.8 + 0.6) = 0.366 \quad (20)$$

Similar calculations for options $(1,3)$ give the following results

$$Sim^{1,2}(1,3) = l(F^1(1,3), F^{2,C}(1,3)) - l(F^1(1,3), F^2(1,3)) = 0.1 \quad (21)$$

$$Sim^{1,3}(1,3) = l(F^1(1,3), F^{3,C}(1,3)) - l(F^1(1,3), F^3(1,3)) = 0 \quad (22)$$

$$Sim^{2,3}(1,3) = l(F^2(1,3), F^{3,C}(1,3)) - l(F^2(1,3), F^3(1,3)) = 0 \quad (23)$$

By aggregating the above values we obtain the similarity for options $(1,3)$

$$Sim(1,3) = \frac{1}{3}(0.1 + 0 + 0) = 0.0333 \tag{24}$$

And, finally, for options $(2,3)$ we have

$$Sim^{1,2}(2,3) = l(F^1(2,3), F^{2,C}(2,3)) - l(F^1(2,3), F^2(2,3)) = 0.2 \tag{25}$$

$$Sim^{1,3}(2,3) = l(F^1(2,3), F^{3,C}(2,3)) - l(F^1(2,3), F^3(2,3)) = 0.2 \tag{26}$$

$$Sim^{2,3}(2,3) = l(F^2(2,3), F^{3,C}(2,3)) - l(F^2(2,3), F^3(2,3)) = 0.15 \tag{27}$$

The aggregation of the above values gives the similarity for options $(2,3)$

$$Sim(2,3) = \frac{1}{3}(0.2 + 0.2 + 0.15) = 0.183 \tag{28}$$

The above results show that the biggest agreement in our group concerns options $(1,2)$ - the similarity measure is equal to 0.75. The smallest agreement concerns options $(1,3)$ - the similarity measure is equal to 0.0333.

Of course, similar calculations can be performed for experts, and the results are:

$$Sim^{1,2} = 0.3666 \tag{29}$$

$$Sim^{1,3} = 0.2666 \tag{30}$$

$$Sim^{2,3} = 0.25 \tag{31}$$

The aggregation of results (29)-(31) gives the similarity measure aggregated both by options and by experts (the general similarity for the group)

$$Sim = \frac{1}{3}(0.3666 + 0.2666 + 0.25) = 0.297 \tag{32}$$

Of course, just the same results will be obtained when aggregating (20), (24) and (28). □

It is worth noticing that the presented method of a group agreement analysis makes it possible to take into account proper weights [in (16)] for pairs of individuals (as some experts can be more important, for instance – competent, than others).

5   Concluding Remarks

We applied a new measure of similarity to assess an extent of agreement in a group of experts giving their opinions expressed by intuitionistic fuzzy preference relations. For intuitionistic fuzzy sets with the additional degrees of freedom – non-memberships, it seems important to use similarity measures taking into account these additional parameters, hence introducing a new quality to, and insight into, the process of assessing similarity. It can be achieved by comparing distances both to an interesting element/preference and to its complement.

References

1. Atanassov K. (1986) Intuitionistic Fuzzy Sets. Fuzzy Sets and Systems, Vol. 20, 87–96.
2. Atanassov K. (1999), Intuitionistic Fuzzy Sets: Theory and Applications. Springer-Verlag.
3. Bouchon-Meunier B., Rifgi M., and Bothorel S. (1996). General measures of comparison of objects. Fuzzy Sets and Systems, Vol. 84, No. 2, 143–153.
4. Chen S., Yeh M. and Hsiao P. (1995). A comparison of similarity measures of fuzzy values. Fuzzy Sets and Systems, Vol. 72, No. 1, 79–89.
5. Cross V. and Sudkamp T. (2002) Similarity and Compatibility in Fuzzy Set Theory. Physica-Verlag.
6. De Baets B. and J. Fodor, Eds. (2003) Principles of Fuzzy Preference Modelling and Decision Making. Academia Press, 2003.
7. Dengfeng L. and Chuntian C. (2002) New similarity measures of intuitionistic fuzzy sets and application to pattern recognitions. Pattern Recognition Letters, Vol. 23, 221-225.
8. Kacprzyk J. (1986) Group decision making with a fuzzy linguistic majority. Fuzzy Sets and Systems, Vol. 18, 105–118.
9. Kacprzyk J. and Fedrizzi M. (1986) 'Soft' consensus measures for monitoring real consensus reaching processes under fuzzy preferences. Control and Cybernetics, Vol. 15, 309–323.
10. Kacprzyk J. and Fedrizzi M. (1988) A 'soft' measure of consensus in the setting of partial (fuzzy) preferences. European Journal of Operational Research, Vol. 34, 315–325.
11. Kacprzyk J. and Fedrizzi M. (1989) A 'human-consistent' degree of consensus based on fuzzy logic with linguistic quantifiers. Mathematical Social Sciences, Vol. 18, 275–290.
12. Kacprzyk J., Fedrizzi M. and Nurmi H. (1992) Group decision making and consensus under fuzzy preferences and fuzzy majority. Fuzzy Sets and Systems, Vol. 49, 21–32.
13. Kang W.-T. (2004) Protest voting and abstention under plurality rule elections. Journal of Theoretical Politics vol. 16, 71–102.
14. Loewer B. and R. Laddaga (1985) Destroying the consensus. In Loewer B. (Guest Ed.): Special Issue on Consensus. Synthese, Vol. 62, 79–96.
15. Pappis C., and Karacapilidis N. (1993). A comparative assessment of measures of similarity of fuzzy values. Fuzzy Sets and Systems, Vol. 56, 171–174.
16. Szmidt E. (2000) Applications of Intuitionistic Fuzzy Sets in Decision Making. (D.Sc. dissertation) Techn. Univ., Sofia, 2000.
17. Szmidt E. and Baldwin J. (2003) New Similarity Measure for Intuitionistic Fuzzy Set Theory and Mass Assignment Theory. Notes on IFSs, Vol. 9, No. 3, 60–76.
18. Szmidt E. and Baldwin J. (2004) Entropy for Intuitionistic Fuzzy Set Theory and Mass Assignment Theory. Notes on IFSs, Vol. 10, No. 3, 15–28.
19. Szmidt E. and Kacprzyk J. (1996a) Intuitionistic fuzzy sets in group decision making, Notes on IFS, 2, 15–32.
20. Szmidt E. and Kacprzyk J. (1996c) Remarks on some applications of intuitionistic fuzzy sets in decision making, Notes on IFS, Vol. 2, No. 3, 22–31.
21. Szmidt E. and Kacprzyk J. (1997) On measuring distances between intuitionistic fuzzy sets, Notes on IFS, Vol. 3, No. 4, 1–13.

22. Szmidt E. and Kacprzyk J. (1998a) Group Decision Making under Intuitionistic Fuzzy Preference Relations. IPMU'98 (Paris, La Sorbonne), 172-178.
23. Szmidt E. and Kacprzyk J. (1998b) Applications of Intuitionistic Fuzzy Sets in Decision Making. EUSFLAT'99, 150-158.
24. Szmidt E. and Kacprzyk J. (2000) Distances between intuitionistic fuzzy sets, Fuzzy Sets and Systems, Vol. 114, No. 3, 505-518.
25. Szmidt E. and Kacprzyk J. (2000) On Measures on Consensus Under Intuitionistic Fuzzy Relations. IPMU 2000, 1454-1461.
26. Szmidt E. and Kacprzyk J. (2001) Distance from Consensus Under Intuitionistic Fuzzy Preferences. Proc. EUROFUSE Workshop on Preference Modelling and Applications, Granada, 73-78.
27. Szmidt E., Kacprzyk J. (2001) Entropy for intuitionistic fuzzy sets. Fuzzy Sets and Systems, Vol. 118, No. 3, 467-477.
28. Szmidt E. and Kacprzyk J. (2001) Analysis of Consensus under Intuitionistic Fuzzy Preferences. Proc. Int. Conf. in Fuzzy Logic and Technology. De Montfort Univ. Leicester, UK, 79-82.
29. Szmidt E. and Kacprzyk J. (2002) An Intuitionistic Fuzzy Set Based Approach to Intelligent Data Analysis (an application to medical diagnosis). In A. Abraham, L.Jain, J. Kacprzyk (Eds.): Recent Advances in Intelligent Paradigms and and Applications. Springer-Verlag, 57-70.
30. Szmidt E. and Kacprzyk J. (2002) Analysis of Agreement in a Group of Experts via Distances Between Intuitionistic Fuzzy Preferences. Proc. 9th Int. Conf. IPMU 2002, Annecy, France, 1859-1865.
31. Szmidt E. and Kacprzyk J. (2004) Similarity of intuitionistic fuzzy sets and the Jaccard coefficient. Proc. 10th Int. Conf. IPMU 2004, Perugia, Italy, 1405-1412.
32. Tversky A. (1977) Features of similarity. Psychol. Rev. Vol. 84, pp. 327-352.
33. Wang X., De Baets B., and Kerre E. (1995). A comparative study of similarity measures. Fuzzy Sets and Systems, Vol.73, No. 2, pp. 259-268.
34. Zadeh L.A. (1965) Fuzzy sets. Information and Control, 8, 338-353.
35. Zadeh, L.A. (1983). A computational approach to fuzzy quantifiers in natural languages. Comput. Math. Appl., Vol. 9, No. 1, 149-184.
36. Zwick R., Carlstein E., Budescu D. (1987). Measures of similarity among fuzzy concepts: A comparative analysis. Int. J. of Approx. Reasoning, Vol. 1, 221-242.

Perceptive Evaluation
for the Optimal Discounted Reward
in Markov Decision Processes

Masami Kurano[1], Masami Yasuda[2], Jun-ichi Nakagami[2], and Yuji Yoshida[3]

[1] Dep of Math., Chiba University, Japan
kurano@faculty.chiba-u.jp
[2] Dep of Math & Infor., Chiba University, Japan
{yasuda,nakagami}@math.s.chiba-u.ac.jp
[3] Fac of Econo. & Business Administ., The University of Kitakyushu, Japan
yoshida@kitakyu-u.ac.jp

Abstract. We formulate a fuzzy perceptive model for Markov decision processes with discounted payoff in which the perception for transition probabilities is described by fuzzy sets. Our aim is to evaluate the optimal expected reward, which is called a fuzzy perceptive value, based on the perceptive analysis. It is characterized and calculated by a certain fuzzy relation. A machine maintenance problem is discussed as a numerical example.

Keywords: Fuzzy perceptive model, Markov decision process, fuzzy perceptive reward, optimal policy function

1 Introduction and Notation

Many contributions to Markov decision processes(MDPs) have been made (cf. [1], [2], [4], [9], [10]), in which the transition probability of the state at each time is assumed to be uniquely given. In a real application of MDPs, the transition probability will be estimated through the measurement of various phenomena. In such a case, the real value of the state transition probability may be partially observed by dimness of perception or measurement imprecision.

For example, in a famous automobile replacement problem [4], the true value of the probability q_{ij} that the car in within age j after six months, given that the car is within age i at that time, may not be observed exactly. Usually, it is linguistically or roughly perceived, e.g., about 0.3, the probability considerably larger than 0.3, etc. A possible approach to handle such a case is to use fuzzy sets ([3], [13]), whose membership function can describe the perception value of the true probability. If the fuzzy perception of the transition probabilities for MDPs is given, how can we estimate in advance the future expected reward, called a fuzzy perceptive value, under the condition that we can know the true value of the transition probability immediately before our decision making.

In our previous work [8], we have tried the perceptive analysis for an optimal stopping problem. In this paper, we formulate the fuzzy perceptive model for

V. Torra et al. (Eds.): MDAI 2005, LNAI 3558, pp. 283–293, 2005.

MDPs and develop the perceptive analysis in which the fuzzy perceptive value for MDPs is characterized and calculated by a new fuzzy relation.

In the remainder of this section, we will give some notation and fundamental results on MDPs, by which the fuzzy perceptive model is formulated in the sequel. For non-perception approaches to MDPs with fuzzy imprecision refer to [7]. Recently Zadeh [14] wrote a summary paper of perception based probability theory.

Let $\mathbb{R}, \mathbb{R}^n$ and $\mathbb{R}^{m \times n}$ be the sets of real numbers, real n-dimensional vectors and real $m \times n$ matrices, respectively. The sets $\mathbb{R}^n$ and $\mathbb{R}^{m \times n}$ are endowed with the norm $\| \cdot \|$, where for $x = (x(1), x(2), \ldots, x(n)) \in \mathbb{R}^n$, $\|x\| = \sum_{j=1}^{n} |x(j)|$ and for $y = (y_{ij}) \in \mathbb{R}^{m \times n}$, $\|y\| = \max_{1 \leq i \leq m} \sum_{j=1}^{n} |y_{ij}|$.

For any set X, let $\mathcal{F}(X)$ be the set of all fuzzy sets $\tilde{x} : \to [0,1]$. The α-cut of $\tilde{x} \in \mathcal{F}(X)$ is given by $\tilde{x}_\alpha := \{x \in X \mid \tilde{x}(x) \geq \alpha\}$ ($\alpha \in (0,1]$) and $\tilde{x}_0 := \mathrm{cl}\{x \in X \mid \tilde{x}(x) > 0\}$, where cl is a closure of a set. Let $\tilde{\mathbb{R}}$ be the set of all fuzzy numbers, i.e., $\tilde{r} \in \tilde{\mathbb{R}}$ means that $\tilde{r} \in \mathcal{F}(\mathbb{R})$ is normal, upper semicontinuous and fuzzy convex and has a compact support. Let $\mathbb{C}$ be the set of all bounded and closed intervals of $\mathbb{R}$. Then, for $\tilde{r} \in \mathcal{F}(\mathbb{R})$, it holds that $\tilde{r} \in \tilde{\mathbb{R}}$ if and only if $\tilde{r}$ normal and $\tilde{r}_\alpha \in \mathbb{C}$ for $\alpha \in [0,1]$). So, for $\tilde{r} \in \tilde{\mathbb{R}}$, we write $\tilde{r}_\alpha = [\tilde{r}_\alpha^-, \tilde{r}_\alpha^+]$ ($\alpha \in [0,1]$).

The binary relation $\preccurlyeq$ on $\mathcal{F}(\mathbb{R})$ is defined as follows: For $\tilde{r}, \tilde{s} \in \mathcal{F}(\mathbb{R})$, $\tilde{r} \preccurlyeq \tilde{s}$ if and only if (i) for any $x \in \mathbb{R}$, there exists $y \in \mathbb{R}$ such that $x \leq y$ and $\tilde{r}(x) \leq \tilde{s}(y)$; (ii) for any $y \in \mathbb{R}$, there exists $x \in \mathbb{R}$ such that $x \leq y$ and $\tilde{s}(y) \leq \tilde{r}(x)$: Obviously, the binary relation $\preccurlyeq$ satisfies the axioms of a partial order relation on $\mathcal{F}(\mathbb{R})$ (cf. [6], [12]).

For $\tilde{r}, \tilde{s} \in \tilde{\mathbb{R}}$, $\widetilde{\max}\{\tilde{r}, \tilde{s}\}$ and $\widetilde{\min}\{\tilde{r}, \tilde{s}\}$ are defined by

$$\widetilde{\max}\{\tilde{r}, \tilde{s}\}(y) := \sup_{\substack{x_1, x_2 \in \mathbb{R} \\ y = x_1 \vee x_2}} \{\tilde{r}(x_1) \wedge \tilde{s}(x_2)\} \quad (y \in \mathbb{R}),$$

and

$$\widetilde{\min}\{\tilde{r}, \tilde{s}\}(y) := \sup_{\substack{x_1, x_2 \in \mathbb{R} \\ y = x_1 \wedge x_2}} \{\tilde{r}(x_1) \wedge \tilde{s}(x_2)\} \quad (y \in \mathbb{R}),$$

where $a \wedge b = \min\{a, b\}$ and $a \vee b = \max\{a, b\}$ for any $a, b \in \mathbb{R}$. It is easy proved that for $\tilde{r}, \tilde{s} \in \tilde{\mathbb{R}}$, $\widetilde{\max}\{\tilde{r}, \tilde{s}\} \in \tilde{\mathbb{R}}$ and $\widetilde{\min}\{\tilde{r}, \tilde{s}\} \in \tilde{\mathbb{R}}$.

Also, for $\tilde{r}, \tilde{s} \in \tilde{\mathbb{R}}$, the following (i)–(iv) are equivalent (cf. [6]): (i) $\tilde{r} \preccurlyeq \tilde{s}$; (ii) $\tilde{r}_\alpha^- \leq \tilde{s}_\alpha^-$ and $\tilde{r}_\alpha^+ \leq \tilde{s}_\alpha^+$ ($\alpha \in [0,1]$); (iii) $\widetilde{\max}\{\tilde{r}, \tilde{s}\} = \tilde{s}$; (iv) $\widetilde{\min}\{\tilde{r}, \tilde{s}\} = \tilde{r}$. We denote by $\mathbb{R}_+$ and $\mathbb{R}_+^n$ the subsets of entrywise non-negative elements in $\mathbb{R}$ and $\mathbb{R}^n$ respectively. Let $\mathbb{C}_+$ be the set of all bounded and closed intervals of $\mathbb{R}_+$ and $\mathbb{C}_+^n$ the set of all n-dimensional vectors whose elements are in $\mathbb{C}_+$. We have the following.

Lemma 1.1 ([5]) *For any non-empty convex and compact set $G \subset \mathbb{R}_+^n$ and $D = (D_1, D_2, \ldots, D_n) \in \mathbb{C}_+^n$, it holds that*

$$GD = \{g' \cdot d \mid g \in G, d \in D\} \in \mathbb{C}_+$$

where x' denotes the transpose of a vector $x \in \mathbb{R}^n$ and for $g = (g_1, g_2, \ldots, g_n) \in \mathbb{R}^n_+$ and $d = (d_1, d_2, \ldots, d_n) \in D$, $g' \cdot d = \sum_{j=1}^{n} g_j d_j$.

Here, we define MDPs whose extension to the fuzzy perceptive model will be done in Section 2. Consider finite state and action spaces, S and A, containing $n < \infty$ and $k < \infty$ elements with

$$S = \{1, 2, \ldots, n\} \quad \text{and} \quad A = \{1, 2, \ldots, k\}.$$

Let $\mathcal{P}(S) \subset \mathbb{R}^n$ and $\mathcal{P}(S|SA) \subset \mathbb{R}^{n \times nk}$ be the sets of all probabilities on S and conditional probabilities on S given $S \times A$, that is,

$$\mathcal{P}(S) \quad := \{q = q(\cdot) = (q(i); i \in S) \mid q(i) \geq 0, \ i \in S, \sum_{i \in S} q(i) = 1\},$$
$$\mathcal{P}(S|SA) := \{Q = (q_{ia}(\cdot) : i \in S, a \in A) \mid$$
$$q_{ia}(\cdot) = (q_{ia}(j), j \in S) \in \mathcal{P}(S), \ i \in S, a \in A\}.$$

For any $Q = (q_{ia}(\cdot)) \in \mathcal{P}(S|SA)$, we define a controlled dynamic system $\mathcal{M}(Q)$, called a Markov decision process(MDP), specified by $\{S, A, Q, r\}$, where $r : S \times A \to \mathbb{R}_+$ is an immediate reward function. When the system is in state $i \in S$ and action $a \in A$ is taken, then the system moves to a new state $j \in S$ selected according to $q_{ia}(\cdot)$ and the reward $r(i, a)$ is obtained. The process is repeated from the new state $j \in S$.

We wish to maximize the expected total discounted reward over the infinite horizon. Denote by F the set of functions from S to A. A policy π is a sequence $(f_1, f_2, \ldots)$ of functions with $f_t \in F$ ($t \geq 1$). Let Π denote the class of policies. We denote by f^∞ the policy $(f_1, f_2, \ldots)$ with $f_t = f$ for all $t \geq 1$ and some $f \in F$. Such a policy is called stationary. We associate with each $f \in F$ and $Q \in \mathcal{P}(S|SA)$ the vector $r(f) = (r(j, f(j)), j \in S)$ and the $n \times n$ transition matrix $Q(f)$, whose (i, j) element is $q_{i, f(i)}(j), i, j \in S$. Then, the expected total discounted reward from $\pi = (f_1, f_2, \ldots)$ is the vector $\psi(\pi|Q) = (\psi(i, \pi|Q), i \in S)$, which is defined, as a function of $Q \in \mathcal{P}(S|SA)$, by

$$(1.1) \qquad \psi(\pi|Q) = \sum_{t=0}^{\infty} \beta^t Q(f_1) Q(f_2) \cdots Q(f_t) r(f_{t+1}),$$

where $0 < \beta < 1$ is a discount factor. For any $Q \in \mathcal{P}(S|SA)$, a policy π^* satisfying that

$$\psi(i, \pi^*|Q) = \sup_{\pi \in \Pi} \psi(i, \pi|Q) := \psi(i|Q) \quad \text{for all} \ i \in S$$

is said to be Q-optimal, and $\psi(Q) := (\psi(i|Q), i \in S)$ is called the Q-optimal value vector. We can state the well-known results.

Theorem 1.1 (cf. [2],[9],[10]) *For any $Q = (q_{ia}(\cdot) : i \in S, a \in A) \in \mathcal{P}(S|SA)$, the following holds:*

(i) *The Q-optimal value vector $\psi(Q) := (\psi(i|Q), i \in S)$ is a unique solution to the optimality equations*

$$(1.2) \qquad \psi(i|Q) = \max_{a \in A}\{r(i,a) + \beta \sum_{j \in S} q_{ia}(j)\psi(j|Q)\} \quad (i \in S);$$

(ii) *There exits an optimal stationary policy f_*^∞ such that $f_*(i) \in A$ attains the minimum in (1.2), i.e.,*

$$(1.3) \qquad \psi(i|Q) = r(i, f_*(i)) + \beta \sum_{j \in S} q_{if_*(i)}(j)\psi(j|Q) \quad (i \in S).$$

In Section 2, we define a fuzzy-perceptive model for MDPs and it is analyzed in Section 3 with a numerical example. The proof of the theorem is given in Section 4.

2 Fuzzy-Perceptive Model

We define a fuzzy-perceptive model, in which fuzzy perception of the transition probabilities in MDPs is accommodated. In a concrete form, we use the fuzzy set on $\mathcal{P}(S|SA)$ whose membership function $\widetilde{Q}$ describes the perception value of the transition probability.

Firstly, for each $i \in S$ and $a \in A$, we give a fuzzy perception of $q_{ia}(\cdot) = (q_{ia}(j), j \in S)$, $\widetilde{Q}_{ia}(\cdot)$, which is a fuzzy set on $\mathcal{P}(S)$ and will be assumed to satisfy the following conditions (i)–(ii):

(i) (Normality) There exists a $q = (q_{ia}(\cdot)) \in \mathcal{P}(S)$ with $\widetilde{Q}_{ia}(q) = 1$;
(ii) (Convexity and compactness) The α-cut $\widetilde{Q}_{ia,\alpha}(\cdot) = \{q = q_{ia}(\cdot) \in \mathcal{P}(S) \mid \widetilde{Q}_{ia}(q) \geq \alpha\}$ is a convex and compact subset in $\mathcal{P}(S)$ for $\alpha \in [0,1]$.

Secondly, from a family of fuzzy-perceptions $\{\widetilde{Q}_{ia}(\cdot) : i \in S, a \in A\}$, we define the fuzzy set $\widetilde{Q}$ on $\mathcal{P}(S|SA)$, called fuzzy perception of the transition probability in MDPs, as follows:

$$(2.1) \qquad \widetilde{Q}(Q) = \min_{i \in S, a \in A} \widetilde{Q}_{ia}(q_{ia}(\cdot)),$$

where $Q = (q_{ia}(\cdot) : i \in S, a \in A) \in \mathcal{P}(S|SA)$. The α-cut of the fuzzy perception $\widetilde{Q}$ is described explicitly in the following:

$$(2.2) \qquad \begin{aligned} \widetilde{Q}_\alpha &= \{Q = (q_{ia}(\cdot)_{i \in S, a \in A}) \in \mathcal{P}(S|SA) \mid \\ & \qquad\qquad q_{ia}(\cdot) \in \widetilde{Q}_{ia,\alpha} \text{ for } i \in S, a \in A\} \\ &= \prod_{i \in S, a \in A} \widetilde{Q}_{ia,\alpha} \end{aligned}$$

for $\alpha \in [0,1]$.

Remark For each $i \in S$ and $a \in A$, in place of giving the fuzzy perception $\widetilde{Q}_{ia}$ on $\mathcal{P}(S)$, it may be convenient to give the fuzzy set $\widetilde{q}_{ia}(j) \in \widetilde{\mathbb{R}}$ $(j \in S)$ on $[0,1]$, which represents the fuzzy perception of $q_{ia}(j)$ (the probability that the state moves to $j \in S$ when the action $a \in A$ is taken in state $i \in S$). Then, $\widetilde{Q}_{ia}(\cdot)$ is defined by

$$(2.3) \qquad \widetilde{Q}_{ia}(q) = \min_{j \in S} \widetilde{q}_{ia}(j)(q_{ia}(j)),$$

where $q = (q_{ia}(1), q_{ia}(2), \ldots, q_{ia}(n)) \in \mathcal{P}(S)$. For any fuzzy perception $\widetilde{Q}$ on $\mathcal{P}(S|SA)$, our fuzzy-perceptive model is denoted by $\mathcal{M}(\widetilde{Q})$, in which for any $Q \in \mathcal{P}(S|SA)$ the corresponding MDPs $\mathcal{M}(Q)$ is perceived with perception level $\widetilde{Q}(Q)$.

The map δ on $\mathcal{P}(S|SA)$ with $\delta(Q) \in \Pi$ for all $Q \in \mathcal{P}(S|SA)$ is called a policy function. The set of all policy functions will be denoted by Δ. For any $\delta \in \Delta$, the fuzzy perceptive reward $\widetilde{\psi}$ is a fuzzy set on $\mathbb{R}$ denoted by

$$(2.4) \qquad \widetilde{\psi}(i, \delta)(x) = \sup_{\substack{Q \in \mathcal{P}(S|PS) \\ x = \psi(i, \delta(Q)|Q)}} \widetilde{Q}(Q) \quad (i \in S).$$

The policy function $\delta^* \in \Delta$ is said to be optimal if $\widetilde{\psi}(i, \delta) \preccurlyeq \widetilde{\psi}(i, \delta^*)$ for all $i \in S$ and $\delta \in \Delta$, where the partial order $\preccurlyeq$ is defined in Section 1. If there exists an optimal policy function δ^*, we put $\widetilde{\psi} = (\widetilde{\psi}(i), i \in S)$ will be called a fuzzy perceptive value, where $\widetilde{\psi}(i) = \widetilde{\psi}(i, \delta^*)$ for $i \in S$.

Now we can specify the fuzzy perceptive problem investigated in the next section. The problem is to find the optimal policy function δ^* and to characterize the fuzzy perceptive value.

3   Perceptive Analysis

In this section, we derive a new fuzzy optimality relation for solving our perceptive problem. The sufficient condition for the fuzzy perceptive reward $\widetilde{\psi}(i, \delta)$ to be a fuzzy number is given in the following lemma.

Lemma 3.1   For any $\delta \in \Delta$, if $\psi(i, \delta|Q)$ is continuous in $Q \in \mathcal{P}(S|SA)$, then $\widetilde{\psi}(i, \delta) \in \widetilde{\mathbb{R}}$.
Proof. From normality of $\widetilde{Q}$, there exists $Q^* \in \mathcal{P}(S|SA)$ with $\widetilde{Q}(Q^*) = 1$, such that $\widetilde{\psi}(i, \delta)(x^*) = 1$ for $x^* = \psi(i, \delta|Q^*)$. For any $\alpha \in [0, 1]$, we observed that

$$\widetilde{\psi}(i, \delta)_\alpha = \{\psi(i, \delta|Q) \mid Q \in \widetilde{Q}_\alpha\}.$$

Since $\widetilde{Q}_\alpha$ is convex and compact, the continuity of $\psi(i, \delta|\cdot)$ means the convexity and compactness of $\widetilde{\psi}(i, \delta)_\alpha$ $(\alpha \in [0.1])$. $\qquad \square$

Theorem 1.1 guarantees that for each $Q \in \mathcal{P}(S|SA)$ there exists a Q-optimal stationary policy f_*^∞ $(f_* \in F)$. Thus, for each $Q \in \mathcal{P}(S|SA)$, we denote by $\delta^*(Q)$ the corresponding Q-optimal stationary policy, which is thought as a policy function.

Lemma 3.2 ([11]) $\widetilde{\psi}(i, \delta^*) \in \widetilde{\mathbb{R}}$ *for all* $i \in S$.

Proof. Applying Lemma 3.1, it is sufficient to prove that $\widetilde{\psi}(i, \delta^*|Q)$ is continuous in $Q \in \mathcal{P}(S|SA)$. For simplicity, for any $Q \in \mathcal{P}(S|SA)$, we put $\psi(Q) = (\psi_1(Q), \psi_2(Q), \dots, \psi_n(Q))$ where $\psi_i(Q) = \psi(i, \delta^*|Q)$ $(i \in S)$. Let $Q = (q_{ia}(\cdot))$, $\emptyset Q = (\emptyset q_{ia}(\cdot)) \in \mathcal{P}(S|SA)$. By Theorem 1.1, we have

$$(3.1) \qquad \psi_i(Q) = \max_{a \in A}\{r(i, a) + \beta \sum_{j \in S} q_{ia}(j)\psi_j(Q)\},$$

$$(3.2) \qquad \psi_i(\emptyset Q) = \max_{a \in A}\{r(i, a) + \beta \sum_{j \in S} \emptyset q_{ia}(j)\psi_j(\emptyset Q)\}.$$

Suppose that $a_i = \delta^*(Q)(i)$ and $\emptyset a_i = \delta^*(\emptyset Q)(i), i \in S$ give the minimum in (3.1) and (3.2) respectively and let $a = (a_i, i \in S)$ and $\emptyset a = (\emptyset a_i, i \in S)$. Then, it yields that

$$\begin{aligned}
\psi(Q) - \psi(\emptyset Q) &\le (r(a) + \beta Q(a)\psi(Q)) - (r(a) + \beta \emptyset Q(a)\psi(\emptyset Q)) \\
&= \beta(Q(a)\psi(Q) - \emptyset Q \psi(\emptyset Q)) \\
&= \beta(Q(a) - \emptyset Q(a))\psi(Q) + \beta \emptyset Q(a)(\psi(Q) - \psi(\emptyset Q)),
\end{aligned}$$

where $r(a) = (r(i, a_i), i \in S)$ and $Q(a) = (q_{ia_i}(j))$ and $\emptyset Q(a) = (\emptyset q_{ia_i}(j))$. Thus, we get

$$(I - \beta \emptyset Q(a))(\psi(Q) - \psi(\emptyset Q)) \le \beta(Q(a) - \emptyset Q(a))\psi(Q),$$

where I is an identity matrix. Since $(I - \beta \emptyset Q(a))^{-1} = \sum_{k=0}^{\infty} \beta^k \emptyset Q(a)^k \ge 0$, we have

$$(3.3) \qquad \psi(Q) - \psi(\emptyset Q)) \le \beta(I - \beta \emptyset Q(a))^{-1}(Q(a) - \emptyset Q(a))\psi(\emptyset Q),$$

Similarly we get

$$(3.4) \qquad \psi(\emptyset Q) - \psi(Q)) \le \beta(I - \beta Q(\emptyset a))^{-1}(\emptyset Q(\emptyset a) - Q(\emptyset a))\psi(Q),$$

where $Q(\emptyset a)$ and $\emptyset Q(\emptyset a)$ are defined similarly as the above. Observing that

$$0 \le \psi_i(Q), \psi_i(\emptyset Q) \le \frac{1}{1 - \beta}\max_{i \in S, a \in A} r(i, a) =: M$$

and $\|Q(a) - \emptyset Q(a)\| \le \|Q - \emptyset Q\|$, $\|Q(\emptyset a) - \emptyset Q(\emptyset a)\| \le \|Q - \emptyset Q\|$,

$$(3.5) \qquad \begin{aligned} &\|\psi(Q) - \psi(\emptyset Q)\| \\ &\le \beta M\|Q - \emptyset Q\|\max\{\|(I - \beta \emptyset Q(a))^{-1}\|, \|(I - \beta Q(\emptyset a))^{-1}\|\}. \end{aligned}$$

When $Q \to \emptyset Q$ in $\mathcal{P}(S|SA)$, $\|(I - \beta \emptyset Q(a))^{-1}\|$ and $\|(I - \beta Q(\emptyset a))^{-1}\|$ are bounded and (3.5) means that $\|\psi(Q) - \psi(\emptyset Q)\| \to 0$. $\qquad \square$

Theorem 3.1 *The policy function* δ^* *is optimal.*

Proof. Let $\delta \in \Delta$. Since $\delta^*(Q)$ is Q-optimal, for any $Q \in \mathcal{P}(S|SA)$ it holds that

$$(3.6) \qquad \psi(i, \delta|Q) \le \psi(i, \delta^*|Q) \quad (i \in S).$$

For any $x \in \mathbb{R}$, let $\alpha := \widetilde{\psi}(i, \delta)(x)$. Then, from the definition there exists $Q \in \widetilde{Q}_\alpha$ with $x = \psi(i, \delta|Q)$. By (3,6), $y := \psi(i, \delta^*|Q) \ge x$, which implies $\widetilde{\psi}(i, \delta^*)(y) \ge \alpha$.

On the other hand, for $y \in \mathbb{R}$, let $\alpha := \widetilde{\psi}(i, \delta^*)(y)$. Then, there exists $Q \in \widetilde{Q}_\alpha$ such that $y = \psi(i, \delta^*|Q)$. From (3.6), we have that $y \ge x := \psi(i, \delta|Q)$. This implies $\widetilde{\psi}(i, \delta|Q) \le \alpha$. The above discussion yields that $\widetilde{\psi}(i, \delta) \preccurlyeq \widetilde{\psi}(i, \delta^*)$.   □

From Lemma 3.2, $\widetilde{\psi}(i) := \widetilde{\psi}(i, \delta^*) \in \widetilde{\mathbb{R}}$ $(i \in S)$, so that we denote by $\widetilde{\psi}_\alpha(i) := [\widetilde{\psi}_\alpha^-(i), \widetilde{\psi}_\alpha^+(i)]$, the α-cut of $\widetilde{\psi}(i)$. The fuzzy perceptive value $\widetilde{\psi} = (\widetilde{\psi}(1), \dots, \widetilde{\psi}(n))$ is characterized by a new fuzzy optimality relation in Theorem 3.2, whose proof is done in the next section.

Theorem 3.2 *The fuzzy perceptive value $\widetilde{\psi} = (\widetilde{\psi}(1), \widetilde{\psi}(2), \dots, \widetilde{\psi}(n))$ is a unique solution to the following fuzzy optimality relations:*

$$(3.7) \qquad \widetilde{\psi}(i) = \widetilde{\max_{a \in A}}\{1_{\{r(i,a)\}} + \beta \widetilde{Q}_{ia} \cdot \widetilde{\psi}\} \quad (i \in S),$$

where $\widetilde{Q}_{ia} \cdot \widetilde{\psi}(x) = \sup \widetilde{Q}_{ia}(q) \wedge \widetilde{\psi}(\psi)$ and the supremum is taken on the range $\{(q, \psi) \mid x = \sum_{j=1}^n q(j)\psi_j, q \in \mathcal{P}(S), \psi \in \mathbb{R}^n)\}$.

The α-cut expression of (3.7) is as follows:

$$(3.8) \qquad \widetilde{\psi}_\alpha^-(i) = \max_{a \in A}\{r(i, a) + \beta \min_{q_{ia} \in \widetilde{Q}_{ia,\alpha}} q_{ia} \cdot \widetilde{\psi}_\alpha^-\} \quad (i \in S);$$

$$(3.9) \qquad \widetilde{\psi}_\alpha^+(i) = \max_{a \in A}\{r(i, a) + \beta \max_{q_{ia} \in \widetilde{Q}_{ia,\alpha}} q_{ia} \cdot \widetilde{\psi}_\alpha^+\} \quad (i \in S),$$

where $\widetilde{\psi}_\alpha^\mp = (\widetilde{\psi}^\mp(1), \widetilde{\psi}^\mp(2), \dots, \widetilde{\psi}^\mp(n))$ and $q_{ia} \cdot \widetilde{\psi}_\alpha^\mp = \sum_{j \in S} q_{ia}(j)\widetilde{\psi}_\alpha^\mp(j)$.

We note that the α-cut of $\widetilde{Q}_{ia} \cdot \widetilde{\psi}$ in (3.7) is in $\mathbb{C}$ from Lemma 1.1, so that $\widetilde{Q}_{ia} \cdot \widetilde{\psi} \in \widetilde{\mathbb{R}}$. Thus, the right hand of (3.7) is well-defined. As a simple example, we consider a fuzzy perceptive model of a machine maintenance problem dealt with in ([9], p.1, p.17–18).

Example: A machine can be operated synchronously, say, once an hour. At each period there are two states; one is operating(state 1), and the other is in failure(state 2). If the machine fails, it can be restored to perfect functioning by repair. At each period, if the machine is running, we earn the return of \$ 3.00 per period; the fuzzy set of probability of being in state 1 at the next step is $(0.6/0.7/0.8)$ and that of the probability of moving to state 2 is $(0.2/0.3/0.4)$, where for any $0 \le a < b < c \le 1$, the fuzzy number $(a/b/c)$ on $[0, 1]$ is defined by

$$(a/b/c)(x) = \begin{cases} (x-a)/(b-a) \vee 0 \text{ if } 0 \le x \le b, \\ (x-c)/(b-c) \vee 0 \text{ if } b \le x \le 1. \end{cases}$$

If the machine is in failure, we have two actions to repair the failed machine; one is a usual repair, denoted by 1, that yields the cost of \$1.00(that is, a return of $-\$1.00$) with the fuzzy set $(0.3/0.4/0.5)$ of the probability moving in state 1 and the fuzzy set $(0.5/0.6/0.7)$ of the probability being in state 2; another is a rapid repair, denoted by 2, that requires the cost of \$2.00(that is, a return of $-\$2.00$) with the fuzzy set $(0.6/0.7/0.8)$ of the probability moving in state 1 and the fuzzy set $(0.2/0.3/0.4)$ of the probability being in state 2.

For the model considered, $S = \{1, 2\}$ and there exists two stationary policies, $F = \{f_1, f_2\}$ with $f_1(2) = 1$ and $f_2(2) = 2$, where f_1 denotes a policy of the usual repair and f_2 a policy of the rapid repair. The state transition diagrams of two policies are shown in Figure 1.

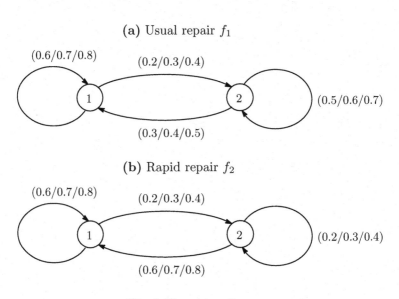

(a) Usual repair f_1

$(0.6/0.7/0.8)$ $(0.2/0.3/0.4)$

1   2 $(0.5/0.6/0.7)$

$(0.3/0.4/0.5)$

(b) Rapid repair f_2

$(0.6/0.7/0.8)$ $(0.2/0.3/0.4)$

1   2 $(0.2/0.3/0.4)$

$(0.6/0.7/0.8)$

Fig. 1. Transition diagrams

Using (2.3), we obtain $\widetilde{Q}_{ia}(\cdot)$ ($i \in S, a \in A$), whose α-cut is given as follows(cf. [5]):

$$\widetilde{Q}_{11,\alpha} = co\{(.6 + .1\alpha, \ .4 - .1\alpha), (.8 - .1\alpha, \ .2 + .1\alpha)\},$$
$$\widetilde{Q}_{21,\alpha} = co\{(.3 + .1\alpha, \ .7 - .1\alpha), (.5 - .1\alpha, \ .5 + .1\alpha)\},$$
$$\widetilde{Q}_{22,\alpha} = co\{(.6 + .1\alpha, \ .4 - .1\alpha), (.8 - .1\alpha, \ .2 + .1\alpha)\},$$

where coX is a convex hull of a set X. So, putting $x_1 = \widetilde{\psi}_\alpha^-(1), \ x_2 = \widetilde{\psi}_\alpha^-(2),$ $y_1 = \widetilde{\psi}_\alpha^+(1), \ y_2 = \widetilde{\psi}_\alpha^+(2)$, the α-cut optimality equations (3.8) and (3.9) with $\beta = 0.9$ become:

$$x_1 = 3 + .9 \min\{(.6 + .1\alpha)x_1 + (.4 - .1\alpha)x_2, \ (.8 - .1\alpha)x_1 + (.2 + .1\alpha)x_2\}$$
$$x_2 = \max\big[-1 + .9 \min\{(.3 + .1\alpha)x_1 + (.7 - .1\alpha)x_2, \ (.5 - .1\alpha)x_1 + (.5 + .1\alpha)x_2\},$$
$$-2 + .9 \min\{(.6 + .1\alpha)x_1 + (.4 - .1\alpha)x_2, \ (.8 - 0.1\alpha)x_1 + (.2 + .1\alpha)x_2\}\big],$$
$$y_1 = 3 + .9 \max\{(.6 + .1\alpha)y_1 + (.4 - .1\alpha)y_2, \ (.8 - .1\alpha)y_1 + (.2 + .1\alpha)y_2\}$$
$$y_2 = \max\big[-1 + .9 \max\{(.3 + .1\alpha)y_1 + (.7 - .1\alpha)y_2, \ (.5 - .1\alpha)y_1 + (.5 + .1\alpha)y_2\},$$
$$-2 + .9 \max\{(.6 + .1\alpha)y_1 + (.4 - .1\alpha)y_2, \ (.8 - 0.1\alpha)y_1 + (.2 + .1\alpha)y_2\}\big],$$

After a simple calculation, we get

$$x_1 = 12 + 4.5\alpha, \ x_2 = 7 + 4.5\alpha, \ y_1 = 21 - 4.5\alpha, \ y_2 = 16 - 4.5\alpha.$$

Thus, we know the fuzzy perceptive value is

$$\widetilde{\psi}(1) = (12/16.5/21), \quad \widetilde{\psi}(2) = (7/11.5/16).$$

4   Proof of Theorem 3.2

For any $\alpha \in [0, 1]$, we define maps $\underline{U}^\alpha, \text{\O} U^\alpha : \mathbb{R}_+^n \to \mathbb{R}_+^n$ by

$$(4.1) \qquad \underline{U}^\alpha u(i) = \min_{q_{ia} \in \widetilde{Q}_{ia,\alpha}} \max_{a \in A}\{r(i, a) + \beta \sum_{j=1}^n q_{ia}(j)u(j)\},$$

$$(4.2) \qquad \text{\O} U^\alpha u(i) = \max_{q_{ia} \in \widetilde{Q}_{ia,\alpha}} \max_{a \in A}\{r(i, a) + \beta \sum_{j=1}^n q_{ia}(j)u(j)\},$$

for $i \in S$ and any $u = (u(i), i \in S) \in \mathbb{R}_+^n$.

In order to prove the theorem, we will prepare two lemmas.

Lemma 4.1   *The following (i) and (ii) hold.*

(i) *The maps $\underline{U}^\alpha$ and $\text{\O} U^\alpha$ are contractions with modulus β;*

(ii) *The extreme point vectors $\widetilde{\psi}_\alpha^\pm := (\widetilde{\psi}_\alpha^\pm(i), i \in S)$ with $\widetilde{\psi}_\alpha = [\widetilde{\psi}_\alpha^-, \widetilde{\psi}_\alpha^+]$ are uniquely given as fixed points of $\underline{U}^\alpha$ and $\text{\O} U^\alpha$ ($\alpha \in [0.1]$) respectively.*

Proof.   The proof of (i) is easy and tedious, so it is omitted. For (ii), let $\underline{\psi} = (\underline{\psi}(1), \dots, \underline{\psi}(n))$ and $\text{\O}\psi = (\text{\O}\psi(1), \dots, \text{\O}\psi(n))$ be fixed points of $\underline{U}^\alpha$ and $\overline{\text{\O}} U^\alpha$ ($\alpha \in [0.1]$) respectively. Then, we have that

$$\underline{\psi}(i) = \max_{a \in A}\{r(i, a) + \sum_{j \in S} q_{ia}(j)\underline{\psi}(j)\}$$

for some $Q = (q_{ia} : i \in S, a \in A)$ with $q_{ia} \in \widetilde{Q}_{ia,\alpha}$. From Theorem 1.1 it follows that $\underline{\psi}(i) = \psi(i, \delta^*|Q)$. So, we get, for all $i \in S$,

$$(4.3) \qquad \underline{\psi}(i) \geq \widetilde{\psi}_\alpha^-(i) = \min_{Q \in \widetilde{Q}_\alpha} \psi(i, \delta^*|Q)$$

Suppose that $\underline{\psi}(i_0) > \tilde{\psi}_\alpha^-(i_0) = \psi(i_0, \delta^*|\underline{Q})$ for some $i_0 \in S$ and $\underline{Q} \in \tilde{\underline{Q}}_\alpha$. Then, the vector $\psi = (\psi_1, \ldots, \psi_n)$ with $\psi_i = \psi(i, \delta^*|\underline{Q})$ $(i \in S)$ satisfies from Theorem 1.1 that

$$\psi(i) = \max_{a \in A}\{r(i,a) + \beta \sum_{j \in S} \underline{q}_{ia}(j)\psi(j)\} \geq \underline{U}^\alpha \psi(i)$$

where $\underline{Q} = (\underline{q}_{ia})$. Applying this iteratively, we have

$$\psi_{i_0} = \tilde{\psi}_\alpha^-(i_0) \geq (\underline{U}^\alpha)^\ell \psi(i_0) \to \underline{\psi}(i_0) \ (\ell \to 0)$$

which contradicts that $\underline{\psi}(i_0) > \tilde{\psi}_\alpha^-(i_0)$, so that from (4.3) it yields $\underline{\psi} = \tilde{\psi}_\alpha^-$. Similarly as the above, we can get $\emptyset\psi = \tilde{\psi}_\alpha^+$. These prove the lemma.   □

Now, we define another maps $\underline{V}^\alpha, \emptyset V^\alpha : \mathbb{R}_+^n \to \mathbb{R}_+^n$ $(\alpha \in [0,1])$ by

(4.4) $$\underline{V}^\alpha u(i) = \max_{a \in A}\{r(i,a) + \beta \min_{q_{ia} \in \tilde{Q}_{ia,\alpha}} \sum_{j \in S} q_{ia}(j)u(j)\},$$

(4.5) $$\emptyset V^\alpha u(i) = \max_{a \in A}\{r(i,a) + \beta \max_{q_{ia} \in \tilde{Q}_{ia,\alpha}} \sum_{j \in S} q_{ia}(j)u(j)\},$$

where $u = (u(i), i \in S) \in \mathbb{R}_+^n$. By the definition of $\emptyset U^\alpha$ and $\emptyset V^\alpha$, it clearly holds that $\emptyset U^\alpha = \emptyset V^\alpha$.

Lemma 4.2 *For any $\alpha \in [0,1]$, the following (i) and (ii) hold:*

(i) $\underline{V}^\alpha$ *is a contraction with modulus β;*
(ii) $\tilde{\psi}_\alpha^-$ *is a fixed point of $\underline{V}^\alpha$.*

Proof. The proof of (i) is easy and omitted. For (ii), we denote by $\phi = (\phi(i), i \in S)$ the unique fixed point of $\underline{V}^\alpha$. Then, for each $i \in S$, we have: $\phi(i) = \max_{a \in A}\{r(i,a) + \beta \sum_{j \in S} q_{ia}(j)\phi(j)\}$ for some $\emptyset Q = (\emptyset q_{ia})$ with $\emptyset q_{ia} \in \tilde{Q}_{ia}$. Using Theorem 1.1, it follows that $\phi(i) = \psi(i, \delta^*|Q)$, which implies $\phi(i) \geq \tilde{\psi}_\alpha^-(i) = \max_{Q \in \tilde{Q}} \psi(i, \delta^*|Q)$ for all $i \in S$. Since $\underline{V}^\alpha \leq \underline{U}^\alpha$, it holds from Lemma 4.1 that $\underline{V}^\alpha \tilde{\psi}_\alpha^- \leq \underline{U}^\alpha \tilde{\psi}_\alpha^- = \tilde{\psi}_\alpha^-$. Applying the above inequality iteratively,

$$\tilde{\psi}_\alpha^- \geq (\underline{V}^\alpha)^\ell \tilde{\psi}_\alpha^- \to \phi \ (\ell \to \infty),$$

which implies $\tilde{\psi}_\alpha^- \geq \phi$, so that $\tilde{\psi}_\alpha^- = \phi$.   □

Proof of Theorem 3.2 For each $\alpha \in [0,1]$, Lemma 4.2 shows that $\underline{V}^\alpha \tilde{\psi}_\alpha^- = \tilde{\psi}_\alpha^-$ and $\emptyset V^\alpha \tilde{\psi}_\alpha^+ = \tilde{\psi}_\alpha^+$, which is same as (3.8) and (3.9) respectively. From this, the assertion of (ii) holds. For (i), for $i \in S$ and $a \in A$, we have:

$$\{1_{r(i,a)} + \beta \tilde{Q}_{ia}\tilde{\psi}\}_\alpha = r(i,a) + \beta \tilde{Q}_{ia,\alpha}\tilde{\psi}_\alpha.$$

So, (3.8) and (3.9) of Theorem 3.2 are clearly the α-cut representation of (3.7). This is what we want to prove.   □

Acknowledgement

The authors wish to express their thanks two anonymous referees for their comments.

References

1. Blackwell,D., Discrete dynamic programming, *Ann. Math. Statist.*, **33**, (1962), 719–726.
2. Derman,C., *Finite State Markovian Decision Processes*, Academic Press, New York, (1970).
3. Dubois,D. and Prade,H., *Fuzzy Sets and Systems : Theory and Applications*, Academic Press, (1980).
4. Howard,R., *Dynamic Programming and Markov Process*, MIT Press, Cambrige, MA, (1960).
5. Kurano,M., Song,J., Hosaka,M. and Huang,Y., Controlled Markov set-chains with discounting, *J. Appl. Prob.*, **35**, (1998), 293–302.
6. Kurano,M., Yasuda,M. Nakagami,J. and Yoshida,Y., Ordering of fuzzy sets – A brief survey and new results, *J. Operations Research Society of Japan*, **43**, (2000), 138–148.
7. Kurano,M., Yasuda,M. Nakagami,J. and Yoshida,Y., A fuzzy treatment of uncertain Markov decision process, RIMS Koukyuroku, **1132**, (2000), 221–229.
8. Kurano,M., Yasuda,M. Nakagami,J. and Yoshida,Y., A fuzzy stopping problem with the concept of perception, *Fuzzy Optimization and Decision Making*, **3**, (2004), 367–374.
9. Mine,H. and Osaki,S., *Markov Decision Process*, Elsevier, Amesterdam, (1970).
10. Puterman,M.L., *Markov Decision Process: Discrete Stochastic Dynamic Programming*, John Wiley & Sons, INC, (1994).
11. Solan,E., *Continuity of the value of competitive Markov decision processes*, J. Theoretical Probability, **16**, (2004) 831–845.
12. Yoshida,Y. and Kerre,E.E., A fuzzy ordering on multi-dimensional fuzzy sets induced from convex cones, Fuzzy Sets and Systems, **130**, (2002), 343–355.
13. Zadeh,L.A., Fuzzy sets, *Inform. and Control*, **8**, (1965), 338–353.
14. Zadeh,L.A., Toward a perception-based theory of probabilistic reasoning with imprecise probabilities, *J. of Statistical Planning and Inference*, **105**, (2002), 233–264.

Cancer Prediction Using Diversity-Based Ensemble Genetic Programming

Jin-Hyuk Hong and Sung-Bae Cho

Dept. of Computer Science, Yonsei University
134 Sinchon-dong, Sudaemoon-ku, Seoul 120-749, Korea
hjinh@sclab.yonsei.ac.kr, sbcho@cs.yonsei.ac.kr

Abstract. Combining a set of classifiers has often been exploited to improve the classification performance. Accurate as well as diverse base classifiers are prerequisite to construct a good ensemble classifier. Therefore, estimating diversity among classifiers has been widely investigated. This paper presents an ensemble approach that combines a set of diverse rules obtained by genetic programming. Genetic programming generates interpretable classification rules, and diversity among them is directly estimated. Finally, several diverse rules are combined by a fusion method to generate a final decision. The proposed method has been applied to cancer classification using gene expression profiles, which is one of the important issues in bioinformatics. Experiments on several popular cancer datasets have demonstrated the usability of the method. High performance of the proposed method has been obtained, and the accuracy has increased by diversity among the base classification rules.

1 Introduction

Genetic programming is a representative technique in evolutionary computation, which has several distinguished characteristics [1]. Especially, interpretable rules obtained by genetic programming provide not only useful information on classification but also many chances to combine with other approaches. Diversity that is important in ensemble might be directly estimated by comparing the rules [2].

Combining classifiers, known as ensemble, has received the attention to improve classification performance [3,4]. The ensemble classifier is obtained by combining the outputs of multiple classifiers, and the diversity among base classifiers is important besides the accuracy. Diversity implies how differently classifiers are formed, while accuracy represents how correctly a classifier categorizes. Many researchers have studied ensemble techniques and diversity measures. Hansen and Salamon have provided the theoretical basis on ensemble [5], while Opitz and Maclin have performed empirical ensemble experiments comprehensively [6]. Zhou *et al.* have analyzed the effect on the number of participating classifiers into ensemble in both theoretical and empirical studies [7]. Bagging and boosting have been actively investigated to generate the base classifiers as popular ensemble learning techniques, while various fusion strategies have also been studied for effective ensemble [3,4,8]. A survey on generating diverse classifiers for ensemble has been conducted by Brown [9]. A hybrid model for efficient ensemble was studied by Bakker and Heskes [10], while Tan and Gilbert applied ensemble to classifying gene expression data [11].

Since ensembling the same classifiers does not produce any elevation on performance [8], selecting diverse as well as accurate base classifiers is very important in

V. Torra et al. (Eds.): MDAI 2005, LNAI 3558, pp. 294–304, 2005.

making a good ensemble classifier [9]. Simple ways to generate various classifiers are randomly initializing parameters or making a variation of training data. Bagging (bootstrap aggregating) introduced by Breimen generates individual classifiers by training with a randomly organized set of samples from the original data [12]. Ensemble classifiers with bagging aggregate the base classifiers based on a voting mechanism. Boosting, which is another popular ensemble learning method, is introduced by Schapire to produce a series of classifiers [13]. A set of samples for training a classifier is chosen based on the performance of the previous classifiers in the series. Examples incorrectly classified by previous classifiers have more chances to be selected as training samples for the current one. Arching [14] and Ada-Boosting [13] are the representative boosting methods.

Some researchers select diverse classifiers to combine for ensemble [3,8]. Diversity among classifiers is estimated by some measures, and the most discriminating classifiers are selected to make an ensemble classifier. In general, the error patterns of classifiers are used to measure the diversity [9]. Bryll proposed a novel approach that employs different sets of features to generate different classifiers [4]. Most studies aim at generating distinct base classifiers, but they hardly provide explicit methods to measure diversity of classifiers and errors might be included into selecting classifiers. An explicit method estimating the diversity among classifiers might be helpful to minimize errors and to prepare a set of diverse base classifiers.

The objective of this paper is to investigate an ensemble approach using genetic programming. Classification rules are generated by genetic programming, while the rules might be interpreted to explicitly measure diversity. A subset of rules is selected based on the diversity to construct an ensemble classifier in which they may be distinct as much as possible from the others. The proposed method is applied to classifying gene expression profiles that is an important problem in bioinformatics. Section 2 describes cancer classification using genetic programming as backgrounds. The proposed method and results are presented in Sections 3 and 4. Conclusion and future work are finally summarized in Section 5.

2 Cancer Classification Using Genetic Programming

Cancer classification based on gene expression profiles is one of the major research topics both in the medical field and in machine learning. DNA microarray technology recently developed provides an opportunity to take a genome-wide approach to the correct prediction of cancers. It captures the expression levels of thousands of genes simultaneously which contain information on diseases [15]. Since finding an understandable classification rule is required beside the accuracy, discovering classification rules using genetic programming was studied in the previous work [16]. Even though the rule is quite simple, it shows a good performance in classifying cancers.

An individual of genetic programming is represented as a tree that consists of the function set $\{+, -, \times, /\}$ and the terminal set $\{f_1, f_2, ..., f_n, \text{constant}\}$ where n is the number of features. The function set is designed to model the up and down regulations of the gene expression. The grammars for the classification rule are: $G=\{V=\{EXP, OP, VAR\}, T=\{+, -, \times, /, f_1, f_2, ..., f_n, \text{constant}\}, P, \{EXP\}\}$, where the rule set P is as the following.

$$EXP \rightarrow EXP\ OP\ EXP\ |\ VAR$$
$$OP \rightarrow +\ |-|\times|\ /$$
$$VAR \rightarrow f_1\ |\ f_2\ |\ \dots\ |\ f_n\ |\ constant$$

The category of an instance is determined by evaluating it with the rule. An instance will be classified into class 1 if the evaluated value is over 0, while it will be classified into class 2 if the value is under 0. Conventional genetic operators for genetic programming are employed for evolution. Crossover randomly selects and changes sub-trees from two individuals, mutation changes a sub-tree into new one, and permutation exchanges two sub-trees of an individual. All genetic operations are conducted according to the predefined probabilities.

3   Combining Classification Rules with Diversity

The proposed method consists of 3 processes as shown in Figure 1: selecting features, discovering multiple rules, and selecting and combining the rules. Based on the previous work, Euclidean distance, cosine coefficient and signal-to-noise ratio are employed to score the degree of association of genes with cancers. With the selected genes, genetic programming works to generate multiple classification rules. Diversity among these rules is estimated by the tree edit distance, and a subset of diverse classification rules is used to construct an ensemble classifier. Contrary to conventional ensemble learning methods that simply combine the outputs of individual classifiers, the proposed method picks up some classification rules that maximize diversity.

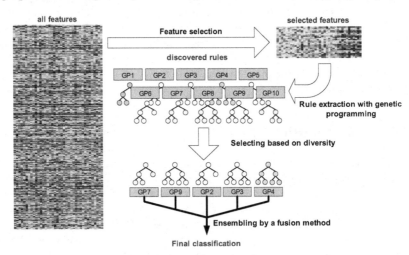

Fig. 1. Overview of the proposed method

3.1   Estimating Diversity in Genetic Programming

Diversity is concerned with the levels and types of variety between individuals in genetic programming. Features such as fitness values and structures are employed to design diversity measures [2]. Moreover, diversity of the population can be controlled during evolution so as to generate diverse individuals.

In genetic programming, diversity often refers to structural differences. Two identical structures might produce the same result, but this does not imply that the two structures with the same results are identical. Even if two individuals with different structures have the same outputs, they should be regarded as different ones possessing different potential characteristics. There are some representative methods for estimating diversity between two individuals such as edit distance, isolated-subtree distance, top-down distance, and alignment distance [17]. Edit distance, one of the most popular methods, measures the similarity between two individuals. It scores a distance of 1 if the nodes have different values, or 0. After scoring for all nodes in two trees, it sums up the distances and normalizes by dividing it by the size of the smaller tree. Sometimes a tree is interpreted as a string by a specific strategy, and the matching score between them is used to employ as the similarity of them.

3.2 Selecting Features

In general, microarrays include the expression information of thousands or even tens of thousands of genes, but only a small portion of them are related to the target cancer. A subset of informative genes should be selected by the feature selection process. Cutting down the number of features to a sufficient minimum is requisite to improve classification performance [18]. Two "ideal" marker gene expression profiles are designed as shown in Figure 2. The first one is a binary vector which is 1 among all the samples in class A and 0 among all the samples in class B, while the second one is another binary vector which is 0 among all the samples in class A and 1 among all the samples in class B. Three popular measures are employed such as Euclidean distance, cosine coefficient and signal-to-noise ratio. Fifty genes are selected by each feature selection method: the first 25 for ideal marker 1 and the rest for ideal marker 2.

The similarity between an ideal marker *ideal* and a gene *g* can be regarded as a distance, while the distance presents how far they are located in. A gene is regarded as an informative gene if the distance is small, while the gene is regarded as an uncorrelated gene if the distance is large. Euclidean distance (ED) and cosine coefficient (CC), where *n* is the number of samples, estimate the distance as follows:

$$ED = \sqrt{\sum_{i=1}^{n} \left(ideal_i - g_i \right)^2} \tag{1}$$

$$CC = \frac{\sum_{i=1}^{n} ideal_i \times g_i}{\sqrt{\sum_{i=1}^{n} ideal_i^2 \times \sum_{i=1}^{n} g_i^2}} \tag{2}$$

Given the mean μ and standard deviation σ from the distribution of gene expressions within their classes, the signal to noise ratio of a gene *g*, SN, is defined as follows:

$$SN = \frac{\mu_{class\,A}(g) - \mu_{class\,B}(g)}{\sigma_{class\,A}(g) + \sigma_{class\,B}(g)},$$

where $\mu_{class\,i}(g)$ is the mean of *g* and *ideal* whose label is *class i*

and $\sigma_{class\,i}(g)$ is the standard deviation of *g* and *ideal* whose label is *class i*

$$\tag{3}$$

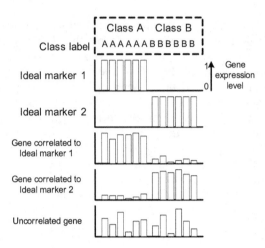

Fig. 2. Illustration of the feature selection

3.3   Generating Multiple Classification Rules

In order to generate multiple classification rules, genetic programming operates in parallel as shown in Figure 1. Each genetic programming obtains a classification rule that consists of a subset of features and arithmetic operators. Four fifths of the whole training data is randomly selected to construct a training set for evolving a rule. Generating a classification rule was described in Section 2.

In evolution process, genetic programming evaluates individuals in classification accuracy, while it also considers the simplicity of rules. The concept of Occam's razor also supports the introduction of simplicity [19]. The accuracy is estimated as correct classification rate for training samples, and the simplicity is measured as the number of nodes used in a rule. The following formula show the fitness function used in this paper, and the weights for each criterion are set as 0.9 and 0.1, respectively.

$$fitness \ of \ individual_i = \frac{number \ of \ correct \ samples}{number \ of \ total \ train \ data} \times w_1 + simplicity \times w_2$$

$$where \ simplicity = \frac{number \ of \ nodes}{number \ of \ maximum \ nodes},$$

$$w_1 = weight \ for \ training \ rate, and \ w_2 = weight \ for \ simplicity$$

3.4   Selecting Diverse Rules

Selecting a subset of attributes is also benefit for learning diverse classifiers as well as constructing a training set dynamically [4]. The classification rules obtained by genetic programming have different structures and use different genes. It signifies that the parallel genetic programming might naturally generate diverse rules by selecting different sets of attributes and structures [20]. Before combining classification rules, diversity is measured by the edit distance of structures and the appearance of genes used. The edit distance between the structures of two rules r_i and r_j is estimated as follows:

$$edit\_distance(r_i, r_j) =$$

$$\begin{cases} d(p, q), & \text{if neither } r_i \text{ nor } r_j \text{ have any children} \\ d(p, q) + edit\_distance(\text{RS of } r_i, \text{RS of } r_j) \\ \quad + edit\_distance(\text{LS of } r_i, \text{LS of } r_j), \\ \quad \text{otherwise (RS : right subtree, LS : left subtree)} \end{cases}$$

$$where \ d(p, q) = \begin{cases} 1, & \text{if } p \text{ and } q \text{ overlap} \\ 0, & \text{if } p \text{ and } q \text{ do not overlap} \end{cases}$$

The appearance of genes in rules is also compared with each other. The diversity decreases when there is the same gene, while it increases if different genes are used. A good ensemble can be made when base classifiers are distinct from one another, so some classification rules are selected to compose an ensemble classifier from 10 rules by the algorithm described in Figure 3. Since some fusion methods might result in a tie, 5 rules are selected for ensemble in this paper.

```
R: A set of extracted rules {r₁, r₂, ..., r₁₀}
S: A set of selected rules {s₁, s₂, ..., s₅}

int calculate_diversity(rᵢ, rⱼ) {
    cfᵢⱼ = common_feature_number(rᵢ, rⱼ);
    dfᵢⱼ = different_feature_number(rᵢ, rⱼ);
    edᵢⱼ = edit_distance(rᵢ, rⱼ);
    return dfᵢⱼ – cfᵢⱼ + 0.5 × edᵢⱼ;
}
For i=1 to 10 {
    For j=i+1 to 10 {
        dᵢⱼ = calculate_diversity(rᵢ, rⱼ);
}}
Find a set S in which rules' diversity is maximized
S = {s₁, s₂, ..., s₅}
```

Fig. 3. An algorithm for selecting 5 diverse classification rules

3.5 Combining Multiple Classification Rules

Four fusion methods are used: Majority vote (MAJ), maximum (MAX), minimum (MIN) and average (AVG) [3]. They are described as the following formula, where m_i is the margin of the classifier i.

MAJ   # of classifiers selecting class1 > # of classifiers selecting class2 ? class1 : class2   (4)

MAX $ABS\_MAX(m_1, m_2, m_3, m_4, m_5) > 0$? class1 : class2   (5)

MIN $ABS\_MIN(m_1, m_2, m_3, m_4, m_5) > 0$? class1 : class2   (6)

AVG $\sum_{i=1}^{5} m_i > 0$? ? class 1 : class2   (7)

4   Experimental Results

4.1   Experimental Environment

Three popular gene expression datasets are used in this paper: Types of diffuse large B-cell lymphoma cancer dataset [21], lung cancer dataset [22], and ovarian cancer dataset [23]. All of them are normalized from 0 to 1 at first.

Diffuse large B-cell lymphoma (DLBCL) is one disease, which is the common subtype of non-Hodgkin's lymphoma [21]. There are various subtypes of lymphoma cancer needed different treatments, but it is not easy to distinguish them clinically. Hence, lymphoma cancer classification using gene expression profiles has been investigated [24,25]. The dataset consists of 47 samples: 24 samples of germinal centre B-like group and 23 samples of activated B-like group. Each sample has 4,026 gene expression levels.

Lung cancer dataset has been exploited in classifying between malignant pleural mesothelioma (MPM) and adenocarcinoma (ADCA) of the lung. There are 181 tissues: 31 MPM tissues and 150 ADCA tissues. Each tissue has 12,533 gene expression levels [22].

Ovarian cancer dataset aims to identify proteomic pattern in serum so as to distinguish the ovarian cancer. It has 91 controls (normal) and 162 ovarian cancer tissues where each sample has 15,154 gene expression levels [23].

Since each dataset consists of few samples with many features, we conduct 5 folds cross-validation. One fifth of samples are evaluated as test data while the others are used as training data, and it is repeated 10 times for the average results, leading to 50 (5×10) experiments in total. The parameters for genetic programming are set as shown in Table 1. We use roulette wheel selection with elite preserving strategy.

Table 1. Experimental environments

Parameter	Value	Parameter	Value
Population size	200	Mutation rate	0.1~0.3
Maximum generation	3,000	Permutation rate	0.1
Selection rate	0.6~0.8	Maximum depth of a tree	3~5
Crossover rate	0.6~0.8	Elitism	yes

4.2   Classification Accuracy

Table 2~4 summarize the predictive accuracy of the proposed method for each dataset; the highlighted values represent the highest accuracy obtained. The result shows that the ensembling improves the performance of classification, while the proposed method that considers diversity obtains the highest accuracy in most cases against the combination of 10 classifiers and the combination of 5 classifiers. The ensemble that uses 10 rules was inferior to the ensemble that uses 5 rules, even though the former procedure includes more information than the latter. This implies that error is increased with increasing numbers of base classifiers. Finally, the proposed approach not only supports the same degree of useful information with the ensemble that uses 10 rules, but also minimizes the increment of the error.

Table 2. Test accuracy on lymphoma cancer dataset (%)

Features	Fusion method	10 classifiers	5 classifiers	5 diverse classifiers	Individual classifier
ED	MAJ	92.2	92.9	**94.4**	
	MAX	96.8	95.7	**100**	88.9
	MIN	78.2	80.1	81.6	
	AVG	96.8	95.4	**98.9**	
CC	MAJ	92.2	93.7	**100**	
	MAX	96.7	95.5	**100**	91.3
	MIN	76.3	82.5	84.3	
	AVG	95.6	94.9	**100**	
S2N	MAJ	95.6	95.4	**99.7**	
	MAX	97.8	96	**99.1**	89.7
	MIN	74.1	80	**96.1**	
	AVG	98.9	96.5	**99.1**	

Table 3. Test accuracy on lung cancer dataset (%)

Features	Fusion method	10 classifiers	5 classifiers	5 diverse classifiers	Individual classifier
ED	MAJ	97.8	**98.3**	97.4	
	MAX	**99.2**	98.9	99	97.5
	MIN	94.2	**95.7**	93.9	
	AVG	**99.4**	98.8	98.2	
CC	MAJ	99.2	99.1	**99.9**	
	MAX	98.9	98.9	**99.4**	97.8
	MIN	94.5	**95.9**	95.8	
	AVG	99.4	99.2	**99.9**	
S2N	MAJ	**99.7**	99.6	99.6	
	MAX	99.4	**99.5**	99.4	99
	MIN	95.3	**96.7**	96.5	
	AVG	**100**	99.8	**100**	

Table 4. Test accuracy on ovarian cancer dataset (%)

Features	Fusion method	10 classifiers	5 classifiers	5 diverse classifiers	Individual classifier
ED	MAJ	96.6	96.8	**97.5**	
	MAX	**97.6**	97	97.3	96.4
	MIN	95.1	95.4	**96.1**	
	AVG	97	96.8	**97.3**	
CC	MAJ	89.3	89.2	**92.6**	
	MAX	90.3	90.1	**91.5**	87.7
	MIN	80.6	83.7	83.4	
	AVG	89.7	89.8	**92.6**	
S2N	MAJ	98.6	98.9	**99.9**	
	MAX	99	99	**99.9**	98.5
	MIN	97.2	97.9	**99.3**	
	AVG	99.2	99	**99.9**	

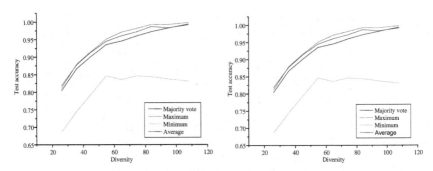

Fig. 4. Test accuracy for diversity for lymphoma cancer (left: CC and right: S2N)

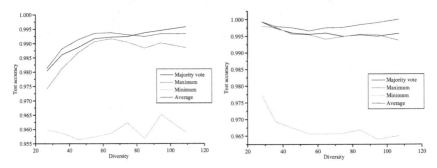

Fig. 5. Test accuracy for diversity for lung cancer (left: CC and right: S2N)

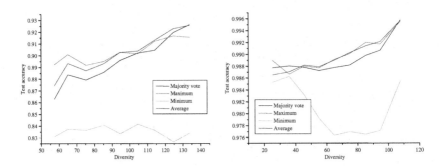

Fig. 6. Test accuracy for diversity for ovarian cancer (left: CC and right: S2N)

4.3 Diversity Performance

The relationship between diversity and performance is also analyzed and shown in Fig. 4-6. The results indicate that classification accuracy increases according to the increment of diversity in most cases. A decline in accuracy occasionally appears, because diversity is apt to increase when there is a peculiar rule. This can be solved by a non-pair-wise approach for estimating diversity in ensemble genetic programming. MIN often selects poor rules among the diverse rules, while the others use mutually cooperative rules from the rule set.

5 Conclusion

In this paper, we have proposed an effective ensemble method with genetic programming. Since gene expression data is composed of a few samples having a number of features, feature selection is applied to reduce the dimensionality. Then, genetic programming generates various classification rules with arithmetic operators based on the genes selected. The classification rules might be comprehensive so as to be possible to directly estimate diversity between them. Contrary to the conventional ensemble learning, the proposed method selects a set of base classification rules whose diversity is maximized. After all, a fusion method combines the diverse rules selected as shown in Figure 7.

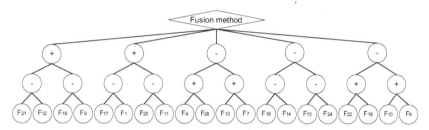

Fig. 7. An ensemble classifier obtained by the proposed method

We have applied the proposed method to cancer classification using gene expression. Especially, 3 cancer datasets have been employed for the demonstration. The proposed ensemble method using genetic programming produces higher performance than the others as presented in the results. Moreover, the experiments show that the diversity calculated by directly matching representations of rules increases the performance of ensembling.

As the future work, we will compare the method with various conventional diversity measures, and extend it by combining ensemble learning methods such as Arcing, Ada-boosting, attribute bagging, etc. Other popular benchmark datasets in bioinformatics will be also investigated with the proposed method.

Acknowledgement

This work was supported by Brain Science and Engineering Research Program sponsored by Korean Ministry of Commerce, Industry and Energy.

References

1. J. Koza, "Genetic programming," *Encyclopedia of Computer Science and Technology*, vol. 39, pp. 29-43, 1998.
2. E. Bruke, et al., "Diversity in genetic programming: An analysis of measures and correlation with fitness," *IEEE Trans. Evolutionary Computation*, vol. 8, no. 1, pp. 47-62, 2004.
3. L. Kuncheva, "A theoretical study on six classifier fusion strategies," *IEEE Trans. Pattern Analysis and Machine Intelligence*, vol. 24, no. 2, pp. 281-286, 2002.
4. R. Bryll, et al., "Attribute bagging: Improving accuracy of classifier ensembles by using random feature subsets," *Pattern Recognition*, vol. 36, no. 6, pp. 1291-1302, 2003.

5. L. Hansen and P. Salamon, "Neural network ensembles," *IEEE Trans. Pattern Analysis and Machine Intelligence*, vol. 12, no. 10, pp. 993-1001, 1990.
6. D. Opitz and R. Maclin, "Popular ensemble methods: An empirical study," *J. of Artificial Intelligence Research*, vol. 11, pp. 160-198, 1999.
7. Z. Zhou, et al., "Ensembling neural networks : Many could be better than all," *Artificial Intelligence*, vol. 137, no. 1-2, pp. 239-263, 2002.
8. D. Ruta and B. Gabrys, "Classifier selection for majority voting," *Information Fusion*, 2004.
9. G. Brown, et al., "Diversity creation methods: A survey and categorization," *Information Fusion*, vol. 6, no. 1, pp. 5-20, 2005.
10. B. Bakker and T. Heskes, "Clustering ensembles of neural network models," *Neural Networks*, vol. 16, no. 2, pp. 261-269, 2003.
11. A. Tan and D. Gilbert, "Ensemble machine learning on gene expression data for cancer classification," *Applied Bioinformatics*, vol. 2, no. 3, pp. 75-83, 2003.
12. L. Breiman, "Bagging predictors," *Machine Learning*, vol. 24, no. 2, pp. 123-140, 1996.
13. Y. Freund and R. Schapire, "Experiments with a new boosting algorithm," *Proc. the 13th Int. Conf. Machine Learning*, pp. 148-156, 1996.
14. L. Breiman, "Bias, variance, and arcing classifiers," *Tech. Rep. 460, UC-Berkeley*, 1996.
15. C. Peterson and M. Ringner, "Analyzing tumor gene expression profiles," *Artificial Intelligence in Medicine*, vol. 28, no. 1, pp. 59-74, 2003.
16. J.-H. Hong and S.-B. Cho, "Lymphoma cancer classification using genetic programming with SNR features," *Lecture Notes in Computer Science*, vol. 3003, pp. 78-88, 2004.
17. J. Wang and K. Zhang, "Finding similar consensus between trees: An algorithm and a distance hierarchy," *Pattern Recognition*, vol. 34, no. 1, pp. 127-137, 2001.
18. M. Xiong, et al., "Feature selection in gene expression-based tumor classification," *Molecular Genetics and Metabolism*, vol. 73, no. 3, pp. 239-247, 2001.
19. M. Brameier and W. Banzhaf, "A comparison of linear genetic programming and neural networks in medical data mining," *IEEE Trans. Evolutionary Computation*, vol. 5, no. 1, pp. 17-26, 2001.
20. Y. Zhang and S. Bhattacharyya, "Genetic programming in classifying large-scale data: An ensemble method," *Information Sciences*, vol. 163, no. 1-3, pp. 85-101, 2004.
21. A. Alizadeh, et al., "Distinct types of diffuse large B-cell lymphoma identified by gene expression profiling," *Nature*, vol. 403, no. 6769, pp. 503-511, 2000.
22. G. Gordon, et al, "Translation of microarray data into clinically relevant cancer diagnostic tests using gene expression ratios in lung cancer and mesothelioma," *Cancer Research*, vol. 62, no. 17, pp. 4963-4967, 2002.
23. E. Petricoin III, et al., "Use of proteomic patterns in serum to identify ovarian cancer," *The Lancet*, vol. 359, no. 9306, pp. 572-577, 2002.
24. M. Shipp, et al., "Diffuse large B-cell lymphoma outcome prediction by gene-expression profiling and supervised machine learning," *Nature Medicine*, vol. 8, no. 1, pp. 68-74, 2002.
25. T. Ando, et al., "Selection of causal gene sets for lymphoma prognostication from expression profiling and construction of prognostic fuzzy neural network models," *J. Bioscience and Bioengineering*, vol. 96, no. 2, pp. 161-167, 2003.

Language Generation for Conversational Agent by Evolution of Plan Trees with Genetic Programming

Sungsoo Lim and Sung-Bae Cho

Dept. of Computer Science, Yonsei University
Shinchon-dong, Seodaemun-ku, Seoul 120-749, Korea
{lss,sbcho}@sclab.yonsei.ac.kr

Abstract. As dialogue systems are widely demanded, the research on natural language generation in dialogue has raised interest. Contrary to conventional dialogue systems that reply to the user with a set of predefined answers, a newly developed dialogue system generates them dynamically and trains answers to support more flexible and customized dialogues with humans. The paper proposes an evolutionary method for generating sentences using interactive genetic programming. Sentence plan trees, which stand for the sentence structure, are adopted as the representation of genetic programming. With interactive evolution process with the user, a set of customized sentence structures is obtained. The proposed method applies to a dialogue-based travel planning system and the usability test demonstrates the usefulness of the proposed method.

Keywords: Dialogue system, Natural language generation, Interactive genetic programming, Sentence plan tree

1 Introduction

In the past few years, as the number of dialogue systems has increased, there has been an increasing interest in the use of natural language generation (NLG) in these systems. Current research on dialogue systems has mainly focused on understanding the input query or controlling the dialogue flow rather than generating dynamic sentences [1]. Canned scripts or templates are usually employed to support answering in those systems, hence they tend to be static, using the same or similar response patterns in the interaction with humans.

In order to support a flexible and realistic interaction with humans, recent dialogue systems attempt to adopt a mechanism generating sentences like natural language generation. NLG is a method which automatically creates sentences based on a non-linguistic information representation [2]. It used to provide information for user in expert systems. NLG is hard because it involves making choices. There may be many possible ways in which a text can be organized and in which words and syntactic constructions can be used to convey the required content.

The traditional natural language is usually based on grammars or templates. Especially the templates are the most popular technique for NLG because it is conceptually fairly easy to produce high quality output that is specific to each dialog situation. Although these methods, grammars and templates, are useful, the developer needs to design proper grammars to prevent from creating wrong sentences or to construct a large set of templates to support various types of sentences. The approaches require the developer to design a number of grammars or templates for every possible sen-

V. Torra et al. (Eds.): MDAI 2005, LNAI 3558, pp. 305–315, 2005.

tence structure which may be impractical for domains where many sentence structures are possible [3].

In order to overcome the limitations, trainable approaches have been attempted recently [3,4,5,6]. Walker et al. proposed the sentence plan tree representing the structure of a sentence while training is conducted by a RankBoost method [4]. A stochastic model generating sentences was presented by Levin et al. while they have applied it to a dialogue-based travel planning system [5]. And Ratnaparkhi has suggested a hybrid model [3], while Bulyko and Ostendorf generated various sentences using a weighted finite state machine [6].

In this paper, we propose an evolutionary method which makes diverse and flexible sentences in dialogue-based system. It uses an interactive genetic programming that adopts the sentence plan tree as the representation of individual sentences. The method composes a sentence by combining basic units with several joint operators, and iteratively interacts with humans to adjust itself to a domain. A dialogue-based travel planning system is constructed with the proposed method for demonstration, and several scenarios and experiments show the usefulness of the proposed method.

2   Natural Language Generation

The study on natural language is largely progressed as natural language understanding (NLU) and natural language generation (NLG). The main goal of NLG is to investigate how computer programs can produce a high-quality natural language text from internal representations of information [7,8]. In recent years, the increasing feasibility of human-computer dialogue systems have prompted the need for better responses by generating diverse sentences.

Many research of NLG systems use generation grammar rules, much like parsers with semantic or syntactic grammars [9]. A good example of a rule-based system is SURGE [10]. In general, well-generated grammar rules enable an NLG system to have wide coverage, be domain independent, and be reusable, proven by many very different applications that use SURGE [9]. However, the grammar-based systems, such as SURGE, need much effort and time for developer to design. It is why the template-based approaches are the most popular technique for NLG, nevertheless grammar-based approaches have better performance than those of template-based.

Templates provide an alternative approach, in which the developer handcrafts a set of templates and canned expressions. In principle, a template-based system can generate every sentence a rule-based system can generate, if the set of templates covers all of the possible sentences the grammar rules can generate. However, in the general case, that is not very practical [9]. But, as mentioned above, this method is easy to construct and to get high performance in specific domains, so most of current systems applied it. However, it has little reusability and also there are some restrictions when rare explicit representations of linguistic structures are presented [11].

Recent studies have attempted trainable approaches to overcome the limitations of grammar-based and template-based systems. Ratnaparkhi proposed four trainable approaches of NLG and evaluated them [4]. The first one is the baseline. It simply chooses the most frequent template in the training data that corresponds to a given set of attributes. The second one is n-gram model. It assumes that the best choice to express any given attribute-value set is the word sequence with the highest probability that mentions all of the input attributes exactly once. And the third one is dependency information. It focuses on the defect of n-gram model which considers only two near words. The search procedure in dependency information generates a syntactic dependency tree from top-to-bottom instead of a word sequence from left-to-right. Finally, the fourth one is a hybrid model which can be viewed as an extension of third one in which the lexical choice is jointly determined by a grammar and statistical learning, whereas in third one it was purely determined by statistical learning.

Except these, Bangalore and Rambow used a dependency grammar with statistical information [12] and Walker at el. proposed a trainable approach for NLG in the air travel domain [4]. And Oh and Rudnicky describe a statistical approach in the air travel domain [9].

In this paper, we propose an interactive genetic programming for generating sentences. In our previous research, we adopted a grammar-based approach for encoding methods [13]. This method was attempted to overcome the difficulty of designing grammars with evolutional methods and to generate user adaptive sentences. However, it has a defect that the method makes wrong sentence if it does not have enough time for evolution. In this paper we use sentence plan trees for encoding genetic trees instead of grammar-based approach. This method prevents the wrong sentences and generates user adaptive sentences through evolution.

3   The Diverse Sentence Generation Using Genetic Programming

Genetic programming is proposed by John R. Koza to create automatically a computer program solving a problem. It is an extension of the genetic algorithm in which each individual in the population is a computer program [14]. In this paper, it generates sentences dynamically and adaptively to the domain.

An object represented as a sentence plan tree (SPT) denotes a complex sentence. In each SPT, each leaf node contains one simple sentence that is corresponding to the unit and parent nodes represent joint operators for combining child nodes. Figure 1 briefly shows the outline of dynamic sentences generation process using genetic programming.

3.1   Sentence Plan Tree

In this paper, we apply sentence plan trees for representing gene trees, which is a binary tree with leaves labeled by pre-defined templates of simple sentences, and with its interior nodes labeled with joint operators (JOs) which combine two sentences.

We define JOs based on the analysis of Korean language. There are 5 operators which are applied differently for each of the 3 cases of combining two sentences: 2 statements, a statement and a question, and 2 questions. JOs are defined as below:

Sentence A = subject (s1) + template-variable (t1) + verb (v1).
Sentence B = subject (s2) + template-variable (t2) + verb (v2).

1. **JO 1:** Combine two sentences of A and B by using conjunction 'and'. The result is 's1 t1 v1 and s2 t2 v2.'
2. **JO 2:** Combine two sentences which have the same subject (s1 = s2). The result is 's1 t1 v1 and t2 v2.'

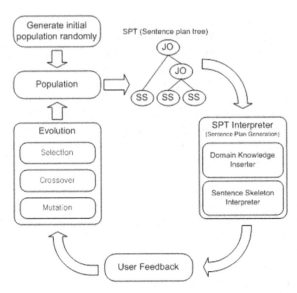

Fig. 1. The procedure of generating sentences by interactive genetic programming

3. **JO 3:** Combine two sentences which have the same subject (s1 = s2) and the same verb (v1 = v2). The result is 's1 t1 t2 v1.'
4. **JO 4:** Combine two sentences which have the same communicative act (t1 = t2) and the same verb (v1 = v2) by making a proper subject (s3). The result is 's3 t1 v1' where s3 is the subject which includes s1 and s2.
5. **JO 5:** Combine two sentences which have the same subject (s1 = s2) and different verbs but can be replaced by a verb v3 which includes the meaning of v1 and v2. The result is 's1 t1 t2 v3.'

Table 1~3 show the examples of combining two SSs with those rules. Since the sentences are translated from the Korean, some sentences might not be matched exactly with JOs in English.

Table 1. Combining two statements

JO	Sentence 1	Sentence 2
	Result Sentence	
JO 1	You go to [aLocation].	He goes to [aLocation].
	You go to [dLocation] and he go to [dLocation].	
JO 2	You like [something1].	You hate [something2].
	You like [something1] and hate [something2].	
JO 3	You leave [dLocation].	You leave at [dTime].
	You leave [dLocation] at [dTime].	
JO 4	He is going to [aLocation].	She is going to [aLocation].
	They are going to [aLocation].	
JO 5	You leave [dLocation].	You are going to [aLocation].
	You are traveling from [dLocation] to [aLocation].	

Table 2. Combining a statement and a question

JO	Sentence 1	Sentence 2
	Result Sentence	
JO 1	You go to [aLocation].	Where does he go?
	You go to [dLocation] and where does he go?	
JO 2	You like [something1].	What do you hate?
	You like [something1] and hate what?	
JO 3	You leave [dLocation].	What time do you leave?
	What time do you leave [dLocation]?	
JO 4	Incorrect sentence	
JO 5	You leave [dLocation].	Where are you going?
	Where are you traveling from [dLocation] to?	

Table 3. Combining two questions

JO	Sentence 1	Sentence 2
	Result Sentence	
JO 1	Where do you go?	Where does he go?
	Where do you go? And where does he go?	
JO 2	What do you like?	What do you hate?
	What do you like and hate?	
JO 3	Where do you leave?	What time do you leave?
	Where and what time do you leave?	
JO 4	Where is he going to?	Where is she going to?
	Where are they going to?	
JO 5	Where do you leave?	Where are you going to?
	Where are you traveling from and to?	

The SPT interpreter in Figure 1 derives a complex sentence from a SPT. The sentence skeleton interpreter makes a skeleton of a complex sentence by combining simple sentences which appears at the leaf nodes. Then the domain knowledge inserter completes the complex sentence with domain-relevant knowledge, subjects and verbs corresponding to it. Figure 2 presents the procedure of interpreting a STP in the sentence skeleton interpreter. [dLocation] and [dTime] represent slots where information about departure location and time can be filled into.

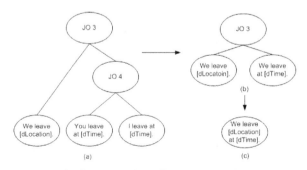

Fig. 2. A procedure of interpreting a STP

The STP in Figure 2 (a) becomes a complex sentence using JO 3 and 4. At first by using JO 4, two SSs, 'You leave at [dTime]' and 'I leave at [dTime],' are combined to form one complex sentence, 'We leave at [dTime].' JO 3 will combine this sentence and 'We leave [dLocation],' finally deriving a complex sentence like: 'We leave [dLocation] at [dTime].'

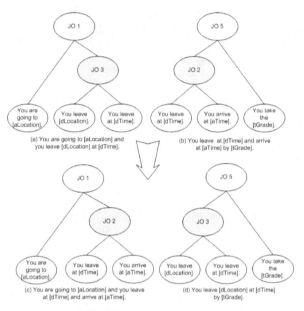

Fig. 3. Crossover operation

3.2 Crossover and Mutation

A variety of sentences can appear from SPTs when genetic programming is applied. Figure 3 and 4 show an idea of how crossover and mutation operations are executed in SPTs. Figure 3 (a) and (b) show two SPTs before crossover operation and the shaded nodes are nodes that are going to be changed by crossover operation. Figure 3 (c) and (d) show the resulting SPTs after crossover. As Figure 3 shows, two complex sen-tences, 'You are going to [aLocation] and you leave [dLocation] at [dTime]' and 'You leave at [dTime] and arrive at [aTime] by [tGrade]' are changed to 'You are going to [aLocation] and you leave at [dTime] and arrive at [aTime]' and 'You leave [dLoca-tion] at [dTime] by [tGrade].'

Figure 4 (a) and (c) show the same SPT with a different shaded node before muta-tion, where the shaded nodes will be changed by mutation. Figure 4 (b) and (d) show the resulting SPTs after mutation. The upper example of Figure 4 illustrates the result of changing JO, and the lower one shows the result of changing CA. As shown above, the sentence 'You leave [dLocation] at [dTime] and take the [tGrade]' is changed to 'You leave [dLocation] at [dTime] by [tGrade]' by changing joint opera-tor. The lower SPT is changed to be interpreted as 'You leave [dLocation] at [dTime] and are going to [aLocation]' by changing CA. With crossover and mutation opera-tions, diverse SPTs might be generated to construct various sen-tences.

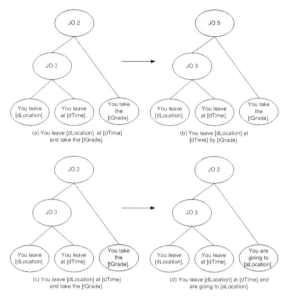

Fig. 4. Mutation operation

4   The Travel Planning Agent

This section introduces a travel planning agent implemented by the proposed method, and shows how the evolution of SPTs works. The travel planning agent makes some conversations with a user to automatically collect the user's required information needed to decide which train to search.

When doing the same job, former "canned-script" systems tended to offer only simple and monotonous conversations, limited by their pool of available expressions and sentences. The presented system makes up a more dynamic and familiar conversations by coming up with a variety of sentences and expressions created in real-time. Figure 5 shows the structure of the train planning agent.

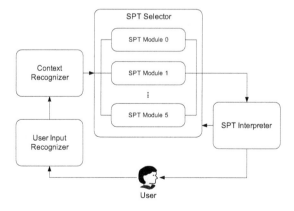

Fig. 5. Structure of the travel planning agent

The context recognizer chooses a SPT group most suitable for creating relevant queries by recognizing the amount of knowledge available. Then the SPT selector randomly chooses a SPT from the given group. Then the selected tree is translated into a sentence by the SPT interpreter, finally being delivered to the user. Lastly, when the user's response has been given, the user input recognizer acquires available knowledge from the response. When enough information is gathered to determine a specific train, the agent will show the corresponding trains.

4.1 User Input Recognizer

The user input recognizer accepts the user's response to the offered query, and extracts relevant information by applying pattern matching with templates: The agent performs a series of pattern matching with prepared templates to find the most similar template, and extracts relevant information from the template. For instance, when the user's response was "I am traveling from Seoul to Pusan," the most similar template will be "I am traveling from [dLocation] to [aLocation]." and the agent will be able to extract the user's place of departure, Seoul and the destination, Pusan.

4.2 Context Recognizer

The context recognizer relies on the amount of information available, namely the following 6 kinds: the user's place of departure, destination, departing date, departing time, arriving time and the seat class, to select a proper SPT group which will be generating a query sentence. In this paper, SPTs are classified into 6 groups where each group represents the number of information the agent has.

4.3 SPT Selector

After the context recognizer chooses a SPT group to produce the query, the SPT selector selects a random SPT among the chosen group, and passes it to the SPT interpreter.

4.4 SPT Interpreter

The SPT interpreter derives a query sentence from a SPT. Table 4 shows examples of SSs which are contained in the leaf nodes of a SPT. We stated above that leaf nodes of a SPT contain the corresponding SS. When there are no restrictions on choosing a SS to print, there are chances that a statement with unknown information tokens is chosen. Awkward query generations arise again when a tree contains statements and questions together, which refers to the same kind of information. In this paper, this problem is solved by only indicating the kind of information involved in each sentence in the corresponding leaf nodes. The agent will automatically select a proper type of sentence (statement/question) by considering the agent knows the relevant information or not.

4.5 Interactive Evolution

SPTs are grouped by the criteria stated in Section 4.1. Each SPT group shows all available information of agent to the evaluator, and the evaluator will give fitness scores (between 0 and 10) to each of the query that the SPTs generated. The fitness is evaluated according to the natural of the queries. Then the evaluated trees evolve to their next generation. Finally, the system converges into the preference of the evaluator.

Table 4. SSs used by a travel planning agent

User Information		Simple Sentence
Departure	Statement	Where do you leave?
Location	Question	You leave [dLocation].
Arrival	Statement	Where are you going?
Location	Question	You are going to [aLocation].
Departure	Statement	When do you leave?
Date	Question	You are leave on [Date].
Departure	Statement	What time do you leave?
Time	Question	You leave at [dTime].
Arrival	Statement	What time do you want to arrive?
Time	Question	You arrive at [aTime].
Seat	Statement	What kinds of seat do you want?
Grade	Question	You take [tGrade].

5 Experimental Results

Ten subjects iteratively interact with the system in 90 generations. Crossover rate and mutation rate are set as 0.6 and 0.2, respectively. Each generation, the subjects evaluate the fitness of all individuals. It needs much effort, so we set the population size as 20.

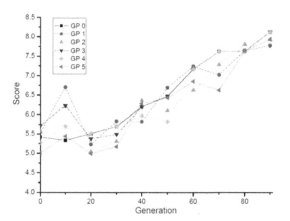

Fig. 6. Score distribution through evolution

Figure 6 represents the changes of average score as generation grows. GP *n* means the fitness of STPs for information type *n* in figure 5. We limit the generation until 90 steps because more steps are the cause of overfitting and decreasing the diversity.

In the result, the score increases rapidly during the first 10 generations and decreases contrarily between the 10th and 20th generations and increases continuously after the 20th generation. This trend is occurred because the subjects felt at first steps of evolution that the unbalanced sentences change to more naturally, so they evaluate relatively high. And they felt in the middle that the changes do not get at the point of their expectation comparing with the first steps, so they evaluate low.

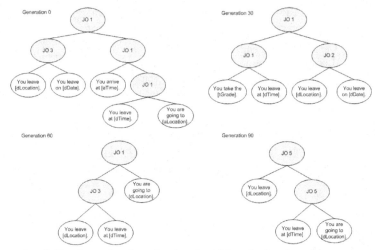

Generation 0: You leave Seoul on October the 10th and what time do you want to arrive? And what time do you leave? And you are going to Pusan.

Generation 30: What kinds of train do you want to take and what time do you want to leave? And you leave Seoul and leave on October the 10th.

Generation 60: What time do you leave Seoul? And you are going to Pusan.

Generation 90: What time do you leave for traveling from Seoul to Pusan?

Fig. 7. Sentences obtained by the system

Figure 7 shows the sentences obtained by the system, especially on the case of the third SPT while the system collects information on the departure location, the arrival location, and the departure data. As shown in Figure 7, the sentence in the initial stage was a little disorderly and complex while the sentence obtained through evolution became refined.

6   Conclusion

We have presented the evolutionary method for natural language generation which uses interactive genetic programming and sentence plan tree. It generates sentences in the interaction with humans and increases the reality and flexibility of a dialogue system. Contrary to our previous method which needs much time and effort for the developer to design the system, the proposed method could construct it with several templates. And the evolutionary method adapts itself to various domains or users. The experiment shows the possibility of user adaptive system.

As the future work, we will expand the join operators to generate further diverse sentences and apply some methods for easy evaluation and on-line evolution to improve the usefulness of the system.

Acknowledgement

This work was supported by Brain Science and Engineering Research Program sponsored by Korean Ministry of Commerce, Industry and Energy.

References

1. V. Zue and J. Class, "Conversational interfaces: Advances and challenges," *Proc. of the IEEE*, vol., 88, no. 8, pp. 1166-1180, 2000.
2. M. Theune, "Natural language generation for dialogue: System survey," *TR-CTIT-03-22*, 2003.
3. A. Ratnaparkhi, "Trainable approaches to surface natural language generation and their application to conversational dialog systems," *Computer Speech and Language*, vol. 16, no. 3-4, pp. 435-455, 2002.
4. M. A. Walker, O. C. Rambow and M. Rogati, "Training a sentence planner for spoken dialogue using boosting," *Computer Speech and Language*, vol. 16, no. 3-4, pp. 409-433, 2002.
5. E. Levin, R. Pieraccini and W. Eckert, "A stochastic model of human-machine interaction for learning dialog strategies,", vol. 8, no. 1, pp. 11-23, 2000.
6. I. Bulyko and M. Ostendorf, "Efficient integrated response generation from multiple targets using weighted finite state transducers," *Computer Speech and Language*, vol. 16, no. 3-4, pp. 533-550, 2002.
7. W. Weiwei, L. Biqi, C. Fang and Y. Baozong, "A natural language generation system based on dynamic knowledge base," *Proc. of the 3rd Int. Conf. on ICSP*, pp. 765-768, 1996.
8. K. McKeown, "Language generation: Applications, issues, and approaches, " *Proc. of IEEE*, vol. 74, no. 7, pp. 905-919, 1986.
9. H. Oh and I. Rudnicky, "Stochastic natural language generation for spoken dialog systems," *Computer Speech and Language*, vol. 16, no. 3-4, pp. 387-407, 2002.
10. M. Elhadad and J. Robin, "An overview of surge: A reusable comprehensive syntactic realization component," *Technical Report 96-03, Department of Mathematics and Computer Science*, 1996.
11. S. Seneff and J. Polifroni, "Formal and natural language generation in the Mercury conversational system," *Proc. of ICSLP*, vol. 2, pp. 767-770, 2000.
12. S. Bangalore and O. Rambow, "Exploiting a Probabilistic hierarchical model for generation," *Int. Conf. on COLING*, vol. 1, pp. 42-48, 2000.
13. K.-M. Kim, S.-S, Lim and S.-B. Cho, "User adaptive answers generation for conversational agent using genetic programming," *IDEAL 2004, LNCS 3177*, pp. 813-819, 2004.
14. J. Koza, Genetic programming, *Automatic discovery of reusable programs*, The MIT Press, 1994.

Optimization of Fuzzy Systems Based on Fuzzy Set Using Genetic Optimization and Information Granulation

Sung-Kwun Oh[1], Keon-Jun Park[1], and Witold Pedrycz[2,3]

[1] Department of Electrical Engineering, The University of Suwon,
San 2-2 Wau-ri, Bongdam-eup, Hwaseong-si, Gyeonggi-do, 445-743, South Korea
ohsk@suwon.ac.kr
[2] Department of Electrical and Computer Engineering, University of Alberta
Edmonton, AB T6G 2G6, Canada
[3] Systems Research Institute, Polish Academy of Sciences, Warsaw, Poland

Abstract. In this study, we propose a fuzzy inference systems based on information granulation to carry out the model identification of complex and nonlinear systems. Information granules are sought as associated collections of objects (data, in particular) drawn together by the criteria of proximity, similarity, or functionality. Information granulation realized with Hard C-Means (HCM) clustering help determine the initial parameters of fuzzy model such as the initial apexes of the membership functions and the initial values of polynomial functions being used in the premise and consequence part of the fuzzy rules. And the initial parameters are tuned effectively with the aid of the genetic algorithms and the least square method (LSM). The proposed model is evaluated with using two numerical examples and is contrasted with the performance of conventional fuzzy models in the literature.

1 Introduction

There has been a diversity of approaches to fuzzy modeling. To enumerate a few representative trends, it is essential to refer to some developments that have happened over time. In the early 1980s, linguistic modeling [2], [3] and fuzzy relation equation-based approach [4], [5] were proposed as primordial identification methods for fuzzy models. The general class of Sugeno-Takagi models [6] gave rise to more sophisticated rule-based systems where the rules come with conclusions forming local regression models. While appealing with respect to the basic topology (a modular fuzzy model composed of a series of rules) [7], [8], these models still await formal solutions as far as the structure optimization of the model is concerned, say a construction of the underlying fuzzy sets – information granules being viewed as basic building blocks of any fuzzy model. Some enhancements to the model have been proposed by Oh and Pedrycz [9], yet the problem of finding "good" initial parameters of the fuzzy sets in the rules remains open.

This study concentrates on the central problem of fuzzy modeling that is a development of information granules-fuzzy sets. Taking into consideration the essence of the granulation process, we propose to cast the problem in the setting of clustering techniques and genetic algorithms. The design methodology emerges as a hybrid structural optimization (based on Hard C-Means (HCM) clustering and genetic optimization) and parametric optimization (based on least square method (LSM), as well

V. Torra et al. (Eds.): MDAI 2005, LNAI 3558, pp. 316–327, 2005.

as HCM clustering and genetic optimization). Information granulation with the aid of HCM clustering help determine the initial parameters of fuzzy model such as the initial apexes of the membership functions and the initial values of polynomial function being used in the premise and consequence part of the fuzzy rules. And the initial parameters are tuned (adjusted) effectively with the aid of the genetic algorithms and the least square method. The proposed model is through intensive numeric experimentation.

2   Information Granulation (IG)

Roughly speaking, information granules [10], [11] are viewed as related collections of objects (data point, in particular) drawn together by the criteria of proximity, similarity, or functionality. Granulation of information is an inherent and omnipresent activity of human beings carried out with intent of gaining a better insight into a problem under consideration and arriving at its efficient solution. In particular, granulation of information is aimed at transforming the problem at hand into several smaller and therefore manageable tasks. In this way, we partition this problem into a series of well-defined subproblems (modules) of a far lower computational complexity than the original one. The form of information granulation (IG) themselves becomes an important design feature of the fuzzy model, which are geared toward capturing relationships between information granules.

It is worth emphasizing that the HCM clustering has been used extensively not only to organize and categorize data, but it becomes useful in data compression and model identification. For the sake of completeness of the entire discussion, let us briefly recall the essence of the HCM algorithm [12].

We obtain the matrix representation for hard c-partition, defined as follows.

$$M_C = \left\{ U \mid u_{gi} \in \{0,1\}, \ \sum_{g=1}^{c} u_{gi} = 1, \ 0 < \sum_{i=1}^{m} u_{gi} < m \right\} \tag{1}$$

[**Step 1**] Fix the number of clusters $c(2 \leq c < m)$ and initialize the partition matrix

$$\mathbf{U}^{(0)} \in M_C$$

[**Step 2**] Calculate the center vectors $\mathbf{v}_g$ of each cluster:

$$\mathbf{v}_g^{(r)} = \{v_{g1}, \ v_{g2}, \cdots, \ v_{gk}, \cdots, \ v_{gl}\} \tag{2}$$

$$v_{gk}^{(r)} = \sum_{i=1}^{m} u_{gi}^{(r)} \cdot x_{ik} \Big/ \sum_{i=1}^{m} u_{gi}^{(r)} \tag{3}$$

Where, $[u_{gi}] = \mathbf{U}^{(r)}$, $g = 1, 2, \ldots, c$, $k=1, 2, \ldots, l$.

[**Step 3**] Update the partition matrix $\mathbf{U}^{(r)}$; these modifications are based on the standard Euclidean distance function between the data points and the prototypes,

$$[\text{Step 4}] \ d_{gi} = d(\mathbf{x}_i - \mathbf{v}_g) = \left\| \mathbf{x}_i - \mathbf{v}_g \right\| = \left[\sum_{k=1}^{l} (x_{ik} - v_{gk})^2 \right]^{1/2} \tag{4}$$

$$u_{gi}^{(r+1)} = \begin{cases} 1 & d_{gi}^{(r)} = \min\{d_{ki}^{(r)}\} \text{ for all } k \in c \\ 0 & \text{otherwise} \end{cases} \qquad (5)$$

[Step 4] Check a termination criterion. If

$$\| U^{(r+1)} - U^{(r)} \| \le \varepsilon \quad \text{(tolerance level)} \qquad (6)$$

Stop; otherwise set $r = r+1$ and return to **[Step 2]**

3   Design of Fuzzy Set-Based Fuzzy Systems with the Aid of IG

The identification procedure for fuzzy models is usually split into the identification activities dealing with the premise and consequence parts of the rules. The identification completed at the premise level consists of two main steps. First, we select the input variables x_1, x_2, ..., x_k of the rules. Second, we form fuzzy partitions of the spaces over which these individual variables are defined. The identification of the consequence part of the rules embraces two phases, namely 1) a selection of the consequence variables of the fuzzy rules, and 2) determination of the parameters of the consequence (conclusion part). And the least square error (LSE) method used at the parametric optimization of the consequence parts of the successive rules.

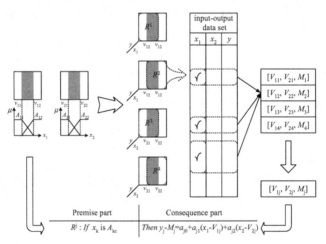

Fig. 1. Fuzzy model based on information granulation; illustrate is a case of the two-input single-output system

In this study, we use the isolated input space of each input variable and carry out the modeling using characteristics of input-output data set. Therefore, it is important to understand the nature of data. The HCM clustering addresses this issue. Subsequently we design the fuzzy model by considering the centers (prototypes) of clusters. In this manner the clustering help us determine the initial parameters of fuzzy model such as the initial apexes of the membership functions and the initial values of polynomial function being used in the premise and consequence part of the fuzzy rules. The design process of fuzzy model based on information granulation for two-input single-output system is visualized in figure 1.

3.1   Premise Identification

In the premise part of the rules, we confine ourselves to a triangular type of membership functions whose parameters are subject to some optimization. The HCM clustering helps us organize the data into cluster so in this way we capture the characteristics of the experimental data. In the regions where some clusters of data have been identified, we end up with some fuzzy sets that help reflect the specificity of the data set. In the sequel, the modal values of the clusters are refined (optimized) using genetic optimization, and genetic algorithms (GAs), in particular.

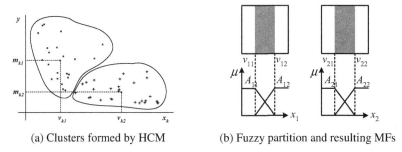

(a) Clusters formed by HCM   (b) Fuzzy partition and resulting MFs

Fig. 2. Identification of the premise part of the rules of the system

The identification of the premise part is completed in the following manner

Given is a set of data $U=\{x_1, x_2, ..., x_l ; y\}$, where $x_k =[x_{1k}, ..., x_{mk}]^T$, $y =[y_1, ..., y_m]^T$, l is the number of variables and, m is the number of data.

[Step 1] Arrange a set of data U into data set X_k composed of respective input data and output data.

$$X_k=[x_k ; y] \tag{7}$$

X_k is data set of k-th input data and output data, where, $x_k =[x_{1k}, ..., x_{mk}]^T$, $y =[y_1, ..., y_m]^T$, and $k=1, 2, ..., l$.

[Step 2] Complete the HCM clustering to determine the centers (prototypes) v_{kg} with data set X_k.

[Step 2-1] Classify data set X_k into c-clusters, which in essence leads to the granulation of information.

We can find the data pairs included in each cluster based on the partition matrix u_{gi} by (5) and use these to identify the structure in conclusion part.

[Step 2-2] Calculate the center vectors v_{kg} of each cluster.

$$v_{kg} = \{v_{k1}, v_{k2}, ..., v_{kc}\} \tag{8}$$

Where, $k=1, 2, ..., l$, $g = 1, 2, ..., c$.

[Step 3] Partition the corresponding isolated input space using the prototypes of the clusters v_{kg}. Associate each clusters with some meaning (semantics), say Small, Big, etc.

[Step 4] Set the initial apexes of the membership functions using the prototypes v_{kg}.

3.2 Consequence Identification

We identify the structure considering the initial values of polynomial functions based upon the information granulation realized for the consequence and antecedents parts.

[Step 1] Find a set of data included in the isolated fuzzy space of the j-th rule.

  [Step 1-1] Find the input data included in each cluster (information granule) from the partition matrix u_{gi} of each input variable by (5).

  [Step 1-2] Find the input data pairs included in the isolated fuzzy space of the j-th rule (refer check marks in Fig 1.).

  [Step 1-3] Determine the corresponding output data from above input data pairs.

[Step 2] Compute the prototypes $\mathbf{V}_j$ of the data set by taking the arithmetic mean of each rule.

$$V_j = \{V_{1j}, V_{2j}, \ldots, V_{kj}; M_j\} \tag{9}$$

Where, k=1, 2, ..., l. j=1, 2, ..., n. V_{kj} and M_j are prototypes of input and output data, respectively.

[Step 3] Set the initial values of polynomial functions with the center vectors $\mathbf{V}_j$.

The identification of the conclusion parts of the rules deals with a selection of their structure that is followed by the determination of the respective parameters of the local functions occurring there.

In Case of Type 2: Linear Inference (Linear Conclusion)

The conclusion is expressed in the form of a linear relationship between inputs and output variable. This gives rise to the rules in the form

$$R^j : If \ x_1 \ is \ A_{1c} \ and \ \cdots \ and \ x_k \ is \ A_{kc} \ then \ y_j - M_j = f_j(x_1, \cdots, x_k) \tag{10}$$

The calculations of the numeric output of the model, based on the activation (matching) levels of the rules there, rely on the expression

$$y^* = \frac{\sum\limits_{j=1}^{n} w_{ji} y_i}{\sum\limits_{j=1}^{n} w_{ji}} = \frac{\sum\limits_{j=1}^{n} w_{ji}(f_j(x_1, \cdots, x_k) + M_j)}{\sum\limits_{j=1}^{n} w_{ji}} = \sum\limits_{j=1}^{n} \hat{w}_{ji}(a_{j0} + a_{j1}(x_1 - V_{j1}) + \cdots + a_{jk}(x_k - V_{jk}) + M_j) \tag{11}$$

Here, as the normalized value of w_{ji}, we use an abbreviated notation to describe an activation level of rule R^j to be in the form

$$\hat{w}_{ji} = \frac{w_{ji}}{\sum\limits_{j=1}^{n} w_{ji}} \tag{12}$$

where R^j is the j-th fuzzy rule, x_k represents the input variables, A_{kc} is a membership function of fuzzy sets, a_{j0} is a constant, M_j is a center value of output data, n is the number of fuzzy rules, y^* is the inferred output value, w_{ji} is the premise fitness matching R^j (activation level).

Once the input variables of the premise and parameters have been already specified, the optimal consequence parameters that minimize the assumed performance index can be determined. In what follows, we define the performance index as the mean squared error (MSE).

$$PI = \frac{1}{m}\sum_{i=1}^{m}(y_i - y_i^*)^2 \tag{13}$$

where y^* is the output of the fuzzy model, m is the total number of data, and i is the data number. The minimal value produced by the least-squares method is governed by the following expression:

$$\hat{a} = (X^T X)^{-1} X^T Y \tag{14}$$

where

$$x_i^T = [\hat{w}_{1i} \ \ldots \ \hat{w}_{ni} \ (x_{1i} - V_{11})\hat{w}_{1i} \ \ldots \ (x_{1i} - V_{1n})\hat{w}_{ni} \ \ldots \ (x_{ki} - V_{k1})\hat{w}_{1i} \ \ldots \ (x_{ki} - V_{kn})\hat{w}_{ni}],$$

$$\hat{a} = [a_{10} \ \cdots \ a_{n0} \ a_{11} \ \cdots \ a_{n1} \ \cdots \ a_{1k} \ \cdots \ a_{nk}]^T,$$

$$Y = \left[y_1 - \left(\sum_{j=1}^{n} M_j w_{j1}\right) \ \ y_2 - \left(\sum_{j=1}^{n} M_j w_{j2}\right) \ \cdots \ y_m - \left(\sum_{j=1}^{n} M_j w_{jm}\right) \right]^T$$

$$X = [x_1 \ \ x_2 \ \ \cdots \ \ x_i \ \ \cdots \ \ x_m]^T.$$

4 Optimization of IG-Based FIS

The need to solve optimization problems arises in many fields and is especially dominant in the engineering environment. There are several analytic and numerical optimization techniques, but there are still large classes of functions that are fully addressed by these techniques. Especially, the standard gradient-based optimization techniques that are being used mostly at the present time are augmented by a differential method of solving search problems for optimization processes. Therefore, the optimization of fuzzy models may not be fully supported by the standard gradient-based optimization techniques, because of the nonlinearity of fuzzy models represented by rules based on linguistic levels. This forces us to explore other optimization techniques such as genetic algorithms. First of all, to identify the fuzzy model we determine such an initial structure as the number of input variables, input variables being selected and the number of membership functions standing in premise part and the order of polynomial (Type) in conclusion. The membership parameters of the premise are genetically optimized.

It has been demonstrated that genetic algorithms [13] are useful in a global optimization of such problems given their ability to efficiently use historical information to produce new improved solutions with enhanced performance.

In this study, for the optimization of the fuzzy model, genetic algorithms use the serial method of binary type, roulette-wheel in the selection operator, one-point crossover in the crossover operator, and invert in the mutation operator. Here, we use 1000 generations, run the GA for 60 populations, consider 10 bits per string, and set up the crossover rate and mutation probability as equal to 0.6, and 0.1, respectively (the choice of these specific values of the parameters is a result of intensive experimentation; as a matter of fact, those are quite similar to the values reported in the literature).

5 Experimental Studies

This section includes comprehensive numeric studies illustrating the design of the fuzzy model. We use two well-known data sets.

5.1 Nonlinear Static System

In this section, we consider a nonlinear static system with two inputs, x_1, x_2, and a single output

$$y = (1 + x_1^{-2} + x_2^{-1.5})^2, \quad 1 \leq x_1, x_2 \leq 5 \tag{15}$$

This nonlinear static equation is widely used to evaluate modeling performance of the fuzzy model. This system represents the nonlinear characteristic. Using Eq. (15), 50 Input-output data are generated: the inputs are generated randomly and the corresponding output is then computed through the above relationship. To come up with a quantitative evaluation of the fuzzy model, we use the standard MSE performance index (13).

We carried out the structure identification on a basis of the experimental data using GAs to design Max_Min-based and IG-based fuzzy model. Because only two input variables are considered, we considered the number of membership functions and consequence type. The number of membership functions assigned to each input of Max_Min-based and IG-based fuzzy model were set up to be 5. At the conclusion part, both models come with the consequence of type 3. For each fuzzy model, we conducted the optimization of the parameters of the premise membership functions.

Table 1 summarizes the performance index for Max_Min-based and IG-based fuzzy model. It becomes evident that the performance of the IG-based fuzzy model is better than the Max_Min-based fuzzy model.

From the Table 1 it is clear that the performance of IG-based fuzzy model is better than that of Max_Min-based fuzzy model not only after identifying the structure but also after identifying optimally the parameters.

Table 1. Performance index of Max_Min-based and IG-based fuzzy model (θ=0.0)

Model	Identification	No. Of MFs	Type	PI
Max/Min_FIS	Structure	5+5	Type 3	0.02253
	Parameters			0.00008
IG_FIS	Structure	5+5	Type 3	$9.790e^{-7}$
	Parameters			$2.330e^{-10}$

Figure 3 depicts the values of the performance index produced in successive generation of the genetic optimization. We note that the performance of the IG-based fuzzy model is good starting from some initial generations; this could have been caused by the characteristics of the experimental data at hand.

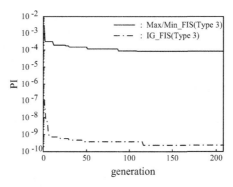

Fig. 3. Optimal convergence process of performance index for Max_Min-based and IG-based fuzzy model

The identification error (performance index) of the proposed model is also compared to the performance of some other models; refer to Table 2. As we know from Table 2, the performance results of the proposed model are quite satisfactory. Compared with approaches presented in previous literatures, our modeling method has much more accuracy.

Table 2. Comparison of identification error with previous models

Model		No. of rules	PI
Sugeno and Yasukawa[14]		6	0.079
Gomez-Skarmeta et al[15]		5	0.070
Kim et al.[16]		3	0.019
Kim et al.[17]		3	0.0089
Oh et al.[18]	Basic PNN		0.0212
	Modified PNN		0.0041
Park et al.[19]	BFPNN	9	0.0033
	MFPNN	9	0.0023
Our Model		10	$2.330e^{-10}$

5.2 Gas Furnace Process

We illustrate the performance of the model and elaborate on its development by experimenting with data coming from the gas furnace process. The time series data (296 input-output pairs) resulting from the gas furnace process has been intensively studied in the previous literatures [9,22,23]. The delayed terms of methane gas flow rate $u(t)$ and carbon dioxide density $y(t)$ are used as six input variables with vector formats such as [$u(t-3)$, $u(t-2)$, $u(t-1)$, $y(t-3)$, $y(t-2)$, $y(t-1)$]. And as output variable $y(t)$ is used. The first one (consisting of 148 pairs) was used for training. The remaining part of the series serves as a testing set. We consider the MSE (13) being regarded here as a performance index.

We carried out the structure identification on a basis of the experimental data using GAs to design Max_Min-based and IG-based fuzzy model. The maximal number of input variables was set to be equal to 2 and 3 from above the type of vector format. The corresponding input variables were picked up to be $u(t-3)$, $y(t-1)$ and $u(t-1)$, $y(t-$

2), y(t-1) for each system. The number of membership functions assigned to each input were set up to be 2. At the conclusion part, Max_Min-based and IG-based fuzzy model for each system come with the consequence type 4 and 3, respectively. For each fuzzy model, we conducted the optimization of the parameters of the premise membership functions.

Table 3 summarizes the performance index for Max_Min-based and IG-based fuzzy model.

From the Table 3 we know that the performance of IG-based fuzzy model is better than the Max_Min-based fuzzy model.

Table 3. Performance index of Max_Min-based and IG-based fuzzy mode

Model	Identification	Input variable	No. Of MFs	Type	PI	E_PI
Max/Min_FIS	Structure	u(t-3)	2+2	Type 4	0.022	0.341
	Parameters	y(t-1)			0.024	0.269
IG_FIS	Structure	u(t-3)	2+2	Type 4	0.020	0.329
	Parameters	y(t-1)			0.020	0.267
Max/Min_FIS	Structure	u(t-1)	2+2+2	Type 3	0.058	0.193
	Parameters	y(t-2) y(t-1)			0.058	0.135
IG_FIS	Structure	u(t-1)	2+2+2	Type 3	0.037	0.559
	Parameters	y(t-2) y(t-1)			0.030	0.134

Figure 4 shows the values of the performance index produced in successive generation of the genetic optimization for Max_Min-based and IG-based fuzzy model with input variables, u(t-1), y(t-2),(t-1). It is obvious that the performance of an IG-based fuzzy model is good due to the characteristics of input-output data.

The model output and resulting prediction error for training and testing data for IG-based fuzzy model with input variables, u(t-1), y(t-2),(t-1) is displayed in figure 5.

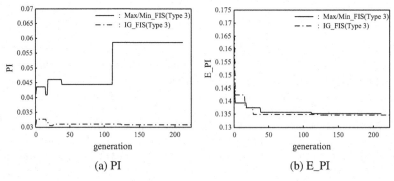

(a) PI   (b) E_PI

Fig. 4. Optimal convergence process of performance index for Max_Min-based and IG-based fuzzy model with input variables, u(t-1), y(t-2),(t-1)

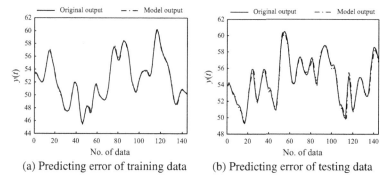

(a) Predicting error of training data   (b) Predicting error of testing data

Fig. 5. The comparison of original and output data for IG-based fuzzy model with input variables, $u(t\text{-}1)$, $y(t\text{-}2),(t\text{-}1)$

The identification error (performance index) of the proposed model is also compared to the performance of some other models in Table 4. The performance of the proposed model is better in the sense of its approximation and prediction abilities than other works studied in the literatures as shown in Table 4.

Table 4. Comparison of identification error with previous models

Model		PI_t	PI	E_PI	No. of rules
Tong's model[20]		0.469			19
Pedrycz's model[2]		0.776			20
Xu's model[21]		0.328			25
Sugeno's model[7]		0.355			6
Oh et al.'s Model[9,22]	Simplified		0.024	0.328	4
			0.022	0.326	4
	Linear		0.021	0.364	6
HCM+GA[23]	Simplified		0.035	0.289	4
			0.022	0.333	6
	Linear		0.026	0.272	4
			0.020	0.264	6
Our model			0.020	0.267	4
			0.030	0.134	6

6 Conclusions

In this paper, we have developed a comprehensive identification framework for fuzzy model based on information granulation realized with HCM clustering. The underlying idea deals with an optimization of information granules by exploiting techniques of clustering and genetic algorithms. We used the isolated input space for each input variable and defined the fuzzy space by information granule. Information granulation with the aid of HCM clustering help determine the initial parameters of fuzzy model such as the initial apexes of the membership functions and the initial values of polynomial function being used in the premise and consequence part of the fuzzy rules. The initial parameters are tuned (adjusted) effectively with the aid of the genetic algorithms and the least square method. The experimental studies showed that the model is compact (realized through a small number of rules), and its performance is better than some other previous models. The proposed model is effective for nonlinear complex systems, so we can construct a well-organized model.

Acknowledgements

This work has been supported by KESRI(R-2003-0-285), which is funded by MOCIE(Ministry of commerce, industry and energy)

References

1. Zadeh, L.A.: Fuzzy sets. Information and Control. **8** (1965) 338-353
2. Tong, R.M.: Synthesis of fuzzy models for industrial processes. Int. J Gen Syst. **4** (1978) 143-162
3. Pedrycz, W.: An identification algorithm in fuzzy relational system. Fuzzy Sets Syst. **13** (1984) 153-167
4. Pedrycz, W.: Numerical and application aspects of fuzzy relational equations. Fuzzy Sets Syst. **11** (1983) 1-18
5. Czogola, E., Pedrycz, W.: On identification in fuzzy systems and its applications in control problems. Fuzzy Sets Syst. **6** (1981) 73-83
6. Takagi, T., Sugeno, M.: Fuzzy identification of systems and its applications to modeling and control. IEEE Trans Syst, Cybern. SMC-**15**(1) (1985) 116-132
7. Sugeno, M., Yasukawa, T.: Linguistic modeling based on numerical data. In: IFSA'91 Brussels, Computer, Management & System Science. (1991) 264-267
8. Ismail, M.A.: Soft Clustering Algorithm and Validity of Solutions. In: Gupta MM, editor. Fuzzy Computing Theory, Hardware and Application. Amsterdam. North Holland. (1988) 445-471
9. Oh, S.K., Pedrycz, W.: Identification of fuzzy systems by means of an auto-tuning algorithm and its application to nonlinear systems. Fuzzy Sets and Syst. **115**(2) (2000) 205-230
10. Zadeh, L.A.: Toward a theory of fuzzy information granulation and its centrality in human reasoning and fuzzy logic. Fuzzy Sets and Syst. **90** (1997) 111-117
11. Pderycz, W., Vukovich, G.: Granular neural networks. Neurocomputing. **36** (2001) 205-224
12. Krishnaiah, P.R., Kanal, L.N., editors.: Classification, pattern recognition, and reduction of dimensionality, volume 2 of Handbook of Statistics. North-Holland Amsterdam (1982)
13. Golderg, D.E.: Genetic Algorithm in search, Optimization & Machine Learning, Addison Wesley (1989)
14. Sugeno, M., Yasukawa, T.: A Fuzzy-Logic-Based Approach to Qualitative Modeling. IEEE Trans. on Fuzzy systems. **1**(1) (1993) 7-13
15. Gomez Skarmeta, A. F., Delgado, M., Vila, M. A.: About the use of fuzzy clustering techniques for fuzzy model identification. Fuzzy Sets and Systems. **106** (1999) 179-188
16. Kim, E. T., Park, M. K., Ji, S. H., Park, M. N.: A new approach to fuzzy modeling. IEEE Trans. on Fuzzy systems. **5**(3) (1997) 328-337
17. Kim, E. T, Lee, H. J., Park, M. K., Park, M. N.: a simply identified Sugeno-type fuzzy model via double clustering. Information Sciences. **110** (1998) 25-39
18. Oh, S. K., Pedrycz, W., Park, B. J.: Polynomial Neural Networks Architecture: Analysis and Design. Computers and Electrical Engineering. **29**(6) (2003) 703-725
19. Park, B. J., Pedrycz, W., Oh, S. K.: Fuzzy Polynomial Neural Networks: Hybrid Architectures of Fuzzy Modeling. IEEE Trans. on Fuzzy Systems. **10**(5) (2002) 607-621
20. Tong, R. M.: The evaluation of fuzzy models derived from experimental data. Fuzzy Sets Syst. 13 (1980) 1-12

21. Xu, C. W., Zailu, Y.: Fuzzy model identification self-learning for dynamic system. IEEE Trans. on Syst. Man, Cybern. SMC-**17**(4) (1987) 683-689
22. Park, C. S., Oh, S. K., Pedrycz, W.: Fuzzy Identification by means of Auto-Tuning Algorithm and Weighting Factor. The Third Asian Fuzzy Systems Symposium(AFSS). (1998) 701-706
23. Park, B. J., Pedrycz, W., Oh, S.-K.: Identification of Fuzzy Models with the Aid of Evolutionary Data Granulation. IEE Proc.-Control Theory and Applications. 148(05) (2001) 406-418
24. Park, H.S. Oh, S.K.: Rule-based Fuzzy-Neural Networks Using the Identification Algorithm of the GA Hybrid Scheme. International journal of Control, Automations, and Systems. **1**(1) (2003) 101-110
25. Park, H.S., Oh, S.K.: Fuzzy Relation-based Fuzzy Neural-Networks Using a Hybrid Identification Algorithm. International Journal of Control, Automations, and Systems. **1**(3) (2003) 289-300

A New Approach to Genetically Optimized Hybrid Fuzzy Set-Based Polynomial Neural Networks with FSPNs and PNs

Sung-Kwun Oh[1], Seok-Beom Roh[2], and Witold Pedrycz[3,4]

[1] Department of Electrical Engineering, The University of Suwon,
San 2-2 Wau-ri, Bongdam-eup, Hwaseong-si, Gyeonggi-do, 445-743, South Korea
ohsk@suwon.ac.kr
[2] Department of Electrical Electronic and Information Engineering, Wonkwang University
344-2, Shinyong-Dong, Iksan, Chon-Buk, 570-749, South Korea
[3] Department of Electrical and Computer Engineering, University of Alberta
Edmonton, AB T6G 2G6, Canada
[4] Systems Research Institute, Polish Academy of Sciences, Warsaw, Poland

Abstract. We investigate a new fuzzy-neural networks-Hybrid Fuzzy set based polynomial Neural Networks (HFSPNN). These networks consist of genetically optimized multi-layer with two kinds of heterogeneous neurons that are fuzzy set based polynomial neurons (FSPNs) and polynomial neurons (PNs). We have developed a comprehensive design methodology to determine the optimal structure of networks dynamically. The augmented genetically optimized HFSPNN (namely gHFSPNN) results in a structurally optimized structure and comes with a higher level of flexibility in comparison to the one we encounter in the conventional HFPNN. The GA-based design procedure being applied at each layer of gHFSPNN leads to the selection leads to the selection of preferred nodes (FSPNs or PNs) available within the HFSPNN. In the sequel, the structural optimization is realized via GAs, whereas the ensuing detailed parametric optimization is carried out in the setting of a standard least square method-based learning. The performance of the gHFSPNN is quantified through experimentation where we use a number of modeling benchmarks-synthetic and experimental data already experimented with in fuzzy or neurofuzzy modeling.

1 Introduction

A lot of researchers on system modeling have been interested in the multitude of challenging and conflicting objectives such as compactness, approximation ability, generalization capability and so on which they wish to satisfy. It is common practice to use various forms of neural networks and fuzzy systems in designing nonlinear system with good predictive abilities as well as approximation capabilities. In particular, when dealing with high-order nonlinear and multivariable equations of the model, we require a vast amount of data for estimating all its parameters that is an important key to determine the model performance. The Group Method of Data Handling (GMDH) [1] introduced by A.G. Ivakhnenko is one of the approaches that help alleviate the problem. But, GMDH has some drawbacks. First, it tends to generate quite complex polynomial for relatively simple systems. Second, owing to its limited generic structure, GMDH also tends to produce an overly complex network(model)

V. Torra et al. (Eds.): MDAI 2005, LNAI 3558, pp. 328–337, 2005.

when it comes to highly nonlinear systems. In alleviating the problems of the GMDH algorithms, Polynomial Neural Networks(PNN) [2], [3] was introduced as a new class of networks. Combination of neural networks and fuzzy systems (or neurofuzzy systems for short) has been recognized as a powerful alternative approach to develop fuzzy systems. We have investigated a new category of neuro-fuzzy networks, Fuzzy Set based Polynomial Neural Networks (FSPNN) and developed Hybrid Fuzzy Set based Polynomial Neural Networks (HFSPNN) composed of multi-layer with two kinds of heterogeneous neurons that are fuzzy set based polynomial neurons (FPSNs) and polynomial neurons (PNs). Although the HFSPNN has flexible architecture whose potential can be fully utilized through a systematic design, it is difficult to obtain the structurally and parametrically optimized network because of the limited design of the nodes (viz. FSPNs and PNs) located in each layer of the network.

In this paper, we study a genetic optimization-driven new neurofuzzy topology, called genetically optimized Hybrid Fuzzy Set based Polynomial Neural Networks (gHFSPNN) and discuss a comprehensive design methodology supporting their development. gHFSPNN is a network resulting from the combination of fuzzy inference system and PNN algorithm driven to genetic optimization. Each node of the first layer of gHFSPNN, that is a fuzzy polynomial neuron (FSPN) operates as a compact fuzzy inference system. The networks of the second and higher layers of the gHFSPNN come with a high level of flexibility as each node (processing element forming a PN). The determination of the optimal values of the parameters available within an individual PN and FSPN (viz. the number of input variables, the order of the polynomial, a collection of preferred nodes, and the number of membership functions (MFs)) leads to a structurally and parametrically optimized network.

2 The Architecture of the Hybrid Fuzzy Set-Based Polynomial Neural Networks

2.1 The Architecture of Fuzzy Set-Based Polynomial Neurons (FSPN) Based Layer of gHFSPNN

The FSPN encapsulates a family of nonlinear "if-then" rules. When put together, FSPNs results in a self-organizing Fuzzy Set-based Polynomial Neural Networks (FSPNN). The FSPN consists of two basic functional modules. The first one, labeled by F, is a collection of fuzzy sets (here denoted by $\{A_k\}$ and $\{B_k\}$) that form an interface between the input numeric variables and the processing part realized by the neuron. The second module (denoted here by **P**) refers to the function – based nonlinear (polynomial) processing that involves some input variables This nonlinear processing involves some input variables (x_i and x_j), which are capable of being the input variables (Here, x_p and x_q), or entire system input variables. Each rule reads in the form

$$\text{if } x_p \text{ is } A_k \text{ then } z \text{ is } P_{pk}(x_i, x_j, a_{pk})$$
$$\text{if } x_q \text{ is } B_k \text{ then } z \text{ is } P_{qk}(x_i, x_j, a_{qk}) \tag{1}$$

where a_{qk} is a vector of the parameters of the conclusion part of the rule while $P(x_i, x_j, a)$ denoted the regression polynomial forming the consequence part of the fuzzy rule which uses several type of high order polynomials besides the constant function forming the simplest version of the consequence; refer Table 1.

Table 1. Different forms of the regression polynomials forming the consequence part of the fuzzy rules

No. of inputs Order of the polynomial	1	2	3
0 (Type 1)	Constant	Constant	Constant
1 (Type 2)	Linear	Bilinear	Trilinear
2 (Type 3)	Quadratic	Biquadratic-1	Triquadratic-1
2 (Type 4)		Biquadratic-2	Triquadratic-2

1: Basic type, 2: Modified type

The activation levels of the rules contribute to the output of the FSPN being computed as a weighted average of the individual condition parts (functional transformations) $P_{(l,k)}$.

$$z = \sum_{l=1}^{\text{total inputs}} \left(\sum_{k=1}^{\text{total\_rules related to input } l} \mu_{(l,k)} P_{(l,k)}(x_i, x_j, a_{(l,k)}) \middle/ \sum_{k=1}^{\text{total\_rules related to input } l} \mu_{(l,k)} \right)$$

$$= \sum_{l=1}^{\text{total inputs}} \left(\sum_{k=1}^{\text{rules related to input } l} \tilde{\mu}_{(l,k)} P_{(l,k)}(x_i, x_j, a_{(l,k)}) \right)$$

(2)

$$\tilde{\mu}_{(l,k)} = \frac{\mu_{(l,k)}}{\sum_{k=1}^{\text{total\_rules related to input } l} \mu_{(l,k)}}$$

(3)

When developing the FSPN-based layer, we use genetic algorithms to produce the optimized network, which is realized by selecting such parameters as the number of input variables, the order of polynomial, and choosing a specific subset of input variables. Especially for the polynomial type of the consequent part, we consider two kinds of input vector formats in the conclusion part of the fuzzy rules as shown in Table 2.

Table 2. Polynomial type according to the number of input variables in the conclusion part of fuzzy rules

Input vector Type of the consequence polynomial	Selected input variables in the premise part	Selected input variables in the consequence part	Entire system input variables
Type T	A	A	B
Type T*	A	B	B

2.2 The Architecture of the Polynomial Neuron (PN) Based Layer of gHFSPNN

As underlined, the PNN algorithm in the PN based layer of gHFSPNN is based on the GMDH method and utilizes a class of polynomials such as linear, quadratic, modified quadratic, etc. to describe basic processing realized there. Let us recall that the input-output data are given in the form

$$(X_i, y_i) = (x_{1i}, x_{2i}, \ldots, x_{Ni}, y_i), \quad i=1, 2, 3, \ldots, n$$

(4)

where N is the number of input variables, i is the data number of each input and output variable, and n denotes the number of data in the dataset.

The estimated output $\hat{y}$ reads as

$$\hat{y} = c_0 + \sum_{i=1}^{N} c_i x_i + \sum_{i=1}^{N}\sum_{j=1}^{N} c_{ij} x_i x_j + \sum_{i=1}^{N}\sum_{j=1}^{N}\sum_{k=1}^{N} c_{ijk} x_i x_j x_k \cdots \qquad (5)$$

Where, $C(c_0, c_i, c_{ij}, c_{ijk}, \ldots)(i, j, k, \ldots: 1, 2, \ldots, N)$ and $X(x_i, x_j, x_k, \ldots)(i, j, k, \ldots: 1, 2, \ldots, N)$ are vectors of the coefficients and input variables of the resulting multi-input single-output(MISO) system, respectively.

The detailed PN involving a certain regression polynomial is shown in Table 3.

Table 3. Different forms of the regression polynomial building a P

Order	No. of inputs	1	2	3
1	(Type 1)	Linear	Bilinear	Trilinear
2	(Type 2)	Quadratic	Biquadratic-1	Triquadratic-1
	(Type 3)		Biquadratic-2	Triquadratic-2

3 Genetic Optimization of gHFSPNN

Genetic algorithms (GAs) are optimization techniques based on the principles of natural evolution [5]. In essence, they are search algorithms that use operations found in natural genetics to guide a comprehensive search over the parameter space. In this study, for the optimization of the gHFSPNN model, GA uses the serial method of binary type, roulette-wheel used in the selection process, one-point crossover in the crossover operation, and a binary inversion (complementation) operation in the mutation operator. To retain the best individual and carry it over to the next generation, we use elitist strategy [6].

As mentioned, when we construct PNs and FSPNs of each layer in the conventional HFSPNN, such parameters as the number of input variables (nodes), the order of polynomial, and input variables available within a PN and a FSPN are fixed (selected) in advance by the designer. This could have frequently contributed to the difficulties in the design of the optimal network. To overcome this apparent drawback, we resort ourselves to the genetic optimization.

4 The Algorithm and Design Procedure of Genetically Optimized HFSPNN (gHFSPNN)

The genetically optimized HFSPNN (gHFSPNN) comes with a highly versatile architecture both in the flexibility of the individual nodes as well as the interconnectivity between the nodes and organization of the layers. Overall, the framework of the design procedure of the HFSPNN based on genetically optimized multi-layer perceptron architecture comprises the following steps.

[Step 1] *Determine system's input variables.*

[Step 2] *Form a training and testing data.*

The input-output data set $(\boldsymbol{x}_i, y_i) = (x_{1i}, x_{2i}, \ldots, x_{ni}, y_i)$, $i = 1, 2, \ldots, N$ is divided into two parts, that is, a training and testing dataset.

[Step 3] *Decide initial information for constructing the gHFSPNN structure.*
a) Stopping criterion, b) the maximum number of input variables, c) the total number W of nodes, d) the depth of the gHFSPNN, e) the depth and width of the gHFSPNN to be selected, f) The decision of initial information for fuzzy inference method and fuzzy identification.

[Step 4] *Decide a structure of the PN and FSPN based layer of gHFSPNN using genetic design*
This concerns the selection of the number of input variables, the polynomial order, and the input variables to be assigned in each node of the corresponding layer. In addition, particularly for the FSPN based layer, we should consider the number of the membership functions. That is why we divide the chromosome to be used for genetic optimization into three sub-chromosomes for PN based layer and four sub-chromosomes for FSPN based layer. The 1st sub-chromosome contains the number of input variables, the 2nd sub-chromosome involves the order of the polynomial of the node, the 3rd (which is used only for the FSPN based layer) involves the number of membership functions (MFs), and the last sub-chromosome (remaining bits) contains input variables coming to the corresponding node (PN and FSPN) and). All these elements are optimized when running the GA.

[Step 5] *Estimate the coefficient parameters of the polynomial in the selected node (PN or FSPN).*

[Step 5-1] *In case of a PN (PN-based layer)*
The vector of coefficients $\mathbf{C}_i$ is derived by minimizing the mean squared error between y_i and z_{mi}

$$E = \frac{1}{N_{tr}} \sum_{i=0}^{N_{tr}} (y_i - z_{mi})^2 \tag{6}$$

Using the training data subset, this gives rise to the set of linear equations

$$\mathbf{Y} = \mathbf{X}_i \mathbf{C}_i \tag{7}$$

Evidently, the coefficients of the PN of nodes in each layer are expressed in the form

$$\mathbf{C}_i = (\mathbf{X}_i^T \mathbf{X}_i)^{-1} \mathbf{X}_i^T \mathbf{Y} \tag{8}$$

[Step 5-2] *In case of a FSPN (FSPN-based layer)*
At this step, the regression polynomial inference is considered. The inference method deals with regression polynomial functions viewed as the consequents of the rules. In the fuzzy inference, we consider two types of membership functions, namely triangular and Gaussian-like membership functions. The consequence parameters are produced by the standard least squares method.

[Step 6] *Select nodes (PNs or FSPNs) with the best predictive capability and construct their corresponding layer.*
The generation process can be organized as the following sequence of steps
Sub-step 1) We set up initial genetic information necessary for generation of the gHFSPNN architecture.

Sub-step 2) The nodes (PNs or FSPNs) are generated through the genetic design.

Sub-step 3) We calculate the fitness function. The fitness function reads as

$$F(\text{fitness function}) = 1/(1+EPI) \tag{9}$$

where *EPI* denotes the performance index for the testing data (or validation data).

Sub-step 4) To move on to the next generation, we carry out selection, crossover, and mutation operation using genetic initial information and the fitness values obtained via *sub-step 3*.

Sub-step 5) We choose several nodes (PNs or FSPNs) characterized by the best fitness values. Here, we use the pre-defined number W of nodes (PNs or FSPNs) with better predictive capability that need to be preserved to assure an optimal operation at the next iteration of the HFSPNN algorithm. The outputs of the retained nodes serve as inputs to the next layer of the network. There are two cases as to the number of the retained nodes, that is

  (i) If $W^* < W$, then the number of the nodes retained for the next layer is equal to z.

  (ii) Here, W^* denotes the number of the retained nodes in each layer that nodes with the duplicated fitness values were moved.

  (iii) If $W^* \geq W$, then for the next layer, the number of the retained nodes is equal to W.

Sub-step 6) For the elitist strategy, we select the node that has the highest fitness value among the selected nodes (W).

Sub-step 7) We generate new populations of the next generation using operators of GAs obtained from *Sub-step 4*. We use the elitist strategy. This sub-step carries out by repeating *sub-step 2-6*.

Sub-step 8) We combine the nodes (W populations) obtained in the previous generation with the nodes (W populations) obtained in the current generation.

Sub-step 9) Until the last generation, this sub-step carries out by repeating *sub-step 7-8*.

[Step 7] *Check the termination criterion.*

As far as the performance index is concerned (that reflects a numeric accuracy of the layers), a termination is straightforward and comes in the form,

$$F_1 \leq F_* \tag{10}$$

Where, F_1 denotes a maximal fitness value occurring at the current layer whereas F_* stands for a maximal fitness value that occurred at the previous layer.

[Step 8] *Determine new input variables for the next layer.*

If (10) has not been met, the model is expanded. The outputs of the preserved nodes ($z_{1i}, z_{2i}, \ldots, z_{Wi}$) serves as new inputs to the next layer ($x_{1j}, x_{2j}, \ldots, x_{Wj}$)($j=i+1$). This is captured by the expression

$$x_{1j} = z_{1i}, x_{2j} = z_{2j}, \ldots, x_{Wj} = z_{Wj} \tag{11}$$

The HFSPNN algorithm is carried out by repeating steps 4-8 of the algorithm.

5 Simulation Study

We demonstrate how the gHFSPNN can be utilized to predict future values of a chaotic Mackey-Glass time series [4], [7], [8], [9], [10], [11], [12]. The time series is
generated by the chaotic Mackey-Glass differential delay equation [13] comes in the
form

$$\dot{x}(t) = \frac{0.2x(t-\tau)}{1+x^{10}(t-\tau)} - 0.1x(t) \qquad (12)$$

To obtain the time series value at each integer point, we applied the fourth-order
Runge-Kutta method to find the numerical solution to (12). From the Mackey-Glass
time series $x(t)$, we extracted 1000 input-output data pairs in the following format:

$$[x(t-24), x(t-18), x(t-12), x(t-6), x(t) ; x(t+6)]$$

where, t=118 to 1117. The first 500 pairs were used as the training data set while the
remaining 500 pairs formed the testing data set. To come up with a quantitative
evaluation of the network, we use the standard RMSE performance index as given
by (13).

$$E(PI \ or \ EPI) = \sqrt{\frac{1}{N}\sum_{p=1}^{N}(y_p - \hat{y}_p)^2} \qquad (13)$$

Table 4 summarizes the list of parameters used in the genetic optimization of the
network.

Fig. 1 depicts the performance index of each layer (FSPN-based or PN-based
layer) of gHFSPNN for each type (Type T*: that is, entire system inputs) according
to the increase of maximal number of inputs to be selected.

Table 4. Summary of the parameters of the genetic optimization

	Parameters	1st layer	2nd to 3th layer
	Maximum generation	150	150
GA	Total population size	60	60
	Selected population size (W)	30	30
	Crossover rate	0.65	0.65
	Mutation rate	0.1	0.1
	String length	3+3+2+30	3+3+30
	Maximal no.(Max) of inputs to be selected	$1 \leq l \leq Max(2\sim5)$	$1 \leq l \leq Max(2\sim5)$
HFS PNN	Polynomial type (Type T) of the consequent part of fuzzy rules	$1 \leq T \leq 4$	$1 \leq T \leq 4$
	Consequent input type to be used for Type T (*)	Type T*	Type T
	Membership Function (MF) type	Triangular Gaussian	.
	No. of MFs per input	$2 \leq M \leq 5$	

l, T, Max: integers, T* means that entire system inputs are used for the polynomial in the conclusion
part of the rules.

Fig. 2(a)-(b) illustrate the detailed optimal topologies of gHFSPNN for 1 layer and
Max=5 in case of Type T*: those are quantified as PI=5.58e-4, EPI=5.61e-4 for triangular MF, and PI=2.74e-4, EPI=3.68e-4 for Gaussian-like MF.

Table 5 gives a comparative summary of the network with other models.

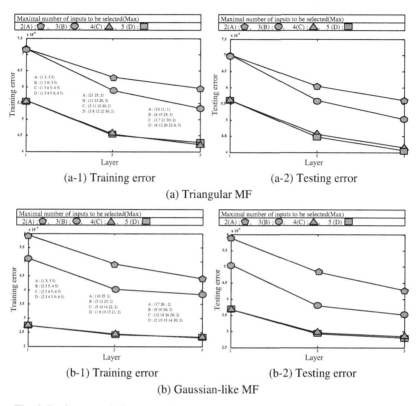

(a-1) Training error   (a-2) Testing error

(a) Triangular MF

(b-1) Training error   (b-2) Testing error

(b) Gaussian-like MF

Fig. 1. Performance index according to the increase of number of layers (Type T*)

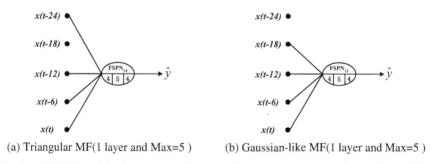

(a) Triangular MF(1 layer and Max=5)   (b) Gaussian-like MF(1 layer and Max=5)

Fig. 2. gHFSPNN architecture in case of using entire system input vector format (Type T*)

6 Concluding Remarks

In this study, the GA-based design procedure of Hybrid Fuzzy Set based Polynomial Neural Networks (HFSPNN) along with its architectural considerations has been investigated. Through the consecutive generation of a layer through a growth process (iteration) of the gHFSPNN, the depth (layer size) and width (node size of each layer) of the network could be flexibly selected based on a diversity of local characteristics of these preferred FSPNs and PNs (such as the number of input variables, the order of

Table 5. Comparative analysis of the performance of the network; considered are models reported in the literature

Model				Performance index			
				PI	PI$_s$	EPI$_s$	NDEI*
	Wang's model[7]			0.044 0.013 0.010			
	ANFIS[8]				0.0016	0.0015	0.007
	FNN model[9]				0.014	0.009	
	Recurrent neural network[10]			0.0138			
SONN**[11]	Basic (5th layer)		Case 1		0.0011	0.0011	0.005
			Case 2		0.0027	0.0028	0.011
	Modified (5th layer)		Case 1		0.0012	0.0011	0.005
			Case 2		0.0038	0.0038	0.016
HFPNN[4]	Triangular		5th layer		7.0e-4	6.0e-4	
	Gaussian		5th layer		4.8e-5	7.1e-5	
Proposed gHFSPNN	Max=5 (Type T*)	Triangular	3rd layer		4.28e-4	4.05e-4	
	Max=5 (Type T*)	Gaussian	3rd layer		2.30e-4	2.80e-4	

* Non-dimensional error index (NDEI) as used in [12] is defined as the root mean square errors divided by the standard deviation of the target series.

** is called "conventional optimized FPNN".

the consequent polynomial of rules/the polynomial order, a collection of specific subset of input variables, and the number of membership functions) available within HFSPNN. The design methodology comes as a hybrid structural optimization (based on GMDH method and genetic optimization) and parametric learning being viewed as two fundamental phases of the design process. The comprehensive experimental study involving well-known datasets quantify a superb performance of the network in comparison to the existing fuzzy and neuro-fuzzy models. Most importantly, through the proposed framework of genetic optimization we can efficiently search for the optimal network architecture (structurally and parametrically optimized network) and this becomes crucial in improving the performance of the resulting model.

Acknowledgements

This work has been supported by KESRI(R-2003-B-274), which is funded by MOCIE(Ministry of commerce, industry and energy)

References

1. Ivahnenko, A.G.: Polynomial theory of complex systems. IEEE Trans. on Systems. Man and Cybernetics. SMC-**12** (1971) 364-378
2. Oh, S. K., Pedrycz, W.: The design of self-organizing Polynomial Neural Networks. Information Science. **141** (2002) 237-258
3. Oh, S. K., Pedrycz, W., Park, B. J.: Polynomial Neural Networks Architecture: Analysis and Design. Computers and Electrical Engineering. **29** (2003) 703-725
4. Oh, S. K., Pedrycz, W., Kim, D. W.: Hybrid Fuzzy Polynomial Neural Networks. Int. J. of Uncertainty. Fuzziness and Knowledge-Based Systems. **10** (2002) 257-280

5. Michalewicz, Z.: Genetic Algorithms + Data Structures = Evolution Programs. Springer-Verlag. Berlin Heidelberg. 1996
6. Jong, D., K. A.: Are Genetic Algorithms Function Optimizers?. Parallel Problem Solving from Nature 2, Manner, R. and Manderick, B. eds. North-Holland. Amsterdam
7. Wang, L. X., Mendel, J. M.: Generating fuzzy rules from numerical data with applications. IEEE Trans. Systems, Man, Cybern. **22** (1992) 1414-1427
8. Jang, J. S. R.: ANFIS: Adaptive-Network-Based Fuzzy Inference System. IEEE Trans. System, Man, and Cybern. **23** (1993) 665-685
9. Maguire, L. P., Roche, B., McGinnity, T. M., McDaid, L. J.: Predicting a chaotic time series using a fuzzy neural network. Information Sciences. **112** (1998) 125-136
10. James Li, C., Huang, T. Y.: Automatic structure and parameter training methods for modeling of mechanical systems by recurrent neural networks. Applied Mathematical Modeling. **23** (1999) 933-944
11. Oh, S. K., Pedrycz, W., Ahn, T. C.: Self-organizing neural networks with fuzzy polynomial neurons. Applied Soft Computing. **2** (2002) 1-10
12. Lapedes, A. S., Farber, R.: Non-linear Signal Processing Using Neural Networks: Prediction and System Modeling. Technical Report LA-UR-87-2662, Los Alamos National Laboratory. Los Alamos. New Mexico 87545. (1987)
13. Mackey, M. C., Glass, L.: Oscillation and chaos in physiological control systems. Science. **197** (1977) 287-289
14. Park, B.J., Lee, D.Y., Oh, S.K.: Rule-based Fuzzy Polynomial Neural Networks in Modeling Software Process Data. Int. J. of Control, Automations, and Systems. **1**(3) (2003) 321-331
15. Park, H.S., Park, B.J., Kim, H.K., Oh, S,K,: Self-Organizing Polynomial Neural Networks Based on Genetically Optimized Multi-Layer Perceptron Architecture. International journal of Control, Automations, and Systems. **2**(4) (2004) 423-434

Genetically Optimized Hybrid Fuzzy Neural Networks in Modeling Software Data

Sung-Kwun Oh[1], Byoung-Jun Park[2], Witold Pedrycz[3,4], and Hyun-Ki Kim[1]

[1] Department of Electrical Engineering, The University of Suwon
San 2-2 Wau-ri, Bongdam-eup, Hwaseong-si, Gyeonggi-do, 445-743, South Korea
ohsk@suwon.ac.kr
[2] Department of Electrical, Electronic and Information Engineering, Wonkwang University
344-2, Shinyong-Dong, Iksan, Chon-Buk, 570-749, South Korea
[3] Department of Electrical and Computer Engineering, University of Alberta
Edmonton, AB T6G 2G6, Canada
[4] Systems Research Institute, Polish Academy of Sciences, Warsaw, Poland

Abstract. Experimental software data sets describing software projects in terms of their complexity and development time have been a subject of intensive modeling. In this study, a new architecture and comprehensive design methodology of genetically optimized Hybrid Fuzzy Neural Networks (gHFNN) are introduced and modeling software data is carried out. The gHFNN architecture results from a synergistic usage of the hybrid system generated by combining Fuzzy Neural Networks (FNN) with Polynomial Neural Networks (PNN). FNN contributes to the formation of the premise part of the overall network structure of the gHFNN. The consequence part of that is designed using genetic PNN.

1 Introduction

Empirical studies in software engineering employ experimental data to gain insight into the software development processes and assess their quality. Data concerning software products and software processes are crucial to their better understanding and, in the sequel, the development of effective ways of producing high quality software. Efficient modeling techniques should allow for a selection of pertinent variables and a formation of highly representative datasets. The models should be able to take advantage of the existing domain knowledge and augment it by available numeric data to form a coherent data-knowledge modeling entity. The omnipresent modeling tendency is the one that exploits techniques of Computational Intelligence (CI [1], [2]).

In this study, we develop a hybrid modeling architecture, called genetically optimized Hybrid Fuzzy Neural Networks (gHFNN). In a nutshell, gHFNN is composed of two main substructures driven to genetic optimization, namely a fuzzy set-based fuzzy neural network (FNN [3]) and a genetic polynomial neural network (gPNN). The role of the FNN is to interact with input data, granulate the corresponding input spaces. In the first case (Scheme I) we concentrate on the use of simplified fuzzy inference. In the second case (Scheme II), we take advantage of linear fuzzy inference. The role of the gPNN is to carry out nonlinear transformation at the level of the fuzzy sets formed at the level of FNN. The gPNN that exhibits a flexible and versatile structure is constructed on a basis of Group Method of Data Handling (GMDH [4],

V. Torra et al. (Eds.): MDAI 2005, LNAI 3558, pp. 338–345, 2005.
© Springer-Verlag Berlin Heidelberg 2005

[5]) method and genetic algorithms (GAs [6]). The design procedure applied in the construction of each layer of the PNN deals with its structural optimization involving the selection of optimal nodes (polynomial neurons; PNs) with specific local characteristics (such as the number of input variables, the order of the polynomial, and a collection of the specific subset of input variables) and addresses specific aspects of parametric optimization. To assess the performance of the proposed model, we experiment with NASA dataset [7] widely used in software engineering.

2 Conventional Hybrid Fuzzy Neural Networks (HFNN)

The architectures of conventional HFNN [8], [9] result as a synergy between two other general constructs such as FNN and PNN. Based on the different PNN topologies, the HFNN distinguish between two kinds of architectures, namely basic and modified architectures. Moreover, for the each architecture we identify two cases. In the connection point, if input variables to PNN used on the consequence part of HFNN are less than three (or four), the generic type of HFNN does not generate a highly versatile structure. Accordingly we identify also two types as the generic and advanced. The design of the HFNN proceeds further and involves a generation of some additional layers. Each layer consists of nodes (PNs) for which the number of input variables could the same as in the previous layers or may differ across the network. The structure of the HFNN is selected on the basis of the number of input variables and the order of the polynomial occurring in each layer.

3 The Architecture and Design Procedure of gHFNN

The gHFNN emerges from the genetically optimized multi-layer perceptron architecture based on fuzzy set-based FNN, GAs and GMDH.

3.1 Fuzzy Neural Networks and Genetic Optimization

We use FNN based on two types of fuzzy inferences, that is, simplified (Scheme I) and linear fuzzy inference-based FNN (Scheme II) as shown in Fig. 1. The output of the FNN is governed by the following expression.

$$\hat{y} = f_1(x_1) + f_2(x_2) + \cdots + f_m(x_m) = \sum_{i=1}^{m} f_i(x_i) \tag{1}$$

We can regard each $f_i(x_i)$ given by (1) as the following mappings (rules).

$$\text{Scheme I} - R^j \colon \text{If } x_i \text{ is } A_{ij} \text{ then } Cy_{ij} = w_{ij} \tag{2}$$
$$\text{Scheme II} - R^j \colon \text{If } x_i \text{ is } A_{ij} \text{ then } Cy_{ij} = ws_{ij} + w_{ij} x_i \tag{3}$$

R^j is the j-th fuzzy rule while A_{ij} denotes a fuzzy variable of the premise of the fuzzy rule and represents a membership function μ_{ij}. ws_{ij} and w_{ij} express a connection existing between the neurons as visualized in Fig. 1. Mapping from x_i to $f_i(x_i)$ in (2) is determined by the fuzzy inferences and a standard defuzzification.

$$f_i(x_i) = \sum_{j=1}^{z} \mu_{ij}(x_i) \cdot w_{ij} \Big/ \sum_{j=1}^{z} \mu_{ij}(x_i) \tag{4}$$

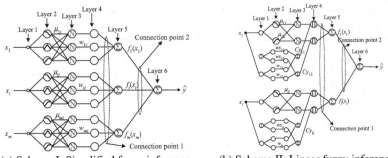

(a) Scheme I; Simplified fuzzy inference   (b) Scheme II; Linear fuzzy inference

Fig. 1. Topologies of fuzzy set-based FNN

The learning of FNN is realized by adjusting connections of the neurons and as such it follows a standard Back-Propagation (BP) algorithm. For the simplified fuzzy inference-based FNN, the update formula of a connection in Scheme I is as follow.

$$\Delta w_{ij} = 2 \cdot \eta \cdot (y_p - \hat{y}_p) \cdot \mu_{ij}(x_i) + \alpha(w_{ij}(t) - w_{ij}(t-1)) \tag{5}$$

Where, y_p is the *p-th* target output data, $\hat{y}_p$ stands for the *p-th* actual output of the model for this specific data point, η is a positive learning rate and α is a momentum coefficient constrained to the unit interval. The inference result and the learning algorithm in linear fuzzy inference-based FNN use the mechanisms in the same manner as discussed above. In order to enhance the learning of the FNN and augment its performance of a FNN, we use GAs to adjust learning rate, momentum coefficient and the parameters of the membership functions of the antecedents of the rules.

3.2 Genetically Optimized PNN (gPNN)

When we construct PNs of each layer in the conventional PNN [4], such parameters as the number of input variables, the order of polynomial, and input variables available within a PN are fixed in advance by the designer. This could have frequently contributed to the difficulties in the design of the optimal network. To overcome this apparent drawback, we introduce a new genetic design approach; especially as a consequence we will be referring to these networks as genetic PNN (to be called "gPNN"). The overall genetically optimization process of PNN is shown in Fig. 2.

3.3 The Algorithms and Design Procedure of gHFNN

The premise of gHFNN: FNN (Refer to Fig. 1)
[Layer 1] Input layer.
[Layer 2] Computing activation degrees of linguistic labels.
[Layer 3] Normalization of a degree activation (firing) of the rule.
[Layer 4] Multiplying a normalized activation degree of the rule by connection. If we choose Connection point 1 for combining FNN with gPNN as shown in Fig. 1, a_{ij} is given as the input variable of the gPNN.

$$a_{ij} = \bar{\mu}_{ij} \times Cy_{ij} = \mu_{ij} \times Cy_{ij} \,, \begin{cases} \text{Simplified} : Cy_{ij} = w_{ij} \\ \text{Linear} \quad : Cy_{ij} = ws_{ij} + w_{ij} \cdot x_i \end{cases} \tag{6}$$

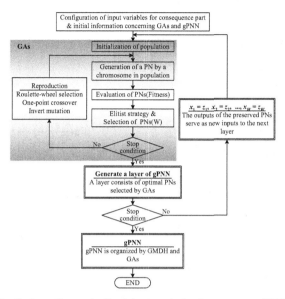

Fig. 2. Overall genetically-driven optimization process of PNN

[Layer 5] Fuzzy inference for the fuzzy rules. If we choose Connection point 2, f_i is the input variable of gPNN.

[Layer 6] Output layer of FNN] Computing output of a FNN.

The consequence of gHFNN: gPNN (Refer to Fig. 2)

[Step 1] Configuration of input variables.
If we choose the first option (Connection point 1), $x_1=a_{11}$, $x_2=a_{12}, \ldots, x_n=a_{ij}$ ($n=i \times j$). For the second option (Connection point 2), we have $x_1=f_1$, $x_2=f_2, \ldots, x_n=f_m$ ($n=m$).

[Step 2] Decision of initial information for constructing the gPNN.

[Step 3] Initialization of population.

[Step 4] Decision of PNs structure using genetic design. We divide the chromosome to be used for genetic optimization into three sub-chromosomes as shown in Fig. 3(a). In Fig. 3(b), 'PN$_n$' denotes the nth PN (node) of the corresponding layer, 'N' denotes the number of inputs coming to the node, and 'T' denotes the polynomial order in the node (Refer to Table 1).

[Step 5] Evaluation of PNs.

[Step 6] Elitist strategy and selection of PNs with the best predictive capability.

[Step 7] Reproduction.

[Step 8] Repeating Step 4-7.

[Step 9] Construction of their corresponding layer.

[Step 10] Check the termination criterion (performance index).

$$E(PI \text{ or } EPI) = \frac{1}{n}\sum_{p=1}^{n}\frac{|y_p - \hat{y}_p|}{y_p} \qquad (7)$$

[Step 11] Determining new input variables for the next layer.
The gPNN algorithm is carried out by repeating Steps 4-11.

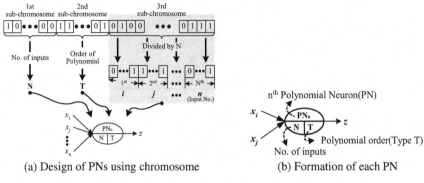

(a) Design of PNs using chromosome   (b) Formation of each PN

Fig. 3. The PN design using genetic optimization

Table 1. Different forms of regression polynomial forming a PN

Number of inputs Order of the polynomial	2	3	4
1 (Type 1)	Bilinear	Trilinear	Tetralinear
2 (Type 2)	Biquadratic-1	Triquadratic-1	Tetraquadratic-1
2 (Type 3)	Biquadratic-2	Triquadratic-2	Tetraquadratic-2

3.4 Model Selection

For the NASA software dataset, our model selection procedure is based on seeking a sound compromise between approximation and generalization errors. The main performance measure that we use in this paper is the MMRE (the mean magnitude of relative error) of (7). For evaluation of generalization ability, many estimates have been proposed in the literature; the most popular ones being the holdout estimate and the k-fold cross-validation estimate [10]. The holdout estimate is obtained by partitioning the dataset into two mutually exclusive subsets called training and test sets. The error estimate on the test set is used to assess generalization ability. On the other hand, the k-fold cross-validation estimate is obtained by a sample reuse technique. The dataset is divided into k mutually exclusive subsets of almost equal size, k-1 subsets are used for training, and the kth is used for prediction. This process is repeated "k" times, each employing a different subset for prediction.

When k is equal to data size, it is called leave-one-out cross-validation (LOOCV) estimate. In this study, we employ the LOOCV estimate of generalization error because of two reasons. First, it possesses good mathematical properties [11]. Second, it seems to be particularly suited for software engineering applications where the best available data are relatively small sets [12]. Thus, our model selection is based on the analysis of LOOCV estimate of generalization error for gHFNN in NASA dataset.

4 Experimental Studies

The experimental studies are concerned with a software effort dataset from NASA [7]. The dataset consists of two independent variables, viz. Developed Lines of Code (DL) and Methodology (ME), and one dependent variable, viz., Effort (Y) in man-months.

The goal is to seek a parsimonious model, which provides a good fit to the DL and Y data of NASA software project data and exhibits good generalization capability. The results of the preferred architectures are summarized in Tables 2.

Table 2. Performance index of gHFNN for 1 system input (DL)

Fuzzy Inference	Premise part No. of rules (MFs)	PI	EPI	CP	Layer	No. of inputs	Input No.			T	PI	EPI
Simplified	2 (2)	0.164	0.180	01	1	1	1			1	0.210	0.232
					2	3	3	4	7	3	0.118	0.202
					3	2	7	14		2	0.105	0.141
Linear	2 (2)	0.145	0.166	01	1	2	1	2		3	0.135	0.167
					2	3	1	53	7	3	0.106	0.153
					3	3	6	13	30	2	0.0747	0.131

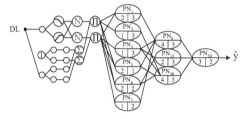

Fig. 4. Optimal topology of gHFNN for 1 system input (Linear, connection 01)

Now we develop effort estimation model based on two independent variables DL and ME. For the simplified and linear fuzzy inference based NFN, the performance indexes of gHFNN are shown in Table 3.

Table 3. Performance index of gHFNN for 2 system inputs (DL, ME)

Fuzzy Inference	Premise part No. of rules (MFs)	PI	EPI	CP	Layer	No. of inputs	Input No.				T	PI	EPI
Simplified	4 (2+2)	0.102	0.114	01	1	2	1	4			3	0.0908	0.118
					2	2	21	29			1	0.0829	0.0984
					3	4	15	22	25	30	3	0.0407	0.0896
				02	1	2	1	2			3	0.0908	0.118
					2	2	5	6			1	0.0829	0.0985
					3	1	25				1	0.0706	0.0799
Linear	4 (2+2)	0.0959	0.119	01	1	3	1	2	4		1	0.117	0.154
					2	4	13	16	21	30	2	0.0117	0.0723
					3	4	2	4	13	17	2	0.00014	0.00307
				02	1	2	1	2			2	0.0916	0.133
					2	2	2	5			2	0.0687	0.0950
					3	3	3	7	14		3	0.0454	0.0719

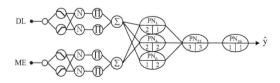

Fig. 5. Optimal topology of gHFNN for 2 system inputs (Simplified, connection 02)

Table 2 and 3 summarize the results of the optimized architectures according to connection points based on each fuzzy inference method. In the table, the values of the performance index of output of the gHFNN depend on each connection point based on the individual fuzzy inference methods. The optimal topologies of gHFNN are shown in Fig. 4 and 5, respectively. Fig. 6 illustrates the optimization process by visualizing the performance index in successive cycles. It also shows the optimized network architecture when taking into consideration gHFNN based on linear fuzzy inference and connection point (CP) 1, refer to Table 3. Table 4 contrasts the performance of the genetically developed network with other fuzzy-neural networks and conventional HFNN studied in the literatures.

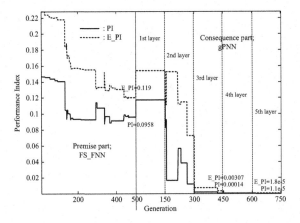

Fig. 6. Optimization procedure of gHFNN by GAs for 2 system inputs (Linear, connection 01)

Table 4. Comparison of performance with other modeling methods

Model			System Input	PI	EPI	No. of rules
Shin and Goel's RBF model [7]			DL	0.1579	0.1870	3 rules
				0.1450	0.1881	6 rules
			DL, ME	0.1470	0.2474	4 rules
				0.0870	0.1907	7 rules
Conventional HFNN	FS based [8]	Simplified	DL, ME	0.0886	0.0907	4 rules/3th layer
	FR based [9]	Simplified	DL	0.175	0.185	2 rules/2th layer
			DL, ME	0.0493	0.0565	4 rules/2th layer
		Linear	DL	0.0877	0.131	2 rules/3th layer
			DL, ME	0.0630	0.0736	4 rules/3th layer
Proposed model	FNN	Simplified	DL	0.164	0.180	2 rules
			DL, ME	0.102	0.114	4 rules
		Linear	DL	0.145	0.166	2 rules
			DL, ME	0.0959	0.119	4 rules
	gHFNN	Simplified	DL	0.105	0.141	2 rules/3th layer
			DL, ME	0.0407	0.0896	4 rules/3th layer
		Linear	DL	0.0747	0.131	2 rules/3th layer
			DL, ME	0.00014	0.00307	4 rules/3th layer

5   Conclusion

The comprehensive design methodology comes with the parametrically as well as structurally optimized network architecture. 1) As the premise structure of the gHFNN, the optimization of the rule-based FNN hinges on genetic algorithms and back-propagation (BP) learning algorithm: The GAs leads to the auto-tuning of ver-texes of membership function, while the BP algorithm helps obtain optimal parame-ters of the consequent polynomial of fuzzy rules through learning. And 2) the gPNN that is the consequent structure of the gHFNN is based on the technologies of the extended GMDH and GAs: The extended GMDH is comprised of both a structural phase such as a self-organizing and evolutionary algorithm, and a parametric phase of least square estimation-based learning, moreover the gPNN architecture is driven to genetic optimization, in what follows it leads to the selection of the optimal nodes. In the sequel, a variety of architectures of the proposed gHFNN driven to genetic opti-mization have been discussed. The experiments helped compare the network with other intelligent models – in all cases the previous models came with higher values of the performance index.

Acknowledgements

This work has been supported by KESRI(I-2004-0-074-0-00), which is funded by MOCIE(Ministry of commerce, industry and energy)

References

1. Pedrycz, W.: Computational Intelligence. CRC Press. FL. (1998)
2. Pedrycz, W., Peters, J.F.: Computational Intelligence and Software Engineering. World Scientific. Singapore (1998)
3. Oh, S.K., Pedrycz, W., Park, H.S.: Hybrid Identification in Fuzzy-Neural Networks. Fuzzy Sets and Systems. 138(2) (2003) 399-426
4. Oh, S.K., Pedrycz, W., Park, B.J.: Polynomial Neural Networks Architecture: Analysis and Design. Computers and Electrical Engineering. 29(6) (2003) 653-725
5. Ivahnenko, A.G.: The group method of data handling: a rival of method of stochastic ap-proximation. Soviet Automatic Control. 13(3) (1968) 43-55
6. Michalewicz, Z.: Genetic Algorithms + Data Structures = Evolution Programs. Springer-Verlag, Berlin Heidelberg (1996)
7. Shin, M., Goel, A.G.: Empirical Data Modeling in Software Engineering Using Radial Ba-sis Functions. IEEE Trans on Software Engineering. 26(6) (2000) 567-576
8. Oh, S.K., Pedrycz, W., Park, B.J.: Self-organizing neurofuzzy networks in modeling soft-ware data. Fuzzy set and systems. 145(1) (2004) 165-181
9. Oh, S.K., Pedrycz, W., Park, B.J.: Relation-based Neurofuzzy Networks with Evolutionary Data Granulation. Mathematical and Computer Modelling. 40(7-8) (2004) 891-921
10. Bishop, C.M.: Neural Networks for Pattern Recognition. Oxford Univ. Press. (1995)
11. Kearns, M., Ron, D.: Algorithmic Stability and Sanity-Check Bounds for Leave-One-Out Cross-Validation. Proc. 10th Ann. Conf. Computational Learning Theory. (1997) 152-162
12. Kemerer, C.F.: An Empirical Validation of Software Cost Estimation Models. Comm. ACM. 30(5) (1987) 416-429
13. Park, H.S. Oh, S.K.: Rule-based Fuzzy-Neural Networks Using the Identification Algo-rithm of the GA Hybrid Scheme. International journal of Control, Automations, and Sys-tems. 1(1) (2003) 101-110
14. Park, H.S., Oh, S.K.: Multi-FNN Identification Based on HCM Clustering and Evolution-ary Fuzzy Granulation. International Journal of Control, Automation and Systems. 1(2) (2003) 194-202

Genetically Dynamic Optimized Self-organizing Fuzzy Polynomial Neural Networks with Information Granulation Based FPNs

Ho-Sung Park[1], Sung-Kwun Oh[2], Witold Pedrycz[3,4], and Hyun-Ki Kim[2]

[1] Department of Electrical Electronic and Information Engineering, Wonkwang University
344-2, Shinyong-Dong, Iksan, Chon-Buk, 570-749, South Korea
[2] Department of Electrical Engineering, The University of Suwon
San 2-2 Wau-ri, Bongdam-eup, Hwaseong-si, Gyeonggi-do, 445-743, South Korea
ohsk@suwon.ac.kr
[3] Department of Electrical and Computer Engineering, University of Alberta
Edmonton, AB T6G 2G6, Canada
[4] Systems Research Institute, Polish Academy of Sciences, Warsaw, Poland

Abstract. In this study, we proposed genetically dynamic optimized self-organizing fuzzy polynomial neural network with information granulation based FPNs (gdSOFPNN), develop a comprehensive design methodology involving mechanisms of genetic optimization. The proposed gdSOFPNN gives rise to a structurally and parametrically optimized network through an optimal parameters design available within FPN (viz. the number of input variables, the order of the polynomial, input variables, the number of membership functions, and the apexes of membership function). Here, with the aid of the information granulation, we determine the initial location (apexes) of membership functions and initial values of polynomial function being used in the premised and consequence part of the fuzzy rules respectively. The performance of the proposed gdSOFPNN is quantified through experimentation that exploits standard data already used in fuzzy modeling.

1 Introduction

Complex plants are difficult to control automatically due to their nonlinear, time varying behavior and imprecise measurement information. Nevertheless human operators can control these complex plants more satisfactorily than conventional automatic control systems based on their some practical experience. When the dimensionality of the model goes up (the number of system's variables increases), so do the difficulties. In the sequel, to build models with good predictive abilities as well as approximation capabilities, there is a need for advanced tools[1].

To help alleviate the problems, one among the first approaches along systematic design of nonlinear relationships between system's inputs and outputs comes under the name of a Group Method of Data Handling (GMDH). Ivakhnenko introduced GMDH in the early 1970's [2]. GMDH-type algorithms have been extensively used since the mid-1970's for prediction and modeling complex nonlinear processes. While providing with a systematic design procedure, GMDH comes with some drawbacks. To alleviate the problems associated with the GMDH, Self-Organizing Neural Networks (SONN, called "SOFPNN") were introduced by Oh and Pedrycz [3], [4,] [5] as a new category of neural networks or neuro-fuzzy networks. Although the SOFPNN has a flexible architecture whose potential can be fully utilized through a systematic

V. Torra et al. (Eds.): MDAI 2005, LNAI 3558, pp. 346–353, 2005.

design, it is difficult to obtain the structurally and parametrically optimized network because of the limited design of the nodes located in each layer of the SOFPNN.

In this study, in considering the above problems coming with the conventional SOFPNN, we introduce a new structure and organization of fuzzy rules as well as a new genetic design approach. The new meaning of fuzzy rules, information granules melt into the fuzzy rules. In a nutshell, each fuzzy rule describes the related information granule. The determination of the optimal values of the parameters available within an individual FPN (viz. the number of input variables, the order of the polynomial, a collection of preferred nodes, the number of MF, and the apexes of membership function) leads to a structurally and parametrically optimized network through the genetic approach.

2 SOFPNN with Fuzzy Polynomial Neuron (FPN) and Its Topology

The FPN consists of two basic functional modules. The first one, labeled by **F**, is a collection of fuzzy sets that form an interface between the input numeric variables and the processing part realized by the neuron. The second module (denoted here by **P**) is about the function – based nonlinear (polynomial) processing. The detailed FPN involving a certain regression polynomial is shown in Table 1. The choice of the number of input variables, the polynomial order, input variables, and the number of MF available within each node itself helps select the best model with respect to the characteristics of the data, model design strategy, nonlinearity and predictive capabilities.

Table 1. Different forms of regression polynomial building a FPN

| Order of the polynomial | No. of inputs | 1 | 2 | 3 |
Order	FPN			
0	Type 1	Constant	Constant	Constant
1	Type 2	Linear	Bilinear	Trilinear
2	Type 3	Quadratic	Biquadratic-1	Triquadratic-1
	Type 4		Biquadratic-2	Triquadratic-2

1: Basic type, 2: Modified type

Proceeding with the SOFPNN architecture essential design decisions have to be made with regard to the number of input variables and the order of the polynomial forming the conclusion part of the rules as well as a collection of the specific subset of input variables.

Where notation **A**: Vector of the selected input variables $(x_1, x_2,..., x_i)$, **B**: Vector of the entire system input variables $(x_1, x_2, ...x_i, x_j ...)$, Type T: $f(A)=f(x_1, x_2,..., x_i)$ - type of a polynomial function standing in the consequence part of the fuzzy rules, Type T*: $f(B)=f(x_1, x_2, ...x_i, x_j ...)$ - type of a polynomial function occurring in the consequence part of the fuzzy rules.

Table 2. Polynomial type according to the number of input variables in the conclusion part of fuzzy rules

Input vector Type of the consequence polynomial	Selected input variables in the premise part	Selected input variables in the consequence part
Type T	A	A
Type T*	A	B

3 The Structural Optimization of gdSOFPNN

3.1 Information Granulation by Means of Hard C-Means Clustering Method

Information granulation is defined informally as linked collections of objects (data points, in particular) drawn together by the criteria of indistinguishability, similarity or functionality [6]. Granulation of information is a procedure to extract meaningful concepts from insignificant numerical data and an inherent activity of human being carried out with intend of better understanding of the problem. We extract information for the real system with the aid of Hard C-means clustering method [7], which deals with the conventional crisp sets. Through HCM, we determine the initial location (apexes) of membership functions and initial values of polynomial function being used in the premise and consequence part of the fuzzy rules respectively.

The fuzzy rules of gdSOFPNN is as followings.

$$R^j : If \ x_1 \ is \ A_{ji} \ and \cdots x_k \ is \ A_{jk} \ then \ y_j - M_j = f_j\{(x_1 - v_{j1}), (x_2 - v_{j2}), \cdots, (x_k - v_{jk})\}$$

Where, A_{jk} mean the fuzzy set, the apex of which is defined as the center point of information granule (cluster). M_j and v_{jk} are the center points of new created input-output variables by information granule.

3.2 Genetic Optimization of gdSOFPNN

Let us briefly recall that GAs is a stochastic search technique based on the principles of evolution, natural selection, and genetic recombination by simulating a process of "survival of the fittest" in a population of potential solutions to the given problem. The main features of genetic algorithms concern individuals viewed as strings, population-based optimization and stochastic search mechanism (selection and crossover). In order to enhance the learning of the gdSOFPNN and augment its performance, we use genetic algorithms to obtain the structural optimization of the network by optimally selecting such parameters as the number of input variables (nodes), the order of polynomial, input variables, and the number of MF within a gdSOFPNN. Here, GAs uses serial method of binary type, roulette-wheel as the selection operator, one-point crossover, and an invert operation in the mutation operator [8].

4 The Algorithm and Design Procedure of gdSOFPNN

The framework of the design procedure of the gdSOFPNN with aid of the Information granulation (IG) comprises the following steps.

[Step 1] *Determine system's input variables.*

[Step 2] *Form training and testing data.*
     The input-output data set $(x_i, y_i)=(x_{1i}, x_{2i}, ..., x_{ni}, y_i)$, $i=1, 2, ..., N$ is divided into two parts, that is, a training and testing dataset.

[Step 3] *Decide initial information for constructing the gdSOFPNN structure.*

[Step 4] *Decide FPN structure using genetic design.*
     We divide the chromosome to be used for genetic optimization into four sub-chromosomes. The 1st sub-chromosome contains the number of input variables, the 2nd sub-chromosome involves the order of the polynomial of the node, the 3rd sub-chromosome contains input variables, and the 4th sub-

chromosome (remaining bits) involves the number of MF coming to the corresponding node (FPN).

[Step 5] *Design of structurally optimized gdSOFPNN.*

In this step, we design the structurally optimized gdSOFPNN by means of FPNs that obtained in [Step 4].

[Step 6] *Identification of membership value using dynamic searching method of GAs.*

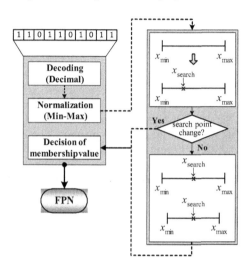

Fig. 1. Identification of membership value using dynamic searching method

[Step 7] *Design of parametrically optimized gdSOFPNN.*

The generation process can be organized as the following sequence of steps

Sub-step 1) We set up initial genetic information necessary for generation of the gdSOFPNN architecture.

Sub-step 2) The nodes (FPNs) are generated through the genetic design.

Sub-step 3) The apexes of MF in the 1st layer are obtained by dynamic searching method of GAs and the apexes of MF in the 2nd layer or higher are obtained by Min-Max method such as the conventional FPNN.

Sub-step 4) We calculate the fitness function.

The fitness function reads as

$$F(\textit{fitness function}) = \frac{1}{E} \tag{4}$$

where E means the objective function with weighting factor($E=\theta \times PI + (1-\theta) \times EPI$).

Sub-step 5) To move on to the next generation, we carry out selection, crossover, and mutation operation using genetic initial information and the fitness values.

Sub-step 6) We choose optimal gdSOFPNN characterized by the best fitness value in the current generation. For the elitist strategy, selected best fitness value used.

Sub-step 7) We generate new populations of the next generation using operators of GAs obtained from *Sub-step 2*. We use the elitist strategy. This sub-step carries out by repeating *sub-step 2-6*.

Sub-step 8) Until the last generation, this sub-step carries out by repeating *sub-step 2-7*.

5 Experimental Studies

We illustrate the performance of the network and elaborate on its development by experimenting with data coming from the NOx emission process of gas turbine power plant [9]. NOx emission process is modeled using the data of gas turbine power plants. Till now, almost NOx emission processes are based on "standard" mathematical model in order to obtain regulation data from control process. However, such models do not develop the relationships between variables of the NOx emission process and parameters of its model in an effective manner. The input variables include AT, CS, LPTS, CDP, and TET. The output variable is NOx. We consider 260 pairs of the original input-output data. 130 out of 260 pairs of input-output data are used as learning set; the remaining part serves as a testing set. To come up with a quantitative evaluation of network, we use the standard MSE performance index.

Table 3. Computational aspects of the genetic optimization of DS_gSOFPNN

	Parameters	1st layer	2nd layer	3rd layer
GA	Maximum generation		100	
	Total population size		300×No. of 1st layer node	
	Crossover rate		0.65	
	Mutation rate		0.1	
	String length		90	
gdSO FPNN	Maximal no.(Max) of inputs to be selected	$1 \le l \le$ Max (2~3)	$1 \le l \le$ Max (2~3)	$1 \le l \le$ Max (2~3)
	Polynomial type (Type T) of the consequent part of fuzzy rules	$1 \le T^* \le 4$	$1 \le T \le 4$	$1 \le T \le 4$
	Membership Function (MF) type	Triangular Gaussian	Triangular Gaussian	Triangular Gaussian
	No. of MFs per input	2 or 3	2 or 3	2 or 3

l, T, Max: integers

Table 4 shows the performance index of the proposed gdSOFPNN.

Table 4. Performance index of DS_gSOFPNN for the Nox process data

Model	Layer M.F Max	Triangular MF		Gaussian MF		Triangular MF*		Gaussian MF*	
		PI	EPI	PI	EPI	PI	EPI	PI	EPI
gdSOFPN N	2	0.016	0.068	0.012	0.180	0.003	0.017	0.002	0.024
	3	0.014	0.036	0.004	0.134	0.002	0.008	0.001	0.023

Fig. 2 illustrates the detailed optimal topologies of the gdSOFPNN for 3 layers (PI=0.002, EPI=0.008).

Fig. 3 shows the membership functions points of each node of 1st layer according to the partition of fuzzy input spaces by a Min-Max method, the HCM clustering method, and GAs.

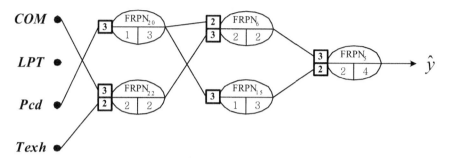

Fig. 2. gdSOFPNN architecture

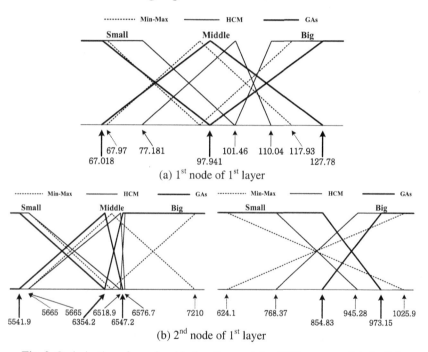

Fig. 3. Optimization of membership functions points of NOx process data by GA

Fig. 4 illustrates the different optimization process between IG_gSOFPNN and the proposed gdSOFPNN by visualizing the values of the performance index obtained in successive generations of GA when using Type T*.

6 Concluding Remarks

In this study, we introduced and investigated a new architecture and comprehensive design methodology of genetically dynamic optimized Self-Organizing Fuzzy Polynomial Neural Networks with Information Granulation based FPNs (gdSOFPNN),

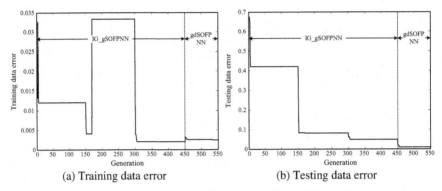

(a) Training data error   (b) Testing data error

Fig. 4. The optimization process quantified by the values of the performance index

Table 5. Comparative analysis of the performance of the network; considered are models reported in the literature

Model				PI_s	EPI_s
Regression model				17.68	19.23
FNN model[10]	GA	Simplified		7.045	11.264
		Linear		4.038	6.028
	Hybrid	Simplified		6.205	8.868
	(GA+Complex)	Linear		3.830	5.397
Multi-FNNs[11]		Simplified		2.806	5.164
Multi-FNNs[12]		Linear		0.720	2.025
gHFPNN[13]	Max=2 (Type T*)	Triangular	3rd layer	0.008	0.082
			5th layer	0.008	0.081
		Gaussian-like	3rd layer	0.016	0.132
			5th layer	0.016	0.116
IG_gSOFPNN[14]	Max=2 (Type T*)	Triangular	3rd layer	0.002	0.045
		Gaussian-like		0.001	0.027
Proposed gdSOFPNN	Max=2 (Type T*)	Triangular		0.003	0.017
		Gaussian-like	3rd layer	0.002	0.024
	Max=3 (Type T*)	Triangular		0.002	0.008
		Gaussian-like		0.001	0.023

and discussed their topologies. gdSOFPNN is constructed with the aid of the algorithmic framework of information granulation. The design methodology comes as a structural and parametrical optimization being viewed as two fundamental phases of the design process. In the design of gdSOFPNN, the characteristics inherent to entire experimental data being used in the construction of the IG_gSOFPNN architecture is reflected to fuzzy rules available within a FPN. Therefore Information granulation based on HCM(Hard C-Means) clustering method was adopted. With the aid of the information granulation, we determine the initial location (apexes) of membership functions and initial values of polynomial function being used in the premised and consequence part of the fuzzy rules respectively.

Acknowledgements

This work was supported by Korea Research Foundation Grant (KRF-2004-002-D00257).

References

1. Nie, J.H., Lee, T.H.: Rule-based modeling: Fast construction and optimal manipulation. IEEE Trans. Syst., Man, Cybern. 26 (1996) 728-738
2. Ivakhnenko, A.G..: Polynomial theory of complex systems. IEEE Trans. on Systems, Man and Cybernetics. SMC-1 (1971) 364-378
3. Oh, S.K., Pedrycz, W..: The design of self-organizing Polynomial Neural Networks. Information Science. 141 (2002) 237-258
4. Oh, S.K., Pedrycz, W., Park, B.J.: Polynomial Neural Networks Architecture: Analysis and Design. Computers and Electrical Engineering. 29 (2003) 703-725
5. Oh, S.K., Pedrycz, W.: Fuzzy Polynomial Neuron-Based Self-Organizing Neural Networks. Int. J. of General Systems. 32 (2003) 237-250
6. Zadeh, L.A.: Toward a theory of fuzzy information granulation and its centrality in human reasoning and fuzzy logic. Fuzzy sets and Systems. 90 (1997) 111-117
7. Bezdek, J.C.: Pattern Recognition with Fuzzy Objective Function Algorithms. New York. Plenum (1981)
8. 8 Jong, D.K.A.: Are Genetic Algorithms Function Optimizers?. Parallel Problem Solving from Nature 2, Manner, R. and Manderick, B. eds., North-Holland, Amsterdam (1992)
9. Vachtsevanos, G., Ramani, V., Hwang, T.W.: Prediction of gas turbine NOx emissions using polynomial neural network. Technical Report, Georgia Institute of Technology. Atlanta. (1995)
10. Oh, S.K., Pedrycz, W., and Park, H.S.: Hybrid identification in fuzzy-neural networks. Fuzzy Sets and Systems. 138 (2003) 399-426
11. Oh, S.K., Pedrycz, W., Park, H.S.: Multi-FNN identification by means of HCM clustering and genetic algorithms. Fuzzy Sets and Systems. (2002) (submitted)
12. Oh, S.K., Pedrycz, W., Park, H.S.: Multi-FNN identification based on HCM clustering and evolutionary fuzzy granulation. Simulation Modelling Practice and Theory. 11 (2003) 627-642
13. Oh, S.K., Pedrycz, W., Park, H.S.: Multi-layer Hybrid Fuzzy Polynomial Neural Networks: A Design in the Framework of Computational Intelligence. Neurocomputing. 64 (2004) 397-431
14. Park, H.S., Oh, S.K., Pedrycz, W.: Genetically optimized Self-Organizing Fuzzy Polynomial Neural Networks with the aid of Information Granulation. International Symposium on Neural Networks. (2004) (accepted)
15. Park, B.J., Lee, D.Y., Oh, S.K.: Rule-based Fuzzy Polynomial Neural Networks in Modeling Software Process Data. Int. J. of Control, Automations, and Systems. 1(3) (2003) 321-331
16. Park, H.S., Park, B.J., Kim, H.K., Oh, S,K,: Self-Organizing Polynomial Neural Networks Based on Genetically Optimized Multi-Layer Perceptron Architecture. International journal of Control, Automations, and Systems. 2(4) (2004) 423-434

NMF-Based Approach to Font Classification of Printed English Alphabets for Document Image Understanding

Chang Woo Lee[1] and Keechul Jung[2]

[1] Dept. of Computer Information Science, Kunsan National University
Kunsan, Jeollabuk-do, 573-701, S. Korea
leecw@kunsan.ac.kr
[2] School of Media, College of Information Science, Soongsil University
156-743, Seoul, S. Korea
kcjung@ssu.ac.kr

Abstract. This paper proposes an approach to font classification for document image understanding using non-negative matrix factorization (NMF). The basic idea of the proposed method is based on that the characteristics of each font are derived from parts of the individual characters in each font rather than holistic textures. Spatial localities, parts composing of font images, are automatically extracted using NMF. These parts are used as features representing each font. In the experimental results, the distribution of features and the appropriateness of use of the characteristics specifying each font are investigated. Add to that, the proposed method is compared with the method based on principal component analysis (PCA), in which various distance metrics are tested in the feature space. It expects that the proposed method will increase the performance of optical character recognition (OCR) systems or document indexing and retrieval systems if such systems adopt the proposed font classifier as a preprocessor.

1 Introduction

Recently, most documents are electronically produced and their paleography is digitalized by imaging, resulting in a tremendous number of electronic documents in the shape of images. Therefore, to process these document images, many methods of document structure analysis and recognition have already been proposed, including font classification [1]. In most published OCR techniques, there is still much room for improvement as regards their recognition accuracy and processing time when font classification is involved. Although font classification is essential in document image analysis and recognition, for example, it can reduce the burden of recognizing characters based on various fonts, essentially allowing single-font character recognition, font classification is only included in a few OCR techniques. In the literature, there have been many reports on font classification, including Khoubyari and Hull [2], Shi and Pavlidis [3], Zhu et al. [4], Zramdini and Ingold [5].

To identify the predominant font and frequent function words, Khoubyari and Hull proposed an algorithm whereby clusters of word images are generated from an input document and matched to a database of function words derived in advance from document images [2]. Meanwhile, Shi and Pavlidis combined font recognition results and contextual information to enhance the accuracy of text recognition [3]. In this

V. Torra et al. (Eds.): MDAI 2005, LNAI 3558, pp. 354–364, 2005.

case, two sources, namely the global page properties, such as a histogram of the word length and stroke slopes, and the graph matching result of recognized short words are extracted as the font information. Plus, the focus is not on the typeface, such as bold, italic, and capital types, but rather on font families, including *seriffed* versus *sans-serif* fonts and *upright* versus *slanted* fonts. In the method used by Zramdini and Ingold [5], a statistical approach based on global typographical features is used to identify the typeface, weight, slope, and size of the text from an image block without any knowledge of the content of that text. However, the classification of a font requires the careful selection of many features and a proper length for the text line. In contrast, Zhu *et al.* presented a texture-analysis-based approach for font recognition without involving a detailed local feature analysis [4]. In this case, without any knowledge of the characters in the document, font classification is performed on the block-level, rather than character- or word-level, yet the cost of forming a uniform block of text is expensive and a different font included in a block is hardly classified.

Recently, a new approach for obtaining a linear representation of data has been proposed which is able to learn part-based representations of objects [6]. This method is called non-negative matrix factorization (NMF) that was used in the work of Lee and Seung to find parts of objects in an unsupervised way. In the view of visual representation of given data, NMF differs from other methods such as principal component analysis (PCA), vector quantization (VQ), by its use of non-negativity constraints. These methods can be compared in the matrix factorization framework. The most significant difference of NMF from other methods is the usage of non-negativity constraint, in that it is based on the idea that negative numbers are against both intuition that parts form a whole and physically meaningless in many data-processing tasks. On other hand, PCA and VQ use a weak orthogonality constraint and a hard winner take-all constraint, respectively [6]. Therefore, PCA allows negative elements in the factorized matrix, lacking intuitive meaning, and only one prototype is needed to represent a given data in VQ.

The current paper proposes a font classification method using the NMF technique that automatically extracts local characteristics from a set of font images. The proposed method consists of two phases: training and testing phases. The character segmentation step in a training phase produces a set of training samples (character images) from the document images containing English alphabets, which are manually generated, printed, and scanned font by font. Feature vectors of the character images are automatically extracted using NMF in the feature extraction step. Using these feature vectors, prototype templates representing each font are constructed using a clustering algorithm in the prototype construction step. In a testing phase, a new character separated from a document image is projected into the NMF-projected space for automatic feature extraction, compared with the prototype templates that consist of training samples used in training phase [7-9]. The character image is finally classified as one of font types. The proposed method is a new approach for font classification using local features and is appropriate for applying to OCR systems because the font classification is experimented on a character-level.

The remainder of this paper is organized as follows: section 2 explains an overview of the proposed font classification method using NMF with clustering, and the experimental results are described in section 3, while section 4 makes some final conclusions.

2 The Proposed Method for Classifying Fonts

As shown in Fig. 1, the font classification can reduce the burden of recognizing mul-tifont characters and has a potential for improvement of the accuracy of character recognition because, if fonts are known in advance, more specific characteristics of characters than general characteristics can be extracted. In this section, first, a method to segment characters from document images and a feature extraction scheme using NMF are presented. Second, a method of prototype template generation from a set of training samples is presented and, last, the proposed font classification method that a new feature vector from a font image is compared with the templates and classified is also presented.

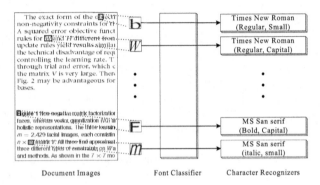

Document Images   Font Classifier   Character Recognizers

Fig. 1. Effects of font classification

2.1 Feature Extraction Using Non-negative Matrix Factorization

The NMF algorithm, devised by Lee and Seung [6], decomposes a given matrix into a basis set and encodings, while satisfying the non-negativity constraints. Given an $n \times m$ original matrix V, in which each column is an n-dimensional non-negative vector and there are m such vectors, NMF decomposes V into W and H in order to approxi-mate the original matrix as in Eq. (1). In those matrices, $n \times r$ is the dimension of W and $r \times m$ is the dimension of H. Each column of W is a basis and each column of H is a encoding of the corresponding column of V.

$$V_{i\mu} \approx (WH)_{i\mu} = \sum_{a=1}^{r} W_{ia} H_{a\mu} \,, \tag{1}$$

where the rank r of the factorization is generally chosen by $(n+m)r < nm$.

The NMF algorithm starts from a random initialization of W and H, and iteratively updates them until they converge. For the convergence of this algorithm, the objec-tive function must be defined. The objective function of the NMF algorithm is then related to the likelihood of generating the original vectors in V from the basis W and encodings H as shown in Eq. (2) that V is drawn from a Poisson distribution with the mean WH.

$$F = \sum_{i=1}^{n} \sum_{\mu=1}^{m} V_{i\mu} \log(WH)_{i\mu} - (WH)_{i\mu} \,. \tag{2}$$

The NMF algorithm is an iterative algorithm with multiplicative update rules that can be regarded as a special variant of gradient-descent algorithms (Eq. (3)) [10].

$$H_{a\mu} \leftarrow H_{a\mu} \frac{(W^T V)_{a\mu}}{(W^T W H)_{a\mu}}, \text{ and } W_{ia} \leftarrow W_{ia} \frac{(V H^T)_{ia}}{(W H H^T)_{ia}}, W_{ia} \leftarrow W_{ia} \frac{W_{ia}}{\sum_j W_{ja}}. \quad (3)$$

Since the proposed method is based on a character-level test, characters from document images are segmented. And then, as a preprocessing, it is needed very large or small character images to be scaled to a standard size because different resolution levels produce different sizes of character images, even though they are in the same typeface and font size.

To obtain test samples from the document images containing machine-printed characters, frequently used document image processing techniques were incorporated to separate a particular character from a document image. First, to segment the text lines from a document image a horizontal projection profile was used to detect the valleys between text lines. Next, a vertical projection profile for each text line was used to separate each character. Thereafter, the boundaries of all the components were adjusted from the boundaries toward the inside, with the size of each component larger than a predefined box size to remove any noise factors. Finally, the size of each component was normalized to 28 × 28, the same size as the training samples.

During the experiments, it was generally assumed that the characters were well separated from each other, based on the results of previous work, including Bae *at el.* [11], Bansal and Sinha [12]. As such, this issue and the skew of a document image are not dealt with in the current paper.

Fig. 2 shows the feature extraction scheme in the proposed method. Since a column vector of the factorized encodings, H, has a one-to-one correspondence to each training sample in the training phase, all the column vectors of the factorized encoding, H, are used as feature vectors composing the prototype template encodings of each font. In the testing phase, a character image obtained from a document image is projected into the NMF-projected space using the same iteration rules as Eq. (3), yet taking the trained matrix W as a constant reference. It results in a new feature vector corresponding to the input font image. In other words, an n-dimensional vector in an image space is projected into one point in the r-dimensional NMF-projected space ($r < \min(n, m)$). In addition, since the elements of the feature vectors are non-negative (i.e. they allow only additive, not subtractive, combinations with the basis), they make it possible to lead the part-based object representation.

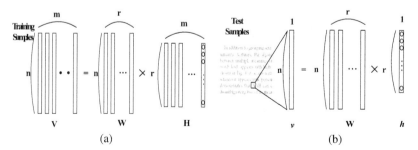

Fig. 2. Feature extraction scheme of proposed font classification method; (a) tranining phase, (b) testing phase

2.2 Prototype Construction Using Hierarchical Clustering Algorithm

There is a set $D = \{\mathbf{x}_1, \ldots, \mathbf{x}_m\}$ of m encodings composed of exactly p disjoint subsets $D_1, \ldots, D_p$ that we want to partition each of which into c clusters. There are many times when clusters have subclusters, these subclusters also have subsubclusters, and so on. Therefore, in this paper, we consider a sequence of partitions of the l samples into c clusters such as $D_1 = \{D_{11}, \ldots, D_{1c}\}$. For a D_i, the first of these is a partition into l clusters, each cluster containing exactly one sample. The next is a partition into $l - 1$ clusters, the next a partition into $l - 2$, and so on until the lth, in which all the samples form one cluster. We shall say that we are at level k in the sequence when $c = l - k + 1$. The level k that we want to stop merging is when clusters properly are grouped.

Hierarchical clustering procedures are among the best known of unsupervised methods [13]. The procedures themselves can be divided according to two distinct approaches: agglomerative (bottom-up or clumping procedure) and divisive (top-down or splitting procedure). For simplicity and effectiveness of the clustering result to our problem, we use agglomerative hierarchical clustering algorithm as follows.

Agglomerative Hierarchical Clustering Algorithm

1	**initialize** T, $\hat{c} \leftarrow m$, $D_i \leftarrow \{\mathbf{x}_i\}$, $i = 1, \ldots, m$
2	**do** $\hat{c} \leftarrow \hat{c}$ - 1
3	find nearest clusters, say, D_i and D_j
4	merge D_i and D_j
5	**until** $d_{\min}(D_i, D_j) > T$
6	**return** $\hat{c}$ clusters

In the algorithm m, $\hat{c}$, and T are the number of data to be clustered, the number of centroids, and the threshold value, respectively. To find the nearest clusters between two clusters D_i and D_j in line 4 of the algorithm, the EMD is chosen as in Eq. (4), in which $\mathbf{m}_i$ and $\mathbf{m}_j$ represents mean vectors of two clusters.

$$d_{\min}(D_i, D_j) = EMD(\mathbf{m}_i, \mathbf{m}_j). \tag{4}$$

The computation of the EMD is based on a solution to the old *Transportation problem*, and can be formulated as the following linear programming problem [8], [9]: Given two signatures that are compact representation of : $\mathbf{p} = \{(p_1, w_{p_1}), \ldots, (p_m, w_{p_m})\}$ and $\mathbf{q} = \{(q_1, w_{q_1}), \ldots, (q_m, w_{q_n})\}$ where p_i and q_j are the cluster centers and the encoding of a test image in our case, respectively, and w_{p_i}, w_{q_j} are the corresponding weights of the points, we now want to seek a set of f_{ij} that minimize overall cost and is the amount of work of p_i matched to q_j, as follows:

$$EMD(\mathrm{p,q}) = \min \frac{\sum_{i=1}^{m} \sum_{j=1}^{n} d_{ij} f_{ij}}{\sum_{i=1}^{m} \sum_{j=1}^{n} f_{ij}}, \tag{5}$$

subject to the following constraints:

$$f_{ij} \geq 0,\ p_i \geq 0,\ q_j \geq 0,\ \ 1 \leq i \leq m, 1 \leq j \leq n \tag{6}$$

$$\sum_{j=1} f_{ij} \leq w_{p_i},\quad 1 \leq j \leq n \tag{7}$$

$$\sum_{i=1} f_{ij} \leq w_{q_j},\quad 1 \leq i \leq m \tag{8}$$

$$\sum_{i=1}\sum_{j=1} f_{ij} = \min(\sum_{i=1} w_{p_i} \cdot \sum_{j=1} w_{q_j}),\ 1 \leq i \leq m, 1 \leq j \leq n \tag{9}$$

$$\sum_{i-1} w_{p_i} \leq \sum_{j=1} w_{q_j} \tag{10}$$

The cost d_{ij} that is the *ground distance* between the element p_i and element q_j is defined as the *Tanimoto distance* between two basis vectors. Constraint (6) allows only for positive amounts of earth to be moved. Constraints (7) and (8) limit the capacity of earth a point can contribute to the weight of the point. Constraint (9) forces at least one of the signatures to use all of its capacity, otherwise a trivial solution is not to move any earth at all. In addition to those constraints, a feasibility condition as Eq. (10) is that the total amount of demand does not exceed the total supply.

With EMD in both the clustering and classification of encodings, *ground distance*, a unit of work, should be defined. In the current paper, the correlations between the basis images are considered. As shown in Fig. 3, it can be seen that learned basis images are able to present non-negligible correlations and other higher order effects. This fact suggests the use of a distance between projected vectors that takes into account this characteristic. Therefore, both in the prototype construction step and classification step, the cost used to weight the transition of one basis vector ($\mathbf{b_i}$) to another ($\mathbf{b_j}$) is defined as

$$d_{ij} = \begin{cases} dist_{Tanimoto}(\mathbf{b_i},\mathbf{b_j}) & if\ i \neq j \\ 1 & otherwise \end{cases}, \tag{11}$$

where $dist_{Tanimoto}(\mathbf{b_i},\mathbf{b_j})=(n_1+n_2-2n_{12})/(n_1+n_2-n_{12})$, and n_1 and n_2 are the number of elements in $\mathbf{b_i}$ and $\mathbf{b_j}$, respectively, and n_{12} is the number that is in both sets. The elements in our case mean the elements having non-zero values in basis images. If we consider the basis in 2-dimensional image space as shown in Fig. 3, two basis images that are learned same spatial position are more correlated. Since, in NMF, it does not ensure that each basis image is orthogonal, furthermore, there does not exist any orders between them, we used *Tanimoto* distance as *ground distance* for EMD instead of *Cosine* distance or *Euclidean* distance. In our case using very well-aligned and size-normalized font images, this metric is suitable and gives some validity to our method by many experiments.

2.3   Font Classification

The basic idea of the proposed method is based on that the characteristics of each font are derived from parts of the individual characters in each font rather than holistic textures. Since NMF does not allow negative entries in and these non-negativity constraints are compatible with the intuitive notion of combining parts to form a whole, basis images provide a more sparse and local representation than the global one provided by a PCA or VQ [6]. Moreover, the NMF basis and encodings contain a large fraction of vanishing coefficients, so both the basis images and image encodings are sparse. In other words, any given character image will not use all the available parts (the basis), thereby resulting in a sparsely distributed image encoding.

The EMD has been used in problems where models were non-negative feature distributions, like color histograms [9] and the NMF-projected space [7], and we use the EMD to measure the similarity between the prototype templates and an encoding of a test image. As shown in Fig. 1, the proposed font classifier is designed such a way that training samples are used to produce the template encodings with clustering, which are then compared with a test image obtained from a document image for classification. If the following Eq. (12) is satisfied, a test image is classified as a particular font type, F_i, in which c is one of the prototype templates of i font type. In Eq. (12), T_{ic} and h represent the cth prototype template of the ith font type and the encoding of a test image. d and l_i represent the number of font types and the number of prototype templates for the ith font type, respectively.

$$F_i = \arg\min_c EMD(T_{ic}, h), \qquad i = 1, \ldots, d \quad c = 1, \ldots, l_i \tag{12}$$

3   Experimental Results

To evaluate our proposed method, six frequently used English typefaces (Courier New (CN), Comic Sans MS (CS), Impact (IM), MS Gothic (MG), Microsoft Sans Serif (MS), and Times New Roman (TR)) combined with four styles (regular, bold, italic, and bold italic) were trained and tested. This means that a test image was classified as one of 48 font types (6 typefaces × 4 styles × 2 (capital and small letter)). The training samples were obtained from both noise-free font images and document images that were scanned as binary images at a resolution of 100, 200, and 300 DPI, respectively, where the number of training images was 4992 character images and the font size was 14. All the training images were normalized at 28 × 28 pixels, then, factorized into the basis and encodings. The prototype encodings were generated from all the encodings of training samples by a clustering algorithm and were used to represent each font type in the testing phase.

The test data were obtained from 144 document images (48 classes × 3 different resolution levels) composed of scanned versions of machine printed documents. The sizes of the document images ranged from 651 × 888 to 655 × 920 at a resolution of 100 DPI, from 1311 × 1737 to 1287 × 1904 at a resolution of 200 DPI, and from 1960 × 2642 to 1960 × 2809 at a resolution of 300 DPI.

The NMF basis and encodings contain a large fraction of vanishing coefficients, so both the basis images and image encodings are sparse. Consequently, it is easily known from Fig. 3 the NMF basis learning of the local parts of font images represents the characteristics of each font. Fig. 3 shows the basis sets used in the experiments according to the number of ranks. As the number of basis images (ranks) increased, both the basis images and image encodings became sparse. Conversely, as the number of ranks decreased, a basis image covered a larger part of the local characteristics of each typeface so that the basis and encodings became less sparse. As such, there is a problem in determining the proper number of ranks, which is partially investigated in the current paper.

For training the basis we processed the task as off-line on PCA and NMF. In the experiments using non-optimized code on Pentium IV 1.7GHz, a test pattern was classified in 0.21, 0.75, 1.42, and 2.66sec for 30, 50, 70, and 100 ranks, respectively, when the EMD distance metric was used, whereas 0.05, 0.07, 0.11, and 0.15sec, for 30, 50, 70, and 100 ranks, respectively, when the L2 distance metric was used. Based on the sizes of the characters in all the document images that was used in our experiments, the size of each character image was determined empirically as $n = 784$ (28×28) during the experiments.

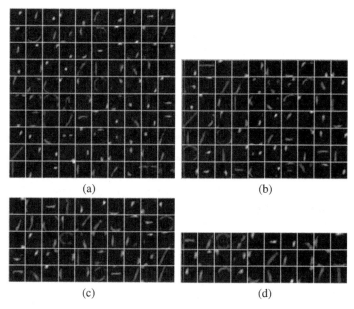

(a)   (b)

(c)   (d)

Fig. 3. Basis sets according to number of ranks; (a) 100 ranks, (b) 70 ranks, (c) 50 ranks, (d) 30 ranks

During clustering each class using hierarchical clustering algorithm, the threshold value T is set to 2.2, 2.5, 2.8, and 3.2 for 30, 50, 70, and 100 rank encodings, respectively. The values are empirically determined after considering trade-offs between the number of prototypes per class and computation speed and classification accuracies. From the clustering results as shown in Table 1 which the number of centroids per class is different, a class having relatively small number of centroids is gathered well in the feature space while the other having relatively large number of centroids is not (dispersed). If we use k-means-like clustering algorithm that the number of clusters is fixed, it is hard to capture this characteristic. Table 2 shows the recognition rates for the 6 different typefaces with 4 styles and two letter types. When the experiments were performed using 100 ranks, the average classification rate was 98.06 %. The lowest classification rate appeared with the regular style MS typeface. As shown in Table 2, it can be seen that most of the confusions are arisen between regular and bold types and this result is caused from the character segmentation step in addition to noise that is added while scanning.

Table 1. The number of clusters (r = 30/50/70/100, columns of W)

	Regular		Bold		Italic		Bold Italic	
	Capital	Small	Capital	Small	Capital	Small	Capital	Small
CN	28/29/25/25	31/28/28/24	30/30/27/23	26/26/24/23	33/31/28/28	32/31/26/28	32/37/33/26	33/32/32/28
CS	43/37/40/37	45/43/36/32	31/32/33/24	33/33/31/23	40/44/36/33	43/43/44/42	44/45/41/40	37/41/32/41
IM	25/21/23/16	23/22/16/16	16/16/16/16	16/16/16/16	16/16/16/16	16/17/16/16	16/19/19/16	19/16/16/16
MG	22/24/23/22	29/32/31/31	30/28/23/22	29/32/33/29	28/24/23/22	32/30/33/32	30/28/25/22	38/36/34/30
MS	22/21/21/19	26/26/26/23	30/24/23/25	27/32/33/28	26/24/25/22	29/28/27/28	27/23/24/21	30/30/28/26
TR	40/38/29/31	36/34/31/28	34/38/31/26	41/43/41/34	41/44/38/33	41/40/38/34	44/43/43/33	49/41/49/44

Table 2. Classification rates using EMD (%, r = 100)

	Regular		Bold		Italic		Bold Italic		Avg.
	Capital	Small	Capital	Small	Capital	Small	Capital	Small	
CN	99.9	98.6	99.5	98.4	100	100	99.8	100	99.53
CS	97	97.4	97.3	97.3	97.8	98.9	98.7	98.5	97.86
IM	96.4	96.2	95.6	95.6	97.0	97.4	98.0	98.8	96.88
MG	96.1	97	96.6	97.3	97.8	98.0	98.7	98.8	97.54
MS	95.2	95.4	96.7	97.8	96.8	97.2	97.5	97.5	96.76
TR	99.3	99.9	99.3	100	99.7	100	100	100	99.78
Avg.	97.32	97.42	97.5	97.73	98.18	98.58	98.78	98.93	98.06

For the evaluation of the proposed method, we compared our font classification method with other methods in the literature. In this paper, we evaluated our method through the partial comparison with other methods (Zhu et al.'s method[4] and Zramdini and Ingold's method [15]) using the results shown in table 2, in which the experiment was performed using 100 ranks with NMF+EMD. The comparison result is shown in Fig. 4, in which 'N/A' stands for 'Not Available' meaning we have no matching font with other methods.

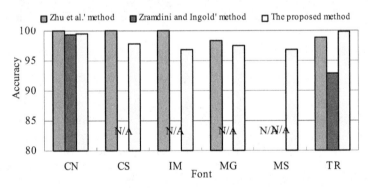

Fig. 4. Comparison results with other methods (%)

As we compared with Zramdini and Ingold's method based on the global typographical features, the proposed method outperformed their method as 0.17% and 6.91% in the accuracy comparison of CN and TR fonts. On the other hand, the accuracy of Zhu et al.'s method was better than our method in most fonts except for TR font. Since the font classification in Zhu et al.'s method is performed on the block-level without any knowledge of the characters in the document, the cost of forming a uniform block of text is expensive and a different font included in a block is hardly classified. Accordingly, it is expected that the accuracy of the proposed method would be improved when word-level test is performed.

The following Fig. 5 shows the average recognition rates of the proposed font classification method, in which the experiments with PCA+L2, PCA+EMD, NMF+L2, and NMF+EMD were performed. With EMD, the cost matrix used to weight the transition of one basis vector to another is defined as $dist_{tanimoto}$ shown in Eq. (11). In case of the NMF, since the basis images are more correlated when the number of ranks is small, in the proposed method that uses EMD as the distance metric, the classification accuracy is low when the lower dimensional feature vectors are used. As shown in Fig. 5, EMD metric is more suitable to use in conjunction with NMF than L2, because NMF+EMD obtains the better recognition rates than NMF+L2 and is also better than PCA+L2.

Although it can be possible to use all the trained encodings as the prototype templates in this case, both the burden of database maintenance and the computation cost is high because the EMD requires a minimization process to obtain the optimal distance between two positive vectors, meaning that EMD is much slower than other distance metrics. Consequently, the experiments reveal that EMD is a more suitable distance metric than L2 in the feature spaces of both NMF and PCA.

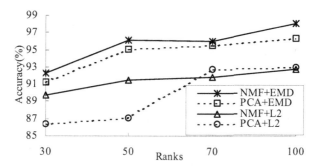

Fig. 5. Results of font classification using document images

4 Conclusions

The current paper presented a new approach for multifont classification using the NMF technique that is able to learn a part-based representation of an image. The proposed font classification method determined the characteristics of a particular font based on the spatially local parts of that font and automatically extracted features corresponding to the input font images. Using a clustering algorithm, first, we strived to maintain the proper size of the prototype templates. These templates, then, were compared with the feature vector of a font image that was segmented from document images. Additionally, it was confirmed EMD is more suitable distance metric in the NMF feature space while testing the proposed method. Experiments were performed at character-level, which were more appropriate for the preprocessing of character recognition systems. The proposed method is expected to improve the performance of OCR systems, document indexing and retrieval systems, when such systems use a font classifier as a preprocessor.

Acknowledgement

This paper was supported by research funds of Kunsan National University.

References

1. Nagy G., "Twenty Years of Document Image Analysis in PAMI," *IEEE Trans. Pattern Analysis and Machine Intelligence* 22, 1 (2000) 38-62.
2. Khoubyari S. and Hull J. J., "Font and function word identification in document recognition," *Computer Vision and Image Understanding* 63, 1 (1996) 66-74.
3. Shi H. and Pavlidis T., "Font Recognition and Contextual Processing for More Accurate Text Recognition," *Proc. Int. Conf. Document Analysis and Recognition* '97 (1997) 39-44.
4. Zhu Y., Tan T. and Wang Y., "Font Recognition Based on Global Texture Analysis," *IEEE Trans. Pattern Analysis and Machine Intelligence* 23, 10 (2001) 1192-1200.
5. Zramdini A. and Ingold R., "Optical Font Recognition Using Typographical Features," *IEEE Trans. Pattern Analysis and Machine Intelligence* 20, 8 (1998) 877-882.
6. Lee D. D. and Seung H. S., "Learning the Parts of Objects by Non-Negative Matrix Factorization," *Nature* 401 (1999) 788-791.
7. Guillamet D. and Vitrià J., "Evaluation of Distance Metrics for Recognition Based on Non-Negative Matrix Factorization," *Pattern Recognition Letters* 24 (2003) 1599-1605.
8. Rubner Y., Puzicha J., Tomasi C., and Buhmann J. M., "Empirical evaluation of dissimilarity measures for color and texture," *Computer Vision and Image Understanding* 84, 1 (2001) 25-43.
9. Rubner Y., Tomasi C., and Guibas L. J.. The earth mover's distance as a metric for image retrieval. *International Journal of Computer Vision* 40, 2 (2000) 99-121.
10. Lee D. D. and Seung H. S., "Algorithms for Non-negative Matrix Factorization," *In Advances in NIPS* 13 (2001) 556-562.
11. Bae J. H., K. Jung, Kim J. W. and Kim H. J., "Segmentation of Touching Characters Using an MLP," *Pattern Recognition Letters* 19, 8 (1998) 701-709.
12. Bansal V. and Sinha R. M. K., "Segmentation of touching and fused Devanagari characters," *Pattern Recognition* 35, 4 (2002) 875-893.
13. Duda R. O., Hart P. E. and Stork D. G., *Pattern Classification*, A Wiley-Interscience, 2000.

Edge-Based Spatial Descriptor
Using Color Vector Angle for Effective Image Retrieval

N.W. Kim, T.Y. Kim, and Jong Soo Choi

Department of Image Engineering, Graduate School of Advanced Imaging Science
Multimedia, and Film, Chung-Ang University
{mysope,kimty,jschoi}@imagelab.cau.ac.kr

Abstract. In this paper we propose a novel approach for image retrieval based on edge structural features using edge correlogram and color coherence vector. After color vector angle is applied in the pre-processing stage, an image is divided into two image parts (high frequency image and low frequency image). In a low frequency image, the global color distribution of smooth pixels is extracted by color coherence vector, and thereby spatial information is incorporated into the proposed color descriptor. Meanwhile, in a high frequency image, the distribution of the gray pairs at an edge is extracted by edge correlogram. Since the proposed algorithm includes the spatial and edge information between colors, it can robustly reduce the effect of the significant change in appearance and shape of objects. The proposed method provides a simple and flexible description for the image with complex scene in terms of structural features from the image contents. Experimental evidence shows that our algorithm outperforms the recent histogram refinement methods for image indexing and retrieval. To index the multi-dimensional feature vectors, we use R*-tree structure.

1 Introduction

The recent explosion in internet usage and the growing availability of multimedia resources on the World-Wide Web have created a demand for effective and flexible techniques for automatic image retrieval and video browsing [1-4]. Since multimedia data have the large capacity, atypical features, and complex structure in contrast to textual data, it is difficult to efficiently manage and retrieve these enormous data by conventional text-based retrieval. Therefore, many researchers have widely studied for implementation of effective content-based image retrieval system [1, 2].

The representative content-based image retrieval method is a color histogram-based algorithm to identify a color image by Swain and Ballad [5]. In this case, three-dimensional histograms are generated for the input and model images in the database. Then an attempt is made to match two images utilizing the histogram intersection method. This method is very simple to implement and produces a reasonable performance. However, the main disadvantage of Swain's color histogram method is that it is not robust to significant appearance changes because it does not include any spatial information. Recently, several schemes including spatial information have been proposed. Huang [6, 7] proposes a color correlogram method, which takes account of the local spatial correlation between colors as well as the global distribution of this spatial correlation. But its computation cost would seem to be a problem for practical applications. Pass et al. [8] suggests partitioning histogram bins based on the spatial

V. Torra et al. (Eds.): MDAI 2005, LNAI 3558, pp. 365–375, 2005.

coherence of the pixels, where a pixel is coherent if it is part of a sizable similar-colored region or incoherent otherwise. A color coherence vector (CCV) is used to represent the pixel classification for each color in an image. However, since an image partition approach highly depends on the pixel positions, most of these approaches are unable to tolerate significant appearance changes.

To cope with significant appearance changes and heavy computation cost, therefore, we use the color and the shape features from edge-processed image together. A pixel classification based on color vector angle [9] is performed first to classify the pixels as either smooth or edge one. Color vector angle is usable, because it is insensitive to variations in intensity, yet sensitive to differences in hue and saturation. For the edge pixels, the distribution of the gray pairs at an edge is represented by edge correlogram. For the smooth pixels, the color distribution is represented by color coherence vector. From this process, we can obtain a set of feature description for whole image and implement the feature-based image retrieval from the color and edge information.

The remainder of the paper is organized as follows. In section 2, we divide an image using color vector angle and propose the feature extraction method using CCV and edge correlogram for the divided images each. And, the experimental results and conclusions follow in Section 3 and 4, respectively.

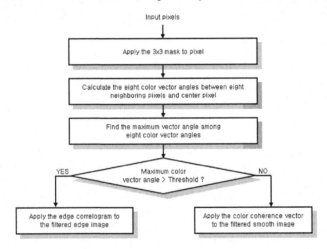

Fig. 1. System block diagram

2   Edge-Based Spatial Descriptor

2.1   Overview of Proposed Descriptor

The problem in conventional color descriptors based on a color histogram [5] is the lack of spatial information. To solve the problem, the edge information is used in the construction of the proposed method. As such, pixel classification based on a color vector angle is performed beforehand to classify the pixels into smooth or edge pixels. A 3 x 3 window is applied to every pixel in an image, where the center pixel and neighboring pixel making the maximum color vector angle are used to detect a color edge. If the center pixel in a 3 x 3 window is an edge pixel, the global distribution of the gray pairs in the edges is represented by the edge correlogram based on colors quantized in *RGB* color space. Conversely, if the center pixel in a 3 x 3 window is a smooth pixel, the color distribution is represented by CCV. The augmented feature map, which consists of both the edge correlogram and CCV, is then used as the edge-based spatial descriptor (ESD). Fig. 1 shows a block diagram of the proposed method.

2.2 Color Edge Detection Using Color Vector Angle

Color vector angles are used to lessen the effect of illumination [9]. A color vector angle is insensitive to variations in intensity, yet sensitive to differences in hue and saturation. As a result of these characteristics, color vector angles are widely used for identifying color edges. The simplest color distance metric is the Euclidean distance in RGB space. However, in the RGB space, the Euclidean distance does not correspond to equally perceptible differences of colors because it is sensitive to intensity variations, yet insensitive to variations in hue and saturation. Fig. 2 shows the usefulness of a color vector angle. Although color pair (C1, C2) appears more perceptually similar than color pair (C3, C4), two color pairs have the same *Euclidean distance*. Since the *Euclidean distance* is very sensitive to intensity variation, two pixels with the same color can have a nonzero distance value. However, the angle of color pair (C3, C4) is larger than that of color pair (C1, C2) due to color vector angle's sensitiveness to differences in hue. Consequently, color vector angle well represents the perceptual color difference. Colors that are separated by an angle, θ, whose sine is calculated as

$$\sin(\theta)_{v1,v2} = \left(1 - \frac{\left(V_1^T V_2\right)^2}{V_1^T V_1 V_2^T V_2}\right)^{1/2}. \tag{1}$$

The color edge is detected based on the eight-connectivity. First, a 3 x 3 mask is applied to every pixel, then the eight color vector angles between the eight neighboring pixels and the center pixel are calculated:

$$\sin(\theta)_{max} = MAX\left[\sin(\theta)_{V_C V_1}, \sin(\theta)_{V_C V_2}, \sin(\theta)_{V_C V_3}, \cdots, \sin(\theta)_{V_C V_8}\right], \tag{2}$$

where V_c and V_i are the center and neighboring pixels in the 3 x 3 mask, respectively.

If the threshold value for maximum vector angle among the eight color vector angles, T, is identified, Fig. 4 shows several edge images by the variation of T. If T has relatively low value, the false detection for edge pixels is largely increased like Fig. 4-(a) or Fig. 4-(b) in the 3rd raw of Fig. 4 which is the edge images for Fig. 3-(c). Conversely, if T has too high value, the missed pixels for edge candidates are seriously increased like Fig. 4-(d) in the 2nd raw of Fig. 4 which is the edge images for Fig. 3-(b). In Fig. 4, we make sure that if T has 0.08~0.09, a better result is achieved. From such result, we classify V_c as an edge pixel which the maximum vector angle is larger than 0.09, or as an smooth pixel otherwise.

2.3 Color Coherence Vector for Spatial Representation

When the pixels are classified by color vector angle as smooth, we apply the smooth pixels to histogram refinement, so-called CCV. The CCV partitions the histogram

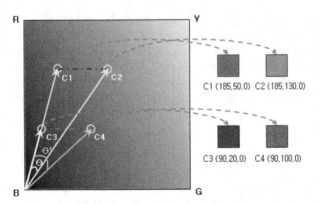

Fig. 2. Visual differences of two color pairs with the same Euclidean distance in the RGB space

bins by the spatial coherence of pixels. A pixel is coherent if it is a part of some "sizable" similar-colored region and incoherent otherwise. The initial stage in computing a CCV blurs the image slightly by replacing pixel value with the average value in a small local neighborhood. Then, it discretizes the color space, such that there are only n distinct colors in the image. The next step is to classify pixels as either coherent or incoherent depending on the size in pixels of its connected component. We obtain thereby the color descriptor for the low frequency image from CCV.

2.4   Edge Correlogram for Shape Representation

If the pixels in 3 x 3 mask are classified as the edge pixels, we apply edge correlogram to the edge pixels. A general correlogram expresses how the spatial correlation of pairs of colors changes with distance. We use not color correlogram but edge correlogram in our method. Edge correlogram improves the storage efficiency and brings down the expensive computation cost.

Let I be an n_1 x n_2 image, quantized into m gray color $c_1,...,c_m$. For a pixel $p=(x, y) \in I$, let $I(p)$ denote its gray color. Let $I_c \approx \{p \mid I(p) = c\}$. Let a distance $d \in [min(n_1, n_2)]$ be fixed a priori. Then, the edge correlogram can be calculated for $i,j \in [m]$, $k \in [d]$ as followings [6,10];

$$\gamma_{c_i,c_j}^{(k)}(I) \underset{p_1 \in I_{c_i}, p_2 \in I}{\triangleq} \Pr \left[p_2 \in I_{c_j} \mid \|p_1 - p_2\| = k \right]. \tag{3}$$

Given any pixel of gray color c_i in the image, $\gamma_{c_i,c_j}^{(k)}(I)$ gives the probability that a pixel at distance k away from the given pixel is of gray color c_j.

2.5   Histogram Comparison Between Spatial Area and Edge Area

Fig. 5 shows the histogram comparison on the spatial and edge area for Fig. 3. As shown in Fig. 5, the histogram for spatial area in a natural image is generally not consistent with that of the edge area. From considering a such gap from areas, we intend to improve the retrieval performance by splitting the feature extraction method into two parts: CCV method in spatial domain and correlogram method in edge domain, respectively.

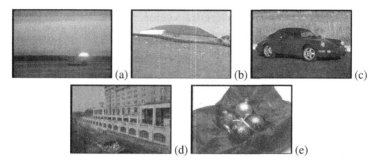

Fig. 3. Test images

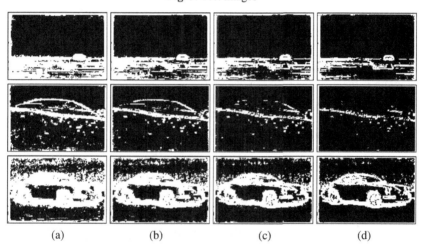

Fig. 4. Edge images by color vector angle in Fig. 3-(a)~Fig.3-(c) : (a) T=0.05, (b) T=0.07, (c) T=0.09, (d) T=0.11

2.6 Similarity Measure

Retrieval systems are based on similarity measurements between a given query (Q) and indexed data (R). Features are considered to be similar if they are in close proximity to each other, and dissimilar if they are further apart.

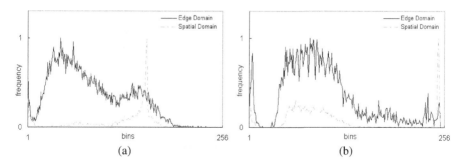

Fig. 5. Histogram comparison for edge and spatial areas in an image: (a) Histogram comparison in Fig. 3-(d) (b) Histogram comparison in Fig. 3-(e)

Similarity Measure for Color Coherence Vector. Let the set of coherence and incoherence pixels for the *j'th* color bucket be (α_j, β_j) in Q and (α_j', β_j') in R. Using the L_1 distance to compare CCV's, the *j'th* bucket's contribution to the distance between Q and R is

$$\Delta simC_{ccv} = \sum_{j=1}^{n} \left| (\alpha_j - \alpha_j') + (\beta_j - \beta_j') \right| . \tag{4}$$

Even though the absolute difference in the pixel count for color bucket j from two pairs of images is the same value in both cases, clearly the difference is more significant for pair of images with lower pixel count for color bucket j. Thus, we use the normalized difference between Q and R as following:

$$simC = \sum_{j=1}^{n} \left| \left(\frac{\alpha_j - \alpha_j'}{\alpha_j + \alpha_j' + 1} \right) + \frac{(\beta_j - \beta_j')}{(\beta_j + \beta_j' + 1)} \right| . \tag{5}$$

Similarity Measure for Edge Correlogram. Using the L_1 distance to compare edge correlogram's, the distance between Q and R is

$$\Delta simS_{correl} = \sum_{i,j \in [m], k \in [d]} \left| \gamma_{c_i,c_j}^{(k)}(Q) - \gamma_{c_i,c_j}^{(k)}(R) \right| . \tag{6}$$

The normalized difference between Q and R is

$$simS = \sum_{i,j \in [m], k \in [d]} \frac{\left| \gamma_{c_i,c_j}^{(k)}(Q) - \gamma_{c_i,c_j}^{(k)}(R) \right|}{1 + \gamma_{c_i,c_j}^{(k)}(Q) + \gamma_{c_i,c_j}^{(k)}(R)} . \tag{7}$$

Our approach associates with two separate vectors for the color feature from smooth pixels and for the shape feature from edge pixels. Hence, two similarity functions are computed, accounting for color and shape respectively: $simC(R,Q)$ and $simS(R,Q)$. The resulting coefficients are merged to form the final similarity function as a linear combination:

$$sim(R,Q) = \alpha \times simS(R,Q) + \beta \times simC(R,Q), \tag{8}$$

where α and β are weighting coefficients (typically, $\alpha = \beta = 0.5$). Fig. 6 shows the intermediate images for the proposed method.

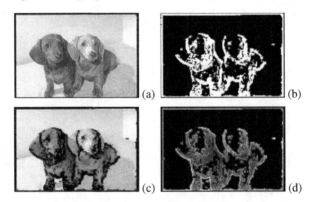

(a)   (b)   (c)   (d)

Fig. 6. Processed Images: (a) Original image (b) Image after color vector angle (c) Image to be operated by CCV (d) Image to be operated by Edge correlogram

2.7 Indexing Structure

We use R*-trees structure [11,12] to index the feature descriptor for the proposed method. R*-trees optimize the tree with respect to overlap, rectangle elongation, and coverage. Since these three values are reduced, the R*-tree is very robust against ugly data distributions. Furthermore, due to the forced reinsert, splits can be prevented, the structure is reorganized dynamically and storage utilization is higher than for other R-tree variants.

3 Experimental Results

Our heterogeneous image database consists of about three thousand color JPEG images with various sizes. The database includes natural scenes, indoor images, plants, animals, landscapes, drama cuts, and paintings etc. The processing time in simulations is measured in a system with Pentium-4 2.8GHz CPU and 512MB RAM in milliseconds. Fig. 7 shows our retrieval system.

Retrieval Accuracy Measure. The retrieval accuracy is measured in terms of the recall, precision, and ANMRR. For each query image q in the database, there are $NG(q)$ similar images. Let n_c, n_m, n_f be the number of correct, missed, and false candidates, respectively, among the first M retrievals. The precision and recall for query image q are defined as

$$Precision = \frac{n_c}{n_c + n_f} = \frac{n_c}{M} \tag{9}$$

And

$$Recall = \frac{n_c}{n_c + n_m} = \frac{n_c}{NG(q)}. \tag{10}$$

ANMRR [13] is the average of the normalized modified retrieval rank over all queries. First, the average rank for query q is as follows:

$$AVR(q) = \sum_{k=1}^{NG(q)} \frac{Rank(k)}{NG(q)} \tag{11}$$

where $Rank(k)$ is the rank of the retrieved image, k, which belongs to the ground truth images. Then, the average rank is modified into

$$MRR(q) = AVR - 0.5 - \frac{NG(q)}{2}. \tag{12}$$

The normalized modified retrieval rank is calculated as

$$NMRR(q) = \frac{MRR(q)}{\max\{4 \times NG(q), \max_{q \in Q}(NG(q))\} + 0.5 - 0.5 * NG(q)}, \tag{13}$$

where Q is the number of all queries. Note that the normalized modified retrieval rank will always be in [0.0~1.0]. Finally, ANMRR is calculated for all queries as follows:

$$ANMRR(q) = \frac{1}{Q} \sum_{q=1}^{Q} NMRR(q). \tag{14}$$

Result. The proposed method is compared with CCV, autocorrelogram and the combination method of CCV and autocorrelogram (AC-CCV). Since the computation cost for correlogram is quite heavy, a color autocorrelogram with {1,3,5,7} for spatial distances is used in the experiments. CCV and correlogram use 128 bins, respectively. AC-CCV and our method use 256 bins, respectively. The bins in CCV represent *sixty-four* distinct colors and their classified buckets as coherent and incoherent. The bins in correlogram represent *thirty-two* distinct colors and their spatial distance with {1,3,5,7}. AC-CCV is the method that extracts the feature vectors from CCV and correlogram each, and combines these features by similarity measure. To compare these approaches fairly, we bring them to a common ground truth images for all the queries in the experiment.

Table I and Table II show the comparison with the other retrieval methods on the query performance and time consumption, respectively. Table I shows that the proposed method produces a better result than the other methods for *ANMRR*, *average recall*, and *precision*. Correlogram relatively shows a good performance for an image with uniform patterns, but not for natural images. And, if most of the colors including an image have a sizable contiguous region, it is difficult to distinguish between the given images using CCV or conventional histogram method. As shown in Table I, all of the proposed ESD method and AC-CCV appear the satisfactory results. However, our proposed method separates the image and extracts the suitable features each for two divided areas unlike AC-CCV which makes twice whole feature extractions for an image. Thus, our approach represents a better performance as well as a fast feature extraction time (FET) rather than that of AC-CCV.

Table II shows the comparison for FET and indexing time of several methods in on-line and off-line. In off-line, the FET of CCV and correlogram is slightly faster than that of our method for time consumption per frame. Being compared with AC-CCV, our method is faster over 15%. For the comparison in on-line, the elapsed time for feature extraction is equal to the time for reading the stored data. It is because the extracted feature information has already been indexed and stored by R*-trees during the first feature extraction. Consequently, as the FET in on-line is only under 1 ms for all retrieval methods, the FET increase of the proposed method compared with CCV or correlogram in off-line doesn't have the significant meaning. The indexing time for the extracted features is under 1ms without regard to on-line or off-line.

Fig. 8 shows the retrieval results for a query and the relevant images, including a camera zoom and change of viewing position. As shown in Fig. 8, the proposed method is very robust to a camera zoom and the appearance changes. Since the proposed method considers color adjacency through an edge correlogram, it is able to produce satisfactory retrieval results even with significant appearance changes. Fig. 9 shows the retrieval result for another query with a new object appearance. Our experiment in Fig. 10 investigates retrieval performance comparisons based on recall and precision effectiveness. Fig. 10 shows the average value for an overall performance comparison. The experiment result shows that ESD performs better than CCV, correlogram, and AC-CCV for query images. The retrieval effectiveness measures shown in Fig. 10 indicate that the relative ordering of the retrieved document set is the best for ESD, followed by AC-CCV, CCV and correlogram (in order). Fig. 11-(a) and Fig. 11-(b) show the retrieval performance comparisons for Fig. 8 and Fig. 9, respectively.

Table 1. Comparison for retrieval performance with other retrieval methods

Method	ANMRR	Recall	Precision
Correlogram	0.425	0.10	0.38
CCV	0.382	0.18	0.47
AC-CCV	0.279	0.24	0.47
Proposed (ESD)	0.223	0.28	0.47

Table 2. Comparison of the elapsed time for retrieval with other retrieval methods. (ms)

Method	Off-line		On-line	
	Feature extraction	Indexing	Feature reading	Indexing
Correlogram	43	0.07	0.12	0.05
CCV	27	0.06	0.15	0.06
AC-CCV	63	-	-	-
Proposed (ESD)	52	0.14	0.17	0.13

Fig. 7. Retrieval System

Fig. 8. Retrieval results with rank: (a) Correlogram (CG) : rank 1, CCV (CV): rank 1, AC-CCV (AC): rank 1, Proposed (P): rank 1 (b) CG : rank 10, CV: rank 7, AC: rank 4, P: rank 6 (c) CG: rank 13, CV: rank 5, AC: rank 7, P: rank 5 (d) CG: rank 23, CV: rank 14, AC: rank 13, P: rank 11

4 Conclusions

In this paper, we have proposed an ESD method that extracts the edge from image using color vector angle and applies the CCV and the correlogram for the smooth area and the edge area, respectively. Since the edge correlogram uses edge pixels, it can effectively represent the adjacency between colors in an image and provide robustness to substantial appearance changes. The CCV method in spatial area can also effectively represent the global color distribution of smooth pixels in an image. The proposed method provides satisfactory image retrieval results even with significant appearance changes and can be applied to image localization through edge histogram backprojection. If the color quantization scheme is improved, a better performance could be achieved with the proposed method.

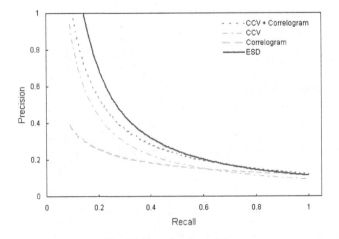

Fig. 9. Additional Retrieval results with rank: (a) Correlogram (CG) : rank 1, CCV (CV): rank 1, AC-CCV (AC): rank 1, Proposed (P): rank 1 (b) CG: rank 4, CV: rank 2, AC: rank 2, P: rank 2 (c) CG : rank 11, CV: rank 7, AC: rank 8, P: rank 6 (d) CG: rank > 30, CV: rank 17, AC: rank 15, P: rank 12

Fig. 10. Recall and precision

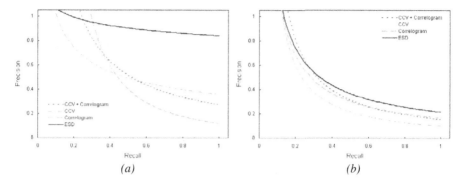

Fig. 11. Recall and precision : (a) for Fig. 8, (b) for Fig. 9

Acknowledgement

This research was supported in part by the Ministry of Education, Seoul, Korea, under the BK21 Project, and by the Ministry of Science and Technology, Seoul, Korea, under the NRL Project (M10204000079-02J0000-07310).

References

1. M. Flickner et al., "Query by image and video content: The QBIC system," *IEEE computer*, vol. 28, no. 9, pp. 23-32, 1995.
2. V. Ogle and M. Stonebraker, "Chabot: Retrieval from a relational database of images," *IEEE computer*, vol. 28, no. 9, pp. 40-48, 1995.
3. J. R. Smith and S.-F. Chang, "VisualSEEK: A filly automated content-based image query system," *in ACM Multimedia Conf.*, 1996.
4. A. Pentland, R. Picard, and S. Sclaroff, "Photobook: Content-based manipulation of image databases," *IJCV*, vol. 18, no. 3, pp. 233-254, 1996.
5. M. Swain and D. Ballard, "Color indexing," *Int. J. Comput. Vis.*, vol. 7, no. 1, pp. 11-32, 1991.
6. J. Huang, S. R. Kumar, M. Mitra, W. J. Zhu, and R. Zabih, "Image indexing using color correlograms," *CVPR*, pp. 762-768, 1997.
7. J. Huang, S. R. Kumar, and M. Mitra, "Combining supervised learning with color correlograms for content-based image retrieval," *in Proc. 5th ACM Multimedia Conf.*, pp. 325-334, 1997.
8. G. Pass and R. Zabih, "Histogram refinement for content-based image retrieval," *IEEE WACV*, pp. 96-102, 1996.
9. R.D. Dony and S. Wesolkowski, "Edge detection on color images using RGB vector angle," *in Proc. Conf. Signals, Systems & Computers*, pp. 687-692, 1998.
10. J. Huang, S. R. Kumar, M. Mitra, and W. J. Zhu,, "Spatial color indexing and applications," *ICCV*, pp. 602-607, 1998.
11. A. Guttman, "R-trees: a dynamic index structure for spatial searching," *Proc. ACM SIGMOD*, pp. 47-57, 1984.
12. N. Beckmann, H.-P. Kriegel, R. Schneider, and B. Seeger, "The R*-tree: An Efficient and Robust Access Method for Points and Rectangles," *Proc. ACM SIGMOD*, pp. 322-331, 1990.
13. "MPEG Vancouver Meeting," ISO/IEC JTC1/SC29/WG11, Experimentation Model Ver.2.0, Doc. N2822, 1999.

Efficient 3D Model Retrieval Method
Using Geometric Characteristics in Intersected Meshes

K.H. Lee, N.W. Kim, and Jong Soo Choi

Department of Image Engineering, Graduate School of Advanced Imaging Science
Multimedia, and Film, Chung-Ang University
{dragonar,mysope,jschoi}@imagelab.cau.ac.kr

Abstract. In this paper we propose a feature extraction method for shape-based retrieval of 3D models, which uses the mutual intersected meshes between model and growing spheres. Since the feature descriptor of 3D model should be invariant to translation, rotation and scaling, we firstly normalize the pose of 3D models using principal component analysis method. We therefore represent them in a canonical coordinate system. The proposed algorithm for feature extraction is as follows. We generate a unit-size circum-sphere around 3D model, and locate the model in the center of the circum-sphere. We produce the concentric spheres with a different radius ($r_i=i/n$, $i=1,2,...,n$). After finding the intersected meshes between the concentric spheres and object, we compute the mean curvatures of the meshes for each growing spheres, and use them as the feature descriptor of 3D model. Experimental evidence shows that our algorithm outperforms other methods for 3D indexing and retrieval. To index the multi-dimensional feature vectors, we use R*-tree structure.

1 Introduction

The use of three-dimensional image and model databases throughout the internet is growing both in number and in size. Using CAD systems, 3D scanners, Web3D and many others that work with 3D data have brought extensive collection of visual data describing 3D objects. These days many contents-based retrieval systems are designed for still image, audio and video, but unfortunately these image-based retrieval systems are not suitable for direct indexing, classification and retrieval of 3D models. So, a number of research groups in the field of computer graphics and computer vision have attempted to find efficient ways of representing 3D objects to identify each object based on its geometric properties.

Content-based 3D model retrieval algorithms proceed in three steps: 1) pose estimation with normalization, 2) feature extraction, 3) similarity comparison. The 3D models are given in arbitrary units of measurement and in unpredictable positions and orientations on 3D-space. The pose estimation step transforms model into a canonical coordinate frame. The goal of this procedure is to make the given 3D model take the same representation for a translated, rotated or scaled copy of the model. In feature extraction step, we capture the features for 3D shape of the objects. Finally, we have listed the top ranking items by using comparing the similarity with 3D objects.

The 3D model retrieval is generally divided into three categories: the graph-based retrieval [1-2], the view-based retrieval [3-4], and the feature-based retrieval [5-8].

First, the graph-based retrieval attempts to extract a geometric meaning from a 3D shape using a graph showing how shape components are linked together. Therefore, it

V. Torra et al. (Eds.): MDAI 2005, LNAI 3558, pp. 376–386, 2005.

has high discrimination, but it has the disadvantages of not having a normalized metric and having a lot of time-cost. Second, the view-based retrieval has the main concept that the 3D models are similar, if they look similar from all view angles. It adopts the 2D image retrieval methods easily. But, it spends a lot of time on searching the compared view angle between 3D models. Finally, the feature-based retrieval spends less time than two previous retrieval methods, because it only extracts the pure geometric characteristic of the shape of 3D model. It usually represents the global characteristic or the local characteristic of 3D model, so it uses the combination of two or three feature extraction methods. In this paper, we propose a feature extraction method representing the global feature and the local feature of 3D model together by using the information for the object meshes with the same distance from the center of model and the mean curvature for intersected meshes at the same time.

The remainder of the paper is organized as follows. In section 2, we introduce a principal component analysis (PCA) to estimate the pose of 3D objects, and propose the feature extraction method using the mean curvature for the intersected meshes between the concentric spheres and object. And, the experimental results and conclusions follow in Section 3 and 4, respectively. Fig. 1 shows the overall flowchart of our system.

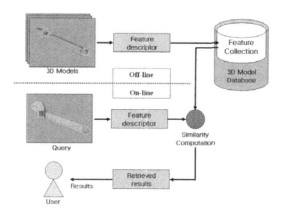

Fig. 1. Overall system flowchart

2   Feature Extraction Using Geometric Information

The 3D models have arbitrary scale, orientation and position in the 3D space. Since the feature descriptor of 3D model should be invariant to these characteristics, it is necessary to preprocess the 3D models to represent them in a canonical coordinate system. We use the PCA method to normalize the pose of the 3D models. Also, we apply it to make the circum-sphere [9].

2.1   Principal Component Analysis

We can calculate the coordinate axes, which is naturally aligned to the set of vertices belonging to each triangle mesh, by using a statistical method called *principal component analysis*. PCA allows us to find a coordinate space in which a set of data composed of multiple variables, such as the x-, y-, and z-coordinates stored in an array of vertex positions, can be separated into uncorrelated components. The primary principle component of the data is represented by the direction in which the data vary the most. To determine the natural coordinate system for an arbitrary set of N vertices $\mathbf{P_1}$, $\mathbf{P_2}$, $\cdots$, $\mathbf{P_N}$, where $\mathbf{P_i}=<x_i,y_i,z_i>$, we first calculate the average position m using Eq. (1).

$$m=\frac{1}{N}\sum_{i=1}^{N}P_i \cdot$$

(1)

We then construct a 3x3 matrix $\mathbf{C}$, called the covariance matrix, as follows.

$$C=\frac{1}{N}\sum_{i=1}^{N}(P_i-m)(P_i-m)^T \cdot$$

(2)

The covariance matrix is a symmetric matrix made up of the following six unique entries.

$$C_{11}=\frac{1}{N}\sum_{i=1}^{N}(x_i-m_x)^2, \quad C_{12}=C_{21}=\frac{1}{N}\sum_{i=1}^{N}(x_i-m_x)(y_i-m_y)$$

$$C_{22}=\frac{1}{N}\sum_{i=1}^{N}(y_i-m_y)^2, \quad C_{13}=C_{31}=\frac{1}{N}\sum_{i=1}^{N}(x_i-m_x)(z_i-m_z)$$

(3)

$$C_{33}=\frac{1}{N}\sum_{i=1}^{N}(z_i-m_z)^2, \quad C_{23}=C_{32}=\frac{1}{N}\sum_{i=1}^{N}(y_i-m_y)(z_i-m_z)$$

The entries of the covariance matrix represent the correlation between each pair of the x-, y-, and z-coordinates. An entry of zero indicates no correlation between the two coordinates used to calculate that entry. If $\mathbf{C}$ is a diagonal matrix, then all three coordinates are completely uncorrelated, meaning that the points are distributed evenly about each axis.

We intend to find a basis to which we can transform our set of vertices so that the covariance matrix is diagonal. If we apply a transformation matrix $\mathbf{A}$ to each of the points $\{\mathbf{P_i}\}$, then the covariance matrix $\mathbf{C'}$ of the transformed set of points is given by

$$C'=\frac{1}{N}\sum_{i=1}^{N}(AP_i-Am)(AP_i-Am)^T$$

$$=\frac{1}{N}\sum_{i=1}^{N}A(P_i-m)(P_i-m)^T A^T \cdot$$

(4)

$$=ACA^T$$

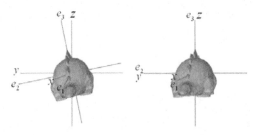

Fig. 2. Coincidence with principal axes and existing coordinate axes

Thus, we require an orthogonal transformation matrix $\mathbf{A}$ whose transpose diagonalizes the matrix $\mathbf{C}$. Since $\mathbf{C}$ is a real symmetric matrix, we know that its eigenvectors are orthogonal. The matrix whose rows consist of the eigenvectors of $\mathbf{C}$ meets our requirements and maps our vertices into a space where their coordinates are uncorrelated.

Let the natural axes of a set of vertices be e_1, e_2, and e_3. The direction e_1 always represents the principal axis, which corresponds to the largest eigenvalue of the covariance matrix. The directions e_2 and e_3 represent the axes corresponding to the second largest and the smallest eigenvalues, respectively. That is, if λ_1, λ_2, and λ_3 are the eigenvalues corresponding to the vectors e_1, e_2, and e_3, respectively, then $|\lambda_1| \geq |\lambda_2| \geq |\lambda_3|$.

2.2 Pose Normalization

As the 3D models haven't an uniform scale, orientation and position in the 3D-space, we replace the 3D models into a canonical coordinate system using PCA and unit-size normalization of object. The process of the pose normalization is as follows. First, the center of 3D model is calculated and the model is translated to the origin. The center of 3D model is the same as the center of the circum-sphere around the model. Additionally, the distance d_{max} between the center of model and the most distant vertex is calculated. Then the model is scaled to an unit size, that is, $d_{max}=1$. At this point, translation and scaling invariance is achieved. In order to achieve rotation invariance, the PCA method is used for each model so as to compute the principal axes of inertia e_1, e_2 and e_3 and their eigenvalues λ_1, λ_2 and λ_3. These principal axes define an orthogonal coordinate system (e_1, e_2, e_3) with $|\lambda_1| \geq |\lambda_2| \geq |\lambda_3|$. Next, the model is rotated around the origin so that the coordinate system (e_1, e_2, e_3) coincides with the coordinate system (x, y, z) as shown in Fig. 2. From such process, the 3D object is robust under transforms as translation, rotation, and scale.

2.3 Calculation of the Mean Curvature

After achieving the pose normalization, we propose the feature descriptor using the curvature of the intersected meshes between concentric spheres and 3D model. Fig. 3 shows the block diagram for our feature extraction method. First, we generate a circum-sphere of unit size. The pose normalized 3D model is located at the center of the circum-sphere. Next, we produce the concentric spheres with n different radius $(r_i=i/n, i=1,2,...,n(=R))$ as shown in Fig. 4.

Here, R is a circum-sphere of an unit size. After finding intersected meshes between 3D model and the n different concentric spheres, we compute the mean curvature for the meshes. To acquire the mean curvature, we bring the intersected mesh and its neighboring meshes in Fig. 5-(a). The center points of center mesh and three neighbor meshes also lie on a circumscribe circle with radius r'' and the four points are circumscribed by a sphere with center O and radius R'' as shown in Fig. 5-(b). Then, let $\mathbf{P}_0$ be a vertex of a simplex mesh have three neighbors $\mathbf{P}_1$, $\mathbf{P}_2$, $\mathbf{P}_3$. The three neighboring points define a plane with normal $\vec{N}_P$. Finally, from the simplex angle [10], θ, between normal $\vec{N}_P$ and the vector $\vec{P_0 P_1}$, we can obtain the mean curvature $\mathbf{H}$

of the surface at the point $\mathbf{P_0}$ by Eq. 5. And, we can get the average mean curvature $\hat{H}$ for the intersected meshes by Eq. 6, where m is the number of the intersected meshes.

$$H = \frac{sin(\theta)}{R} \; , \; \hat{H} = \frac{\sum H}{m} \cdot \tag{5),(6}$$

As applying the proposed algorithm to the concentric spheres repeatedly, we can get the n dimensional feature descriptor. In this paper, we use the following n feature vectors, $<\hat{H}_1, \hat{H}_2, \cdots, \hat{H}_n>$ to describe the 3D model.

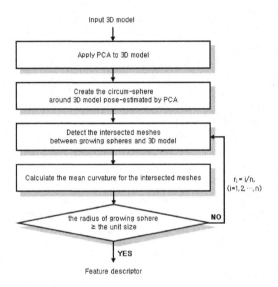

Fig. 3. Block diagram for proposed curvature feature extraction method

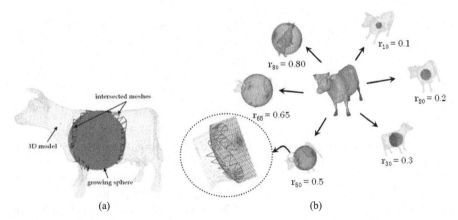

Fig. 4. The intersected meshes between sphere and model (a) 3D model and growing spheres (b) The representation of growing spheres

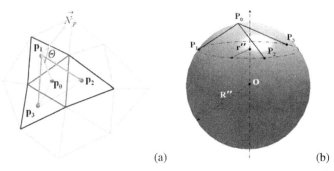

Fig. 5. The mean curvature calculation: (a) configuration of meshes for computing the mean curvature (b) the circum-sphere of radius R'' that includes the four points

2.4 Indexing Structure

We use R*-trees structure [11,12] to index the feature descriptor for the proposed method. R*-trees optimize the tree with respect to overlap, rectangle elongation, and coverage. Since these three values are reduced, the R*-tree is very robust against ugly data distributions. Furthermore, due to the forced reinsert, splits can be prevented, the structure is reorganized dynamically and storage utilization is higher than for other R-tree variants.

3 Experimental Results

We have tested the proposed algorithm with a various kinds of 3D models. Table I represents the category and the number of 3D model. In simulation, we have used total 520 models. They have averagely 3,690 vertexes and 6,260 meshes. Fig. 6 represents the example of 3D model. The processing times in simulations are measured in a system with Pentium-4 1.6GHz CPU and 512MB RAM in milliseconds.

Retrieval Accuracy Measure. ANMRR [13] is the average of the normalized modified retrieval rank over all queries. First, the average rank for query q is as follows:

$$AVR(q) = \sum_{k=1}^{NG(q)} \frac{Rank(k)}{NG(q)} \tag{7}$$

where $Rank(k)$ is the rank of the retrieved image, k, which belongs to the ground truth images. $NG(q)$ represents the number of the similar images for the given query. Then, the average rank is modified into

$$MRR(q) = AVR - 0.5 - \frac{NG(q)}{2}. \tag{8}$$

The normalized modified retrieval rank is calculated as

$$NMRR(q) = \frac{MRR(q)}{\max\{4 \times NG(q), \max_{q \in Q}(NG(q))\} + 0.5 - 0.5 * NG(q)}, \tag{9}$$

where Q is the number of all queries. Note that the normalized modified retrieval rank will always be in [0.0~1.0]. Finally, ANMRR is calculated for all queries like Eq. 10. The results have a good performance as the value of ANMRR is small.

$$ANMRR(q) = \frac{1}{Q}\sum_{q=1}^{Q} NMRR(q) \cdot \tag{10}$$

Result. The proposed method is compared with other conventional methods. The first one is a curvature index method, introduced by Koenderink [6], which uses a local index and is invariant to geometric transformations. The second one, Osada's method [7], is a global index which is invariant to geometric transformations and is also robust to noise. Jeong-jun's method [5] is the object-centered feature extraction which utilizes surface normal distribution and distance distributions between object surface points and origin. Finally, Zhang's method [8] is another local index which is invariant to geometric transformations and robust to noise, but not very discriminative as a stand-alone index.

Table II shows the number of vertexes and meshes for 3D models in Fig. 6. In Table III, we shows the comparison of ANMRR between above mentioned methods and proposed method for Fig. 6. For the experiment, we use one hundred bins. That is, we create one hundred growing spheres, and extract the one hundred mean curvature values from the intersected meshes between growing spheres and model. And other methods use 1,024 bins. As shown in Table III, the proposed algorithm has the best performance among several methods, although our method uses relatively small bins.

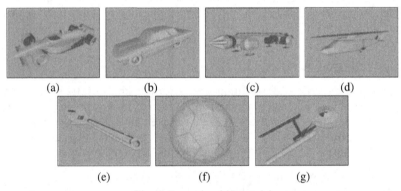

(a)   (b)   (c)   (d)

(e)   (f)   (g)

Fig. 6. Example of 3D model

Table 1. The category and the number of 3D model

Group	No.	Group.	No.
Car	71	Plane	64
Electronics	43	Flying	37
Knife & Tool	62	Bike	29
Table	27	Helicopter	26
Animal & Bug	19	Chair	24
Man	23	Etc	95
-	-	**Total**	**520**

Table 2. Vertexes and meshes for 3D models in Fig. 6

	(a)	(b)	(c)	(d)	(e)	(f)	(g)
Vertex	11,106	8,972	2,546	1,762	3,300	4,032	567
Mesh	21,122	14,462	4,648	3,051	4,076	7,932	1,070

Fig. 7 shows the result of Table III by the graph with the style of radiation. As the proposed algorithm has the small variations and values than other methods, we know that our feature descriptor is more robust than that of other methods for various 3D models.

Fig. 8-(a)~Fig. 8(e) and Fig. 8-(f) represent the retrieval results and the ground truth images for Fig. 6-(a), respectively. In Fig. 8, the retrieved results have the lowest rank at the left-top of the window and has the highest rank at the right-bottom. Be comparing with other methods, our approach in Fig. 8-(e) represents a good outcome, because the proposed method uses efficiently the geometric characteristics in general 3D models. Fig. 9 shows the retrieved results from our algorithm for other models in Fig. 6.

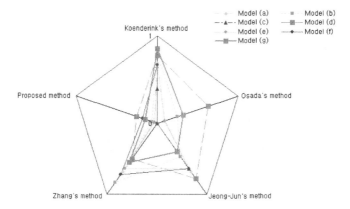

Fig. 7. Comparison of NMRR between conventional and proposed method

Table IV shows the comparison for feature extraction time (FET) and indexing time of several methods in on-line and off-line. In off-line, the FET of Osada's method and Zhang's method is faster than that of our method for time consumption per model, as they have the relatively simple feature extraction method by only computing with the vertex information of mesh. Koenderink's, Jeong-Jun's and our method spend a lot of time, but it is because these algorithms should compute the vertex information of mesh, the configuration of mesh in 3D space, the collision between a line and a mesh, and the collision between a sphere and a mesh, etc.

Table 3. Comparison of ANMRR between other methods and proposed method

	Koenderink's method	Osada's method	Jeong-Jun's method	Zhang's method	Proposed method
(a)	0.69	0.10	0.69	0.69	0.04
(b)	0.79	0.25	0.47	0.83	0.06
(c)	0.39	0.00	0.64	0.00	0.00
(d)	0.78	0.63	0.78	0.50	0.26
(e)	0.64	0.09	0.64	0.63	0.03
(f)	0.67	0.00	0.64	0.73	0.18
(g)	0.85	0.32	0.40	0.55	0.15
ANMRR	0.69	0.20	0.61	0.56	0.10

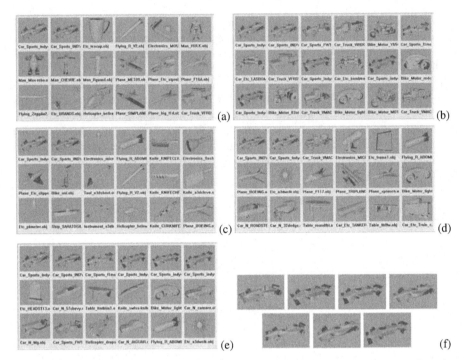

Fig. 8. The first eighteen retrieval results and ground truth images for Fig. 6-(a): (a) Koenderink's method (b) Osada's method (c) Jeong-Jun's method (d) Zhang's method (e) proposed method (f) ground truth images

For the comparison in on-line, the elapsed time for feature extraction is equal to the time for reading the stored data, because the extracted feature information has already stored during the first feature extraction. Fig. 10 shows the comparison results of the retrieval time between proposed method and other methods in off-line and on-line. In Fig. 10-(b), the gap between our approach and other methods is occurred by the size of bins. It is because that the feature dimension of the proposed method is 100 bins, but that of other methods is 1,024 bins. The FET of proposed algorithms therefore spent less time than that of other methods when they read the data from database on the on-line.

Table 4. Comparison of the retrieval time between proposed method and other methods (without R*-trees)

	Koenderink's Method	Osada's Method	Jeong-Jun's Method	Zhang's Method	Proposed Method
Off-line (s)	4.99	1.09	5.52	0.68	5.66
On-line (ms)	3.51	3.58	3.63	3.57	0.72

Additionally, in case of using R*-trees, the retrieval time of all of them in on-line is only under 1 ms for all retrieval methods. Consequently, the FET increase of the proposed method compared with Osada's method and Zhang's method in off-line does not have the significant meaning.

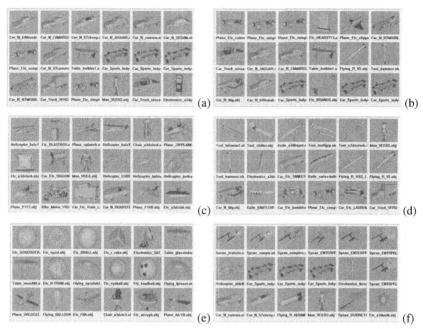

Fig. 9. The first eighteen retrieval results from our algorithm for several models: (a) in Fig. 6-(b) (b) in Fig. 6-(c) (c) in Fig. 6-(d) (d) in Fig. 6-(e) (e) in Fig. 6-(f) (f) in Fig. 6-(g)

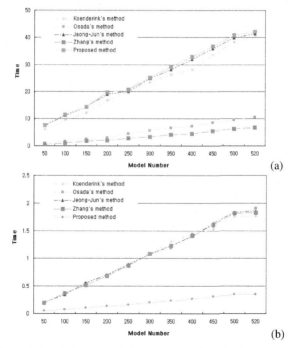

Fig. 10. Comparison of the retrieval time between proposed method and other methods: (a) off-line (b) on-line

4 Conclusions

In this paper, we have proposed the novel feature descriptor using the geometric information extracted by the shape of 3D model. The proposed algorithm represents the local characteristic and the global characteristic of the 3D model together by using an information of the object meshes with the same distance from the center of model and the mean curvature characteristics of their meshes. Our method is the feature-based method in a fixed d-dimensional space, no restrictions on the kind of shape model are imposed and in general the descriptor computation is fast. Also, the indexing using R*-tree is implemented efficiently. The proposed method provides satisfactory the retrieval results than other retrieval methods. But, our approach has the limitation when the mesh is not regular for the level of detail. We are working to improve the approach with a preprocessing step which uses multi-resolution.

Acknowledgement

This research was supported in part by the Ministry of Education, Seoul, Korea, under the BK21 Project, and by the Ministry of Science and Technology, Seoul, Korea, under the NRL Project (M10204000079-02J0000-07310).

References

1. S. Biasotti, S. Marini, M. Mortara, and G. Patané, "An overview of properties and efficacy of topological skeletons in shape modeling," *Int. Conf. on Shape Modeling and Applications 2003*, pp. 245-254, 2003.
2. M. Hilaga, Y. Shinagawa, T. Kohmura, and T.L. Kunii, "Topology matching for fully automatic similarity estimation of 3D shapes," *Siggraph 2001*, pp. 203-212, 2001.
3. D. Y. Chen, X. P. Tian, Y. T. Shen, M. Ouhyoung, "On visual similarity based 3D model retrieval," *Eurographics 2003*, vol. 22, no. 3, pp. 223-233 2003.
4. J. Löffler, "Content-based retrieval of 3D models in distributed web databases by visual shape information," *Int. Conf. on Information Visualization*, pp. 82-87, 2000.
5. J. J. Song, F. Golshani. "3D object feature extraction based on shape similarity," *International Journal on Artificial Intelligence Tools*, vol. 12, no. 1, pp. 37-56, 2003.
6. J. J. Koenderink and A. J. van Doorn. "Surface shape and curvature scales," *Image and Vision Computing*, vol. 10, no. 8, pp.557-565, 1992.
7. R. Osada, T. Funkhouser, B. Chazells, and D. Dobkin. "Matching 3D models with shape distributions," *In Proc. of Shape Modeling International 2001*, pp. 154-166, 2001.
8. C. Zhang and T. Chen. "Efficient feature extraction for 2D/3D objects in mesh representation," *Int. Conf. on Image Processing*, vol. 3, pp. 935-938, 2001.
9. E. Lengyel, "Mathematics for 3D game programming computer graphics," *Charles River Media Inc.*, pp. 182-185, 2002.
10. H. Delingette, M. Hebert, and K. Ikeuchi, "Shape representation and image segmentation using deformable surfaces," *Image and Vision Computing*, vol. 10, pp. 132-144, 1992.
11. A. Guttman, "R-trees: a dynamic index structure for spatial searching," *Proc. ACM SIGMOD*, pp. 47-57, 1984.
12. N. Beckmann, H.-P. Kriegel, R. Schneider, and B. Seeger, "The R*-tree: An Efficient and Robust Access Method for Points and Rectangles," *Proc. ACM SIGMOD*, pp. 322-331, 1990.
13. "MPEG Vancouver Meeting," ISO/IEC JTC1/SC29/WG11, Experimentation Model Ver.2.0, Doc. N2822, 1999.

Bipolar Queries Revisited

Sławomir Zadrożny

Systems Research Institute, Polish Academy of Sciences
ul. Newelska 6, 01-447 Warszawa, Poland
zadrozny@ibspan.waw.pl

Abstract. The concept of bipolar query, recently proposed by Dubois and Prade, is studied. A broader context for this concept is provided based on earlier approaches of other authors. Some properties of the aggregation operators involved are analyzed.

1 Introduction

Recently, Dubois and Prade [1] introduced a concept of *bipolar query*. Such a query is composed of two types of conditions: *required* and *preferred*. The former define constraints that the tuples have unconditionally satisfy, while the latter are of secondary importance. The interrelation between two types of conditions may be interpreted in various ways. Basically, Dubois and Prade adopt a lexicographic order based view of this interrelation. More generally, the way these conditions are jointly taken into account may be treated as the question of a definition/selection of an appropriate aggregation operator to be applied. It turns out, that in the literature this problem has been studied under a different name (and sometimes in a slightly different context) by many authors.

The aim of this paper is to bring together all this various interpretations of the interplay of required and preferred conditions known in the literature. We provide for a thorough discussion of the problem of the bipolar queries definition and interpretation, both for the crisp and fuzzy case.

This topic is a part of a broader area of the *flexible querying of databases*. The flexibility is to be obtained by the use of linguistically expressed conditions and non-standard aggregation operators. The linguistically expressed conditions are modelled using fuzzy predicates. This requires an appropriate interpretation of the classical as well as newly proposed logical connectives. In fact, the concept of bipolar query may be studied from the point of view of a proper interpretation of a new logical connective, which will be referred to as "and possibly". In order to provide a proper ground for the study of this concept we briefly discuss now the basic concepts relevant for flexible querying, notably logical connectives used to combine elementary conditions in a query.

There are several possible fuzzy interpretations of the classical logical connectives. Among them, the most commonly adopted are the following, originally introduced by Zadeh:

V. Torra et al. (Eds.): MDAI 2005, LNAI 3558, pp. 387–398, 2005.

$$x \wedge y = \min(x, y) \tag{1}$$

$$x \vee y = \max(x, y) \tag{2}$$

$$\neg x = 1 - x \tag{3}$$

for conjunction, disjunction and negation connectives, respectively. The most commonly used fuzzy implication operators are the following:

$$\text{Kleene-Dienes: } I(x, y) = \max(1 - x, y) \tag{4}$$

$$\text{Łukasiewicz: } I(x, y) = \min(1, 1 - x + y) \tag{5}$$

$$\text{Gödel: } I(x, y) = \begin{cases} 1 \text{ if } x \leq y \\ y \text{ otherwise} \end{cases} \tag{6}$$

$$\text{Goguen: } I(x, y) = \min(y/x, 1) \tag{7}$$

Let us illustrate the idea of flexible querying on an example:

$$\textit{Find employees who are \underline{young} and have \underline{high} salary} \tag{8}$$

The semantics of the underlined, vague, natural language terms is provided by appropriate fuzzy sets. The main question is how the matching degree for the whole query should be computed. Let ψ denote the matching function and Q the condition of a simple query of the of type $A = \mathcal{F}$, where A is an attribute (e.g., "age") and $\mathcal{F}$ is a vague (fuzzy) term (e.g., "young"), whose semantics may be represented by a fuzzy set F. Then, for a tuple t and the condition Q the value of the function ψ is defined as:

$$\psi(Q, t) = \mu_F(u)$$

where u is $A(t)$, i.e. the value of the attribute A in the tuple t.

The matching function ψ may be easily extended to cover more complex conditions (queries) involving logical connectives. For example, for the conjunction, using (1), one obtains:

$$\psi(Q1 \wedge Q2, t) = \min(\psi(Q1, t), \psi(Q2, t))$$

Another extensions of the standard query condition form consists in taking into account different importance of its parts. Namely, some weights of importance (numbers from the interval $[0, 1]$) may be associated with particular conditions. The interpretation of such importance weights may vary and many schemes for their aggregation has been studied in the literature. Dubois and Prade [2] studied the question of conditions Q_i with importance weights w_i forming together a compound condition Q via the conjunction. They came up with a general formula covering different interpretations of such importance weights:

$$\psi(Q, t) = \min_i(w_i \rightarrow \psi(Q_i, t)) \tag{9}$$

where Q is an overall condition being a conjunction of conditions Q_i, each with an importance weight w_i. Now, depending on the type of implication operator assumed, one obtains various interpretations of importance weights. For example, using the Gödel (6) or Gougen (7) implications, one obtains the *threshold interpretation* of importance weights (details may be found in [2]).

2   Bipolar Queries

The concept of bipolar queries has been introduced by Dubois and Prade [1] in 2002 (the roots of this concept may be traced back to earlier works of Dubois and Prade as well as other authors, cf., e.g., [2]). The idea is to distinguish in a query two types of conditions: *required* and *preferred*. The former have to be unconditionally met by a tuple, while the latter are to some extent optional and less important. However, the facultative character of the latter is rather subtle and cannot be directly grasped with the notion of importance weights as discussed in the previous section (9).

Let us assume the following notation: $T = \{t_j\}$ is a set of tuples to be queried; $C(\cdot)$ and $P(\cdot)$ are, fuzzy in general, predicates corresponding to the required and preferred conditions, respectively. We will identify in a usual way these predicates with fuzzy sets and $C(t)$ and $P(t)$ will denote their membership function values. Then we can linguistically express a bipolar query as follows:

"Find tuples t satisfying C and possibly P"

Hence, the set of tuples sought may be more formally described as follows:

$$\{t : C(t) \ and \ possibly \ P(t)\} \tag{10}$$

Thus, after Yager [3, 4] as well as Bordogna and Pasi [5], we will interpret the merits of bipolar query using a special aggregation operator labelled *and possibly*.

Originally, Dubois and Prade [1] define bipolar query as a set of pairs (C_i, P_i) corresponding to a set of some selected attributes $\{A_i\}_{i=1,k}$, where C_i and P_i are fuzzy sets corresponding to the required and preferred conditions, respectively, imposed on values of attribute A_i. These partial conditions are combined to yield overall conditions C and P in the following way:

$$(C, P) = (\times_i C_i, +_i P_i) \tag{11}$$

where $\times_i C_i = C_1 \times C_2 \times \ldots \times C_k$, $+_i P_i = (P_1^c \times P_2^c \times \ldots \times P_k^c)^c$ and X^c is a complement of the set X. Thus, the evaluation of such a query involves conjunctive aggregation of required conditions and disjunctive aggregation of preferred conditions, what may be more evident when we express (11) as $C(t) = \min_i C_i(t)$ and $P(t) = \max_i P_i(t)$. For our purposes, it will be more practical to treat C as an atomic condition even if it is defined as a Boolean combination of various conditions referring to several attributes. In case of P we will be later interested in its structure, but for a moment we will assume that it is given as an atomic condition, too.

We should also consider what do we expect as a result of such a condition evaluation: merely an *ordering* of the tuples according to their satisfaction of the condition or a *matching degree* of a tuple and the condition? The latter option is much more attractive as it secures the compositionality of such a condition: it may be easily combined with other Boolean or bipolar conditions within the same query.

2.1   Atomic Conditions

Let us start with an analysis of the *and possibly* operator (10), where both conditions C and P are treated as atomic. A query of this type may be exemplified with:

$$\text{Find a house cheaper than 150 000 \$ and possibly located not} \atop \text{more than two blocks from a railway station} \tag{12}$$

Thus, the required, strict condition concerns the price and the preferred condition refers to the distance to a railway station. A fuzzy version of such a query may be exemplified with:

$$\textit{Find a cheap house preferably near a railway station} \tag{13}$$

Lexicographic Interpretation. Basically, Dubois and Prade [1] adopt an interpretation of bipolar queries leading to the lexicographic ordering, $\preceq$, of the tuples, i.e.,

$$t_1 \preceq t_2 \Longleftrightarrow (C(t_1) < C(t_2)) \vee ((C(t_1) = C(t_2)) \wedge (P(t_1) \leq P(t_2))) \tag{14}$$

It is not possible to define a "unique scalar ranking" corresponding to lexicographic order, in general when defined on $R \times R$, cf. e.g., [6]. However, under certain reasonable assumptions, it is possible to come up with such a scalar ranking, see, e.g., Fishburn [6] for a more general discussion or Bosc and Pivert [7] for a querying-related context. In case of crisp conditions such a scalar ranking may be obtained using the following function ψ:

$$\psi_1(C, P, t) = (2 * C(t) + P(t))/3 \tag{15}$$

Then, obviously, $\psi_1(C, P, t) \in [0, 1]$ and:

$$t_1 \preceq t_2 \Longleftrightarrow \psi_1(C, P, t_1) \leq \psi_1(C, P, t_2) \tag{16}$$

In fact, Dubois and Prade [1] do take into account also another interpretation of a bipolar query exemplified by (12) and discuss other potential scalar rankings. As it is closely related to the second interpretation of bipolar queries we discuss in this paper, it will be analyzed in the next subsection.

Possibilistic Interpretation. The second interpretation of (12) is as follows. We are looking for a house that:

- has to be less expensive than 150 000 \$
- if there is a house closer than three blocks from a railway station then other houses satisfying just the first condition are of no interest

The concept of the queries with such an interpretation has been originally proposed by Lacroix and Lavency [8] in 1987. These authors considered such queries only in the crisp context. This interpretation may be more formally expressed by the following description of the set of tuples sought ([8]):

$$\{t \in T : C(t) \wedge (\exists s(C(s) \wedge P(s)) \longrightarrow P(t))\} \tag{17}$$

In order to cover also fuzzy predicates C and P we will express the characteristic/membership function of this set, $\gamma_1(C, P, t, T)$, in the following form:

$$\gamma_1(C, P, t, T) = \min(C(t), \max(1 - \max_{s \in T} \min(C(s), P(s)), P(t))) \tag{18}$$

In this formula min and max correspond to logical conjunction and disjunction in (17), while $\neg x = 1 - x$ is used for negation and Kleene-Dienes version of fuzzy implication operator (4) is assumed.

The very same formula (18), in a slightly different context, has been proposed by Yager [3, 4, 9]. He considers an aggregation of the criteria represented by fuzzy sets C and P, such that: "P is required to be satisfied if it does not interfere with the satisfaction of C". Intuitively, it is completely equivalent to the requirement that "C and possibly P" should be satisfied. The interference of P with C is measured as the possibility of the event that a tuple satisfies P under the condition that it satisfies C, which may be expressed as $\text{Poss}(P \mid C) = \max_t \min(C(t), P(t))$. The higher such a possibility the lower the interference, i.e., there are tuples satisfying both conditions C and P.

As observed by Yager [3, 9], the aggregation scheme (18) may be interpreted in terms of weighted conjunction (9) as soon as we assume *context-* or *content-dependent* weights. Namely, (18) may be expressed as:

$$\gamma_1(C, P, t, T) = \min((1 \rightarrow C(t)), (w \rightarrow P(t))) \tag{19}$$

where w is equal to the truth value of the formula $\exists_{s \in T}(C(s) \wedge P(s))$ or, equivalently, $\text{Poss}(P \mid C)$. Thus, we may interprete (18) as a weighted conjunction where a weight of the required condition C is equal 1 and the weight of the preferred condition P depends on the content of the database. Obviously, in the crisp case, it boils down to the requirement that both conditions have to be met as soon as there exists at least one tuple satisfying both of them.

The characteristic feature of the interpretation represented via (18) is that the value of matching degree, $\gamma_1(C, P, t, T)$, for a tuple t depends not only on t, but also on the whole set of tuples T (what is appropriately accounted for by introducing the fourth parameter, T, of γ_1).

In fact, Dubois and Prade [1], even if advocating the lexicographic order, studied also a formula very similar to (18) and found it unsatisfactory. Namely, they considered the following aggregation scheme:

$$\psi_2(C, P, t) = \min(C(t), \max(1 - \min(C(t), \alpha), P(t))) \tag{20}$$

The following properties of (20) may be easily verified [1]:

$$C(t) \leq 1 - \alpha \Rightarrow \psi_2(C, P, t) = C(t) \tag{21}$$

$$C(t) \geq 1 - \alpha \wedge P(t) \leq 1 - \alpha \Rightarrow \psi_2(C, P, t) = 1 - \alpha \tag{22}$$

$$C(t) \geq 1 - \alpha \wedge P(t) \geq 1 - \alpha \Rightarrow \psi_2(C, P, t) = \min(C(t), P(t)) \tag{23}$$

Dubois and Prade criticize the second property (22), i.e., that the value of (20) cannot increase with C when C is relatively high, but P is small. Let us observe, that in the above approach the value of parameter α has to be assumed arbitrarily. However, in the context of (17) and (18), a clear interpretation of parameter α is obtained. Namely, denoting $\max_{s \in T} \min(C(s), P(s))$ in (18) with α we obtain a formula very similar to (20). Analyzing the properties of (18) one may easily observe that (21)-(23) still hold. However, having a clear interpretation of α we might argue that the property (22) is acceptable. Namely, if α is high, meaning that there are tuples well satisfying both required and preferred conditions, then tuples failing to satisfy preferred conditions, i.e., such that $P(t) \leq 1 - \alpha$ are rejected. Thus, according to the advocated in this paper interpretation of the bipolar queries, we do not care for distinguishing among them. On the other hand, when α is low (i.e., no tuple well satisfies both conditions) then the lack of distinction happens only for tuples best satisfying required condition (i.e., those which, anyway, will be ranked high and listed first in the answer to the query).

Bosc and Pivert's Interpretation. This is historically the first fuzzy interpretation of the Lacroix and Lavency approach. However, Bosc and Pivert [7, 10], adopt the following interpretation of bipolar query, exemplified with (12):

- find houses that are less expensive than 150 000$ (or more generally, satisfy C)
- order them in the answer in such a way that those closer than three blocks from a railway station go first (or more generally, order them according to their satisfaction of the condition P)

Thus, for them the question of combining the satisfaction of C and P is secondary. They are mainly concerned with various, non-Boolean forms of the condition P (cf. next section). Anyway, in [10] Bosc and Pivert propose the following formula for the aggregation of both types of conditions:

$$\gamma_2(C, P, t, T) = \min(C(t), \max(P(t), \min_{s \in T}(P(s) : P(s) > 0) - \epsilon)) \quad (24)$$

where ϵ is some small value. Basically, this formula corresponds to the conjunction, $C(t) \wedge P(t)$, modified so as to avoid 0 matching degree for a tuple satisfying C but not P. This is obviously quite different from the concept of Lacroix and Lavency.

Comparison of Interpretations. Let us compare three interpretations of bipolar queries with atomic form of the preferred condition P on some simple examples. In the following we will refer to this interpretations in the following order:

  I. possibilistic, cf., (18),
 II. Bosc and Pivert's, cf. (24),
III. lexicographic order, cf. (14)

Let us start with a "crisp example" where both required and preferred conditions may be either satisfied or not satisfied, as in classical logic. In Table 1 a table with four tuples is assumed. The second and the third column indicate if given tuple satisfies (1) or not (0) required (C) and preferred (P) conditions, respectively. Next columns show what rank and matching degree get particular tuples according to three interpretations considered. The matching degrees are computed using the functions γ_1 (18), γ_2 (24) and ψ_1 (15) for possibilistic, Bosc and Pivert's, and lexicographic interpretations, respectively. According to the possibilistic interpretation, in case of data given in Table 1 only the first tuple satisfies the query and the rest of them should be rejected. Bosc and Pivert's approach "promotes" tuple 2, what is in agreement with their understanding of condition P as serving for ordering purposes only. The last column shows that the lexicographic order "artificially" distinguishes all tuples.

Table 1. Comparison of interpretations: the crisp case

No	C	P	I		II		III	
			$rank$	γ_1	$rank$	γ_2	$rank$	ψ_1
1	1	1	1	1.0	1	1.0	1	1.0
2	1	0	2	0.0	2	$1-\epsilon$	2	0.66
3	0	1	2	0.0	3	0.0	3	0.33
4	0	0	2	0.0	3	0.0	4	0.0

Let us now analyze an example for fuzzy case, i.e., when both predicates C and P are fuzzy, given in Table 2. This time we omit the matching degree values for the lexicographic order, even if it is possible to compute them along the lines proposed by Bosc and Pivert [7].

Table 2. Comparison of interpretations: the fuzzy case

No	C	P	I		II		III	
			$rank$	γ_1	$rank$	γ_2	$rank$	
1	0.9	0.7	2	0.7	2	0.7	2	
2	0.8	0.8	1	0.8	1	0.8	3	
3	0.7	1	2	0.7	2	0.7	4	
4	1	0	3	0.2	3	$0.7-\epsilon$	1	

This example confirms that the lexicographic interpretation rather does not comply with the logic of bipolar queries. Bosc and Pivert's interpretation yields results similar to these obtained due to possibilistic interpretation. However, what is worth noticing is a relatively high matching degree obtained using γ_2 function for the fourth tuple in Table 2. It is again the result of general assumption of Bosc and Pivert's interpretation that the condition P serves only as a basis for the ordering and it is the condition C which is decisive for the acceptance or rejection of a tuple. However, such a result may be misleading if given bipolar query is just a part of the whole query. In such a case, unfairly high matching degree of a bipolar query combined with the partial matching degrees of other parts of the overall query may yield wrong results.

The formulae for γ_1 and γ_2 are somehow similar, what provides for a similar behaviour of both interpretations in terms of ranking of the tuples. In particular, γ_2 function, similarly to γ_1, also takes into account the whole set of tuples when combining $C(t)$ and $P(t)$ for a given tuple t. However, the use of γ_2 may lead to the counter-intuitive results what is illustrated in Table 3. Here, both the ranking and the matching degrees yielded by γ_2 might be reasonably argued as wrong. The third tuple hardly satisfies the required condition C, but is selected as the best matching the whole bipolar query according to Bosc and Pivert's interpretation.

Table 3. Comparison of interpretations: counter-intuitive results for γ_2 function

No	C	P	I		II	
			rank	γ_1	rank	γ_2
1	1.0	0.0	1	0.9	2	$0.1 - \epsilon$
2	0.8	0.0	2	0.8	2	$0.1 - \epsilon$
3	0.1	0.1	3	0.2	1	0.1

In fact γ_1 and γ_2 functions are in some sense opposite. This may be best seen after transforming both functions to the weighted conjunction form, as in (19):

$$\gamma_i(C, P, t, T) = \min((1 \to C(t)), (w_i \to P(t))) \qquad i = 1, 2 \qquad (25)$$

The weights w_i for both functions take the following forms, respectively: $w_1 = \max_{s \in T} \min(C(s), P(s))$ and $w_2 = 1 - (\min_{s \in T}(P(s) : P(s) > 0) - \epsilon)$. Now, let us assume that there are some tuples satisfying C and all tuples well satisfy P. Then, w_1 is high indicating importance of the condition P, while w_2 is low. In such a case, the value of γ_2 may be too high for some tuples (as illustrated by tuple 4 from Table 2), however the resulting ranking should be in agreement with the intuition and the possibilistic interpretation.

On the other hand, when no tuple satisfies the condition P well (as in Table 3), then w_1 is low, properly indicating that the condition P may be neglected, while w_2 is high, incorrectly downgrading the matching degrees of tuples satisfying C and producing an improper ranking at the same time, as illustrated in Table 3.

2.2   Compound Preference Conditions

Both types of conditions C and P might be complex combinations of elementary, atomic conditions. As long as these combinations are of standard Boolean type the previous interpretations are readily applicable. Namely, the matching values of these conditions may be computed separately and then combined using approaches from the previous section. However, the very nature of bipolar queries calls for the study of other, non-Boolean combinations of elementary conditions forming C and/or P. In fact, this problem has been quite intensively studied in case of preference condition, notably by Bosc and Pivert [7, 10]. Thus, in this section we will assume multiple preferred conditions, P_i, to be combined in some non-standard way. Basically, in the literature two types of such a combination are considered: based on cardinality of the set of satisfied conditions P_i and based on a varying importance of these conditions. There are many methods proposed for such task in a broader context of, e.g., multicriteria decision making. In what follows we will focus on those seemingly more useful in case of bipolar queries.

Cardinality Based Aggregation. Lacroix and Lavency [8] consider the case where we have a set $\{P_i\}$ of preferred (crisp) conditions and a tuple t is deemed to satisfy containing them bipolar query "C and possibly $\{P_i\}$" if:

- it satisfies the required condition C, and
- there is no tuple s satisfying C and more conditions P_i that t satisfies

This case is distinguished by Lacroix and Lavency as the case of a set of *equally important* preferred conditions. It may be formally expressed with the following, similar to (17), description of the set of tuples sought (two equally important preferred conditions are assumed), cf. Lacroix and Lavency [8]:

$$\{t : C(t)\wedge$$
$$(\exists s(C(s) \wedge P_1(s) \wedge P_2(s)) \longrightarrow P_1(t) \wedge P_2(t))\wedge \qquad (26)$$
$$(\exists s(C(s) \wedge (P_1(s) \vee P_2(s))) \longrightarrow P_1(t) \vee P_2(t))\}$$

For a greater number of preferred conditions the formulae are extendible in an obvious way. This formula may be expressed in a form explicitly tackling with the fuzziness of the involved predicates in a usual way, as it is the case with the formulae (17) and (18):

$$\gamma_3(C, P, t, T) = \min($$
$$C(t),$$
$$\max(1 - \max_{s \in T} \min(C(s), P_1(s), P_2(s)), \min(P_1(t), P_2(t))), \qquad (27)$$
$$\max(1 - \max_{s \in T} \min(C(s), \max(P_1(s), P_2(s))), \max(P_1(t), P_2(t))))$$

It is worth noticing that this formula effectively rejects all tuples satisfying less conditions P_i than the "best" one.

Bosc and Pivert [7] deal mainly with the question of various ways of the aggregation of preferred conditions P_i. In order to determine an ordering of tuples Bosc and Pivert first characterize them using a sequence of subsets, $\{T_i\}$, of the set of tuples $T_C = \{t : C(t)\}$, i.e., a set of all tuples satisfying the required condition C. For a set of equally important preferred conditions, the following sequence of sets T_i is defined:

$$T_0 = \{t : t \in T_C \wedge \|\{i : P_i(t)\}\| = 0\}$$
$$T_1 = \{t : t \in T_C \wedge \|\{i : P_i(t)\}\| = 1\} \qquad (28)$$

$$\cdots\cdots\cdots$$

$$T_n = \{t : t \in T_C \wedge \|\{i : P_i(t)\}\| = n\}$$

where $\| \cdot \|$ denotes the cardinality of a given index set. Then, for each tuple t, the index of a set T_i to which it belongs is defined as $\text{ind}(t)$:

$$\text{ind}(t) = i \iff t \in T_i \qquad (29)$$

Finally, the rank-order of the tuples is defined as follows:

$$t_i \ll t_j \iff \text{ind}(t_i) \geq \text{ind}(t_j) \qquad (30)$$

where $\ll$ means that t_i precedes (is not worse than) t_j in the resulting ranking of tuples. The answer to the query is assumed to be a non-empty set T_i with a highest index.

The sequence of sets T_i (28) and the ranking procedure based on it is well-defined for crisp predicates P_i. In order to generalize it for fuzzy predicate, Bosc and Pivert [7] propose to use the following scalar index: $\mu_{P_1,\ldots,P_n}(t) = (1 + \sum_{i=1}^{n} P_i(t))/(n+1)$. Then, $\mu_{P_1,\ldots,P_n}$ is directly used to order the tuples. This scheme of aggregation yields similar results as (27) in terms of ranking, but not in terms of absolute degrees of matching values obtained, as it does not reject/discriminate enough tuples satisfying smaller than maximum possible number of preferred conditions.

The formula for $\mu_{P_1,\ldots,P_n}(t)$ directly refers to the cardinality of a fuzzy set of conditions P_i satisfied by given tuple t. In this case, the scalar cardinality of fuzzy sets is employed. Dubois and Prade [1] propose to use an operator more in the spirit of fuzzy cardinality of fuzzy sets. Namely, they propose to represent each tuple t with a vector: $(C(t), P_{\sigma(1)}(t), \ldots, P_{\sigma(n)}(t))$ where σ is such a permutation (for given tuple t) of the indices of the preferred conditions P_i that $P_{\sigma(1)}(t) \geq \ldots \geq P_{\sigma(n)}(t)$. Then, the lexicographic order of these vectors is used to rank-order the tuples. This aggregation scheme is known as *leximax*, cf. Dubois et al. [11].

Importance Based Aggregation. The preferred conditions P_i may be assigned some importance weights and then aggregated in an appropriate way. This may be done in many ways, assuming different interpretations of these importance weights. For example, one may use numerical weights and proceed with the aggregation as mentioned in the introduction (9). On the other hand, just some ordering of these conditions may be assumed and/or some interrelations between them. In what follows, we will focus on the approaches proposed specifically in the context of bipolar queries.

Lacroix and Lavency [8] considered the use of a linearly ordered set of the conditions P_i and come up with the following logical formula for their aggregation (in case of two preferred conditions, such that P_1 is more important than P_2):

$$\{t : C(t) \wedge$$
$$(\exists s(C(s) \wedge P_1(s) \wedge P_2(s)) \longrightarrow P_1(t) \wedge P_2(t)) \wedge$$
$$(\neg \exists s(C(s) \wedge P_1(s) \wedge P_2(s)) \wedge \exists s(C(s) \wedge P_1(s)) \longrightarrow P_1(t)) \wedge \qquad (31)$$
$$(\neg \exists s(C(s) \wedge P_1(s) \wedge P_2(s)) \wedge \neg \exists s(C(s) \wedge P_1(s)) \wedge$$
$$\exists s(C(s) \wedge P_2(s)) \longrightarrow P_2(t))\}$$

For a greater number of preferred conditions the formulae are appropriately extended (in fact, formula (31) might be slightly simplified, but in the present form it better illustrates the underlying scheme applicable for greater number of preferred conditions). It may be made more explicitly applicable for fuzzy predicates in a usual way, cf., e.g., (26) and (27). It may be easily noticed that (31) is equivalent to the lexicographic order of the vectors $(C(t), P_1(t), \ldots, P_n(t))$.

Bosc and Pivert considered weighted preferred conditions in the framework of the sequence of sets T_i as in case of equally important conditions (28). For a set of linearly ordered conditions, these sets take in their approach the following form:

$$T_0 = \{t : t \in T_C \wedge \neg P_1(t)\}$$
$$T_1 = \{t : t \in T_C \wedge P_1(t) \wedge \neg P_2(t)\}$$
$$T_2 = \{t : t \in T_C \wedge P_1(t) \wedge P_2(t) \wedge \neg P_3(t)\} \qquad (32)$$
$$\ldots \ldots \ldots$$
$$T_n = \{t : t \in T_C \wedge P_1(t) \wedge P_2(t) \wedge \ldots \wedge P_n(t)\}$$

assuming the following order on preferred conditions: $P_1 \succ P_2 \succ \ldots \succ P_n$. The rank-order is defined like in the previous case, i.e., using (29) and (30).

It may be easily observed that the ordering defined by (32) and (29)-(30) is different from the interpretation of a linearly ordered set of P_i defined by (31). This may be illustrated with the following example. Let us consider two tuples, t_1 and t_2, satisfying C and such that $\neg P_1(t_1) \wedge \neg P_2(t_1)$, and $\neg P_1(t_2)$, but $P_2(t_2)$. Then, according to (32) both tuples belong just to T_0 (i.e., $\text{ind}(t_1) = \text{ind}(t_2) = 0$) and are indistinguishable by the ordering defined with (30). On the other hand, according to (31), definitely t_2 belongs to the query answer, while t_1 does not. In other words, according to (30), if P_i is more important (is higher in a hierarchy) than P_j and P_i is not satisfied for a given tuple then satisfaction of P_j does not matter at all for the ordering of this tuple. In case of (31), if there is no tuple satisfying P_i then satisfaction of P_j may play a decisive role in ranking a tuple. This is a quite important property of ordering relation defined with (32) and (29)-(30), which led Bosc and Pivert [10] to propose a specific scalar aggregation operator, *Hierarchical Combination Operator*, yielding exactly such a rank-ordering.

3   Concluding Remarks

The concept of bipolar queries as proposed by Dubois and Prade [1] is closely related to the earlier concept of Lacroix and Lavency [8]. The latter has been later adapted for the fuzzy case by Bosc and Pivert [7]. Still, a direct fuzzification of the original crisp concepts of Lacroix and Lavency, advocated in this paper, provides for a more intuitive interpretation and is equivalent to the combination of fuzzy criteria proposed earlier by Yager [3] and employed by Bordogna and Pasi [5] for information retrieval tasks.

References

1. Dubois D., Prade H.: Bipolarity in flexible querying. In Andreasen T. et al., ed.: FQAS 2002. Volume 2522 of LNAI. Springer-Verlag, Berlin, Heidelberg (2002) 174–182
2. Dubois D., Prade H.: Using fuzzy sets in flexible querying: why and how? In Andreasen T. et al., ed.: Flexible Query Answering Systems. Kluwer Academic Publishers (1997) 45–60
3. Yager R.R.: Higher structures in multi-criteria decision making. International Journal of Man-Machine Studies **36** (1992) 553–570
4. Yager R.R.: Fuzzy sets and approximate reasoning in decision and control. In: Proceedings of the IEEE International Conference on Fuzzy Systems (FUZZ-IEEE), San Diego, USA, IEEE (1992) 415–428
5. Bordogna G., Pasi G.: Linguistic aggregation operators of selection criteria in fuzzy information retrieval. International Journal of Intelligent Systems **10** (1995) 233–248
6. Fishburn P.C.: Lexicographic orders, utilities and decision rules: a survey. Management Science **20** (1974) 1442–1471
7. Bosc P., Pivert O.: Discriminated answers and databases: fuzzy sets as a unifying expression means. In: Proceedings of the IEEE International Conference on Fuzzy Systems (FUZZ-IEEE), San Diego, USA, IEEE (1992) 745–752
8. Lacroix M., Lavency P.: Preferences: Putting more knowledge into queries. In: Proceedings of the 13 International Conference on Very Large Databases, Brighton, UK (1987) 217–225
9. Yager R.R.: Fuzzy logic in the formulation of decision functions from linguistic specifications. Kybernetes **25** (1996) 119–130
10. Bosc P., Pivert O.: An approach for a hierarchical aggregation of fuzzy predicates. In: Proceedings of the Second IEEE International Conference on Fuzzy Systems (FUZZ-IEEE'93), San Francisco, IEEE (1993) 1231–1236
11. Dubois D., Fargier H., Prade H.: Refinement of the maximin approach to decision-making in fuzzy environment. Fuzzy Sets and Systems (1996) 103–122

A Decision Support System for Rheumatic Evaluation and Treatment in Oriental Medicine Using Fuzzy Logic and Neural Network

Cao Thang[1], Eric W. Cooper[2], Yukinobu Hoshino[3], and Katsuari Kamei[3]

[1] Graduate School of Science and Engineering, Ritsumeikan University, Japan
thangc@spice.ci.ritsumei.ac.jp
[2] 21st Century Center of Excellence, Ritsumeikan University, Japan
cooper@se.ritsumei.ac.jp
[3] College of Information Science and Engineering, Ritsumeikan University, Japan
{hoshino,kamei}@ci.ritsumei.ac.jp

Abstract. In this paper, we present an application of soft computing into a decision support system RETS: Rheumatic Evaluation and Treatment System in Oriental Medicine (OM). Inputs of the system are severities of observed symptoms on patients and outputs are a diagnosis of rheumatic states, its explanations and herbal prescriptions. First, an outline of the proposed decision support system is described after considering rheumatic diagnoses and prescriptions by OM doctors. Next, diagnosis by fuzzy inference and prescription by neural networks are described. By fuzzy inference, RETS diagnoses the most appropriate rheumatic state in which the patient appears to be infected, then it gives an oriental prescription written in suitable herbs with reasonable amounts based on neural networks. Training data for the neural networks is collected from experienced OM physicians and OM text books. Finally, we describe evaluations and restrictions of RETS.

1 Introduction

Rheumatism is an arthritis disease widespread in all Vietnamese population groups, unfortunately influencing socioeconomic aspects of Vietnam. Among all soft tissue diseases, rheumatism accounts for 15% and the most common rheumatic type, joint degeneration, accounts for 10% [1]. In Vietnam, therapeutic treatments for rheumatism are physical methods, anti-inflammatories and oriental medicine (OM). Among these, OM is an indispensable part because it has fewer side-effects than western medicine and gives good treatment results. Besides, herbal prescriptions are easy to find and relatively cheap in comparison with western drugs. The number of Vietnamese patients treated by OM is about 50%.

Accurate diagnoses have an important role in treating diseases. Building a successful decision support system such as RETS based on knowledge from experienced OM physicians will help moderate evaluations in rheumatic diagnoses, which tend to be subjective. It will indirectly help physicians to provide the right treatment to the right patients, improving the quality of the health care services as a whole. It also will help qualified and experienced physicians in OM to maintain and share their profound knowledge with colleagues and to assist medical students or young physicians, especially those living and working in rural areas.

V. Torra et al. (Eds.): MDAI 2005, LNAI 3558, pp. 399–409, 2005.

2 Outline of RETS

In the last 50 years, the advent of the computer has greatly stimulated developments of Expert System (ES) and Decision Support System (DSS), which perform the roles of a specialist or assist people in carrying out works requiring specific expertise. There are many domains in which ES and DSS have been successfully applied, such as medicine [2 - 6], geology [9, 10], chemistry [11, 12] and business [13].

According to OM, each disease has specified states and each disease-state is cured by standard herbal prescriptions. Such a prescription is easily found in medical text books or OM reference books. With a patient, standard prescriptions become much more efficient and effective if physicians add more suitably additional herbs to it and then adjust all of its herbal amounts. The herbal adjustments are often based on the severities of observed symptoms on the patient, and their effects mainly depend on physicians' treatment experience. Only experienced physicians can give patients suitable prescriptions with reasonable adjustments.

In OM, rheumatism primarily consists of 12 disease states and 32 typical clinical symptoms. The number of rheumatic treatment herbs is 63 [7]. Based on the severities of observed symptoms, doctors diagnose and classify rheumatic states, then give a corresponding herbal prescription with reasonable amounts in grams. Fig. 1 shows the process of diagnosing and prescribing rheumatism by OM doctors. Such a process can be suitably assisted by a DSS or an ES as shown in Fig. 2 [8].

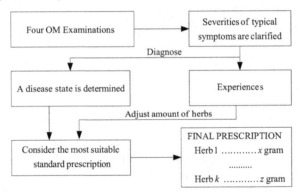

Fig. 1. Diagram of diagnosing and prescribing rheumatism by OM doctors

Roles of the functional parts in Fig. 2 are as follows:

Knowledge Acquisition: Surveys symptoms, prescribing rules, explanations and sample prescriptions.

Knowledge Base: Consists of symptoms, disease states, inference rules, training data and explanations.

Fuzzy Inference: Checks rules, calculates weights and advises the most serious rheumatic state.

Neural Networks: Gives prescriptions with reasonable herbal adjustments.

Interface: Obtains symptoms and their severities from users and shows inferential results.

Explanation: Helps users to understand OM, rheumatism, and explains the results.

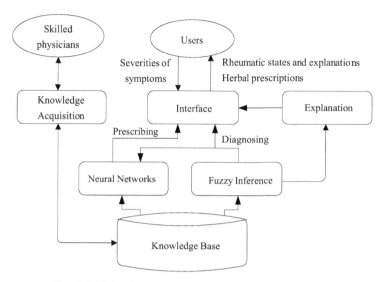

Fig. 2. DSS for diagnosing and treating rheumatism in OM

3 Diagnosing by Fuzzy Inference

In OM, physicians usually give herbal prescriptions based on the severities of clinical symptoms such as high fever, slightly numb joints, moderately yellow urine etc. These ambiguous expressions of symptoms make it unsuitable for traditional quantitative approaches to build a DSS for OM. Fuzzy sets, known for their abilities to deal with vague variables using membership functions rather than with crisp values, have proven to be one of the most powerful approaches to resolve this problem. They also enable developers to use linguistic variables and build friendly user interfaces. OM physicians usually explain diagnosing procedures with such expressions as "this patient has these typical symptoms with these severities, so I prescribe these herbs with these amounts." These expressions can be represented quite naturally in IF-THEN fuzzy rules. In addition, fuzzy rules can give expert-like explanations, making it easier for doctors to understand the DSS.

So far, based on fuzzy logic many practical applications in both western and oriental medicine have been built [2], including rheumatic disease [3, 4].

In the diagnosing stage of RETS, based on observed severities, fuzzy inference is used to decide which rheumatic states the patient has. Then in the prescribing stage, the fuzzy severities will be put into a corresponding neural network to get an appropriate herbal prescription.

3.1 Symptom and Rule Expression

Suppose that rheumatism has m clinical symptoms, l rheumatic states. A rheumatic state is determined by n clinical symptoms.

Let $S^O = (S_1^O, ..., S_m^O)$ be a set of observed symptoms on a patient where S_i^O is a fuzzy proposition representing a symptom.

Let $H = (H_1, ..., H_l)$ be a set of the rheumatic states.

Let $S^{R_j} = (S_1^{R_j}, ..., S_n^{R_j})$ be a set of symptoms in premise of rule $R_j (j = 1, ..., l)$ where R_j is generally described in the following form:

$$\text{IF } S_1^{R_j} \text{ and } S_2^{R_j} \text{ and } ... \text{ and } S_n^{R_j} \text{ THEN } \textit{the rheumatic state is } H_j . \tag{1}$$

Let the two following fuzzy values in S_i^O and $S_i^{R_j}$ be defined:

- $\mu_{S_i^O} \in [0,1]$: truth value of S_i^O given by doctors when diagnosing. $\mu_{S_i^O} = 1$ means S_i^O clearly appears on the patient, $\mu_{S_i^O} = 0$ means S_i^O does not appear on the patient, and $0 < \mu_{S_i^O} < 1$ means S_i^O appears on the patient with severity $\mu_{S_i^O}$

- $\mu_{S_i^{R_j}} \in [0,1]$: importance value of $S_i^{R_j}$ for rheumatic state H_j given by skilled doctors via survey in advance, where

$$\sum_{i=1}^{n} \mu_{S_i^{R_j}} = 1 . \tag{2}$$

$\mu_{S_i^{R_j}} = 0$ means $S_i^{R_j}$ totally does not affect H_j, $\mu_{S_i^{R_j}} = 1$ means $S_i^{R_j}$ is the only significant symptom affecting H_j, and $0 < \mu_{S_i^{R_j}} < 1$ means $S_i^{R_j}$ affects H_j with fuzzy importance $\mu_{S_i^{R_j}}$.

3.2 Fuzzy Inference Process

If an observed symptom S_i^O is found in the premise of rule R_j, premise weight $w_{S_i}^j$ of S_i^O in R_j is calculated as:

$$w_{S_i}^j = \mu_{S_i^O} \otimes \mu_{S_i^{R_j}} . \tag{3}$$

Where $\otimes$ is a t-norm operator, $x \otimes y = (x \times y)$ in RETS.

If symptoms S^{R_j} of R_j match with observed symptoms S^O, weight w_{R_j} of R_j is calculated as:

$$w_{R_j} = \bigoplus_{S_i \in \{S^{R_j} \cap S^O\}} w_{S_i}^j . \tag{4}$$

Where $\oplus$ is a t-conorm operator, this t-conorm should be compatible with (2), $x \oplus y = (x + y)$ in RETS.

Then RETS finds the most serious state H^* having the largest w_{R_j} value among l rheumatic states

$$H^* = \{h_m \mid w_{R_m} = \max_j w_{R_j}\}. \tag{5}$$

Fig. 3 shows the diagram of the inference procedure in RETS. When the inputs, severities of observed symptoms, are matched with one or more rheumatic states, the system finds the most appropriate rheumatic state H^* corresponding with these inputs. If the inputs are not enough to match with any rheumatic state, RETS gives advice about the closest rheumatic state. In this case, the patient may have diseases other than rheumatism.

4 Prescribing by Neural Networks

NN is an effective technique to help doctors to analyze, model and make sense of complex clinical data across a broad range of medical applications [5]. It enables intelligent systems to learn from experience, examples and clinical records, improving performance of the systems over time. Based on knowledge accumulated from experienced doctors and hospital information systems, NN can wisely give doctors good decisions, helping to moderate subjective evaluation in diagnosing and prescribing diseases.

So far many useful NN applications have been developed [5, 6]. In RETS, trained by rheumatic treatment knowledge collected from skilled OM doctors, NN is used to give herbal prescriptions with reasonable amounts. Fig. 4 illustrates steps of applying NN in herbal prescribing stage of RETS.

An important point in preprocessing training data is to select the right sets of input and output features. Raw data are prescription rules and herbal treatment prescriptions with typical observed severities gathered from experienced doctors. Features should be reasonably chosen so that from trained NNs we can get appropriate prescriptions in accordance with observed symptoms and diagnosed rheumatic states.

There are two types of symptoms. The first type is associated with Boolean values: Yes (true, coded by 1) and No (false, coded by 0). Observed severities in the second type are associated with 5 linguistic values in company with fuzzy intervals: no (0.00), slightly (0.25), moderately (0.50), relatively (0.75) and clearly (1.00).

There are two main kinds of herbs in a prescription, treating and conducting herbs. Treating herbs directly cure the infected symptoms while conducting herbs help patients' organisms to easily absorb herbal effects. The total number of herbs in a prescription is from 9 to 15. Amounts of treating herbs are often adjusted by severities of the observed symptoms whereas amounts of conducting herbs are normally unchanged as in the standard prescriptions. The number of observed symptoms used to adjust herbs in a standard prescription is often from 6 to 12. In training data for NNs of RETS only symptoms that affect herbal adjustments are used for inputs and all of treating and conducting herbs are used for outputs.

For the same rheumatic state, prescriptions by different doctors might not look similar because some doctors use some herbs but others prefer equivalent herbs that also give the same effects but come in different amounts. To avoid using many

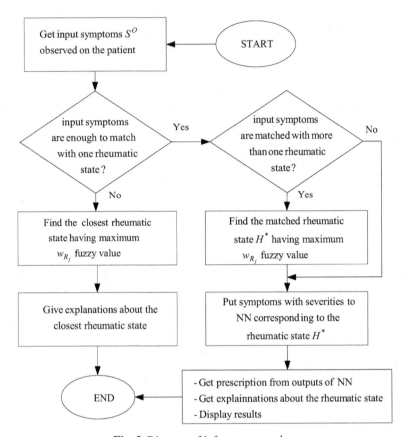

Fig. 3. Diagram of inference procedure

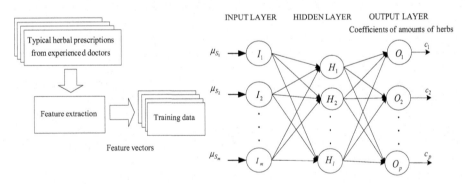

Fig. 4. Neural Network for prescribing applications in OM

equivalent herbs for the same prescriptions in training data, lists of herbs in the standard prescriptions from text books of Hanoi Medicine University are used and clarified by experienced doctors. For user reference, equivalent herbs are written in the description part of sample prescriptions.

Depending on each rheumatic state, the amounts of herbs in prescriptions vary from 2 to 60 grams. The error in the adjusted amounts of an herb accepted by doctors is usually 0.5 gram for small amounts and 1.0 gram for large amounts. Since the output range of NN is chosen from 0 to 1, amounts of herbs are normalized as coefficients. The coefficient c_k of amounts of herb k in training data, and the actual amount W_k^P of herb k in the prescriptive results is calculated as:

$$c_k = W_k^T / W^*. \tag{6}$$

$$W_k^P = c_k \times W^*. \tag{7}$$

Where W_k^T is amount of herb k in training data and W^* is the maximum amount of a herb in the prescription

5 Explanations

One of indispensable features of ES and DSS is capabilities to offer explanations. Logical explanations of RETS can help users, especially young doctors or medical students, to deeply understand inference results. Explanations also make it easier for experienced doctors to revise related sample cases in training data. Currently RETS has general and detailed explanations about rheumatic states and prescriptions.

- *General explanation:* after fuzzy inference process, from the knowledge base RETS obtains a general explanation about the most serious rheumatic state, then shows a fuzzy graph of all related states and fuzzy weights w_{R_j} of rules.

- *Detailed explanation about similar cases:* in training data RETS finds similar cases that have same severities of observed symptoms and same infected rheumatic states with the diagnosed patient, then shows prescriptions of these cases and their explanations from experienced doctors.

6 Implementation

Based on the text books, a preliminary survey and real rheumatic prescriptions from experienced doctors in Thaibinh OM College, we have assessed important fuzzy values of symptoms in rheumatic states, chosen standard prescriptions from the text books, clarified additional and equivalent herbs, selected specific symptoms that affected herbal adjustments, then generated 12,000 doctor-like prescriptions with combinations of severities of the state-specified symptoms using doctor-prescribing rules and linear methods with ranges of herbal adjustments. Training data for NN are the generated prescriptions together with 460 real rheumatic prescriptions from the experienced doctors.

Since most of herbs are written in Chinese and Vietnamese, some herbs have English or French names and some do not, in RETS the names of herbs are written in Vietnamese. Symptoms and general explanations are written in both Vietnamese and English. Detailed explanations with oriental medicine terms are written in Vietnamese.

There are 12 networks corresponding with 12 rheumatic states. Each NN has 3 layers as shown in Fig. 5. Inputs to NNs are state-specified symptoms $S_i^O (i = 1,2,...,m)$ with $\mu_{S_i^O}$ and outputs from NNs are coefficients $c_k (k = 1,2,...,p)$ of amounts of herbs. The number of neurons in the hidden layer is equal to the number of output neurons $(l = p)$. NNs are back-propagation networks adopting sigmoid or hyperbolic tangent activated functions. To accelerated training, adaptive learning and momentum term are also used. Fig. 6, 7 and 8 show the interfaces of RETS for knowledge acquisition from experienced OM doctors, diagnosis by fuzzy inferences, and prescription results, respectively.

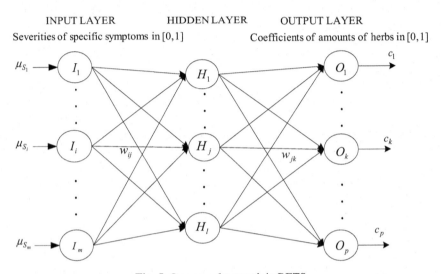

Fig. 5. One neural network in RETS

7 Evaluations

Combining NN and fuzzy inferences, we can have a more powerful and effective DSS with learning, reasoning and explaining capabilities for evaluating and treating rheumatism.

The inference rule given by (1) is equivalent to the following rule form:

IF fuzzy severities of symptoms

$$S_1^{R_j} \text{ is } \mu_{S_1^{R_j}} \text{ and } S_2^{R_j} \text{ is } \mu_{S_2^{R_j}} \text{ and } ... \text{ and } S_n^{R_j} \text{ is } \mu_{S_n^{R_j}} \qquad (8)$$

THEN *rheumatic state is H_j* with certainty factor w_{R_j}.

Using the rule form (8), a DSS may need thousands inference rules with many combinations of symptoms in premises. Not only do they take much time for developers to accomplish the rule acquisition but also much effort for domain experts to revise all of the rules. Using the rule form (1) with (2), RETS uses just 12 inference rules. Experienced doctors have confirmed that the inference results are quite good and it is easy to review the knowledge presented by the rules.

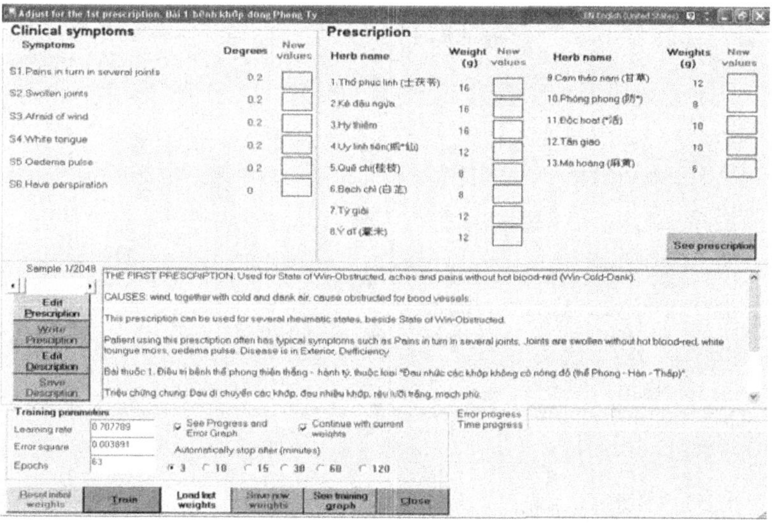

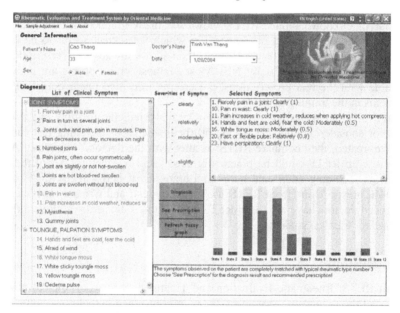

Fig. 6. Interface of knowledge acquisition

Fig. 7. Interface of diagnosis

In our experiment, we randomly split training data into two parts of 70% and 30% and used the former for training and the later for testing. All of nonlinear relations (real prescriptions and rules of prescribed herbs) as well as linear relations (ranges of herbal adjustments) were well learnt by NNs. Depending on the number of inputs and outputs, each NN can learn about 1000 prescriptions within an accuracy of 10^{-2} mean squared error with both training and testing data (equivalent to error of 0.1 gram for each herb).

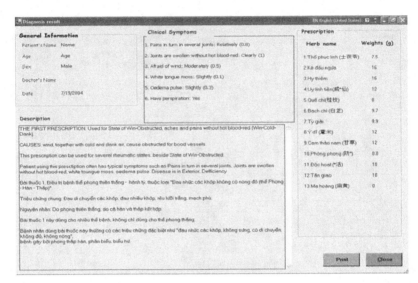

Fig. 8. Interface of prescription results and explanations

In case of unknown inputs, RETS shows the fuzzy graph of infected rheumatic states, recommends the most proper state in which the patient seems to be infected and gives explanations by fuzzy inference, then shows the advised prescription with appropriate amounts of herbs by NN. Most of these prescriptions are completely compatible with the real prescriptions, prescribing rules and linear ranges of herbal adjustments in the training data.

In an evaluation with doctors in Hanoi Oriental Medicine Institute, we asked the doctors for considering and then giving 50 rheumatic cases including real cases that they have treated, then compare RETS' results with the doctors' opinions. "All prescriptions from RETS could be practically used" said by doctors. About the herbal adjustments including additional herbs and amounts of herbs in the final prescriptions, 94% prescriptions from RETS are totally agreed and 6% are fairly accepted. Experienced doctors have also used RETS to illustrate treatments of clinical rheumatism cases for medical students.

8   Conclusions

We built RETS: Rheumatic Evaluation and Treatment System in oriental medicine, and showed the diagnosing system by fuzzy inference and herbal prescribing system by NN. We confirmed that RETS has high performance and high applicability for diagnosing and prescribing rheumatism. Unfortunately, like other DSS and ES which are restricted to a narrow domain of expertise, RETS is developed for diagnosing and prescribing rheumatism only. It lacks much real knowledge of human philosophy [14]. If a patient has other diseases besides rheumatism, doctors cannot solely rely on this system since they do not have evidence to control potential effects of the herbal prescriptions on the other concurrent diseases. Hence, it is recommended that the system be used only for patients with rheumatism alone, not for those with other concurrent diseases.

References

1. Le Anh Ba, Treating reality rheumatism, Medicine and pharmacy journal HCMC, June 2001
2. Maysam F. Abbod, DiedrichG. von Keyserlingk, Derek A. Linkens; ., Mahdi Mahfouf, Survey of utilisation of fuzzy technology in Medicine and Healthcare. Fuzzy Sets and Systems 120 (2001) 331–349
3. M. Belmonte-Serrano, C. Sierra, R. Lopezde-Mantaras, RENOIR: an expert system using fuzzy logic for rheumatology diagnosis, Internat. J. Intell. Systems 9 (11) (1994) 985–1000
4. K. Boegl, F. Kainberger, K.P. Adlassnig, G. Kolousek, H. Leitich, G. Kolarz, H. Imhof, New approaches to computer-assisted diagnosis of rheumatologic diseases, Radiologe 35 (9) (1995) 604 – 610
5. Richard Dybowski and Vanya Gant, Clinical applications of Artificial neural networks, Cambridge University Press 2001
6. A. Bezerianos, S. Papadimitriou, and D. Alexopoulos. Radial basis function neural networks for the characterization of heart rate variability dynamics. Artificial Intelligence in Medicine, 15(3):215–234, 1999
7. Tran Thuy, Pham Duy Nhac, Hoang Bao Chau, Hanoi Medical University - Lectures in Oriental Medicine, Medicine Pub. Hanoi 2002 (2), 160-165
8. John Durkin, Expert System, Design and Development, Prentice Hall Inc, New York 1994
9. Duda, R, O, Et Al, "A Computer Based Consultant for Mineral Exploration." SRI International Menlo Park, CA, September 1979
10. Meksown, D.M., Wilson A.H., "Automating Knowledge Acquisition for Aerial Image Interpretation", Computer Vision Graphics, 1990
11. Feigenbaum EA, Buchanan BG. DENDRAL and META-DENDRAL: Roots of knowledge systems and expert system applications. Artificial Intelligence 1993; 59:223–240
12. Zlatina, L. A., Elyashberg, M. E., Generation of stereoisomers and their spatial models corresponding to the given molecular structure, MATCH, 1992, 27: 191
13. D, V. Pigford, Greg Baur, Expert Systems for Business: Concepts and Applications. International Thomson Pub. Company, 1995
14. Michael Negnevitsky, Artificial Intelligence – A Guide to Intelligent Systems, Pearson Education Limited 2002, 12

Modeling Designers' Color Decision Processes Through Emotive Choice Mapping

Eric W. Cooper[1], Yuko Ishida[2], and Katsuari Kamei[2]

[1] Ritsumeikan University, Computer Science, 21st Century COE Project, 525-8577 Japan
cooper@se.ritsumei.ac.jp
[2] Ritsumeikan University, Computer Science, Soft Intelligence Laboratory, 525-8577 Japan
{yuko,kamei}@spice.ci.ritsumei.ac.jp
http://www.spice.ci.ritsumei.ac.jp/index.html

Abstract. Color selection support systems require a quantitative model of the color design decision-making process in order to support color selection strategies that further the specified goals of the designer without obstructing the unspecified goals. The system described in this paper models the color selection decision process based on the current state of the design, the desired state of the design, which is based on specified and unspecified designer goals. The specified goals are quantified as subjective responses to completed designs. In the main study discussed, seven novice designers independently designed 20 web pages and, in the process, every color selection was recorded. Adjective pairs selected from monologues provided semantic differential for evaluation of the resulting designs. A neural network-based inference system models designer selection based on the eventual results and the current state of the design to form designer strategies for color design support. This research is relevant in a variety of interactive applications but is of special interest for systems that work in close conjunction with human creativity.

1 Introduction

With the advent of the modern desktop computer, more people than ever are beginning to create new media and these novice designers have more viewers than ever before in the history of media. Color selection is at the heart of this creative process and here too the desktop computer offers more selections and accurate color rendering through color management. However, for the novice designer, effective color selection remains one of the most difficult challenges of the design process. This problem is one of the general set of problems involving the assistance of human decision-making in the creative process.

The general dilemma common to all support systems is evident in the example of the color template, a common form of color selection support. A template is simply a set of colors prepared beforehand that, when applied, automatically selects all of the colors (and often other design elements) to the prepared values. Using template simply means selecting on from a group of templates so the interface is easy to use. The designer may gain an attractive design and one that meets some of his needs. In this case, the facile interface and the satisfaction of some designer goals come with the sacrifice of originality. In presentation design, this trade-off between ease-of-use and creativity has even been called a kind of "tyranny." [1] Templates and other forms of color decision support are discussed in more detail in the following section. In this

V. Torra et al. (Eds.): MDAI 2005, LNAI 3558, pp. 410–420, 2005.

paper, *design* is used to mean static 2D designs but since color selection is a part of every visual design, many of the concepts discussed are applicable in all areas of design. Similarly, the concepts of support systems may be applicable to a wide variety of systems that work in conjunction with human creativity.

The goal of this research is to build a color decision support system, based on data from actual designs and their evaluations, and construct its reasoning such that it is able to look ahead to changes in design and anticipate problems that may occur during the color placement process. In line with the dilemma mentioned above, supporting creative processes without suppressing them, and building upon previous color support interface studies [2], [3], the interface is constructed to allow a high degree of user control without losing the support effectiveness. Section 2 describes some important issues of color selection support, Section 3 describes our development process, Section 4 describes the current system construction and its results, and Section 5 presents conclusions drawn from this study.

2   Color Selection Support Systems

The objective of a color selection support system is to assist designers during the design process to further the goals of the designer. Designer goals related to color may include a wide variety of different factors with complex interrelationships. However, we define any goal as any factor that may be evaluated by viewer experience, that is, any aspect of color placement that independent viewers can evaluate, by either subjective or objective means.

The purpose of the support system is to support the goals of the designer but, at the same time, the concept of "support" recognizes that there are many contributions that the designer makes to the design that the support system cannot, or is not meant to support. One reason for this limitation on support systems is mentioned above: the preservation of designer originality. There are also other goals that cannot be specified because the no system can possibly be prepared for every situation. For example, local cultures and individual preferences resent difficulties in both definition and scope. Similarly, although developers may be reluctant to admit it, there are many aspects of human emotive response that are not yet quantifiable. Therefore, any support system must be constructed so that it helps the designer reach specified goals without interfering with unspecified goals. This section discusses several color support systems as well as some of the major issues.

2.1   Lessons from Palettes

Most desktop computers offer millions of colors in various media but in color selection it is common to limit this number to a smaller number for ease of selection, in the form of a color palette. Many palettes now take this concept slightly further by segregating previous selections and by allowing selective palette expansion or reduction. Why should reducing the number of colors immediately available assist the designer? The reason is that, for most designers, design is a process of trial and error.

It has been shown that chess masters actually consider far fewer moves than chess novices. Masters are able to ignore inferior moves without so much as considering them. Similarly, experienced designers are able to quickly eliminate a large number of color selections and therefore may be able to handle large color selection spaces. Novices, on the other hand, need to try different colors to see which ones "work", i.e. which ones meet the designer's goals. Similarly, our objective is to build a support system capable of eliminating bad choices and looking ahead to optimal outcomes.

The process of trial and error implies that novices are unable to imagine what a particular color selection will look like until after it is made. In other words, a common comment from novice designers is: "I know how I want it to appear but I don't know how to make it look that way." After some time many designers get tired or move on to something else, make no further selections, and improvement stops. So a reasonable goal for color selection support systems is to either reduce this process of trial and error or to make it more effective in reaching designer goals.

2.2 Supporting Overlooked Goals

There are several designer goals that even professionals miss easily without some support. For example, the goal of good visibility for colorblind viewers is more complex than most design education programs acknowledge; it is not simply a matter of avoiding certain color combinations. This is not a trivial factor, as viewers with color vision anomalies are estimated variously between 5 and 10 percent, depending on gender and demography. Based on common color vision anomalies, simulations are now available to give designers an idea of how designs appear to people with these color difficulties. As an example, let us consider the process of a user interacting with such a system. The designer selects colors then performs an interaction to activate the color vision anomaly simulation. She is not satisfied with the appearance. Does she continue to select while viewing the simulation or will this interfere with goals related to normal vision? Again, we find the designer returning to the process of trial and error. Recently released palettes for color vision anomaly support do address this problem better than previous systems but still do not address the problem raised here of reducing the trial and error process while working closely with designer processes.

2.3 Templates

Some of the advantages and disadvantages of templates have already been discussed in Section 1. It should now be apparent why templates are so widely used. They significantly reduce the trial and error process. Instead of selecting between an astronomical number of color combinations (explored in more detail below), the designer selects from relatively small number of designs prepared by another designer. Besides the main problem of originality, this has other drawbacks. For example, the designer cannot be sure that these templates have already been checked for easily overlooked goals, such as color vision anomalies. There is generally no support given for selecting the right template for the present goals. Altering a template to fit one's own needs may be easier than selecting every color from scratch but this process would also benefit from selection support.

2.4 "Warning" the User

When building a first support system, many developers quickly adopt a defensive type of system, a "warning system." This may simply take the form of notifying the designer of a problem during the process [2], which may leave the user befuddled as to what the problem is, or may even identify specific problems or the areas concerned. While we think it is a good idea to identify problems that are easy to overlook, we have found these types of systems to be very ineffective because they do nothing to reduce or assist the actual selection process. [3] The user sees and understands the warning but does not know how to eliminate the problem. Therefore, for the most part we have abandoned warning systems as a means of support. However, they do offer a less intrusive method of access to the support system.

2.5 Intelligent, Dynamic Palettes

The authors have developed systems that alter the number of colors that appear in the palette depending on optional selections by the user. For example, if the user wants to improve the overall balance of the colors, he may select "Contrast" from a menu and the palette shows only the selections that will not improve this factor when applied the current color area. This solution is flexible without being intrusive. It allows the palette support to have intelligence without forcing changes on the designer.

However, these systems did lack one important feature, the ability to look ahead at further changes in the design. A good example of where this can be a problem is in the selection of a background. If the background is selected first, a novice may assume that the color of the background will determine the emotive content of the design and he may select a highly chromatic color. Later, when he is selecting a foreground color, text for example, he finds that the visibility of the foreground is unnecessarily limited. None of the colors in the palette or color space available can overcome the colorful background. This is one of many situations that are avoidable if the system can look forward to future possible states of the design, in just the same way a game-playing program eliminates bad moves and looks forward to find promising outcomes.

The color selection process can be viewed as a succession of choices in which the "game space" is determined by the size of the palette. When a color is selected, the state of the design changes and this puts restraints on the selections that follow. This navigation process is what makes trial and error so difficult. Even with a modestly sized palette, the number of possible outcomes is huge. The vast majority of color selections are so opposed by common sense that they will not be considered. Skilled color designers will also ignore even more, perhaps because they can imagine the selection without trying it or they have some set of conceptual rules. For support, we have been working on implementing the method of passing different selections through the support system to assist the user in navigating the color selection space. The basic palette interface is just as in our previous systems but with a richer variety of selections for palette support.

3 Development Process

In this study, we are developing a color support system with the following process. First, we collect samples of color design. These web pages are analyzed and converted for color placement. Then we ask experiment subjects, novice designers to select colors for the designs. The completed designs are then evaluated by another

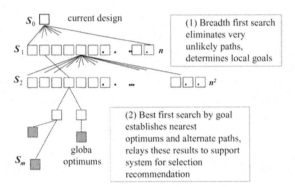

Fig. 1. Every time a color is selected, the state of the design changes. The number of colors in the palette is n and the number of colors selected is m. The number of possible outcomes is very large but most outcomes will not even be considered. Current systems generally either make all selections at once or support a single selection and a single state. Supporting the search methods described above requires that the system understand something about the state of the design when only a few colors have been selected. [7]

group of subjects, the evaluators. The data from the designs and their respective evaluations are then combined to develop a model that infers achievement ratings for many possible design states. This model provides a method for the support system to not only ascertain the current state of the design but to also look ahead to possible changes in the design that may further improve or hinder the designer's specified goals. This section discusses the process of design and evaluation.

3.1 Design Preparation

We selected web design because the web is quickly becoming the most common method of media-based communication and because the development of a web page involves many of the designer goals discussed. The web pages were selected from various public and private institutions, pages we thought would capture the essence of the design problem, and groups we thought would most probably benefit from color support as they would most be likely to have a wide audience without the budget required to hire professional designers. We also thought these groups would be likely to want a high degree of originality and freedom in the design process.

We separate each of these designs into areas of color to be selected and areas to remain unselected. Areas to remain unselected may include photographs, logos and other graphics, GUI widgets, and other items we assume to be either out of the designer's reach or not intended for color change. Next, we separate the areas to be selected into groups of pixels individual color areas we call color planes. For example, all text of one color would constitute one plane as would all of one background color's pixels. We classify each plane based on classifications considered to be readily available to an application such as a web page design system or a browser. Except for the areas to remain unselected, the original color selections of the color planes (selectable color areas) as the designs appeared on the web are not used in the experiments described here, only the colors selected by our designer subjects. The designs and their basic attributes are listed in Table 1.

Table 1. Font sizes of headings. Table captions should always be positioned *above* the tables. The final sentence of a table caption should end without a period

Description	Number of assignable colors
Page layout with image, title, text	5
Hobby description	6
Links to public libraries	8
Map of college campus	8
Schedule for subway trains	13
Clinic schedule with pattern background	5
Links to pages about Canada	15
University sign language club	9
Health sciences department	4
Children's workshop page	6
Sports event for elementary school	4
Example math problem, middle school	12
University department layout	11
Ears, nose, and throat office schedule	6
Day care home page	10
Simple entry page for web log content	3
Bulletin board entry page	5
Hobby description	6
College soccer events schedule	6
Page about jazz music albums	6

3.2 Placement Experiment

In the next part of the process, we asked a group of seven novice designers to select colors for these designs using an ordinary color palette. In this experiment, all of the selectable color planes are set to a middle grey and the largest selectable area blinks dark and light grey until the initial selection is made. (Previous studies using this process used black and white blinking but we thought this could possibly be uncomfortable to some subjects.) The designer may try any number of different colors before selecting the "Okay" button on the palette interface. At this point, a small dialog appears to allow the subject to begin a short voice recording. The subject starts the recording and speaks freely and conversationally about the reasons for the selection. These recordings provide data about the selection process for future studies as well as emotive terms and concepts for the present research.

Fig. 2. The audio selection interface, left, allows the subject to record the reason for the current selection

After all of the colors of one design have been selected, the designer is given the opportunity to reselect any of the selectable color areas for re-selection. When the designer is satisfied, the image, the designer's interactions, and the voice data are all

stored and the experiment moves on to the next design. The designers all had little or
no design experience. The purpose is to model a range of color placement skill and
we have found in previous studies that skills vary widely among novices [3]. These
seven designers, two women and five men, were paid for the time required to complete the designs.

3.3 Design Evaluation

Using information from past studies and the voice data, we selected 17 (Japanese)
adjective pairs for a study of goal achievement evaluation. The interface for this experiment is shown in Fig. 3.

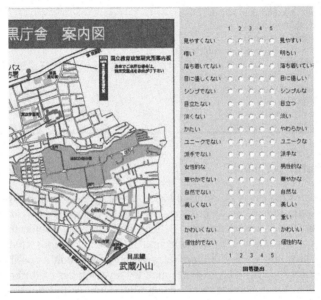

Fig. 3. The evaluator in this experiment looks at the design and selects responses from the
semantic differential scale on the right of the screen. Each scale has a pair of opposite adjectives

A rough translation of the pairs is included in the following section. The use of adjectives, usually in semantic differential surveys such as the one described below, is
part of a group of methods known as *Kansei*, the Japanese word meaning a range of
responses to sensual stimuli. *Kansei engineering*, as it has come to be known, is the
study of the modeling and application of these emotive responses for product design
or other applications. [7] While the objectives of Kansei engineering are to model
emotive response, the methods are generally practical in nature, relying on subjective
data collected from subjects, as we have done here. Each design was evaluated by a
total of five different subjects, all graduate and undergraduate students. The use of
evaluation alone as criteria for achieving designer goals is a method of taking advantage of the principle learned from observing the designer process of trial and error,
that novices are capable of evaluating completed designs but not able to find those
states easily.

4 System Construction and Results

The main objective of this system is to infer the currents state of a color design. The system is then able to perform various changes in the color selection to look a few steps ahead to eliminate unlikely or unproductive selections and then to look further ahead to find optimal solutions, as described in section 2.

4.1 Neural Network Construction

Constructing the system around individual states means that the effectiveness of the system depends in large part on how well the system can assess an individual state of the design. However, at early stages of the design, the system must perform evaluations based only on the few selections that have been made. Therefore, we developed a system that evaluates the emotive response to the current color selections based on their attributes. The method of inference is a set of neural networks, one for each adjective pair. The input for each neural network is two colors from the completed designs from the placement experiments described in the previous section. The target data for each neural net is the average SD response to its respective adjective pair, in which the SD response is set as a response in the interval [0, 1]. The structure of each neural network is a standard back-propagation neural network with sigmoid firing functions, ten inputs, six hidden nodes in the first layer, three in the second layer, and a single output for the average SD response ($10 \times 10 \times 3 \times 1$).

The process the system uses to infer the state of design i for the Kansei emotive response k is as follows. The first six inputs are the RGB values of two color areas in the design, c_1^i and c_2^i. Next there are four inputs describing quantitative factors of the two color areas. The area of the two colors in the image is given as

$$w(c_1^i, c_2^i) = \frac{A_1^i + A_2^i}{total\_A^i} \tag{1}$$

where A_1 and A_2 are the areas (in pixels) of color areas A_1 and A_2 respectively and $total\_A$ is the total area for the image, including areas not selected by the designer, such as images and logos. This total area of the two colors $w(c_1^i, c_2^i)$ is also used as weight for the weighted average of repeated iterations of the neural net output, as described below. The next input is the relative sizes of the two colors, given as

$$z(c_1^i, c_2^i) = \frac{A_1^i}{A_1^i + A_2^i}. \tag{2}$$

The target output used to train the network is the average response to adjective pair k for all evaluators who viewed image i.

Since each image has $_{n\_colors}C_2$ combinations of two colors each, the network is applied this many times and the output is the weighted average for all outputs based on the size of the input colors in pixels as compared to the total number of pixels in the design. This is weighted by the total size of the two colors in the design as

$$\hat{y}(k)^i = \frac{\sum o(c_a^i, c_b^i)_k \cdot w(c_a^i, c_b^i)}{\sum w(c_a^i, c_b^i)} \tag{3}$$

Table 2. The inputs and output of the network used to infer the average emotive response $\bar{y}^i(k)$ for the adjective pair number k to a specific two-color combination (c_2^i, c_2^i)

Input	Computation	Output for training
1	Color area c_1^i RGB *red* value c_1^i	
2	Color area c_1^i RGB *green* value c_1^i	$$\bar{y}(k)^i = \dfrac{\sum_j y(k)_j^{\,i}}{n}$$
3	Color area c_1^i RGB *blue* value c_1^i	
4	Color area c_2^i RGB *red* value c_2^i	
5	Color area c_2^i RGB *green* value c_2^i	$\bar{y}^i(k)$: average response for image i on adjective pair k with total evaluators n
6	Color area c_2^i RGB *blue* value c_2^i	
7	$w(c_1^i, c_2^i)$	
8	$z(c_1^i, c_2^i)$	
9	is_foreground(c_1)	
10	is_background(c_2)	

where $o(c_a^i, c_b^i)_k$ is the actual output of the network k, the network for the Kansei adjective pair k.

Since the alternate pairs of colors in a given design are selected by the same designer, these networks learn two things: 1) The influence of one pair of colors in a design on the emotive content of the design, 2) Color pairs likely to be selected by designers who are successful at infusing their designs with specific emotive traits. So the system is constructed to learn not only how colors influence emotive content, but also the color combination selections of designers who achieve these goals.

4.2 Network Training

The results of the neural network training are shown as correlation coefficients for the total weighted average for 70 training designs and 70 removed designs. Most of the adjectives evaluated had a good correlation for the

5 Conclusions

This paper discussed the problem of developing a color selection support system and interface. Previous work in this area and an examination of the more common systems on the market show that the difficulty is compounded by the need for support systems to give effective assistance without interfering with unspecified user's goals, including creativity and originality.

Our solution to this problem has been to construct a color support system that has a built-in understanding of both color and how it influences designer goals, as well as an ability to look ahead and see the process of a design. In order to do this effectively, the system we discuss in this paper uses a minimum of colors to assess the current state of the design. This system is currently able to infer trends in the emotive state of

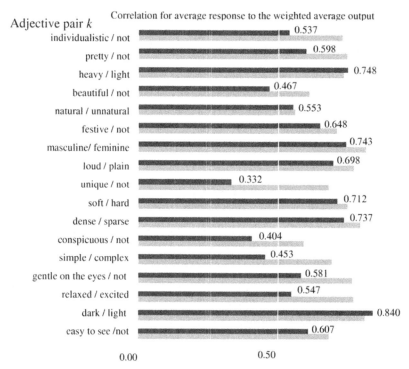

Fig. 4. This bar graph shows the results of neural network training for the 17 adjectives. The dark bars show the data that was unknown to the network at training time and the numbers are that set of data's correlation coefficient for average response $\bar{y}^i(k)$ to inferred response $\hat{y}^i(k)$. The adjectives are translated from Japanese and are not exact translations

a design for most of the adjective pairs examined. The objective of this study was to introduce new methods applicable to the concept of color state space navigation through inference of color design states.

The simplicity of this model leaves several problems to be solved. This system has not yet been tested on designs other than the twenty designs used for training and testing so future work will require a further examination of the system's ability to work on unknown designs. In addition to the inference given here, the system would also benefit from global inference based on the state of all of the colors in the design. Another remaining problem is the simplicity of the dynamic palette interface itself. There may be a limitation to what can be done with adjectives and many color design factors are required that involve more detailed studies of color visual factors and their relationships. Also, while the use of adjectives may improve the ease of input in the final interface, some aspects of design may not be expressed easily in terms a novice will readily understand. Solving this type of problem and others related to comparing novices to experts will require more studies with experienced designers, studies the authors are currently conducting. Also, there are a number of usability issues with the interface, for example, implementing a method of controlling the number of colors to be shown that works smoothly with the dynamic palette concept.

The authors envision a day when all desktop computers are both intelligent visual designers and cooperative assistants with their human users. When you design a web page, a presentation, or any media in the future, your desktop computer will offer help as you select colors and work with the other elements of design. Such systems will be as common and as easy to use as spelling checkers. The most successful of these systems will not interfere with the creativity of the user but will instead examine the user's specified goals and look ahead to foresee changes in the design that will further these goals.

References

1. Tufte, E., The Cognitive Style of Powerpoint, Graphics Press, Connecticut (2003)
2. Kitahara, Y.: Research Activities of Kansei Media in HITACHI Central Research Lab, Proceedings of the 13th Annual Fuzzy System Symposium, pp. 897-902. (1997) Japanese
3. Cooper, E., Kamei, K., Development of a Color Balance Support System, J. of Human Interface Society, vol. 1, no. 4 (1999) 73-80
4. Cooper, E., Kamei, K., A Study of Color Conspicuity for Ease-Of-Use Inference in Visualization, Color Research and Application, vol. 27, no. 2. (2002) 74-82
5. Cooper, E., Kamei, K., Modeling Designer's Color Placement Processes in Web Designs, Proc. of Intl. Conference on Artificial Intelligence in Eng. and Tech. Sabah, Malaysia (2004) 308-312
6. Cooper, E., Kamei, K., Kansei Modeling of the Color Design Decision Process in Web Designs, 2005 IEEE Networking, Sensing and Control Proceedings, Tucson, (2005) 615-620
7. Nagamachi, M., Kansei Engineering: A New Ergonomic Consumer-Oriented Technology for Product Development, International Journal of Industrial Ergonomics, vol. 15, no.1, (1995) 3-12

An Automatic Rule Creating Method for *Kansei* Data and Its Application to a Font Creating System

Hajime Hotta and Masafumi Hagiwara

Department of Science and Technology, Keio University
3-14-1 Hiyoshi, Kohoku, Yokohama, 223-8522, Japan
{hotta,hagiwara}@soft.ics.keio.ac.jp

Abstract. In this paper, we propose a method for creating fuzzy rules of *Kansei* data automatically. This method consists of 3 steps: (1) Generation of pseudo data of *Kansei* data by a General Regression Neural Network; (2) Clustering the pseudo data by a Fuzzy ART; (3) Translating each cluster into a fuzzy rule and extracting important rules. In this experiment, we applied this method to "a Japanese font creating system reflecting user's *Kansei* ." From the result of the experiment, although we have used the same algorithm for drawing font outlines, the system employing our method can reflect *Kansei* better than the conventional one.

1 Introduction

Recently, *Kansei* engineering has been used in various aspects of commerce. *Kansei* means the sensibility of humans and *Kansei* engineering aims at the analysis of *Kansei*. *Kansei* engineering has been used for comfortable function design, appearance design, design of advertising media and so on. Furthermore, there have been proposed many designing systems reflecting *Kansei* such as fonts, posters, 3-demensional virtual spaces, interior layouts, human illustration and music[1]-[5].

In general, we obtain *Kansei* data by questionnaires to quantify human's *Kansei* . However, there are mainly two problems to analyze *Kansei* data. First, they are basically subjective and tend to contain large noise. The noise is caused by the differences among individuals. Second, *Kansei* data are non-linear. This nature makes difficult to analyze with statistic methods. Therefore, fuzzy logic, which can express non-linear function easily, has often been used in *Kansei* engineering. compatibility with language is alsoone of the features of fuzzy logic. Created *Kansei* rules can be used in many systems refs. in [4]-[5].

In this paper, we propose a method for creating fuzzy rules learning *Kansei* automatically. It consists of 3 steps as follows.

(1) Generation of pseudo data phase.
(2) Clustering phase.
(3) Translating phase.

V. Torra et al. (Eds.): MDAI 2005, LNAI 3558, pp. 421–430, 2005.

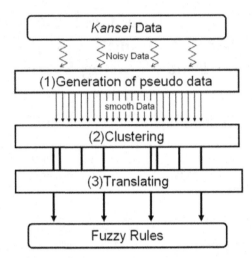

Fig. 1. A flow chart of the proposed method

In Generation of pseudo data phase, pseudo data concerning *Kansei* is generated by GRNN (General Regression Neural Network)[6]-[7]. It is suitable to process noisy data such as *Kansei* data because of robustness. In clustering phase, the pseudo data are clustered by Fuzzy ART(Adaptive Resonance Theory)[8]-[9]. In translating phase, each cluster is translated into one fuzzy rule and then important rules are extracted.

This paper is organized as follows. Section 2 describes details of the proposed method. Section 3 describes an experiment and the results. Section 4 concludes the paper.

2   Proposed Method

2.1   Overviews

Proposed method intends to generate *Kansei* fuzzy rules from *Kansei* data. The aim for generation of rules is to estimate the degree of impression by inference.

Target *Kansei* data need to be obtained by the following way. At first, experimenter presents subjects some target images such as pictures or fonts. Then he/she asks the degree of impression concerning some adjectives such as warm, cool, old and new.

Fig. 1 shows a flow chart of the system. The proposed method consists of 3 steps as follows.

Step 1 Generation of pseudo data phase
All of *Kansei* data are analyzed by GRNN algorithm. After the analysis pseudo data are generated.

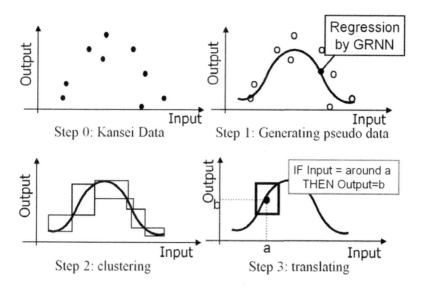

Fig. 2. Status of data in each step

Step 2 Clustering phase
The pseudo data is clustered by Fuzzy ART.

Step 3 Translating phase
Each cluster is translated into one fuzzy rule and important rules are extracted.
    Fig. 2 shows the states of data through this method. Through those steps we can get fuzzy rules from *Kansei* data even if these data contain strong noisy components.

2.2   Fuzzy Logic

For output rules, fuzzy logic is employed in this method. A fuzzy rule is defined as follows.

$$\text{Rule } r : \text{ if } x_1 \text{ is } L_{1r} \text{ and } x_2 \text{ is } L_{2r} \; \ldots \; \text{ then } y = y_r \tag{1}$$

where $x_1, \ldots, x_n$ are input variables, y is an output variable, $L_{1r}, \ldots, L_{nr}$ are labels of the membership functions and y_r is a constant value. Gaussian function is chosen as the membership function, i.e.,

$$\mu_{mr}(x) = \exp\left(-\frac{(x - a_{mr})^2}{\sigma_{mr}^2}\right) \tag{2}$$

where l_{mr} is a representative value and σ_{mr} is a constant that decides the extent of this function. Fig.3 shows an example of membership function.

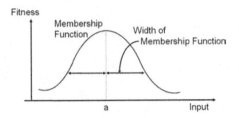

Fig. 3. An example of membership function

Fitness of the rule r is evaluated by

$$w_r = \prod_{m=1}^{n} \mu_{mr} \tag{3}$$

where $\prod$ means minimum operator.

After evaluated fitness values of all the rules, output value is estimated by defuzzification as

$$y = \frac{\sum_{r} w_r y_r}{\sum_{r} w_r}. \tag{4}$$

2.3   Generation of Pseudo Data Phase

The purpose of this phase is to reduce noisy components from *Kansei* data. The proposed method employs GRNN[6] algorithm. It is one of the statistic algorithms that can analyze non-linear data. GRNN is a non-parametric neural network model with Parzen window and have ability to create regressive functions by the following equation After learning from *Kansei* data, it can generate pseudo data.

2.4   Clustering Phase

The purpose of this phase is to cluster generated pseudo data having same features. For this purpose, the proposed method employs Fuzzy ART (Adaptive Resonance Theory)[9]. It is one of the self-organizing neural networks and it clusters data in rectangle.

The input vector to the Fuzzy ART is defined as follows.

$$X = [x_1, x_2, \cdots, x_n, 1 - x_1, \cdots, 1 - x_n, y, 1 - y] \tag{5}$$

This is a united vector of input and output of the pseudo data and complement coding is used. Since $x_1, \ldots, x_n$ and y in equation (5) are required to satisfy $0 \leq x_n \leq 1$ and $0 \leq y \leq 1$, pseudo data must be normalized within [0,1] before inputting to the Fuzzy ART.

Table 1. The examples of font parameters

category	parameter
thickness	horizontal, vertical, start, middle, end
size	width, height
noise	outline noise
slope	horizontal, vertical
typography	Gothic, Mincho, Reisho, Roundish gothic

2.5   Translating Phase

In this phase, each cluster is translated into one fuzzy rule and then important rules are extracted. According to the Fuzzy ART algorithm, each cluster is rectangular and is expressed as

$$C = [x_1, x_2, \ldots x_n, \sigma_1, \ldots \sigma_n, y, \sigma_y] \tag{6}$$

where $x_1, \ldots, x_n$ and y are the values of the center of the cluster and $\sigma_1, \ldots, \sigma_n$ and σ_y are the values of the width of the cluster. Then membership function is expressed as

$$L_r : \mu_{ij}(x) = \exp\left(-\frac{(c_{ij} - x)^2}{\sigma_{ij}^2}\right). \tag{7}$$

This corresponds to equation (2). Thus, every cluster is translated into one rule like equation (1) where y_r in equation (1) is corresponding to y in equation (6).

After the translation, importance of each rule is decided depending on the importance. If inference accuracy does not deteriorate without some rule, the rule is eliminated.

3   A Japanese Font Creating System

In order to verify the effectiveness of the proposed method, we have carried out an experiment with a Japanese font creating system reflecting user's *Kansei* .

3.1   Overviews

Fig. 4 shows the flow chart of this system. First, a user inputs desired impression. We can input some words of impression like warm and cool and the degrees of words. For example, "very warm", "slightly cool", or "not warm at all" can be inputted. Then the system calculates various font parameters to reflect the user's input in *Kansei* to Parameter phase. Font parameters determine the feature of fonts such as thickness and inclination by 32 parameters. Examples of the font parameters are shown in Table 1. In Parameter to Font phase, the system reflects the values of parameters to each character.

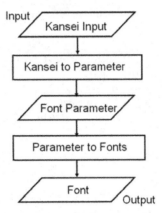

Fig. 4. Flow Chart

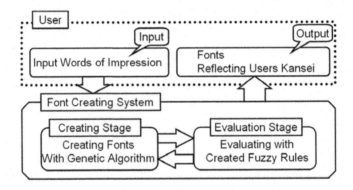

Fig. 5. *Kansei* to Parameter Phase

3.2   *Kansei* to Parameter Phase

Fig.5 shows the structure of *Kansei* to Parameter phase. In this phase, genetic algorithm (GA) is employed. Prototypes of chromosomal composition are shown in Fig.6. Font parameters are determined by combination of 2 chromosomes, a chromosome of basic font parameters and a chromosome of decoration font parameters. All parameters are expressed in 8 bits.

For calculating the degree of reflection of *Kansei* , the system uses fuzzy rules. In case of the conventional system, rules are written by designers. Whereas the new system uses rules generated by the proposed method.

The fitness values of chromosomes are calculated by the following way. First, the degree of reflection of each *Kansei* word is inferred by fuzzy rules about the word. Then the fitness of the chromosome is calculated by

$$f = \sqrt{\sum_w (I_{Uw} - I_{Sw})^2} \tag{8}$$

A Chromosome of Basic Font Parameters

A Chromosome of Decoration Font Parameters

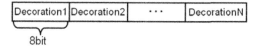

Fig. 6. Prototypes of chromosome

Table 2. A List of Impression words

warm	cool
antique	innovative
common	unconventional
unfashionable	elegant
imposing	light
calm	lively

Table 3. A List of parameters

Parameter	Value
Radius of GRNN	0.2
Viligence parameter of Fuzzy ART	(input)0.65
	(output)0.8
Learning rate of Fuzzy ART	1
Generations for GA	50
Individuals for GA	100
Mutation probability of GA	0.05

where I_{Uw} is an impression level specified by a user and I_{Sw} is an impression value inferred by fuzzy rules.

3.3 Examples of the Generated Rules

Kansei data for the proposed method were obtained from 62 subjects who are students over 20 years old. Table. 2 shows an impression word list. Here are examples of the generated rules.

1. If horizontal thickness is *very low* and vertical thickness is *low*
   THEN warmth is *very low*.
2. If horizontal thickness is *very high* and vertical thickness is *very high*
   THEN imposingness is *very high*.

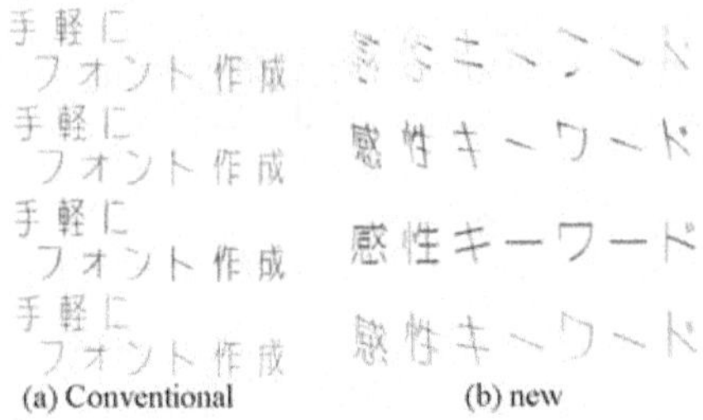

Fig. 7. Font example: light, unconventional

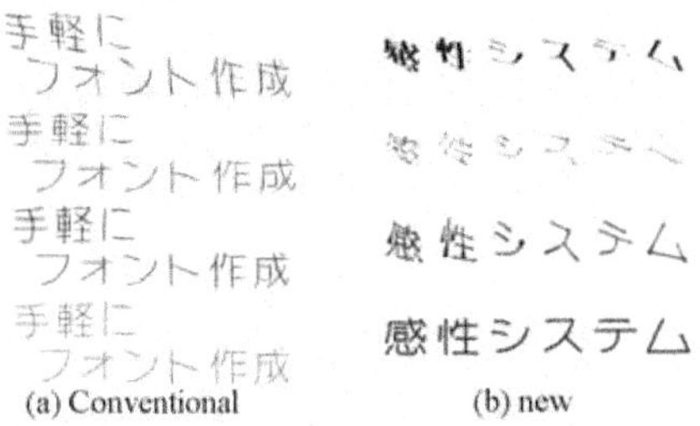

Fig. 8. Font example: lively, innovative

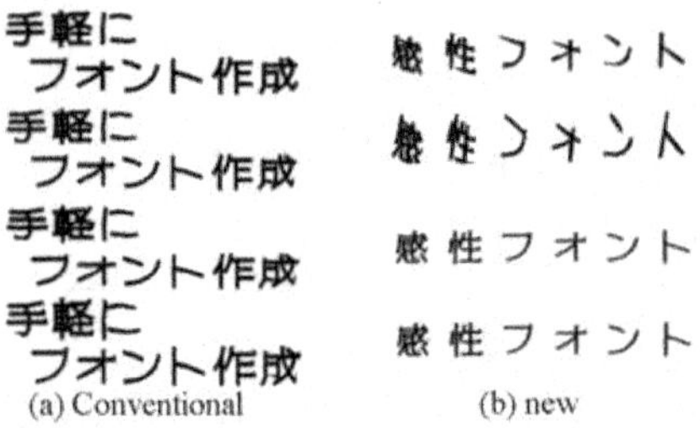

Fig. 9. Font example: imposing

3. If horizontal thickness is *high* and vertical thickness is *very high*
   4mmand width is *standard* and height is *very low*
   THEN antiquity is *very high*.
4. If horizontal slope is *very high* and vertical slope is *very high*
   THEN liveliness is *very high*.
5. If noise is *very high*
   THEN elegance is *very high*.
6. If horizontal thickness is *very high* and vertical thickness is *very low*
   THEN commonness is *very high*.

Actually, all the level words such as "very low", "low", "standard", "high" and "very high" are expressed by membership functions in the system. The average number of rules is 128.1. The 3rd example shows the feature of the font

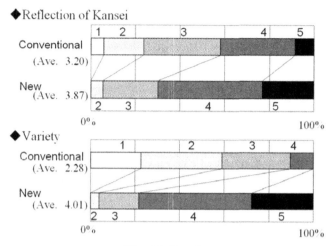

Fig. 10. Results

called "Reisho", which gives an old impression generally. The 6th example shows the feature of the "Mincho" font, which is most commonly used in Japan.

4 Experiment

4.1 Experimental Process

In the experiment, the new system was compared with the conventional one in two points below. The first point is the degree of reflection of *Kansei* . The second point is the degree of variety. Each evaluation is done in 5 levels. "1" means the worst and "5" means the best. Subjects are 15 students and they evaluated 8 kinds of *Kansei* words sets such as "light, unconventional" and "lively, innovative."

Table 3 shows the parameters of the systems.

4.2 Reflection of *Kansei* and the Degree of Variety

Examples of the created fonts with both systems are shown in Figs.7-9. Fig.10 shows the degree of reflection of *Kansei* and the degree of variety. The results show that the new system excels to the conventional one from bothpoints of view. Therefore, the fuzzy rules generated by the proposed method are valid from the result.

5 Conclusions

In this paper, we proposed a new method for generating fuzzy rules of *Kansei* data automatically. And we applied the generated rules to the font creating system to evaluate the proposed method. In the experiment, the new system excels to the conventional in respect of reflection of *Kansei* and the variety.

References

1. Motoki Korenaga and Masafumi Hagiwara: "An interior layout support system with interactive evolutionary computation", Information Processing Society of Japan Journal, Vol.41, No.11, pp.3152-3160, 2000.
2. Takeshi Ikezoe, Yoshinobu Kajikawa and Yasuo Nomura: "Music database retrieval system with sensitivity words using music sensitivity space", Information Processing Society of Japan Journal, Vol.42, No.12, pp.3201-3212, 2001.
3. Maki Kataoka and Masafumi Hagiwara: "An illustration drawing system reflecting impression of a face", Kansei Engineering International, vol.3, No.2, pp.7-16, 2002.
4. Takayuki Miyazaki and Masafumi Hagiwara: "A poster creating support system to reflect *Kansei* ," Information Processing Society of Japan Journal, Vol.38, No.10, pp.1928-1936, 1997.
5. Akio Wada and Masafumi Hagiwara: "A Japanese font creating system reflecting users' *Kansei* ," Jarnal of Japan Society of *Kansei* Engineering, Vol.5, No.2, 2005.(Planned)
6. Donald F. Specht: "A general regression neural network", IEEE Transatcions on Neural Networks, vol.2, No.6, pp.567-576, 1991.
7. Eric W.M.Lee, Chee Peng Lim, Richard K.K. Yuken, and S.M.Lo: "A hybrid neural network model for noizy data regression:", IEEE Transactions on System, Man, and Cybernetics-PartB:Cybernetics, Vol.34, No.2, pp.951-960, 2004.
8. G.A.Carpenter and S.Grossberg: "The ART of adaptive pattern recognition by a self-organizing neural network", Special Issue on Artificial Neural Systems, Vol.21, pp.77-88, 1988.
9. G.A.Carpenter, S.Grossberg, N.Markuzon, J.H.Reynolds, and D.B.Rosen: "Fuzzy ARTMAP: A neural network architecture for incremental supervised learning of analog multidimensional maps", IEEE Transations on Neural Networks, Vol.3, pp.698-712, 1992.

Video Motion Capture for Virtual Characters

Atsushi Nakano and Junichi Hoshino

Systems & Information Engineering, University of Tsukuba

Abstract. Video motion capture is useful for computer animation because we do not need expensive sensing systems to capture complex motion. However the conventional motion analysis techniques can be failed due to the partial occlusions. In this paper, we propose a robust tracking method by minimizing both intensity change and joint torque applying to the body parts along the long image sequences. We also developed the object-oriented software systems working on many platforms.

1 Introduction

Tracking human body from video is important for many applications such as creating digital actors and merging graphics with video[9]. If we can estimate 3D human motion from video, we would be able to use it as a motion capture method without expensive sensors.

Human body tracking has been investigated mostly in the computer vision field. These methods use image features such as gradient, silhouette, color segments, and image contours [1,2,3,4,5,6]. Each algorithm is important from the image processing point of view. However, the video motion capture is still not practical for computer graphics applications.

One of the problems is the robustness of the algorithm. When the intensity information is partly missing due to the occlusions, the parameter estimation becomes unstable. The similar problem occurs for silhouette based methods because hands and legs need to be separated from body to obtain best results.

The possible solutions for the problem of occlusion may be using multiple views taken by many cameras. However, using many cameras requires specialized studio setup that may be too costly for personal applications. In addition, it is still difficult to capture the whole appearance when the multiple people exist within the same camera view.

The other problem may be the completeness of the tracking software. Human body tracking typically consists of many image and signal processing modules. It is generally difficult to imagine the module configurations from the image processing algorithm to duplicate the results.

In this paper, we propose a human motion estimation method by minimizing both intensity difference and joint torque along the long action trajectory. The minimum joint torque criterion adds extra constraints during the motion estimation. We optimize the whole motion trajectory along the long image sequences to increase the robustness of the estimation.

This paper presents the theoretical background, and also experimental results that demonstrate the robustness of the tracking. We show that the complex, dynamic human action such as dance sequences can be captured from video.

V. Torra et al. (Eds.): MDAI 2005, LNAI 3558, pp. 431–441, 2005.

Fig. 1. Tracking results of two person and application for manipulating digital actors

Our video motion capture software is implemented using JAVA Swing and JAVA3D which can be executed on the most of the computational platform including Windows, Linux, and SGI IRIX.

2 Overview

Fig.2 shows the concept of our tracking algorithm. We integrate the following four techniques to achieve practical stability for video motion capture.

1) Minimum intensity and joint torque: We increase the robustness of the tracking by minimizing both intensity differences and joint torques along the motion trajectory.
2) Global optimization over long image sequences: estimation of human motion from just one or two frames is inherently unstable. We increase the robustness of estimation by using long image sequences.
3) Parametric representation of continuous motion trajectory: We represent the continuous angler motion in a few parameters using the hermite interpolation to decrease the degree of freedom. The parameter reduction also helps the faster convergence and the increases in the stability.
4) Robust estimate for rejecting outliers: Robust statistics are used to suppress large intensity errors due to the partial occlusions.

We use the human body model in Fig.3 to calculate dynamics of human body. The body models are approximated by a polyhedron made by CAD modeler. The model has a tree structure with a root at the trunk, and has a local coordinate system whose origin is located at a joint. The dynamic model of human body can be derived from Newton-Euler method.

In the following sections, we explain the detail of the dynamic modeling of the human body, and the optimization of joint torque along the motion trajectory.

3 Dynamic Modeling of Human Body

Newton-Euler formulation desribes the motion of the links in terms of a balance of forces and moments acting on it [7,8]. Consider the generic augmented link of the human body kinematic chain. Newton equations for the translational motion of the center of mass can be written as

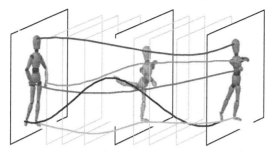

Fig. 2. Concept of the human body tracking using long image sequences and minimum torque criterion

$$\mathbf{F} = m\dot{\mathbf{v}} \qquad (1)$$

The Eular equations for the rotational motion of the link (referring moments to the center of mass can be written as

$$\mathbf{N} = \mathbf{I}\boldsymbol{\omega} + \boldsymbol{\omega} \times (\mathbf{I}\boldsymbol{\omega}) \qquad (2)$$

where

$\mathbf{F}$: force exerted on link
m: is a mass of augmented link
$\dot{\mathbf{v}}$: linear velocity of center of mass
$\mathbf{N}$: moment of inertial of rotator
$\mathbf{I}$: inertia tensor of augmented link
$\boldsymbol{\omega}$: angular velocity of link

Once the joint positions, velocities and accelerations are known, one can compute the link velocities and accelerations, and the Newton-Euler equations can be utilized to find the forces and moments acting on each link in a recursive fashion, starting from the force and moment applied to the end effectors. On the other hand, also link and rotor velocities and acceleration can be computed recursively starting from the velocity and acceleration of the base link. In sum, a computationally recursive algorithm can be constructed that features a forward recursion relative to the propagation of velocities and accelerations and a backward recursion for the propagation of forces and moments along the structure.

Let the human body has s branch, and branch k has $n_k\ (k = 1,...,s)$ links. The calculation of the joint torque can be done in the following steps.

1) The acceleration, angular velocity, angular accelerations of blanch 1, 0th link can be specified as

$$\dot{\mathbf{v}}_0^1 = -\mathbf{g}\ ,\ \boldsymbol{\omega}_0^1 = 0\ ,\ \dot{\boldsymbol{\omega}}_0^1 = 0 \qquad (3)$$

2) Compute $\mathbf{v}_c^1, \boldsymbol{\omega}_c^1, \dot{\boldsymbol{\omega}}_c^1$ from $c = 1$ to n_1 for branch1.

3) The initial value of the angular velocity and angular accelerations of branch $k\ (k = 2,....,s)$ can be obtained as

$$\dot{\mathbf{v}}_0^k = \left(\mathbf{B}_R^k\right)^T \left\{\dot{\mathbf{v}}_{col}^{cob} + \dot{\boldsymbol{\omega}}_{col}^{cob} \times \widetilde{\mathbf{B}}_p^k + \boldsymbol{\omega}_{col}^{cob} \times \left(\boldsymbol{\omega}_{col}^{cob} \times \widetilde{\mathbf{B}}_p^k\right)\right\} \qquad (4)$$

$$\boldsymbol{\omega}_0^k = \left(\mathbf{B}_R^k\right)^T \boldsymbol{\omega}_{col}^{cob} \tag{5}$$

$$\dot{\boldsymbol{\omega}}_0^k = \left(\mathbf{B}_R^k\right)^T \dot{\boldsymbol{\omega}}_{col}^{cob} \tag{6}$$

where $\mathbf{B}^k$ is a 4x4 coordinate transform matrix from a parent branch to a child branch in a homogeneous coordinate system. $\mathbf{B}_R^k$ shows the left-above 3x3 matrix of $\mathbf{B}^k$, and $\tilde{\mathbf{B}}_p^k$ is a right-above matrix of $\left(\mathbf{B}^k\right)^{-1}$. cob is a branch number of branch k, and col is a link number of branch k.

4) Calculate $\mathbf{v}_c^k, \boldsymbol{\omega}_c^k, \dot{\boldsymbol{\omega}}_c^k$ for branch k $(2,...,s)$ from $c=1$ to n_k

5) Calculate force $\mathbf{f}_c^k$ and moment $\mathbf{n}_c^k$ for blanch $k(s,...,1)$ from $c = n_k$ to. The joint torque $\boldsymbol{\tau}_c^k$ can be estimated as follows

$$\boldsymbol{\tau}_c^k = \mathbf{z}_0^T \mathbf{n}_c^k \qquad : \text{Revolute joint} \tag{7}$$

$$\boldsymbol{\tau}_c^k = \mathbf{z}_0^T \mathbf{f}_c^k \qquad : \text{Slide joint} \tag{8}$$

The equation of the human motion dynamics can be represented as follows:

$$\boldsymbol{\tau} = \mathbf{M}(\mathbf{q})\ddot{\mathbf{q}} + \mathbf{h}(\mathbf{q},\dot{\mathbf{q}}) + \mathbf{g}(\mathbf{q}) \tag{9}$$

where $\mathbf{M}(\mathbf{q})$ is inertia tensor matrix, $\mathbf{h}(\mathbf{q},\dot{\mathbf{q}})$ represent centrifugal and Corioli's force, $\mathbf{g}(\mathbf{q})$ is a gravity term, $\mathbf{q}$ is a joint angle.

Right side of eq. (9) consists of constant values except angler velocity and angler accelerations. Therefore we can obtain the joint torques by specifying them as described in Sec. 4.2

We have implemented the above motion equations by ourselves because current system is in Java3D. However, in general, we can also use commercial software such as SD/Fast[15], and other free multi-link physical simulator in C/C++.

4   Optimizing Motion Trajectory

In this section, we show the motion tracking method using the minimum torque criterion. We optimize the joint torques along the whole motion trajectory, and also the least squares difference of image intensity.

4.1   Initial Estimate of Motion Trajectory

First we obtain initial estimate of motion trajectory by using the sparsely estimated 3D pose and the simple interpolation technique. We use the silhouette-based pose alignment algorithm[9] for the initial estimation. This type of pose estimation technique is only useful when the hands and legs are clearly separated from the

Fig. 3. Human joint model

body. Therefore we still need the global optimization technique to estimate continuous human motion at every frames.

We use the curve fitting by the piecewise hermite interpolation using the 3rd order bezier-spline. We need to specify the sample point and tangent vectors to estimate the curve. Let the node of $E+1$ be $\mathbf{Q}_0, \mathbf{Q}_1, ..., \mathbf{Q}_E$, we can obtain the tangent vectors by

$$\mathbf{l}_0 = \frac{\mathbf{Q}_1 - \mathbf{Q}_0}{|\mathbf{Q}_1 - \mathbf{Q}_0|}, \mathbf{l}_E = \frac{\mathbf{Q}_E - \mathbf{Q}_{E-1}}{|\mathbf{Q}_E - \mathbf{Q}_{E-1}|},$$

$$\mathbf{l}_e = \frac{\mathbf{Q}_e - \mathbf{Q}_{e-1}}{|\mathbf{Q}_e - \mathbf{Q}_{e-1}|}, (e = 1,2,....,E-1) \tag{10}$$

Then we obtain the interpolated curve $\{P(t) \mid 0 \le t \le E\}$ where t is a frame number. We use $P(t)$ as an initial value for the pose estimate. Such parametric representation also has the advantage of decreasing the degree of freedom to stabilize the estimation.

4.2 Obtaining Angular Velocity and Acceleration

To estimate joint torque using eq. (9), we need an angular velocity and angular acceleration of the joint angle. The velocity $\dot{q}_f$ and the acceleration $\ddot{q}_f$ of f th frame are obtained by

$$\dot{\mathbf{q}}_f = \frac{\frac{\mathbf{q}_{f+1} - \mathbf{q}_f}{H} + \frac{\mathbf{q}_f - \mathbf{q}_{f-1}}{H}}{2} = \frac{\mathbf{q}_{f+1} - \mathbf{q}_{f-1}}{2H} \tag{11}$$

$$\ddot{\mathbf{q}}_f = \frac{\frac{\mathbf{q}_{f+1} - \mathbf{q}_f}{H} - \frac{\mathbf{q}_f - \mathbf{q}_{f-1}}{H}}{H} = \frac{\mathbf{q}_{f+1} - 2\mathbf{q}_f + \mathbf{q}_{f-1}}{H^2} \tag{12}$$

where

H : frame time interval
f : frame number
$fMax$: total frame number
$\mathbf{q}_f$: joint angle of f th frame

4.3 Evaluation Function and Optimization

The total of joint torques $\boldsymbol{\tau}_r$ at r th link $Link\_r$ can be calculated using the torque value $\mathbf{T}_f$ at f th frames:

$$\boldsymbol{\tau}_r = \sum_{f=1}^{fMax-2} \mathbf{T}_f \tag{13}$$

f is from 1 to $fMax - 2$ because the velocity and acceleration can be only estimated within these frames from eq. (11), (12). The resulting $\mathbf{T}_f$ has the same range.

The total of the intensity value $\mathbf{D}_r$ of $Link\_r$ can be obtained as

$$\mathbf{D}_k = \sum_{f=1}^{fMax-2} \sum_{u=0}^{uMax} \sum_{v=0}^{vMax} w(u,v)\left(i_f(u,v) - i_{f-1}(u,v)\right)^2 \tag{14}$$

where intensity value of (u,v) is $i_f(u,v)$. $W(u,v)$ is a weighting function of robust statistics. In this paper, we use the following function.

$$w(u,v) = \begin{cases} (1 - (|\Delta\eta|/\sigma)^2)^2 & if\,|\Delta\eta| < \sigma \\ 0 & if\,|\Delta\eta| > \sigma \end{cases}$$

The occlusion by the body parts can be judged by using the 3d body model and z-buffer.

By using eq.(13), (14), the evaluation function can be written as

$$\alpha_r \tau_r + \beta_r \mathbf{D}_r \rightarrow \min \tag{15}$$

where α_r, β_r is a weight functions. We use the greedy method to optimize eq. (15). By perturbing the control points of spline curve around the small neighborhoods, we find the motion trajectory which minimize eq.(15). In our experiments, this simple optimization algorithm works well for complex actions.

4.4 Adding Extra Constraints

Adding extra constraints can be integrated with our methods. Constraints can be represented as error functions, and added to eq.15 for the global minimizations. We show the example of points and planar constraints. The other constraints can be integrated in the same mammer.

1) Point and Motion Constraints
Point constraints may be useful because we can fit body model to marker positions. Using only markers are not practical because it can also suffer from partial occlusions. The point constraints can be represented as a following error function

$$\mathbf{D}_{po\,int} = \left(p_i - p_m\right)^2 \tag{16}$$

where p_i is a point on the body model projected onto 2D image plane, and p_m is a point in the video image.

The motion direction constraints can be also represented by changing the p_i and p_m to the velocity vectors.

2) Planar Constraints
Planar constraints represent points on the model contact to a plane in 3D environment. It would be useful when the persons are moving on the floor or slope. The point constraints can be represented as a following error function

$$\mathbf{D}_{plane} = \left(\left(p_p - p_m \right) \bullet n \right)^2 \tag{17}$$

where p_p is a point on the plane, p_m is a point on the body model, and n is a normal vector of the plane.

4.5 Using Multiple Cameras

We prefer to use a single camera because it is cheaper in practice. However, when we capture the motion of multiple people, it would be useful for using multiple cameras for reducing occlusions. Our method can be extended into a multi-camera version by calculate D_p from the different camera positions, and apply minimization of eq.15.

5 Implementation Details

We have developed object-oriented software packages for video motion capture (Fig.4). The software architecture is simple, yet flexible enough to apply the video motion capture for multiple humans.

5.1 Swing and Java3D

In this paper, we use Java Swing for GUI, and Java 3D for 3D model display and implementation of motion estimation algorithm. Java Swing component is packages for developing GUI. Java3D is using Direct3D or OpenGL as low-level API incorporating hardware accelerations. The advantage of using Swing package is that many GUI descriptions become easier such as tree structure descriptions, menu descriptions, dialogue box, and sliders. By combining Java Swing and Java3D, it will be much easier to build GUI software packages with hardware accelerations than using C language and OpenGL.

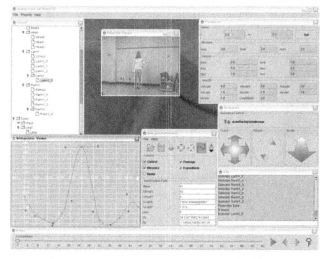

Fig. 4. Screen shot of the video motion captuer software

5.2 System Configurations

The prototype system consists of five packages: *Spatio-Temporal Interpolator, Video Manager, Dynamics Controller, 3D Parts Manager, Human Body Tracker* (Fig.5). The advantage of the system is that the local updates does not affect the whole functions. The role of each packages are as follows:

- Spatio-Temporal Interpolator: spatio-temporal interpolation and editing functions
- Video Manager: processing intensity images considering the occlusions of human body
- Dynamics Controller: calculating dynamics of human body
- 3D Parts Manager: describing structures and physical property of human body
- Human Body Tracker: Managing of above four modules

1) Spatio-temporal Interpolator
Spatio-Temporal Interpolator package is performing interpolation of pose values along time sequences. We use hermite interpolation using bezier-spline curve for the current implementation. The package also has an interactive editing function of spatio-temporal action trajectory.

2) Video Manager
Video Manager package extracts intensity values from video and calculate least squares errors corresponding to the each body parts.

3) Dynamics Controller
Dynamics Controller package holds dynamic equations of human body, and provide them to the management package.

4) 3D Parts Manager
3D Parts Manager describes the structural relationship of the human body, and also the physical property of the position and velocity.

5) Human Body Tracker
Human Body Tracker package manage above four packages. Human Body Tracker package describes the structures of human body model. The proposed tracking method was implemented by using the message passing between four modules.

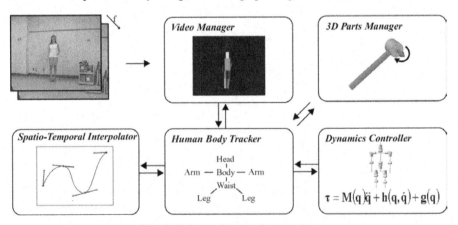

Fig. 5. Software System Compostion

5.3 Sequence of the Pose Estimation

Motion estimation process can be realized by the following steps:

1. Generate necessary 3D Parts Manager and setting initial values.
2. Communicate with Spatio-Temporal Interpolator package, and automatically or interactively edit pose data.
3. Handing parameters in 3D Parts Manager to Video Manager and Dynamics Controller via Human Body Tracker Video Manager and Dynamics Controller returns the intensity values and joint torques.

   Evaluate intensity value and joint torque.

6 Experiments

We have implemented our algorithm using standard PC to test the effectiveness of the tracking. Fig.6 show the result of tracking using the video sequence including complex and dynamic behavior.

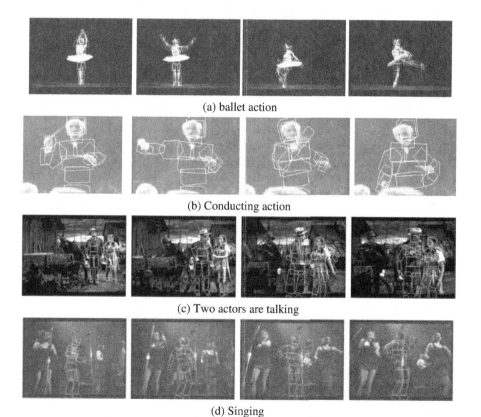

(a) ballet action

(b) Conducting action

(c) Two actors are talking

(d) Singing

Fig. 6. Tracking examples

7 Conclusions

We proposed a human motion estimation method by minimizing both intensity change and torque applying to the body parts. The minimum torque criterion adds extra constraints during the motion estimation. We also demonstrated the performance of our algorithm using the complex behaviors such as dance sequences. In future, we extend our algorithm to estimate articulated and non-rigid motion such as animals.

References

1. Bregler. C., Malik, J.: Tracking people with twists and exponential maps. *Proc. IEEE Comput. Soc. Conf. Comput.Vision and Pattern Recogn.* (1998) 8–15
2. Gavrila, D., and Davis, L.: 3d model-based tracking of humans in action: A multi-view approach. *Proc. IEEE Comput.Soc. Conf. Comput. Vision and Pattern Recogn.* (1996) 73–80
3. Kakadiaris, I., Metaxas, D.: Model-based estimation of 3d human motion. *IEEE Trans. PAMI*, 22(12) (2000) 1453–1459
4. Rehg, J. M., Kanade, T.: Visual tracking of high DOF articulated structures: An application to human hand tracking. *Lecture Notes in Computer Science*, 800 (1994) 35–46
5. Wren, C., Azarbayejani, A., Darrell, T., Pentland, A., Pfinder: Real-time tracking of the human body. *IEEE Trans. PAMI*, 19(7) (1997) 780–785
6. Yamamoto, M., Koshikawa, K.: Human motion analysis based on a robot arm model. *Proc. IEEE Comput. Soc. Conf. Comput. Vision and Pattern Recogn.* (1991) 664–665
7. Kawasaki, H., Shimizu, T.: Development of Robot Symbolic Analysis System ROSAM II. Proc. of Int. Conf. Of Japan-USA Symposium on Flexible Automation (1998) 1121-1128
8. Luh, J. Y. S., Walker, M. W., Paul, R. P. C.: On-Line Computational Scheme for Mechanical Manipulators. IEEE Int.Jour. of Dynamic Systems, Measurement, and Control, No. 102 (1980) 69-76
9. Hoshino, J., Hirofumi, S.: A Match Moving Technique for Human Body Sequences. ICASSSP2001, Conference Proceedings CD-ROM, IMDSP-P3.1 (2001)
10. Popovic, Z., Editing Dynamic Properties of Captured Human Motion. in IEEE International Conference on Robotics and Automation (2000)
11. Popovic, Z., Witkin, A.: Physically Based Motion Transformation. in Computer Graphics SIGGRAPH (1999)
12. Gleicher, M.: Motion Path Editing. Proceedings of the 2001 ACM Symposium on Interactive 3D Graphics (2001)
13. Gleicher, M.: Retargetting Motion to New Characters. Proceedings of SIGGRAPH 98. In Computer Graphics Annual Conferance Series (1998)
14. Gleicher, M.: Motion Editing with Spacetime Constraints. Proceedings of the 1997 Symposium on Interactive 3D Graphics (1997)
15. Michael, G., Hollars, Dan E., Rosenthal, Michael, A., Sherman.: Sd/fast. Symbolic Dynamics, Inc (1991)
16. Hodgins, J. K., Pollard.: Adapting simulated behaviors for new characters. SIGGRAPH 97, (1997) 153-162
17. Jessica, K., Hodgins, Paula, K., Sweeney, David, G., Lawrence.: Generating natural-looking motion for computer animation. In Proceedings of Graphics Interface 92, (1992) 265-272
18. Faloutsos, P., Panne, M., Terzopoulos, D.: Composable Controllers for Physics-based Character Animation. Proceedings of ACM SIGGRAPH 2001, (2001)
19. Wilhelms, J., Brian, A., Barsky.: Using dynamic analysis to animate articulated bodies such as humans and robots. In Graphics Interface ' 85 (1985) 97-104

20. Cohen, M.: Interactive spacetime control for animation. Proc. SIGGRAPH'92, Vol.26, No.2 (1992) 293-302
21. Nago, J., Marks, J.: Spacetime constraints revisited. Prof. SIGGRAPH'93 (1993) 343-350
22. Witkin, A., Kass, M.: Spacetime Constraints. Proc. SIGGRAPH'88, Vol.22, No.4 (1988) 159-186
23. Williams, D. Shah, M. A Fast Algorithm for Active Contours and Curvature Estimation. CVGIP: Image Understanding. Vol. 55, No. 1 (1992) 14-26

Picture Languages in Medical Pattern Knowledge Representation and Understanding

Marek R. Ogiela and Ryszard Tadeusiewicz

AGH University of Science and Technology, Institute of Automatics
Al. Mickiewicza 30, PL-30-059 Kraków, Poland
{mogiela,rtad}@agh.edu.pl

Abstract. In the paper, there will be presented the new way of application of structural methods of pattern recognition, in the form of picture languages, for creation of knowledge representation for medical pattern analysis and understanding. Specialist medical databases storing data in visual form constitute a large group among multimedia databases; those patterns originate from numerous diagnostic examinations of practically all organs of the human body. One of the main problems in the fast accessing and interpretation of such visual information is the way of transformation of these visual data into a form enabling intelligent analysis and understanding of medical meaning of these patterns. The basic problems leading to achieve this goal is the method of representation and indexing the important objects constituting the data contents. In the paper we describe some examples presenting ways of applying picture languages techniques in the creation of intelligent cognitive knowledge representation for selected class of medical images.

1 Introduction

One of the most challenging problems in the tasks of accessing and fast search for semantic information in medical databases is the creation of a method of representation and indexing of important objects (organs and lesions) constituting the data contents. Generally the task of semantic search for important information was discussed a number of times and to some degree is solved for databases including texts exclusively [10]. Unfortunately, the introduction of multimedia databases has demonstrated once again that the search for useful information on the basis of their content is a problem to which a practical solution is still impossible to find. Everything seems to suggest that techniques of syntactic pattern analysis with especially picture languages, used in computer-aided medical diagnosis, can be very useful also in the tasks of creation knowledge representation for automatic search of visual data [7, 9].

In interpretation of medical images the shape of anomalies or lesions can vary between the cases due to the fact that human organs vary between individuals [4, 7, 9]. On the other hand, every type of disease leads to some characteristic changes in the shapes of visualised organs; therefore this type of information, obtained owing to the application of the method of structural pattern analysis, will constitute information label determining the image content [1]. Techniques proposed in [9] allow the change of a pattern into its syntactic description in such a way that the automatically generated language formula transforms precisely the basic pattern content: the shape of the examined organ and its anomaly caused by disease. Those formalised, automatically

V. Torra et al. (Eds.): MDAI 2005, LNAI 3558, pp. 442–447, 2005.

generated knowledge representation in the form of shape descriptors for analysed objects, allow for separating the indexing process from the secondary formal features of the recorded patterns. Accordingly, the description is focused on the most important contents.

2 Linguistic Knowledge Representation

Graph grammar description algorithms as presented further expand the traditional methods of computer-aided analysis through the interpretation of possibilities directed at tasks supporting medical diagnostics [2]. Additionally, semantic information enables the use of such techniques in tasks of semantically-oriented search for some concrete disease cases in medical image data bases. In practice such tasks were difficult to implement, sometimes even impossible due to difficulties in creating indexing keys that describe image semantics [3, 6, 8]. Expanding analysis possibilities by meaning interpretation allows us to find an answer to questions concerning the medical meaning of the analysed image, semantic information specified by the features of the examined image and classification possibilities of disease units based on lesions on the image. The analysis of images conducted in this paper will go in the direction pointed out by the formulated questions. Its objective will be, in particular, to present and evaluate the possibilities of expansive graph grammar application for the recognition and intelligent meaning analysis of wrist and bones radiogrammes.

The idea presented here and associated with creating indexing keys allows for an efficient search and categorisation of both information specifying the type of medical imaging or the examined structure and meaningful semantic information specifying the looked-for object within the framework of one database. In a special case, apart from the main indexing key allowing the search or archiving of a specified type of medical images (e.g. coronograms or spinal cord images [9]), it is possible to create additional indexing labels specifying successive layers of semantic details of image contents. First of all, this information tells us about the progress of a disease detected with the use of the grammars and semantic actions defined in them. The indexing information is also a description of the external morphology of the imaged organ. This type of description takes the form of a terminal symbol sequence introduced while grammars are defined for individual types of images and organs visible on them. Finally, the lowest level of information useful for a detailed search are the types of recognized lesions and linguistic derivation leading to the generation of a semantic description of those lesions.

3 Semantic Description of Selected Visualization

The approach to the generation of structural-semantic representation of medical patterns in multimedia databases with the use of context-free and EDT graph grammars [5] presented in this study is a new solution. Preliminary research reveals that such approach proves to be an extremely efficient and universal tool enabling visual data compression and unambiguous data representation. An important point is that the proposed indexation technique has been optimised with an aim to find diagnostic information, easily observed in the shape of organs visible on patterns and dependent on disease symptoms. Real examples of images showing pathological lesions in the form of wrist bone necrosis and calcification have been shown on Figure 1. Such irregularities are to be detected and interpreted correctly by the syntactic image recognition method described in this paper [4].

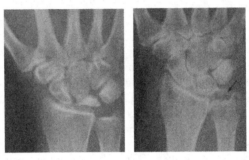

Fig. 1. A) A case of avascular necrosis of lunate (Kienbock's disease). B) Image showing calcification (arrow) in the region triangular of the wrist

For making the representation of the examined structures in the form of EDG graphs [9] it is necessary to define an appropriate linguistic formalism that is an appropriate graph grammar defining a language. The language is defined in such a way that one could describe using it, without any ambiguities, every image representing a spatial system composed of elements similar to the wrist bone system. In this way we create a tool describing all possible shapes and locations of wrist bones, both the correct and pathological ones. After defining such a grammar, every X-ray image will be converted into a linguistic formula built in accordance with the rules of that grammar. The effective parsing of that formula conducted by the computer, compliant with the rules of the created grammar will lead to an automatic assessment of photograph contents. This will make it possible in particular to determine whether the built of a wrist falls within the norm or whether it has pathological deviations.

For the analysis of wrist radiogrammes an expansive graph grammar was defined.

$$G_{exp}=(N, \Sigma, \Gamma, P, S)$$

Non-terminal set of peak labels

N= {STS, u s, l, t, p, tm, tz, c, h, m1, m2, m3, m4, m5}.

Terminal set of peak labels Σ={r, u s, l, t, p, tm, tz, c, h, m1, m2, m3, m4, m5}

Γ - edge label set {s<p<q<r<s<t<u<w<x<y<z}

Start symbol S=STS

P – is a finite production set presented on Figure 2.

Possibilities to describe image cases showing additional wrist bones can be obtained by enriching the above-presented set of rules introducing the formulas of the analysed grammar by productions defined on Figure 3. Set of non-terminal labels N will then contain also an additional peak label, 'Acc Bone' standing for the reasoning tree for the new object/bone appearing on the image (in the first series) and located in accordance with the labelled directions.

Image showing other pathology forms in wrist image: synostoses or bone defects can be recognised with the use of alternative rules specified on Figure 4. In this case an additional 'Fuss' peak appears and stands for the introduction of an additional bone, originating from the merger of two neighbouring ones.

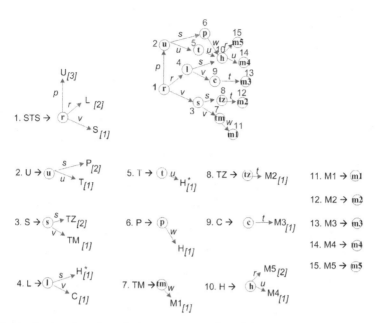

Fig. 2. Production/graph set introducing a representation of the correct build and the number of bones in the wrist

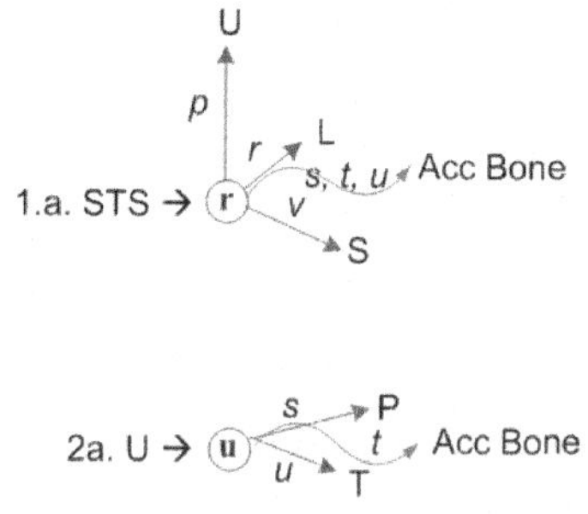

Fig. 3. Production set describing additional bones in wrist radiogrammes. For simplification, in these productions peak and graph ordinals as well graph location, operators were omitted

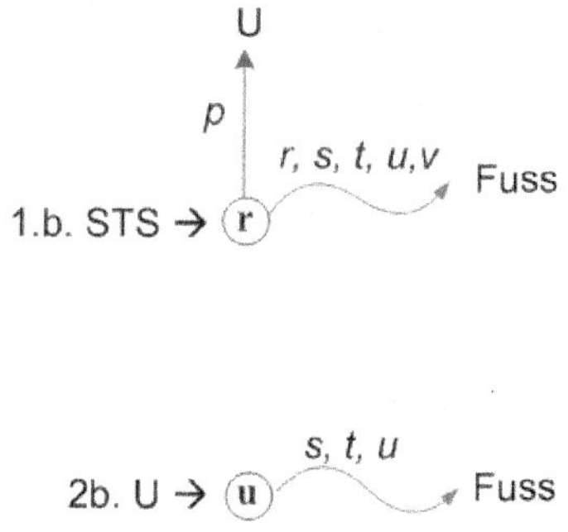

Fig. 4. Production set describing bone defects caused by bone joints or by bone dislocation

4 Selected Results

The prepared method of knowledge representation were aimed at building an automatic detection and semantic interpretation system for detected regularities as well as the diagnosed irregularities in the carpus bones. It is worth notice, however, that the test data set used for defining the output rules in the presented grammar was composed of only about 30 radiogrammes. Despite such an insignificant representation and, owing to a great descriptive and generation power of the used graphs, it is possible to classify practically any number of analysed images. The initially assessed efficiency exceeds the 90% threshold. On the other hand, the appearance of difficult and ambiguous cases can be quickly considered by enriching grammar formalisms by new (so far not considered) reasoning rules and by specifying the meaning interpretation or such new cases. This is also the direction that will be followed in the conducted research.

The main strength of the proposed structural methods for indexation and search for data in medical visual databases is its high efficiency due from small memory complexity of semantic representation generated to represent patterns; besides algorithms used to search for similar patterns are not time-consuming. Accordingly, such search boils down to comparing the sequences of symbols representing the semantic content of analyzed images, involving the search for the descriptions most similar to that of a given object in database (it is done as visual query). This type of search operations are unaffected by minor disturbances (noise) or geometrical transformations of patterns as these factors are independent of the generated syntactic and semantic representation.

Those properties result from unambiguity of representation generated for various semantic contents. In practical terms the result of computer implementation of the syntactic analysis algorithms provided here is a developed system allowing for structural analysis of the discussed medical patterns targeted at creation of semantic representation defining various disease symptoms. The research confirmed the highest potential of developing the description of visible deformations of shapes as well as semantic categorisation and database mining of various disease symptoms. Those descriptions are arrived at as a result of intelligent lesions recognition. Yet, from the point of view of knowledge engineering, they may also serve as data for deeper reasoning and be used by Computer-Aided Diagnosis systems.

Acknowledgement

This work was supported by the AGH University of Science and Technology under Grant No. 10.10.120.39.

References

1. Albus, J.S., Meystel, A.M.: Engineering of Mind: An Introduction to the Science of Intelligent Systems. Willey (2001)
2. Bankman, I. (ed.): Handbook of Medical Imaging: Processing and Analysis. Academic Press (2002)
3. Berchtold S., Keim D. A., Kriegel H-P., Seidl T.: Indexing the solution space: a new technique for nearest neighbor search in high-dimensional space. IEEE Transactions on Knowledge & Data Engineering, 12(1) (2000) 45-57

4. Burgener, F.A., Kormano, M.: Bone and Joint Disorders. Thieme, Stuttgart (1997)
5. Flasinski, M.: On the parsing of deterministic graph languages for syntactic pattern recognition. Pattern Recognition, 26 (1993) 1-16
6. Martinez A. M., Serra J. R.: A new approach to object-related image retrieval. Journal of Visual Languages & Computing, 11(3) (2000) 345-363
7. Meyer-Baese, A.: Pattern Recognition in Medical Imaging. Elsevier (2003)
8. Pietka, E. (et al.): Computer-Assisted Bone Age Assessment: Image Preprocessing and Epiphyseal/Metahyseal ROI Extraction. IEEE Trans. On Medical Imaging, 20/8 (2001) 715-729
9. Tadeusiewicz, R, Ogiela, M.R.: Medical Image Understanding Technology. Springer, Berlin-Heidelberg (2004)
10. Torra, V., Miyamoto, S., Lanau, S.: Exploration of textual databases using a fuzzy hierarchical clustering algorithm in GAMBAL system. Information Processing and Management, 41(3) (2005) 578-598

Loading Problem in Multiple Containers and Pallets Using Strategic Search Method

Shigeyuki Takahara

Kagawa Prefectural Industrial Technology Center, Takamatsu 761-8031, Japan
takahara@itc.pref.kagawa.jp

Abstract. An optimal loading in multiple containers and pallets is considered. In this paper, a strategic search method using meta-heuristics and strategic procedure is proposed. This method gives the loading sequence of packages and selection sequence of containers and pallets to utilize them. The meta-heuristics determines the sequence of packages, and the strategic procedure determines the sequence of containers and pallets with reference to search process. Therefore, this method is realized to find optimal sequences. The effectiveness of the proposed method is compared with other methods, such as local search and simulated annealing. The experimental results show that the present method is superior to other methods.

1 Introduction

Container loading problem and pallet loading problem arise in a variety of distribution modes, such as truck, railway, ship and aircraft. Several approaches have been taken to solve these problems. However, most of them deal with a single container and pallet, not multiple containers and pallets.

Ivancic *et al.* [5], Bischoff and Ratcliff [1], Terno *et al.* [8] and Eley [2] deal with the loading of packages in multiple containers and pallets. These researches deal with one kind of same size container and pallet and its objective is to find a minimal number of containers and pallets. Hence it cannot correspond to load the packages in a variety of kinds of containers and pallets.

In the present paper, a strategic search method using meta-heuristics and a strategic procedure is proposed. In this method, cooperation between decision of package loading sequence and decision of container and pallet (C/P) selection sequence is realized. This method employs the meta-heuristics, such as local search (LS) and simulated annealing (SA), to decide the package loading sequence and uses the strategic procedure to decide the C/P selection sequence.

This method is applied to container loading problem of packages of rectangular-shaped box in multiple containers. The experimental results show that the present method is superior to other methods.

2 Loading Problem in Multiple Containers and Pallets

2.1 Problem Description

Assume that n packages are loaded in m containers and pallets. Moreover, each package correspond to integer 1,2...n and each container and pallet correspond to integer 1,2...m. Namely; the package set P and the container and pallet set S are denoted by

V. Torra et al. (Eds.): MDAI 2005, LNAI 3558, pp. 448–456, 2005.

$$P = \{p_1, p_2, ..., p_n\}$$
$$S = \{s_1, s_2, ..., s_m\} \tag{1}$$

The present paper uses a sequence-based approach when package solution represents a loading sequence and container and pallet solution represents a selection sequence. A collection of permutation of packages and a collection of permutation of containers and pallets are denoted by

$$\rho = \{\sigma = (p_1, p_2, ..., p_n)\}$$
$$\lambda = \{\mu = (s_1, s_2, ..., s_m)\} \tag{2}$$

Permutation $\sigma \in \rho$ is a sequence for determining the loading position of packages and permutation $\mu \in \lambda$ is a sequence for determining selection of containers and pallets. The optimal solution is found by changing these permutations.

A package loading algorithm A and a criterion must be prepared for the container loading problem and the pallet loading problem. This algorithm uses heuristics and determines the loading position of each package according to the sequence σ. Therefore, the criterion F is denoted by $F(A, \sigma, \mu)$. The optimality implies that useless space of the containers and pallets is minimized. Thus, the loading problem in multiple containers and pallets is denoted by

$$\min_{\sigma \in \rho, \mu \in \lambda} F(A, \sigma, \mu) \tag{3}$$

where $F(A, \sigma, \mu)$ is the objective function.

Assume that the volume of package p_i is $V(p_i)$, and the capacity of container and pallet s_j is $V(s_j)$, ratio of the useless space R is defined by

$$R = 1 - \sum_{i=1}^{n} V(p_i) \bigg/ \sum_{j=1}^{k} V(s_j) = 1 - V(P) \bigg/ \sum_{j=1}^{k} V(s_j) \tag{4}$$

where k is the number of the containers and pallets that is loaded the packages. Thus this paper takes $F(A, \sigma, \mu) = R$.

2.2 Loading Procedure

Two kinds of loading procedures in multiple containers and pallets using the loading algorithm A are considered.

- Package priority procedure: This procedure determines the loading position of package p_i according to the C/P selection sequence μ.
- Container and pallet priority procedure: This procedure determines the layout of container and pallet s_j according to the package loading sequence σ.

Moreover, cooperation between decision of package loading sequence σ and decision of C/P selection sequence μ is realized.

The container and pallet priority procedure is shown in Fig.1. In this procedure, at first decide a package loading sequence σ, and then select a container and pallet that determines a layout according to a C/P sequence μ. This procedure finishes when all packages are loaded.

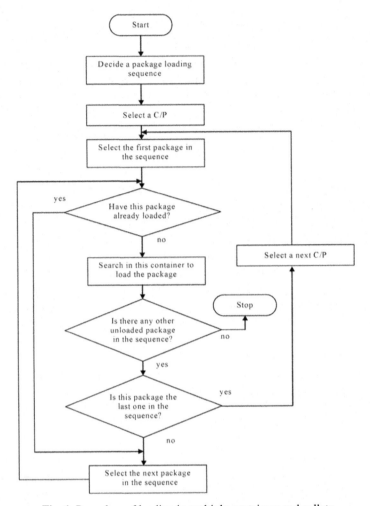

Fig. 1. Procedure of loading in multiple containers and pallets

2.3 Strategic Search Method

A strategic search method that enables cooperation between decision of the package loading sequence and the C/P selection sequence is proposed. The present search mechanism with the following components is illustrated in Fig. 2:

- Controller
- Selector
- Observer

These details are shown below.

1) Decision method of package loading sequence: In order to decide a package loading sequence, the meta-heuristics method that is based on a neighborhood search, such as LS and SA, is adopted. A solution is represented by (2). The neighborhood of a solution is denoted by $N(\sigma)$. The controller decides the neighborhood and selects the solution using the meta-heuristic method.

Moreover, observer monitors the search process and gives instruction to the controller. Hence, it is possible to realize an adaptive search [7].

2) Decision method of C/P selection sequence: A selector determines the C/P selection. This selector has next two modes and one option, and an observer gives instructions for switching these modes and using this option.

- Fixed mode: The selector does not change the C/P selection sequence. The aim of this mode is that optimal solution is found by only changing the package loading sequence whereby a strongly local search is realized.
- Free mode: The selector selects the C/P selection sequence freely according to a certain strategy, such as meta-heuristic method, heuristics, and ranking selection. The aim of this mode is to escape from the local minima and realize global search.
- Restriction option: The selector changes a current C/P selection sequence so that the rest of the packages may be loaded efficiently in a container and pallet. Therefore, the current C/P selection sequence is changed by the exchange operation or the insertion operation. The aim of this option is to utilize a container and a pallet when the unloaded packages have decreased.

The restriction option is used in both the fixed mode and the free mode. Hence conditions when to use the option must be defined. One is the condition of switching the fixed mode and the free mode. This mode switching condition is considered as follows:

- Regular switching
- Switching when the search falls into local minima with no improvement
- Random switching

The other is the condition of using restriction option within the fixed mode or the free mode. This option switching condition uses a functional relation of the unloaded packages and the rest of the containers and pallets, and also the layout of other containers and pallets. Assume that s_h is currently selected containers and pallet to determine the layout, a collection of the unloaded packages is P_h, a collection of the rest of the containers and pallets is S_h, and the ratio of the useless space of l_{th} layout, which is already determined, is R_l. The option switching condition is given by

$$V(P_h)\big/(1 - \max_{1 \leq l \leq h-1} R_l) \leq \max_{s_j \in S_h} V(s_j) + \min_{s_j \in S_h} V(s_j) \tag{5}$$

If this condition is satisfied, the observer orders the selector to use the restriction option. Next, the selector selects the container and pallet that satisfies the following condition.

$$\min_{s_k \in S_h} \left| V(s_k) - V(P_h)\big/(1 - \max_{1 \leq l \leq h-1} R_l) \right| \tag{6}$$

Thus, s_h in the C/P selection sequence is exchanged by s_k. Some other conditions can also be considered. If unnecessary, the selector may not use to the restriction option.

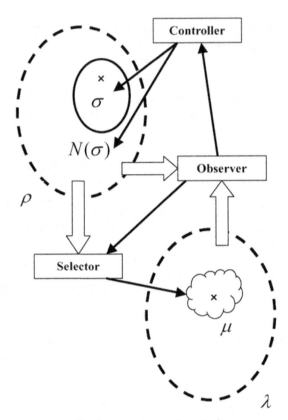

Fig. 2. Strategic search method

3   Experimental Results and Discussion

3.1   Configuration

The proposed method is applied to the container loading problem in multiple contain-ers. Three sample package data sets form Data1 to Data3 and a sample container data set have been used. Data1 includes 10 kinds of different packages, which has 250 each. Data2 includes 50 kinds of packages, which has 50 each. Data3 includes 100 kinds of packages, which has 25 each. Moreover, the container data set includes 5 kinds of containers, which has 5 each. Table 1 shows the package data set Data1 and the container data set.

1) Loading algorithm: "Branch heuristics [6]" is used as the package loading algo-rithm *A*. This algorithm is shown below.

Step 0. Decide a package loading sequence $\sigma = (p_1, p_2, ..., p_n)$; define an initial branch L_0; set $k = 0$ as index for the current package.

Step 1. Take the package *k* for loading.

Step 2. Scan the branch L_k. If a non-overlap loading position is found, go to *Step 4.*

Step 3. Else set $k = k + 1$. Go to *Step 5.*

Table 1. Sample data set

Packages   (Data1)

Package size (mm/mm/mm)	Qty	Package size (mm/mm/mm)	Qty
920 × 1130 × 330	250	590 × 1190 × 390	250
370 × 520 × 280	250	520 × 540 × 490	250
330 × 570 × 290	250	450 × 750 × 350	250
370 × 990 × 300	250	680 × 790 × 440	250
640 × 920 × 330	250	490 × 1160 × 470	250

Containers

Container size (mm/mm/mm)	Qty	Container size (mm/mm/mm)	Qty
2270 × 3642 × 2252	5	2330 × 11998 × 2197	5
2330 × 5867 × 2197	5	2256 × 12054 × 1970	5
2388 × 5908 × 2072	5		

Step 4. Load the package on the selected position by *Step 2*. Set $k = k + 1$. Update the branch L_k.

Step 5. If $k < n$, then go back to *Step 1*, else stop.

The branch is a set of the spaces that can be loaded packages. This algorithm is able to realize "*wall-building approach* [3]" and "*stack-building approach* [4]" by changing the order of the search in the branch L_k in *Step2*. This algorithm determines a layout in a container or a pallet. Therefore, in the case of loading packages to multiple containers and multiple pallets, the loading sequence is reconstructed using the unloading packages in *Step0*.

2) Decision method of package loading sequence: The meta-heuristics is used to decide the package loading sequence. The basic LS and SA using the exchange neighborhood $N(\sigma)$ are used. This neighborhood is based on the exchange operation, that is, two numbers indicating the corresponding two packages are exchanged in the sequence. In the case of SA, the initial temperature is 100, the end temperature is 0, the temperature deduction ratio is 0.85 and the number of searches at each temperature is the number of packages. The initial solution is given by the sorted sequence of the decreasing order of the volume of the packages.

3) Decision method of C/P selection sequence: When the observer should give instruction for switching the fixed mode and the free mode and using the restriction option is important. At the time when a search starts, the selector is in the fixed mode. If the search does not improve in 50 times of the iteration, the observer switches to the free mode. The selector is in the free mode until the search improves, then the observer switches to the fixed mode. Moreover, the condition of (5) and (6) is used as the condition to use the restriction option. The strategy in the free mode is the SA, which is same as the method used by the package loading sequence decision. The initial solution is given by the sorted sequence of the decreasing order of the capacity of the containers.

3.2 Experimental Results

Differences between the determination method of package lading sequence and the determination method of C/P selection sequence are compared. The proposed method (PM) is compared with other method, such as local search (LS), simulated annealing (SA) and a heuristic that is given by the sequence the sorted sequence of the decreasing order of the area (HU) as the determination method of C/P selection sequence. The determination method of package loading sequence is LS and SA.

Table 2. Results of experiment

(a) Data1

LS	HU	LS	SA	PM
Average [%]	14.23	13.18	13.05	11.40
Best result [%]	14.23	12.92	12.92	10.55
SA	HU	LS	SA	PM
Average [%]	14.23	12.26	12.35	11.27
Best result [%]	14.23	10.70	11.56	10.31

(b) Data2

LS	HU	LS	SA	PM
Average [%]	13.82	13.37	13.60	12.73
Best result [%]	13.82	12.84	13.07	12.23
SA	HU	LS	SA	PM
Average [%]	15.75	13.05	13.50	12.56
Best result [%]	13.82	11.82	12.82	11.72

(c) Data3

LS	HU	LS	SA	PM
Average [%]	13.75	13.33	13.54	12.85
Best result [%]	13.75	12.11	13.07	12.19
SA	HU	LS	SA	PM
Average [%]	13.75	13.39	13.38	12.78
Best result [%]	13.75	12.37	12.97	12.27

The results are shown in Table 2. A simulation has been done 10 times for each case, and the simulation time is 10min for each method in the case of Data1, 20min for each method in the case of Data2, and 100min for each method in the case of Data3 on a Pentium 4 2.8GHz PC with 1GB memory. The average of the ratio of the useless space in 10 trials and the best result among them are shown in this table.

Fig. 3 shows a layout example using Data2 and the used container list. The ratio of useless space is 11.72%, and the number of the used containers is 17 in this example.

The results show that the proposed method PM is better than other methods: LS, SA and HU, as the determination method of C/P selection sequence. LS and SA is not efficient because of the independent decisions between the package loading sequence and the C/P selection sequence. It has also been observed that LS is better than SA as the determination method of the package loading sequence. If the search does not cooperate the decision of package loading sequence with the decision of C/P selection sequence, LS is more effective than SA. Thus it seems that optimization of the decision of package loading sequence and the decision of C/P selection sequence separately does not lead to the total optimization.

However, using the proposed method, SA is better than LS as the determination method of package loading sequence. Thus it is possible to improve the search efficiency by using the proposed method and employing a more effective meta-heuristics as the determination method of package loading sequence.

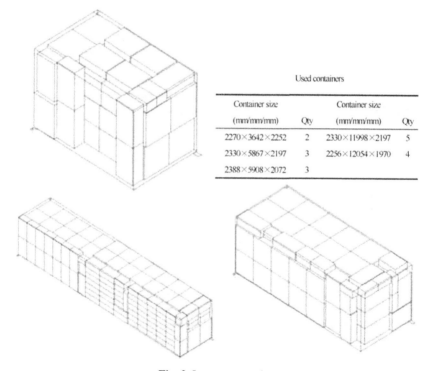

Used containers			
Container size		Container size	
(mm/mm/mm)	Qty	(mm/mm/mm)	Qty
2270×3642×2252	2	2330×11998×2197	5
2330×5867×2197	3	2256×12054×1970	4
2388×5908×2072	3		

Fig. 3. Layout examples

4 Conclusions

The method of strategic search using meta-heuristics and a strategic procedure is proposed. This method realizes cooperation between the decision of the package loading sequence and the decision of the C/P selection sequence. It employs the meta-heuristics to determine the package loading sequence and uses the strategic procedure to determine the C/P selection sequence. The strategic procedure uses components of observer and selector that simulate human strategies in the search.

The performance of the proposed method has been tested using simulation experiments. The results show that this method is superior to other methods.

Acknowledgments

The study has been supported by the Program for Promoting Fundamental Transport Technology Research from the Japan Railway Construction, Transport and Technology Agency (JRTT), *Project Number 2004-1*.

References

1. Bischoff, E.E., Ratcliff, M.S.W.: Loading multiple pallets. JORS. 46 (1995) 1322-1336.
2. Eley, M.: Solving container loading problems by block arrangement. EJOR. 141 (2002) 393-402.
3. George, J.A., Robinson, D.F.: A heuristic for packing boxes into a container. Computers Ops. Res. 7 (1980) 147-156.
4. Gilmore, P.C., Gomory, R.E.: Multistage cutting stock problems of two and more dimensions. Opns. Res. 13 (1965) 94-120.
5. Ivancic, N., Mathur, K., Mohanty, B.B.: An integer-programming based heuristic approach to the three-dimensional packing problem. J. Manuf. Ops. Mgmt. 2 (1989) 268-298.
6. Takahara, S., Miyamoto, S.: An adaptive meta-heuristic approach to three-dimensional packing problems. Proc. of AFSS2000. (2000) 278-283.
7. Takahara, S., Kusumoto, Y., Miyamoto, S.: Solution for textile nesting problems using adaptive meta-heuristics and grouping. Soft Computing. 7 (2003) 154-159.
8. Terno, J., Scheithauer, G., Sommerweiß, U., Riehme, J.: An efficient approach for the multi-pallet loading problem. EJOR. 123 (2000) 373-381.

Meta-data: Characterization of Input Features for Meta-learning

Ciro Castiello, Giovanna Castellano, and Anna Maria Fanelli

CILab - Computational Intelligence Laboratory
Computer Science Department, University of Bari
Via E. Orabona, 4 - 70126 Bari, Italy
{castellano,castiello,fanelli}@di.uniba.it
http://www.di.uniba.it/~cilab/

Abstract. Common inductive learning strategies offer the tools for knowledge acquisition, but possess some inherent limitations due to the use of fixed bias during the learning process. To overcome limitations of such *base-learning* approaches, a novel research trend is oriented to explore the potentialities of *meta-learning*, which is oriented to the development of mechanisms based on a dynamical search of bias. This could lead to an improvement of the base-learner performance on specific learning tasks, by profiting of the accumulated past experience. As a significant set of I/O data is needed for efficient base-learning, appropriate meta-data characterization is of crucial importance for useful meta-learning. In order to characterize meta-data, firstly a collection of meta-features discriminating among different base-level tasks should be identified. This paper focuses on the characterization of meta-data, through an analysis of meta-features that can capture the properties of specific tasks to be solved at base level. This kind of approach represents a first step toward the development of a meta-learning system, capable of suggesting the proper bias for base-learning different specific task domains.

1 Introduction

Common learning procedures proposed in the realm of machine learning are characterized by a fixed form of bias (base-learning paradigm), that forces the learner to specialize in a limited domain. This is a common circumstance in the base-learning paradigm, where different learning models perform well in some context, but appear to be inadequate in others. Meta-learning is a novel field of investigation intended for overcoming the limitations of traditional base-learning approaches by performing a dynamical search of bias [1], [2]. In other words, meta-learning is aimed at improving, by means of learning, the performance of a base-learner.

Different strategies can be cast within the meta-learning paradigm and several approaches have been proposed in the literature (see [2] for a comprehensive survey). A large amount of the research efforts have been addressed to investigate methods for adaptively selecting a particular learning model (among a pool of

V. Torra et al. (Eds.): MDAI 2005, LNAI 3558, pp. 457–468, 2005.
© Springer-Verlag Berlin Heidelberg 2005

candidates) that could prove to be best suited for a given task or an application domain [3], [4]. This kind of *model selection* approach moves from the assumption that every single learning algorithm can be considered as a form of bias. In this sense, meta-learning is achieved by studying the performance of several models when applied to different problems. A number of research projects have produced results in this area, prominent examples include STATLOG [5] and METAL [6] projects.

Our peculiar conception of meta-learning is aimed to dynamically adjust the bias characterising a specific learning model. This kind of approach, distinct from selection and combination of models, belongs to a potential avenue of research claiming that a learning algorithm should be able to change its internal mechanisms according to the task under analysis [2], [7]. In this way, a meta-learning strategy is centred on the extensive analysis of the special capabilities of a single base-learner, favouring the continuous accumulation of meta-knowledge useful for indicating the most appropriate form of bias for each problem. This means that a meta-learner should improve the learning performance of the base-learner by exploiting experience accumulated on previous tasks, which has to be retained as a form of meta-knowledge.

Of course, as for any standard base-learner, the success of a meta-learner is greatly dependent upon the quality of the (meta-)data chosen; especially it depends heavily on the input features used to describe the problem. Thus, a fundamental problem to be addressed in meta-learning is how to find appropriate meta-features that capture the properties of specific tasks to be solved through base-learning. Various strategies for defining these meta-features have been proposed [5], [8], [9]. Most of them are oriented to describe base-level tasks by means of a set of measures, including general measures (e.g. number of attributes, number of classes), statistical measures (e.g. mean and variance of numerical attributes) and information theory based measures (e.g. average joint entropy of classes and attributes). The description of a dataset in terms of its statistical/information properties appeared for the first time within the framework of the STATLOG project [5]. However, to date, there is no consensus on how good meta-features should be chosen.

In this paper, we proceed with a careful analysis of the most commonly employed meta-features, discussing their intrinsic properties in a systematic way. We suggest guidelines to select the most informative measures and we introduce new features that are transformations of existing ones. As a result of our analysis, a set of selected measures is suggested, that can be conveniently used as meta-features to compile a meta-dataset.

2   Meta-data Characterization

The idea underlying meta-learning is to identify a meta-knowledge apparatus that could be useful in supporting the search for a suitable bias when applying a base-learner to solve a specific task. Practically, the ordinary base-learning tasks are tackled by a learner $\mathcal{L}_{base}$ on the basis of a dataset $\mathcal{T}_{base}$, containing observational data related to the problem at hand. We assume that $\mathcal{T}_{base}$ can be expressed as a set of K samples, each of them can be decomposed in a couple of input-output vector, respectively indicated by $\mathbf{x}_k = (x_{k1}, \ldots, x_{km})$ and $\mathbf{y}_k = (y_{k1}, \ldots, y_{kn})$, namely:

$$\mathcal{T}_{base} = \{(\mathbf{x}_k, \mathbf{y}_k)\}_{k=1}^K \qquad (1)$$

The knowledge derived after base-learning concerns the particular task under study. The meta-learning process, instead, is performed by a learner $\mathcal{L}_{meta}$ which starts from the analysis of meta-data, or equivalently a meta-dataset $\mathcal{T}_{meta}$, and ends up by formulating a meta-knowledge that describes the correlation between the specific task (described by a set of meta-features) and the proper bias to be used during base-learning of the task. $\mathcal{T}_{base}$ and $\mathcal{T}_{meta}$ have a different nature, that leads to the main distinction between base-learning and meta-learning. Whilst the dataset $\mathcal{T}_{base}$ is simply drawn up on the basis of the available data, representing the task tackled by the base-learner, the meta-dataset $\mathcal{T}_{meta}$ has to be carefully built up by analyzing the characteristics of each single task and exploiting the accumulated past experience.

The goal of meta-learning is to let the meta-learner discover the relationships between categories of tasks and base-learner bias configurations. Hence, in order to arrange the meta-data, particular attention must be paid in defining the distinguishing meta-features of every task. Successively, the identified meta-features should be correlated with the most appropriate bias employed by $\mathcal{L}_{base}$ to efficaciously solve a particular class of tasks.

The definition of a proper bias involves an analysis of the free parameters engaged in the particular base-learning algorithm adopted, and it is out of the scope of this paper. This paper focuses essentially on the characterization of meta-features, which is independent on the particular base-learner adopted. In the following section we provide a characterization of the meta-features in terms of the most common measures found in the literature.

3   Characterization of Meta-features

In order to collect meta-features about a given learning task, it is necessary to perform an analysis of the information embedded inside a dataset associated to it. Obviously, this means that a dataset, besides banally providing information concerning the data (related to mean values, standard deviations, and so on), could be able to furnish a somewhat precise knowledge of the particular task underlying the dataset at hand. Therefore, meta-features can be conceived as specific collections of morphological characteristics of a dataset, that jointly affect the performance of a learning algorithm when it is applied to the particular task represented by the dataset. The main assumption is that the information codified in the meta-features should exhibit some kind of general hints (related, for instance, to the task complexity), other than the self-evident information content embedded in the particular dataset at hand (simply related to the data configuration).

Generally speaking, for the purpose of meta-learning, an adequate set of meta-features must satisfy mainly two basic conditions. Firstly, it should prove to be useful in determining the relative performance of individual learning algorithms. Secondly, it should not be too difficult to calculate. A number of measures have been proposed to characterize data for meta-learning and a common practice has been established in focusing over general, statistical and information-theoretic measures (see for example the meta-features employed in the STAT-LOG [5] and the METAL [6] projects). In the following we describe in more details the most frequently adopted meta-features.

3.1   General Meta-features

General meta-features include general information related to the dataset at hand and, to a certain extent, they are conceived to measure the complexity and/or the size of the underlying problem. The following general meta-features can be distinguished:

Number of observations: it represents the total number K of samples in the dataset (i.e. the cardinality of the dataset T_{base} defined in (1)).

Number of attributes: it represents the total number m of attributes in the dataset (i.e. the dimensionality of the input vector $\mathbf{x}_k$ in (1)).

Number of output values: it represents the total number n of output values in the dataset (i.e. the dimensionality of the output vector $\mathbf{y}_k$ in (1)).

Dataset dimensionality: it represents the ratio between the number of attributes and the number of observations constituting the dataset, i.e. $dim_{data} = \frac{m}{K}$.

3.2   Statistical Meta-features

It is straightforward to make use of standard statistical measures to describe the numerical properties of a distribution of data. By means of particular statistical meta-features it could be possible also to define the properties of the numerical subspace where a task domain evolves. Therefore, statistical meta-features can be employed to take into account the number of properties which enable a learner to discriminate the degree of correlation of numerical attributes and estimate their distribution. The following statistical meta-features can be distinguished:

Standard deviation: this quantity estimates the dispersion of a random variable $X = x_1, x_2, \ldots, x_K$ with respect to its mean $\overline{X} = 1/K \sum_{k=1}^{K} x_k$. It is computed as $std_X = \sqrt{\frac{1}{K} \sum_{k=1}^{K} (x_k - \overline{X})^2}$. In (1), the components of each sample represent particular instances of random variables. Therefore, from being $\mathbf{x}_k = (x_{k1}, \ldots, x_{ki}, \ldots, x_{km})$, a number of m random variables in the dataset assume the values $(x_{1i}, \ldots, x_{Ki})$, for $i = 1, \ldots, m$. As observed before, since the standard deviation depends on the size of the dataset and on the range of the data, it should be convenient to include the minimum and the maximum value of std_X as measures of a single dataset, or equivalently the mean standard deviation evaluated over all the attributes of the dataset, that is:

$$\overline{std_X} = \frac{1}{m} \sum_{i=1}^{m} (std_{X_i}),\tag{2}$$

Coefficient of variation: it evaluates the normalization of the standard deviation of a random variable X with respect to its mean value: $VarCoeff_X = \frac{std_X}{\overline{X}}$. As a measure of the coefficient of variation of an entire dataset, the average of $VarCoeff_{X_i}$ over all the m numerical attributes could be considered:

$$\overline{VarCoeff_X} = \frac{1}{m} \sum_{i=1}^{m} (VarCoeff_{X_i}).\tag{3}$$

It should be pointed out that the standard deviation is independent from the scaling of an attribute, while the coefficient of variation is not influenced by translations. Indeed, random variables X and αX possess the same coefficient of variation, while X and $X + \alpha$ have the same standard deviation. These properties should be taken into account whenever the meta-features should help a learner to discriminate for similar translation and/or scaling.

Covariance: the covariance extends the variance concept to the bidimensional case. In fact, it expresses the linear relationship between two random variables $X = x_1, \ldots, x_K$ and $Y = y_1, \ldots, y_K$, defined as:

$$Cov(X, Y) = \sum_{k=1}^{K} \frac{(x_k - \overline{X})(y_k - \overline{Y})}{K - 1}.\tag{4}$$

In our dataset formalization, the covariance could be evaluated for each pair of input variables, $\mathbf{x}_k$, $\mathbf{x}_l$, for $k \neq l$. As a measure of the covariance of an entire dataset, the average of $Cov(X, Y)$ over all the possible distinct pairs of numerical attributes could be considered.

Linear correlation coefficient: correlation analysis attempts to measure the strength of a relationship between two random variables X and Y. The linear correlation coefficient shows the linear association strength between X and Y by means of a single value. The coefficient of linear correlation can be estimated by the following formula:

$$\rho_{X,Y} = \frac{Cov(X, Y)}{\sqrt{std_X \, std_Y}}.\tag{5}$$

The values of $\rho_{X,Y}$ range in the interval $[-1, 1]$. The linear correlation coefficient could be evaluated for each pair of input variables. As a coefficient of the entire dataset linear correlation, the mean of the absolute values of the correlations between all distinct pairs of attributes could be evaluated.

Skewness: it measures the lack of symmetry in the distribution of a random variable X. Negative skewness values indicate data that are skewed left, while positive skewness values denote data that are skewed right. By skewed left (respectively, right) we mean that the left tail is heavier than the right tail (respectively, the right tail is heavier than the left one). An estimator of the skewness is represented by the third moment of the distribution of a random variable X, divided by the third power of standard deviation, i.e. $Skew_X = \frac{1}{std_X^3} \frac{\sum_{k=1}^{K}(x_k - \overline{X})^3}{K}$. As a measure of the skewness of an entire dataset, the average of $Skew_{X_i}$ over all the m numerical attributes could be considered:

$$\overline{Skew_X} = \frac{1}{m} \sum_{i=1}^{m} (Skew_{X_i}). \tag{6}$$

Kurtosis: it measures the peakedness in the distribution of a random variable X. The kurtosis can be estimated by the ratio of the fourth moment of the distribution of X to the fourth power of the standard deviation, i.e. $Kurt_X = \frac{1}{std_X^4} \frac{\sum_{k=1}^{K}(x_k - \overline{X})^4}{K}$. As a measure of the kurtosis of an entire dataset, the average of $Kurt_{X_i}$ over all the m numerical attributes could be considered:

$$\overline{Kurt_X} = \frac{1}{m} \sum_{i=1}^{m} (Kurt_{X_i}). \tag{7}$$

1-D variance fraction coefficient: this coefficient indicates the relative importance of the largest eigenvalue of the attribute covariance matrix and it measures the representation quality of the first principal component. In principal component analysis (PCA), methods for transforming a given dataset into a new dataset of reduced dimensions are studied, to concentrate the information about the differences between samples into a small number of dimensions [10]. In the PCA context, the first principal component is an axis in the direction of maximum variance; the variance of this principal axis is given by the largest eigenvalue of the covariance matrix of the original data. The fraction of the total variance retained in the 1-dimensional space can be computed as the ratio between the largest eigenvalue λ_1 of the covariance matrix S (whose elements are the covariances of the considered random variables) and the sum of all its eigenvalues:

$$Frac1 = \frac{\lambda_1}{trace(S)} \tag{8}$$

where $trace(S)$ is the trace of the covariance matrix S. In order to evaluate this meta-feature for a dataset formalized as in (1), the covariance matrix has to be extracted from the attribute matrix, whose elements are x_{ki}, for $k = 1, \ldots, K$ and $i = 1, \ldots, m$.

3.3   Information-Theoretic Meta-features

Information-theoretic meta-features are particularly appropriate to describe discrete (categorical) attributes, but they also fit continuous (numerical) ones.

Firstly, we define the entropy of a discrete random variable X as a measure of the randomness in the variable, evaluated by:

$$H(X) = -\sum_{i=1}^{n} q_i \log_2(q_i) \tag{9}$$

where $q_i = p(X = x_i)$ denotes the probability that X assumes the ith value x_i, for $i = 1, \ldots, n$. Conventionally, logarithms are to base 2 and entropy is then said to be measured in units called "bits" (binary information units). The highest entropy value is $\log_2(n)$, when n distinct values of X could appear with an equal probability. Therefore, the entropy values range in the interval $[0, \log_2(n)]$ and they are strictly connected with the degree of uniformity of the distribution of a variable.

The entropy definition given in (9) assumes that the random variable X is characterized by discrete values $(x_1, \ldots, x_n)$. In order to deal with continuous real-valued random variables, we should replace the summation term with an integral and the probabilities q_i with the probability density function $p_{\mathcal{D}}(\mathbf{x})$, being $\mathcal{D}$ the distribution of probability employed to draw the instances of X from an instance space. Whenever the distribution probability is unknown, in order to apply the formula (9), it is necessary to discretize the numerical data. A number of n equally spaced intervals have to be determined and then the relative frequency histogram for the i-th interval can be adopted as an estimate of q_i. It can be observed that, when dealing with classification tasks, the dataset expressed in (1) can be considered as a collection of values for m continuous random variables (corresponding to the m input attributes), together with the n values of a discrete random variable (corresponding to the output class, which can assume n distinct and discrete values). For the sake of simplicity, in the following we are going to describe the information-theoretic meta-features by referring to a classification problem, assuming the discretization process performed over the input attribute values.

Normalized class entropy: the entropy value $H(C)$ of a class variable C indicates how much information is necessary to specify one class. The value $H(C)$ can be evaluated using (9), where $q_i \equiv \pi_i$ defines the prior probability for a class (being π_i the relative frequency of occurrence of a particular class value). When we suppose that each class value in a dataset has the same probability to appear, then the theoretical maximum value for the class entropy is $\log_2(n)$. Therefore the normalized entropy can be computed as:

$$H(C)_{norm} = \frac{H(C)}{\log_2(n)} = -\frac{\sum_{i=1}^{n} \pi_i \log_2(\pi_i)}{\log_2(n)}. \tag{10}$$

Normalized attribute entropy: the attribute entropy value $H(X)$ of a random variable (which could be represented by one of the m discretized attribute input) measures the information content related to the values that X may assume. Since $\log_2(n)$ represents the maximum value for the attribute entropy, the normalized entropy can be computed as $H(X)_{norm} = \frac{H(X)}{\log_2(n)} =$

$-\frac{\sum_{i=1}^{n} q_i \log_2(q_i)}{\log_2(n)}$. As a measure of the attribute entropy of an entire dataset, the average of $H(X_i)_{norm}$ over all the m input attributes could be considered:

$$\overline{H(X)_{norm}} = \frac{1}{m} \sum_{i=1}^{m} (H(X_i)_{norm}). \tag{11}$$

Joint entropy of class and attribute: it measures the total entropy of the combined system of variables, i.e. the pair of variables (C, X), which could be represented by a class variable and one of the m discretized input attributes, respectively. If p_{ij} denotes the joint probability of observing the i-th value of attribute X and the j-th class value, the joint entropy is defined as $H(C, X) = -\sum_{ij} p_{ij} \log_2(p_{ij})$. As a measure of the joint entropy of an entire dataset, the average of $H(C, X_i)$ over all the m input attributes could be considered:

$$\overline{H(C, X)} = \frac{1}{m} \sum_{i=1}^{m} (H(C, X_i)). \tag{12}$$

Mutual information of class and attribute: it measures the common information shared between two random variables C and X. If C and X respectively represent a class variable and one of the m discretized input attributes, then the meta-feature measures the information conveyed by the attribute X about a class value and describes the reduction of uncertainty for C due to the knowledge of X. The mutual information of class and attribute can be evaluated by $MI(C, X) = H(C) + H(X) - H(C, X) = \sum_{ij} p_{ij} \log_2(\frac{p_{ij}}{\pi_i q_j})$. As a measure of the joint entropy of an entire dataset, the average of $MI(C, X_i)$ over all the m input attributes could be considered:

$$\overline{MI(C, X)} = \sum_{i=1}^{m} MI(C, X_i). \tag{13}$$

Equivalent number of attributes: when we refer to classification tasks, the information required to specify the class is $H(C)$ and no classification scheme can be completely successful unless it provides at least $H(C)$ bits of useful information. This information has to come from the attributes taken together, and in the simplest (even if often unrealistic) case that all attributes are independent, we would have:

$$MI(C, X) = MI(C, X_1) + \ldots + MI(C, X_m).$$

In this case, we could count up how many attributes would be required, on average, by taking the ratio between the class entropy $H(C)$ and the average mutual information $\overline{MI(C, X)}$. The meta-feature expressing the equivalent number of attributes, therefore, can be evaluated by:

$$EN_{attr} = \frac{H(C)}{\overline{MI(X, C)}}. \tag{14}$$

This meta-feature furnishes a rough information about the complexity of a problem, specifically it indicates if the number of attributes in a given dataset is suitable to optimally solve the classification task (under the assumption of independence among attributes).

Noise-signal ratio: it measures the amount of irrelevant information contained in a dataset. If we consider $\overline{MI(C,X)}$ as a measure of useful information about class, and $\overline{H(X)} - \overline{MI(C,X)}$ as a measure of non-useful information (where $\overline{H(X)}$ represents the mean of the attribute entropy), the meta-feature can be evaluated by:

$$NS.ratio = \frac{\overline{H(X)} - \overline{MI(C,X)}}{\overline{MI(C,X)}}. \tag{15}$$

The above listed ensemble of measures represents a set of candidates which could be employed as meta-features in a meta-learning task.

4   Selection of Meta-features

Despite many works in literature explicitly admit that the choice for particular input meta-features does not necessarily relies upon preventive analyses (see, for instance, [8]), it is our opinion that, in order to choose the meta-features to be employed for discriminating across different tasks, a deeper analysis is necessary. Moving from these considerations, in this section we revisit the above listed meta-features on the basis of an analysis having a twofold goal: (i) deepening the understanding of the employed meta-data and (ii) taking into account the particular application domain.

Since we are interested in discriminating among different learning problems, we resolved to extract numerical meta-features from the available observational data related to each task. Obviously, these kinds of information could provide both knowledge connected to the data alone and the different ways they have been collected, and knowledge which more directly concerns the underlying task and its intrinsic "difficulty". Even if there is no doubt that the process of learning a particular task could become much more complex in dependence of the configuration of the adopted dataset (which could reveal itself to be inadequate for the presence of excessive noise, missing values, and so on), we consider that a meta-learning system should be able to discriminate among different problems in terms of their inherent characterization, renouncing to taking account also of data arrangement. This represents, therefore, a further assumption for our analysis: the meta-features employed to characterize a learning problem should furnish pieces of information as unrelated as possible to the dataset configuration, and should attempt to capture, instead, the actual complexity of the task under consideration. In this sense, we could undertake a brief revisitation of the ensemble of meta-features described in section 3.

Among the general meta-features, we suggest the only use of *number of attributes* and *number of output values*, since the *number of observations* and the *dataset dimensionality* provide information related to the dataset configuration.

Moreover, the *number of output values* could be discarded if the application domain involves only concept learning tasks, each one characterized by two output values.

As concerns the statistical meta-features, we observe that, while the *mean standard deviation* and the *mean coefficient of variation* appear to be strongly related to low-level information pertaining to dataset configuration, on the other hand *covariance, linear correlation coefficient, skewness* and *kurtosis*, even if they evaluate purely statistical information, could be computed in a slightly different way, in order to furnish some kind of high-order task information. In fact, the computation of statistical meta-features is generally performed by employing only the input attribute variables of a dataset; it could be possible to obtain some more information if we could exploit also the knowledge related to the class membership[1]. Therefore, we suggest to discard the *mean standard deviation* and the *mean coefficient of variation*, and to proceed in evaluating the remaining statistical meta-features on a *"per class"* basis, that is by separately computing the meta-features values for each group of samples belonging to different output classes, and then retaining the average value (over the number of classes) as the final meta-feature value. A further consideration regards the *mean covariance*, which determines a value strongly dependent on the range of the data. For the sake of generality, we decided to discard such a feature, considering that a similar information can be obtained by the *mean linear correlation coefficient*, with the additional advantage that this results to be independent on the ranges of input data (in fact its range is [-1,1]). Finally, the *skewness* and the *kurtosis* lose their discriminating character when evaluated on uniformly distributed data, thus such features can be discarded if the application domain involves data with uniform distribution.

In order to analyze the information-theoretic meta-features, it is important to recall that, from (9), the entropy values of any random variable X range in the interval $[0, \log_2(n)]$, being n the number of the distinct values that X may assume. Higher and lower values of $H(X)$ depend on the more or less uniformity in the distribution of the values of X. Therefore, even if the information provided by the *normalized class entropy* and the *mean normalized attribute entropy* could potentially be useful for deriving some kind of high-order task knowledge, it is unsuitable for application domains involving dataset characterized by the uniform distribution. As concerning the *mean mutual information of class and attribute*, we considered that the average computed in (13) could waste the greater part of the information content embedded in this meta-feature. Therefore, we propose to refer to the maximum value of the c/a mutual information, instead of considering the average over all the m input attributes:

$$maxMI(C, X) = \max(MI(C, X_1), \ldots, MI(C, X_m)). \qquad (16)$$

---

[1] Obviously, this kind of approach is applicable only for classification tasks.

Table 1. The set of selected meta-features

Meta-feature	Notation
General meta-features	
Number of attributes	m
Number of output values	n
Statistical meta-features	
Mean linear corr. coeff. (on class basis)	$\rho_{X,Y}^{class}$
Mean skewness (on class basis)	$Skew_X^{class}$
Mean kurtosis (on class basis)	$Kurt_X^{class}$
1-D var. fraction coeff. (on class basis)	$Frac1^{class}$
Information-theoretic meta-features	
Normalized class entropy	$H(C)_{norm}$
Mean normalized attribute entropy	$\overline{H(X)}_{norm}$
Max. norm. mutual info. c/a	$maxMI_{norm}(C,X)$
Equivalent number of attributes	$EN.attr$
Noise-signal ratio	$NS.ratio$

The obtained value could be normalized for the sake of generality by the following formula:

$$maxMI_{norm}(C, X) = \frac{maxMI(C, X)}{\min(H(C), H(X_l))}, \qquad (17)$$

where $H(C)$ is the class entropy, $H(X_l)$ is the attribute entropy evaluated for the l-th input attribute and $l = \arg\max_i(MI(C, X_i))$. In this way, the new value computed for such meta-feature expresses the portion of information that would be retained if the task under consideration were analyzed only on the basis of the most relevant (in sense of information content) input attributes.

Table 1 summarizes the set of selected meta-features that we considered suitable for meta-learning applications.

5   Conclusions and Future Works

Similarly to what happens with the employment of any standard machine learning algorithm, the success of a meta-learning strategy greatly depends on the quality of the (meta-)data to be used during learning. In order to characterize meta-data, firstly a collection of significant meta-features, discriminating among different learning tasks, is to be identified. In this paper we have presented a characterization of meta-features, through a systematic analysis of the most frequently used measures. As a result of such analysis, new features that are transformations of existing ones have been proposed, and some guidelines have been delineated to select the most informative ones. The selected set of meta-features represents a first step toward the design of a meta-learner, capable of suggesting the proper bias for base-learning different specific task domains. In order to develop such a meta-learning system, our current research activity is addressed to evaluating the selected meta-features appropriateness in characterizing different learning domains, each one including groups of related tasks. The aim is to relate each set of meta-feature values (properly derived from a dataset representing a base-learning task) to a bias configuration. Particulary, the bias configuration should be identified as the base-learner parameter setting yielding the best performance results for the considered task. Such pieces of information, gathered from different base-learning experiences, will permit the compilation of a proper set of meta-data, useful to derive meta-knowledge through a meta-learning process.

References

1. Giraud-Carrier, C., Vilalta, R. and Brazdil, P.: Introduction to the special issue on meta-learning. Machine Learning, **54** (2004) 187–193.
2. Vilalta, R., and Drissi, Y.: A perspective view and survey of meta-learning. Journal of Artificial Intelligence Review **18**(2) (2002) 77–95.
3. Merz, C.J.: Dynamical selection of learning algorithms. In: Fisher, D., Lenz, H.J. (eds.): Learning from data: Artificial Intelligence and Statistics, Springer-Verlag, Berlin Heidelberg New York (1995).
4. Brazdil, P.B.: Data transformation and model selection by experimentation and meta-learning. Proceedings of the ECML98 Workshop (1998) 11–17.
5. Michie, D., Spiegelhalter, D., and Taylor, C.: Machine learning, neural and statistical classification. Ellis Horwood, New York (1994).
6. Kalousis, A. and Hilario, M.: Model selection via meta-learning: a comparative study. Proceedings of the 12th International IEEE Conference on Tools with AI. IEEE Press (2000).
7. Soares, C., Brazdil, P.B. and Kuba, P.: A meta-learning method to select the kernel width in support vector regression. Machine Learning, **54** (2004) 195–209.
8. Brazdil, P., Soares, C., and Costa, J.: Ranking learning algorithms: Using IBL and meta-learning on accuracy & time results. Machine Learning **50**(3) (2003) 251–277.
9. Linder, C. and Studer, R.: AST: Support for Algorithm Selection with a CBR Approach. Proceedings of the 16th International Conference on Machine Learning, Workshop on Recent Advances in Meta-Learning and Future Work. (1999).
10. Bishop, C.M.: Neural Networks for Pattern Recognition. Clarendon Press, Oxford (1995).

Author Index

Lecture Notes in Artificial Intelligence (LNAI)